THE
MONTESSORI
CHILD

THE
MONTESSORI
CHILD

A PARENT'S GUIDE TO RAISING CAPABLE CHILDREN
WITH CREATIVE MINDS
AND COMPASSIONATE HEARTS

SIMONE DAVIES AND **JUNNIFA UZODIKE**

WORKMAN PUBLISHING | NEW YORK

Workman
Workman Publishing
Hachette Book Group, Inc.
1290 Avenue of the Americas
New York, NY 10104
workman.com

Workman is an imprint of Workman Publishing, a division of Hachette Book Group, Inc.
The Workman name and logo are registered trademarks of Hachette Book Group, Inc.

Design by Galen Smith and Hiyoko Imai

Constructive Rhythm of Life chart (p. 24) and The Bulb chart (p. 207) © Association
Montessori Internationale (AMI)

The publisher is not responsible for websites (or their content) that are not owned by
the publisher.

Workman books may be purchased in bulk for business, educational, or promotional use.
For information, please contact your local bookseller or the Hachette Book Group Special
Markets Department at special.markets@hbgusa.com.

First edition March 2024

Printed in China on responsibly sourced paper.

10 9 8 7 6 5 4 3 2 1

ON CHILDREN

Kahlil Gibran (1883-1931)

And a woman who held a babe against her bosom said, Speak to us of Children.
And he said:
Your children are not your children.
They are the sons and daughters of Life's longing for itself.
They come through you but not from you,
And though they are with you yet they belong not to you.

You may give them your love but not your thoughts,
For they have their own thoughts.
You may house their bodies but not their souls,
For their souls dwell in the house of tomorrow, which you cannot visit,
    not even in your dreams.
You may strive to be like them, but seek not to make them like you.
For life goes not backward nor tarries with yesterday.
You are the bows from which your children as living arrows are sent forth.
The archer sees the mark upon the path of the infinite, and He bends you with
    His might that His arrows may go swift and far.
Let your bending in the archer's hand be for gladness;
For even as He loves the arrow that flies, so He loves also the bow that is stable.

CONTENTS

ONLINE RESOURCES

GO TO WORKMAN.COM/MONTESSORI FOR:

40 Ways to Build Self-Discipline and Intrinsic Motivation

A Caterpillar's Journey

The Montessori Adolescent at the Montessori Centre for Work and Study, Rydet, Sweden

How does Montessori work?

Activity starter kits

Activities listing based on interest

An introduction to the Great Lessons

How to make a booklet

Play dough recipe

What to look for in a Montessori school

What the Montessori program looks like for the 3–6 and 6–12 child at school

If they don't want to go to school and other common questions

When parents are separated

Further reading

INTRODUCTION

1

WHY WE NEED MONTESSORI AT HOME

What if there was an easier way to raise children? As parents, we are juggling demands from work and home, trying to find time to enjoy ourselves and our family, and to contribute to our community, all while fending off serious concerns about humanity, the impact of technologies, and the future of our planet.

We (Junnifa and Simone) believe that Montessori is the antidote to this juggling act. We can learn the tools to understand our children, see from their perspective, and raise them with joy. Even, and especially, for a future full of uncertainty.

The Montessori approach offers what Junnifa and Simone like to affectionately call the "triumvirate."

First, there is raising our child in the spirit of respect, love, and understanding. As parents and caregivers, we are our child's guide, not their boss or servant. We are on their side, and we are on this journey together. A journey where everything (good or bad) is an opportunity for learning and growth.

Second, there is the prepared environment. We can set up our homes intentionally (and introduce our child to the world outside our home) so that our child can be capable, feel like they belong, and become a meaningful member of our family and the community.

Third, there are activities that meet the needs of our unique child to support their development in a holistic way—cognitively, emotionally, socially, and spiritually.

Dr. Montessori developed this approach to children's development over 100 years ago. We might wonder how it is still relevant in today's world. To that we would remind the reader that the needs and characteristics of children have not changed. Children need to move, to express themselves, to connect with others, and to learn about the world around them. In Montessori, we want children to learn, not because someone is forcing them, but because there is an intrinsic desire and flame inside them that is being protected and stoked. In addition, Montessori is an approach that has worked for all types of children around the world for more than a century. It is a philosophy that allows every child to develop uniquely on their own timeline, with their own way of learning, and with their unique interests.

Our children can benefit from the Montessori approach whether or not they attend a Montessori school when we apply the Montessori principles in our homes. In fact, this makes Montessori accessible, equitable, and culturally responsive as we apply the principles for our unique family and circumstances.

Many people might say, "Well, I turned out okay without Montessori." That may be true for a handful of folks who had families who were able to offer unconditional support and opportunities or who were able to take care of themselves in spite of their circumstances. Far more often we think that we are doing okay; however, if we dig a little deeper, we may have dreams we never fulfilled; or we may have followed a path set by our parents or societal expectations; or perhaps we feel like we cannot be 100 percent ourselves; or we may hold resentment and anger toward people who think differently from us (be it politics, religion, interests, cultural background, economic status, etc.) or our own family members; or we never learned how to express our emotions, or to set kind and clear boundaries with others; or we have old wounds and unresolved trauma. So, we think we turned out okay, but we are only beginning to unpack that we also would have benefited from a Montessori upbringing.

Montessori is booming in popularity not because it's a trend but because we are looking for a way to raise our children to be creative and critical thinkers, who know how to live in society with others, and to be caretakers of the Earth.

We cannot promise you that your child will become a tech giant like the Google guys (although they do credit a lot of their creativity to attending a Montessori school). What we will do is share with you all the secrets we know about raising capable children with creative minds and compassionate hearts. Children who become self-aware adults who are kind and respectful and who care for themselves, others, and our planet. They will go into society in any role that they desire—be it a mechanic, a CEO, a parent, a scientist, a programmer, a farmer, an educator—and make their contribution to society.

We'll be referring to the child, the adult, and the environment a lot. There is a dynamic relationship among these three things. We'll learn to understand the child and how we can prepare ourselves and our environment to support them. We'll see that the principles are quite commonsense and intuitive, yet many of us have forgotten them. We'll learn how to observe, how to respond rather than react, how to understand the needs and characteristics of children as they grow, and so much more.

Let's learn more about The Montessori Child.

WHO WE ARE

Junnifa is an Association Montessori Internationale (AMI) 0–3, 3–6, and 6–12 trained teacher, a wife, and mother to four children, all raised with Montessori principles from in utero. Junnifa is the founder and head of school of Fruitful Orchard Montessori school in Abuja, Nigeria, serving children from 15 months to 12 years old; she is an AMI board member and also trained in the Resources for Infant Educarers (RIE) approach.

Junnifa feels blessed to have found Montessori education before her first child was born. It allowed her to start her parenting journey empowered with an understanding of her children's needs and the tools she needed as a parent. She has continued to learn with her children as they have passed through the planes of development. Parenting her children, leading the school, guiding the elementary classroom, and supporting the families in her community and around the world continue to reinforce her trust in Montessori principles. She believes them to be a foundation for building a good life and a cohesive society founded on respect and stewardship with everyone learning to care for and support themselves, others, the environment (both tangible and intangible), and the society as a whole.

As a Montessori educator and parent, Junnifa sees the gift in every child she works with. At home, she trusts her children, guides them, and fosters a strong sense of independence while building a tight-knit family unit and community. She applies Montessori principles in a culturally relevant way and has participated in Montessori trainings in the United States, Italy, India, and South Africa.

Simone is an Association Montessori Internationale (AMI) 0–3 teacher, holds 3–6 and 6–12 AMI assistant certificates, and is a Positive Discipline educator. She's been working in Montessori classrooms since 2004 and running her own parent-child classes at Jacaranda Tree Montessori in the Netherlands since 2008.

Simone raised her two children (now young adults) applying Montessori principles. Disillusioned with the traditional educational system, she sent her children to a Montessori playgroup and preschool in Castlecrag, Australia, and then to a public Montessori school in the Netherlands until they were 12 years old. Even after they entered regular high school and then university, Simone continued to use Montessori principles at home.

She has seen how the Montessori principles lay the foundation for empathetic, kind, curious children. She has had a respectful relationship with her children: She hasn't needed to threaten them to get cooperation; they helped prepare meals and learned to be great bakers; they each played a sport, taught themselves the keyboard, spent time with friends, and enjoyed hours stretched out on the living room floor making comic books and signs for secret clubs inspired by their favorite books. Living in a Montessori way extended to family vacations spent running around a farm, creating a dam at a beach, or exploring museums in different cities. Simone is the first to acknowledge that there was a lot of privilege in having been able to offer all this to her children. And she assures you that Montessori does not mean raising perfect children—her children also experienced their difficulties and struggles during these years, and she will share how such situations were navigated as we go further in the book.

We have found so much peace, joy, and connection with our children from applying the Montessori principles in our home, and we hope you do too.

ABOUT THIS BOOK

After Simone wrote *The Montessori Toddler* and Junnifa and Simone wrote *The Montessori Baby* together, people kept requesting a book for the later years. This book is the result. We have collected wisdom from Dr. Montessori, our Montessori training, our experience with our own children and many families, a lot of research, professional education, training courses, podcasts, workshops, and many other Montessori educators who have contributed to this book and compiled it into a guide for Montessori families with children from 3 to 12 years old.

The goal of this book is not to set up our homes as a Montessori classroom. In fact, we would advise against it. And this is not a book about Montessori homeschooling. It's about how you can apply the Montessori principles at home whether your child goes to a Montessori school or not.

You can read this book from cover to cover or open it to any page to find some wisdom you can put into practice today. Our hope is that you can use this book as a scaffold. You can absorb the principles, and over time, they will become second nature. Then you can remove the scaffold and stand on your own (and revisit the book when you need a refresher or when difficult situations arise).

Whether you are reading about Montessori for the first time or you've been practicing Montessori since before your children were born, we hope you will walk away with confidence, a deeper understanding of your children, and a stronger connection with your family. If you have never practiced Montessori before in your home, we like to say it's never too early to start with Montessori, and it's never too late. It might feel at first like a huge shift to observe, prepare your home and yourselves, and support your child's development in a new way, but know that your investment will pay off. Montessori is not a quick fix. It is a long-term approach.

NOTE: We have preserved the original quotes from Dr. Montessori's writings, which are mostly gendered he/him as representative of her time and place.

FURTHER READING

For the science behind the Montessori approach and the ideas shared in this book, we refer the reader to:

- the comprehensive yet accessible work of Angeline Stoll Lillard, *Montessori: The Science Behind the Genius*
- the online appendix, "How Does Montessori Work?" by Mira Debs and Angela K. Murray (workman.com/montessori)

MONTESSORI IS FOR EVERY CHILD

We believe that Montessori can be applied in any home, with any child from any background, anywhere in the world, and regardless of their family constellation. Montessori is about learning how every child is unique, supporting their individual development, and making adjustments as necessary.

Montessori is not only for children who can sit quietly and bring their activity back to the shelf. It's also, and particularly suited, for children who need to move. They can move as they play, they can dance and sing, make music, discover rhythms, and make big and small movements. Montessori is for all types of learners. Those who are visual learners or aural learners or kinesthetic learners (those who like to touch and feel things to get to know them). It's for children who like learning through doing, and it's also for children who like learning through observing.

Dr. Montessori observed the potential in all children, including those who are neurodivergent (e.g., are autistic, twice exceptional, gifted, or have ADHD, sensory issues, or learning differences), have a disability (intellectual or physical), are deaf or blind or have (selective) mutism.

WHAT WE LOVE ABOUT
THE 3- TO 6-YEAR-OLD CHILD

The 3- to 6-year-old child is curious. While we might like to stay in bed all day, our 3- to 6-year-old cannot stop learning and moving. They have so many new things to discover and constantly ask "What?" and "Why?," hungry to understand the world around them. They want to know the names of things, relationships between people, and simple explanations of how things work.

The 3- to 6-year-old child picks things up effortlessly. Dr. Montessori described the child's mind at this age as an *absorbent mind* able to pick things up effortlessly like a sponge. We see children of this age learn multiple languages without any formal lessons; they absorb how to move and how to communicate and listen; they start to explore symbols like letters, numbers, maps, and flags; and they take in the social life of others. Where the absorbent mind of the child younger than 3 years old is *unconscious*, taking everything in without conscious effort, the mind of the 3- to 6-year-old is *conscious*, aware of what they are taking in and eager to crystallize all they have learned in earlier years.

The 3- to 6-year-old child takes things literally. They understand the world in a very concrete way based on what they see around them. This reality-based understanding is an important foundation for their growing imagination. It can make for some fascinating conversations too. For example, if you ask them what would happen if you didn't have a brain, a common response might be that your head would look squashed!

The 3- to 6-year-old child loves to communicate and express themselves. By the age of 3 years old, a child has mostly learned to express themselves verbally. From ages 3 to 6, there is increased vocabulary and an informal introduction to grammar. By around age 6, many children can express themselves (speaking and writing) and understand others (listening and reading). They also love to express themselves with dance, with music, and with art.

The 3- to 6-year-old child is busy matching, sorting, grading, and classifying impressions in the world around them through their senses. They are still a sensorial learner. This means they will learn and take in information through touching, smelling, hearing, seeing, and tasting everything they come across. Verbal instructions or lectures are less interesting; invitations for explorations to make their own discoveries are much more exciting. They are exploring the qualities of materials they come across—rough and smooth, long and short, soft and loud, hot and cold, light and dark.

The 3- to 6-year-old child will repeat and repeat a task. When a 3- to 6-year-old is working to master something, they will repeat it many times until it is mastered. In the classroom, we can witness a child tying bows, undoing them, and tying them all over again, or coming back to the same activity every day for 2 weeks and then moving on from it.

The 3- to 6-year-old child loves to be involved in daily life. Children of this age love what we call *practical life activities*. They like to learn how to look after themselves by brushing their hair, looking after plants or pets, or setting the table for family meals. They are learning a sequence of steps and refining their coordination and movements, and they love making a contribution. Through these daily life activities, they are also exposed to their culture through everyday objects (like the utensils we use to eat) and customs (like how we say hello).

The 3- to 6-year-old child is capable of more than we expect. They are able to cook pancakes, tie their shoelaces, make a map of Africa and label each country, and sew a decorative pillow. When they have an environment set up for them to be successful, the freedom to choose what they like, a patient adult or older child to ask for help if they get stuck, and the time to practice and master skills, children can take on and complete time-consuming and detailed tasks.

The 3- to 6-year-old child mostly lives in the present moment. While they are starting to get a better understanding of time than when they were toddlers, for them "yesterday" could be any time in the past and "tomorrow" any time in the future. They remind us to stay present, in the here and now, and not too focused on the past or future. They have things they are doing right now that are far more important.

WHAT WE LOVE ABOUT THE 6- TO 12-YEAR-OLD CHILD

We can have a lot of compassion for the 6- to 12-year-old child. They are often criticized for being rude, disorderly, and answering back. We may wonder what has happened to our sweet child. Our child is entering a new stage of development (the *second plane*), and they will need to be supported differently.

The older child is driven by reason, imagination, and their developing moral values. They are attracted to working in, being in, and belonging to groups that aren't family. But adults still play an important role. They have an increased stamina and thirst for knowledge, and they want to make a difference in the world.

The 6- to 12-year-old child is more stable. The rapid rate of physical growth of early childhood begins to slow, and they become more stable and less volatile. They are losing their baby teeth and their round faces, and their legs are getting stronger. They are becoming more adventurous and daring and will share their feats with us.

The 6- to 12-year-old child has an enormous sense of justice. They want to make things as equal as possible for everyone. If there are ten cookies and six children, they would prefer that each child get one cookie and leave four on the plate than some children get two cookies. As they thrive on law and order, we can ask them to help create agreements for the home, which they will be happy to uphold and enforce. This also means they are trying to be truth tellers, eager to let us know when someone has done something wrong. They are trying to follow the rules and distinguish right from wrong.

The 6- to 12-year-old child loves being part of a group. They are learning how to be a contributing member of the group, exploring the idea of fairness, learning how others think, developing empathy, and feeling protective of those they perceive as "weaker." They are practicing being members of society and may need our help navigating some of these natural instincts toward sociability.

The 6- to 12-year-old child has an interest in secret languages. They may be fascinated by ciphers and hieroglyphics, or might invent their own language, a way for children to feel independent and separate from their family while creating their own society with friends.

The 6- to 12-year-old child is capable of big work (and big mess!). They will want to do work if it has a purpose, if it is with and for their group, and if it is aligned with their interests. They love sharing new knowledge and discoveries. They now need a wider environment to explore; they are not satisfied with only the home and school. We can give them the universe—not just math and grammar, but subjects like biology, history, geography, astronomy, and mechanics. They are learning that everything is interrelated and that everything in the universe (from a bacterium to a spider to themselves) has a *cosmic task* and its own special role to play.

The 6- to 12-year-old child uses their imagination to explore the universe. They are moving beyond exploring with their senses and can now apply their imagination to understand other cultures, environments, and things they cannot physically touch or see. Simone once heard this described as using "the eyes of the mind, not just the body." They might do this by inventing something, thinking of ways to solve a problem like pollution, or using their imagination to put themselves in another's shoes.

The 6- to 12-year-old child is building the foundations to grow into a contributing adult of society and be of service to others. They are learning that they can be of service to their class, their classmates, their family, and others in society; for example, by mowing the lawn for an elderly neighbor or writing a letter to the local authority to ask them to fix a crack in the pavement that might disadvantage those in a wheelchair.

WHAT OUR CHILDREN ARE TRYING TO TELL US

THE 3- TO 6-YEAR-OLD CHILD

THE 6- TO 12-YEAR-OLD CHILD

When they say, "No, you do it," they are ACTUALLY saying, "Will you get me started?" or "Will you sit with me while I do it?"

When they argue and yell, "It's not fair!," they are ACTUALLY trying to understand justice and how things really work.

When they ask, "What?" or "Why?," they are ACTUALLY wanting to take in everything about the world around them. Encourage them to do this.

When they tattle constantly, they are ACTUALLY checking the limits and consistency of right and wrong.

When they say, "But I don't want to go to bed!," they are ACTUALLY saying, "Do you mean it's really bedtime or are you so tired that you are going to let me stay up?"

When they make big messes, they are ACTUALLY exploring and making big work and are often putting ideas in order, though it may be hard to see.

When they cry, they are not pretending. They are ACTUALLY saying, "I'm not doing well right now. Can you help me to regulate myself? Then I'll fix what I've broken."

When they cry, they are not pretending. They are ACTUALLY saying, "Even though I'm older, I'm still not doing well right now. Can you help me to regulate myself? Then I'll fix what I've broken."

When they ask for help, they are ACTUALLY saying, "Help me to do it myself," so they can learn to take care of themselves, others, and the space around them.

When they ask deep questions, they are ACTUALLY asking us to help them think for themselves and give them tools and frameworks for exploring ideas and finding answers.

When they are not listening, they are ACTUALLY saying, "What you are saying to me does not align with what I want to do right now. Can you let me finish and then ask me again in a way that makes me want to do it?"

When they seem like they are not listening, they are ACTUALLY always listening. They might not respond or follow directions, but they did hear.

IMPORTANT MONTESSORI PRINCIPLES FOR THE 3- TO 12-YEAR-OLD CHILD

2

A BRIEF HISTORY OF MONTESSORI

Dr. Maria Montessori was an Italian medical doctor, anthropologist, and scientist who was interested in everything from women's rights to geometry and botany—and especially children.

Born in 1870, Dr. Montessori received an education and opportunities that were unusual for women of her time. She earned her medical degree and began working with special-needs children (then referred to as "delinquent children"), producing extraordinary results. (After working with the children, Dr. Montessori registered her students for a state exam. The majority passed, some receiving higher marks than the children without special needs.) As a result, Dr. Montessori thought children without special needs could be doing better.

In 1907, Dr. Montessori had the opportunity to test her ideas in the Italian educational system. She opened the first Casa dei Bambini (Children's House) for the children of working parents living in a low-income housing estate in the slums of San Lorenzo, Italy. The school became Dr. Montessori's laboratory. She observed the children, documented everything she saw, and supported their development. If the children appeared interested in something, she would provide it. If they stopped showing interest in something, she would replace it with something else. She followed their natural tendencies and modified the environment accordingly. Contrary to the commonly accepted belief at the time that children were stubborn, selfish, and unwilling to share, Dr. Montessori found that when children were in the right environment and their needs were being met, they were caring, capable, and eager to learn.

Dr. Montessori was unique in that she learned about children not by guessing, theorizing, or making assumptions but by simply observing them. What we call the "Montessori method" could really be thought of as the "children's method" because the children transmitted—through Dr. Montessori's observations—what they liked, what they preferred, and their characteristics at different ages.

Dr. Montessori worked with children around the world, testing, refining, and improving her method, until her death in 1952. News about her work spread, and the people (educators, parents, government officials, dignitaries) who came to observe and learn from her returned home and replicated her methods—setting up the environment, observing the children, and meeting their needs. Her methods were hailed for their positive and replicable results.

Today, over a century later, educators, parents, and caregivers around the world have applied the same approach and have found that the underlying characteristics of children—their human tendencies and their needs—haven't changed. Children are independent and capable; they are able to listen, they are able to follow instructions, they are able to share, and they are able to care. In fact, these traits are part of their nature. These methods are therefore as relevant today as they were during Dr. Montessori's life.

WHAT IS MONTESSORI?

One of the most frequent, and most challenging, questions asked by anyone encountering Montessori for the first time is "What is Montessori?" Montessori encompasses so much: It is an outlook, a lens, an attitude, and a form of wisdom.

> Montessori is a philosophy of life. A way of living, and of being with others but specifically, being with children.

Montessori as an outlook

The Montessori outlook or perspective is one of awe and wonder. It is living in awe of ourselves and those around us—including animals and plants, big and small. It is appreciating the Earth and its components, animate and inanimate; the universe; and the intricacies that contribute to our existence. It is wondering how everything came to be, what else is out there, and how it all works together.

This awe and wonder are often accompanied by joy. Montessori is joy. We (Junnifa and Simone) have experienced this joy in our parenting, in our work as educators, and, more generally, in our day-to-day activities because of this expanded view of life.

The Montessori outlook centers on stewardship and responsibility. On an understanding that there is an interdependence between things, and that our actions, conscious and unconscious, affect everyone and everything. It is the intention of approaching life with this awareness and acting with responsibility for ourselves, others, our society, and the environment. It is knowing to first look at ourselves before looking at others, especially children, when trying to solve problems.

This outlook affects everything we do because it colors the way we look at our interactions, homes, and the way we raise our children and the opportunities we explore for ourselves, our children, and beyond. It becomes the lens through which we view our children.

Montessori as a lens

When we look at children through the Montessori lens, we don't view
them as empty vessels, ready to be filled up or made into whatever
we desire. Instead, we view them as human beings, full of potential,
deserving of respect, and capable of participating in their own
development. Our role as educators, parents, and caregivers is to try
to understand, nurture, and bring out what our children already contain.

We view children as unique, with their own individual strengths, personalities,
capacities, and interests. We recognize that their journey, pace, and experience will
be different from those of others. We do not see them as replicas of us or define them
by their age and other general descriptors. We don't try to force them to conform
to the actions of others or compare them to one another. Instead, we recognize and
nurture their individuality.

We view children as capable. They are capable of constructing their own unique
personalities and of doing so much for themselves at every stage. We recognize that
they are capable of constantly improving upon their capacity. Instead of doing things
for them, we give them the opportunity to do what they are capable of, and when they
need help, we help them do it for themselves.

We view our children with awe and wonder. We notice their little conquests and are in
awe of their amazing abilities. This awe and wonder make parenting and caregiving a joy
instead of a chore.

Because we view children differently, **we also come to view ourselves and our role
differently**. We are not sculptors or creators but gardeners. We are more guides than
teachers. As Kahlil Gibran says in "On Children" (see the dedication page), "You are the
bows from which your children as living arrows are sent forth."

Montessori as an attitude

Montessori is an attitude toward children as well as life in general. It is an attitude of
respect, humility, constant curiosity, openness and acceptance, patience and trust.

Montessori is an attitude of respect. We approach the child first as a human being
that deserves to be addressed and treated with respect. We allow even the youngest
child to have and express their opinions, choices, and preferences. Instead of judging,
we are open and try to understand. When a child is crying, for example, instead of
seeing it as an annoying disruption, we try to understand what the child might be
trying to communicate. Montessori encourages respect for the child's unique process
of development and learning, their capabilities, and their growth.

We communicate with respect in both our tone and words. We are not patronizing. We don't label children or call them names. We don't speak harshly to them. We are conscious of the effects of our words. We also give them space to speak while we listen and consider, without talking over them. We give them opportunities to participate, and we acknowledge their contributions.

Respect is also evident in the way we handle and touch our child. We ask, first, for their permission and then use soft, gentle, noninvasive hands that consider their experience (unless their safety is at risk). We show respect by preparing our spaces in such a way that considers our child's needs and accommodates them accordingly.

Montessori is an attitude of humility and constant curiosity. Dr. Montessori's own curiosity and humility, her constant questioning to understand children, fueled the development of the Montessori philosophy. As the adults, we do not see ourselves as "sages on the stage" who have all the answers and fill our child with knowledge. Instead, we are "guides on the side," staying curious as we walk beside and collaborate with our children, learning from them and with them and staying open to new possibilities. And we stay humble, allowing our child to make their own discoveries and develop their intelligence.

Montessori is an attitude of openness and acceptance. We accept and welcome the children in our care the way they are, with curiosity about their needs and a willingness to modify our environments and expectations to allow them to bloom.

Montessori is an attitude of patience and trust. We are slow and deliberate in our interactions, taking time to model activities and behavior. We also wait and watch, so we can observe what our child is showing us. We give them time and space to do the things they've mastered, and opportunities to practice the things they have not. We are patient as they develop at their own pace.

Just as the gardener prepares the soil, trusting that the plant will sprout; feeds the soil, trusting that the plant will grow; weeds, waters, prunes, and cares for the plant, always with trust; we, too, trust that the child will develop. We prepare the environment and nurture the child with trust and with patience. We trust their abilities to do, to think, to be. We work with them to develop these abilities, and then we trust them to use them.

> Montessori is a belief in the potential and the abilities of the child. The belief that children are always capable given the opportunity and the right environment. The belief in the innate goodness of children and their ability to learn.

Montessori as wisdom

Of the many gifts that Montessori has given us, the most critical one is wisdom: understanding how children develop and how we can support them through their own metamorphosis.

The Montessori approach helps educators, parents, and caregivers understand and recognize the stages of our child's development. It teaches us to identify all changes— even when the signs are barely perceptible. The *human tendencies* and the *planes of development*, both Montessori terms, provide a valuable framework to help us understand, guide, and support our children as they grow and transform toward adulthood.

Dr. Montessori used the analogy of a caterpillar's metamorphosis from egg to caterpillar to chrysalis to butterfly to describe the child's development. Children go on a similar journey; at each stage, they are like completely different beings. They grow and change, physically and psychologically. Sometimes the changes are obvious, and other times, they are barely noticeable. Sometimes the changes are uncomfortable—for the child and for us—and hard to understand. But these changes are part of the natural path of development on the way to adulthood. To unfurling their wings to fly. (For a beautiful story about Junnifa and the children watching a butterfly's development, read "A Caterpillar's Journey" found in the online appendix at workman.com/montessori.)

THE HUMAN TENDENCIES

"One of Dr. Montessori's great contributions to the subject of child study was that of the human tendencies. . . . The human tendencies are innate in man. They are the characteristics, the propensities which allowed the human being, from his first inception on earth, to become aware of his environment, to learn and understand it. . . . Each child, as he is born, enters, as did the very first human being, an environment created for him but unknown to him. If he was to live his life securely within it, he had to have a way of making a knowledge of it. This way was through the human tendencies."

—Margaret E. Stephenson, "Dr. Maria Montessori—A Contemporary Educator?"

"Human tendencies" are the universal natural inclinations of human beings—the ways we think, act, and respond to adapt to our environment and meet our material and spiritual needs. When the human tendencies are nurtured, they aid our child's self-construction (how they take in and discover everything around them to create their personality) and "adaptation" (how our child becomes a citizen of their time, place, and culture). Human tendencies are a cornerstone of the Montessori practice. Our role as caregivers is to ensure that conditions are right for the human tendencies to be expressed and to remove any obstacles that might interfere with them.

What are the human tendencies?

Imagine for a moment that we have just gotten off a plane in a new country. What might we do first? Maybe we'd meet our family members or friends before getting a taxi to our hotel. We might then check in to our hotel, rest a bit, and head out to explore. We might visit places of interest, try the local cuisine, listen to some music, or go to a museum. We might stop at the store on our way back to our hotel and buy some things—we'd most likely do the currency conversions to make sure the prices make sense. We might plan to return to our hotel, so we can text our family back home to share some of our experiences. But imagine that when we came back, our hotel was no longer where we'd left it. We might hesitate to explore further until we had sorted out the situation.

This journey we just went on illustrates many of the human tendencies: exploration, orientation, order, communication, the mathematical mind, imagination, abstraction. We'll explore these further below along with the other human tendencies of movement, work, exactness, repetition, self-perfection, social development, and expression.

Exploration

We humans explore to become familiar with our environment. We search, investigate, and experience through movement, our senses, our intellect, and our imagination.

Physical, cognitive, social, and spiritual exploration comes naturally to children. In the early years, most exploration is physical—a newborn searching for their mother's nipple, a toddler touching everything in reach, a child climbing furniture. As our child gets older, their exploration becomes more cognitive and social and then, later, spiritual. It is through exploration that our child gains the reference points they need to explore even further.

There is so much that children need to know and explore as they go through childhood. *What are those things? How do I get around? How do I read? Write? What is appropriate? What do I enjoy? What is safe? How much of this is fun? How was this made? Oh, there were people even before my grandparents? How did they live? There are other countries, continents, planets? Where are they? What happens there?*

Children explore their environment to understand and master their place, time, and culture. To orient themselves. Once they adapt to their environment, they can work to change it or improve it.

Our role: We can support our children by providing resources to aid their exploration. When our child is jumping on the sofa, instead of simply stopping them, we can try to understand what they are exploring—perhaps the capacity of their body, or the sound of their jumping, or even what is allowed or not allowed. Then we can provide appropriate alternatives for their exploration.

Dr. Montessori believed that we should provide the child younger than 3 years old with the home, the 3- to 6-year-old child with the world, and the 6- to 12-year-old child with the universe. As the child gets older, we can incorporate new tools, agreements, or boundaries, as well as proper guidance, for exploration.

Orientation

Orientation is the tendency and ability to align or anchor ourselves—to place ourselves physically or psychologically in relation to our environment or situation. Orientation is usually the first step in exploration. When a child is oriented, they feel secure and have a starting point for exploration.

Humans have a need to know where they are and what to expect. It's important to observe our children and understand how much orientation they require to feel safe.

A newborn's point of reference is their mother's heartbeat or voices familiar from the womb. A young child in the park might look behind them for their parent or caregiver to orient themselves before gaining confidence and exploring more freely. If a child is starting a new school, they will want to be oriented on the first day to things like the toilets, where they store their belongings, eat lunch, and the general order of the day. An older child gains more points of reference, not just physical ones—they orient themselves with what they already know or believe about a subject they've previously explored as well as orienting themselves with rules or expectations.

Our role: We can prepare the physical, cognitive, social, and spiritual environment that our child will orient themselves around. We can provide opportunities for exploration so that our child develops even more points of reference. We can help our child understand the expectations and limits of their environments and ensure that they have anchors to count on throughout their day—in their home, their classrooms, and their interactions. We can be as predictable as possible in our reactions and interactions so that they can know what to expect.

Order

In Montessori, we often say "a place for everything and everything in its place."
When there is physical order, we are more likely to have internal—psychological and
cognitive—order. Order can also be a logical, predictable sequence in the child's daily
life, one that they can rely on and that anchors them. For younger children, an anchor
may be an action, like a song sung every morning. For an older child, the anchor might
be a regularly scheduled event, like dinner at six o'clock. Order includes the tendency to
classify and organize what we know and learn, including ideas, values, and feelings.

Our role: We create order in the child's environment and help our child create, maintain,
and restore order. We can help them build skills, create systems, and guide them. We can
ensure that they have daily, weekly, and seasonal rhythms and rituals, so they experience
predictability.

Communication, expression, and social development

Communication is the natural inclination to share our ideas, experiences, and concerns,
as well as to listen to and understand those of others. It supports the human tendency for
social relations and collaboration. Babies are often born able to suck, swallow, and cry as
a form of communication. By the time the child is 3 years old, they have usually learned
the language(s) of their community and can express their thoughts fluently. Then the
child develops the ability to read, write, sing, gesture, and create art and poetry, and may
learn to speak additional languages.

We have a human tendency for expression, the desire to express ourselves through art,
music, and dance. They are sources of happiness. Even babies move to the rhythm when
they hear music. Most children from 3 to 12 years old are naturally drawn to open-
ended art activities. They seem to naturally want to draw, paint, or arrange rocks and
petals into designs. All of these are forms of expression.

As mammals, we have a desire to be part of a group, and we have a human tendency for
social development. We have a need to belong and to collaborate. The social environment
grows with the child—a baby is part of their family; then it extends to other caregivers;
then perhaps to a nursery or a playgroup; then to preschool, grade school, and other
activities and groups. We will look at their social development in detail in chapter 6.

Our role: Children absorb language easily, so we can prepare a language-rich environment
by talking (or signing) to our children, reading to them, singing to them, sharing stories,
and letting them watch while we interact with others. As our child grows, we can use
even more precise and rich language—instead of "flower," we can say "red hibiscus
flower." When our children want to share their experiences, thoughts, or questions, we
can give them our time and attention.

We can provide opportunities for artistic expression and also the tools of expression, like pencil and paper, paintbrushes and paint, and music players, song lyrics, and instruments.

We can support the child's social development by teaching the expected rules, behaviors, and culture in our family and community. We can support our children as they learn how to interact and be members of our family group and then with other individuals and groups.

The mathematical mind

Humans are born with a very logical mind. We use our mathematical mind when we go to the store and keep a running tally of our items in our head. We see it in the baby estimating where and how far to reach to pick up an object. We see it when we offer a child two cookies and they pick the bigger one. The mathematical mind is always at work, and it supports and works with two other tendencies, imagination and abstraction.

Our role: We can provide opportunities for our children to use their mathematical mind. Opportunities for them to solve problems, to estimate, to guess, sort, categorize, measure, and engage in activities that require analysis.

Imagination

Imagination is the ability to see things that aren't in front of us, to create solutions that do not currently exist, and to meet our needs. This starts at a very early age. A young child will learn that they still have a parent or caregiver even when they are not present in the room. Older children are able to imagine what life was like for people in early civilizations or in other places even if they have never been there. And early humans noticed animals had thick fur that protected them from the elements and imagined clothing that would do the same—they pictured it and then they created it.

Our role: Imagination is built on concrete experiences. We can support our child's imagination by providing lots of activities for hands-on exploration and discovery of the world around them in the first 6 years. For our older children, we can share stories about life and times that are different from theirs and invite them to use their imagination.

Abstraction

Abstraction is imagination's cousin. It is the ability to take the essence of something and apply it to other things. It is the ability to see beyond the concrete, to interpret, and to generalize. While abstract thoughts are present in younger children, they become very active as the child gets to be 6 years old. Abstraction and imagination are optimized once a child has a strong understanding of reality. For example, when a younger child is doing addition with golden beads in a Montessori classroom, they put 5 beads and 4 beads together and count that there are 9 beads in total. An older child will be able to abstract when they see the numbers and a plus sign and will know to add them together to get the answer.

Our role: We can help them gain understanding of key concepts, provide them tools to understand, and revisit the concepts as much as they need to until they internalize it; for example, offering concrete objects, dictionaries, etc. We can also allow the child to use their imagination to create or bring their ideas to life. This is a form of abstraction.

Movement

Movement is the ability and need to use our bodies in our environment. This is how we explore our environment and eventually improve it. This tendency is very evident in children. How many times do we comment on how our child cannot sit still? The innate drive to move helps the child's development.

Manipulation, another kind of movement, is an important form of exploration. Dr. Montessori called the hands "the instruments of the intelligence." Our hands are an important tool in our mastery of our environment, and in our ability to modify, work with, regenerate, and improve it.

Our role: Instead of being an obstacle to the child's movement and activity, we can provide opportunities and activities that help develop and refine their motor skills. We can give them room and space to jump and run. We can offer them items to manipulate that require increasing abilities.

Work, exactness, repetition, and self-perfection

It is through *work* that we improve our environment and ourselves. Once we understand our environment, our mathematical minds usually see ways to modify it to better meet our needs. We can imagine these modifications and then bring them to reality through work. This could be as easy as oiling a squeaky chair or fabricating a toolbelt with pockets that hold special items.

Along with our inclination to work, humans have a tendency toward *exactness* and *self-perfection*. We have a need for precision. We see this in children learning to ride a bike, write, climb, or acquire any new skill they desire. Even when they fall or fail, they try again. Self-perfection is the desire to continually improve ourselves and do the best for ourselves and for others. We see exactness in the child's questioning. They keep asking, seeking for exact answers around what things are and how they work.

Repetition helps us master an activity. Mastering an activity gives us control of the environment and leads to confidence and contentment. When our children reach for the same activity over and over, they are acting on their human tendency, and we can appreciate the value of this repetition. An older child between 6 and 12 years old will also repeat but may not want to repeat it in the same way each time. Instead, they will look for ways to repeat with variations.

Our role: We can provide activities that are on the edge of our child's ability—not too easy and not too hard, and constantly adding new levels of difficulty—to support our child's work toward self-perfection. Children are often more focused on the process than on the product. We can support this by resisting the urge to help when they struggle and allowing them to repeat steps. Repetition requires time, so we can make sure the child has blocks of time in which they can explore and repeat without interruption.

OBSERVATION TO SUPPORT THE HUMAN TENDENCIES

- Observe our child to see which tendencies are at work and how the child is acting on them.
- Prepare our environment to be rich with opportunities and activities that support the tendencies.
- If, over time, we do not observe a particular tendency at work, look for obstacles impeding it and try to remove them.
- Evaluate ourselves and our environment to see if and how our child's tendencies are being supported. What can we change or do better?

THE FOUR PLANES OF DEVELOPMENT

Dr. Montessori's *four planes of development* is a framework to describe how humans develop from birth to maturity (around 24 years old). We can use the four planes to understand the characteristics of our child at every age, so we can support them through every stage. Each plane is around 6 years long: ages 0 to 6 years (infancy), 6 to 12 years (childhood), 12 to 18 years (adolescence), and 18 to 24 years (maturity). Interestingly, Dr. Montessori included the ages 18 to 24 in childhood years before studies on the brain found that the prefrontal cortex (where rational decision-making is located) is still developing into our mid-twenties.

Dr. Montessori used the word "rebirth" to describe the changes that occur in the child as they move from one plane to the next. At each stage, it can feel like a new and different child emerges, one with new characteristics and needs, one who acts on their human tendencies in new ways and learns in new and different ways. Just like a caterpillar goes through many physical and behavioral transformations on its way to becoming a butterfly, so does our child as they mature.

Each plane builds on the previous one, with the acquisitions of each plane preparing and laying a foundation for the next. It is important to know that while Dr. Montessori noted that each plane lasts for about 6 years, the moment of transition is different for every child. For example, some children start to show the signs of switching to the second plane at 5.5 years and others at 7 years. Transitioning from one plane to the next is usually gradual, with the child sometimes having one leg in one plane and the other in the next. We can use the ages as guides and look out for the other signs and characteristics of transitioning, which we will discuss, to recognize when our child is moving from one plane to the next.

When we have an understanding of each plane, we can adapt our method, environment, and response to meet our child's needs. Our role as parents, caregivers, educators, or loving adults changes as our child moves through the planes of development.

CONSTRUCTIVE RHYTHM OF LIFE

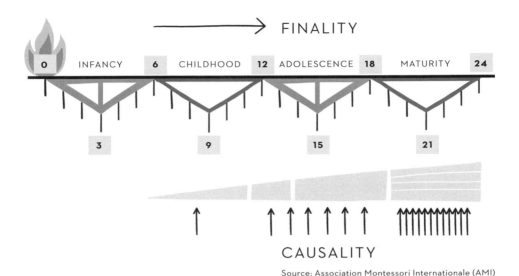

Source: Association Montessori Internationale (AMI)

This diagram was presented by Dr. Montessori in Perugia, Italy, in 1950 to explain the four planes of development.

- We see four repeated triangles. Each triangle represents a plane that consists of 6 years.

- The first and third planes are subdivided into subplanes; for example, the first plane of development is made up of the 0-3 subplane (the acquisition phase) and the 3-6 subplane (the refinement and consolidation phase).

- Dr. Montessori observed that humans develop in cycles, with periods of rapid development followed by periods of consolidation. This was counter to the more commonly held belief of the time that human development follows a linear or straight path where the youngest learners learn the least and the older learners are capable of learning the most. This traditional view of development is shown in the lower half of the diagram (blue triangles showing the amount of education starting from 6 years and increasing into the college years).

- The planes share similarities. The first and third planes have thick orange lines because they are dynamic, explosive, and dramatic periods of physical and psychological growth. The second and fourth planes have thin blue lines because they are calmer periods of steady growth. This is what we call in Montessori "parallel planes."

The first plane: 0 to 6 years, infancy

The first plane of development is marked by explosive growth and significant physical, cognitive, and psychological changes. The child at 6 years old looks very different from the newborn and knows so much more.

The child in the first plane is a sensorial explorer. They receive sensorial impressions from the environment and use them to build their intelligence and personality.

Because the child in this plane is focused on constructing themselves, while they may like being around others, they prefer to work on their own or side by side with another person. This will change radically in the second plane, ages 6 to 12.

The child in the first plane has what Dr. Montessori called an *absorbent mind*. From birth until age 6, the child takes everything in without effort and without discrimination. They absorb the sights, smell, tastes, behaviors, and culture around them. This is an unconscious process that doesn't involve our child's choice or effort. It happens automatically and with ease. Their mind is like a sponge that soaks up whatever liquid it is immersed in. It cannot decide what part of the water to absorb—it takes it all in. The things that our child absorbs become a part of their personality and their self.

The first subplane (0 to 3 years)

A child does so much in these years. They learn how to walk, talk, act, and be a person of their time and place. It is a period of great physical growth and transformation. Our child goes from having no teeth to a full mouth of teeth, from only drinking milk to being able to eat everything, from crying as a newborn to possibly speaking multiple languages. During these years, they go from instinctively kicking their legs to rolling, crawling, standing, walking, running, jumping, and enjoying a wide range of movement. From batting their hands to using a refined pincer grip (holding something between their thumb and index finger) for specific tasks like sewing and writing. From peeing and pooping by instinct to controlling the process and using the toilet independently. They go from not knowing much about the world to knowing how things work in their home and the world around them. They know how to think and solve some problems. They know some of the norms and cultures of their group and are beginning to understand what is appropriate. They can make connections and draw some conclusions.

The child at 3 years old, especially if they have been given the right environment, is a creator who has already accomplished so much. They have created what Dr. Montessori called their *psychic organs*—language, movement, culture, intelligence, and a will. The amazing thing is that they have done all this without realizing it or even remembering the process. This is why Dr. Montessori called the child at this stage *the unconscious creator*.

continued on page 28

SENSITIVE PERIODS

"A sensitive period refers to a special sensibility which a creature acquires in its infantile state, while it is still in the process of evolution. It is a transient disposition and limited to the acquisition of a particular trait. Once this trait, or characteristic, has been acquired, the special sensibility disappears."

—Dr. Maria Montessori, *The Secret of Childhood*

A sensitive period is a time or stage in the child's life when they seem to be drawn to a certain aspect of the environment. We notice them constantly returning to an activity or repeating an action. Through this work over a period of time, they acquire a new skill or ability. The child may be able to make the acquisition at a different time, but it will require a lot more effort.

Sensitive periods are extremely active and concentrated in the first plane of development. Dr. Montessori called them *beams of light*, *vital impulses*, and *creative sensibilities*. While the absorbent mind allows the child to take in everything in the environment indiscriminately, the sensitive periods, like beams of light, focus the child on one aspect of the environment. The skills acquired in each sensitive period helps the child act on their human tendencies.

SENSITIVE PERIODS ARE TRANSIENT. They eventually disappear, whether or not the skill is acquired. This work can be done tangibly (physically) or intangibly (mentally).

SENSITIVE PERIODS WILL OCCUR NATURALLY FOR EVERY CHILD. However, they need an adult to support them by preparing the right environment and encouraging activity within the environment. For example, a child in a sensitive period for language is drawn to language and has the ability to develop language skills. However, if there is no language in the environment, they won't acquire the skill, and, eventually, the sensitive period will pass.

RECOGNIZING SENSITIVE PERIODS. Sensitive periods happen around the same time for most children, so they can be anticipated and identified by observation.

Some things that can be observed during a sensitive period are:

- An attraction to a certain element of the environment

- Increased activity and repetition leading to concentration

- A feeling of refreshment and satisfaction at the end of work

The sensitive periods that manifest strongly in the first plane are:
- Language
    - Spoken language: in utero to 2.5–3 years
    - Writing: from 3.5 years to 4.5 years
    - Reading: 4.5 years to 5.5 years

- Weaning: 6 months to 12 months

- Order: birth to 5 years (peaking between 1.5 years and 2.5 years)

- Tiny detail and small objects: from 1 year to 4 years

- Movement
    - Acquisition: from birth to 2.5 years
    - Refinement and coordination: from 2.5 years to 4.5 years

- Sensorial exploration and classification
    - Acquisition and accumulation of impressions: in utero to 3 years
    - Classification and organization of impressions: 2.5 years to 6 years

- Numbers and mathematics: from 4 to 6 years

- Manners and courtesies: 2.5 years to 6 years

- Assimilation of images (storing images/details in their mind): birth to 6 years

- Music: 2 years to 6 years

NOTE: 1. Ages are for guidance only; all children develop on their own timeline.
2. If a sensitive period is missed, the child will still be able to learn the skill but it will take more effort (like learning a foreign language as an adult).

The second subplane (3 to 6 years)

In the second subplane, our child goes from an unconscious creator to a conscious worker. Guided by the tendencies of repetition, exactness, and self-perfection, our 3- to 6-year-old child makes a more intentional and deliberate effort to refine and master the abilities they acquired in the first subplane.

From the ages of 3 to 6, our child is active, seeking to use their hands and master their environment. Dr. Montessori called this "the age of play" and described play as the child's work. Our child wants more precise language, more precise movement; they want to understand the world around them better and do things for themselves. If they could express what they want from us, they would say, "Help me to do it myself." They want tools that they can use, and they want to participate in life around them. These children are constantly asking "What?" and "Why?." They want to know the names of things and what they do. They want to do what they see the adults around them doing. They want to perfect the construction of themselves as an individual and forge independence through the ability to care for themselves—like eating and dressing themselves and using the toilet independently.

The adult and environment for the first-plane child

Our role during this stage is to give the child security and unconditional love, and prepare our home as recommended by Dr. Montessori in a way that allows our child to feel oriented and provides predictability. A home is a love-filled nurturing environment with a consistent caregiver. The environment is prepared with beauty and order, filled with rich language and sensorial impressions. Things for the child to see, touch, smell, taste, and hear. We can ensure that there are opportunities for the child to explore through movement, manipulation, and their senses, with opportunities to freely explore both the indoors and the outdoors.

In the first plane, our child will:

- Develop coordinated movement.
- Develop intelligence (an understanding of "What?," "Where?," and some "How?" around their immediate world). They are ready for the universe.
- Learn to order and classify their impressions (e.g., lightest to darkest, smallest to biggest, smoothest to roughest).
- Refine their sensorial perceptions in order to make judgments.
- Develop the language(s) of the environment.
- Develop functional independence (e.g., to dress themselves, care for their body).
- Develop a unique character and personality and adapt to their time, place, and culture.

Second plane (6 to 12 years): childhood

Unlike the busy, fast-moving first plane, the second plane is, according to Dr. Montessori, a "calm period of uniform growth." It begins with significant physical changes. Our child starts to lose their baby teeth and grow permanent teeth. They become leaner and taller, with more balanced proportions. Their hair texture changes and their feet grow bigger to balance their growing height. Most of the early childhood illnesses are behind them, and the hormones of adolescence have yet to kick in. So our child is strong and generally happy. Their body is capable of so much, and they know it, so they test and push their bodies. They want to see how fast they can run, how high they can climb, how many cartwheels they can do.

There are also psychological changes:

Social. Our 6- to 12-year-old child is confident and secure in their family, so they begin to seek more time with others. They want playdates and sleepovers. They want to be part of groups and are influenced by their peers. They want to explore farther away from home in the community. They may also lose some of their sweetness. Dr. Montessori and many of us who have children this age notice that they can exhibit a kind of hardness or toughness that can come off as unkind and even rude. (Dr. Montessori called this "the age of rudeness.")

As a younger child at the end of the first plane, they enjoyed being part of a social group and knew largely how to act within the group. The child in the second plane wants to create their own group, to determine the hierarchies, the roles, and the rules. At times, we may need to remind them of, and uphold, our family agreements (the freedoms and limits of our home), which provide them guidance and security about how to behave in social groups.

This is also a period of hero worship, as our child finds people to admire and be inspired by.

Cognitive. The child in the second plane outgrows the absorbent mind. Now they can move, speak, act, and express the culture of their environment. They are strong and capable, independent and intelligent, confident and articulate. They are a person of their time and place. They now need and use their *logical, reasoning mind.*

Our child is no longer a sensorial explorer; they are an intellectual explorer. They spend a lot of time abstracting and imagining, and there is no limit to their exploration— they only need opportunities and the right conditions. Adults tend to underestimate the abilities of the child in this plane. We can offer them wider contact with the environment to feed their hunger for knowledge and culture.

Dr. Montessori said that this is the plane for optimal learning, and she invited adults to sow as many seeds of interest as possible, to give our child culture, and offer them the universe to explore. Our child has the advantage of physical strength, good health, and interest driven by their logical inquiring minds. We are to share with them the world of nature and the accomplishments of humans over time. We tell stories and build their interest and curiosity, while also helping them make connections between concepts and ideas, and eventually building their own understanding of the universe.

Our child not only wants to know "what," they also want to know "why" and "how."

Moral. While the child in the first plane mostly accepts whatever we tell them is not appropriate, the child in the second plane wants to know what it means to be appropriate and why something is not okay. It may feel like they are always tattling and reporting someone for doing the wrong thing, but they are trying to understand what is right and wrong and what is fair and just. *Why is it right? When is it right? All the time or sometimes? How does one respond? Do they respond this way sometimes or all the time?* They are instinctively trying to develop their moral compass.

This is a sensitive period for justice. We hear them say "It's not fair" so many times. It is because they have a heightened sense of justice and want things to be fair. They have intense feelings and rebel against injustice, including to animals.

This is also a time when the adult must be conscious of being honest and morally correct in front of the child. Lying to the child while they're in this plane can break the child's trust in them. The child in this plane is a cultural explorer who encompasses the right and the wrong, the good and the bad. They don't just absorb the world around them; they seek answers.

Emotional. Children in this plane have an understanding of reality and how things are meant to be. They practice adapting their behavior to circumstances. They now have self-control, can self-regulate, and can delay gratification. When these factors are working together, the child becomes an integrated personality. They are able to research and learn things, control themselves, and question things while staying regulated.

While in the first plane the child had a high sense of physical and external order, the second-plane child may seem disorderly as their focus moves to internal, intellectual order. The first-plane child also exerted maximum physical effort, wanting to use a lot of energy, but the second-plane child with their logical mind wants to be efficient. They want to exert minimum effort for maximum results. The second-plane child's maximum effort is more intellectual and social.

The adult and environment for the second-plane child

We can sow seeds of interest and provide resources and opportunities for our child to pursue these interests. We can tell them stories and encourage them to use their imagination and their logical, reasoning mind. They need a lot of intellectual stimulation.

Our role is to still provide the love and security of home while also trusting and giving the child freedom and opportunities to explore beyond home. We can prepare them for interactions with other groups. School is a great way to extend the child's community, but they also need environments beyond school, like scouting groups or musical groups.

The second-plane child needs physical activity and social interaction, so this is a great time for group sports. They also need good role models and people to look up to. We can provide opportunities for the child to be a part of groups that work together on projects or activities. This allows them to learn how to work within a team and also figure out group dynamics. It is also a rich field for moral exploration. We can act as a guide for social interactions and help the child work through the inevitable conflicts that arise as a result of being part of a social group.

Our child will have come to the end of the second plane when we recognize that:

- They are strong and stable both physically and mentally.
- They are gregarious and have good peer relationships. They love being part of a pack.
- They are a social being able to participate and associate positively in groups.
- They can control their will and self-regulate and therefore also listen to instructions and adjust their behavior.
- They have developed a logical, reasoning mind. There will be critical thinking, cognitive flexibility, a great imagination, and love for exploring abstraction, whether in the form of ideas, formulas, or concepts.
- They are confident, knowledgeable, and responsible.
- They have a strong sense of justice and a strong moral compass and the ability to distinguish between right and wrong.
- They have a rich knowledge of the world and the universe. They can make connections and see interdependences—how things affect others— and out of this grows a sense of responsibility and stewardship.
- They have achieved intellectual independence. They have interests and the ability to explore and enrich them.

Third plane (12 to 18 years): adolescence; Fourth plane (18 to 24 years): maturity

The third plane is another explosive and creative period, similar to the first plane. This time, it is the adult that is being created. The fourth plane is the period between childhood and adulthood when our child enters the world, the *unprepared environment*. This again is a more stable period with fewer physical changes.

We'll look at the third and fourth planes more in chapter 9, "What's Next."

FIRST PLANE	SECOND PLANE	THIRD PLANE	FOURTH PLANE
0–6 years	**6–12 years**	**12–18 years**	**18–24 years**
We are planting the seeds.	The stem is growing tall and strong.	Leaves and blossoms unfurl, nearing maturity.	The plant is fully grown.
• physical and biological independence • absorbent mind • concrete understanding of the world • sensorial learner • working in parallel with small amounts of collaboration • rapid growth and change	• mental independence • using their logical, reasoning mind; developing their moral sense and exploring how things work and connect • more abstraction • learning through imagination • working in groups • more stable period	• social independence • developing social policy (how they would change the world) • sharing ideas and ideals with others • enormous physical and psychological changes (similar to the first plane)	• spiritual and moral independence • giving back to society • reasoning, logical mind • more stable period (similar to the second plane)

RAISING THE MONTESSORI CHILD

3

BEING THEIR GUIDE

Montessori educators are called "guides," not "teachers." This is central to the Montessori philosophy. A Montessori guide observes the children in the class, sets up the classroom environment to meet their needs, helps connect the children to it, and makes adjustments as needed. This is different from a teacher deciding what each child needs to learn based on an arbitrary timeline or curriculum and teaching it to them.

Similarly in the home, we are not our child's boss (nagging or deciding what they have to learn, do, or be) or their servant (doing everything for them) or laissez-faire (letting them do whatever they want).

Instead, we are the child's guide.

We want our children to feel involved in the home. We want them to become independent and responsible. We want them to learn how to contribute to the family and their community. And we want to cultivate a love of learning within them. They are so capable when we allow it.

- A guide prepares a safe physical and psychological environment.
- A guide develops agreements together with the child.
- A guide observes the child and seeks to understand their needs.
- A guide fosters independence and responsibility.
- A guide sparks the child's wonder in the world around them.
- A guide nurtures connection.
- A guide builds trust.
- A guide is a model for them.
- A guide cultivates slowness.
- A guide respects the child, loves them, and accepts them.
- A guide helps them become a member of the family and society.

There is now so much research showing that children who are engaged in their own learning are more likely to develop into independent, self-directed, and lifelong learners. Children who are respected learn to respect themselves, others, and their environment. And instead of having to conform to familial or societal expectations, our children are allowed to become their true selves.

It takes practice to let go of some control. To step back and only step in when our child really needs support. To allow them to experience all of their feelings and provide support if needed, like rubbing their back or helping them make amends once they are calm. To give them time to develop skills like dressing themselves, preparing their own lunch, writing a thank-you note, or making a repair with a friend.

It can feel brave to step in and calmly and clearly set a limit to keep everyone safe. To let them know that something they are doing or saying is unkind or hurts, not in an angry way, but by modeling how to set boundaries with others that are kind and clear.

It requires patience. This is a long-term approach, not a quick fix. We are laying a foundation of trust and connection so that our child knows they can come to us even when they are not at their best, that we will love them at their worst and guide them to become independent so that they can help themselves, others, and the world.

We will need to navigate the contradictions of raising children: keeping them close yet giving them space; sparking an interest but letting them take it further on their own; allowing them freedom while setting clear limits and responsibilities; fostering a secure attachment and also letting them go.

Our role as a Montessori parent or caregiver then is to allow the child to develop naturally to their optimal potential while helping them adapt to their family and society.

> "It is necessary for the teacher to guide the child without letting him feel her presence too much, so that she may always be ready to supply the desired help, but may never be the obstacle between the child and his experience."
>
> —Dr. Maria Montessori, *Dr. Montessori's Own Handbook*

LAYING A STRONG FOUNDATION

1. Make agreements for our home

In Montessori classrooms, there are clear freedoms and limits. These freedoms and limits—these agreements—are known to everyone and are predictable. In the 6 to 12 classroom, the children are involved in deciding what the agreements should be. Kim Anh Nguyễn Anderson, a Montessori educator of over 15 years, says that this process of making agreements together makes the learners feel safe and like they belong.

Together with our children, we can make agreements for our home. The more involved our child is in making the agreements, the more likely they are to be intrinsically motivated to keep to them. The goal is that everyone in the family agrees on, contributes to, and understands the agreements. Being specific helps. If an agreement is, "We treat each other with respect," we can clarify what "respect" means—waiting for someone to finish speaking before speaking ourselves, using a gentle tone of voice with each other, not making fun of each other, and so on.

These agreements provide a clear base to refer to. We can ask the child, "What's our agreement about rough play?" There is not much to argue with when they have been involved in making the agreements.

Make too many agreements, and it will be hard to keep track of them. And we should be mindful of changing them too often—our children need the agreements to be predictable rather than dependent on our mood or how much sleep we had the night before. However, they are living documents, and we may need to revise them if they are not working and as our children grow. If that's the case, change the agreements at a neutral (ideally, planned) moment, like at a family meeting.

Family meetings. For children from 3 to 12 years old, having regular but informal family meetings can be helpful. The family meeting can be a space in which to develop clear house agreements, to discuss what's going well for our child and where they may need help, or to look at what's coming up for the week ahead. Some families like to add something fun to the meeting, like popcorn, or have a family meal or movie after the meeting.

With a 3- to 6-year-old, the meeting is going to be short and more adult-led, but they may have ideas about where they'd like to go on an outing or their favorite meal as a dinner suggestion. We can practice respecting and valuing their contribution. By the age of 5.5 to 6 years old, they will be well on their way to being able to participate fully in the meetings.

EXAMPLES OF FAMILY AGREEMENTS

- **WE ARE KIND TO EACH OTHER.** Even if we disagree, we will not hurt each other physically or tease each other. This teaches children to respect themselves and each other and find ways to solve disagreements through discussion.

- **WE GET PERMISSION BEFORE TOUCHING ANYONE.**

- **WE SIT AT THE (DINING) TABLE TO EAT.** This keeps food to one area of the home and helps limit mindless eating while playing. It also gives families a regular time to be together and have conversation and allows us to get to know each other's friends better, too, when they are visiting.

- **WE CONTRIBUTE TO THE HOUSEHOLD.** No matter what our age, we help around the house, and our help is valued.

- **WE ENGAGE IN ROUGH PLAY ONLY BY MUTUAL CONSENT.** This is a mouthful for young children, but they understand its meaning. If someone says "stop," they are saying that they are not having fun anymore and the game needs to end.

- **WE ARE RESPECTFUL AND SAFE TOWARD OURSELVES, EACH OTHER, AND THE ENVIRONMENT.** That could mean singing as long as it doesn't bother others, uplifting and encouraging others, or using a bookmark rather than folding pages in order to care for our books.

If we are raising children with a partner or co-parent, it can be a good idea to have a separate meeting once a week to discuss things between the adults. Going over all the practical things that come up in the family during the week—appointments, commitments, meal planning, transportation arrangements—can bring calm to the upcoming days. It also allows any invisible load to become visible and equitably distributed. Periodic meetings can also be arranged with a grandparent or caregiver who regularly looks after the child or children to keep everyone on the same page (as much as possible).

Ad hoc agreements. Dr. Jane Nelsen, author of the Positive Discipline books, also suggests making ad hoc agreements, which we can kindly and gently hold them to. For example, if our child has some work they need to do, we can ask them what time they'd like to get it done. They love to choose exact times, like 5:33 p.m. If they need reminding, we can say, "It's 5:33" and wait for them to process what we have said. If they ignore us or say, "But . . . ," we can calmly repeat ourselves: "It's 5:33." We can hold them to the agreement they made in a kind and clear way.

2. Prepare the physical and psychological environment

Physical environment. We can set up a physical environment where our child feels welcome, where they can find everything they need, where they know where things belong and can put them away, where they can be independent, where they can find ways to entertain and challenge themselves, and where they can learn to care for these spaces. The environment will be adapted as our child grows. We go into this in more detail in the next chapter.

Psychological environment. We are also responsible for preparing the psychological environment of our home. This means a space in which our child feels emotionally safe and free to explore. We can ensure that our child feels safe coming to us when they are having a hard time. And we can be predictable, clear, and consistent, so they know what to expect. We want to create a home where they can feel "seen, safe, soothed, and secure," as described by Daniel Siegel and Tina Payne Bryson in their book *The Power of Showing Up*.

Safety and supervision. Our child relies on us to provide physical safety and supervision. Their prefrontal cortex, the part of the brain responsible for rational decision-making, isn't fully developed until their early twenties. So "it is our job to keep them safe," a phrase we learned from our Montessori friend Jeanne-Marie Paynel.

This doesn't mean wrapping them up in bubble wrap or being a helicopter parent, but we can find ways for them to do what they'd like to do and keep them safe at the same time. If a child wants to climb a tree, rather than saying no, we can help them choose a tree that is the appropriate size and has sturdy branches, explain how to test a branch, and show them how to climb down. We can allow our children to have friends over and make their own pizza. We can supervise to make sure they are safe but allow them to burn the pizza if they forget to turn on the timer, or ask them to wash up at the end even if the dishes don't get perfectly clean.

A child of 6 to 12 years old may want to do more on their own outside of the house. If we live in a city, we will likely need to supervise, but we can still offer our child more freedom. For example, we can let them research their route on public transportation, go with them but allow them to get on the bus going in the wrong direction, and then let them work out how to fix their mistake.

Removing obstacles. We can also identify and remove any obstacles to our children's development. We can address physical obstacles, such as placing their plates, glasses, and snacks in a low drawer so they are easily accessible or placing their toothbrush, toothpaste, and a mirror at their height to encourage toothbrushing.

A child from 3 to 6 years old might still be hanging on to things like a pacifier, a diaper, or a stroller that may be keeping them from moving on to the next stage of development. For a child from 6 to 12 years old, we might find that too many scheduled activities or too much screen time is limiting their development.

Other obstacles may include too many interruptions (we can set up a space where our child can choose to be alone), limited opportunities for hands-on discovery (we can provide some new and exciting opportunities for exploration), and too many new things competing for their attention (we can limit the number of activities available at one time).

Sometimes, *we* are the obstacle to our child's development. For example, by telling them what they should wear; not allowing them space to develop their own ideas; doing their homework for them; nagging them constantly; not allowing time for conversation, free play, or time outdoors; or not making them feel safe and accepted.

3. Nurture connection with our child

As Simone wrote in *The Montessori Toddler*, "Without connection, we get very little cooperation."

From the time our child is in utero, we begin to build a connection with them. We are learning who they are, and they are learning about us too. But within a few years, our relationship may become less about connection and more about accomplishing tasks and delivering instructions to get through a busy day. It is not surprising then that our child stops listening to us. If instead most of our daily interactions with our child are rooted in connection, then our (less frequent) requests for cooperation are more likely to be heard. As our child gets older and their world and social circles expand, it's even more important to maintain a strong connection.

Connecting with our child can look like:

- Snuggling up with some books first thing in the morning, before getting ready for the day
- Taking time for family meals and sitting at the table together (no screens allowed)
- Showing an interest in our child's passions even if we don't necessarily share them
- Finding time for conversation, particularly in instances where we don't need to make eye contact—while biking or in the car, cooking or washing dishes
- Not judging what they tell us so they feel they can come to us without being subjected to a lecture or unsolicited advice
- Making a list of things we enjoy doing together—and then doing them
- Putting on music to dance to in the kitchen or sing along to together

- Having family rituals—Sunday-morning pancakes or a weekly outing with the whole family
- Creating a set of family values (e.g., being environmentally friendly, connecting with nature, or giving to the community), perhaps made into a poster and hung on the wall
- Turning off our phones, putting them away, and being truly present with our family
- Responding in a predictable way in moments of conflict
- Being a reliable guide when outside the home ("Use your eyes to look at the fragile things in the store.")
- Finding moments of one-on-one time with each child in the family
- Allowing space for them to finish what they are saying ("I'll first finish listening to Oliver and then I'd love to hear what you have to say, Emma.")
- Having a sense of humor (including some potty humor!)

4. Build trust with them

A large part of raising a Montessori child is trust—if we show our child that we trust them, they build trust in themselves and learn to trust their environment.

Learning to trust themselves might look like a baby batting a ball and making it move (*I did it!*), a toddler wiping up some milk they spilled (*I can clean it up!*), a preschooler feeding the family pet (*I can care for others!*), a school-age child developing ways to help society (*I can make a change!*).

As the adult, we show our child we trust them by:

- Allowing them to do things for themselves (e.g., fetch something from a tree while we hold the ladder).
- Giving them opportunities to do things they are capable of (e.g., serve a cup of tea to a visiting grandparent).
- Respecting their opinions (e.g., by making them feel heard).
- Giving them responsibilities and not nagging them (e.g., for a younger child, trusting that they will brush their teeth when they are ready; and for an older child, letting them decide when to do their homework and follow through by themselves).
- Letting them overhear us telling others that we trust them (e.g., standing up for them if someone does not believe them). One morning at church, Junnifa's son missed out on sweets that had been passed around. When he asked for one, he was told by the caregiver that he had already had one. Junnifa stepped in to say that she trusted her son, and if he said he had not yet received one, she believed him. This was a huge deposit in the trust bank with her son.

- Valuing them as contributing members of the family (e.g., relying on them to empty the trash or to help ready the home for visitors).
- Involving them in making and sticking to agreements (e.g., about whether they are allowed screen time and how much).
- Allowing them times to be in charge (e.g., for a younger child, to choose on the map which animals we will visit at the zoo; and for an older child, to use a map to lead the way on a hike).
- Being understanding about their mistakes (e.g., doing our best to stay calm if our child breaks something while giving them an opportunity to repair the object and make it up to us).
- Resisting the urge to rescue our child when they make a mistake (e.g., delivering a forgotten sports bag or nagging them to do their homework so they don't get in trouble at school). We can trust that the child will feel the consequences and learn to adjust their behavior for themselves.
- Being honest with our child (e.g., giving them age-appropriate, clear, and direct answers to their tough questions about things like death, divorce, sex, race). See chapter 7 for more of these conversations.

For those of us used to taking control, we can take the role of hands-off supervisor rather than micromanaging boss. We can let go of societal expectations about how and when our child should develop and trust that they are growing on their own timeline. It takes trust to believe that our child will become interested in reading or mathematics or sports even if we don't force it. We can focus on how they are developing as a whole human and contributing in the way they were meant to.

5. Be a model for them

We ask our children to be kind to each other, to speak softly, to wait their turn, to be honest, and more. But remember, our actions speak louder than our words.

Here are some examples of things we can do to be a model for our child:

- Care for ourselves and our environment, such as by keeping our clothing and spaces neat and organized.
- Take time to move and care for our bodies.
- Rest and have some items in our home to invite resting, like an eye pillow, a cozy blanket, a yoga mat, or a floor cushion.
- Care for others—bake something for a friend or neighbor, stop to talk with someone asking for money, help an elderly person with some shopping or housework.
- Be mindful with our movements (difficult for some of us). We can apologize if we bump into someone.

- Resolve conflicts in front of them so they learn how we repair a rupture.
- Let them know when we learn that something we thought was true is actually misinformation. Learning, unlearning, relearning.
- Take and give space in terms of how we use our voices, how we pause and listen.
- Spend less time looking at our screens and more time looking into others' eyes.
- Be careful how we talk about our work and friends. Our children will observe our work and social habits, our focus, and our joy.
- Say thank you, accept compliments, and graciously receive feedback.
- Apologize when we get it wrong ("What I should have said is . . . " or "What I should have done is . . .").
- Be lifelong learners and exhibit a love of learning.

LEARNING WHO OUR CHILD IS

1. Observe them

As a parent, it's hard to be objective about our own child because we are so connected with them. Observing allows us to step back and more clearly see who our child is, how they are unfolding, how their needs are changing, what skills they are practicing, and which skills they still need to learn.

It's easy to get activated by our children (they don't seem to listen to us, do something careless, or appear to lack appreciation), and observing can give us the space to pause, see things clearly, and respond rather than react.

Observing is not easy. In the *1921 London Lectures*, Dr. Montessori talked about the need to prepare our eyes to observe, to draw a bead across a string every time we want to interfere, to practice being silent and motionless, to observe everything in our field of vision, to be patient, and to pay attention to uninteresting things (because we don't know what will become interesting).

"It is not always imperative to see big things, but it is of paramount importance to see the beginnings of things. At their origins there are little glimmers that can be recognized as soon as something new is developing."

—Dr. Maria Montessori, *Education and Peace*

SOME THINGS TO OBSERVE

When we observe, we see our child with fresh eyes without any preconceptions or judgments. We can take a notebook and pen and do a 5-minute observation, pretending to be a scientist who has never met our child before. We can make a running record of what we see, be like a video camera recording all the details. Even the smallest moments can provide valuable information. Some ideas what to look for:

· MOVEMENT: how they walk, stand, sit, climb, skip, etc.; how they hold a pencil, a book, scissors, or an object they are using, etc.

· COMMUNICATION: aspects of their speech; their articulation; the speed at which they talk; their vocabulary; their body language, etc.

· SOCIAL DEVELOPMENT: how and when they interact with ourselves and others; their body language; whether they initiate contact or reply when spoken to, etc.

· INDEPENDENCE: when they ask for help; what they can manage by themselves; if/how they react when something they are doing themselves becomes difficult, etc.

· ACTIVITIES: what engages them; what they do if they are bored; what breaks their concentration (sometimes this is us interrupting), etc.

· EMOTIONAL DEVELOPMENT: how they react when they are sad, happy, frustrated, or angry; how they solve problems, etc.

· SELF-OBSERVATION: how we react/respond to our child; how our hands move; what activates us, etc.

· IN CHALLENGING MOMENTS: e.g., how our child reacts; how they calm down; what helps them; when this happens; whether there are any patterns, etc.

From these observations, is there something new we learned about our child? Is there anything we would like to change as a result? Something in the environment? Another way we can support them? Obstacles we can remove? Including our own intervention? Observe joy!

2. Understand their needs

As we explored in chapter 2, the needs of a child in the first plane of development can be quite different from those of a child in the second plane of development. They will still have the same human tendencies, but these will look quite different.

When we have a child transitioning between planes of development, we may observe characteristics of both. For example, Simone remembers a friend talking about her 6-year-old. Sometimes the child was asking for more responsibility and sometimes they were being very emotional about something that seemed very small. They wanted to be "big" and "small" at the same time.

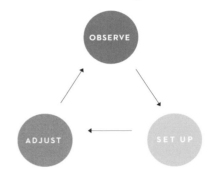

We observe the child to understand their needs, we set up our environment and prepare ourselves to support them, and then keep adjusting.

3. Respect them

Respecting children is a fundamental part of the Montessori approach.

Some examples of this respect are:

- How we physically handle them when needed: gently and with their consent
- How we step back when they can manage themselves and are available when they need guidance
- How we allow them to develop their full potential, without projecting onto them our own ideas of who they should be
- How we allow them to speak for themselves
- How we listen to them with our whole body and heart
- How we communicate kindly with them
- How we find ways to cultivate cooperation rather than using threats, bribes, or punishment
- How we work with them rather than making demands all day
- How we are clear and kind when communicating limits
- How we solve problems together so that everyone in the family can have their needs met

4. Love them

We can love our children deeply, show them empathy, and allow space for everyone in the family in a fair and equitable way.

Love is infinite and can be shown in so many ways. We recommend reading *The Five Love Languages* by Gary Chapman to remind ourselves that people receive love in different ways—and not always in the ways we give it.

If we find it fun to show love through food or presents or taking our children places, then we give and do these things unconditionally. Unconditionally means we are not doing it for their thanks or their love, to be a good parent, or so they do something for us in return. Giving with resentment is not how we show anyone our love.

We do these things because we love giving in this way or we love how others light up when they receive in this way.

5. Accept them

We accept our child for who they are. We are not molding them. We believe in, respect, and value our child and their unique potential. We are their guide as they explore who they are. We let them be themselves.

Accepting means dropping judgment or catching ourselves when we're judging. Accepting means not testing them ("What color is this?"), showing them off ("Tell Grandma what you just won"), or comparing them to other children ("Why can't you be more like _____?").

To accept our child fully is to also allow them all their feelings. If we were raised in a more traditional way, we may have been told "Don't worry," "It doesn't matter," "Don't cry," or "It's not so bad." We may have learned not to express our feelings or to feel understood by our loved ones, or how to manage emotions like anger and sadness when they come up. Instead, we try to see things from our child's perspective. Because all behavior is communication.

The Montessori approach to raising children can be described as being in service to our child's spirit. We prepare ourselves and the home intentionally, then allow them to *construct themselves*. They are laying down their personalities, finding out how the world works, and discovering their abilities.

We are learning to "follow the child." To let them unfold into their full capacity. To support their interests. To blow flames on their fire, not dampen their spirit. To be their guide when there are skills to build in difficult areas. To give them clear limits when needed.

We let them lead the way in their life, we lead the way in ours, and we travel the path together, alongside each other.

"I have helped this life to fulfill the tasks set for it by creation."

—Dr. Maria Montessori, *The Absorbent Mind*

SELF-DISCIPLINE AND INTRINSIC MOTIVATION

When we observe a Montessori classroom, there are children working in different parts of the classroom, on different activities; some by themselves, some in pairs or, in a classroom of 6- to 12-year-olds, in larger groups. There is a hum of activity and movement that looks to the observer like a dance as the children go about their work, the adult quite inconspicuous in the classroom. For someone who went to a school where we sat in a classroom with the teacher at the front telling us what to do, it's hard to believe that no one is telling these children what they need to learn, that they are choosing to work on long division, or taking care to walk around another child's work that is laid out on a floor mat, or watering the plants and wiping up any spills they may make.

This system works because it's not freedom *from* rules. It's freedom *to* do things—to move, to choose, to express themselves—with the associated responsibilities. The children are being told that they can do something, rather than that they can't. For example, they can move freely as long as they are not hurting themselves, someone else, or the space. They can choose what they want to work with as long as it isn't being used by someone else. They can express themselves by talking, writing, or even singing and dancing, as long as they do not use words that are hurtful, use a volume that is okay with everyone, and do it in a space where others won't be disturbed. Carla Foster, an AMI Montessori trainer, refers to these options as "rules, not prohibitions."

In our homes, we can also offer such freedom and responsibilities and prepare an intentional space for our children to explore. The child can make themselves a snack when they are hungry, or help themselves to a glass of water when they are thirsty, and leave the area tidy when they are finished. They can play quietly if they wake up early, as long as they don't disturb others. They are free to talk and contribute their views at mealtimes, waiting for others to finish talking and taking their turn.

Rewards, bribes, and punishment are extrinsic motivations—our child complies with our wishes only to avoid being punished or to receive the bribe or reward being offered. While we all may have used them, these strategies do not build self-discipline. In the Montessori approach, one of our roles as their guide is to cultivate the child's intrinsic motivation. We want our child to do things because they feel capable, they want to contribute, or they want to help another. We give the child freedom, and they learn that with that freedom comes responsibility.

Did you know that the root word of "discipline" is "disciple," meaning "to teach and learn"? Every time something happens, be it a fall, an argument, a disappointment, or a child lying, we don't have to be afraid. Instead, we can see it as a fresh opportunity for learning for our children and us.

The Montessori approach to raising our child is all about building self-discipline and encouraging their intrinsic motivation. It is a different, very respectful way to approach the child. To assume the best in them, to make and uphold family agreements, and to have clear conflict resolution strategies.

FOSTERING INDEPENDENCE AND RESPONSIBILITY

Dr. Montessori heard a child say, "Help me to help myself," and this phrase was soon adopted as a tenet of Montessori education and one we can use at home. We can help our child learn that they are capable and in charge of themselves and their bodies (*physical independence*) and that they can think for themselves (*mental independence*).

When a child is independent, they also learn responsibility for themselves, others, and their environment. They will want to make a contribution to the family and society. They learn to wait their turn, help a friend, or take care of a plant. They are intrinsically motivated to do so.

Self-discipline arises when we create opportunities for independence and mastery and when children learn the skills to be in community with others. We show our child we trust them, and they thrive on the chance to be responsible. It could be carrying their own plate to the table for their meal; using a sharp knife once they have learned to do so safely (with supervision); thinking to prepare something special for a child with a food allergy when inviting them to a birthday celebration; learning to light candles safely at dinnertime; or being in charge of looking up the train times for a family outing and buying the tickets from the ticket machine.

"Following some inner guide, they occupied themselves in work different for each that gave them joy and peace, and then something else appeared that had never been known among children, a spontaneous discipline. This struck visitors even more than the explosion into writing had done; children were walking about, seeking work in freedom, each concentrating on a different task, yet the whole group presented the appearance of perfect discipline. So the problem was solved: to obtain discipline, give freedom."

—Dr. Maria Montessori, *Education for a New World*

Scaffold skills. Children do not learn skills overnight. We might start with modeling, then collaborating, then allowing them to take over more steps themselves. As they master things, we can add more difficult steps. If our child forgets some steps they knew before, we can show them again until they have mastered them. Skills take practice before they become fully integrated.

Break skills into small parts. We can break down the skill they are learning into small parts that are easier to master. For example, for a younger child, by slowly showing them the steps for undoing and doing up a button or tying their shoelaces; older children can follow a note with instructions to get dinner started when they arrive home.

Step in as little as possible, and as much as necessary. It takes practice to trust, to observe, to wait, to let children make mistakes. Then we are rewarded by those moments of satisfaction, or deep concentration, or when they clap for themselves, skip off happily, or smile, having mastered something themselves (*I can do it*).

If we see that they are struggling and are about to become too frustrated to get further, instead of taking over, we can first ask, "Would you like some help?" or "Would you like me to show you?" or "Would you like me to give you a tip?" Then we can give the smallest amount of help, and let them continue.

Some children will refuse our help, and we do our best to be okay with that, too, knowing that they will keep trying and will get it in their own time.

Set up the environment for success. Our children can help themselves independently when they can access a choice of clothing, or reach the plates to set the table, or have their activities arranged in baskets or trays, or have a broom or mop at the ready. Older children will know where to find their sports equipment or musical instruments and have art materials like scissors, a stapler, and paper at the ready.

Allow time. It takes more time for a child to dress themselves, to have them help prepare dinner, or to stop to listen to a long story they want to share. When our schedules are less full, we are allowing more time for them to master skills, make discoveries for themselves, engage in rich conversation, and connect with us and others. They need time to get bored, to get creative, and (particularly for older children) to work on big projects.

Slow hands, omit words. When we are showing a 3- to 6-year-old child how something works (e.g., opening a combination lock on a bike, putting on an item of clothing), we can say, "Look!" then stop talking and make very slow and precise movements to demonstrate. This makes it simpler for them to learn. Jeanne-Marie Paynel, a Montessori parent educator, uses the acronym SHOW (slow hands, omit words) as a friendly reminder. Once our child is 6 and older, we can use a lot of words!

Help them become a member of the family and society. We want our child to become the best version of themselves while being respectful of others and the environment. Raising children in a Montessori way does not mean letting them do whatever they like (e.g., letting noisy kids run around a restaurant is disrespectful to the other people eating there). Nor does it mean being so strict that the child has little autonomy and either becomes subservient, passive, or compliant or goes behind our backs so as not to get caught. We are offering freedom with responsibilities, supporting them to become members of the family and society. We'll explore this more in chapter 6.

RAISING CURIOUS CHILDREN

As a child's guide, we can inspire them, wonder with them, and spark their curiosity. We can also provide them with a community of folks they can learn from, including our family, friends, peers, experts, and those in the local community.

Respond with curiosity to their questions. Rather than always giving our child the answer, it's fun to say, "Let's find out together." It's easy to look something up on the internet, but it can be a richer experience to look it up in a book or encyclopedia (we can come across wonderful things while we are searching), call an expert/ professional/grandparent/family friend with knowledge of the subject, or plan a visit to a museum. Children will learn that when they don't know the answer, they can find it out.

The 3- to 6-year-old child has a *conscious* absorbent mind and therefore has lots of questions. They ask us, "What is this?" and "Why?" They are looking for simple explanations for the things they see around them. We can respond patiently even if they repeatedly ask the same question, because we want them to never stop being askers of questions! We could reply, "I remember speaking with you about that earlier. Do you remember what I said?" or "Why do you think?"

The 6- to 12-year-old child has a reasoning mind and the power of imagination, so their questions are now around "How?" and "Why?" They want to know not only the facts but the cause and effect of things. Dr. Montessori wrote in *The Absorbent Mind* that the 6- to 12-year-old "is not satisfied with a mere collection of facts; he tries to discover their causes."

When our child asks questions about topics like race, sex, war, or violence in the news, it can be hard to know how to answer. Britt Hawthorne, an antiracist and antibias educator, speaker, and advocate, suggests we do the following:

- Ask them what they already know.
- Ask them what they are wondering.
- Tell them we are glad they asked.
- And if we don't know the answer ourselves, agree on a time to come back to them to discuss it together. See chapters 6 and 7 for more help with answering tough questions.

A "wonder wall" is another idea we love. It comes from Julie Bogart's book *Brave Learner,* which we learned about from Montessori educator Pilar Bewley. When our child asks a question, rather than giving them the answer or immediately looking it up on the internet, we can write it down on a sticky note and put it on our wonder wall. Then these questions become topics to do a deep dive into, use as inspiration, or seek answers to at a later time.

Respond with curiosity to their statements. Sometimes children will repeat things they hear or say something we know not to be true, or we think they are saying one thing when they mean something else entirely.

It's easy at these times to shame them or correct them, but this could cause them to say less, or be scared to talk about these things in the future, or make them think we don't talk about these things. Britt Hawthorne suggests that if we instead respond with curiosity, they'll know that there is no embarrassment in getting things wrong; we can help them to correct it, or we may find that we simply misunderstood what they were saying. They will also learn to check whether they understood something correctly themselves.

WAYS TO RAISE CURIOUS CHILDREN

ASK OPEN-ENDED QUESTIONS:

"I wonder what would happen if . . . ?"

"Can you guess what that is/does?"

"I'm curious about _____. Why do you think that's the case?"

WHEN READING A BOOK TOGETHER, WE MIGHT ASK:

"What do you think the characters are thinking?"

"What do you think might happen next?"

WHEN THEY SHOW US SOMETHING THEY MADE, WE CAN ENCOURAGE THEM TO SAY MORE:

"Ooh. Tell me about it."

WE LIKE TO AVOID QUIZZING OR TESTING CHILDREN. We could instead use this question from Paula Lillard Preschlack's book *The Montessori Potential*:

"What do you remember about . . . ?"

We could ask, "Could you say more about that?" or "Let me just check that I understood you correctly; what did you mean when you said _____?" They may need more information, they may need to know that we don't say unkind things about people's ethnicity or skin color. For a 6- to 12-year-old child, we can explore further; for example, by asking, "Can we think about it in a different way?" or saying, "Let's consider how this might impact _____." Or we may have misunderstood what they meant and find that they weren't saying anything problematic. Curiosity allows us to clarify what support is or isn't needed.

Challenge them to question things and become critical thinkers. We can help them be critical thinkers about the media that we consume, to learn how to find reliable sources, and to question information from different perspectives. This applies not just to information but also to societal expectations and systemic thinking.

Children from 3 to 6 years old will see us being agents of social justice, and together, we can question things around us. From the ages of 6 to 12, children will become even more active in these conversations and may feel inspired to take action. (For more on moral development, see chapter 6.)

Become a storyteller. This may not come naturally to everyone, but we can learn to be a storyteller. Storytelling has the power to spark a child's curiosity and capture their imagination. When sharing information, our family history, or our sense of wonder about the world around us, let's think of how we can create an engaging and meaningful story. It may take some practice, but we have plenty of time to develop our storytelling skills. We can also use concrete objects, books, and art as springboards for our stories.

Our child may then be inspired to make their own storybook, comic strip, or stop-motion film. They might do some research at the library, conduct a survey, or interview a neighbor. Or they might just enjoy a good story, well told (and perhaps aspire to become an interesting storyteller too).

Link them to the environment. In *The Absorbent Mind*, Dr. Montessori described the prepared adult as one who offers "warmth, enlivens and invites." We can link children to things in our homes; to the wonders of nature; to the community, society, and eventually the world and the universe.

We never force them to do something, but we can introduce new ideas through conversation, with concrete materials, by working on something ourselves, or perhaps by presenting some well-selected media like an article or TED-Ed talk. We can fill our home with a curated selection of books, encyclopedias, beautiful objects, and artwork to inspire further research or inquiry.

Then we can encourage creativity by making time for free exploration, interrupting as little as possible, and leaving it up to our child how and with whom they might like to explore these ideas.

Teach by teaching, not by correcting. Who hasn't had someone correct them and immediately felt their heart sink? If we are working from an understanding that our child is doing their best and that mastery requires practice, then when we see them make an error, we can make a note of the skill they are missing and make time to teach it to them again. This could apply equally to a cognitive skill (e.g., how they've divided up their marbles) or a behavior (e.g., slamming a door, which we could have fun showing them how to close it as quietly as possible at a more neutral moment later). They are learning to be friendly with making mistakes.

If necessary, we can scaffold the skills, and teach them one step at a time. If we notice a 3-year-old with their shoes on the wrong feet, we could say, "I see you put on your shoes all by yourself!" Then at another time, we find a way to show them how to put their shoes on the correct feet. Then, we might make them a mat with the outline of each shoe to use as a guide.

Go slow. Slowing down is one of the easiest places to start. It allows us to:

- Take the time to observe and see things clearly—not just what we think we see.
- Pause before stepping in to help them with something they can manage themselves or allow them to learn from their mistakes.
- Respond (by pausing first) rather than reacting (acting before we think).
- See details that we would otherwise miss.
- Show our child how something works by slowing down our movements, talking less.
- Make time for connection, conversation, exploration, independence.
- Look after ourselves so we can more fully show up to care for others.
- Listen completely (to their words, their actions, their facial expressions).
- Be intentional in setting up our home and activities.
- Incorporate calmness into our homes.
- Move at the child's pace.
- Make an investment in the future by giving the child the time to learn to do things to care for themselves, others, and the environment (this takes longer in the short term but yields long-term gains).
- Model for family and other caregivers how we give our child time to master things for themselves.

> "Slow down . . . the small steps lead to extraordinary outcomes."
>
> —Catherine McTamaney, *The Tao of Montessori*

The Montessori principles we have discussed in this chapter help our child move from seeking extrinsic motivation (looking outside themselves) to nurturing their intrinsic motivation (doing something because they want to do it, they want to master a skill, or they want to care for someone or the environment). We are helping them become self-motivated citizens of the world. For more about supporting their intrinsic motivation, see the online appendix "40 Ways to Build Self-Discipline and Intrinsic Motivation."

JUNNIFA, UZO, SOLU, METU, BIENDU, NALU

Nduoma Montessori
Nigeria

"Montessori to our family is our enjoyment of the little things and the little moments. In our observation of the world around us. Noticing the buds and the bugs, the changes in season, the bird building its nest and working with its partner to watch their eggs, noticing the nestling and the fledgling. Noticing the eggs, the caterpillars, and the butterflies and truly enjoying the experience. Montessori has made us more mindful, intentional, and peaceful in our daily lives."

"I also really enjoy observing my children. I am fascinated by human development and just watching to understand them. I like to see how their unique personalities reflect in their everyday life as they act and also in their interactions with each other. Observing them helps me understand them and appreciate their individuality."

"We spend a lot of time with our extended family and in so doing share our culture, values, and customs. We attend a lot of cultural events around music and art. Concerts, exhibitions, celebrations, fairs, and just things that introduce our children to aspects of our culture and bring up questions that can be dug into. In our home, we play music, put up art, have clothing and food that reflect our culture while still exposing them to other cultures through travel and other experiences. We also share stories and read books. My dad enjoyed sharing stories of his childhood."

SETTING UP
OUR HOME

4

Our home is our child's base, the soil in which they put down roots and from which they take nutrients and sprout. It is the base from which they explore all other environments, the anchor that keeps them grounded. When we prepare our home intentionally to meet our child's needs, they can take all they need from it and blossom. The environment we prepare for our child can be a way to demonstrate our love, regard, and respect for them.

Dr. Montessori said that the absorbent mind takes indiscriminately from the environment and uses whatever it takes to construct the child. The things our child absorbs from the environment become a part of our child. Knowing this, we can consider what our child will see (colors, shapes, cleanliness, beauty, and order); what they will smell (plants, other natural scents); what they will hear (quiet, sounds of nature outside, wind chimes); and what they will feel (the temperature, the ambience).

Just as our children grow and change, our prepared environment can adapt to our growing child and their changing needs.

THE PREPARED ENVIRONMENT FOR EACH STAGE

THE NEEDS OF OUR CHILD FROM AGES 3 TO 6:

- Movement
- Space and opportunities for physical exploration
- Order
- Rich sensory input for all senses
- Opportunities to absorb our culture—through art, objects, and so on
- Beauty
- Encouragement toward functional independence

THE NEEDS OF OUR CHILD FROM AGES 6 TO 12:

- Systems to support order
- Space and provisions for big work
- Resources for intellectual exploration
- Items and spaces to spark their curiosity

THINGS TO CONSIDER IN PREPARING THE PHYSICAL ENVIRONMENT

Accessibility: Our homes can be set up to encourage our child's autonomy and help them feel confident and respected. We want our child to be able to see, reach, and use the things in our space. When possible, we can have child-sized furniture and tools, or we can adapt things to support, encourage, and ensure accessibility: providing a stable stool or portable stair to use in reaching higher surfaces, lowering light and fan switches and door handles if needed, adding faucet extenders, placing their items on low shelves, and choosing furniture that is light enough that it can be picked up and moved by our child when necessary.

We can be aware of the way our child will interact with our space and the things in it. We want them to be able to move through their space with ease and not have too many areas that are out of bounds or things that we must constantly prevent them from touching or using. Things that are not appropriate for kids—such as fragile family heirlooms or expensive computer equipment—can be moved to less trafficked areas of the home. If a child has a physical disability, we can ensure that the space is adjusted to allow them as much independence as possible.

Functionality/independence/autonomy: Our homes can be a place where our children learn to act, think, and make choices for themselves. We want them to be able to open doors; turn lights on and off; and reach dishes, cutlery, snacks, clothes, toys, paper, pencils, paint, and tape. We want them to be able to take care of their basic needs: get water when they're thirsty, make a snack when they're hungry, and rinse their plate and cutlery. We want them to be able to solve simple problems for themselves, like getting a Band-Aid for a small cut. We can create possibilities for movement and exploration, both physical and intellectual. For example, a child who encounters a word they don't understand can have a dictionary in reach to check its meaning. We can provide them with things to touch and feel, to wonder about, to measure, to inspire them, and to use.

From age 3, a child begins to develop their personality and sense of self separate from their parents or caregivers. When we provide opportunities for independence, we acknowledge this separateness and support their development. As they acquire more awareness of their capabilities and capacities, they become better able to assess their limits and assess risks.

From ages 6 to 12, our child is very capable and can do a lot for themselves and for others. Our home can be designed to support these capacities and stretch the child's abilities. They can be given opportunities to use knives; cook on a stove; employ a tool to fix something; change a light bulb; run the washing machine, dishwasher, and other appliances; and use an iron.

Comfort: We can make choices that will allow both adult and child to feel equally comfortable in our home—this can include paying attention to furniture and the way our space is organized, ventilated, decorated, and lit.

Beauty: Beauty is subjective and can be a way to transmit culture to our children. We can create our spaces with elements that reflect our culture, our preferences, and our values, and in so doing, transfer these to our children. From ages 3 to 6, our child is still in the period of the absorbent mind and so this beauty will become one of the building blocks for their personality. From ages 6 to 12, our child is exploring the world. Their imagination is in full bloom, and so our home can become a canvas for this exploration and creation.

Order: A core Montessori principle is "a place for everything and everything in its place." This means designating different spaces for different activities: a place to cook, a place to eat, a place to sleep, bathe, and so on. And establishing a place for our everyday objects and possessions: a place for shoes, a place for books, a place for the sponge and for the soap.

Our spaces can have consistent points of reference to meet our child's need for orientation and a sense of order. (The couch is always in the same place even if the pillows might change.) Consistency and predictability lend a sense of safety to children. When changes need to be made, we can notify our children and involve them in the process. It can be an opportunity to contribute to the home and practice decision-making.

The 3- to 6-year-old child has a need for external order—we can support this by preparing the space so they can find everything and know where to return things, and can begin to take responsibility for keeping the house tidy for everyone. The 6- to 12-year-old child places less importance on external order, but it will come more easily to them if they understand where things go.

Simplicity: A simple space often encourages order. It also supports independence in our children because it is usually easier to maintain. We can avoid clutter and choose items for our home which are both beautiful and functional. We can have storage for things that are needed but not currently in use. Toys can be rotated, and extra supplies can be stored neatly away. When we prioritize simplicity and a minimalist outlook, we also start to see new uses for the things we already have. When we bring into our home only the things we need (making sustainable choices when we can), we are also showing our children to limit overconsumption.

Richness of sensorial feedback: Children from 3 to 6 years old are interested in categorizing and classifying, comparing and contrasting. We can provide opportunities for this in our home. We can choose sheets, curtains, or containers that show a gradation of colors; planters, light fixtures, or containers with different geometric shapes; a set of nesting tables that are graded in height and size; rugs, couches, and blankets with different textures; kitchen containers made of different materials. We can plant different flowers that have a range of colors, leaf shapes, and scents. All of these differences provide an opportunity to enrich our child's language as we give them specific vocabulary for them.

Accommodation: Every room in the home can accommodate both adult and child, supporting our child's need to communicate, socialize, and spend time with their loved ones. They may not want to interact with us all the time, but they do want to be close and feel our presence.

Safety: We will want to keep hazards such as poisonous substances, electrical wires, choking hazards, sharp objects, and medication out of reach. However, the 3- to 6-year-old is very capable and reasonable and can be shown how to use things appropriately. Instead of eliminating danger, our goal is to help our child become masters of their environment, making good judgments about what is and is not safe. We do this by watching, guiding, and showing. We can label things a safety hazard and show our child what is okay to use and what is not, how to use it and how not to, and in doing so, we can allow them opportunities to learn, grow, make judgments, and build and understand capacity through practice. Children in Junnifa's school have access to a room with sharp tools, and even the 3- to 6-year-old children learn how to use the tools safely, with care and consideration for themselves and others.

Storage: In order to have calm and engaging spaces, effective storage will be an important part of our home. We keep out only a few well-selected activities for each child in the family and store things that are not being used (or for a younger child to use when they get older). Ideally, this storage will be easy to access and keep organized. When things are difficult to reach, we are less likely to store and rotate the activities. Toy rotation can continue until the children are no longer playing with toys (around 12 years old).

ROOM BY ROOM

Here are some ideas and considerations for preparing each room of our home. These lists encourage us to look at our spaces with fresh eyes to see what we may be able to add, adjust, or perhaps subtract.

Entryway

This is a space that welcomes every member of the family into the home and bids them farewell on their way out. It could have:

- A place to sit to take off shoes and a place to store them.
- A place for keys and to hang up bags and coats/jackets/raincoats.
- A basket for umbrellas.
- A full-length mirror to check themselves in before heading out the door.
- Tissues and sunscreen at the ready.
- Plants to add color and a natural ambience.
- A place to pause, set down the burdens of the outside world, and transition into the refuge of home. It could be a doormat to wipe our feet on, indoor shoes or slippers to switch into, or a sign or piece of art that reminds us that we are home.

Living room

The living room can be the heart of the home, the locus of family connection. Every member of the home feels welcome here and has a sense of ownership of this space. Play spaces can be created in the living room as this is the space where the family "lives" and spends their time, which means children often spend their time here playing. There may be space for a separate play room, but it is not necessary. The living room could have:

- Comfortable seating for adults and children to sit or lie down on for conversation, reading, watching a family movie, hanging out with guests, or spending time together.
- A low table for games and other shared activities.
- A music player and/or instruments for shared experiences with music and dancing.

- Toys and other items that promote collaboration, such as building blocks, train sets, puzzles, Legos, games, supplies for drawing or painting, and books that can be enjoyed by old and young. These can be kept accessible on a low shelf.
- A place to display our child's art—both made and found. This can be a designated spot on the wall for hanging art, or a table, basket, frame, or shelf for displaying found items. We can display them for a while, then replace them with new treasures.
- A flower, rock, or leaf arrangement that showcases our child's creativity and (found) seasonal items while also adding beauty and character to the space.
- Plants that can be taken care of by our children
- If the family has a TV, monitor, or projector, it can be in this space but preferably not as the focal point. Specific shows can be watched together as a family and discussed. As our children get older, the family can choose to have designated shows or screen time, but more time can be given to other activities that actively engage the senses.
- A rug and/or the ability to easily move furniture to open up the floor space for floor play, "indoor camping" and other floor-based activities, and big work for a 6- to 12-year-old.
- Floor mats that can be rolled out to mark an area where the children are playing. Using a mat also keeps blocks, Legos, and loose parts in a contained area.
- Items that lend comfort and coziness, like blankets and pillows.

WHEN THERE IS MORE THAN ONE CHILD

- We can use lower shelves for items that are safe for any younger siblings, such as blocks, baskets of animals, vehicles, and Magna-Tiles and higher shelves for things for an older child that may have small or fragile parts.

- For small parts, use containers that are difficult for a younger child to open.

- Create clear spaces where each child can go to be alone; for example, the dining table or a tent made from a blanket and two chairs with a sign that says "Do not disturb."

See also pg. 67: Considerations for small, shared, and large rooms.

ELEMENTS OF A PREPARED ENVIRONMENT

Here are some ideas to incorporate into our spaces in the way that works best for our family with our space, budget, and style.

Kitchen sink with a modification to allow child to reach water

Sectional sofa in living room that can be moved around

Accessible art/craft materials

Instruments at the ready to play

Shelves—three or four shelves are useful.

Table and chairs appropriately sized for our child

Large spaces to play/work

Somewhere to keep shoes, bags, and keys in the entryway

A place to hang a daily routine, timetable, or calendar

Uncluttered storage for sports equipment and musical instruments

Accessible wardrobe with labels

Shelves above the bed for our child's special things or collections

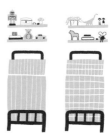

A display of some of of their schoolwork as artwork

A work/study area

Space to move

A place to read

A workshop

Accessible cleaning supplies

Kitchen and dining area

The kitchen is an important space in the life of our child. So much learning, sensorial experience, and connection can happen in the kitchen. It is another space that can be shared by and adapted to every member of the family. We can set up our kitchen to allow collaboration with our children, and nearness when not collaborating. Meals are opportunities to connect and share—we can share our culture, history, and values with our children, and we can learn about their experiences and foster trust. Our kitchen can be set up to include:

- A work space that allows for our child's participation. This can be a low table or a stool to extend our child's reach.
- Child-sized tools and utensils like a cutting board, serrated knife, choppers, and other tools, like an egg slicer or carrot peeler.
- Tools for the older child to explore, like a blender, mixer, juicer, mechanical peeler, pasta maker, bread maker, ice cream maker, toaster/toaster oven, or measuring scale.
- Access to the oven and stovetop (with supervision).
- A snack area in a low cupboard or on a low shelf to encourage independent snack making. A level in our fridge can also be assigned to things our child needs for snack preparation. We can also have a snack table that is our child's size. They can set the table for a snack, pour drinks for themselves or siblings, and wipe up when done.
- If possible, a space for our child to sit with an activity when not participating in meal preparation. This is especially helpful for families with multiple children.
- Plates and utensils suitably sized for children and available at their height.
- Access to the dishwasher if we have one, or a cart for dirty dishes if the washing-up area or dishwasher is not accessible to a child.
- Ingredients for our child to use in making simple meals kept in accessible areas of the kitchen cabinets, pantry, and refrigerator. We can make sure containers are easy to open and a suitable size. For example, a small jug of milk for a younger child instead of a gallon jug.
- An accessible area with cleaning supplies like a broom, brush and dustpan, napkins, a feather duster, sponges, a mop, and rags to allow our child to contribute to the care of the home and clean up after themselves.
- An adjustable chair like the Stokke or a cushion or booster to help our child eat in a comfortable position when sitting at the dining table for family meals.
- Supplies to set the table for meals, again at their level. These can include tablecloths or place mats, dishes, and cutlery. Special table runners, flower arrangements, candles, and name cards can add ritual and ceremony to the process. Children who are learning to read and write will enjoy making and placing the name cards. Older children might enjoy learning different and more challenging ways to fold napkins.

Children will like the responsibility of making a meal and making it feel like a special occasion. They will also remember the ritual of setting the table when relatives or friends are visiting for a meal. It is a chance to add more cutlery for different courses like soup and dessert.

- Drinking water that our child can reach independently during the day. This could be in a dispenser, a refillable pitcher, or a water bottle.

- A large calendar where important dates and appointments can be noted, and also an interactive one for younger children where they can turn a disc or a block daily, weekly, and monthly. This supports their growing awareness of time and also provides an anchoring ritual.

- A clock to use in keeping track of time and routines.

Child's bedroom

If choosing a room for our child in a new home, we can consider our child's view from the windows and choose a room with good light and opportunities to observe nature, such as trees swaying, birds (and possibly birds' nests), the changing light as the day passes, the moon, and the signs of the seasons. If building a house, consider lower windows and even bay windows when possible.

The design and layout of our child's room can convey warmth, security, and comfort. This room is our child's space, where they can feel most centered, anchored, and balanced. We can consider what will transform the room from being any child's room to being our specific child's room. It can reflect their preferences and interests as much as possible. These can come through in color choices, fabric choices (sheets, curtains), wall hangings, art, and accessories. The room can be arranged simply and in an orderly manner with a consistent place for everything.

> "We must give the child an environment that he can utilize by himself: a little washstand of his own, a bureau with drawer he can open, objects of common use that he can operate, a small bed in which he can sleep at night under an attractive blanket he can fold and spread by himself. We must give him an environment in which he can live and play; then we will see him work all day with his hands and wait impatiently to undress himself and lay himself down on his own bed. He will dust the furniture, put it in order, take care to eat well, dress by himself, be gracious and tranquil, without tears, without tantrums, without naughtiness."
>
> —Dr. Maria Montessori, *The Child in the Family*

Preparing the environment for sleep

- An accessible bed allows our child to climb in and out on their own. A small twin frame is great for the 3- to 6-year-old child, or a bunk bed for a shared room. A larger bed can accommodate shared experiences like cuddling with or sleeping with a sibling, or lying together with us while we're reading bedtime stories or putting them to bed.
- A comfortable chair or rug could provide a spot for shared time with us and other adults.
- A fitted sheet and a simple blanket or quilt allow our child to make their own bed. If our child is still working on nighttime toilet independence, a waterproof sheet would protect the mattress and support independent cleanup.
- A bedside lamp is cozy for reading, and a night-light is useful for helping our child navigate any middle-of-the night visits to the bathroom.
- An end table or nightstand can hold accessories, a book that is being read at night, a cup or bottle of water for the night, or any belongings by the bed.

Getting dressed

- A regular closet can be modified with most of the clothes hanging or folded higher up and a few options for them at our child's eye level. We don't want the closet to be cluttered or too full; it should be easy for our child to take out and put away their clothes.
- It helps our child's sense of order to have a designated place for each category of clothing, such as shirts, sweaters, pants, skirts, dresses, socks, and shoes. Drawers, baskets, or boxes are great for this categorization. They can be labeled with pictures, name tags, or both.
- It is useful to have a few clothes that go together, like a capsule wardrobe that can be combined in different ways. This allows our child to make choices that are suitable for the season and occasion.
- A small chair, stool, or rug for sitting on to put on clothes can be helpful. As always, observe what works best for our child.
- A laundry bag or basket for dirty clothes accessible to our child. As our child gets older, we can provide options for sorting laundry into white clothing, colored clothing, dark clothing, and delicate items.
- A mirror that allows our child to see their full self from head to toe supports independent dressing as well as a sense of self.

Considerations for play, work, and other activities

- A music player to listen to and enjoy music and audiobooks.
- A place for books, maybe a small reading corner. Some options include a small standing shelf with a comfortable seat, a floating shelf on the wall for a few books, pockets hanging from a bed or chair, or a book basket.

- If the bedroom is also a play space, a shelf for a few (quiet) toys or activities that can be rotated.
- A table and chair, and a rug or open floor space for playing.
- A few pieces of furniture that are easy for a child to move so they can create forts, tents, and tea parties. These self-made spaces can be opportunities for a child to use their imagination and create private retreats.

Considerations for small, shared, and large rooms

- If the room is a shared space, each child can have some designated space that feels like theirs alone. We can paint the wall by each child's bed a different color or add wallpaper. They can each have a shelf by their bed for their special things, artwork near their bed around their interests, a special blanket on their bed, and a selection of books that they are reading on their bedside table. Dressers can have assigned drawers.
- In a small room, the bed can be elevated like a top bunk and the space underneath can be used as a work/play area.
- A large room can be arranged to still feel cozy and personal. Nooks and corners can be created for different purposes, like reading, resting, and sleeping.
- In a room shared by children in different planes of development, their individual needs will have to be considered. The older child could have belongings on higher shelves that cannot be reached by the younger child. Tables can be adjustable or have different levels to be used by different-age children or to grow with them.
- In a shared room, we can provide opportunities for privacy (especially as the children get older), like a curtain that can be drawn or a sign to indicate when they do not want to be disturbed.
- In small spaces, hang sports equipment, shelves, storage systems on the walls; remove pieces of furniture that are not used often; look for furniture that can be used for multiple purposes; paint storage cupboards the same color as the walls to make the space feel larger.

Adjustments in the bedroom for 6- to 12-year-old children

All of the above also applies for the 6- to 12-year-old child, but there are some extra things to consider as they grow.

The 6- to 12-year-old will want to be involved in setting up their room. They may have opinions about the furniture, colors, fabrics, layout, and art. If it is possible to make changes to their room as they grow, we can include them in the decision-making.

At around age 6, or when our child begins to tell time, they can have a wall or tabletop clock that is easy to read. A weekly or monthly calendar to note the passing of time and keep track of dates important to them such as birthdays, activities, and due dates could be added to the room.

It is also lovely to have something living they can care for. It can be a plant, a terrarium, or a family pet. A small animal like a fish, turtle, or hamster can live in their room or in other shared spaces.

If our child has toys or games in their room, a shelf with compartments will help maintain order. Our 6- to 12-year-old child is working on creating mental order and is not as concerned with external order. This means that they can be messy! Knowing this, we can create systems that help our child maintain their room in an orderly way. They can have fewer things and keep them in labeled containers. A time can also be agreed on (daily and weekly) when they tidy up and return their belongings to their designated places. They may need us to guide them in this process to break it down into smaller manageable tasks if they are feeling overwhelmed.

If our child has specific clothing, equipment, instruments, or materials for their extracurricular activities, we can provide designated storage spaces for these items with a checklist to help them stay organized.

Bathroom

The bathroom is a space that our child uses multiple times daily. We want it to be comfortable and offer support for our child's developing independence and sense of self. We need to ensure that it is accessible and safe. We can provide:

- For a younger child, a stable step stool to use in reaching the sink and low hooks or rods for a towel, washcloth, and other hanging items.
- A wall-mounted or pedestal mirror to use when brushing their hair and teeth.
- A small container for accessories and pocket treasures that might be removed in the bathroom.
- A container or accessible shelf to keep self-care tools like soap, a toothbrush, toothpaste, tissues, toilet paper or wipes, and a shower cap within their reach.
- A few water toys or other things that make bath time enjoyable, such as a hand shower, bubble bath, and bath bombs.
- A small bin that can be managed by our child.
- A toilet brush, mop or towel, and any other tools needed to clean up the toilet and bathroom after use.
- In a shared bathroom, visual prompts to remind each person to flush the toilet, wipe the seat, put down the lid, and wash their hands. Different-colored toothbrushes, hairbrushes, and hand towels can also help each child find the one that belongs to them.

Adult's spaces

Even older independent children who have their own room enjoy spending time with their parents or caregivers. This is usually in the morning, at the end of the day, and on weekends. Accommodations can be made to allow our children to feel welcome in our rooms, such as our work space or our bedroom. We may want them to feel comfortable in bed with us and/or provide a rug, a couch, or a chair where they can read a book or do an activity. That way, they are close.

Part of preparing our personal spaces for our children is setting and sharing our expectations and limits with them. There might be a time before which they are not allowed to enter our room or an expectation that they will knock and wait for a response before they enter or that they only enter when the sign on the door says they can. We need to communicate this to them. We can also provide some guidance for when it's time to leave or when privacy is wanted. These boundaries need to be defined.

If our children have access to our rooms, it is important to consider things in our room that might be unsafe or inappropriate for them; these will need to be out of our child's view and reach. We can also set boundaries around what they are allowed to touch in our room.

Considerations for a shared room (parents and child)

- In Montessori, independence extends to sleeping. However, some families choose to have a family bed or share a room with their children. This is a personal decision for each family.
- In the room where adults sleep, we can add a sleeping corner with a mattress that can be folded up or a convertible couch. Our child can come to sleep on this during the night if they are feeling sick or scared or are having trouble sleeping.
- In a shared family sleeping room, we can think about how each child can have their own space if needed, including clothes storage, a space to go to if they want to be alone, and a place to get dressed. The same can be done for the adults who share the space.

Playroom

If space allows, the considerations in setting up a playroom for our child are the same as in the other areas in our home, including beauty, order, and accessibility:

- Each activity has its own place. Toys with multiple pieces can be put together in a basket or container; keeping the components together allows our child to manage for themselves and makes it easy for our child to put them away when they are finished.
- We can provide seating and floor options for play and work, as well as a table and work surface.

- We can factor in the kinds of activities our child will be doing in this space. Perhaps we put a rug in part of the room and leave the floor bare where they do activities that might require cleanup, like painting or clay.
- Shelves can be used to display toys and games and art supplies. With children of mixed ages, we can designate the lower shelves for items suitable for all of our children, and activities with smaller pieces or fragile items can be placed on higher shelves out of reach of the younger children.
- Shelves don't always need to be placed side by side along the walls. We can create areas and nooks by placing shelves at a right angle to each other, creating cozy corners within the room. We can designate areas for different kinds of activities, such as making art or playing musical instruments.
- We can create an art supply area where they can find paper, pencils, a stapler, tape, yarn, and so on (see the Activities Appendix for ideas for activities' supplies).
- Art on the walls where our children can see it, sculptures they can touch, and found art from nature can become inspiration for their art.

For the 6- to 12-year-old child, we may not need to prepare activities. Instead, we can display interesting items for exploration and trays or baskets for gathering them. That said, it can still be valuable to display activities for older children rather than expect them to open a cupboard to find something of interest.

Outdoors

The outdoors is an important part of the home environment and can be prepared for our child's enjoyment, development, and safety. It's nice to have space and opportunities for movement and activities such as walking, running, riding a bike, skating, jumping, skipping, climbing, and playing catch and other ball games.

We can look to make space for a small atelier or woodworking shed where our child can build, create, and use their imagination, as well as their growing mathematical and analytical skills. We can hang safety goggles and tools at the ready, with a clear place for everything to be safely stored, such as a hammer, drill, saw, gloves, measuring tape, wood glue, and containers for small nails and screws. We show our children how the tools are used safely, we collaborate, then we step back and let them manage independently, providing supervision as needed. Woodworking can also be an opportunity for collaboration and shared activity with an adult.

Also allow space and opportunity for observation, exploration, and appreciation of nature. This can be in the form of:

- A vegetable garden or container garden to tend to while observing the life cycle of plants, their parts, and their functions, as well as the needs of different plants, and their soil.

- A flower garden or a few flowerpots to attract birds and insects and offer the beauty, colors, shapes, and scents of flowers
- Logs that can be climbed on or lifted to find little ecosystems such as frogs, worms, ants, termites, and other living things like mushrooms, moss, and algae

A small outdoor space can include potted plants, flowerpots, a bird feeder or birdbath, and other things that attract and reflect nature. If you have no outdoor space, make time to get to the local park, woods, or any nature spot nearby to offer these experiences.

We can provide ways for our child to document their observations, express their imagination, or capture inspiration found from being outdoors with materials, such as: art supplies for drawing and painting, an analog or digital camera, a nature journal, a leaf or flower press, and a jar in which to keep rocks, shells, or sticks.

We can provide places to rest and relax outdoors, for example, the shade of a tree, a hammock, a shaded outdoor space, a chair to sit in to read or simply to enjoy looking around, mats to lay out, or grassy space to lay on.

We can provide specialized equipment like a swing set, jungle gym, trampoline, bicycle, scooter, skateboard, wheeled cart, rollerblades, or roller skates. If we are near the seaside, we could look for a secondhand boogie board or surfboard. If there is a place to ice-skate in the winter, ice skates or strap-on skates could be useful.

Other tools to aid interaction with and care for the outdoors could include gardening tools (such as a watering can and a child-size rake, hoe, and spade), a water hose, a wheelbarrow, binoculars, a telescope, a magnifying glass, a bug catcher and holder, or a microscope to use in examining samples found outside.

Activities like painting, weaving, woodworking, gardening, upcycling, or crafting with recycled objects are great for the outdoors.

As much as possible, we can make the outdoor area safe so that children can be given freedom to explore it independently. We can prepare or provide appropriate clothing for different weather conditions to allow our children to enjoy the outdoors in every season. We can provide sunscreen, bug repellent, hats, and any other items that make for safe enjoyment of the outdoors accessible.

As our child gets older, the outdoor environment is not limited to the immediate space outside their home. They might visit friends, use community parks or playgrounds, ride their bikes or skate down the street, walk to a neighborhood shop, or hike a nearby trail. At this stage, part of the preparation of the outdoor environment becomes preparing our child to use and enjoy the outdoors.

We can show them how to:

- Pack a bag for an outing, perhaps helping them make their own checklists so they don't forget anything
- Safely cross the road
- Ride a bike
- Take a bus or other public transportation
- Greet people and ask for directions
- Spot signs of danger
- Take action in times of uncertainty or danger
- Memorize important phone numbers and addresses

Ideas for enhancing outdoor space in our home environment include:

- A walking path, either paved or made of rocks or stone slabs. At a Montessori school in rural Mexico, educator Meg McElwee used smooth rocks to create a beautiful spiral, labyrinthine walking path. At the entrance, there was a small chair where the children would sit and take off their shoes before entering the labyrinth barefoot.
- A sand pit.
- A balance beam made with a log, a wood plank, or a raised board.
- Hand-built hills or other variations to the land.
- Climbable trees.
- An easel for doing artwork outside.
- Space to play sports, like soccer, basketball, or badminton.
- A water source.
- Containers for collecting water.

In cases where there is minimal access to an outdoor space, here are some suggestions:

- A balcony can be set up be to child-friendly and safe. It can include an easel, or a table to sit at and paint or play, some plants to care for, a bird feeder, or a simple chair to sit in and watch the world go by.
- A little window garden or compost bin can bring some nature in.
- A younger child might be able to ride a small bicycle in our home's hallways.
- Soft balls to kick or throw into a basket or hoop or to one another, which can be used inside.
- Pillows, cushions, rugs, and other floor coverings can bring opportunities for gross-motor movements into indoor living spaces. These can be used to set up obstacle courses. An area can be provided for practicing cartwheels, somersaults, or yoga. A small trampoline or climbing wall can be added to the space.

PSYCHOLOGICAL PREPARATION

The psychological environment is the intangible part of our home. The atmosphere within our home, how our child and others feel there—this, too, needs to be prepared.

Love: Our home can be a place of emotional safety for our child. The love is tangible and intangible. We can express our joy and enjoyment in our children through the time we spend with them and our attitude on seeing them and being with them. We smile, laugh, have conversations, hug them, listen to them, and are present, in the moment, with them.

Acceptance and belonging: We can create a feeling of acceptance by the way we prepare our home with consideration for our child in each space. Also by the way we speak to and react to our children. Accepting them for who they are and not trying to change them into who we want them to be. Involving them in decisions that affect them as well as the family.

A friendly attitude toward mistakes: Our attitude toward mistakes also affects the psychological environment. We want our home to be a place where it is okay to make mistakes. Accidents happen, and we help our child learn how to fix it and try again.

Trust: Our trust in our child's ability as well as their trust in us also constitutes the psychological environment. We show our trust in them in the way we encourage them to build their independence by allowing them to do things they feel they are capable of instead of insisting on helping. We also allow them to participate and contribute to our home even when it is not convenient and their effort is not perfect. Most times it is easier, faster, and more efficient to do things ourselves, but when we include our children, they build trust in themselves and in us.

Our emotional and mental state: Another part of the psychological environment is the adult's emotional and mental state as well as the relationship between the adults in the home. When we are stressed, angry, unhappy, anxious, fearful, or frustrated, our child feels and absorbs these emotions. Children are very perceptive and sense when things are not okay. It is important to know this and ensure that we take care of ourselves and our relationships to promote a positive atmosphere and make sure they see us resolve any conflicts.

We will discuss this preparation in detail in chapter 8, "Preparation of the Adult."

NUSAIBAH & NOAH

Rumi Montessori
UK & Malaysia

"There's a huge emphasis in the Montessori philosophy about respecting and trusting the child. For me, as a Muslim, I see this as part of our faith; we should already trust and respect the child. With my work in Islamic Montessori, it's not so much about trying to make Montessori Islamic, but more about trying to understand that all these Montessori principles of love and respect are already part of the teachings of our Prophet. As Muslims, we should be people who have this trust, love, honor, and respect for the child, and we should strive to follow the natural development of the child, their fitrah."

"I knew he was autistic from when he was quite young. I decided to take his autism as a gift, and embrace it positively with all that it comes with, rather than taking it on as a challenge. I found the art of observation to be the best tool that's helped me as a mother to an autistic child. When observing, we learn to be objective; we get to find out what is really happening rather than seeing our own narrative. This is where I learned so much about Noah's needs and how I can support him. He was interested in birds of prey for 2 years, we had so much fun exploring this interest. He was very unique and did many things differently. Through observing, we got to find his triggers and understand his challenges. It was always interesting for people to observe him and say, 'I've never seen anyone do anything like that.' It was truly amazing."

"The fruits of all the work we put in as Montessori parents really blossom in the adolescent years. When you have an adolescent who has been through the Montessori philosophy from birth, they're very self-directed: They know who they are, they know who they want to be, and they don't get swayed by peer pressure as much because they have their own concept of who they are and what's right and what's wrong. They have a strong moral sense and clarity on what they want to do and not do. It becomes a pleasure to see them grow into these wonderful young adults who are ready to take part in society and make a positive impact."

MONTESSORI
ACTIVITIES
FOR CHILDREN

5

In the previous chapters, we learned about our child, their characteristics and needs, and how they develop. Now we are going to look at how we can support their development. Our goal is not to replicate a Montessori classroom. We are looking to find ways to support our child's interests, seize upon learning moments that occur naturally through daily life in a fun way, and encourage our child to become a lifelong learner.

When many think of Montessori, they think of specific materials and toys. While these Montessori activities are valuable, there are more important things that can't be purchased but can make all the difference in our child's development. That is where we'll start.

CONSIDERATIONS FOR SUPPORTING OUR CHILD'S DEVELOPMENT

Time

The first way we can support our child's development is by giving them time. Just like a plant that grows from a seed, our child needs time, nurturing, and warmth to grow and thrive. We can set aside some time each day to connect with and focus on each of our children. This time spent together is how they learn to feel secure in our love.

Children need time to explore. This is time when they are free to choose how to occupy themselves, indoors or outdoors (and ideally both). This is undirected free time when they can follow their inner guides. They need time to explore their environment with all of their senses. To make messes, chase butterflies, and roll in the grass. To sit quietly and read a book, or work on an activity, or share a game of hide-and-seek. To get to know themselves and others. To make friends, build relationships and memories.

Children need time to experience boredom. We might worry about our child being bored and feel like we need to entertain them or ensure that they are always engaged in an activity—but children actually need periods when they have nothing to do. This is when they can reflect and figure out for themselves how to fill their time. As children get older, and especially from ages 6 to 12, time to be bored is usually what spurs big work. So when our child comes to us and complains of boredom, we can tell them it's okay to feel that way and that it's a good time to come up with new ideas.

Children need time to observe. As we know, the child from 0 to 6 years old has an absorbent mind that soaks in everything they observe. For the 6- to 12-year-old child, observation is how they make connections and find things to question and understand. Junnifa remembers her children stopping during walks to watch ants carrying food, watching a stock person stack boxes at the grocery store, or watching a plumber fix a leak in their house. This observation is part of their self-construction, so it's okay to slow down for them to observe and not interrupt them. When our child observes us, we can be conscious of our movements and do things carefully so that they can take in the details when we're working, cleaning, cooking, or writing

Children need time to repeat. Repetition is the way that humans perfect their skills and abilities. Many times, we'll notice our child finish doing something and choose to do it again immediately. Children, especially those from 3 to 6 years old, are less focused on the outcome than on the process, so they will repeat an activity over and over again, or possibly repeat just one step of the activity. We might see a child tie a shoelace and immediately untie it to try again, or ask us to read the same book over and over. Repetition can be a clue to what sensitive period they might be in or to an interest they might be working on. It can be a sign that they are concentrating. The 6- to 12-year-old repeats, too, but not necessarily in the same way each time; they often repeat with variations, like making paper airplanes again and again but making them slightly different each time.

Children need time to solve their problems. Dr. Montessori said to "never help a child with a task at which he feels he can succeed." This means that we first assess whether the child actually thinks they can do it. There's usually a thin line between struggle and frustration, especially with younger children. We observe our child when they are struggling, and if it seems they are tipping over into frustration, we can step in and ask if we can help. If they accept our help, then we need to *help them to help themselves*—giving just enough help and showing them how to do it themselves. For example, an older child might be struggling with an idea or question that they're trying to understand. Instead of giving the answer, we can show them how to use a dictionary or encyclopedia. A young child might be getting frustrated trying to unbuckle their shoes. If they accept our offer to help, instead of taking off the shoes completely for them, we can show them how to pull the strap to undo the buckle. We can encourage them if they need it: "I think you can do it!" or "Keep trying" or "You can do hard things." We offer just enough help to still allow the child to experience and own their success.

Children need time to rest. They need time to sleep, to be quiet and still. A lot of consolidation happens while children rest and sleep. We can build quiet time into our child's day. This can be a nap or just a time to lay down and rest their bodies. As much as possible, it is also important for children to go to bed early. For children between 3 and 12 years old, 7:00 to 8:30 p.m. is a reasonable time in general.

Children need time for communication and connection with us. We stop to listen, to take turns in conversation, to ask questions, to allow them to ask questions, to use rich language, to be together, and to be a safe place for them to express themselves. We will also need time to practice grace and courtesy, which we will cover more in chapter 6.

Purposeful activity

Children need purposeful activity. Dr. Montessori wrote in *The Absorbent Mind* that the child from 3 to 6 years old needs such hands-on purposeful experiences to perfect, enrich, and understand all they absorbed in the first 3 years and to see their effect on the environment. We can set up our environment to encourage spontaneous and natural activity as well as prepare activities based on our child's needs and interests; for example, their need at this age for movement, language, and refinement of the senses.

When we offer purposeful activities, we see our child find meaning in their work; they feel like they are making a contribution, we see deep concentration, and when we offer them real objects and experiences, they know we trust them.

> "So we must have interest first and then work with an intelligent purpose, work which is freely chosen by the individual."
>
> —Dr. Maria Montessori, *The 1946 London Lectures*

Purposeful work for the 6- to 12-year-old child involves thought, problem-solving, and the building of new understanding and connections. The child's goal is intellectual independence, so purposeful work helps direct and strengthen thought. For example, pre-measured ingredients for baking might be purposeful for a child younger than 6 years old, but a more purposeful setup for a 6- to 12-year-old would involve them figuring out what ingredients are needed. This can be by reading a recipe, gathering the ingredients, and figuring out the measurements.

Process versus product

Notice that when doing activities, the child from 3 to 6 years old is more interested in the process than the product, and they will often focus on one part of the process, repeating it many times.

The older child from 6 to 12 years old is different. They are no longer driven by just the desire for movement; they are interested in the product or result. They like responsibility and can be given freedom to execute tasks in ways that reflect and display their abilities. They want to be involved in aspects of running the family, like creating a meal plan for the week, researching a vacation, making a list for grocery shopping, or planning the daily routine or schedule. All of these tasks also provide opportunities for the child to acquire and refine physical, cognitive, and social skills. They build responsibility and prepare the child for life.

Follow the child

An important note: There are so many ways we can support our child's development; it can seem overwhelming! The suggestions outlined in this book are not meant to be done all at once or even at all. Remember, we follow our child's interests and their timeline, and use them as a starting point for exploration. That said, a child does not leave school for the day and stop learning. We hope to give you support on how you can help your child develop a true love of, interest in, and wonder at the world around them and want to make a difference in it.

Other tips

- At home, children might choose to work with multiple activities concurrently and might not return each activity before bringing out a second one. This is fine as long as they do not have so many things out that it becomes chaotic, disorderly, or overwhelming to clean up. We can set limits on the maximum number of things that can be out before we pack some up and help them notice and recognize when things are getting out of hand.

- A younger child may want to have everything they need on a tray and at the ready. Then we will notice when they are also able to collect the things they will need onto a tray themselves. For example, fetching a tray, choosing some paper and a pencil, and bringing the tray to the table to work.

Choosing toys

When choosing toys, it's ideal to choose "passive" toys that the child needs to actively manipulate and explore. Avoid "active" toys, which are designed to entertain the child and the child is mostly passive, like a toy that sings a song when the child pushes a button.

We also want to select toys that are aiding their development. We can look at what skills our child is showing interest in and working to master. We prefer toys made from natural materials, which are often more environmentally friendly than those made from plastic and also provide more and richer sensorial qualities in areas like color, weight, size, and texture.

We want to choose toys (and furniture) that will grow with our child, items that can continue to be used over time, can be used in a new way, and can later be sold or passed on to another family. We can look for toys that invite both individual and collaborative play with friends and/or siblings; encourage thinking, problem-solving, and analysis; and foster concentration and focus.

We want to be mindful of consumption and not buy lots of materials. Most of the suggestions in this chapter and the Activities Appendix to support our child's development do not require additional materials or can be made using things we already have in our homes.

We can buy secondhand, go to thrift stores, reuse packaging for art materials, rent rather than buy toys, set up a sharing community, search freecycle groups, borrow items from the library and share with friends, and repair rather than replace.

Our favorite way to source materials is to head out into nature and find items there. Have fun being creative while inspiring our children to be caretakers of our Earth.

WHY MONTESSORI ACTIVITIES ARE IMPORTANT

Dr. Montessori said that the child develops through "means of their own activity." We can support this by making a wide range of activities available to our child. When choosing activities, we call to mind our knowledge of the *human tendencies*, the characteristics of the *planes of development* that our child is in, and the *sensitive periods* we observe them in.

We see children in Montessori classrooms calm, focused, and at ease. When a child is engaged in an activity that meets their needs and interests, they experience what psychologist Mihaly Csikszentmihalyi calls a flow state. When in a flow state, a child is calm and regulated. The more often they experience a flow state, the easier it is for them to come back to calm when dysregulated. If we do not find activities to challenge our children, they will challenge us.

Activities for the 3- to 6-year-old child

We know that the human tendencies for exploration, orientation, order, communication, movement, work, repetition, and self-perfection are dominant in the first plane. We also know that the child from 3 to 6 years old is consciously working on refining the acquisitions they made in the period from 0 to 3 years old and that they are in the sensitive periods for movement, language, and the refinement of senses. All of these are considerations when providing opportunities and activities for our 3- to 6-year-olds.

We can provide our child with opportunities to experience things with all of their senses. They can classify the world around them: grading pine cones from biggest to smallest; refining their sense of smell with smelling jars or while cooking in the kitchen; or putting on a blindfold and exploring different textures.

When they ask us "what?" we can give them rich vocabulary to understand the world they are absorbing. When they ask us "why?" we can help them look up the answer in a book or encyclopedia, or find an expert to ask, or create hands-on experiences for them to discover the answer for themselves.

Introducing a new activity to a 3- to 6-year-old

Some of the activities we set up for our child will be intuitive and easy for them to figure out on their own. Others will require us to model or demonstrate to get them started. The following are some considerations and steps for modeling or introducing new activities.

- Ensure that we have set up all the required items or parts of the activity and that they are logically arranged. These may be displayed on a tray or for the child to fetch the parts needed.
- Practice in advance to make sure we understand the sequence we want to follow.
- Set up the activity on a shelf or where we would like it to go.
- Choose a time when our child is calm and when we have the time and attention to immerse ourselves fully in the activity.
- Invite our child: "I have something interesting I want to show you." We shouldn't force them to join us; we should respect their decision not to if they are not interested.
- Go with them to retrieve the activity from its location so they know where to return it to when they are finished.
- Let the child know that we will show them and then they will get a chance to do it too. This encourages them to wait patiently while we show them the activity.
- Sit in such a way that the child has a good view of our hands. Ideally, they sit on our nondominant side because we will mostly be using our dominant hand.
- Introduce them to the activity, giving vocabulary for the activity, parts, and steps.
- Demonstrate the activity, making sure to minimize words when demonstrating so that the child can focus on the actions.
- Let the child have a turn. Be careful not to correct or interrupt. If we notice something that needs correction or emphasis, wait until they are done, then ask to take another turn and emphasize the necessary steps.
- When the child is working independently, step away and allow them to repeat the activity as many times as they want. We can remind them to pack up and put it away when done.
- We can observe from a distance.

Activities for the 6- to 12-year-old child

The 6- to 12-year-old child now uses their logical, reasoning mind, which asks "Why?" and "How?" They want to understand how the world works, how things fit together, the origin of things, and the workings of the universe. Their imagination is active, and they are able to conceive of a different time and place. This is a great time to:

- Encourage big work (projects that take a long period of time and/or take up a lot of space).
- Go out into the community to learn about areas of interest.
- Challenge and promote their critical thinking skills: Ask them questions; explore their questions with them; get them to back up their opinions; encourage them to research and debate topics arising in current affairs.
- Share stories (including fantasy stories).
- Help them develop their language for classification and observation.
- Honor their love of hero worship by delving into history, civilization, great inventions, and people who made or make a difference.

Cosmic education

For the 6- to 12-year-old child, cosmic education becomes very important. Cosmic education is the idea that everything in our cosmos—people, animals, plants, etc.— has a purpose (its cosmic task), and that everything in the universe is interconnected. The child learns to develop respect for, and be gentle with, all living things (even those that may sometimes annoy them like flies, wasps, ants, or spiders).

With their love of big ideas and big work, curiosity, imagination, and interest in social and moral development, the 6- to 12-year-old will enjoy exploring this concept. They will also learn that they have a special role to play, as well as an opportunity to make a difference in the world, be it in their family, school, or local or global community.

We can begin to introduce these concepts to the 3- to 6-year-old child. We can discuss with them what plants need to grow and why we are gentle with insects they find, and talk about the water cycle, the sun and moon, and anything else they show interest in as they explore the world around them.

An example of cosmic education would be talking with our child about the food we eat and all the people and factors that made it possible. The person who planted the seeds and nurtured them. The soil in which it grew, the water that nourished it, the worms that made the soil nutritious, the insects that pollinated it. The person who harvested it, the one who transported it for processing, the person who processed it, packaged it, sold it,

WHAT WE CAN OBSERVE

- Interests: topics they talk about; observations they make while exploring; which activities they are drawn to, etc.

- What movements they are mastering: how they hold their pencil; how they climb, swing on monkey bars, etc.

- Activities they choose: how long they work with each activity; how much of the activity they do; what they do with the materials; whether they have mastered the activity.

- Where they use the activity: how they retrieve the activity from the shelf; how they carry it to a mat or table; whether they return it to the shelf when finished.

- Independence: whether they choose activities independently; what aids their independence; any obstacles (including ourselves) to independence; how they ask for help; if they accept help, etc.

- Focus: Look for moments when they are deeply focused as well as when they are distracted by someone or something but still able to come back to the activity. Note when their breathing is smooth; when they are regulated; when they look satisfied at completion.

- Concentration: what breaks their concentration; where they concentrate best; how we support their concentration (mostly this is by not interrupting; at times we can step in to help a little then step back again to let them get further).

- Repetition: if they repeat an activity; if they repeat in the same way or with variety.

and cooked/prepared it. The person who will pick up the trash when we throw away the leftovers, the bugs that will break it down. They can learn all these interdependencies and that everyone has a role. They will enjoy finding more connections like this.

Interdisciplinary education

While in many non-Montessori schools, subjects are taught separately, in our Montessori classrooms, we recognize that all subjects are interconnected. For example, while focusing on science, we also touch on math, geography, culture, language, and more. We can help the child to realize that everything in life is interrelated.

TYPES OF MONTESSORI ACTIVITIES

IN THE ACTIVITIES APPENDIX, which begins on page 232, we provide dozens of activities for everything from reading and writing to sensorial experiences to learning about the natural world to music and art. We can pick the ones that speak to our child's interests at the moment and return to the list when we see that they've entered a new interest, sensitive period, or stage of development.

IF YOU'D LIKE INSPIRATION BASED ON THEIR INTERESTS, you can refer to the online appendix titled "Activity appendix based on interest" at workman.com/montessori to get you started. Montessori is a truly holistic approach to the child, and one area of interest can be a springboard for many areas of development. For example, an interest in rainbows could cover art, science, language (vocabulary, books, poetry), etc.

SOME COMMON QUESTIONS ABOUT SUPPORTING OUR CHILD'S DEVELOPMENT

How can we nurture our child's concentration?

We can help build their concentration by:

- Minimizing interruptions—we can wait as long as possible before interrupting them to offer them help, to ask them a question, or call them for a meal.
- Allowing boredom—long blocks of unscheduled time allow them to get bored, come up with creative ideas, and take these ideas deeper and further.
- Minimizing devices—limiting the availability of screens will keep them as active learners for more of the day.
- Modeling concentration—we can take time to pursue our own hobbies, like sewing, gardening, or building.
- Observing—when the choices available in our home follow their interests based on our observation, they will be more focused on these activities.
- Learning what concentration looks like for our child—for example, is their breathing smooth when they are concentrating? Do they stick out their tongue? Do their eyes stay focused on the activity and do they not notice what is going on around them? Do they go back to their activity even after being distracted?
- Preparing the environment—have a table facing a wall, a place they can go where they won't be disturbed, or a work mat that can keep everything together for them to focus on.

How can we make the activities inviting?

How we arrange the activities in our home will often determine how our child uses them. Here are a few helpful tips:

- **Storage.** It helps to have a place to store toys that are not currently in use. We can use tubs or boxes to separate different categories by types, interests, and ages.

- **Shelves.** It helps to have open shelves where our child can easily see what is available. This is preferable to a big toy box, where it can be difficult to see what's available and often the contents get dumped out onto the floor, leaving a mess.

- **Order.** We can arrange the activities on the shelf from easiest to hardest. This helps the child orient themselves. If an activity is too difficult, they can try an easier one to the left; if it's too easy, they can try a harder one to their right. We can also arrange materials so that our child's movements are from left to right as indirect preparation for reading and to give them practice crossing the midline. In countries where we read from right to left, we can set up the activities for the child to move from right to left.

- **Group similar items together.** This helps them to know where things belong, and it can also help manage the energy in different parts of our home. We may have a quiet reading area next to activities for fine-motor-skill coordination like puzzles and some climbing equipment near other activities with larger movements like music.

- **Less is more.** It is easier for the child to choose an activity when there is a curated selection for them to choose from. If we have everything stored in a cupboard or toy box with things on top of other things, it is difficult to see what is available. Similarly, having too many toys out at one time makes it more difficult to choose and find those things that are available. We could select as few as six toys per child and rotating those activities that are not being used.

- **Containers.** Look for baskets, trays, and boxes to display the activities that are made of natural materials and that the child can manage themselves. We can use clever wall storage to hold jars filled with materials for arts and crafts.

How can we help our child with homework?

If our child is at a non-Montessori school and receives homework, we may need to help them from time to time. Our goal is to provide as little help as possible and as much as necessary.

If our child is having a problem understanding their homework, we can look to create a hands-on opportunity for them to understand it more clearly; help them create a science experiment to bolster their comprehension of the topic; go to the library or find an expert whom they can interview to find out more about the subject.

Helping them with homework will then take longer than answering the question for them because we are helping them to understand the concepts and learn how to find answers to things they don't know.

Depending on our child we can check in daily or weekly to see if they need help with their planning. We can scaffold these skills until they are able to plan their homework and any study independently.

How can we cultivate imagination and creativity?

Some people have the impression that Montessori limits creativity because of the focus on activities with defined purposes and because we focus on reality over fantasy in those first 6 years. In fact, Dr. Montessori spoke a lot about imagination. One of our favorite quotes of hers on the topic appears in *To Educate the Human Potential*: "The secret of good teaching is to regard the child's intelligence as a fertile field in which seeds may be sown, to grow under the heat of flaming imagination. Our aim therefore is not merely to make the child understand, and still less to force him to memorize, but so to touch his imagination as to enthuse him to his inmost core."

Here are some ideas for cultivating creativity and imagination in our child:

Start with reality. In the first 6 years, we help our child explore the real world with all the senses. They are still working out the difference between reality, pretend, and fantasy, so when we come across a book with a dog driving a car, we can help guide them. "Do dogs really drive cars? No, that's pretend." Once they have a strong foundation in reality in the first plane, everything they have explored will become a springboard for their imagination in the second plane. If in the first plane the child has seen many towers in person and in books, in the second plane they may come up with a design for their own tower that is beyond anything they have seen or experienced.

Allow them to process all they have taken in. We will see the 3- to 6-year-old child doing a lot of pretend play with objects around them. They will pretend to bake a cake, go to school, nurse the baby, or be a dog. We don't discourage this play. We observe them and see them processing and making sense of what they have absorbed around them. We also don't have to give them prescriptive items for such play, like a doctor's kit or a firefighter's hat. We can give them open-ended items like scarves or blocks for them to explore in their own way.

Let them explore with the eyes of the mind. Once they are 6 years old, the children want to explore the universe, beyond what they can touch and feel and instead explore with their imagination. This has been described as using the eyes of the mind, not just the body—such a rich description of the 6- to 12-year-old child's imagination.

Encourage them to solve their own problems. Montessori children learn to solve problems for themselves. They are not given solutions or formulas but come up with these themselves from manipulating materials, doing calculations, and undertaking research and experiments. When they don't know an answer, they look for ways to find out.

Promote working with others. They also look to come up with creative solutions with others. In chapter 6, we explore this social development in detail, learning to be part of and to serve their community.

Provide a rich environment. In our homes, we set up interesting invitations and materials for them to make discoveries, and as much as possible, we have beautiful, good-quality art materials for them to use. There is beauty around them in the form of flowers, plants, and artwork. We include a lot of natural materials, and they also have opportunities to connect with nature outside the home. They have their culture represented as well and perhaps access to a workshop or atelier. All this makes their environment a space for creativity and using their imagination.

Avoid prescriptive workbooks and coloring books. A variety of papers and materials will help them come up with their own ideas, rather than follow someone else's. We don't prescribe to them that the sky has to be blue or the grass green. We show them how materials are used and then let them use their own imagination.

Prepare ourselves. We can ask, not tell. "Would you like to tell me about what you made?" We can allow long stretches of uninterrupted time to play and get bored, a breeding ground for creative ideas. We can focus on the process rather than the result. "I see you were working for a long time positioning things carefully and gluing them in place." And we can be okay with things being a little messier as the child gets creative.

Go outside. Spending time outdoors or in nature provides endless inspiration and can be a source of interesting treasures that can be brought home and used in projects. We can also attend dance and music performances and visit art galleries and other cultural spaces to admire others' work, meet creative people, and get new ideas.

YULIYA, KLAAS-WILLEM, YVANN, NATASHA

Welcome to Montessori
Netherlands & Ukraine

"Now that our children are in the second plane, we can really see how their world is expanding. Our 10-year-old is particularly interested in world affairs and news. He's trying to understand how and why certain things happen, is more curious about travel to places he learns about, etc. It's magical to watch his world grow from our small village to the whole world, and more!"

"Our home is a mixture of so many cultures and languages at any time. My first language is Russian (I speak this to the children), my husband speaks Frisian (a regional language in the Netherlands), and when we are all together, we tend to speak English. I cook Russian/Ukrainian food at home, we watch movies and read books in Russian, and we keep up with some traditions that I grew up with, too. We just try to offer exposure without forcing anything."

"Our family has benefited from Montessori in so many ways, especially after I became paralyzed. We really see the independence and trust that comes with Montessori at home. When I was first injured, I lost my independence and had to relearn how to do everything. I saw how so many people would take over tasks for me or make assumptions about what I could or could not do. My husband and I talked so much about this, and he helped to set up our home in a way that allowed me to be completely independent. Especially when one is in a wheelchair, the

limited mobility can mean that our spaces will look different or we need help with preparing the environment. It's okay to do things differently than what one sees on social media."

SUPPORTING OUR CHILD'S SOCIAL AND MORAL DEVELOPMENT

6

Montessori is known for fostering independence in children. Less understood is that the purpose of raising independent children is to build a stronger society. In this chapter, we will explore how our child can become a person in society, confident in themselves, aware of and accepting of others, able to recognize injustice, and empowered to take action.

> "One can speak of a true community only when each member of the group feels sufficiently free to be himself, while simultaneously restricting his own freedom for the sake of adjustment to the group. It is in seeking an optimal solution to this tension between personal independence and dependence on the group that the social being is formed. Too much individual freedom leads to chaos, too much uniformity, imposed by adults, leads to impersonal conformity or to rebellion."
>
> —Mario M. Montessori Jr., *Education for Human Development*

FOSTERING SOCIAL DEVELOPMENT

The day our child is born, they are in community with others. Their first community is their immediate family. Then comes their extended family, any other caregivers, and the people they meet in their daily life (at the library, the market, a playgroup, etc.). When our child is between 3 and 6 years old, their community will often expand to include their preschool, where they are working out how to live in a mini society with others. They may also visit friends' homes and attend classes or participate in activities with or without us. From ages 6 to 12, our child sees their society extend to their school, neighbors, friends, and the wider community.

Our child's *social development* is how they interact with others, how they get along with others, and how they understand other people and their needs.

Children learn social behavior from their environments. Ideally, our child is spending time in caring environments and experiencing positive social interactions. We can prepare them to navigate new or different environments by offering them lessons in grace and courtesy. We can help them learn how to be respectful, how to understand the social norms of our culture, and how to behave in certain social situations. As the adult, we can also model these things—being intentional with the language we use and in our daily manners, and when showing respect and care for ourselves, our child, and others.

OBSERVING OUR CHILD

To understand how we can best support our child with their social development, we can observe the following:

- **HOW THEY INTERACT WITH OTHER CHILDREN.** Do they initiate play or conversation? Do they prefer parallel play? Do they seek out others to play with? How do they respond when children would like to play with them?

- **HOW THEY RESPOND TO NEW SITUATIONS.** Do they take time to warm up in social situations? Do they walk in and immediately find something or someone to play with?

- **HOW THEY RESPOND TO US AND OTHER ADULTS.**

- **HOW THEY RESPOND IN A GROUP.** Do they listen to instructions? Do they like doing group sports? Do they know how to wait their turn?

- **HOW THEY RESOLVE CONFLICT.** Do they find solutions with their siblings/friends/other children on the playground? Do they need assistance? Do they come to ask for help when needed?

- **HOW THEY TAKE OTHERS INTO CONSIDERATION.**

- **WHAT OPPORTUNITIES THEY HAVE FOR SOCIAL DEVELOPMENT.** This can be friends of the same age or different ages, siblings, cousins, adults, after-school activities, visits to the playground or community center, volunteer work (for younger children, volunteering with us; for older children, perhaps helping a neighbor or working at an animal shelter).

Dr. Montessori talked about the importance of developing *social cohesion*—when a community works together for the good of everyone. We can help our child consider not just what is good for them but also what is good for others around them—children on the playground, people in the supermarket, passengers on the train, or our neighbors.

We can help our child explore their cosmic task—a Montessori term that broadly means "one's purpose"—and the cosmic tasks of others. We can help them understand how all life on Earth is interdependent. We can help our child think beyond their role in our family or their classroom. We can encourage them to think about the planet and their responsibility to protect it; to serve others in our community and, as the child gets older, further afield; or to participate in such events as the Montessori Model United Nations—a forum where children from around the world act as ambassadors of different countries and present their policies—if the resources or a scholarship are available.

FOSTERING MORAL DEVELOPMENT

"Moral education is the source of the spiritual equilibrium on which everything else depends and which may be compared to the physical equilibrium or sense of balance without which it is impossible to stand upright, or move into any other position."

–Dr. Maria Montessori, *From Childhood to Adolescence*

As parents, we want to raise children who have a strong moral compass, who can discern between right and wrong. We want our child to do the right thing even when it is difficult. We want them to do the right thing because it is right and not because they want to be praised for doing it. We want to raise our child to have a strong character and to listen to their inner guide. We want our child to be secure in their beliefs and their abilities. To have a strong awareness of self and the ability to relate to others.

During the first plane of development, our child is absorbing more than just language and culture—they are also soaking in the values and beliefs that will become the foundation of their moral development. If we want our child to be kind, polite, courteous, patient, determined, generous, honest, optimistic, charitable, flexible, and inclusive, we must reflect these values in our attitude toward them and toward others. We can try to ensure that the communities where our child spends time—school, friends' houses, religious spaces—also share our values.

We can also explicitly tell our child what we expect of them. Different societies have different behavioral expectations—we are responsible for helping our children understand the expectations of our family and community. Of course, no one is perfect (even parents!), so we can also expect our child to hold us accountable when we do not live up to our values. We can encourage our children to question things they don't understand, to not blindly obey, and to learn to make good judgments.

If we have religious beliefs, these will also become a part of our child's moral development. We can share our beliefs with our child and help them develop their own sense of right and wrong.

EXTRA CONSIDERATIONS FOR THE 6- TO 12-YEAR-OLD CHILD'S SOCIAL AND MORAL DEVELOPMENT

The time from ages 6 to 12 is when our child's morals are solidified, but first they go through a period of testing and questioning our rules and values, poking to find any holes and exceptions. Our older child uses their logical, reasoning mind. They want to understand the whys and hows. The "how much" and "how often." They want to know the limits, conditions, and exceptions to all things, including morals.

Dr. Montessori called the years from ages 6 to 12 "the age of rudeness." We may observe that they are inclined to "tattle" or report on others. This is exploration—our child wants to see our response to help them judge whether something is right or wrong. They also may push the limits, with rude behavior and language. When this happens, it is important for us to respond respectfully and consistently with the understanding that they are experimenting and collecting data that will help them make their own choices in the future. We want to take time to explain the whys, give them opportunities to listen and act on their inner voice, and allow them to experience natural consequences as much as possible.

Children from 6 to 12 years old also have a strong sense of justice and are very concerned with fairness. As adults, we want to be fair and consistent, because our child is a keen observer and will catch any trace of injustice. This is a good time to have conversations about equality vs equity and fairness. (There is an excellent graphic made by the Robert Wood Johnson Foundation that shows how giving all members of a family the same bike would be an example of equality but not equity. Equity would look like a balance bike for a toddler, a child's bike for a school-age child, a three-wheeled bike for someone in the family with a disability, and an adult-sized bike for an adult.)

The 6- to 12-year-old child is very social. Belonging to a group or participating in group activities helps our child see the effect their actions or choices have on others. In addition to the group work and play they will likely do at school, we can provide them with opportunities to collaborate in and outside of our home. This is a great time for team sports or groups like scouts or guides. They will learn social skills, how to compromise, how to lead, and how to follow.

The child from 6 to 12 has the gifts of their logical, reasoning mind, and an imagination. We can invite them to empathize, to analyze, and to explore different behaviors, actions, reactions, and possibilities. They can explore events in the news and in politics and discuss different sides or viewpoints. Books (including mythology) and movies are also opportunities for discussions. We can introduce our children to good literature, music, and art that reflect the values we want them to acquire. We can talk about what we are reading and seeing and listen to our child's impressions, helping them fine-tune their understanding of complex issues.

In a Montessori classroom for 6- to 12-year-olds, particular attention is paid to people's contributions to the world and how they are connected. This interconnectedness is something we can highlight at home, developing gratitude for others and cultivating in our child a desire to contribute. We can wonder about the engineer who installed the traffic light that helps us drive safely or the farmer who planted the cotton from which our clothes were made or the person who invented the light bulb. We can help our child see that they, too, can work to have an impact on others in their community and the world. In this way, they start to explore their cosmic task.

As our child learns about people who have made an impact on the world, they will start to identify mentors and people who can be examples and models to them. Hero worship is a characteristic of the second plane, and our child may seek out idols who inspire them. Knowing this, we can expose them to models, whether fictional or real, who align with our family's values. We can also help them explore how humans can have both a positive and negative impact on the world around them. We can discuss what it means to use one's power responsibly.

An important part of supporting our child's moral development is giving them the opportunity and freedom to make their own decisions. This freedom means that they will likely make some bad decisions, and this is okay. It is better for them to make these decisions while they are still in our care, so we can walk through the repercussions together. This practice in decision-making and taking responsibility for one's choices will prepare them for the bigger decisions they will make down the road. Experience, not words, is the best teacher.

FOSTERING GRACE AND COURTESY

In Montessori classrooms, the children are given lessons on what is called *grace and courtesy*. The 3- to 6-year olds learn that while they have individual freedom, that freedom is limited by the needs and preferences of the group. For example, our child might like to sing loudly while knitting, but this might disrupt others. These lessons help the children learn how to respect one another and how to act around one another.

At home, we can help our child begin to recognize that they have to consider others in their choices and decisions. We can show our child how to recognize and express their feelings. We can show them how to respond to common situations, both positive and negative. What do you do when you want to do an activity that someone else is using? How do you react if someone offers you something you do not like? Or something you really like? Instead of assuming that our child "should know better," we can take the time to share with them what they need to know. We can practice these skills with them at neutral times and keep practicing until they become natural for our child. It does not need to be forced, and the best way for them to learn is for them to see us using these social graces and courtesies.

> "The adults do not insist on manners and courtesies but maintain an attitude of mutual respect and model expected manners and courtesies."
>
> —Judi Orion, AMI trainer, lecture in Switzerland, 2018

Grace and courtesy lessons still apply for the 6- to 12-year-old child, but they will look different. Our older child may be interested in the reasons behind the skills they are acquiring. For example, where did the custom of shaking hands come from? (It was a way for early people to show they didn't have a sword in their hand and meant no harm!) There is also less overt "teaching" with the 6- to 12-year-olds. Instead, we can make observations: "I've noticed that there are towels on the bathroom floor after you shower." We can see if they have observed the same, and invite them to explore the best way for their towel to dry. We can ask them to report back at the end of the week to let us know how it's going. When we hand the responsibility over to our child and give them space and time to sort it out for themselves, eventually it will come naturally to them.

As the adult, we define for our children the boundaries of appropriate behaviors. Grace and courtesy will reflect our family values, our culture, and our time and place. If we observe our child being rude to a friend or a caregiver or even to us and we ignore it, we have communicated to them that it is appropriate behavior. It is important to set limits and be consistent in maintaining these boundaries. When we do this, we are helping them develop knowledge and confidence in their world. There is a security that comes from knowing what is appropriate and what is not.

It is okay to say no to our child and stop them from behaving in a way that is antisocial. It is okay to take our child and leave the store or park if they are not behaving appropriately. We don't have to lose our cool or yell. We can count to 10 in our head to calm ourselves down first. We can say, "We are leaving now because this is inappropriate behavior/ because there are other people here whom we need to consider/because the library is a space for people to read and study quietly."

When possible, we can prepare our children in advance so that these kinds of situations are avoided. Before visiting a friend, we can orient them by telling our child how we will let them know when it's time to go. We can then give them advance notice when it will soon be time to leave and allow time for transitioning.

Grace and courtesy lessons we can give at home:

How to greet family members, friends, and strangers. We can model how to greet people in a way that is appropriate for our specific culture and environment. We can practice these greetings with our child. If in the moment of greeting someone, our child forgets, we can gently remind them. If they purposely refuse, instead of putting them on the spot or getting into a power struggle, we can discuss it with them at a later time.

How to welcome a friend or visitor. We can show our child how to welcome a friend or a special guest into our home. They can make a flower arrangement or a nice welcome sign. If culturally appropriate, we can show them how to offer a handshake, a hug, or a bow.

How to tell a friend you would rather not share a special toy. We can respect our children's wishes when they prefer not to share. We can show them how to put their special toys away before a guest comes over. We can teach them how to politely say they would rather their friend not use that toy. We can show them how to offer an alternative to their friend.

How to own up to a wrongdoing. Sometimes it can be hard to own up to a wrongdoing. We can help our child feel more comfortable by role-playing with them and showing them different ways to take responsibility for their actions.

How to apologize. We can show our children ways to apologize that communicate genuinely that they are sorry. In Junnifa's family, they are encouraged to say, "I am sorry that I _____ . I was wrong. Next time I will _____ . What can I do to make you feel better?" (For more on helping children make a repair, see page 154.)

How to express gratitude. We can make appreciation part of our family culture. We can start with saying thank you. Then we can teach our children to write thank-you notes or make little thank-you gifts. They can thank people for things like a meal or a gift; or they can thank the people in their life, like a postal worker who delivers packages.

How to give constructive feedback. Children can be blunt with their feedback, which can come across as insensitive. In our Montessori classes, we teach a "sandwich" approach, which can also be used at home. First, we acknowledge what we like or what the person did well; then we point out something they can improve upon, with specifics on how; and then we end with positive feedback. (For example, "Look how colorful your painting is. Maybe you could try to stay more on the paper next time. I can tell you worked really hard on it. You look pleased with it.")

OTHER GRACE AND COURTESY ACTIVITIES

MANNERS

- How to say please, excuse me, sorry, thank you, and pardon me

- How to open and close doors quietly

- How to excuse themselves from a group

- How to get the attention of a friend, parent, or stranger

- How to hold the door while someone passes through

- How to sneeze (into one's elbow)

- How to graciously accept or decline a hug, a gift, or an invitation

- How to express excitement

- How to disagree

- How to question a thought they don't agree with

- How to invite a friend to an event

- How to accept rejection

- How to give and receive a compliment

- How to talk or not talk about another person's features

- How to introduce oneself to an audience

MOVEMENTS AND INTERACTION

- Walking carefully (e.g., around furniture or where someone is working)

- Opening and closing a door or window

- Striking up a conversation

- Offering someone something

- Getting past someone who is in their way

- Meeting someone for the first time

DINING

- Setting the table

- Dining etiquette

- Manners—saying please and thank you

- Asking someone to pass them something

- Not speaking while eating

- Excusing themselves from the table

- Pulling out and pushing in chairs

GOING OUT

An important part of supporting our child's development
is in going out into the community. In a Montessori class
for 6- to 12-year-olds, the children arrange their own outings and an adult accompanies
them as a chaperone. The children are responsible for making appointments, booking
tickets, looking up transportation routes and timetables, and sending thank-you notes.

We can allow our children to do this as well. Some ideas include visiting a museum,
the library, the train station, a bank, or the post office; doing community service or
volunteer work or helping a neighbor; visiting an expert, a local business (e.g., a bakery),
or a recycling depot. They learn so much from getting out into the community, expanding
their horizons, and taking on the organizational responsibilities.

HOW TO HANDLE COMMON MORAL
AND BEHAVIORAL CHALLENGES

The following are some moral and behavioral challenges that often come up in childhood.

Lying

Somewhere around the age of 3, children start to experiment with lying. For a 3-year-
old, the lies may be very obvious or over the top. It is still important to address these lies
and help our child practice telling the truth. If we address the behavior when they are
young, it will likely stop for a while. But we shouldn't be surprised if the inclination to
lie appears again in the 6 to 12 age range as our child begins to explore morality.

When our child lies, it is usually not malicious. Sometimes it is spontaneous self-preservation.
Sometimes they are testing us to see if they can get away with it. Sometimes we know our
child is lying, and we may be inclined to confront them or put them on the spot.

Junnifa learned this lesson the hard way in her elementary class. A child who had very
neat handwriting was working on a project and for some reason wrote very messily on

it. When Junnifa saw it, she said, "This couldn't possibly be Karina's." Karina was put on the spot, so she lied and said it wasn't hers. Karina later found Junnifa and confessed that it *was* hers, explaining that she had been embarrassed because Junnifa had already announced that it couldn't possibly be hers. It's in this way that we can unintentionally put our children in positions where they feel uncomfortable and then resort to lying.

However, it's important not to punish, overreact, or embarrass our child, especially if we see that they were lying to try to protect themselves. Instead of asking, "Did you do this?" we can help them verbalize it on their own in a nonthreatening way: "I see that the vase got broken. Let's talk about what we can do to make it better." We can offer alternative ways to handle the situation, always emphasizing the importance of honesty and trust. It is also important to show children how to make amends or restitution when they have done something wrong. (See more about making repairs on page 154.)

It is also important for us to model honesty by always telling our children the truth and also keeping our word. "I said I'd be home by 5:00 p.m., and I wasn't. That's not okay. I understand if you are upset, and I'd like to make it up to you." It is important not to exaggerate and to be careful when we are joking because the child may take our joke literally and think we are lying.

Siblings

Sibling relationships are some of the most important and lasting relationships our child will develop over the course of their lives. Here are some ways to support the development of a positive sibling relationship:

Start early. We can start while the younger sibling is still in utero. We can involve the older sibling or siblings by having them talk to the baby and read books and sing to the baby in the womb. We can involve our older child in the preparation for the new baby's arrival, such as helping to set up the baby's spaces. When the baby arrives, we can find age-appropriate ways to involve them. Allow them to carry the baby (for older children) and have them help with the care of the baby (for any age sibling). All of these actions build a bond with the baby.

Nurture our connection with the older sibling/s. When the baby is young, we can find ways to nurture our relationship with our older children while also helping them understand the needs of the baby. We can make sure to have some daily quality time when we are focused on our older child or have our partner and other family members give them more time and attention. We can also be careful not to give them too much responsibility. We can say things like "Can you look after each other while I visit the bathroom?" reminding them to care for each other regardless of birth order.

Do not compare them to each other. Each child is unique and will develop their own unique personality. Our own personalities can also affect the way we perceive our different children. We may be drawn to the child who is more like us or be activated by a child who reflects something we don't like in ourselves. Whatever our feelings are, it is imperative to not compare our children. When we do that, we give one child the impression that we prefer the other child, which can sow seeds of discord. We can encourage their uniqueness and strengths without putting anyone down.

As they grow, provide opportunities for them to do things together. While individual rooms might be attractive, a shared space is a lovely way to support sibling relationships. They will negotiate, discuss, laugh, play, and grow together. We can also provide activities that invite collaboration. Routines and rhythms, celebrations and rituals also support positive sibling relationships. We can develop family rituals around birthdays, holidays, or even meals, eating together, conversing about our day, and acknowledging each other's experiences.

Remain neutral when they disagree. It is normal for siblings to disagree or bicker, and it is important not to take sides or blame one child (often the older one). We can resist the temptation to interfere or to moderate every argument. When we do step in, we can try to remain neutral, acknowledging everyone's feelings, help our children clarify what they are feeling, and help them sort out the issue for themselves. All parties can be responsible for the solution. This avoids any resentment, and the children learn that they are part of a family that works and solves problems together.

It can also be helpful to have house rules or agreements about how members of the family interact with each other. (See page 36 for more on making agreements and page 153 for resolving conflicts.)

Connect with each child on an individual basis. When children aren't getting the attention they need, they will seek it by any means—including negative behavior. (See page 39 for ideas on how to connect.)

Prioritize equity over equality. We want to be fair, but instead of equality, we can aim for equity (see page 93). Sometimes one child needs more attention at a particular time, and that's okay. We can learn how each of our children perceives love and make sure to give them what they need. Some children need more touch, others more quality time, others words of affirmation, other acts of service, and others gifts; sometimes they need a combination. (For more on love languages, read *The Five Love Languages* by Gary Chapman.)

Encourage them to express their feelings to each other. We can give them the words: "I love you." "I appreciate how you _____." We can have discussions about what each child values, their love languages, and the language of apology. We can help each child learn how to fill the other's tank.

Observe when there is a lot of arguing. If our children always seem to be bickering and disagreeing, it is important to take time to observe and see what might be leading to the disagreements. Sometimes, when children are in different planes, their needs and perspectives are just different. Our once loving 6-year-old might become quite impatient with a younger sibling. We may need to provide them with tools to act better or modify our environment to ensure that each child has what they need. We can provide opportunities to be together as well as time apart; shared spaces and private spaces. (See chapter 4 for more tips about setting up the environment for siblings.)

Sharing

In a Montessori classroom for 3- to 6-year-olds, there is only one of each activity, and the children must take turns with it. They know an activity is available when it is back on the shelf, complete and ready for the next person. Dr. Montessori believed that this encourages the children to develop patience and to learn to respect someone else's work, whilst eliminating competition.

In our homes, if we have similar clear agreements about how things are shared, the children know what to expect and are able to solve problems with each other.

- What is the agreement about sharing activities in our home?
- What about special items for each child?
- Before visitors come over, can we involve our child in setting aside anything special they do not feel like sharing that day?
- How do we solve conflicts when they arise?

We can help our children learn how to negotiate sharing outside the home. For example, at the playground, we can help them learn how to stand up for themselves: "It's my turn next. You can wait behind me." "That's my bucket. You can have a turn when I'm done." We can also help them understand that there may be different rules at the playground than at home, and we let everyone have a turn. "Let's count down from ten so that someone else can have a turn on the swing now."

For a younger child, if they have taken something from another child and that child is upset, we may need to step in to translate for both parties. To the other child, we can say, "It looks like you are sad. That's your toy, and you weren't finished playing with it? I'm sorry my child took your toy. They really wanted to play with it, but it was not okay for them to take it." Then to our child, we can say, "This child was still playing with this, but it will be available soon. Can you please give it back, or do you need my help to give it back?" Similarly, if our child wants to bring a toy to the playground, we can remind them that other children may want to use it and check to see how that feels to them.

For the 6- to 12-year-old children, they are likely to come up with their own collaborative solutions, particularly if we encourage this and do not interfere.

How to interrupt politely

From the age of 3, a child can learn ways to interrupt us politely if we are in the middle of something. We can teach them to put their hand on our shoulder while they wait for us to finish. We can then put our hand on their hand to connect with them and acknowledge that they are waiting for us. We can keep our hand there until we are ready to give them the attention they need. This is something we can practice—for example, role-playing making a phone call and letting them practice getting our attention. When they forget (and they will), we can quietly tap our shoulder to remind them.

We can also be mindful of how we interrupt our child to tell them it's time to leave or that it's time for dinner or to ask them a question. Is it possible to wait until they are finished with what they are doing before saying anything? If we do need to interrupt them, how might they like to be interrupted? With a knock on the door? By our playing some music? With a timer or alarm? By placing our hand on their shoulder? How much time do they need in advance to transition from what they are working on?

If our child has a tendency to talk over us or others, we can help them learn to wait their turn by saying, "I'll finish my turn, and then you can talk." Or "We want to hear what you have to say once your brother has finished talking."

How to apologize or make it up to someone

Junnifa once observed the following exchange in a classroom: Toward the end of the day, as a child was carrying an activity back to the shelf, he got distracted looking out the window and bumped into another child. She began to cry and said, "Aslam bumped into me!" Aslam just stood there. A teacher asked him if he would like to apologize, and he did not respond. The teacher then said, "Emame is hurt. Would you like to bring some ice for her?" Aslam immediately went to get the ice. When he brought it to Emame, he looked concerned for her and helped her press it to the spot that hurt. He then said to her, "I really didn't mean to bump into you. I saw my mom's car go past, and I was distracted. I didn't even see you." And she replied, "It's okay. I feel better now." No one said the word "sorry," but both children had a clear understanding of what had happened and how the other person felt, the conflict was resolved, and each person left feeling better.

Often when children are forced to say they're sorry, they may not mean it, and it may not mean anything to the person on the receiving end of the apology. Instead of forcing our child to say they're sorry, we can encourage them to talk through their conflicts and guide them in coming to a resolution. When we feel an apology is necessary and our child is not being forthcoming, we can apologize on behalf of our child and then talk to our child later. Sometimes our child may need time to process an event before they can take responsibility. (More on repairs on page 154.)

Bullying

What if our child is being bullied? If our child complains about being bullied, we can first empower them to speak up for themselves. We might guide them on how to bring the issue up to their teacher if it is happening in school or directly to the perpetrators if it is happening elsewhere. If we do need to step in, we can do it in such a way that our child still feels empowered and is part of the conversation (e.g., we can ask them if they would like us to go with them to speak to their teacher to support them if necessary), instead of being relegated to the position of victim (we speak to the teacher for them). In a Montessori school, we recognize that a child who bullies generally does not feel like they belong. If possible, we can work with the school to make sure that they find a way for the other child to be seen, heard, and understood, so our child can be safe there.

What if our child is the bully? It is important to get to the root of the behavior. Children who hurt others are often feeling hurt themselves. Perhaps our child is feeling insecure or disempowered. It is important to address these needs as well as make our child understand that bullying is unacceptable. We can also hold them accountable and guide them in making a repair.

When our child appears bossy or shy

Some children enjoy telling everyone—including the adults—what and when and how to do things. These children may have a spark, initiative, and leadership qualities that we do not want to quash. But we also want them to build the skills they need to live and work harmoniously with others—to learn to wait, to respect and listen to others, to understand that everyone has their own will. Rather than labeling our child "bossy" (which can be a hard label to grow out of), we can help them identify their underlying need and build any skills they still need to learn.

Similarly, with a child who hides behind our leg in new situations, takes time to warm up to new people, or needs a lot of time alone after social engagements, we can accept them for who they are while still helping them build the skills they will need to live in society. We can help them learn to say hello in a way that makes them feel comfortable, to ask if they can join a group to play, and to excuse themselves for some quiet time when needed. We can stop calling them "shy" (again, such a label can become self-fulfilling) and instead guess how they may be feeling: "Do you need some time to warm up right now? Would you like to say, 'I need a bit more time to watch first'?"

Friendships

Children start to cultivate friendships in the first plane. We can provide opportunities for them to interact with others. They can also observe us modeling the elements of building positive relationships. We offer them language and opportunities for communication, showing our child how to express themselves, empowering them to stand up for themselves respectfully, and encouraging but not forcing collaboration.

Ideally, by the time our child has reached the second plane of development, we have helped them set a good foundation of values and morals that will guide them as their friends begin to have more influence over them. We can remind them of their values and discuss the choices that they're making. In order for these conversations to have an impact, we need to have built a relationship based on connection and open communication.

When we see signs of changes in our child's behavior with a particular friend.
We can bring these changes to our child's attention and have a conversation about them. We can listen to how they feel when they are with the child and why they might behave differently around them. Perhaps we need to do some work with them on their sense of self or give them tools to help them when they feel pressure from this friend. If this doesn't improve things, we can consider limiting their time with the friend by having more family time or playdates with other children. We can be careful not to come across as punitive, as this can also lead to rebellion or resentment from our child. As much as possible, we can remind our child of the values that matter in our home so they can have something to measure or compare other people's behavior against.

When things go wrong. When our children do something wrong in the presence of others, it's important to be calm and we can wait until we are alone with them to have a conversation with them about their behavior. It's important to always check our motives and make sure that we want our children to do the right thing because it's right and not because we want them to conform or because we care what others will say. Children are perceptive, and they absorb everything, including a feeling of wanting to please others.

Helping our child build skills with friends. If we observe that our child might need to develop some skills, we can play or practice with our child. For example:

- If our child likes to give hugs, we can teach them to check with the other person that they would like one.
- We can teach them to say "Stop" or "I don't like that" if someone does something they don't like or they want to stop rough play.
- If our child is sad that their friend doesn't want to play with them, we can teach them to ask if they would like to play another day, about games they can play by themselves, how they can ask to join another group's game, while also acknowledging our child's feelings.
- We can help them learn when to ask for help from an adult.

The competitive child

There is nothing wrong about a child enjoying competition. It is only a problem if our child has difficulty losing, or when their competitive spirit negatively affects other children. The Montessori classroom creates a noncompetitive peer learning environment. Even with the youngest children, we nurture working together as a community. Encouraging collaboration over competition reinforces the idea that everyone belongs and contributes.

If we have a child who is showing competitive behavior at home, we can look at the following:

Are we encouraging competition in our home? Do we ask, "Who can get ready first?" "Who can be my best helper?" "Who ate all their dinner?" Instead, could we encourage collaboration? "Let's see how quickly we can get ready for school." Those who are ready first can help the last ones if they need help.

When they compare themselves to others, can we focus instead on the individual? When our child moans, "It's not fair; they got two and I only got one," instead of lecturing or moralizing—for example, by saying, "Things don't always go our way"— we can acknowledge how they feel: "It sounds like you really wanted more. I can see why it must have been frustrating that there weren't enough for everyone to get two." When they boast, "I'm the fastest/strongest," we can respond without building up competition and focus on the individual: "It sounds like you love running fast/feeling strong!"

Can we focus on the process, not the result? This can help a child who wants to be best to focus on all the steps along the way, not only the outcome. "You've been training hard for the competition this weekend and not missed a single practice."

Does our family have an abundance mindset? In a Montessori classroom, every child can achieve their best and it's not at the expense of someone else. There is enough time to learn, there is enough space for each child, and every child is valued. This is an *abundance mindset*.

Can we practice sporting conduct—whether we win or lose? When children are playing a sport or a game, we have an opportunity to teach them sporting conduct—balancing their desire to do their best and build the skills to excel while keeping in mind ideas like equity and fairness. We can focus on playing our best, trying to improve ourselves, rather than always needing to win. We can practice the grace and courtesy of saying "Congratulations" to the winner and "Better luck next time" to the loser. We focus on how we all played, rather than on who won. This takes a lot of repetition and practice! If our child is upset when they lose, we can offer comfort: "It's hard to see you sad when you lose" or "It can be hard to lose when you really tried your best." This can help you to maintain connection even when they are having a hard time.

BECOMING SOCIAL CITIZENS

In our Montessori classrooms, we see every child as unique, we accept every child for who they are, and we ensure that every child feels they belong in our community. We can do similar work in our home. Raising antiracist, antibias children is intrinsically linked with raising a Montessori child. It stretches from how we spend our money, to how we show up in our communities, to finding ways to take action in the face of injustice.

A helpful framework for this work is the four antibias education goals developed by Louise Derman-Sparks and Julie Olsen Edwards.

Goal 1: Each child understands and values their own identity. We are all made up of an intersection of identities, including race, ethnicity, gender, religion, economic class, family structure, neurodiversity, differing abilities, languages, and so on. The child from 3 to 6 years old with their absorbent mind will pick up attitudes (positive, neutral, or negative) about parts of their identity from us and others around them. The 6- to 12-year-old child takes this further and will question how they or their family are the same and different from others.

To build a strong sense of self, we can help our child see themselves (their skin color, hair type, family structure, language, etc.) represented in:

- Books and storytelling
- Artwork, posters, and photographs
- Toys, such as dolls and puzzles
- Art materials, such as skin-tone crayons or paints they can mix to replicate their own skin tone
- Songs, dance, music, and instruments

Part of understanding who they are is also recognizing any privileges they have. Which of their identities gives them access, ease, or "invisibility" and which identities do not?

Goal 2: Each child understands and values others' identities. We can build on the work we have done on Goal 1 by helping our children get to know other people in our community, through real experiences.

We can look for toys, books, artwork, exhibitions, and other media that represent human diversity and centers stories about children and families whose lives and identities are different from our own.

"Children learn prejudice from prejudice—not from learning about human diversity. It is how people respond to differences that teaches bias and fear."

—Louise Derman-Sparks and Julie Olsen Edwards, *Anti-Bias Education for Children and Ourselves*

We can go further and try to ensure that our friends, doctors, and other people in our daily life and communities represent a broad spectrum of identities. We can venture outside our communities to other neighborhoods or towns that are different from our own. We can notice what things are the same and what might be different.

Our 3- to 6-year-old children will take all of this in with their absorbent mind. The 6- to 12-year-old child will explore the similarities and differences under the lens of their moral compass and their intellectual growth, and ties to their interest in how people live in different places and at different times in history.

Goal 3: Each child can identify injustice and recognize that it hurts. We can help our child recognize injustice, unfairness, and stereotypes that are aimed at them or others. We can help them become critical thinkers by asking questions like "Who is not in the room?" or "Who does this disadvantage?" We can model asking questions when we hear something in the news, read an article or social media post, walk past a billboard, or overhear our children talking. Antibias educator Britt Hawthorne encourages us to help our child identify the problems in the system rather than the individual. When our child asks, "Why do those people live under a bridge?" it is an opportunity to talk about things like the cost of living in our city and how our city hasn't invested in affordable housing.

We can help our child challenge binary categories and learn to center others. They can learn to appreciate other cultures, not appropriate them. We can acknowledge the native stewards and caretakers of the land where we live and explore ways in which individuals and society can redistribute resources. As our child learns about who holds power in society, they can also learn to critically analyze the effects.

Goal 4: Each child feels empowered to take action in cases of injustice. We can ask our child what action they'd like to take. We can help them draft a letter to the local government. We can encourage them to stand up for themselves or someone else if they see prejudice or discrimination. "That's unkind." "That hurts me/them when you say that." In times of crisis, they may want to donate money they have saved or find hands-on ways to help and support individuals in our community who may be living on the margins.

We can help our 6- to 12-year-old child develop their sense of fairness and empathy. But these conversations can happen far earlier, with our babies, toddlers, and preschoolers. As their adults, we need to educate ourselves so that we can guide them in these critical conversations and model calling people in and out when we see or experience injustice.

Here are some useful phrases from *Speak Up at School* by Learning for Justice:

- "That offends me."

- "I don't find that funny."

- "I'm surprised to hear you say that."

- "What do you mean by that?"

- "What point are you trying to make by saying that?"

- "Did you mean to say something hurtful when you said that?"

- "Using that word as a put-down offends me."

- "Using that word doesn't help others feel safe or accepted here."

A note on books

We learned from Britt Hawthorne that there are different types of book collections. There are affirming books (in which children sees themselves represented), books for diversity (which represent many types of different children, people, and families), books for social justice (including books that include harmful stereotypes or other content that we want to critically analyze together with our child), and books for activism (about how others have taken action in the past and how we can take action now). We can think about the purpose of the books and how we will use them as we add to our book collections and when visiting the library. Some books we will want to make sure we read with our children so we can discuss what we see, and others we will be able to leave on the shelf for our children to explore on their own.

FURTHER READING

- *Raising Antiracist Children: A Practical Parenting Guide* by Britt Hawthorne (written by a Montessori-trained anti-bias, antiracist educator and includes lots of activities to do with our children)
- *The Antiracist Kid: A Book About Identity, Justice, and Activism* by Tiffany Jewell (also written by a Montessori-trained educator, for children 8 to 12 years old)
- *Anti-Bias Education for Children and Ourselves* by Louise Derman-Sparks and Julie Olsen Edwards
- *Speak Up at School* by Learning for Justice
- *Cultivating Genius: An Equity Framework for Culturally and Historically Responsive Literacy* by Gholdy Muhammad

BUILDING OUR FAMILY CULTURE

We can build a conscious family culture in our home. Colleen Wilkinson, of Trauma Informed Montessori, writes of mirror neurons: "We are a social species; if one animal senses danger, the entire group becomes alert, survival increases; calmness, safety, well-being are also contagious." We can be intentional then to offer our children such calmness, safety, and well-being.

- We want our children to feel safe in our home, physically and psychologically.
- They will receive our care, and they will learn to show the same care to others in the family.
- We can develop clear family agreements (see p. 36).
- We can talk about what respect means, such as using kind words, listening to each other, using our bodies to listen, and giving each other space to talk, move, and rest.
- And we can have fun. Simone knows a 10-year-old who who came up with a new way for their family to connect through pizza. Each person wrote down what toppings they wanted on their personal pizza and placed the paper in a hat. Everyone picked someone else's request and made it for them.
- We can ensure that each member of the family feel like they are special and belong in our family.

JOSHUAA, KALEB, KATERI

@ndnslp & Faculty of Johns Hopkins
Bloomberg School of Public Health
Diné & Acoma Pueblo, New Mexico,
on the Navajo Nation

"There's been a lot of problem-solving activities that I've done with my kids, like taking them outdoors and showing them cause and effect through the irrigation canal, like what happens when you fill up the water and it flows over."

"I also think about how I teach vocabulary to my kids, like being in the Kiva as Pueblo people, or out hunting and using those opportunities to tell them about what's happening and to provide that language facilitation through real-life conversations."

"I think Montessori is like real-life learning. Learning by doing, learning by experiencing, and learning by feeling and eating, by actually seeing it too. So that's really how I would explain Montessori and coming from an Indigenous lens to it, we're all about connection. Connectedness is such a key piece of our existence as humans, is connection to our children, and the other way around, connection to our parents, and then even connection to what's around us, living things, nonliving things, to Earth, all these things."

"Children that have been given those opportunities to learn a skill set, like starting a fire, respecting it, learning about it, why we do it, and how it's used, at a very early age, start to do some of those things on their own. Like putting the fire together, like being able to know what needs to be dried, starting with small pieces, and when to use something big."

"As a speech language pathologist, and as a parent, this approach works very well for young Native children, who are very unique learners and are in this stage of learning more about their culture, relearning their language, but also working through generations of trauma as well to where inadequate learning spaces were a contributor to increased anxiety and reduce academic self efficacy."

PUTTING IT
INTO PRACTICE

7

PART ONE

APPLYING MONTESSORI IN DAILY LIFE

DAILY RHYTHMS

Children thrive on knowing what comes next, which gives them a measure of control in their otherwise unpredictable days. Studies show that children have better cognitive and psychosocial outcomes when they have choice and control in their day, with predictable times for things like getting dressed, eating meals, and going to bed.

Often life seems to sweep us along, but it can be useful to be intentional about what our days, weeks, and months look like. Rather than the word "routine" or "schedule," we like using the word "rhythm," which we learned from Eloise Rickman, author of *Extraordinary Parenting*. Rhythms allow some flexibility to be able to follow the child's pace, with the predictability of knowing what comes next and how it will be carried out.

Most children like to know what the general plan is for the day. During breakfast, we can check in with the family to see what the day is going to look like. On vacations or weekends, this morning check-in can also help our child plan their activities. If we are heading out in the afternoon, they know they have the morning to themselves. If we have the whole day free, they might start work on a bigger project that needs more time and space. This gives them some choice in and control over their days.

When plans change (and they will), we can give them a heads-up. "You know how we were planning to go out soon? I've just seen that there is a delivery coming before lunch, so would it be okay if we go after lunch instead?"

TO OBSERVE

- Is there a clear rhythm in our home on weekdays?
- How is this similar/different on weekends?
- Is there enough time? Or are we always in a rush?
- What can we take out of our schedule to allow more free time in our week?

A daily rhythm

A daily rhythm is not a rigid schedule but more like large blocks of uninterrupted time for certain activities, with mealtimes at pretty regular times every day.

It's hard to generalize because families vary so much, but here is an example of what a daily rhythm might look like for a child of 3 to 12 years old:

WAKING

- Reads or plays quietly on waking
- Cuddles and reads or talks with parent

GETTING READY

- Brushes teeth, combs hair, washes face
- Gets dressed
- Helps prepare breakfast and eats with the family
- Packs lunch (if needed)
- Packs schoolbag

LEAVING THE HOUSE

- Puts shoes on
- Adds layers of clothing—coat, hat, gloves, scarf—if needed
- Applies sunscreen if needed
- Takes schoolbag and anything else they'll need for the day (clothes for playing a sport, a musical instrument, library books to return, etc.)

MORNING

- Attends preschool/school/a morning activity
- Lunch—eats at school or at home or has a picnic lunch

AFTERNOON

- Engages in after-school activities, such as:
  - Spending time in nature—going to the playground, park, beach, mountain, or forest
  - Spending time with the community—visiting family or friends, volunteering in the neighborhood, or going to the library
  - Playing sports or having a music lesson (not too many days in the week)
  - Engaging in free-play at home—reading, exploring, inventing, building, baking

LATE AFTERNOON

- Helps prepare dinner
- Sets the table
- Does any homework
- Tidies up

DINNER

- Eats with the family at the table (this will include learning grace and courtesy practices and engaging in family conversation)

AFTER DINNER

- Enjoys quiet activities or family walk
- Takes a bath or shower
- Brushes teeth
- Gets into pajamas

BEDTIME

- Reads books or tells stories in bed
- Debriefs about the day
- Snuggles
- Lights out

There are so many opportunities in our daily rhythm for our child to build their independence, take responsibility for themselves, and make their own choices.

We also check the needs of our child. If we have a child who prefers to be at home and we have had a lot of outings, scheduling a pajama day will give them time to decompress. If our child is overtired, we can look at our rhythm and see how we can create more rest for them.

When problems arise in our daily rhythms

It can be quite frustrating when our toddler who was interested in dressing themselves and getting ready now shows disinterest or seeming laziness, or expects us to help them. This is common from the age of 2.5 to 3 years and older. They no longer find it an interesting challenge to master, yet also want more autonomy over themselves. It can be a frustrating stage for both adult and child.

Always start first with observation to collect some objective information, including looking for any bottlenecks—points of resistance—that recur on a daily basis.

It might be that after breakfast, they need to go back to their room to get dressed, but they get distracted by the toys in the living room. We might be able to change the order so they get dressed upon waking, and then help prepare their breakfast.

It might be that siblings wind each other up and distract each other. We could try to have them get ready separately until the skills are in place again and then move toward their being able to get dressed at the same time.

Lessen the battles by being clear about what is happening (such as when we'd like to leave and what needs to be done), using positive ways to encourage cooperation, and not taking on the problem as our own. (See pages 141–146 for tips to cultivate cooperation.)

Slow down the pace and allow enough time. Both the 3- to 6-year-old child and the 6- to 12-year-old child generally do not like being rushed. They want to feel in control of how they leave the house. It can be a useful exercise for our child to record how long it takes to do everything to get out of the house (a younger child might need our help with this). We can then allow an extra 5 minutes on top in case someone cannot find their gloves or something unexpected arises.

Make a checklist or use routine cards. With a child from 3 to 6 years old, one way to ease morning and evening rhythms is to have the child help make a checklist of everything that needs to be done. (It's important to choose a neutral time to make this list, not when we are trying to rush out the door or they are bouncing around in their pajamas avoiding bedtime.)

Together, we can think of all the necessary steps that need to be done and document them. We can write a list, make a chart with simple drawings, print out some routine cards, or print photos of our child doing each step. These visual cues can be hung with tape, on a string with clothespins, or on a magnetic board that allows the child to choose or change the order of the routine. Then, instead of having to nag them, we can simply point to the chart, ask "What does the chart say is next?" and let them take responsibility for getting ready. We are working together. Often after a week, the rhythm has been restored and our child will rely less on the checklist.

For children ages 6 to 12, we could discuss at our family meeting ideas to help everyone leave on time in the morning. They might choose to set a series of alarms, agree to an earlier bedtime, organize things the evening before, or ask us to check if they are awake. Then we can make a time to come back to see how the new plan is working out.

Prepare the environment. We can review the principles in chapter 4 to prepare the enviroment so that the child knows where everything can be found, everything looks appealing, and they can do things with less help. The child younger than 6 years old likes it when everything is in the same place each time they look for it; and the 6- to 12-year-old needs some order in the external environment as it doesn't come so naturally to them.

To get out the door on time, observe the following:

- Is it easy for our child to choose clothing for themselves?

- Are the cupboards or drawers too full so it's hard for them to see what is available?

- Do we need to store out-of-season items to make it easier for them to choose appropriate clothing?

- Do they need a special place to sit to get ready?

- Would they find it fun to choose some clothes the night before and lay them out in the shape of a person?

- Is everything that they will need to leave by the front door? Shoes? Bags? Sunscreen in warmer months? Gloves and hats in colder seasons?

- Would a checklist of things they need to pack in their bags, including sports equipment or a musical instrument, be useful?

Help them to do it themselves. It may initially take a little longer to teach our child how to put on their shoes and tie their shoelaces than to do it for them, breaking it into small steps for them to practice. In the long run, however, we will then have a child who can do these things by themselves and no longer needs our help.

Give as little help as possible (and as much as necessary). We start by scaffolding the skills, but we can take down the scaffold when it is no longer needed.

For an older child around 5 years old, if they still need cues like "Now you need to put on your shoes," we may have forgotten to take down the scaffold. As we make the transition to doing less, we might need to keep ourselves busy. Our role is to support, not make it all happen. We can be responsible for things like ensuring that our child has clean clothes available and that there's healthy food in the fridge. Then we can trust our child to manage getting ready with just a little help like saying "bag" if we see that they are headed out the door without it.

Let them learn by experiencing consequences. A child leaving the house without their coat on will feel cold. A child who jumps in puddles will learn that their feet get wet. A child might go to school in their pajamas if they are not dressed in time—warn the school beforehand so they can provide support on their end and try to act completely normal so as not to shame the child but let them learn from the natural consequences. We do not need to lecture (avoid "See, I told you so"); we can let the consequences speak for themselves.

Get their agreement. Make it clear what the departure time is and ask if they need anything from us to make it happen. Let them know when it's 5 minutes before departure. Instead of calling from another room, go over to where they are, and, as much as possible, try not to interrupt them. Wait until they have finished their activity so they will be more likely to hear us. If it looks like they may not have time to finish what they are working on, we could say, "It is leaving time in 5 minutes. Would you like to start finishing up your game? Or you can put it somewhere to finish it when we get back."

Some last tips

- A playful reminder ("5 minutes, bakers!" if they have ever seen a cooking show) can be less stressful than a demand to hurry up.
- Allow time for them to process any requests. It is worth counting to 10 slowly in our head (not aloud, which can stress out our child) before repeating ourselves. While we think they are ignoring us, they may still be processing what we said.
- For the most relaxing start to the day, wake up half an hour earlier. Even better if it's before the rest of the family wakes up—we then have time to ourselves to shower, get dressed, and be ready to help the others if they need it.

Continued on page 118

TALK IN A WAY THAT HELPS THEM LISTEN

GIVE THEM A CHOICE	"Would you like to put on your coat or shoes first?"
GET THEM TO THINK	"What do we need to do before we leave?" "Where are your shoes kept?"
DESCRIBE THE PROBLEM (WITHOUT JUDGMENT) AND LET THEM WORK OUT THE REST	"I see you have bare feet, and we are about to go outside."
USE ONE WORD INSTEAD OF A LONG EXPLANATION	"Shoes" (if they need to put on their shoes). "Light" (as a reminder to turn off the light). "Plate" (if they have forgotten to take their plate to the sink).
WHISPER	This is a surprising way to get their attention and to bring down the energy levels in the house.
WRITE A NOTE	"Please don't forget me!" (taped to a pair of shoes) (Even if the child can't read, they are sure to ask you what it says.)
USE A CLOCK OR TIMER	"Let's see if we can get ready before the big hand gets to the 12/before the beeper goes off." We can see how fast we can go as a family (avoid a competition between children) and those ready first will be able to help the slower ones, even us—the adult—if we are the last to be ready.

- Fill their emotional bucket first thing in the morning—snuggle in bed, read books, give lots of hugs and tickles. Those lovely minutes spent connecting with our child will pay off in cooperation during the morning routine.
- Prepare the night before—it can help to pack lunches, lay out possible clothes choices, and check the weather. Rise and shine, and we will be ready to go.
- We can ask our child how they would like us to remind them if we notice they are short of time. It's hard to watch them be late, but we can stay calm knowing we have helped them, and they will do the rest.
- If a child is refusing to go to school, we can be clear that not going to school is not an option and be compassionate at the same time. "It sounds like there's something going on that is making you not want to go. We'll work together to make it as easy as possible for you to get to school."

If there is still resistance . . .

- Do not get into a power struggle.
- Remain calm.
- Let them know it's time to go using a kind and clear voice: "We need to leave now, and it's important for us to leave together." Please do not threaten the child by saying, "I'm leaving without you." This erodes the connection we are building.
- Assist a younger child if needed: "You tried to put on your shoes all by yourself. We've run out of time today, so I'll help you finish, and you can try again tomorrow."
- If the child becomes upset, we can give them a cuddle, and guess at their feelings. But as hard as it is, keep moving forward. We could say, "It looks like you wish you had longer to finish that" as we keep moving with them toward the door.

We can show appreciation for their cooperation by describing what they have done. "I see someone who is ready to go out and play in the park. You have your shoes on, your coat done up, and your mittens and hat on to keep you warm. It was helpful how you got yourself ready while I packed our bag. We make a good team, huh?"

SEASONAL RHYTHMS

Who remembers the smell of their favorite dish cooking at a special time of year? Or the sounds of crunchy autumn leaves? Or going on a scavenger hunt to find signs of spring? The taste of salt on our lips at the ocean? The touch of cold snow on our tongues or hands? Seasonal rhythms provide foundational memories for our child.

Our seasonal rhythms will depend on where we live and the places we visit. They will also reflect our culture and beliefs. We can be mindful to build our culture into our seasons. To think about the music we play, the food we cook and eat, the songs we sing, the dances we teach, the art on our walls, the poetry we read, the sacred places we visit, and the stories we tell. No Montessori family will be the same, but our seasonal rhythms can reflect our past, our present, and our future.

In Junnifa's family, they study their bibles and pray together every evening. They travel to their hometowns every Easter and December to spend the vacation with the extended family. On Christmas Day, they cook and bake and share with members of their community who do not have the means for a Christmas dinner.

Incorporate rituals

Rituals can be built into our daily, weekly, or monthly rhythms, from a slow Sunday breakfast to birthday traditions practiced year after year and cultural celebrations like Shabbat, Eid, Christmas, and Holi. As with rhythms, the child enjoys the familiarity of these events happening in the same way each time and imprints them into their soul.

We can also make space for surprise or novelty—filling up their room with balloons on their birthday, slipping a poem into their lunch box, or dressing up to go for afternoon tea.

Birthday celebrations

Celebrating birthdays is a beautiful opportunity to create rituals in the family. Our child does not need much to feel special on their big day. Here are some ideas to get you started:

- Make a birthday crown from felt with the age they are turning on it.
- Use a wooden candleholder, adding a candle every year.
- Make their favorite cake.
- Hang up birthday bunting for decoration.
- Go for a meal at a favorite local café or restaurant.
- Arrange a party for a handful of their close friends—one suggestion is to invite as many friends as the age the child is turning.
- Some of the best parties are at home with either nothing planned or activities to explore or a scavenger hunt.

GIFTS

We want to teach our children to be thoughtful about what we consume. Instead of new toys, we can give our child an experience, like an annual pass to a local museum or art gallery, or a trip to a water park with a friend or two.

It's harder to navigate gifts from other people that may not align with the Montessori approach. We can first try to prevent this by sending out a wish list or guidance in advance when the gifts are anticipated, such as for birthdays and graduations. We can do this in a gentle way, advising that these are things we are saving toward. If there is a theme, this may help people focus on things that would be helpful to receive; for example, things for the garden, crystals or rocks, animal figurines for our child's collection, or items related to the solar system. It is helpful to include a variety of price options as well as a variety of both material items and activities—for example, books, toys, sports, and outings.

If our child does receive a gift that doesn't align with our values:

- We can remember that if a family member or friend chooses their own gift, they have done so with good intentions and because it is something they think our child will like.

- It is important to still appreciate the gift and model gratitude to our children. They can call or write a note to say thank you.

- We can then decide what we want to do with it.

- Some gifts can be kept for a while and then taken out of rotation.

- Some gifts can be repurposed to have a more Montessori friendly use; for example, some battery-powered toys can become passive if batteries are not put in. When an item is taken apart, a piece of it might serve a different purpose.

- We can save for later what is not age appropriate. If it is something that might become obsolete, like an iPad or smartphone, we might explain that the child is not old enough for it yet and suggest an alternative.

- We can regift or donate what we think others might appreciate.

- If it is completely unacceptable or inappropriate, we can donate it or dispose of it.

EATING AND MEALTIMES

We can impart to our children a few important principles around food.

We respect food. Children learn to respect food when they learn how much goes into having fresh food available for their meals. We can smell the food at the market and get excited by the delicious array our local stores provide. We can talk about who grew the food and all the steps it takes to get to us. We can prepare only as much food as we will eat so as to not waste food. We can be clear at mealtimes that food is not to be played with; it is for nourishment. We can express gratitude for our food. We can grow our own food to show our children the time and labor that goes into providing food.

Meals are for connecting with the family. Meals are as much a social occasion as they are a time for eating and nourishing our bodies. Connecting every day at the table means that we are prioritizing our connection and relationship as our children grow. We are passing on oral histories, checking in with each other, and learning to listen and take turns in the conversation, as well as having family jokes and building memories. The research shows positive outcomes for children in families that eat meals together, with children feeling better physically and mentally.

As much as our schedule allows, we can try to have as many family meals as possible. As our children grow and may wake later on the weekend, we can join them at the table with a coffee or tea (or a second breakfast) while they eat.

We learn to listen to our own bodies. Rather than insisting that our child finish everything on their plate, we can help them listen to cues from their body that tell them that they are hungry or full. Rather than preparing a plate, we can place the food on serving dishes and have everyone help themselves. They can take as much as they would like (considering others, too) and serve themselves more if they are still hungry.

Mealtimes are opportunities to practice grace and courtesy. We can model grace and courtesy at every mealtime by saying please when we ask someone to pass a plate and saying thank you when they do; eating with our mouth closed; waiting to finish our mouthful before talking; taking turns to talk; staying at the table and learning to excuse oneself; expressing gratitude for our meal; using cutlery; and asking people if they'd like any more of a dish before taking the last portion.

We can also respectfully remind our child of manners; for example, if they talk with their mouth full, we can say, "I didn't hear you so well. Do you mind repeating yourself once you've finished your mouthful?"

Children enjoy food they have helped prepare or prepared themselves. Junnifa's family has inspired many to cook their own omelets. Working by the stove requires adult supervision and lessons in how to use the stove safely, how to pick up a hot pan, how to chop vegetables, and which utensils to use to turn over the omelet. We can simplify the processes for younger children and allow older children to do more and more themselves, being available to offer help if needed.

Similarly, in Simone's home, Oliver was about 10 years old when he wanted to cook dinner for the family every Sunday night. He selected a recipe from a cookbook (an easy, tasty recipe with not too many ingredients), and together they made a shopping list and bought the ingredients. They read through the recipe together to see if there was anything he wasn't sure about, and Simone acted as sous-chef (although Oliver never needed much help at all). His cooking skills improved that year, and he was really proud of himself.

Cooking with friends can be a fun hobby for a 6- to 12-year-old child. They might enjoy going to a cooking class where they learn to cook or bake with friends; some learn this at scouts, and others learn from relatives—particularly if we don't enjoy cooking ourselves.

There are many learning opportunities around food. When we prepare and eat food together, there is so much our child can learn. In the Activities Appendix, which begins on page 232, we can find many ideas for learning vocabulary, fine-motor and gross-motor skills, practical life skills, how to grow food, sensorial experiences, as well as how their bodies work, how to make balanced food choices, and what helps bodies grow.

Food can provide cultural experiences. One of the most important parts of preparing food is learning about our family culture. There are recipes, traditional foods, ways of eating, and rituals around food from our culture that we can honor in our home. It could be making a braided challah bread for Shabbat, eating with chopsticks, or cooking paella to share with friends. In this way, we pass on our cultural heritage and traditions. We can also learn about other cultures by visiting restaurants run by people of that culture, visiting friends from different cultures, or, if means allow, traveling to other places around the world and tasting the food, from Berber pancakes in Morocco to roti canai (a typical flatbread) in Malaysia.

Our own attitudes and behavior around food are being absorbed. If we speak about being too fat or thin, are often on a diet, or have disordered eating, our children will be absorbing this—the 3- to 6-year-old child with their absorbent mind and even the 6- to 12-year-old through their intellect. We may need to do some internal work on healing our relationship with food for our children to develop healthy attitudes and behaviors around food.

Allow time and lower expectations. This can be easier said than done. Cooking with kids has many benefits, yet speed and cleanliness are not always among them. If we work full-time, we may wish to spend more time cooking with the children on the weekends at first so we can allow more time to make a family meal. We might like to make a special Sunday-night dinner of homemade pizzas, wraps with toppings for everyone to help themselves, or homemade sushi.

Problems at mealtimes

When we worry about what/how much they are eating

If we are worried about how much our child is eating, we can use an observation journal to note down every day for one week:

- What and when they eat and drink, including snacks and drinks while they're out and about.
- Where they eat. Are they sitting at a table to eat? Or playing at the same time?
- With whom they eat. Are they eating alone or with others?
- What eating time looks like. Is the table clear of other things? Is it set beautifully, maybe with flowers or candles? Is it free of screens, including our phones?

We can then see if they are filling up on snacks or drinks between meals, what their appetite is actually like over a whole week, what their favorite foods are, and what foods we would like to introduce.

Remember that we cannot make a child swallow their food. We can decide when mealtimes will be, what will be offered at mealtime, and where we will sit to eat. They decide how much they eat, and we are there to be their guide if needed. "It looks like you are all done. Would you like some help to take your plate to the kitchen?"

If they refuse to try a new food, we can keep offering it to them without any expectations and without too many words. Often when we want to encourage them to try something, we end up making it a big deal and we can make them wary. Children have a good sense of whether they are being manipulated. Instead, make the food look inviting, offer food with all the colors of the rainbow, invite them to help in the kitchen, and, above all, keep things relaxed at mealtimes.

If we have bigger concerns about our child's diet, we can seek help from a dietician or medical professional.

When we want to avoid using dessert as a bribe

If we want our child to eat more vegetables or we worry that they'll wake up hungry if they haven't eaten their dinner, we may end up bribing them: "If you eat your dinner, you can have dessert." However, this strategy does not allow our child to explore whether they are full. As Megan McNamee and Judy Delaware of Feeding Littles say, we are also unconsciously "ranking food," implying that dessert is more special. Instead, we can help our child learn that we eat lots of types of food—sometimes it's cookies, sometimes it's yogurt, sometimes it's fruit. Or we might ask them if they are all done: "Are you feeling satisfied? Do you have room for some yogurt or fruit?"

When our child refuses to eat what we have made and asks for something else

When our child demands something else for their meal, they may protest when we kindly and clearly say, "We are having this meal tonight. We can have that another day." We stay calm knowing that we have decided what to serve and they can decide how much of it they eat. As hard as it is for us, they may not eat anything. However, when we respond in a predictable way each time, they will learn that we aren't going to change our mind based on their demands. Some children like to be able to make a choice, and we can offer one when we are preparing the food: "Would you like peas or carrots tonight or both?" They might like to help us do some meal planning and assist us with the shopping. Or we might decide to have a small selection of food on the table that we are happy for them to choose from.

We can also see things from their perspective. "I hear you. It sounds like you really wanted that for dinner tonight. Maybe tomorrow." We can make a note so they see that we have heard them, and then we can make sure to prepare that meal when we can.

When they want to get up from the table as soon as they've finished eating

A 3-year-old may not want to stay at the table once they are finished. We might make an agreement with them that they may get down from the table and take their plate to the kitchen while others continue eating. Older children can learn to stay at the table until everyone is finished—although we may need to practice telling interesting stories and asking good questions to keep them engaged in the conversation.

Simone has a self-confessed bad habit of needing to get up to fetch things in the kitchen during mealtime. If our child is having a hard time staying at the table, we can observe how often we also get up during mealtime and work to have everything we need on the table so we can model staying seated at mealtimes.

When our child has a case of mealtime sillies

At the end of a long day, we want to relax and eat our meal in relative peace. Our children, on the other hand, can be a little tired and silly, and one child seems to wind up another until they are doing silly things with their food or just laughing uncontrollably and not eating.

Honestly, this is part of life with family. Junnifa will observe, and if they are happy and not being disrespectful, then she'll let it go. If we feel impatient, we might want to take ourselves out of the room to get ourselves a glass of water, breathe, and check in with ourselves about why we are feeling activated. Maybe we wait until most of the laughter has died down (as long as we know everyone is safe). Maybe we can find our sense of humor, come back, and laugh along. However, if the behavior is inappropriate or unkind, Junnifa reminds them that we respect ourselves, each other, and our food and asks them to compose themselves.

When we want to avoid screens and other distractions during mealtimes

In order to taste the food and enjoy all the social and sensorial aspects of mealtime, we leave toys, phones, and other screens away from the table. There may be some protests at first, but our children quickly learn to enjoy the connection and conversation. It might be the adults who have the most difficulty leaving our phones in silent mode in a basket or another room while we eat. Yet our children are watching, and we are an important example to them.

When our child still wants us to feed them

If our child is used to us feeding them, we could plan a conversation with them at a neutral time (not at mealtime itself) when we discuss with them that we did this for them when they were younger, and now they can learn to feed themselves. This may be a call for connection, so we can make sure there is some lively mealtime conversation that they can join in. They may eat less at first than they would if we fed them. They are learning to listen to their bodies. It can often go more easily than we expect when we stop feeding them. It may be that we were more attached to feeding them so we knew they'd had enough to eat rather than them needing us to feed them.

When they throw food

By showing our children how we respect food (see "We respect food," on page 121), we teach them to appreciate the meals we are able to make in our home. Children older than 3 years old can learn that food is not for throwing. If they have finished their meal, a 3-year-old can tell us they feel full and ask to leave the table to put their plate in the kitchen. We can let them know to leave anything they don't like on the edge of their plate (or to get a bowl to put it in if they can't stand it on their plate).

If they are having difficulty, we can support them through their feelings but set a limit kindly and clearly: "It looks like you are all done. Let me help you get down from the table so you can bring your plate to the kitchen."

FURTHER READING

- The Feeding Littles website (feedinglittles.com)
- *First Foods to Family Meals* by Sarah Moudry

SLEEPING

Montessori children are not allowed to stay up as late as they like. Our role is to help with the where, when, and how. But we cannot make our child's eyes close to fall asleep.

WHERE
- A calm sleeping environment.
- A consistent, cozy, and relaxing space for them to sleep.

WHEN
- A consistent bedtime for our 3- to 6-year-olds.
- An agreed-upon consistent bedtime for our 6- to 12-year-olds.

HOW
- By offering a predictable bedtime rhythm—including reading stories at bedtime, even for school-age children.
- By coming up with agreements with them—for example, about what to do if they wake in the middle of the night or early in the morning.
- By checking our attitudes about sleep and the energy we might be bringing to bedtime—for example, can we picture our children going happily to bed rather than expecting a battle? How can we be a calm and clear guide even at the end of the day when we are exhausted? Can we have a predictable bedtime so that we have some time to rest ourselves?
- By being clear about expectations—stepping in kindly and clearly if they are making a lot of noise or turning the lights on and off.

PROBLEMS AROUND BEDTIMES

If our child is getting up out of bed, having troubles falling asleep, refusing or stalling bedtime, waking up early, or experiencing any other sleep issues, we can observe:

- What the bedtime routine looks like

- What helps to relax them

- What winds them up or makes them overexcited

- How they fall asleep, and how they wake up

- What time they lie down in their bed and whether they talk or read once they're in bed and for how long

- What time they fall asleep

- What their sleeping environment looks like

We can problem-solve with our child and find a way that works for all of us. We might like to consider the following:

- **What are they digesting?** Not just the food they eat, but everything they take in: the music they listen to, the media they watch, the books they read, the friends they spend time with, and the atmosphere at home and at school. All these things can result in poor sleep, nightmares, or fear of the dark or monsters.

- **Are they getting enough time outdoors?** Fresh air can promote sleep.

- **Are there sustainable ways for them to get to sleep?** White noise helps some children. Listening to the same audiobook every night can give their brain something to focus on while being familiar enough to not overactivate their brain or keep them awake. Older children may be able to learn relaxation techniques or a meditation that we can do with them. Some children need a deep-pressure massage or a weighted blanket to help them decompress. Others find that wrestling before bedtime gets out the last of their energy.

- **Do they have breathing issues that could be affecting their sleep?** These can be assessed by a sleep specialist.

- **How do they process their day?** A bedtime conversation can help them let go of the day's events. Older children may enjoy writing or drawing in a journal.

- **Can we offer gratitude as part of our bedtime rhythm?** It can be calming to end the day by thinking about the things we appreciate—from something tasty they ate to something kind someone did for them.

- **Is there a cue to help them know when to get up in the morning?** A clock that lights up in the morning at a time you set (like Groclock) can be great for young children; a regular alarm clock works for older children.

- **What does the weekend rhythm look like?** From around 5 years old, children are generally happy to let us sleep longer while they get up to play and help themselves to a piece of fruit if they are hungry while waiting for the family breakfast. We could put a note on the door as a reminder not to wake us, "Please play quietly until 9 a.m. Help yourself to a piece of fruit if you are hungry."

- **Is the light making it difficult to sleep in summer months?** Closing the curtains in the living room after dinner is a helpful visual cue that we are starting to wind down for our bedtime rhythm, regardless of the light outside. Investing in blackout curtains will be useful too.

- **Is the darkness making it hard to wake up in the winter months?** An alarm with a wake-light may be of help, or our child might come up with their own solution.

Note: For preschoolers still using a pacifier at bedtime, look for other ways for them to relax their nervous system, like sucking yogurt through a straw, blowing bubbles, holding on to a book or soft toy, a brisk towel rub after bath, deep-pressure bear hugs, kneading dough, squeezing bath toys, or a slow and firm back rub. Agree to a time to say goodbye to the pacifier; for example, passing it on to a family with a new baby could be helpful. Then be patient and supportive as they make the transition. Mostly it goes more smoothly than expected, and we see that we were just as attached to the pacifier as they were.

TOILETING AND STAYING DRY AT NIGHT

Learning to use the toilet

If our child has not yet learned to use the toilet, we can support their transition. Here are some steps we can take to scaffold the skills they will need:

- Set up spaces for them to be able to reach their own underwear and clothing if they get wet; have cleaning cloths and spray at the ready for them to use in cleaning up if they wet their clothes; have a bucket available in the toileting area for their wet clothes.

- Have them practice pulling down their trousers or pulling up their skirt and pushing their underwear down, then repeating those actions in reverse.
- Choose clothes that are easy for them to manage themselves when toileting (avoid overalls, tight jeans, etc.).
- Offer the potty at each diaper change so they get used to sitting on the potty.
- Start offering the potty at regular times, like on waking, after meals, before leaving and after returning home, at bath time, and before bed.
- Teach them to flush the toilet and wash their hands.
- Let them choose some underwear they like at the store.
- Begin by having them wear underpants under the diaper so they start to feel wet when they pee or poop or use training pants (padded underwear).
- Let them choose a date on the calendar when they will stop using diapers.
- On the agreed-upon date, say thank you to the diapers, pass any that are left on to another family with a baby, and begin to use the underpants.
- Continue to offer the potty at regular times.
- Our child will eventually start to feel when they are peeing or pooping; then they will begin to transition to knowing when they need to go; and then they will make it to the potty or toilet by themselves without being reminded. This is a process and can take more time depending on the child.
- Show them how to fold the toilet paper and wipe from front to back. They can wipe themselves first, and we can offer to finish off the wiping for them. Then over time the child can manage this more and more for themselves.
- If they wet themselves, we don't need to shame them. We treat them with respect just as we would want to be treated in the same situation. We can wait until they finish what they are doing and say to them, "I see that your clothes are wet. You can change your clothes and come back to clean up." They can clean themselves up and then wipe the floor, at first perhaps with some support and then taking over the whole process. It may take them more than 15 minutes to do this. We don't need to rush them as this is valuable time learning to care for themselves, but we can offer help if we see they are having difficulty. It's no different from what we do if they break a plate—we show them how to make it right again and move on.

- It can be most difficult for them to stay dry when they are in the middle of working on something. There's a struggle for them between leaving what they are doing and needing to use the toilet/potty. This comes with maturity and being able to hold on longer, until they are able to choose to come back to what they are doing or complete what they are doing and get to the toilet/potty in time.

Staying dry at night

The child may be able to transition to using underwear at night at the same time as learning to use the toilet or potty. Here are some tips:

- We can set up their bed to have a protective cover on the mattress and can tuck in a towel across the bed or use a pad on the bed to absorb any wetness.
- They can learn to go to the toilet/potty before bed and immediately upon waking.
- We can show them how to clean up their sheets and open windows if they are wet during the night.
- If they wet the bed, we can make observations as to when and how often to notice any patterns. Again, we don't shame the child, and we equip them with the skills to deal with whatever is causing a problem and empowering them with solutions. These could be setting an alarm clock to wake themselves up during the night to use the toilet or limiting their water intake in the evening. Or if, for example, we notice that they wet the bed on cold nights, we can anticipate it and offer to wake them during the night to avoid this.

If we have concerns about our child's toileting or ability to stay dry at night, we can see a specialist.

FURTHER READING

- *Toilet Awareness* by Sarah Moudry

CARE OF TEETH

As children move into the second half of the first plane of development, at around 3 years old, they will be taking over more responsibility for their oral hygiene. Caring for their baby teeth helps build a foundation for caring for their adult teeth. We can be there to supervise and perhaps to finish off their brushing; the rest they can manage by themselves.

We can help them take on this responsibility by reading books about cleaning our teeth and why it is important to look after our teeth and gums. We might like to brush our teeth while they clean theirs. For reluctant brushers, we can sing a song while they brush

("This is the way we brush our teeth . . ."), or a sand timer or music box might give them a visual or aural cue while they brush.

Their first trip to the dentist can be very casual. They could come with us to our next dental appointment and watch while we have our teeth cleaned. The dentist might allow them to sit in the chair and make it go up and down. They could open their mouth while the dentist looks inside, and that can be enough to orient them to the idea for their first visit. Reading books about going to the dentist will also help them prepare themselves and understand the process.

If they often forget to brush their teeth, we can help them come up with ways to remind themselves, from a sticky note on the bathroom mirror to following the same sequence in the morning and evening to make it automatic.

When an older child refuses to brush their teeth, it can help to appeal to their reasoning mind by exploring the importance of tooth care. Then we can make a plan to research human teeth, teeth in different animals, how we care for them, and how animals take care of their teeth. We might go to the library to look up information about what happens when we don't brush. Information from the dentist at regular checkups will likely be more readily received than information from us as they are the expert. The dentist can also give the child extra tips on cleaning any hard-to-reach spots or what to do if there is any gum disease.

Regina Lulka, who was the head of a Montessori school in Toronto for many years, has a lovely suggestion for the early second-plane child who loses their first tooth: They can learn about different cultural traditions surrounding this event; for example, by reading *Throw Your Tooth on the Roof: Tooth Traditions from Around the World* by Selby B. Beeler and learning that children in Botswana throw their tooth on the roof, and in Afghanistan, they drop their tooth down a mousehole!

PART TWO

PRACTICAL QUESTIONS

WHEN TO HELP OUR CHILDREN . . . AND WHEN NOT TO

When to step in

Many people think that Montessori children can do whatever they like. However, Dr. Montessori was clear.

We will step in to stop them if:

- They are hurting themselves.
- They are hurting others.
- They are hurting the environment.

This could be if they are causing harm verbally or physically (whether intentionally or not) or creating a disturbance.

These situations need to be immediately addressed without shaming the child but showing them how they can do better; for example, by saying things like:

- "I can't let you bang your head. You look frustrated. Can you show me with this paper and pencil instead?"
- "I can't let you hit your friend. I'll help you calm down, and then we can come up with some words to tell them why you are angry."
- "Those flowers are fragile. This is how we care for them."

When to wait and observe

Then there are far more times when we can stand back to observe to allow our child to learn from the experience.

We can observe and wait a little longer if no one is in danger and the child:

- Will learn from the natural consequences
- Is trying to master something
- Is trying a different way to do something
- Is expressing themselves
- Is testing the limits of their body

In these moments, we try not to comment or react. As long as it is not an emergency, we can wait and show them at another time when they will be more receptive to learning from us.

A couple of examples:

1. With a child who is learning to write, we don't correct their spelling. We continue to model spelling and careful writing when we are writing something for them.
2. If a child slams a door in anger, we can make a mental note and later show them in a fun way how we close the door slowly and quietly. "Can we do it as quietly as possible? Did you hear it?"

When to help our child

Sometimes helping our child is giving them just the smallest amount of assistance so they can get further.

Help might look like:

- A verbal cue
- Asking if they'd like help
- Telling them they can ask us if they'd like help at any point
- Asking if we can have a turn to show them something, then stepping back to see if they can get further
- Setting up an activity to help them learn a skill they are missing

Imagine a 6-year-old is cutting out a model of a paper house. We can see that they are about to cut off a piece that they will need. Can we wait to see if they correct themselves? Can we wait to see if they cut it off and then work out how they will fix it? Or we might give the smallest verbal cue—"I can see that flap looks like it is about to be cut off"—and then wait to see what they do with that information.

As children get older, they can manage more and more themselves. These questions from Dr. Christine Carter, a sociologist, author, and speaker, can be helpful to assist them:

- What's your plan?
- You're going to do that later? What does that look like?
- How will you remind yourself?
- What would you like me to do if you ignore your alarm?

INSTEAD OF "GOOD JOB"

Many adults believe that if we praise our children ("Good job," "Good boy," "Good girl") or offer them rewards, it will motivate them to learn or behave. However, by praising them, we teach them to look outside themselves rather than fostering their own intrinsic motivation. For those wanting to find out more about the effect of praise, we recommend reading Alfie Kohn's article "Five Reasons to Stop Saying 'Good Job!'"

So what to say instead? We can instead give them feedback using objective language, to help them build a picture of themselves. Adele Faber and Elaine Mazlish's book *How to Talk So Kids Will Listen & Listen So Kids Will Talk* has some helpful suggestions:

- Describe what they did. "Look at that! You carried that bucket of water all the way up the hill to make the moat you are building." (Rather than saying "Good job!")

- Describe their effort. "You've worked every night on that report, and it's nearly done." (Rather than focusing on its not being complete yet.)

- Describe what they might be feeling. "You look really excited/pleased/proud of yourself." (Rather than saying, "I'm so proud of you.")

- Sum it up with a word: "You helped Grandma all the way up the stairs. That's what I call being thoughtful/kind/patient!" (Rather than saying, "Good girl.")

- Say how we feel. "I enjoy cooking dinner with you." (Rather than saying, "Good boy.")

For older children, Terrence Millie (an experienced Montessori elementary teacher and trainer) likes to engage the child in self-reflection by asking questions here, too, like: "I noticed you _____. How did that make you feel?"

HOW TO ENCOURAGE INDEPENDENCE

We have talked in this book about the benefits of our child's being able to care for and think for themselves. For the children who resist and want us to continue to do things for them, we can scaffold the skills of independence. It might be that they never clean up after themselves, or that they won't wipe their own bottom, or pull up their trousers. They might expect us to sit next to them while they play.

Remember, the more we force them, the more they will resist. Instead, here are some tips to encourage independence:

- **Inspire them.** Make the task interesting and engaging for them, follow their interests, get them involved.
- **Look for and remove obstacles.** Look for distractions and perhaps physical obstacles (ourselves included) and remove them.
- **Observe.** How long can they play by themselves? How close do we need to be? What self-care activities can they manage by themselves? Do we need to stay in the same room doing something else to keep them accountable?
- **For something difficult for them, do it together first.** Then the next time, we can help them get started with the first step, and then let them take over.
- **Build up slowly.** Let them get used to leading the play. Then step out to another room to do a job and come back. Build up the time they are playing independently.
- **Leave the problem with them.** Let's stop rescuing them. We can set up the environment, we can help them make a plan, and then we can let them feel the natural consequences.
- **Assess whether they have the skills.** How can we support them to learn them? Can we break the activity into smaller steps they can manage?
- **Make the task age appropriate and scaffold skills.** For example, we don't let a young child ride their bike through the city by themselves. First, they start in a park with us running alongside them. Then they might soon be riding on their own in a bike lane or on the sidewalk. As they acquire more skills, they learn to bike on the road with us on our bike at their side. Then we bike a lot through the city together over the years to give them more experience. By the time they start high school, they have enough experience to go alone, with a mobile phone in case of emergency.

When our child demands our help

Our child might shout at us, "I can't!" or demand, "You do it. I don't want to!" We can observe to see if there is an obstacle that could be removed. They may be seeking connection with us in this moment (we could offer a small amount of help and let them get further; e.g., by saying "I'll do this one, and you can do that one"). Or perhaps they are feeling rushed (we can look at how our mornings could be restructured to allow them more time), or that there is too much that's out of their control (how can we give them control over more parts of their day?).

We don't need to accept their shouting. We can calmly and clearly guide them to learn ways to request our help without demanding. We like the phrase in Jane Nelsen and Chip DeLorenzo's book, *Positive Discipline in the Montessori Classroom*: "How can you ask me in a way that I can hear and understand you?" We can reassure them that we are doing our best to support them and will be available if they get stuck (we might do some self-reflection here if we are indeed doing too much for them).

For more, refer back to page 47, "Fostering independence and responsibility."

STAYING HOME BY THEMSELVES

It will be some time before we leave our child at home by themselves. In many states in the US, there is a legislated age; in some states, from 12 years old. In the meantime, we can build skills they will need.

Here are some things to consider:

- **Safety.** What would they do in case of a fire, accident, or other emergency? Teach them how to contact emergency services. Have important contact numbers readily accessible.
- **Strangers.** What do they do if someone knocks on the door or if the phone rings?
- **Snacks.** What can they eat while we are out?
- **Security.** Keep any alcohol, cleaning materials, and lighters out of reach.
- **Distance.** How far away are we?
- **Contact information.** Are we reachable by phone?
- **Time.** How long are they okay by themselves?
- **Community.** What kind of community do we have around us? Do we know our neighbors? Can our neighbors look out for them? Do we live in a big city?

If our child has a friend who is allowed to be home alone and we don't feel comfortable with our child playing there, we can discuss it with the child's parent or invite their child to our home instead.

Children around 6 years old will want more independence and risk, so we can find ways for them to play with friends with less supervision. For example, we could take them to an adventure playground in our neighborhood and stay in the café area while they explore, climb, and take greater risks in a controlled environment. There may be community groups like scouting where they can practice more advanced activities like learning to start fires and sleeping under the stars.

TRAVELING WITH KIDS

If we are lucky enough to have the resources to travel with our children, Montessori principles can also be packed in the bag with us.

- **Get the children involved from the time we start planning.** They may not get to decide our final destination, but we could let them pick from a couple of places we have come up with or from two accommodation options. We can also go to the library together to do some research on the area, people, food, and culture of our destination before we go.
- **Have a physical map of the area.** It will be easier for them to concretely understand where we are staying and the places we are visiting, and the children can help us plan any public transportation we will be using with a transit map. They can also decorate the map with colored stickers to mark highlights from the trip or glue entrance and travel tickets onto special places from our stay.
- **Children like to have an idea of, and be involved in making, the plan.** We can give our child a heads-up the night before of the following day's plans and get their suggestions for things they might like to add in to make sure that everyone has a say in what's happening. We could also make a visual calendar of the days ahead if this helps them.
- **Make a travel journal.** It could be a combined family journal or a notebook with a lock for recording events and inspiration from their travels. We can add photos when we get back home.
- **Appreciate, don't appropriate.** To be mindful of how we spend our time and money, we can seek out tours from locals rather than large companies and avoid buying cheap trinkets from the markets and instead buy fewer but better-quality and more authentic items made by local or Indigenous people. We can teach our child that appropriation begins when people profit from what they saw, learned, or bought on their travels.

- **Plan some downtime.** Think about how we can bring unscheduled time to our travels. Likely one or more members of our family will need some time to decompress during the trip. Schedule a pajama morning or day off or some time each afternoon to read books and play, or visit a park or playground between museum tours to allow some big movement. We might pack our current favorite board game to play as a family.

- **Get packing.** Find child-sized luggage that they can manage themselves. A 3-year-old can pack and carry their own backpack, and a 10-year-old can lay out everything they need to take for us to check and give any feedback, then pack the items into their bag. Children might make their own checklists or ask how many sets of underwear, pairs of socks, and items of clothing they will need.

- **Think about food.** Finding accommodations with a kitchen can be useful. We can prepare some food for during the day to take with us or mark on a map some cafés near places we are visiting so that we don't have tired and hungry children on our hands.

- **Practice the language before arrival.** Learn some phrases to use in greeting people and saying thank you and goodbye. If we will be traveling abroad for a long stay, we could consider attending classes with our children or practicing with a friend or neighbor who speaks the language.

- **Provide alternatives to screens.** While we may choose to allow our children access to screens on travel days, as much as possible, look for hands-on activities that fit in their backpack or suitcase. If possible, include a notebook and pen, a secondhand camera, a pack of cards, a book to read, and maybe some travel watercolor paints. For some old-fashioned games to play on long trips, check out the Activities Appendix organized by interest online at workman.com/montessori.

- **And remember to look for ways to reduce our impact on the Earth as we travel.** Consider destinations that can be reached by shorter train travel over long-haul flights, make less frequent trips, find eco-friendly lodgings, take reusable bottles and cutlery, and avoid buying disposable souvenirs that will soon get dusty.

BILINGUALISM/MULTILINGUALISM

The child from 3 to 6 years old with their absorbent mind will absorb any language we use in our home. Common ways to introduce languages are one parent, one language (OPOL) or domains of use. In OPOL, each parent uses their native language with the child, and a family language is chosen to be used between parents. Applying domains of use means that we have consistent times (e.g., a day of the week or mealtime) and/or places (e.g., inside or outside the home) when and/or where each language is used.

About 30 percent of our child's waking hours need to be in a particular language for it to become a literacy language (meaning the child is proficient enough to study in this language). We can look for ways to increase exposure to a language like finding additional caregivers who speak the language, asking a neighbor who speaks it to read books with our child, or planning longer holiday visits to our country of origin.

A child from 6 to 12 years old can start to learn another language; however, they no longer have the assistance of an absorbent mind or sensitive period for language. Instead they will apply their conscious, logical, reasoning mind. We can make it useful and fun for them to learn a language—for example, we can use the new language to make films or write poetry, or read translated editions of their favorite books.

FURTHER READING

For more on this topic, read Eowyn Crisfield's book
Bilingual Families: A Practical Language Planning Guide.

MONTESSORI FOR CHILDREN WITH A DISABILITY OR NEURODIVERGENCE

As we touched on in the first chapter, Montessori is for every child. We meet each child where they are and make adjustments where needed. There are now Montessori courses for children with disabilities, and while it's beyond the scope of this book, here are some general examples to get you started:

- A child with a physical disability often has similar cognitive ability to that of other children their age. We can look at ourselves and the environment to adapt them so the child gets the opportunity to master the same skills as other children though they may need additional support in some areas. For example, a child with less muscle tone may not be able to carry a tray or to speak, so we can look for ways for them to be able to access the materials (e.g., having everything at floor height) or to express themselves (e.g., by using a computer program to assist).
- A child who is deaf has a need to communicate, and we want to give the child the opportunity to express themselves and to understand others. We can offer rich language experiences from sign language and spoken language from birth, get their attention first before communicating, use our body language and gestures to add more meaning, and be mindful of acoustics and lighting in our spaces.

- For a child who is blind, we can be intentional about how we set up the room and stay with the same arrangement. We can have braille books and tactile or braille labels where needed. Any siblings can be shown how to guide the blind child. And we can allow more time for them to navigate the room themselves.

- A child who is neurodivergent may need more practice in some areas of learning like motor skills, language, sensory processing, and emotional regulation. We can let them focus on their strengths and give them opportunities to practice the skills they find difficult as well as seek any necessary additional support from experts and therapists.

- A child with ADHD may benefit from an environment with fewer distractions and less clutter. We can look for those activities that help them self-regulate, including many of the practical life activities.

- An autistic child may have a strong need for order in their environment and their day, and we can make things as predictable as possible (and help them build skills around uncertainty and adjusting to changes as they grow). Some may benefit from additional support and learning in social situations and in communicating. We will observe the child and make adaptations accordingly based on their unique needs.

As the adult supporting them, we need to remember to support ourselves. It can take a lot of energy to advocate for our child, to help them as little as possible and as much as necessary, to get them to extra appointments and assessments, and to support their emotional journey. Look for community, and look for ways to get sufficient rest, to get a break, to exercise, and to eat well.

Every child's timeline will look different. There will be individual challenges to navigate. All children deserve to be treated as the beautiful human being they were put on Earth to be. Let's look at capability and help them build skills and adapt ourselves and the environment where necessary.

FURTHER READING

- For families with neurodivergent children, we recommend *Differently Wired* by Deborah Reber.
- Learn about the signing community from the website What Dad Did with Ashton Jean-Pierre (whatdaddid.com.au).

PART THREE

WHEN DIFFICULT SITUATIONS ARISE

Raising our children in a Montessori way doesn't mean there will never be any conflict; instead, our children are learning to work with others and to solve conflict in a respectful way. For us to be their guide during these difficult situations, we need to notice when we are activated by a situation and how we can regulate ourselves (see chapter 8 about preparing ourselves).

CULTIVATING COOPERATION

We might find ourselves saying, "They just won't listen to me!" They are tired, overscheduled, and want to do things in their own way, on their own time, and do not want us to nag them. In these moments, remember that this is often when the "good stuff" happens.

Let's see it as an opportunity:

- To cultivate cooperation in our family
- For our child to learn something new about themselves or others
- For us to help them build the skills to face difficult situations
- To maintain the relationship with our child that we have built

Know that it's not too late to learn new ways to cultivate cooperation. We can start today to be more respectful with our child. We can explain to them that we have been learning some new skills, that we want to be in a better relationship with them. It usually doesn't take long for our children to like this new approach. After all, we are now working together, on each other's side. Not against each other.

WHEN OUR CHILD DOESN'T COOPERATE

Let's learn to be a proactive guide, rather than a boss or servant. When we're trying to cultivate cooperation with our child, here are eight questions we can ask ourselves:

1. WHAT CAN WE OBSERVE/WHAT INFORMATION CAN WE OBJECTIVELY COLLECT?

We often feel that our child never listens to us or never tidies up or never goes to bed on time. What can we observe to see the situation more clearly?

For example:

- What time does it happen?
- How often does it happen?
- Is the child tired or hungry?
- Are there any changes in our family?
- What communication do they use?
- What are they doing when it happens?
- Is anyone else involved?

2. WHAT IS THEIR NEED/WHAT IS OUR NEED?

Nonviolent communication can be a very helpful tool in a Montessori home. We want to respect the child and solve problems with them, and we want to find solutions that work for everyone.

An important part of Montessori is to "follow the child," letting them develop in their unique way. Yet this can sometimes be misunderstood to mean that everything is about the child. We may have conversations with our friends or our partner constantly interrupted by our child; we may make plans only around the children without making time for our own interests and hobbies; and we might forget to look after and nourish ourselves. Instead, being a Montessori family means meeting the needs of our child while also having our own needs met. Below are some examples:

> "It sounds like you are really interested in going out with your friends. And it's my job to keep you safe. I wonder if we can come up with a plan that addresses my concerns about safety and still allows you to go. If not, I'll have to say no, but I'd really like to see if we can come up with something."

"It sounds like you want to sing loudly, and I have a headache. How can we solve the problem?" (They help us lie down on the couch with a cup of tea and go into their room to sing with headphones on.)

Even when they seem too young, we can ask them to be involved in coming up with a solution by asking, "How can we solve the problem?" It's amazing some of the creative ideas they come up with.

3. HOW CAN WE KEEP THEM SAFE WHILE THEY HAVE THEIR NEEDS MET, IF APPLICABLE?

We might stand at the entrance to the store while they make a purchase by themselves; we might encourage them to invite their friends to our home to hang out; or we might first review a game, book, or film so that we can guide them if needed through any possibly scary or adult parts.

4. HOW CAN WE FIND A WAY TO WORK WITH THEM IN THIS SITUATION (VS BRIBING, THREATENING, PUNISHING, OR LECTURING)?

In his book *Unconditional Parenting*, Alfie Kohn talks about getting children to help come up with ways to solve problems ("working with") rather than using extrinsic means that come from us like bribing, punishing, or threatening ("doing to"). When we work with our child, we acknowledge that we have something that needs to happen and that we want this to align with what our child wants to happen (see the Venn diagram below showing this sweet spot). When they are involved in the process, they feel empowered and capable.

WHAT OUR KID WANTS TO DO

WHAT WE WANT OUR KID TO DO

THE SWEET SPOT

Depending on the age of our child, this might be doing some brainstorming with them, writing down the ideas they come up with, or suggesting some ideas for them to choose from or as a springboard for their own ideas. For a 2.5-year-old, we may need to help them create a visual schedule to get ready for bed that they can follow. For a 10-year-old, we may need to gently remind them that it's 8:03 p.m. and we cannot hear the shower running.

5. ARE WE SUPPORTING THEIR DEVELOPMENT?

This is a useful question we learned from Alison Awes to reflect on. We can look at the direction our child is headed in and the skills they will need to move in this direction. We may need to scaffold skills, but let's not keep them in a stage of development that they have outgrown. Let's ask ourselves if we are keeping them in an earlier stage of development or if something they are doing (e.g., overreliance on technology) is not supporting their development.

6. HOW CAN I SET A KIND AND CLEAR LIMIT IF NEEDED?

We are the child's guide. We give them freedom within limits. We can remind them of agreements that we have made and help them follow through (see page 150 on setting kind and clear limits).

7. WHAT CAN THE CHILD (AND WHAT CAN WE) LEARN FROM THIS SITUATION?

Even though it can be difficult to see our child having a hard time, they are growing from these experiences. They may be learning to overcome their fears, to make plans and stick to them, to regulate themselves when they are anxious or worried, or to see that they can solve problems. We are likely to learn more about our child and ourselves too.

8. HOW CAN I MAINTAIN CONNECTION WITH MY CHILD IN THIS SITUATION?

Again, we come back to the importance of connection when getting their cooperation. We try not to get frustrated. We try to be a calm and clear guide. Yet if there are times when we get frustrated, we can apologize and try again. "What I should have done is _____." "What I should have said is _____." "Let's try it again."

If they won't listen

Instead of blaming them for not listening to us, we want to look for ways to communicate so we will be heard. What comes to mind is the Walter B. Barbe quote "If you've told a child a thousand times and he still doesn't understand, then it is not the child who is the slow learner."

Here are some ideas we use in our classrooms; many we have learned from the book *How to Talk So Kids Will Listen & Listen So Kids Will Talk* by Adele Faber and Elaine Mazlish. (Also, refer to page 117, "Talk in a way that helps them listen.")

Keep them involved in coming up with a solution. Offer questions to activate their brain, like "What could you do?" or "What could you try?" or "What is our family agreement about _____ ?"

Allow time for them to process our request. We all need some time to switch activities. So ideally, we can wait until they have finished what they are doing or allow them time to process our request ("tarry time"). It works well to count to 10 silently in our head (not out loud), allowing time for a child to respond. Try it. Often by the time we have counted to around 8 in our head, they are starting to finish up what they were doing and are ready to listen or respond.

Use positive language and tell them how to be helpful. When we use "no" or "don't," the child hears first what we don't want them to do. Then they have to work out what to do instead (if they work it out at all). Instead, there is always a way to say things in a positive way; telling them what we want them to do, not what we don't want them to do. For example, say, "Be gentle with the baby" rather than "Don't hit;" "Use two hands" instead of "Don't spill;" and "Let's sit to eat" rather than "Don't leave the table."

Instead of saying no, we can also use "yes, when . . ." For example, "Yes, you can have another cracker when you've finished the one you are eating." If there are no more crackers, we could say, "Yes, you can have another one when we've been to the store tomorrow."

We can say "Let me think about it." Sometimes we automatically say no to our child's request. Instead, we can say we'll think about it to see if we can make it work (as long as we remember to come back to them).

Actions speak louder than words. Children can tune out long explanations or instructions given from across the room. We can stand up and go over to them or show them where something goes by tapping a shelf and saying, "It goes here."

Give information. We might respectfully tell them, "Diego, the door is open," "I see a lunch box on the table," or "Milk goes bad if we leave it out of the fridge." Then we let them work out what needs to be done. We avoid using a patronizing or sarcastic tone, modeling respect for each other.

Provide age-appropriate choices. A 3- to 6-year-old can decide what they would like to have for lunch based on some healthy options, and a 6- to 12- year-old can decide if they would like to play first or do their homework first, as long as it gets completed.

Use one word. If we need to remind our child of something they already know well, often a lecture or constant nagging will be ignored. Instead, saying "lunch box" or "shoes" in a kind tone might prompt a child to check if they have forgotten something or remind them gently of the next step. Again, they are invited to think for themselves, rather than passively receive an instruction.

Talk about how we feel. We can model clear boundaries with our child (without giving a guilt trip). "When you hit me, it hurts me. I'm going to move over here. I'd like you to be gentle with me."

Write a note. When something is written down, it gives it some authority. Use this option sparingly, but do use it. "Please put me away" placed on an experiment left on the table; "Please let us sleep until 9:00 a.m." stuck on the bedroom door; "Please use tiptoes" along the hallway where the downstairs neighbors complain about noisy feet can all be effective. For children who can't read, we can add a picture or tell them what it says. "It says 'Fragile.' Let's be gentle with that glass cabinet." "It says 'Private.' I think your brother wants to be by himself. Let's do something together." Or "It's time to turn the oven on. Let's put a sign on it that says 'Hot' to remind us."

Use humor. A little humor can go a long way. With a young child who is resisting putting on their shoes, we can pretend to put their shoe on our foot and say, "Ah, it seems to be too small. What's going on here? Why doesn't it fit me?" Or we can use the wrong name/color and let them correct us. They'll delight in telling us, "Those shoes are not blue! They're purple." This can lighten the mood, and they may then be willing to put on the shoes. With an older child, we might substitute some silly lyrics for the usual ones in a favorite song or put on some music to clean up to together.

WHEN OUR CHILD IS UPSET

Allow all feelings

Our child's feelings help them (and us) understand what is important to them, judge situations, have empathy for others, and make sense of the world around them. When we hold space for our child's feelings, we are learning to see things from their perspective while not jumping in to solve things for them. It's not our role as parents to take away the hard stuff for our children. Our role is to be there to support them in the joy and the sorrow. We need to let them have their own experience.

When our child is feeling big emotions, we can help them by:

Guessing how they are feeling. By responding in this way, we are showing our child that we are available to help them even when they are having a hard time. We aren't telling them they are angry—the child will usually retort with an angry "I am *not* angry!" But when someone touches on a feeling we may be experiencing, we can feel seen and supported.

Here are some of our favorite stem sentences to use:

- "It sounds like you _____."

- "Are you maybe feeling _____?"

- "You really wish you could _____?"

- "I can understand if you were feeling _____ right now."

- "When _____ happened, it could be upsetting."

- "Of course you'd feel _____."

- "That's understandable. I can imagine that could have been _____?"

- "That makes sense. I can understand why you might feel _____."

Helping them process their emotions. When we try to distract a child or cheer them up quickly before they have processed everything, it's like we are putting on a Band-Aid. But as soon as the Band-Aid comes off (i.e., something else happens), the wound will still be there, and the emotions will resurface. In *The Whole Brain Child*, Daniel Siegel and Tina Payne Bryson talk about "naming it to tame it." We can help our child process their feelings (from the right brain) by talking about them (using the left brain); for example, helping them retell a story about something that happened. Similarly, if they have fears, we want to accept their concerns, not dismiss them; we seek to understand them and then help make them manageable for our child. (See page 157 for more on managing fears.)

Helping them regulate themselves. There are times when our child flips their lid and is no longer able to access their prefrontal cortex (the part of the brain used for rational decision-making, planning, self-control, and control over emotions). The reptilian brain (what Siegel and Payne Bryson refer to as the "downstairs part of the brain," which contains the brain stem, limbic region, and amygdala) has kicked in, and they become dysregulated. This might look like a tantrum or when they are completely out of control of their emotions. They won't be able to hear us until their lid is closed again and they are calm.

We first help our child come back to regulation and then, only once they are calm again, talk to them about what happened and help them take responsibility if needed.

Ideas for self-regulation:

- They choose to take themselves to their room when they are upset.
- They choose to go to their calm space (see page 149).
- They allow us to co-regulate (e.g., allow us to give them a cuddle, rub their back, breathe with them). When we are regulated, we can imagine "lending them" our nervous system.
- They rock or sway their body or hum.
- They move their body (e.g., by doing jumping jacks, running, or cleaning).
- They do a breathing exercise (e.g., breathe in, smell the flower, breathe out, blow out the candle, or breathe in for 3 seconds, hold for 3 seconds, breathe out for 6 seconds).
- An older child may be able to look for five things they can see, four things they can touch, three things they can hear, two things they can smell, and one thing they can taste.

FURTHER READING

- *Self-Reg: How to Help Your Child (and You) Break the Stress Cycle and Successfully Engage with Life* by Stuart Shanker

Staying calm. There may be times when our child looks like they are out of control, but this time they are using what Siegel and Payne Bryson refer to as the "upstairs part of their brain" (including the prefrontal cortex). We might, for example, see that they are able to stop crying to argue or talk. Then we can stand firm—we do not negotiate—while acknowledging that it can be hard to hear no. We are kind and clear.

All behavior is communication, and our child may be expressing a need for attention or affection or other. Again, we stand firm, we do not change our mind, but we will look for any underlying reasons to understand what is going on for them.

Creating a calm space. A calm space can be useful anytime they are upset (an idea from Dr. Jane Nelsen's Positive Discipline books). For children from around 2.5 to 3 years, we can create a space in our home with them (usually in a common area of the home) where they can go to calm down when they are upset. "What might make you feel nice at times when you're upset?" They may choose to have some books there, a favorite soft toy, some fairy lights, cushions, trains or cars; anything that makes them feel good. It's different from a time-out, when the child is sent away as punishment. Going to a calm space is sometimes referred to as a time-in. They can choose to go to self-regulate, and they can stay as long (or as briefly) as they like. If tempers are high and they don't want to go, we can always go to the space ourselves to calm down or go there with them. They are learning how to bring themselves back to calm.

Have a notebook available for each child. When they are having big feelings about something, another way for them to feel heard is to have us write down what they are upset about. When we write it down, it feels very important to them; they feel acknowledged. If a child wants to juice oranges but there are none left, we can write it down so we can let them know when there are oranges again. For older children, we can encourage them to write down any reminders for themselves in their own notebook. (This also works well if they are nagging us to buy something in a store. We can write it in our notebook as an option for a birthday or special occasion.)

Help them talk

Sometimes it's hard for them to talk to us. As we mentioned earlier, some of the most difficult conversations happen most easily while we are doing something else, doing a job around the house ("Come talk to me while we fold some laundry"), sitting side by side on the bus, building Legos together, or throwing a ball.

We can ask them what is going on for them and what they need (not what they want). Their ability to articulate their needs (e.g., reassurance, a hug, space, connection) will improve as we continue to practice this with them.

Amanda Morin, author of *What Is Empathy?*, talks about being a detective, gathering information, making sure we understand the situation correctly, listening, and affirming.

- "You looked kind of grumpy, and I wonder how you are feeling now."
- "What I hear you saying is _____? Did I get it right?"
- "Tell me what you need me to know/what you need to tell me."
- "Is there something I can help you with?"

If they lash out at us, Morin says we can be clear:

- "I don't feel good when you shout at me."
- "I can't fix this for you, but I can be that person that you can talk to about it."

Remember not to take it personally, especially with 6- to 12-year-olds, who notoriously talk back and are rude. They want mental independence and are showing us they can think for themselves. And we will let them know what language is okay and what is not okay for us, perhaps coming back to it at a later time when everyone is calm.

SETTING KIND AND CLEAR LIMITS WHEN NEEDED

In those moments when things have escalated or someone may get physically or emotionally hurt, as the adult, we need to be the child's prefrontal cortex. We can use the phrase we learned earlier: "It's my job to keep everyone safe." It's calm and clear and takes ownership of our responsibility as the parent/caregiver.

We might then refer to one of our agreements, "We agreed to no biting, hurting, or teasing in our home" or "We agreed to eat food at the table."

Sometimes the child will protest: "It's not fair. _____ is allowed to _____." We will not negotiate on one of the agreements in the moment, but we can add it to our list to discuss at another, neutral time or at the next family meeting so we can weigh the pros and cons and make a balanced decision. "It sounds like it's important to you that we review that agreement. Let's write it down to come back to on _____."

If needed, we can give them a respectful choice ("We agreed to no screens this weekend. Would you like to turn off the TV, or shall I do it?"), and if they don't respond, we follow through kindly and clearly.

"If you say it, mean it, and if you mean it, follow through."

—Jane Nelsen and Kelly Gfroerer, *Positive Discipline Tools for Teachers*

We need to be careful of our tone so it doesn't come across as a threat, and we also need to be careful not to be too weak. ("Shall we put these away?" we ask timidly.) Instead, we need to be kind and clear, and follow through. ("I expect the floor to be clear of muddy footprints by dinnertime.")

If they become upset when we set a limit, we can help them come back to calm as we learned earlier. We show them that we see their struggle and that we are not overwhelmed by their discomfort (nor do they need to be). They might shout at us for setting a limit. "I hate you!" They might go to their room and slam the door. We have to be okay with them not liking us in that moment and look for ways to regulate ourselves if needed.

When everyone has calmed down, we can make a repair (see "Making a Repair" on page 154).

The period from 6 to 12 years, as we've said earlier, is more stable. When setting limits for children in this age group, we can appeal to their rational mind and their moral and social development. If we don't want them to run inside, we need to give them a reason or two. "If you run inside, there is a chance you will bump into the table with the vase from Grandma, which is special to me, and it's noisy for your brother, who is studying for his exam tomorrow." They may not be happy about it, but they will respect it.

Additionally, if we have already been practicing Montessori in earlier years, then our children will already know that when we say yes, we mean yes; when we say no, we mean no; and when we say, "Let's see," we'll be sure to think about it some more.

Children in the Montessori approach aren't allowed to do everything they like. They have a lot of freedoms, but we are there to guide them, set clear limits if needed, and keep them safe.

PROBLEM-SOLVE TOGETHER

There are times when we'll need to make a time to sit down to resolve a problem that keeps coming up.

In a Montessori school, if a child keeps coming to school late, instead of being punished, they have a meeting with their teacher to work out the reason for the lateness. Is it because they are having trouble getting out of bed? Maybe there is something going on in the family? How can we help remind them so they'll be on time? The teacher is working with the child to find a way to get them to come to school, rather than punishing them and making the child not want to come to school at all.

We can use a similar idea at home if our child is having trouble waking up in the morning for school. We can have a meeting and brainstorm a list of ideas (even silly ones), for example:

- Setting an alarm
- Setting a series of alarms
- Putting the alarm clock across the room so they need to get out of bed to turn it off
- Not going to school at all
- A parent coming to check on them

Once we have a long list with everyone's suggestions, we can go through and remove the ones that definitely won't work ("Not going to school isn't an option, so let's cross that one off.") and then choose one to try.

After that, we can make a plan to review how it's going (usually around a week later) to see what's working and if anything needs to be changed.

RESOLVING CONFLICT BETWEEN TWO PARTIES

When our child experiences conflict with another person, we can allow them space to resolve it on their own, and we are there if they need support. In this case, experience is the best teacher. In *The Absorbent Mind*, Dr. Montessori wrote, "Apart from exceptional cases, we ought to leave such problems to the children. We can then study their behavior objectively. . . . It is through these daily experiences that a social order comes into being."

When our support is needed

In the article "Did You Say 'Sorry?': Seeing Through Montessori Eyes," Donna Bryant Goertz does not force a child to say sorry. Children are guided to listen to each other, understand what the other child didn't like that they did, and come up with a way that would work for both of them. The child causing the conflict is not seen as a problem, but supported to do the right thing and to feel like they belong.

When we see that our children are having a hard time, we can involve them in the problem-solving process. They listen to each other, we are there to act as a neutral guide if needed, and they come up with their own solution. They will feel supported, loved, and more engaged in following through with the solution. The process may need to be revisited, adjusted, or refined, but the children are involved and taking responsibility for the solution.

When there is a basis of trust, Bill Conway, head of Montessori East in Sydney, Australia, for many years, likes to ask older children, "What do you think you could have done differently in this situation?" They are often very aware of how they could have done better and what to do to make it up to anyone else involved.

Solving problems by themselves

As our children get practice in conflict resolution, we can remove the scaffold of our support. We can offer young children the opportunity to solve the problem for themselves: "One of you wants to play, and the other wants to be by themselves. I'm curious how you will work this out."

Older children will begin to solve more of their disputes and may want to tell us about it later. Or if we hear arguing, we can stand on the side in view so they see that an adult is watching; and if needed, we can offer our help: "You both sound angry right now. Let me know if you need any help."

MAKING A REPAIR

When a child breaks something or hurts someone, whether physically or with words, we can offer them an opportunity to *repair with dignity* (this is a phrase we learned from the Nautilus training with Public Montessori in Action International). This teaches the child to think, *I know how to fix things that are broken*, and the other party receives the care they need. If the child doesn't take responsibility, the victim may continue to feel hurt and the child may continue to carry the guilt or shame too.

First, make sure all parties have calmed down. Then we can help them make the repair. It might be offering a tissue or wet cloth to a child that they pushed; fixing a toy that was broken; or making them a picture or card. These are more meaningful repairs than a hollow "Sorry."

For a child from 3 to 6 years old, it's best to make a repair right away while the incident is fresh in their mind. With a child from 6 to 12 years old, we could wait for a more neutral moment later in the day. We can say, "You know earlier, when you said _____ to me?" They will often respond with a spontaneous apology: "I'm sorry. I don't even know why I was so angry."

In Junnifa's family, she tries not to force her children to apologize. She suggests and encourages as needed but gives them time to think about it and come to it themselves, because only then will they be willing to give a genuine apology.

In Simone's family, in times of conflict, they would discuss together how they could make it up to the other person. One time, Oliver played a prank on Emma and her friend having a sleepover, setting their alarm for 4:00 a.m. To make it up to them, he agreed to cook them French toast for breakfast. They were happy, he was pleased with himself for making amends, and he also never pranked them again.

When there is not another child involved, our child may learn to take responsibility through natural or logical consequences. Natural consequences might be, for example, that if they don't want to put on their coat, they'll feel cold outside. If they eat their snack first thing in the morning, there will be no more snack for them to eat. If they don't remember their sports bag, they won't be able to participate in sports practice, or their teacher may not be happy with them.

Sometimes we may apply a logical consequence in a kind and clear way. If the child has borrowed our tools and left them out in the rain, they may find that the next time they come to use our tools, there is a lock on the box. If they are kicking a ball inside, the ball might be put away until we head to the park, and we can invite them to kick a punching bag or jump on an indoor trampoline instead. If children are fighting in the car, we might pull over until it's quiet so we can concentrate on driving. We can talk to them about what we could do next time so that they can eventually use our tools again, leave their ball somewhere inside, or keep themselves occupied in the car so the driver can concentrate.

These are not done in a shaming way ("See, I told you you would get cold") or by threatening them ("If you do that again, I'll _____"). Once they have learned the lesson, we need to drop it too. **They are learning to take responsibility, not to feel guilt.** If the same situation arises, we can remind them what happened last time so they can make a better choice this time.

One reason that a partner or family member might think that the Montessori approach is too soft or that children are allowed to do whatever they like is that people often miss this step. Do not skip this step. Help children make a repair and take responsibility—this is how they grow.

SOME COMMON PROBLEMS

When there is throwing, hitting, biting, or meanness

If our child is upset, we cannot allow them to hurt themselves or others, or act out on something in our home or the environment. If a child throws things, hits, bites, or is being mean:

- We connect with them and stop any dangerous behavior. If they are physically hurting someone, we can say, "I can't let you hurt them," and separate them. If they are hitting something, we can smile at them and say, "You're really giving that thing a hard time. Can you come inside for a minute for me to check something with you?"

- We seek to understand them and help support them to find ways for their needs to be met or build any lagging skills. For example:
  - Do they need some physical activity to get out some energy or frustration? Can we provide opportunities for them to exert this energy in acceptable ways, from a punching bag, to chopping wood, to going for a swim or run?
  - Are they having trouble expressing themselves with words? Can we ask them if they need help to talk to their friend or sibling? Or can we practice at neutral moments until they are integrated?
  - Do they feel seen and like they belong? If not, they may look for other ways to be seen or belong in the family or group.
  - If they are throwing their activities at home, are the activities meeting their needs? Are they too hard or too easy? What are they interested in right now?
- We help them make a repair if needed (see page 154).

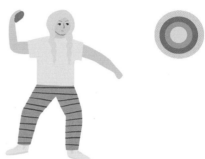

When a child whines

A whining child is telling us something—we can be like a detective to uncover what is going on. As a child, Simone had the nickname Moany Macaroni because she would complain a lot. Her family owned a store, and one day she was so bored. Simone lay behind the cash register kicking her legs in defiance. She wanted out of there. Simone eventually learned to pack a bag of books and knitting to keep herself busy. Her parents also gave her jobs around the store, which made her feel like she was contributing.

We can observe our child: When do they whine, and why do they whine? Are they missing any skills? Can we teach them how to interrupt politely? (See page 102.) Can we see what needs are not being met? Are there moments when they are engaged and able to communicate calmly? Can they practice at neutral times how to ask for help? Can we find time for them to tell us about their woes?

A parent in Simone's classes allows her three children to have "grievance time" when they can talk about things that are bothering them, particularly with their siblings, which helps them get rid of their frustrations and sometimes even come up with solutions.

How to manage fears

A preschooler might have a fear of things like monsters under the bed, the dark, dogs, or learning to bike or swim. Children ages 6 to 12 may also begin to fear things like bad things happening to those they care about or not being liked by other children.

We may not be able to get rid of their fears, but we can help them begin to manage them by:

- Being a safe place for them to talk about it. We can allow all feelings and listen to them without enabling their fear (e.g., we don't play along by squirting water under the bed to keep the monsters away).
- Finding practical solutions with the child to help them manage the anxiety (e.g., by providing a night-light and leaving the door open for a child who is scared of the dark).
- Looking for any input that could be adding to their fears (e.g., television programs or books like fairy tales with witches or monsters).
- Assisting them in building up practical skills slowly. We could visit a dog park regularly for them to learn about dogs from a distance (for a child scared of dogs); they could sit on the side of the swimming pool to watch for a few weeks of classes (for a child frightened of water); and we could find a balance bike so they can touch their feet to the ground to move and slowly learn to glide when they are ready to release their feet (for a child scared of falling off their bike).
- Staying calm ourselves. If we scoop up our child at every loud noise or have some uncertainty ourselves, our child will feel it. We can model how we might approach a dog or tell them about a fear we learned to overcome.
- Offering a security object. They may wish to choose a soft toy or blanket to sleep with or keep with them if they are scared of the dark or monsters.
- Researching things together. If they are scared of storms, we can find out what they are and the safest things to do in a storm.
- Simone recommends using the rainbow ritual to help them feel connected to us at night or if they have difficulty separating from us. We send the colors of the rainbow from our heart to their heart ("I'm sending the color red—the color of strawberries, tomatoes, roses, and fire engines—from my heart to your heart. Now the color orange . . ."). This rainbow ritual was developed by the Quest for Life Foundation to help children deal with sad or difficult news. Children feel connected to us by this rainbow, which can feel very concrete to a young child.

PART FOUR

DISCUSSING SENSITIVE TOPICS

Most people would say that they find honesty and telling the truth important. Yet children ask tricky questions, and at times we aren't sure what to say. Answering questions around sex and death can be some of the most difficult conversations—not for the children but for us. We may have shame around these topics, remember embarrassing experiences from our own childhood, or not know the right thing to say. Yet if we avoid answering our children's questions about sensitive subjects, then our children learn that we don't talk about these things or that there is some shame around them.

So what to do instead?

Be a model of honesty

Telling our children to tell the truth and telling the truth ourselves might sometimes be at odds. For example, do our children ever hear us telling a little white lie? Our example is being absorbed by our child. And what we do is more powerful than what we say.

Instead of saying, "Let's just tell them you are only 3 years old so you don't have to pay for a train ticket," we can be honest: "Now that you are 4, we'll need to buy you a children's ticket."

Give age-appropriate factual answers or look them up together

In Montessori, we like to answer children's questions with the correct facts. We don't have to give them all the information straightaway. It might be sufficient to answer a 3- or 4-year-old's question with a few simple, clear sentences. In response to the question "Why don't they have a daddy in their house?" we could answer, "There are many types of families, some people have only a mommy and others have only a daddy. Some have two mommies and others have two daddies, while some have a mommy and a daddy." We can talk about the possible reasons for the different constellations while discussing our family's values and modeling respect for others. If they don't ask any further questions in the moment, we can follow up later to see if they have more questions.

Books can also be a great way to facilitate these discussions. If we don't have a book on hand, we can tell them we could have a look at the library for a book about their question and write ourselves a note so we don't forget.

Older children will likely have more detailed questions. Be open, be honest, and don't shame them or be embarrassed. We want them to learn to trust us with their questions so they will continue to come to us and not get their information from less reliable sources.

If it's not a good time to talk, plan a time to come back to their question

Similarly, if we don't have the time or answers right now, we can tell them we'd like to give their question some thought or do some research before answering. Even better, we can agree to seek out the answer together. Then be sure to make a time to come back to it so they see that we value their question and are not avoiding it.

Respond with curiosity if we hear something that does not sound kind or appropriate

If we hear something that sounds racist or is unkind about someone, we can respond first with curiosity. It may have been an innocent mistake, or we may need to tell them that it's not kind to exclude someone based on how they look.

Even though the situation may be uncomfortable, if we don't say anything, the children miss a learning opportunity. We can also empower children to stand up for themselves or for others: "It hurts me when you say _____" or "It's not kind to say that to _____."

We highly recommend Britt Hawthorne's book *Raising Antiracist Children* and the book *Anti-Bias Education for Young Children and Ourselves* by Louise Derman-Sparks and Julie Olsen Edwards, both of which have useful examples of how to have discussions with children about race, gender, class, and ability. For more on this, see chapter 6.

Similarly helpful is the important message shared by Lucy and James Catchpole (of the Catchpoles website) that disabled adults and children are not teachable moments; they deserve the same privacy and common courtesy as everyone else. So if our child says something like "What happened to you?" to a person in a wheelchair, we can mouth "Sorry" to the other person, tell our child we all look different, and remind them that we don't ask personal questions of people we don't know.

IS SANTA REAL?

Being radically honest with our children means that for those celebrating Christmas, some people are starting to talk about Santa as a cultural symbol but choosing not to lie about who brings the presents. Christmas can still be a cozy celebration full of surprise and wonder, just as birthday celebrations are magical occasions, too. For those who would like to keep their own childhood memories alive and continue the story of Santa, Simone heard a mother answer the question if fairies and Santa were real with "I haven't seen them myself. Have you?"

If one does have Santa in the home, be careful not to threaten the children to be good or Santa won't come. Or to use the Elf on the Shelf to keep an eye on them. These hollow threats and forms of bribery conflict with our goal in Montessori for our children to develop self-discipline, not to only behave so they get something.

Setting limits around sensitive topics

Parents and caregivers ask us about setting limits when there is a sensitive topic. As hard as it is, we use the same kind and clear approach in these areas too. When we do this, we don't bring any shame to the child, we give the information needed in an age-appropriate manner, and we respect and model our boundaries too.

As easily as we might say, "We eat at the table. I'll put your cracker here for you when you are done playing," we can set a kind and clear limit with sensitive topics. "Remember we respect each other, so if you need to fart, please go to the bathroom. Sometimes it is an accident, and in that case, we can apologize to those around us."

FURTHER READING

- Little Parachutes books for children about sensitive topics like grief, divorce, and disabilities.

TALKING ABOUT DEATH

Losing a family member, a friend, or a pet is one of the hardest experiences we suffer as humans. Our children will see us sad and might have questions. The best thing we can do is give honest, accurate, and age-appropriate answers. Here are some suggestions:

- Instead of telling them that our deceased loved one is having a long sleep, we can use accurate language and say, "They died," or use terms that we use in our culture to express this, like "transitioned from the physical plane."
- When they ask us what happens when we die, we can answer, "Some people think _____ and other people think _____. What do you think might happen?"
- If a pet dies, we might want to cheer our child up by getting a new one straightaway. Yet sitting with sadness and grief will allow the child to reflect on their time with their pet and understand that life has a beginning, middle, and end. We can offer them compassion and understanding and allow them to have all their feelings.

We can make a photo album, book of memories, or video about the person or animal who has died to celebrate their life. We can honor their passing by preparing their favorite meal, playing their favorite songs, or taking photos of places they loved. Involve your child in these activities as much as they are interested. Children's books can be a good way for children to process what they are feeling.

If our child is talking a lot about death, they are likely seeking answers to the questions of life or trying to process their feelings. We can listen, we can share our own experience, and we can get them help if needed.

As young children live very much in the present moment, they may not talk about a loved one's death much at all. If one of their parents has died and we would like to keep their parent's memory alive, we can find ways to celebrate them so that the young child will build a strong memory of them. We can find natural ways to do this, like talking about their favorite food if we see it at the supermarket, and we can also do this in a more intentional way by visiting some of their favorite places, displaying photos of them, making a simple book about them that we can read at bedtime, and celebrating their birthday or other special days by making a card for them together.

TALKING ABOUT SEX

Talking about sex is not a one and done conversation. Through honest and open dialogue with our children, we can help them have a healthy relationship with their body, to respect others' bodies, and help break any taboos or trauma that we might have picked up in our own childhood. In addition to our Montessori training, the work of Melissa Pintor Carnagey of Sex Positive Families has been so helpful to us in framing these conversations with our children. Our culture and beliefs will also be a part of this conversation.

Children will learn about sex and relationships in many ways. Whether we like it or not, they are and will be receiving and exposed to information, images, and conversations about sex. If we can be the first point of contact or introduction for our children, then our children are more likely to check what they hear against what we have told them instead of vice versa. We also have the opportunity to frame it within our value system. Here are some things to consider:

How they will learn about consent. It starts in the first year, as we ask them before handling their bodies, saying, "I'm going to pick you up," then pausing to allow them time to process this and give us permission. We touch their bodies gently, with respect. We ask our child if they would like a hug or a kiss, modeling consent from the earliest ages. We use gentle hands when buckling them into their car seats. We guide them rather than pulling them by the hand.

When washing babies and children, we can also use the same gentle touch on all parts of their body, including their vulva, penis, or bottom. This helps them complete their body schema—how their body is made up.

Simone also had a rule in their house: "Rough play by mutual consent." If anyone wasn't having fun when roughhousing, the word to use was "Stop!" and then it was clear that the rough play was over. If Simone heard someone not enjoying rough play, she would ask, "Does someone need to say stop?" or she'd say, "I heard someone say stop," if needed.

Naming their body parts with accurate language. When we name our child's body parts, we can use the correct names; for example, "vulva" (for the external sex organs—clitoris, vaginal opening, urethra, labia minora and majora), "vagina" (for the canal that connects the vulva to the cervix and uterus), and "penis."

We are giving our children the tools to be able to communicate clearly to their adults (parent, doctor, caregiver) if there are any problems. And there won't be any shame as they get older, when they will already be using the correct terminology for their parts.

Babies don't grow in tummies. They grow in uteruses. We can use this language with our children, who we have already learned are capable language learners.

How we interact with our partners. Young children observe how we speak to each other, how we show love, how we respect each other, and how we resolve any conflicts that come up. They will learn to be in healthy relationships by seeing healthy relationships around them.

Following their interest in baby animals. On a farmyard, our children can see and feed baby animals and sometimes even witness animals being born. In Dutch schools, they talk about "lentekriebels" ("spring fever") in animals when children are around 5 or 6 years old. This is a natural way to talk about where babies come from. The 6- to 9-year-old child is already interested in reproduction and biology. We can introduce human reproduction in the same way as we would the reproductive patterns of insects, birds, rabbits, or farm animals.

Consider beginning the conversation before puberty. Depending on our comfort level, we can choose to talk with them earlier than later, because once a child enters puberty, they can become more self-conscious about their body and may be more embarrassed to talk with us.

Consider using gender-inclusive and ideas. Gender encompasses a person's body, expression, and identity. To make everyone feel most affirmed, we may wish to consider:

- Keeping our language gender-inclusive; for example, by saying, "You're becoming an adult" (instead of "You're becoming a man/woman").
- Modeling using our pronouns when we introduce ourselves: "My name is Simone and my pronouns are she/her." This will show how we feel most affirmed and help others reflect on the pronouns they use to feel most affirmed.
- Questioning the idea that pink is for girls and blue is for boys, that toy stores have toys for girls or boys, and that clothing stores have girls' or boys' clothing.
- Allowing children of any gender to show emotion, dress up in their parent's clothing, wear clothing that they feel comfortable in or would like to experiment with, play sports or not, and consider any career path of their choosing.

Answering their questions or finding out the answers together. They may have questions about their body because they want to know if they are normal. They may ask questions about something they see. Simone remembers walking with her family through the red-light district in Amsterdam to a café. Oliver—then around 10—asked why there were women standing in the windows in their underwear. Simone didn't avoid the question and instead gave a simple answer about prostitution and what it was. He didn't ask anything further, and they continued on to the café.

If we ignore our child's questions or seem embarrassed, they will learn that this is something we don't talk about. If we feel embarrassed, we can be honest about it. "I'm noticing that I'm feeling embarrassed talking about this topic. I never had anyone to talk to about this stuff. But I want you to feel comfortable asking me anything. I'd like to find out some more before we talk about it. Can we make a plan to talk tomorrow after school?"

Teaching all children about menstruation. Some people feel comfortable having their children, regardless of gender, in the bathroom while they are menstruating— for example, while changing a pad, tampon, or menstrual cup—so that all children learn that menstruation is a natural cycle. Other families may mention that someone is having their period if they are needing more rest or feeling sensitive. We all live in community with people who menstruate, and our children will learn about this in a natural way.

Allowing them to learn from our stories. As our child gets older, we can be vulnerable and share our experiences. Even if these were not perfect, we can reflect on how we wish they had been better. Being open with our children will show them that we are comfortable with them coming to us when they have questions.

Offering them an understanding of a wide range of experiences. If we live in a cisgender, heteronormative family, the child will have absorbed this as normal in the first six years. Regardless of our family constellation, we can teach them to respect all types of families. Our child will also want to see their own family constellation represented in the books, media, and online resources we offer to feel most affirmed.

FURTHER READING

- The Sex Positive Families website (sexpositivefamilies.com)

Some books for children:

- *What Makes a Baby* by Cory Silverberg is inclusive and educational when it comes to explaining where babies come from to young children
- *Sex Is a Funny Word* by Cory Silverberg is for older kids, around ages 7 to 11, and discusses touch (of others, of oneself) and consent
- *Making a Baby* by Rachel Greener

TALKING ABOUT BODIES

In addition to teaching them about their changing bodies and sex, we also want to help our children accept their bodies and all bodies in their diversity. This includes hair texture, skin color, height, and shape. Children are looking to answer the question, "Am I okay as I am?"

Here are some ideas that Junnifa and Simone apply in their homes and classroom:

- With children from birth through 3–6 years old and into 6–12 years old, we work on building their self-identity. This involves their having an understanding of their culture (their race, ethnicity, family history, etc.) and seeing themselves represented in their surroundings, including in books, art, and media. (For more detail on building identity, see chapter 6.)
- Practicing self-care in the home and classroom—learning to care for our bodies.
- Being grateful for our bodies—wondering and learning about the role of every cell in our body.
- Being careful not to focus only on appearances; for example, when we meet a child, instead of saying, "That's such a pretty dress," we can say, "I'm so happy to meet you."
- Focusing on the person and their characteristics and/or efforts when we give feedback rather than on what people look like: "I saw you working really hard together today. I'm so curious what you learned."

- Being kind about our own bodies and eliminating negative self-talk or saying, "I shouldn't have had that cake today" or "I've got to go out for a run" when these come from a place of guilt or shame.
- Modeling intuitive eating—eating just what our bodies need; listening to our bodies after each bite to see if it still feels good (see more about eating on page 121).

In her book *Raising Antiracist Children*, Britt Hawthorne shares a powerful message about beauty from Trisha Moquino (a highly respected Indigenous Montessori educator): "You don't need to wear makeup to be beautiful. Our grandparents taught us not to rush into wearing makeup. They stated that our creator made me the way I was supposed to be and that I was fine that way, I was beautiful that way." This is one of the messages Trisha has shared with her girls when talking about self-love in their family over the years.

The same book also has us think critically with our children:

- About corporations selling products to make us look "right."
- About the use of Photoshopped images and the messaging in advertisements.
- About setting boundaries around body-shaming—that no one is allowed to make fun of someone's body size or shape. We can say, "Bodies are just bodies. All bodies are worthy bodies. It's not okay to comment on someone's body."
- About valuing all bodies, including bodies of all colors, abilities, and genders.
- About saying, "I love my body; it belongs to me" if someone comments on our body.
- About how everyone is allowed to choose what they wear.
- About learning to have respect for disabled bodies and to recognize where we have privileges and immunity and how we can advocate for others in the community.
- About how disability can be both visible and invisible.
- About learning more about body positivity from *The Body Is Not an Apology* by Sonya Renee Taylor.

We are living in a world of commercialization, and it can feel like we have little control. In an interview on the *Tilt Parenting* podcast, Zoë Bisbing and Leslie Bloch of the Full Bloom Project, which promotes body positivity, said that we can create an environment in our homes to buffer the effect. We can take away the morality around food, diet culture, healthy food, and junk food. And it is never too late to make adjustments in our home. We can talk with our child, tell them we've learned something new and what we are going to try instead.

All that said, our children live in society, and we can help them build the skills to feel safe in their body. If they feel under someone's gaze, they may choose to put on a jacket over what they are wearing; if someone puts down what they are wearing, they can practice saying, "It's not your business what I wear. My clothes make me feel like me."

TALKING ABOUT MONEY

One part of raising children is teaching them about money.

The 3- to 6-year-old child is beginning to understand abstract concepts; for example, that a note or coin is a representation of a sum of money that we give in exchange for an item or service. As so much money is now exchanged digitally via a card at checkout or online, it is more difficult for them to see concretely. It can be nice for us to have cash available for them to see us pay for groceries and receive change. They also enjoy handing over the money and receiving the change, and we can do simple grace and courtesy lessons to practice this.

Like any skill they learn, much of what our children will learn about how to manage money starts with our own example. The 3- to 6-year-old child with their absorbent mind will absorb our attitudes to money in our daily life: when we are at the grocery store, how we react when we receive bills, how we talk about finances and taxes.

We can look at our own attitude to money. How do we feel about money? Do we have an abundance or scarcity mindset? Do we spend a lot? Are we careful with money? Do we put money aside for savings? How do we model charity in our family? How do we redistribute wealth to under-resourced communities? None of these questions have a right or wrong answer, but they help us to consider what values we want our children to associate with money.

The 6- to 12-year-old child may start to become more interested in the idea of money, and they can learn about the origins and history of money, different types of currency around the world, physical cash, and electronic money. They may have questions for us about how we earn money, how other people earn money, where money is kept, and how we manage our budget.

One way of learning about money is through practice—both earning and spending money. We can open a bank account with them so they learn how to keep track of their money. Some young children can be quite entrepreneurial and want to set up a lemonade stand, do jobs for neighbors to earn money, or do jobs for us to earn extra allowance. However, an interest in earning money and having some economic independence is mostly seen in the following plane of development, from ages 12 to 18.

Some people like giving children an allowance so the child learns how to save, spend, invest, and donate money. Traditionally, an allowance is given if a child does chores at home. However, in a Montessori home, we have the child take part in doing things around the home to contribute to and be part of the family. Giving an allowance in return for chores then is at odds with the Montessori approach.

Educators like Michael Grose (not a Montessori educator but an Australian parenting expert very aligned with the Montessori approach) advocate for giving an allowance as a right, not tied to any behavior or chores. The amount could be nominal, to use in purchasing an occasional ice cream or to save up for a toy. Or the child may receive as much as they would need to buy their own clothing, gifts for friends, and any additional snacks that they want. This can be quite a significant amount, and if they spend too much at the beginning of the week or month, they will naturally experience that there is not enough for the end of the month.

Simone's children didn't receive an allowance at all before they were 12 years old, with the idea that if there was something they needed, it would be purchased by the family. If someone needed a new pair of shoes, these would be bought with the family budget in mind. There was not a lot of spare money, so the children understood the value of what was bought and were not always asking for more stuff. They sometimes received some money for their birthday and had the opportunity to practice saving and spending. With regard to giving money to causes, the family had discussions about current causes they wanted to support and would make a family donation.

When her children were 12, they were given €5 a week each to buy lunch at school if they wanted. Quickly, Oliver and Emma realized that they could make their lunch at home and save the money. Around the age of 15, they were given a clothing allowance every 3 months. They also obtained part-time jobs, Oliver at the cinema and Emma helping out Simone from time to time with administrative tasks as well as briefly working at a store.

Now, at university, they receive a student loan and manage their budget independently. When Simone asks if they need any money or help, they ask for advice occasionally but otherwise refuse any help and want to manage by themselves. True characteristics of Montessori children.

If an allowance is given, guidelines can be agreed upon with the child about what money can be spent on as well as putting some aside for saving, giving (e.g., making a charitable donation), and investing. It can be very frustrating to have them save up for plastic toys that don't align with our values of being mindful of consumption and the environment.

TALKING ABOUT STEALING

Stealing provides a thrill, the risk of being caught; or stealing can be about a child wanting something they aren't allowed. There may be a friend inviting them to take part. They may be the ringleader themselves. We are not going to get the truth by being angry or asking direct questions. We need to understand that they must be very dysregulated to think that stealing is okay.

As difficult as it may be, we want them to know we are on their side. That everything can be worked out. We don't need to rush into a conversation. "I'm concerned about what has happened, but I need some time to calm myself down and prepare myself for this conversation. Can we come back together tonight to talk about it?"

We will want to understand what their needs are and if we can find other thrill-seeking ways for them to meet them. If they are getting into trouble with a particular friend or friend group, we can't stop them from seeing each other, but we could have limits on the number of sleepovers per month or time they spend together during the week. We can use this time to reconnect with our child and help them come back to their path. If it's about not being allowed things, we can review if we are being too top-down about certain things and how we can hand back control over parts of their lives.

We also must make sure that the child takes responsibility for their actions, owning up to what they have done, apologizing for their mistake, and returning the item to the store/owner or paying for it.

We can also use opportunities when they arise to discuss this with our child to prevent such situations occurring. For example, if we read an article about shoplifting, this could open a conversation with our child. We can talk about why some children feel they need to steal. We could discuss with them what they could say to a friend who might encourage them to steal. We also might cover what they could do if they hear someone else they know has been stealing.

TALKING ABOUT TECHNOLOGY

Technology has become part of our lives. We want to use it in our homes as a tool rather than an obstacle to our child's development.

Here are some things to consider when it comes to technology:

Some ideas for technology by age. As sensorial learners, 3- to 6-year-olds will still learn and understand best through hands-on exploration of concrete materials.

At home consider:

- Limiting the use of technology to video calls with family; for example, when a loved one might read a book with them
- Instead of using the internet to look up their favorite construction vehicle, going to the library to find a book about one or watching one at a building site
- Rather than asking an AI chatbot the answer to a question, choosing a concrete way to find the answer (using a set of encyclopedias or writing the question on a Post-it Note to make a "wonder wall" of things to investigate further)
- Instead of using a screen to entertain them at a café, taking a notebook to draw in or a book to read, having a family conversation, or playing "I spy"
- Allowing them to use our camera or phone to take photos and edit them
- Using concrete materials to learn about patterns and sequencing, which later could be used as building blocks for coding and programming if they show interest
- If the child is exposed to screens, consciously choosing the programming: shorter programming, slower edits, and, as much as possible, based in reality rather than fantasy (avoiding wicked witches, dragons, pirates, etc. for children under 6 years); having an adult available to support their understanding and answer any questions that come up; and referencing websites like Common Sense Media when making media choices

For 6- to 12-year-olds, who are seeking to understand the universe, we can talk to them about using technology actively as a tool rather than passively to consume content or to copy information. Some examples:

- Using computers for research—we can guide the child how to evaluate the information found as well as assess what information is the most reliable; our favorite websites can be saved as bookmarks on the toolbar for easy access; and we can encourage the child to think about media literacy, such as by visiting the News Literacy Project website

- Learning how to make a summary of information found, how to note their sources, and how not to simply copy and paste text into their work
- Encouraging them not to rely only on online search information but also to seek out books in the public library or find experts to interview
- Using specialized software like 3D modeling and architecture programs, or learning coding basics, how to create a presentation or video, or how to build a website
- Connecting with an expert overseas or possibly other (Montessori) schools in different parts of the world

- Making a difference in the world like raising money for a cause
- If they are interested in social media, having a shared family account, maybe about our family pet or our cooking experiments, to try out social media together
- Making a family film night a social occasion by inviting friends over, hanging up an old sheet, and projecting a film onto it. It will make for a memorable evening.

In his article "Technology and Montessori," Montessori educator Mark Powell adds:

- Taking photos with a digital camera.
- Making stop-motion films.
- Creating digital stories (recording a voice-over and images and then cutting them together with movie editing software).
- Recording digital audiobooks for younger children.
- Using technology like a ProScope (a lighted handset held over an animal/object to project it onto a computer screen) to make photos, videos, and time-lapse recordings, for instance, of a plant growing).
- Watching well-produced educational videos (e.g., about volcanoes) or listening to inspirational historical speeches, such as by Dr. Martin Luther King Jr.

> "We want the playground experience whereby children learn to think creatively, reason, and collaborate. We want the emphasis to be on collecting, analyzing, evaluating, and presenting information."
>
> —Alison Awes (an elementary AMI Montessori trainer)
> "On Building Character: The Elementary Child's
> Moral Development in the Digital Age"

The needs of the child. The child needs to move, to be social, to be creative, and to get good sleep. We can ensure:

- The child has enough movement (3 hours a day according to the World Health Organization)
- Screens in our lives are not affecting face-to-face communication with our child
- The child has lots of unstructured time to explore the real world, play with friends in person, and come up with their own ideas (rather than passively watching television or playing a computer game or spending time on social media)
- Screens are not affecting their sleep (no screens in the bedroom or within an hour or two of bedtime)

Agreements. There is interesting research by the Royal College of Pediatrics and Child Health in the UK showing that children themselves recognize that technology can be both useful and harmful. So we can invite them to help develop agreements for their tech use and and give them credit for sticking to them. For the 3- to 6-year-old child, the family agreements are likely to be made by the adults. For 6- to 12-year-olds, these agreements become more collaborative. The agreements would cover:

- Whom they can communicate with and for how long.
- Where they can engage with screens—ideally, any computers and other devices will be kept in the living area so an adult can see the screen to supervise if needed.
- What technology options/apps/games are considered okay—do they align with our family values? Do they require the child to be active in coming up with solutions? Are there opportunities for the child to move their body?
- Any safety considerations (see "Safety" below).
- Avoiding snacking during screen time.
- Whether they need a cell phone to catch public transportation.
- Whether there are different rules when the family is traveling on longer trips.

If the agreements are broken, the child is showing us that they do not yet have the skills or enough practice to master abiding by them. We can come back to see how we can help them follow the agreements, or review them if necessary at the next family meeting. We can involve the child in reading the latest research on screens and ask them what they think should happen. Sometimes they are harder on themselves than we would be.

Note: If there is an older sibling in the home with more access to screens, we can discuss what is appropriate for any younger sibling to see. We can make family arrangements; for example, that they watch a film in the evening after the younger child is asleep.

Grace and courtesy. We want our children to learn how to communicate online respectfully, use technology wisely, and recognize any suspicious behavior online. We call this digital grace and courtesy. For example: How do we interpret emojis? How do we read someone's tone? What is the etiquette around communicating on different channels like email, text, and social media? How do we make space and take space in conversations online? Would we say this to the person directly?

Research by data journalist Alexandra Samuel showed that children who were mentored by adults when learning to navigate the digital social environment got into less trouble in digital spaces than children who had no guidance.

Safety. Ericka Sóuter, author of *How to Have a Kid and a Life: A Survival Guide*, has some useful questions around digital safety. Does our child know who to trust? Do we know who they are talking to? What does spam look like? What do scams look like? How can they protect their digital footprint? What are they sharing? Has the child gotten permission from an adult to make an online purchase? What to do if we see inappropriate content? What are the guidelines if we allow the child to play online games with friends? How do we manage passwords?

We also need to think about safety issues with location services and people being able to know where our children are at any moment.

Be an example. Our children observe how we interact with technology. We can use our phones and devices purposely; for example, telling them what we are doing when we pick up our phone or are on our computer: "I'm going to send a message to let them know we are here." And when we use it as a break: "I'm going to go online for 10 minutes to check my social media." We can also get their permission before posting any photos of them or information about them.

Other considerations. In her article "On Building Character," Alison Awes also mentions:

- Questioning with our children stereotypes found in online media, especially idealized images.
- Letting them explore the history of technology. How was it developed? By whom? How did we listen to music before computers?
- Talking about setting boundaries, including with friends, on text and social media.
- Inappropriate content. If a child sees pornography, Awes writes, "Parents will want to discuss how that is different from real sex in a loving relationship, explaining why they feel the content is demeaning or promotes a narrow view of sexuality." Or if they come across some disturbing news while watching a weather video, "The adult can apologize that the child found something that was not meant for children."

Artificial intelligence. We can raise our children to use AI as an additional tool in the same way we teach them to use the internet. We want to help them become critical users of AI (for example, questioning the ethics around AI-generated art) and to discuss when it's appropriate to use it (and when it's not). We (Junnifa and Simone) suspect that AI will mean that many schools will move towards a Montessori approach to learning in the classroom—where children are learning by doing, not generating their answers via a chatbot.

Making changes. If we have not been intentional with the use of technology in our family, we can start a conversation with our child. In her course Montessori Homeschool by Design, Jana Morgan Herman suggests adding things rather than taking things away. For example, thinking of other activities to do in the evening instead of being on screens, like playing a game together or going for a walk after dinner. It will take some time to change habits, and we can move step-by-step toward making new agreements.

FURTHER READING

- "On Building Character: The Elementary Child's Moral Development in the Digital Age" by Alison Awes
- "Technology & the Elementary Student," www.creoschool.org/blog/kidsandtechnology
- *Screenwise: Helping Kids Thrive (and Survive) in Their Digital World* by Devorah Heitner

TALKING ABOUT GUN PLAY

The most helpful Montessori perspectives on gun play are offered by Donna Bryant Goertz and the late John Snyder of Austin Montessori School. Snyder spoke of children trying out power in their play, from throwing rocks, snowballs, and dirt to pretending to use guns or spears. When children use sticks, their finger, or Legos to "shoot" at people, the adult offers the phrase, "We don't pretend to shoot people."

As Montessori families, we want to instill an attitude of solving problems with others in nonviolent ways and not have guns in our home. We can redirect our child's play toward other ways to try out power with activities that involve noise and (possibly) shiny objects. These could include making a "volcano" with vinegar, dishwashing liquid, and baking soda and watching it "erupt"; banging pots and pans with a hammer; playing with water balloons (yet not throwing them at people or animals); making a go-kart; or launching their own DIY rockets to the moon.

We can also look at where their need to explore guns is coming from. Is it from books, television, video games, and other stories with "good guys" and "bad guys"? From other children at preschool and school? Wouldn't it be nice if we could move away from these types of stories as a society? We can be the ones to start.

There is also an opportunity to have discussions with our children around war, fighting, and international diplomacy between people, groups, or nations having opposing views. Speak often of peace, and compassion, and foster finding solutions in our homes so that everyone's needs are met.

TALKING ABOUT WAR AND CLIMATE CHANGE

In March 2022, following the outbreak of war in Ukraine, Lead Montessori hosted a conversation called "How to Talk to Children about What Is Happening?" with three AMI Montessori trainers—Madlena Ulrich, Tiina Suominen, and Carla Foster—and Dinny Rebild, a longtime Montessori educator who worked for 5 years at the Red Cross asylum center Kongelunden in Denmark. The information shared can be applied to any difficult world events, from war to the climate crisis to natural disasters to a school shooting. Harrowing events happen around us, and we can help our children process them even when we ourselves may find it difficult to comprehend them.

The first thing to say is that we have to take care of ourselves before we take care of the children. It helps to have a safe person or circle we can talk to so that, as much as possible, we can show up for our families. We don't have to pretend to be happy. We can be authentic. We can tell the children that this is upsetting for us, too. When we have done some of our work already to process the event, we will find it easier to stay grounded to hold space for, and help, our children. We don't want to burden them with our problems.

With children younger than 3 years old, we do our best not to expose them to information that can harm them or their minds. We need to be their guardians and be careful about the information coming in around them to protect them as much as possible. We want to provide them with physical and psychological security so they know they can trust us. We can keep our routines as stable and normal as possible, including with predictable mealtimes and bedtimes. We want to be careful not to pass on our own feelings of doubt or fear to the children.

The 3- to 6-year-old child may hear something from our conversations, at preschool, or school, or they might see a newspaper or the news on television. We can start by observing whether they show signs of unusual behavior. We can say, "You don't look yourself. Is there anything worrying you?" We can let them know that it's okay to feel sad or worried, we can ask them what they know, and we can answer any questions that come up for them. Remember that if they see a newsclip played again and again on the news, they may think that it is happening over and over rather than being replayed, and they may also feel like it is happening nearby or could happen to them or our families.

We could model and involve them in doing something to help. They might do some fundraising, offer help to an affected neighbor, or assist us with anything we are doing to help, from making a donation, to baking for a bake sale, to knitting blankets being collected. We can also let them know of things that are being done to help in the international community and any peacekeeping talks being held to find solutions and restore peace.

For the 6- to 12-year-old child, Carla Foster mentions Dr. Montessori's call for the united nations of humanity, not individual countries. Foster says, "Pride in our culture is not nationalism." We can share how humans' hearts, minds, and hands have been able to solve problems over the course of history. We respond to a threat by coming to action together in community, not aggression. Where they may want to stamp "good" or "evil" onto any party involved, we can help them instead explore the question of how humans can deal with the dilemmas that we come up against and find better solutions. They can help alleviate suffering by finding ways to offer support, such as via an NGO or international organization.

Most of all, we can be available. We can again start by asking what they have heard and answering questions they have. Keep information factual, find information from different perspectives, and look critically at information to find out what is reliable. We can correct any misunderstandings they might have and look on a map to see where the conflict is happening. They might like to process what is going on through making art or music.

We can remind our children that these things are rare. We don't have to lie to our children and say that everything is going to be okay. But we can assure them that everyone is doing their best to make things as safe as possible. As Mister Rogers would say, "Look for the helpers. You will always find people who are helping."

When we are directly affected by events, we do our best to cope, to tell our children in an age-appropriate way what is going on, and to make things in their daily routine as predictable as possible. Again, we don't want to make any promises we can't keep, but we can offer them reassurance that we are doing our best, that others are helping to make sure that we will be safe and secure, and that we are doing it together.

The same principles can be applied to conversations about the climate crisis. We can acknowledge the facts, let them know what is being done, tell them we also sometimes feel worried about it, and make a plan for what we would like to do as a family to combat climate change. (For more, see p. 266, "Connecting with and feeding Earth.")

TALKING ABOUT FAITH

Our beliefs and faith are personal to ourselves and our families. Children younger than 6 years old will absorb the beliefs we share with them. From 6 to 12 years old, they will become interested in what their friends believe in and how this is similar to or different from our own family.

For some of us, this is an important part of our culture, and we will include our child in our rituals and ceremonies. Or we may not be religious but still be spiritual. Regardless of our faith, we can pass on to our children in their early years a love for all humanity and the concept that every living thing has a cosmic purpose. We can show respect for others' beliefs: "Some people believe _____ and other people believe _____. In our family, we believe _____." Or "I believe _____. What do you believe?"

For those interested in a Montessori-based approach to religious education, there is the Catechesis of the Good Shepherd. This program was developed in 1954 by Dr. Sofia Cavalletti and professor Gianna Gobbi based on Dr. Montessori's pedagogy. In this approach, the Atrium is a prepared mixed-age learning environment where the child can ask, "Help me come closer to God by myself." The principles are based in Catholicism but have also been used in other Christian denominations, Islam, and other religions to share their faith with children.

FURTHER READING

- *The Child in the Church* by Dr. Maria Montessori
- *The Religious Potential of the Child* by Sofia Cavalletti

PART FIVE

WORKING WITH OTHERS

There's an African saying that it takes a village to raise a child. We can't raise our children in isolation. We work with others, including immediate family members like our partner (if we have one) and other children; extended family members like our siblings, parents, in-laws, uncles, and aunts; our chosen family, those friends and neighbors in our trusted circle; and other caregivers who help us care for our children and teach them, such as nannies, au pairs, schoolteachers, enrichment program teachers, and religious guides. We also work with the parents and caregivers of our children's friends, other neighbors, and sometimes even people whom we've met in parks or shops.

Many times we will be working with people who do not share our philosophy. They may not know what Montessori is, or some of them may know of it but not necessarily have a positive opinion of it or agree with us. How do we interact with these people and communicate our beliefs to them? How do we get them to buy in to or at least respect our opinions with regard to how we want our children to be raised?

General principles for working with others

Inform. Be clear about our beliefs. Communicate our limits and nonnegotiables clearly and respectfully. If others are open, we might go into detail about the whys. With some people, it might actually be better to focus on the principle and not even mention Montessori. For example, Junnifa's children are not exposed to screens during their early years. This stems from Montessori recommendations for more sensorial experiences for young children. We also know that research and most medical bodies agree, so she tells people that her children are not allowed to watch TV or use phones, and when they ask why, she refers to research or WHO recommendations because she has found that people are more open to that source than to Montessori.

Educate. It is especially important to educate those with whom our child will have a long relationship or spend a lot of time with about the core Montessori principles. People are more likely to buy in to what they understand. We can help them understand topics like:

- What Montessori is.
- Key principles: respect, independence, freedom with limits, cooperation with our child
- The outcomes: short- and long-term goals we have for our child
- Our values

- How to support independence
- The importance of talking to and listening to children

We can also share practical information like:

- "What to say instead of"
- Why we don't praise or say "Good boy/girl" or "Good job"
- What to do when the child is upset or throwing a tantrum
- Activities to keep the children busy or what to do instead of watching TV
- How to set limits

Some of the ways that we can educate others:

- Sharing what we know in conversation or writing it down.
- Sharing information: articles or text images, podcasts, memes, reels, or social media posts with small pieces of relevant messages.
- Sharing books. We can read the same book and discuss if they are open to it.
- If we are connected to a Montessori school or community, we might invite them to adult education sessions.
- We can gift them Montessori e-courses or invite them to webinars. Both Junnifa and Simone have enjoyed having partners, grandparents, and other caregivers on their e-courses.
- Modeling and explaining later why we did what we did.

Model. We can model what we want to see. We can model how to interact with our children, how to talk to them, treating them with respect, not interrupting them, allowing and supporting their independence, listening to them when they speak. We can also model teaching instead of correcting, Instead of "Why are you always making a mess?" say, "It's time to clean up your room. What would you like to pick up first?" We can model positive discipline principles, limit setting, collaboration in the kitchen and bathroom, slowing down and being present with our children, patience, and any interaction we want to see with our children.

We can also model respect in our interactions with others, not just our children. So treating our partner (if we have one), caregivers, other children, and others that we interact with respectfully will make people even more likely to treat our own children with respect.

Share joy. When we see ways that Montessori made a difference, we can share them, but not gloatingly. Notice when the child shows independence or reflects values that our beliefs nurtured because of our Montessori choices. "They look so happy to be folding their own clothes from the basket." Gabriel Salomão of Lar Montessori talks about sharing joy when he is at the playground with extended family. He doesn't mention the word *Montessori*; instead he points out what the child has mastered and is enjoying. We can also share experiences from Montessori families in our community who have older children who reflect the values we aspire to.

Offer alternatives. We could also discuss their challenges with maintaining the freedoms or limits we have set and find ways to help them be successful. For example, we can send activities with our children when they are visiting a place where they are usually offered screens for entertainment.

Be patient and give them time. It often takes time for people to first digest and understand Montessori. It is important to give grace and be patient. Acknowledge small efforts and continue to model, guide, and encourage as much as possible.

Have regular check-in meetings with caregivers. It is reasonable if they are looking after our children a lot that we try as much as possible to have a similar approach. We can set aside time each week or month to discuss any problems they are having and come up with solutions together.

Look for their strengths. Our children benefit, too, from different perspectives and skills. We could invite others to take our children to the community garden, play sports together, visit an animal shelter, or bake together, depending on what the friend, relative, or caregiver also loves to do.

SOME SPECIFIC RELATIONSHIPS

Our partner

Ideally, our partner (if we have one) would be on the same page with us, and we would have a plan together of how our children are being raised based on the Montessori philosophy. We can set goals and dream together about the kind of home environment we want for our children and the future we envision for them. However, many times this is not the case. So how do we proceed knowing that we would ideally present a united front to our child?

At a comfortable, happy, neutral time, have conversations about our hopes for our child's future and what kind of humans we want to raise. Ensure that we listen to our partner's views as we share ours. Also identify what we don't like or want, and how we don't want to be. Hopefully, we can find some alignment. Perhaps we both want happy children who grow up to be confident, independent, creative, responsible, kind, respectful, and good stewards of the world. Point out how the Montessori principles can take our child to that desired future. The great thing about Montessori is that its outcomes are long-term and are usually tied to many of our hopes for our child's life as an adult. Focus on the big picture and why we would choose it as a family. We might also talk about the application. What are some of the differences that this choice will make for how we already raise our child, or for the ideas that our partner may have previously held about raising children? This will probably not be a onetime discussion; it can be revisited often as we go on our journey together.

What do we do when our partner wants us to be stricter or maybe our partner corrects our child harshly, yells at them, or even punishes or spanks them? How do we react?

First, remember that they are probably doing what they think is best. It is important to remind ourselves of this so that we can respond logically.

Next, remember that it is best not to argue or disagree with our partner in front of our children. This can be hard, so it might be better to leave the room when something we don't feel comfortable with is happening (unless our child is in danger). This minimizes the chance of a confrontation. We can then have a conversation later, making sure not to come across as an expert or as judgmental. We can mention what we felt did not go well, offer alternatives for how it might have been handled differently as respectfully as we can, and then let it go. We might be able to convince them, or not, but often we have sown a seed, and seeds take time to grow. We will have opportunities to water these seeds and plant more, and over time, our partner will hopefully start to shift.

They can also have their concerns heard in the moment. Let's say we go to the park and our child wants to climb a tree, and our partner immediately says, "It's not safe; you can't climb it." But the child has done it before and we know they can, so what do we do? We might say, "It *can* be unsafe to climb trees," acknowledging our partner's point of view. "What if I stand close by and help make sure they are safe?" That way the child gets a chance, and the partner's concerns are not ignored. If the partner still says no, we could redirect the child to another activity and then have the conversation with our partner later to better understand and allay their concerns.

Sometimes a disagreement may happen in front of the child. Then it is best to show our children how we resolve conflict. So often we do this part when the child is not around. They need to see us making repairs with each other, too, when they see a conflict.

As mentioned in the general principles, we can do our best to educate our partner. It's great to find courses that we take together, discuss, and implement together. It is fun to try out our learnings, to observe and celebrate wins together.

Build community. Identify families whose values align with ours so that we can do things together and grow together. We could find them to be models for ourselves and our partner. Junnifa has found this to be very helpful for her family. Oftentimes, hangouts with family friends open doors to conversations about raising our children. If we belong to a Montessori school, building connections with other families in the community provides our child with friends from families who share the same values.

Reinforce what they are doing well. It is tempting to only have a discussion with our partner when they do something out of line, but we have to remember that what we water is what grows so we can try to highlight what they are doing right. We can excitedly share the effect of something they did right and encourage even small efforts or changes.

Again, it is a process, and we want to be patient. Everyone is on their own journey, doing the best they can, developing on their own timeline just as the child is.

Extended family

With our extended family, it helps to first remember that they usually mean well and also to remind ourselves that our child will benefit from a relationship with their loved ones. This helps us put things in perspective when things don't go as we wish.

It is helpful to make our beliefs clear and set limits from the very beginning. We can do this respectfully and kindly but also firmly, especially when it comes to the big things that mean a lot to us. For some it might be respect or punishment, for others it might be screen exposure, and for another it might be processed foods or sugar. Whatever our big things are, we can communicate them. We can also educate, but what we have found to be the most effective tool for extended family members like grandparents is modeling. It might take a while, and that's okay. Remember, we want to be patient. Seeds take time to grow. People often come around when they start to see the difference in the children. Ana-Kay of Pickneys at Play shared that her family came on board when her family witnessed her twins doing practical life activities. They could not believe how capable they were at such a young age.

We can also advocate for our children in situations where it is necessary. For example, if we are visiting family and our child is expected to hug or kiss their relatives and they don't want to, we can explain that we do not force our children to hug or be touched by people. We ask our child's permission and respect their choices about their body. In this way, we are teaching our child body autonomy and consent and that it's okay to say no, even to another adult. And we are teaching our family members about an important boundary.

It can be especially challenging to get grandparents on board because often they feel like they successfully raised their own children and may not then want to be told what to do. Some may also feel like our new choices are a challenge to or judgment of their own methods. There are several areas that may represent challenges:

- Discipline
- Allowing things we would rather not allow, like TV, sweets, plastic noisy toys, phones, and digital devices
- Encouraging dependence and hampering independence
- Being overprotective and not allowing exploration
- Being laissez-faire and not supervising the child

Sometimes we need to reach a compromise with grandparents because, many times, they will do what they want to do. But by reaching a compromise, we let them do what they want within the limits that we have set. It might be that instead of not being allowed to watch any TV, our child can watch TV for up to 1 hour. We can involve our child in holding to this limit also when we are not present. We can discuss the value of integrity and doing what is right even when we are not there and letting them know our expectations.

If issues arise with grandparents, we can focus on what we appreciate about them and the value they bring to our children. We can prioritize the issues, address the big things, and let go of the small things.

Caregivers

We can ensure that we go through a thorough process when selecting caregivers, and once they've been hired, we can educate and train them.

We can be explicit in how we want them to interact with our children and what our expectations are. Let them know what we want our children exposed to and how we would prefer for them to speak to our children. In addition to telling them, we can show them and outline it in a document for reference. We could arrange for them to follow a Montessori course or pass on this book to them to read. We can also check with our children if our caregivers align to our values when we are not present.

To encourage respect from our child, avoid correcting the caregiver in front of the child and speak respectfully. Also avoid speaking negatively about the caregiver in front of the child.

An alternative offered by Trina of DIY Corporate Mom is to give very little instruction to a caregiver except to say, as Dr. Montessori said to her first assistants, "Do not interrupt." She adds, "Relax and observe my child . . . just relax and observe." Then Trina also prepares their home environment with things like knives and glasses accessible to the children, so any caregiver would soon be on board with the Montessori approach in their home.

Our child's teachers

We view our child's teachers as partners in supporting our child's development. In every partnership, communication and trust are keys to success, so we ensure that there is open, honest, and respectful communication. We can discuss preferred means and times of communication. Most teachers would prefer a scheduled meeting or conversation over a spontaneous one. We also work toward building trust. Take time to reflect on what would help us trust our child's teacher and communicate this to them. Engage with them for both positive and challenging reasons so that we are not coming to them with only complaints or challenges. Express genuine care for them. Before jumping into a conversation about our child, we ask how they're doing. Acknowledge their efforts and appreciate them. Share examples of how we see their work reflected in our child at home.

We can attend parent-teacher conferences and other school events. Teachers often put a lot of work into these gatherings, and attending is a way of showing appreciation. We show interest in the child's work in school, ask questions, give feedback, offer our time, help, and expertise when possible.

It can also be respectful to include the child in any meetings at the school. They can express for themselves what they enjoy and what they find difficult, and when there are problems, they can be involved in finding solutions.

Other teachers (enrichment, religious)

We can work to ensure that the enrichment options we choose for our children are in line with our values and that, as much as possible, the other children and families also share our values. This is of course not always possible, so we can supervise and communicate any preferences, limits, and considerations to the teacher from the beginning. Our children should also know these and be empowered to speak up when necessary. We can also have conversations with our children about their experiences and give feedback to the teacher respectfully.

Friends' parents or caregivers

If our child has a friend whose parents or caregivers offer options that are not in line with our preferences, we can make our homes the safe place where our children and their friends gather, and we can be on-site during these gatherings so that we can observe, supervise, and provide guidance as necessary. The advantage of this is that we get to know our children's friends, and our children get an opportunity to positively influence others. We can also follow the general principles discussed earlier.

In a situation where our child has a disagreement with another child and their parent or caregiver confronts us, we can calmly address the complaint and suggest that our children work it out themselves where possible. If not, we can offer to be an impartial mediator, mostly to ensure that each side is being heard. For example, at the park or a party, another adult might expect our child to share a special toy or do something that is not in line with our beliefs. We can help our child advocate for themselves, giving them words to say if they are stuck, or if needed, we can explain to the adult respectfully.

JASMINE, ANDREW & THEIR
3 CHILDREN AGED 1, 9, 10

Three-Minute Montessori
Singapore & UK

"Montessori is less about the physical materials and more about the attitude to life and learning. It looks like setting high expectations while providing enough freedom for them to manage their home responsibilities (e.g., washing dishes and tidying their own bedroom) and school responsibilities (e.g., homework and test prep). It looks like providing enough unstructured downtime to balance out the rigor of a school day, so children can still be children. They love Legos, collecting gemstones, reading, and exercising."

"I used to dread helping them with their homework. Now I've developed a respectful, Montessori approach to provide enough homework guidance, but also enough freedom for them to plan how and when they will complete their homework, make mistakes, and correct their own mistakes."

"During Lunar New Year, watching lion dances is a favorite activity. When younger, children may need earplugs, and we warn them in advance that there will be loud drums and huge crowds, so they do not get overstimulated. When older, this yearly activity becomes firmly cemented as part of their childhood memories around Lunar New Year. It may also spark curiosity about the origins or variations of the lion dance, which serves as a springboard to further research and reading."

"Having done Montessori parenting for a number of years, the payoff becomes more evident in the long term. The children are quietly confident in their abilities. It is not a false confidence built on external rewards or people's praises, but on experiencing for themselves that they are capable."

PREPARATION
OF THE ADULT

8

As we start our Montessori journey, our focus is usually on our child and how to support their development. We soon realize that to do this we, the adult, need to work on preparing ourselves. Dr. Montessori talked about our preparation as not just intellectual (learning more about child development) but also emotional (understanding ourselves) and spiritual (seeing our role in the bigger picture).

Preparing ourselves to bring Montessori into the home inspires significant transformation in us and in our relationship with our child, and will likely extend to how we show up with others in our lives, from members of our community to coworkers. In this chapter, we will explore the work needed to prepare ourselves as we embrace Montessori.

> "Now, if the child is to receive a different treatment from what it receives today, in order to save it from conflicts endangering its psychic life, there is a first, fundamental, essential step to be taken, from which all will depend— the modification of the adult."
>
> Dr. Maria Montessori, *The Secret of Childhood*

HOW WE SHOW UP FOR OUR CHILD

As the adult, we have a responsibility to be on our child's side and to see things from their perspective. This may come naturally to us, or it may take some work.

Understanding, trusting, and guiding our child

Every child is capable and unique. We can learn to see our child with fresh eyes every day, from an objective point of view, so that we can understand their needs and support them. Much like the idea of *unconditional positive regard* in psychology, we see our child as doing their best given their life experience, and we seek to understand them rather than judge them, and allow them to be whoever they wish to be.

Even while our child is still a mystery to us, their full potential still unknown, we honor their way of viewing the world, as well as their rhythm, pace, intellect, emotions, and spirit.

We see them, accept them, and seek to understand them (without unloading on them our expectations, dreams, or unlived childhoods). When we do this, we become guardians of our children and help them flourish and grow.

In Montessori, our role is to trust that with their natural desire to learn, our unconditional love and support, and a prepared environment, our child will have the opportunity to develop to their full potential. We don't need to force them to learn. We don't need to worry ourselves over their meeting every developmental milestone or skill according to a standardized timeline. We need only be their guide on their unique path.

Those of us who like to control everything may need to practice letting go, being more flexible, and improvising when needed. When raising children, things are not always going to go as expected, but we can resist our instinct to control the situation by thinking of a time in our lives when we were flexible (perhaps while traveling as a young adult, unsure how plans would unfold) and applying the same skills with our children.

Looking for the joy

By viewing the world through our child's eyes and being next to them as their guide, we can find so much joy. The joy of:

- Watching our child making a discovery for themselves
- Their delight as they look up to the pine trees or out to the ocean or down at the crunchy leaves
- Their hugs and tears and pain and love that we will experience together
- Seeing them offer a tissue to a friend who is sad
- A homemade cake that is not perfect but made by our child's hands
- Being engaged in rich discussion and debate around a kitchen table
- Winter nights cozied up under blankets and summer nights looking up to the clear starry sky
- Adventuring in our own city or exploring new lands
- Critical minds that seek to make a change in the world toward social and environmental justice
- Reading books together because we are never too old for someone to read to us
- And so much more

Wondering together

One of our favorite things to do with the children we work with and our own children is to wonder with them. We can set aside our expertise and look at things with a childlike curiosity so we can make discoveries and imagine together with our child.

Tammy Oesting, a Montessori educator of nearly 20 years who has a passion for studying awe and wonder, suggests activities like going outside, asking exploratory questions, studying morally inspiring people, dancing or making music together, or going to an art museum, all of which support sparking a sense of awe that leads to the state of wonder.

> "The laws governing the universe can be made interesting and wonderful to the child, more interesting even than things in themselves, and he begins to ask: What am I? What is the task of man in this wonderful universe? Do we merely live here for ourselves, or is there something more for us to do? Why do we struggle and fight? What is good and evil? Where will it all end?"
>
> —Dr. Maria Montessori, *To Educate the Human Potential*

Always learning and modeling curiosity

One thing we can continue to model for our children is our role as a lifelong learner. We can learn more about raising children (reading this book is part of that education) and finding what matches our family values. We can listen to podcasts, attend workshops, follow Montessori training, find inspiration on social media (and stop following accounts that make us feel inadequate), or join an online learning community.

We can also inspire our children by pursuing our own interests. Whether it be ceramics, religion, permaculture, activism, sports, playing guitar, or skydiving, we can model taking lessons, practicing, and sometimes failing. Even if we are not good at something, we can show that we are having fun learning, regardless of our ability or the outcome.

The practice of discernment is also integral to continued learning. Do not follow any philosophy, guidance, or text (even this book!) blindly. Don't yield to the latest toy or activity trending online. We need to make sure that what we adopt suits our family by considering our child, the activity, and our values.

HOW WE SHOW UP FOR OURSELVES

As parents and caregivers, we must remember that our children want to see us happy. No one wants to hang out with someone who does not want to be there. Therefore, let's consider how we can meet our own needs and receive care from others, so that we can bring joy to our role as our child's caregiver.

Filling our own cup

To be able to show up for our child and our family, we need to have a full cup. If we are tired, or haven't eaten a nutritious meal, or haven't taken time for ourselves, it is hard to be patient and kind. Looking after and caring for ourselves might look like:

- Drinking a cup of coffee or tea before the children wake up
- Meditating, perhaps while lying in bed in the morning
- Getting into nature, such as at the park or in the woods
- Soaking in a bath in the evening with the door locked
- Going away for a weekend
- Watching a film, reading a book or newspaper, or listening to a podcast or audiobook
- Gardening, woodworking, or crafting
- Sleeping

We can be creative in our pursuit of our favorite activities: Find a friend who can do a babysitting swap; if we have a parenting partner, schedule time alone and time together each week; or hire a teenager in the neighborhood to read books or play games with our child while we work on filling our cup.

Those of us who put others before ourselves may need to put these moments to look after ourselves as can't-miss appointments on our calendars. We show up for appointments with others; now it's time to show up for ourselves.

We don't have to wait for time off to fill our cup, especially when life is full. We can light a candle at mealtime, put on some essential oil to relax us, sit down to have a cup of tea and reconnect with the family at the end of our day, play music as we get some chores around the house done, have moments of silence when we gaze out the window at the passing clouds or droplets of rain on the window, or take a pause as we transition from one activity to the next, even if this is just sitting in the car for a minute or two before getting out.

Making intentional decisions about our time

By intentionally (re)assessing how we spend our time and what we find important, we can examine whether our family is honoring our values and priorities. If nature is on the list, make time to be out in nature on a daily, weekly, or monthly basis. If we want to spend less time in the car, we can research our options and find a local school, grocery store, or yoga class within walking distance.

When we pare down our schedules and focus more deeply on what is left, our children benefit. This gives them time to focus on their favorite interests and people, as well as unscheduled time for exploration, conversation, connection, boredom, and creativity.

When circumstances do not allow

Some people are not in a position to make big life changes. We see you. We hope that you can find small conscious and intentional ways to bring joy to your days at times when some things in your life are difficult.

> "Grant me the serenity to accept the things I cannot change, courage to change the things I can, and the wisdom to know the difference."
>
> —Reinhold Niebuhr

Cultivating calm

From a place of calm, we can be the best guide to our children. We can do things to help ourselves stay calm (preventative) and things to help us come back to calm when needed (restorative). Some things might do both. Below are lists of some of our favorite ways to cultivate calm to use as inspiration.

Preventative. Be prepared. Wake up before the rest of the family. Meditate. Practice yoga. Go for a run. Spend time with a friend. Light a candle at mealtime. Put on some music. Eat nourishing food. Take a nap. Have a bath. Dance. Drink water. Burn some incense or put on some essential oil. Keep a gratitude journal. Go to bed early. Stay up late.

Restorative. Step away. Make a cup of tea. Go to the bathroom. Ask someone for help. Put on music to dance or shake it out. Rock or sway from side to side. Do some primal screaming with our child or with our friends. Find pillows to hit. Laugh at ourselves.

Finding a community where we feel at home

We live in a time when we often no longer reside under the same roof as our extended family, and may, in fact, live far from any loved ones. Contact with our family or friends may be occasional or rare. But we do not raise children alone. We need support from elders and friends who can listen, hold us in hard times, and offer advice if we seek it. We need people to share in the ferrying of children to school, to sports, and to other activities. We need others who can inspire our children with their craft, their wisdom, their grace, or their music. We need people around us who can feed our child if we are held up in traffic or needing a night off from cooking.

Can we find like-minded families in our school or in the wider community? Is our community diverse and a source of different experiences and perspectives to our children? Are there online communities where we can find folks to inspire us and be inspired by us? Can we reconnect with the land and support the Indigenous people? Can we volunteer in our community in a way that we find fun?

If what we are looking for does not yet exist, we can create it and invite others to join us. We have friends who have moved to find their community. Others have moved back to their hometowns to be closer to family. Junnifa and Simone both built schools to create Montessori communities that didn't previously exist near them.

Communities hold us, and we hold them. Communities challenge us, and we challenge them. Communities celebrate with us, and we celebrate with them.

Aiming for connection, instead of perfection

We might feel that the goal of Montessori is perfection—the perfect response, the perfect space, and so on. While we do strive to be more intentional, to be constantly evolving to be better, and to be present with our family, we do not have to be perfect. It's about supporting our children, having fun with them, and remembering to smile when we take it all too seriously. We are doing our best.

Simone knows that she has a tendency to get excited in a conversation and cut people off; she still moves faster than she would like in the classroom; she catches herself talking while showing a young child an activity when it's easier for them to absorb if she shows them slowly and clearly without words; and there are always gray areas in knowing whether to step in to help or not. Yet despite these imperfections, the children know that she is a safe place and that she accepts them for who they are.

We are real. The Japanese concept "wabi-sabi" (roughly translated as perfectly imperfect) describes it well. If we are only perfect or demand perfection from our children, they may become scared of trying or of doing something wrong. We can model acceptance, trying again, and seeking forgiveness when we've made mistakes, because mistakes are not failures. Can we offer ourselves the same grace we are trying to offer to our child?

Taking care of our mental and physical health

Raising our children and thriving ourselves can be in opposition if we are not careful. Let's avoid burnout: Take care of our mental health; nourish our bodies, minds, and souls; and model true self-care for our children.

Let's sit down to eat. Find exercise we love. Look at what we are taking in, including media, people we spend time with, and any chemicals in our home. Cultivate moments of silence.

Let's do less in order to be more; the lure of having it all is slowly making us exhausted parents and caregivers. Both Junnifa and Simone have had to prioritize more time for family and themselves in their week. They still work, care for others, and do their best, but they do enough, not always more.

It is also important to receive care from others. To allow others to look after us—by cooking for us, making space to listen to us, or holding us. We can also visit a specialist like an osteopath, chiropractor, acupuncturist, reflexologist, or massage therapist. And get help from a mental health professional when we know it shouldn't be this hard.

HOW WE GROW

Being the adult requires us to go on our own personal internal journey. According to Dr. Shefali Tsabary in *The Conscious Parent*, raising children can be a spiritual journey. Similar to peeling away the layers of an onion, once we master one aspect, there is always more to unpack.

Being open to understanding and healing ourselves

We have all been there. Our child says or does something, and we find ourselves being activated. It could be because of our mood that day, because there is a lot going on, or because it touches on the memory of an old wound from our past. If we notice when we're being activated, we can work out what the root issue is—there is room for us to hold it gently, mourn it, and heal it.

For example, when we feel like our child isn't respecting us, it may remind us of times when we weren't respected in the past or when we weren't respecting ourselves or others. We might then be able to apologize (including sometimes to a younger version of ourselves), do over a situation, or write a letter to someone about how they made us feel, a letter that we may never send but that helps us own our emotions and move toward healing.

We can also be activated when our child hands us their problem. Let's say they are always late for school. Instead of getting upset about it and trying to solve the problem for them, we can hand it back to our child. A mother in Simone's workshop did just that. The mother made a plan with her 5-year-old daughter so that she could get to school on time, and the daughter then took responsibility for getting ready herself. The mother was no longer activated, the daughter didn't have her mother nagging her, and everyone was a lot calmer.

What activates us? What are we ready to unpack? Is there a problem we need to hand back to our child?

Exploring ways to heal

By healing ourselves, we can be free to guide our children without our past interfering. Some people like talk therapy, others like to process things with friends. We might choose to move our body by cleaning the house or going for a run, or we might take some space to be alone. Meditation and yoga can help us regulate our nervous system and connect to our body, and they can be practiced either on a daily basis or when things come up.

More and more research shows that trauma and past experiences are held in the body, and there are techniques aimed at accessing and soothing these "old wounds." Eye movement desensitization and reprocessing (EMDR), hypnosis and self-hypnosis, Rapid Transformational Therapy (RTT), tapping, kinesiology, breathwork, and somatic work can all help.

Simone uses a technique called "bean bag releasing," which she learned from Bella Lively, a modern-day spiritual guide. It uses our pure awareness to clear past activations from our body. It eliminates the charge of the active emotion so we can respond rather than react. While this is by no means an expert explanation, these are the basic steps:

1. Recognize when we are activated (whether by a recurring thought, an ongoing issue, or a pushed button).
2. Feel where we are activated in our body (e.g., our neck, our heart, our arm).
3. Describe how big the feeling is in our body and what it feels like (e.g., the size of an orange, spongy inside).
4. Observe the feeling, hold it gently, and acknowledge it ("Of course I'd feel that way").
5. Keep observing in awareness (not judgment or analysis) until it becomes smaller or completely melts away.

FURTHER READING

- *The Body Keeps the Score* by Bessel van der Kolk

Helping others understand our needs with healthy boundaries

When we are clear on what is important to us and let others know if something is bothering us in a kind and respectful way, it's amazing how much peace it can bring to our lives and our family. Boundaries help others understand our needs. And they allow our children to see healthy boundaries in action. When we feel resentment, it's a sure sign that our boundaries are being crossed. Those of us who didn't grow up with adults who were able to set kind and clear boundaries with us or others may need to start from scratch and learn.

> "Boundaries are expectations and needs that help you feel safe and comfortable in your relationships."
>
> —Nedra Glover Tawwab, *Set Boundaries, Find Peace*

Using "I" language and stating how we ourselves feel helps our message be heard, particularly if someone is feeling defensive. "When you walked away, the way I took it was _____" or "When you shouted, I felt scared." Avoid language like "You made me feel _____" or "When you attacked me, _____."

We might choose to delay the conversation too: "Let's make a time to talk about it when we are both feeling calm" or "It's important for me that we stick to our house agreements. We can discuss any changes at our next family meeting." We need to remember that people may not immediately respect the boundaries we are communicating or may forget them. We can remind them of a boundary by restating it kindly and clearly.

Once we learn about boundaries, we might find ourselves going from having *porous* boundaries (when we are unclear or do not act in accordance with what we say) to having *rigid* boundaries (where we show no flexibility and can put up a wall between ourselves and others). Instead, therapist and relationship expert Nedra Glover Tawwab encourages having *healthy* boundaries, which allows us to consider the current circumstances and our values, know our limits, and be able to say no and to hear no without taking it personally. For example, a healthy boundary might be allowing our child a moderate serving of cake at a fiftieth wedding anniversary celebration for their grandparents, rather than never allowing sweets (rigid) or giving in to their demands for sweets instead of a balanced dinner (porous).

FURTHER READING

- *Set Boundaries, Find Peace* by Nedra Glover Tawwab.

Addressing our biases

In her article "Understanding Implicit Bias: What Educators Should Know," Cheryl Staats tells us that everyone—regardless of our race, ethnicity, gender, or age—has implicit biases, "the attitudes or stereotypes that affect our understanding, actions, and decisions in an unconscious manner." Our unconscious mind will operate faster and contribute to decisions we make before our conscious mind is even aware.

The good news is that we can do something about our implicit biases. First, we can identify where our conscious ideals differ from our automatic implicit reactions, and bring them into closer alignment. Second, we can increase our contact with people of different religions and ethnicities, as well as people who identify in ways other than we do. When we don't encounter these people in our community, we might follow people on social media with different beliefs, backgrounds, and experiences to ensure that our perspective remains as broad as possible. Last, we can seek exposure to folks who show up in nonstereotypical ways, including those who break occupational gender norms and those with lived experiences that are different from our own.

Our aim is to eventually reduce the difference between our implicit and conscious understanding of the world. This is important work to reduce our biases and allow our children and any child in society to reach their full potential.

Digging deeper

As Montessori adults, we aim to cultivate more patience, more compassion, more empathy, and more forgiveness for the child. Less anger and pride. More love and acceptance.

Remember that the teachings of Dr. Montessori encourage us to dig deeper by being constant in our willingness to learn and grow as individuals, families, and communities. In her article "Grace and Courtesy and the Adult," Catherine McTamaney of *Montessori Daoshi* challenges us as adults to aspire to the same social cohesion that happens in a Montessori classroom—respecting others; understanding that when we take something (materials, resources, or time), there is less for another; practicing our own grace and courtesies; offering to be of service to others; and being conscious of and caring for our environment.

HOW WE CULTIVATE A PRACTICE OF SELF-REFLECTION

We have learned so much from Andy Lulka and Pamela Green, two of the most experienced Montessori educators in North America, about the important practice of self-observation and self-reflection in our preparation as the adult. We have talked a lot about observation in this book. It also plays a critical role in this chapter as we work on ourselves.

Self-observation

It's easiest to practice self-observation in calm moments. Then we can build up our skills to manage in moments where we are activated. It's like going on a meditation retreat. It may be easier to find peace and calm when in a quiet place up in the mountains. Then we build up to maintaining that peace and calm back in the haste of our busy lives.

Here are some ideas for observing ourselves. We can make a column on the side of our paper as we observe our child to note anything coming up for us. Or we can do an observation with the focus being solely on ourselves.

- What are our hands doing?

- What are we thinking?

- What are we feeling?

- What comes up for us as we observe?

- Can we stay in our body? Or are we only in our mind?

- Is our view of the world changing?

- Are we present?

- Do we need support?

- Are we listening to our bodies?

- What do we need to care for ourselves?

- How do we react when our child does something we wouldn't expect them to be ready for?

- How do we react when our child does something we expect they would already know?

Reflection

After observing comes reflection:
- What things are going well?
- What could be improved?
- What is one thing that could be changed that would make everything else easier or unnecessary?

Reflecting on our childhood

Part of our self-reflection will be on our own childhood. We carry this experience into our role as parents and caregivers. The memories of laughter and joy, sadness and pain.

Some questions to ponder. Did we feel seen? Did we feel trusted? Were we raised with a lot of freedom or very strictly? What happened when we made mistakes? What was important to our caregivers: creativity, school marks, independence? What qualities did our caregivers pass on to us: a love of travel, artistic talent and expression, a sense of humor, stubbornness? From these reflections, we can make intentional decisions about which lessons and values we choose to pass on to our children.

Reflecting on our childhood allows us to be gentler with ourselves. We might say to ourselves: "Of course I would find it hard to let go," "I understand why I don't like change," or "No wonder I find it hard to trust my child." Recognizing these things in ourselves is the first step in making a change. Reflection also allows us to understand our children better. Mister Rogers wisely said, "I think that the best thing we can do is to think about what it was like for us and know what our children are going through."

Accepting our journey

Perhaps reading this book brings up feelings like "I wish I'd known about this earlier" or "Why wasn't I raised this way?" Our story is our journey. Everything that we have experienced, the good and the bad, has made us the person we are today. Simone considers having had children in her twenties a very positive experience as she felt like she grew up right alongside them. There are things she could have done differently, but instead of wanting to change them, she is grateful for the mistakes she made along the way and accepts them as part of the journey.

We may have had a difficult relationship with our parents or not known them at all. This experience then often shows us how we would like to show up for our own child and break generational cycles if necessary.

Being a safe adult to whom our child can turn

Through self-reflection, we can examine what would make our children feel safe to come to us with a problem. We can practice acceptance, vulnerability, and being friendly with mistakes. Being predictable and responding, not reacting, are helpful to becoming a safe adult. If this doesn't come easily to us, another option is making sure there's an adult in our child's life whom they can turn to without fear of judgment or punishment.

Seeking guidance

Self-reflection reminds us not to forget ourselves. It means looking at ourselves to see where we can do better. Just as we help children build skills in lagging areas, we can identify our own difficulties and get help to build these skills. We can look for a mentor, attend a workshop, ask a friend to give us feedback, or seek advice from those in our community who support us.

Connecting to self and nature

Self-reflection requires us to get quiet, connect with ourselves, and listen to what we are feeling. We might put a hand over our heart, put our feet on the ground, and find a place in our body that is calm (toes are usually a good place to try if we feel discombobulated).

Taking a moment to drink a cup of coffee on the front steps, listen to the birds, and watch the clouds; taking the family on a hike; going to the beach and putting our feet in the sand; breathing some mountain air; or otherwise getting into nature can be restorative ways for us to turn inward.

HOW WE LET THEM FLY

Being our child's guide also means knowing when to give them space to spread their wings. The key here is knowing when to be together and when to give distance, when to fill our cup and when to fill our child's.

Enjoying every age and every stage

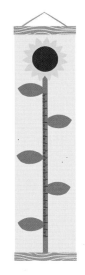

When Simone's children each turned 18, she reflected back on their years as children. People said to her, "It goes so fast." Instead, Simone felt like she was really able to enjoy every age and every stage of her children as they grew up by showing up and being as present as she could along the way.

It's easy to want to rush through moments and milestones: We may feel eager to put our child in school so we'll have more time to ourselves, or we might roll our eyes when driving our child to an early-morning sports practice. Honestly, it's impossible to be in the mood to act as the adult every day. But when Simone looks back, she is glad for every chance she had to connect with her children and witness their growth and development, as well as for the stray Lego bricks and rained-out sports days.

We also want to be having fun; our children know when we aren't enjoying being with them. Simone made a list of things she loved to do with her children—things like baking, playing board games, building Legos—and had it on the fridge; if they wanted to do something together, they'd choose something off the list rather than a game Simone was not able to enjoy. Everyone's needs can be met at every age and stage.

For Junnifa, enjoying every stage is embracing the understanding that her children will continue to change. Accepting each of them, their needs, and unique behaviors at each stage helps her enjoy every age. Knowing that while her toddler might want to pick up and put everything in order, her 6- to 12-year-old seems to enjoy making more of a mess, and that's expected.

Being their rock

When our child is having a hard time, the best thing we can do is to stay grounded while we support them. If we were on a boat in a storm, a captain's calmness and confidence would help moderate our feelings of panic. Similarly, we can be our child's rock, strong and steady when their world is shaking.

As hard as it is, when they attack us, we try to not take it personally. Instead, we can see that they feel safe with us, knowing we will keep loving them even if they lash out. If need be, we can also tell them (perhaps at a later moment) that their words hurt us.

When our child has these big feelings, it can be helpful to practice equanimity. Someone once described equanimity to Simone like this: *Imagine you are sitting in traffic. Instead of getting worked up about it, you imagine yourself in a large marshmallow. The marshmallow acts as a buffer between you and what is going on outside of your car. You don't get stressed by the traffic. You are in your marshmallow.* We can imagine being in our own marshmallow when our child is having a hard time. Not only is it likely to make us smile, it might help us stop reacting to what they are saying so we can stay solid and offer empathy and support.

Attaching and then letting go

By planting roots, we help our child unfurl their wings. But letting go is not easy for some of us. We can be gentle with ourselves, have people to support us (not our children), and let our children shed another layer as they get closer to becoming their beautiful butterfly.

Letting go is . . .

. . . having other people in their lives. This means selecting people we trust to teach, model, and care for our children. Their world gets richer by having others in it from whom to learn. At preschool, grade school, sports, clubs, and friends' homes, they can trust in others as much as their own family.

. . . letting them climb a little higher. By letting them take some risks, go further, or simply do things for themselves, we encourage our child to listen to their own body and make judgments about their capabilities. We stand ready if they need us but allow them to explore their limits.

. . . supervising, not abandoning. We can give them a lot of independence (when possible) and access to the things they need, but we'll be available to guide them.

. . . observing when they're ready. We can help our children scaffold skills so that over time they become more independent. Then remove the scaffold when ready.

. . . showing our child that we have confidence in them or in a new situation. If our child can see and feel that we are comfortable in a situation, they will trust our judgment and feel safer.

. . . constantly discovering who our child is. We see them for who they are, right now, and in every moment, without trying to change them. We let them become themselves.

. . . allowing them to make mistakes and learn from them. We try not to fix things for them but provide guidance and support. They are working out how to solve problems and taking responsibility if they get it wrong.

. . . standing on our own two feet so that our child can have wings. We are better caregivers when we fill our own cup. When we are happy in our own right, we are ready to support our child and be their guide.

Practicing simplicity, patience, and compassion

"If we build our classrooms on simplicity, they are free to find our common soil. If we build our classrooms on patience, they are free to grow at their own pace. If we build our classrooms on compassion, they are free to wind together, climbing higher for the support we offer each other."

—Catherine McTamaney, *The Tao of Montessori*

These words from Catherine McTamaney can be a guide in our homes too:

- Let our homes be simple and invite calmness, exploration, conversation, and connection. Let them be host to our unconditional love.
- Let us develop patience so we can let our children unfold on their own timeline. May we practice pausing to respond rather than react. May we take time to look at things from their perspective. May we allow a moment more for them to manage by themselves.
- Let us practice compassion so that our children feel supported and learn how to support others. May our home be open and accepting to all, and a place where our children feel safe to express their ideas, hopes, and dreams. May we be a shoulder to cry on.

SVETA, JOHANN, MAYA, NINA

It's a practical life
USA

"We try to balance developing the girls' skills and interests (piano, art, and tennis are their favorites) and finding lots of time to just be. If anyone complains of boredom, we say, 'You're welcome!' We prioritize having dinner together every night and don't schedule extracurricular activities that interfere with the flow of the evening. This is getting increasingly challenging for our 15-year-old, but thus far, we've been successful."

"I contend that Montessori environments are microcosms of society—they represent the 'real world' better than traditional environments—so that when children leave their Montessori schools, they are better equipped to be purposeful and responsible citizens of the world. I notice in Maya and other adolescents who have graduated from Montessori schools a love of learning, resilience, self-assuredness, and a genuine desire to figure out who they are called to be in this world."

"One of the biggest challenges when sending your children to a Montessori school or following the philosophy at home is having to explain yourself to family and friends with a more traditional mindset."

WHAT'S NEXT

9

In this chapter, we look ahead to the third and fourth planes to see what to expect in the coming years. We can be reassured that through every plane, many things remain the same for raising our Montessori children—connection, joy, respect, love, understanding, trust, and acceptance. Hold these values close, and the rest we can work out alongside our children.

It's fascinating that Dr. Montessori stated that childhood ends toward 24 years old, at the end of the fourth plane of development. Most people believe that childhood ends at around age 18. But brain science now confirms that the prefrontal cortex—the area of our brain that helps us make rational decisions—is still developing until the early twenties, supporting Dr. Montessori's observations on childhood.

TRANSITIONING TO THE THIRD PLANE OF DEVELOPMENT

The first time Simone's children rolled their eyes at her, she feared the teenage years were not far ahead and bought books like *How to Talk So Teens Will Listen & Listen So Teens Will Talk* and *Positive Discipline for Teenagers*. She started reading and immediately felt relieved. The approach recommended in these books was much the same as the Montessori approach she had already been using in raising her children. She built that strong base over the first two planes. This is the foundation we have helped lay as our child moves into the third plane.

We want to assure you that you don't have to fight with your teenagers, that they are great company, and that your parenting job doesn't end when they enter middle school and high school. Yet they are changing and now need support in a different way.

There are questions about when adolescence starts these days, as some children experience early puberty. Jenny Marie Höglund, one of the most experienced AMI trainers for 12- to 18-year-olds, views the characteristics and ideals aligning with the third-plane adolescent still becoming evident in children closer to 12 years old. The child is leaving childhood and entering adulthood. They are now asking, "What will my role be?" and "How can I contribute?" In practice, it's a gradual transition to be aware of. Sometimes the child will exhibit characteristics of the second plane, and other times those of the third plane.

WHO IS THE THIRD-PLANE CHILD, THE ADOLESCENT?

Teenagers, like toddlers, are largely misunderstood. Society paints them as difficult, self-absorbed, temperamental, and selfish. They stay up late, they sleep in, they lay about, they are out with friends, or they hide in their room.

In Montessori, we view adolescents in a different light. Teenagers are working out who they are—they might put on a brave face, but really, they are very vulnerable, doubting and questioning themselves and others. They can be enormously capable given the right environment, guidance, opportunities, and challenges. They can also be fun to be around, with their especially interesting conversations about how they would change the world.

If you've ever thought that toddlers and teenagers are alike, Dr. Montessori would agree. Remember how the first plane and the third plane are seen as parallel planes? (See the orange triangle in both of these planes in the diagram on page 24.) Both present enormous physical changes; both are very volatile periods of development; and in both, children are seeking independence (moving away from their parents in the first plane, and preparing to move into society in the third plane). We can also see this in The Bulb diagram, below. See the large orange area during the adolescent years, smaller yet still enlarged as in the first plane.

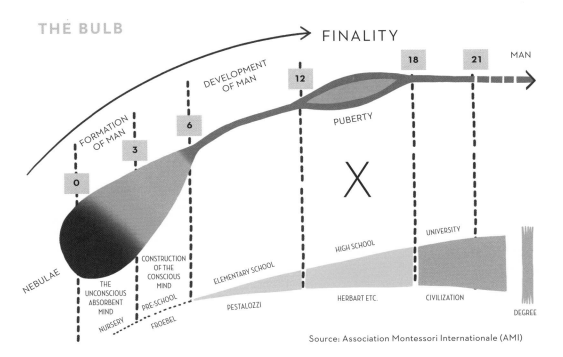

Source: Association Montessori Internationale (AMI)

Let's take a closer look at how we view adolescents in Montessori.

Adolescents are as fragile as newborns. This is a vulnerable time. They are very self-critical about their appearance and abilities, they can be irrational, and they can isolate themselves in their room. They are working out "Who am I?" and "What is expected of me?" Rather than criticizing them, we can "hold" them as gently as a baby, being a safe person with whom they can explore these big questions.

Adolescents are going through an enormous amount of change. During the first 2 years of adolescence, their bodies are preparing; during the second 2 years, their bodies are blossoming; and during the final 2 years, their bodies are perfecting themselves. There are huge hormonal changes, making it an emotional period. With so much growth and change, adolescents are more fragile and get sick more easily. It is also a time of fatigue, when they like to stay up late and will eat whatever and whenever food is available. It is ideal for them to do physical work or exercise outdoors to strengthen their body and mind and challenge themselves physically.

Adolescents appear not to be studious. An adolescent's brain is in so much flux, which makes it seem like they have less academic capacity. Psychologist David Elkind calls this "pseudostupidity." They are actually still very capable and are now able to see a problem from different perspectives. But instead of making life easier, it makes it more complicated for them, as there is often no longer one simple answer. Their brains are wired for metacognition—learning about how they learn—like wanting to be involved in deciding what they are learning and how. They also enjoy studies that are meaningful to them and being able to practically apply things they learned in the earlier years.

Adolescents need protection. As their prefrontal cortex continues to develop, we need to provide an environment that feels secure and safe, that they can rely on. However, the adolescent does not want to be controlled. We need to show them we trust them, set up agreements and systems with them, and discuss options and solutions together, so that they can have their freedom with the accompanying responsibilities. All that said, sometimes we as their caring adults will need to make a decision they are not happy with to keep them safe. When they know we have explored all the options, they may not be happy but will understand that it's our job to keep them safe.

Adolescents need to understand society. We can have higher expectations for our adolescents and give them the opportunity to prepare themselves as young adults. Rather than just doing schoolwork, hanging out with friends, or having us take them to sports practices or drama or dance classes, adolescents need to have experiences of being in society. Whereas from ages 6 to 12, the child was interested in exploring the whole universe with their imagination, the place of exploration for the adolescent is getting hands-on experiences in their home, their school setting, and the wider community as practice for entering adult life. Practice in a prepared environment before they go out into the unprepared environment in the following fourth plane.

Adolescents seek economic and social independence. More than being given pocket money, adolescents want to take part in society to earn their own money. We think, "They should just be kids; they don't need to get a job yet." Yet there is a fire in their belly that is less about making a lot of money than about exploring how to function in this time and place in society. They begin to be financially independent and have an impact in the world. They also want to make decisions about how to spend the money they earn, with some guidance from us.

Adolescents need to belong and be part of a bigger purpose. At such a vulnerable age, they seek to be like others, want to work out how they can contribute to their group, and often have high ideals. As such, they can be part of self-organizing groups of like-minded adolescents who are working toward a bigger goal—it might be setting up a permaculture farm for their neighborhood, fundraising for a cause or community, making music as part of an orchestra or band, or visiting the elderly in nursing homes. This gives them a cause to support while working with others.

Adolescents need to differentiate themselves. At the same time as wanting to belong, they are also figuring out how they want to be different. They are navigating how to be themselves and how they'd like to fit into the group.

Adolescents say, "Help us to do it by ourselves." The first-plane child says, "Help me to do it myself." The second-plane child says, "Help me to think by myself." The third-plane child says, "Help us to do it ourselves." The adolescent, placing importance now on their community, wants to work with their peers and manage for themselves. This empowers them, gives them confidence, and provides them with real-life experiences.

Adolescents have a sensitive period for justice. They are developing their moral compass further. The adolescent continues to explore the morality that they began to acquire in the second plane, but it's no longer about things being only equal. They can see people's strengths and needs and consider what is right. They are also ready to think about systems and if they are fair or systems of oppression and power. This combined with their growing self-awareness and love for being in community makes them ready to be activists for change.

Adolescents have a sensitive period for dignity. They experience personal dignity when they make a contribution and feel like they matter. Dr. Montessori referred to this as *valorization*, how the adolescent finds their place in the world. Both dignity and justice are things that cannot be taught but must be lived. For the adolescent, this is by being in community.

Adolescents are drawn to risky behavior. *Valorization* also refers to valor's second meaning: to be brave. Research shows that the adolescent's brain seeks risk and reward and that they need to experience risk to experience valorization, that feeling of bravery. We need to help them manage the risk, though, as they are not yet able to assess risk very accurately. Instead we can guide them toward relatively safe activities like rock climbing and riding roller coasters where they can still experience a feeling of risk.

> "It is the 'valorisation' of the personality, to become aware of ones [*sic*] own value. Without this, as many psychologists say, the child only feels his own value if he is loved. This is another 'valorisation'—he is independent, he is sure of his own actions and knows how to act."
>
> —Dr. Maria Montessori, *Citizen of the World*

WHAT DID DR. MONTESSORI ENVISION FOR ADOLESCENTS?

Dr. Montessori proposed that adolescents from 12 to 15 years old attend a farm school, an "Erdkinder." It's hard to imagine our adolescents living away from us, but in this way, they are able to begin the application of knowledge learned to real-life situations with real-life consequences. To take responsibility with the other students to look after the animals and the farmhouse, to have a store and a guesthouse. All this in a prepared environment with a few prepared adults to support them.

The goal is not "success" or to prepare them for a career as a farmer or to get a good job. It's for every child at the end of this plane to be prepared to do something meaningful to them. We are, again, not filling them with facts or focused only on their intellectual development; we also want to help them meet their social, emotional, and spiritual needs, offering them experiences that show them what adult life could be like.

The prepared environment plays an important role in this plane of development, as it did in earlier planes. Both indoor and outdoor environments—the store, the guesthouse, the land—are essential. The young adolescents are practicing in this carefully prepared environment, which is safe and predictable, before they will move into the unprepared

environment as a young adult. This time away from home offers them the opportunity to do great things and to learn to live in a social group in an environment where they feel confident and secure, where they can find inner ease and balance while learning to adapt to not only their group but also the wider environment and groups.

The farm belongs to the adolescents. They work hard as a community to maintain the farm, learn to live with others, and see that everyone has a role to play. When they love their work, they care for their environment and become responsible for it. They take responsibility for their lives, from shopping to cooking and cleaning. They also experience the consequences of self-management; for example, that they will not have light if no one changes a bulb that's gone out or that they will run out of money at the end of the month if they do not budget well for their meals and other expenses.

In addition to doing farmwork, they study topics that are relevant to their life on the farm. They are applying what they learn in the classroom (theoretical) to real-life situations (practical). Their work and study cover self-expression (music, art, language); psychic development (moral development, mathematics, and language); and the study of Earth and life (human development, civilizations, and the history of humanity).

Alongside the "farm school" models, there has been a lot of work done—including by Mario Montessori and Mario Montessori Jr. (Dr. Montessori's son and grandson)— to develop Montessori adolescent programs in urban settings. They will involve a lot of community work, with the students working collaboratively.

A fun example is Embark Education in Denver, Colorado, a micro-school applying Montessori principles in a bike store and café. Some schools run a CSA (community-supported agriculture) project, growing and selling produce, and holding fundraising events for the school or charities. Other schools encourage their students to look at their gifts and skills to come up with and run their own micro-businesses. At the middle school program at Montessori Jewish Day School in Toronto, Canada, the money earned goes toward a two-week trip to Israel prior to graduation and to a charity carefully selected by the students.

The best of these programs offer meaningful work, incorporate outdoor communal work, are led and staffed by adults prepared to guide the adolescents, and take an interdisciplinary approach to their studies (i.e., by exploring the intersection of math, history, geography, and other subjects). The students are not just following a textbook at their own pace.

For more on life at an Erdkinder, refer to the case study "The Montessori Adolescent at the Montessori Centre for Work and Study, Rydet, Sweden" found in the online appendix. It is incredible to learn about all that adolescents are capable of there.

HUMAN TENDENCIES OF THE ADOLESCENT

Remember the human tendencies from chapter 2? These are still present in the adolescent, but they'll show up in different ways.

The adolescent's **orientation** is now to the larger society outside their family and to their peers. They explore not just the physical space but also their role in their family, their friend group, and school as well as who they are, including their gifts, their passions, and their values. And they observe adults and peers to see if we behave in line with our values.

Abstraction can be seen when they begin to look at things from others' perspectives. They are now aware of their thought processes and begin to understand the patterns behind them. They have a more global perspective, and they want to solve big problems, at first with big ideas and then later in the plane with more precise and realistic plans.

They use their **imagination** to look for ways they could make life better, from how a subject is taught at school, to what the future could look like, to how to improve their environment or make life on the planet sustainable for us all. Sometimes they'll feel small and insignificant; other times they'll feel powerful and that they can effect change.

Their **work** still requires their head and their hands to work together, this time with academic studies alongside practical experience (like working on the farm or being involved in a community project). They are working no longer just for themselves but also for their community and trying out different roles through their work. Through making or growing goods and selling them, they are connecting with the adult world, taking part in both the social aspects and commerce. They still strive for maximum effort, taking on work that is challenging and with a definite purpose as long as it is related to them and makes sense to them. The results of their work are not instant—for example, the time for vegetables to grow from seeds—and they learn to work not only with their preferred partner or group but with anyone in the community as practice for their adult life.

There are many opportunities for them to **calculate** now in real-life situations, such as when buying groceries or determining how much paint to buy if they are decorating their room. When making decisions, they are capable of assessing possible outcomes or consequences for themselves, others, and possibly their environment.

The human tendencies to **perfect**, to **be exact**, and to **repeat** are observed in adolescents as they aim to understand everything they do. They perfect what they are good at and refine these skills. Rather than allow them to be only outwardly focused on what others think of them, we can help them explore what they find important and be okay with who they are. We do this by helping them recognize their strengths and build skills in weaker areas. If we ask an adolescent to do a self-assessment around a task, they are often more critical of themselves than we are of them.

Communication is hard work for an adolescent. They are learning to express their ideas, try them out on others, and participate in discussions with peers and adults. They continue to learn how to collaborate with others, live peacefully in a social group, make decisions, and try out different perspectives. They can have some big emotions to let out, and communicating makes them feel alive.

THE MONTESSORI ADOLESCENT AT HOME

In some ways, we could say that our expectations of teenagers are too low. Or that we are asking too much from them in areas that are not important to them. Rarely are we offering them opportunities for adult work, thinking that it is too hard for them or that we don't want to weigh them down with the responsibilities too soon.

Yet when we see all they are capable of in the Erdkinder environment (see the case study in the online appendix), we can think about what prepared environment we can offer our adolescents, what their needs are, the atmosphere we want to create, as well as the experiences they will benefit from.

In *From Childhood to Adolescence*, Dr. Montessori wrote about adolescents having two needs: "If puberty is on the physical side a transition from an infantile to an adult state, there is also, on the psychological side, a transition from the child who has to live in a family, to the adult who has to live in society. These two needs of the adolescent: for protection during the time of the difficult physical transition, and for an understanding of the society which he is about to enter to play his part as an adult, give rise to two problems that are of equal importance concerning education at this age."

From this we see that our task is to be their safe space (giving them physical and psychological safety) and to support them as they transition in society from child to adult.

The prepared environment

The prepared home environment for adolescents is less about Montessori shelves with activities and more about the idea of their having a place to practice being a citizen in the safety of their family and wider community.

Here are some thoughts about the physical space:

- The adult helps them set up the environment with order, and the adolescent is then responsible for maintaining it. They may still need some assistance from time to time, like a prompt to do a seasonal inventory of their closets for clothing that can be sold, donated, or passed down to a younger sibling, or to make space to study by storing or recycling work that is no longer needed.

- The adolescent often expresses their need for privacy, and we'll want to create spaces where they can be by themselves, also during waking hours. If our home does not allow for them to have their own room, we can provide privacy with a room divider or curtain or half wall. Some people may be able to build a studio in their garden if they have one.

- "A place for everything and everything in its place" can still be helpful at this age when they are less organized; we can help them put it into practice by designating a storage area near the front door for sports gear or musical instruments.

- We can create a reading nook with an armchair, a lamp, and a table with books on it so they are drawn to sit down with a book rather than scroll on their phone.

- We can make board games accessible so they can play with family or friends. It can be fun to have a chess set, a mini-pool table, ice hockey table, or Ping-Pong table in a common area to create an opportunity for them to socialize in a way that is not centered around screens.

- Consider having a space in our home where they can gather with their friends. If we make it inviting for their friends to come over, we will be able to meet their friends and observe the group dynamics. We may be limited by space, but even having a table in the kitchen where they can eat snacks or play games means they always feel welcome.

- The environment can also be adjusted based on their interests. If possible, we can dedicate a corner of the home to encourage these interests, such as by setting up an easel for painting; a lightbox area for photographing items to sell online; an area for practicing piano, drums, or guitar; a woodworking area; or a table at which to make stop-motion films.

- As mentioned earlier in the discussion of the Erdkinder, adolescents have a need for physical work. They may be able to help mow the lawns of neighbors; have a paper route; help paint the house, sand the floors, and do practical repairs around the home; or help out in a community garden or a family garden. Look for opportunities that align with their interests. We can also hang a punching bag, ropes, or rings from the ceiling for them to use in channeling excess or emotional energy.

- They are busy with social relationships, and practical matters like locking the front door or turning out the lights are low on their list of priorities. Look for easy ways for them to remember these things, like a sign on the front door that says "Lights and lock" so they remember to turn off the lights and lock the door if they are the last to leave the house.

- Don't forget the outdoors. We can offer them opportunities to be outdoors and out in nature. If it doesn't happen daily, we can make time to go hiking on the weekends or camping on vacation, or make a vegetable patch in raised beds that they can help with. If we have an outside space, we can hang a hammock that they can lie in to watch the clouds and contemplate life.

The prepared environment is also their safe psychological space. Things we can do to create this space include:

- Helping them navigate their studies—not doing their homework for them but checking in as often as needed (daily or weekly) to make sure they have enough time to complete their tasks.
- Holding space for them emotionally as they navigate relationships with themselves and others.
- Observing when they are mentally overloaded and helping them assess their schedule and modify it if needed.
- Creating agreements around practical tasks like laundry, cooking, and cleaning—how much they do themselves, how much will be done collectively.
- Giving guidance when requested around logistical arrangements for things like making health appointments or getting to places further afield.

Developing agreements

Just as we did with the second-plane child, we establish with our adolescent a code of conduct. What is expected, how we do things safely, with respect for each other, and in a way that is predictable and consistent.

Our job as their parent or caregiver is to keep them safe. Their job as the adolescent is to keep stretching themselves, which may look like seeing how far they can push us. Instead of this being a battle, it can be done in collaboration.

They are not going to be told the rules. These agreements need to be developed with them. One family may opt for weekly family meetings. Others might have more casual conversations at mealtimes.

When we have made a new agreement, such as around use of screens in our family (including for the adults), the last step is to make a time to come back to review how it's going and see what could be improved. (More on screens on page 223.)

The agreements may need to be adjusted over time. But never when the adolescent is wound up and wants to change the rules on the spot. We can calmly say, "It sounds like you aren't happy with the current agreement that we have. Let's write it down to review when we are all calm."

Freedom and limits

The adolescent has an enormous amount of freedom based on trust built up over the years. They may have their own cell phone, be able to choose the subjects they study at school, and get themselves to where they need to go (depending on where you live, the safety of the area, and accessibility to transportation).

They also have the freedom to be themselves, as they have in previous planes. It can be easier for us to accept them for who they are when they are toddlers and preschoolers and the stakes are lower. Adolescents will remind us that they want to express themselves, not blindly follow what we might choose for them. This could be what they study, the sports they play, the hobbies they pursue, the clothes they wear, the music they listen to, their religious beliefs, their gender identity, or whom they are attracted to. With their freedom also comes our acceptance.

Having more freedom does not mean they have license to do whatever they like. They also have responsibilities arising from this freedom; for example, to let us know if there is a change to the plan, to do their part in contributing to the family, and to use their phones in a way that is safe and responsible.

If the trust gets broken, then there will need to be a repair. It might be that there is less freedom for a while until we can trust each other again.

Most of the time, we'll be able to collaborate with them to find a solution that works for the whole family. For example, when 14-year-old Emma wanted to go to a concert alone with a school friend, Simone said something like, "You want to go to that concert, and it's my job to keep you safe. How can we find a way that you can go to the concert and I know that we've done as much as we can to keep you safe?" The agreement they came up with was that the girls would eat pizza at Simone's house before the concert (so Simone could meet Emma's friend), that Simone would cycle with them to the venue and make sure they got in okay, that they understood the risks inside the venue with alcohol and drugs, and that Simone would cycle to meet them after the concert—she wasn't the only adult there—and the girls were able to attend the concert.

At times, we as the adult might need to set a limit and say no and, if so, there will be a good reason. Our children have learned over the years that if we say no, we have given their request a lot of thought, we have discussed it with them to try to find a way that would work for us both, and we have been unable to come up with one. They may not be happy about it and may rage against us, but sometimes we will see that they are relieved and can blame us while not losing face with their friends.

It's okay to have boundaries, and it's helpful for them to see us model boundary setting. If they say something rude to us, we can say, "I don't like it when you speak to me like that" or "Let's talk about this tomorrow when we are all feeling calm."

Do you see how the principles of working together (rather than threatening and bribing) and setting limits when needed are the same with younger children and teenagers? We are being their guide.

Handling big emotions

We've talked about helping our children process their emotions as babies, toddlers, preschoolers, and 6- to 12-year-olds. We can build on that foundation and continue to guide our adolescents through their big feelings. They are subject to hormones and changes they do not understand.

We can have compassion for them, remember to not take it personally if they lash out at us, and understand that they are actually going through a vulnerable transition in their life. It can be a good idea to remember that Dr. Montessori considered adolescents to be as "fragile as a newborn."

Hormonal adolescent outbursts are not so dissimilar to toddler tantrums. In the moment:

- We might be able to rub their back and ask what they need.
- We can offer them a glass of water and be there if they want to talk.
- We can offer to hold space while they let out their emotions. Some adolescents will be able to name the emotion and let us know where they feel it in their body. When they center their awareness on that place, they can help the emotion move through them, maybe assisted by their shaking their body, sighing, exhaling deeply, rocking back and forth, or crying.
- Some of them may want to move their bodies by going for a run or hitting a punching bag.
- Some will want to take some space and retreat to their room to calm down.

Unlike with toddlers, who need us to close the circle in the moment, with adolescents, we have the luxury of time. We can come back later in the day to ask about what happened, or to ask them to make amends if they said something unkind or hurt someone. As uncomfortable as these moments are, there is growth here. Our connection is made stronger. They learn that we love them even at their worst.

Contributing to others

In a Montessori Erdkinder, the adolescents get a lot of meaning out of being an important part of farm life. They work so as not to let the group down. They begin to make choices for the group, not just themselves.

Even if they are not living in an Erdkinder, they can look for ways to contribute to their community. For example, by being of service in their school community. They might visit the younger children's classes to read books or do planting with them, make materials for the younger children's classes, help fix things around the school, work in the school kitchen if there is one, or help with maintenance jobs like mowing the lawn. The younger students admire the adolescents, and the adolescents provide an example of what will come next to both the young children and their families.

They also need to feel part of something bigger than themselves. Outside of school and home, they can find a cause that aligns with their passions and join a group to help raise awareness or funds. The cause might be animal welfare, human rights, climate change, or peace for war-torn areas. Imagine them meeting each week with like-minded adolescents to plan a bake sale or festival to raise money. It means they'll need to work with others; everyone has a role, and they'll need to problem-solve, be financially responsibile, and give back to society. There are local councils that will give funds to youth groups who want to create a community project. They could come together to write an application to get their group some funding, and the parents and caregivers could offer to come to share their expertise as needed.

In vacation periods, there are opportunities to volunteer in other communities, look after the neighbors' children or pets, or take part in a community garden project.

Earning money

> "Productive work and a wage that gives economic independence, or rather constitutes a first real attempt to achieve economic independence, could be made . . . a general principle of social education for adolescents and young people."
>
> —Dr. Maria Montessori, *From Childhood to Adolescence*

Where the preschooler sought functional independence and the school-age child mental independence, the adolescent seeks economic independence. They want to experience at least a "real attempt" at working for money, earning money, and spending money. Earning money is a way they can practice being in society in these adolescent years.

Work involves learning new systems, following instructions, working as a team member, interacting with customers and colleagues, and asking for help when needed. They will be practicing time management by fitting in work around school, homework, sports, family and social commitments. There is also self-organization around reading rosters, being on time, and making arrangements during vacations.

If they work at a cinema, they'll be trained to perform various tasks like cleaning the screening rooms, selling tickets, checking tickets and ages for entry to certain films, and selling snacks at the concession stand. They'll need to make visitors feel welcome, as well as turn away someone who's underage or help calm a volatile situation. A manager would also have the additional responsibilities of building and organizing the team.

In exchange for their time, they receive money—money they can spend on things they save for. If they spend all their money on food and going out with friends, there may not be enough for an item of clothing they would like to purchase. If they want a video game, rather than asking us for it, they learn to save up for it. It is all an experience in earning, spending, and saving money, including having their own bank account.

As part of their financial education, we can introduce them to the idea of saving and investing money, including where we can put our money to save it, the concept of compound interest, and the risks of investing, all while modeling our own investment choices. Some families will be living paycheck to paycheck. Our children will then be learning how to manage the family budget to meet our immediate needs. When they begin to earn money, we can ensure that they put some aside to contribute to people, organizations, or causes they believe in. They are learning to be part of the financial ecosystem and a member of society.

As mentioned earlier, with money now being mostly digital, it's less concrete to understand than cash. We can observe our child to see if they understand the idea behind digital money or if we need to scaffold these skills with them by using cash to demonstrate how amounts are transferred between parties. Rather than labeling a child "bad with money," we can keep teaching them.

There are different approaches to pocket money. Some families cover the costs of everything the child needs, and the child saves money for more discretionary purchases. Other families opt for a monthly or quarterly allowance. In a Montessori home, an allowance is not generally tied to jobs they need to do around the home. This is how they have always contributed to, and continue to contribute to, the family. However, when they do a job that we would otherwise have to pay someone for, like doing the bookkeeping for the family business or helping paint the living room, then they could earn some extra money on top of their allowance.

For a younger adolescent, an allowance could be a smaller amount for them to buy lunch at school (they quickly learn that if they make their lunch at home, they can save their money for other things) or a larger amount for a clothing allowance to buy the clothing they will need (some children will choose to save up for a higher-priced item; others will go to thrift stores to stretch their money further).

Stay connected with them

It's easy for our adolescents to be pulled away from our guidance by the attraction of their peer group. In his book *Hold On to Your Kids*, Gordon Neufeld calls this *peer orientation*. Peers are great for helping adolescents find out who they are, have meaningful connections, and share interests. Yet left in the hands of their peers, adolescents are in danger of developing themselves only to please others and be liked in a superficial way, rather than to fulfill their human potential. Neufeld encourages us not to let our children slip away amid the power of peers and instead to keep our connection with them strong throughout these years.

We want to stay connected with them during these adolescent years so that we can continue to be a positive influence and someone they look to for feedback, counsel, and support. If we have little connection, our attempts to provide guidance will be ignored or be responded to with resistance and/or defiance. In these years, it's less about attempting to shape and correct their behavior and more about building our relationship.

How we now connect with our children will depend a lot on their unique interests and the relationship we have built over the years. Some examples from families we know include:

- Asking them to keep us up to date with the football results and how their favorite team is doing.
- Planning annual family visits to nostalgic places like an amusement park or a hiking trail.
- Making time to connect at the beginning and end of the day.
- Listening to music they like or music they play, or having a ritual of Sunday-night music evenings with the family and an old record collection.
- Hanging around the kitchen when they get in from school or we get home from work to have a cup of tea and debrief their day.
- Knowing their friends' favorite foods so their friends feel welcome and enjoy spending time in our home.
- Reading a longer book about a shared interest together at night—one of Simone's friends calls home while he's on business trips so he and his child can still read together.

- Having a tradition of Sunday-night dinners that they can invite friends to join.

- Doing ongoing larger art and crafts projects together like knitting, sewing, origami, or painting.

- Watching a series or film on television—where once we wanted to be screen-free, a show once a week can be time to connect, to cozy up on the couch together and build a shared interest.

- Traveling during school holidays to make special memories—adolescents can help research places to visit or spots they want to photograph; they can pack for themselves; and they can walk for miles when fueled with water and gelato.

- Having fun together rather than only giving out instructions all day.

- Eating meals together—food continues to be a perfect space for open conversation and connection. Eat breakfast and dinner together as often as possible; eat at the kitchen or dining table, rather than in front of the TV; switch off the phones; and offer simple, nutritious, home-cooked food. On the weekends, Simone would have a second breakfast with her adolescents when they woke up or a cup of tea to join them. On those days when they are happy to hang out chatting after a meal, we make sure not to rush off to do another job but stay and enjoy all the company we can get.

- Continuing the family rituals established in earlier planes, like special Sunday breakfasts or cake for family birthday celebrations.

- Attending any drama, music, or school performances or sports events—being there in the audience or on the sidelines to show support.

- Listening when they talk, even when we don't agree.

- Having them cook one or two nights a week—they can pick up any ingredients they need and delight us with new recipes they are trying.

- Showing interest in their passions, whether they be computer games, football, marine biology, designing fonts, or making short films. Ask them questions about it, remember to follow up on conversations, and perhaps do something together around their interests.

- Asking, "Do you want company or would you rather be alone right now?" if they are feeling moody.

We also build connection when, just as in earlier years, we show up to support them in hard times. Having a continued secure attachment provides space where they can make mistakes, practice, try out different identities, and learn. We can grow alongside them, sharing our own ups and downs. They observe how we navigate life, relationships, and challenges while we also model how to be vulnerable. In this way, they can find out for themselves what is the right or wrong thing to do, and how to build their own safe and healthy relationships.

We continue to trust them. We will not know everything they are up to. We can give them information to keep them safe, educate them about alcohol, drugs, sex, and being streetwise. Tell them to be with sensible friends if they want to try anything unsafe. Let them know they can call us at any hour to help them. Then trust and send a guardian angel to keep watch over them.

Timing is everything

Even though connection is important, adolescents may not appreciate being bombarded with questions the minute they walk in the door. They need a lot of alone time. They need time to transition from school to home. They need to open up to us when they are ready.

Junnifa compares being the parent of an adolescent to being like a potted plant. We hang around a lot in common areas of the home (like the kitchen and living room) to show we are available. We are careful to give our children their space, while making our presence known. Then when our adolescent comes in and wants to talk, to ask us a question, or to simply flop down next to us, we are available to them. We may have a busy work life during this period of their lives, so, we can let them know when we get home from work. We might make it a habit to have a cup of tea together or to prepare dinner together or wash up together after our meal, connecting at the end of the day side by side.

The social newborn

In Montessori, we describe the adolescent as a social newborn. They are learning how to step over the threshold from their family into society. We can help this transition by including them in the social life of the family and giving them responsibilities (instead of allowing them to retreat to their room). They can greet visitors, offer beverages, ask and answer questions, and learn the social graces of our culture.

Offer them opportunities to meet a variety of people with different backgrounds, jobs, ethnicities, and religions. They will learn about different experiences and may get inspiration about a profession they might like to pursue in the future.

Allow them to get themselves around the city or area by bike or public transportation so they can begin to discover how society works. They will run into problems, go the wrong way, run out of money, get a flat tire. They will find ways to solve these problems and see what it takes to live in a social group and eventually find their place in it.

So often when our adolescent is having a difficult time, we want to take away their pain, jump in and solve their problem for them, empathize for a hot second and then get into ways they can make it better, or share what we have learned in our extra decades on the planet so they don't have to go through it.

"It's hard to see you having a hard time." This is something that Simone says a lot and that is particularly useful during the adolescent years. Because one of the wisest things Simone learned in these years was, as painful as it is to bear witness, to let them have their experience.

Instead of jumping in, we can be there as their anchor to hold space for all their emotions as they suffer, wallow, grieve, ache, hurt, laugh, cry, learn, and grow.

Teach lagging skills

Sometimes we think, "They should know better!" They leave the back door open, forget their sports clothes, or leave some food in their room to grow moldy. Instead of being activated, we can recognize that they would do better if they could do better. Or as Ross Greene says in *The Explosive Child*: "Behaviorally challenging kids are challenging because they're lacking the skills to not be challenging."

Our teenagers need us to see that they are not trying to give us a hard time. They either don't yet have a certain skill or need more practice. We can think to ourselves, *What is the skill they are missing? What is getting in the way?*

Then we take the time to build these skills with them. It might be coming up with a system for unpacking their bag as soon as they arrive home. Or recognizing that they flop when they get home and would do better if they unpacked their school bag at dinnertime. We don't decide for them but work out a way with them to help them do better.

Technology and teenagers

Technology is a tool. It is not all bad—it is a matter of how we use it.

Where we might have once chatted with our friends on the phone for hours, this generation is connecting in group chats, on social media, and while gaming with friends, and most of this is happening and available to them in their pocket no matter where they are. Many hobbies might be online, from drawing tutorials to learning to play an instrument.

In the second plane, we helped introduce how to use screens safely, where to find accurate information, and how to have a limited but balanced approach to screens. In the third plane, the adolescent is ready to take on more responsibility in this area, as in other areas of their lives. They have reached a certain level of maturity where they are capable of using technology in a way that supports their development rather than undermining their self-esteem or using it to disconnect. This will not happen overnight, but we are available along the way to guide them.

We can apply the same principles of making agreements with them and preparing the environment (both physically and emotionally) to help them manage using screens. Here are some things we can do:

- Establish agreements about when there are no screens—for example, at mealtimes, when we have visitors, during important discussions.

- Educate them about digital safety—ensure that they know not to meet strangers via the internet and to get our permission before joining a new social network; agree for us to have their passwords, not to spy on them but for ad hoc checks if required.

- Discuss what information to keep private online—their real name, school, current location—and remind them of the responsibility and possible consequences of having a permanent digital profile for any text or email sent or social media post.

- Inform them about the power of words—discuss online bullying and unkind comments; make it clear that they are to alert us if they are a victim of online bullying or if something online makes them uncomfortable or is inappropriate.

- Make a space in the common area for screens to sleep at night, ideally stopping screen use an hour or two before bed.

- Model ourselves how we would like them to use screens—rather than scrolling aimlessly, we can say, "I'm going to have a 15-minute social media break" or "I'm going to look up the train times for tomorrow" or "I'm sorry. I don't usually check my phone during family time, but I received an urgent text. Let me step out to handle this and I'll be back in 5 minutes."

- Discuss what apps they use and how they can use them safely.

- If they are falling behind with schoolwork or not contributing to the home or fulfilling other responsibilities, have a meeting to help them come up with a plan to manage their screen time.

- Invite them to look up information at the library, arrange a face-to-face conversation with an expert, or attend a seminar on a topic they are interested in rather than using the internet as a first resource.

- Help them be critical thinkers about the information they find on the internet, even from reliable sources. We can ask them questions like "Who created this information?" and "For what purpose?"

- Familiarize ourselves with the social media they are using so we can assess risks, show them how to use it safely, and understand the input they are taking in.

- Encourage the use of timers for gaming sessions.

They are learning to navigate technology the same way adults do—turning off notifications so they can get their homework done, practicing communicating clearly with friends so that they can make plans to meet up, and finding the balance between online and offline life. We are there to help them navigate it, and we can step in to guide them if they need some limits.

If they are comparing themselves to others or getting lost in negative conversation threads and their mental health is being affected, set a time to discuss it with them and make a plan. Be sure to review the plan regularly to see if it is helping.

In *From Childhood to Adolescence*, Dr. Montessori wrote, "Children should learn to use machines habitually as part of their education. The machine is like an extra adaptable limb. . . . But beware." Let's help our children prepare for the world they live in. Provide plenty of time for real face-to-face social interactions, make sure they are joining for (screen-free) family meals, provide opportunities for concrete learning experiences, make sure they get exercise (cycling to school is great where possible), and they can supplement with technology when they are able to manage the associated responsibility appropriately.

THE ADOLESCENT AND SCHOOLWORK

It can be hard to motivate adolescents to do their homework if the work is not meaningful to them or is not challenging.

Tony Evans, the director of Dundas Valley Montessori School in Canada, sums it up succinctly: "Give them dignity, give them deadlines, and give them work that needs them to be working at a high level. You don't teach the adolescent maths. You reverse engineer: How can they care about learning maths?"

The adolescent needs to feel purposeful, to feel challenged, and needs goals to work toward. It might be preparing food for forty-five people in a soup kitchen or going on a canoe trip with their class. They need to be doing real work, not just receiving lessons.

The transition from middle school to high school is an enormous adjustment for many adolescents. We can prepare them by discussing what the expectations are at the new school, like being on time, completing homework assignments, and studying for tests. Many adjust quite easily. Others may take more time.

If we are not able to access a Montessori school for adolescents, we can still support them in their schooling in a Montessori way. Here are some ideas:

- We can help give meaning to their work by talking with them about the practical application of the skills they are learning in class.
- If they have tests at their school, they can learn to see these as an opportunity to find out which areas of a given subject they still haven't completely mastered or fully understood.
- If our child needs help with planning, we can sit with them once a week while they map out their timetable, sport commitments, assignments due, and rest time; we can check in with them to see if they are on track or if they are feeling overwhelmed.
- We can show interest in their studies—ask how they felt about their test, check that they have enough time to do their homework—but, unless they need help, leave it up to them to study for their tests and work on their projects. We can still apply the philosophy of giving as little help as possible and as much as necessary.
- If they are feeling overwhelmed, we can help them break down what needs to be done into manageable steps.
- Rather than our getting in the habit of nagging them, let them take responsibility for their studies and experience the consequence of not studying for a test or arriving late for class.
- When our child is having a hard time getting to school on time or is relying on us to be their personal alarm clock and rouse them from bed, we can sit down with them to make a plan. The idea is not to punish them (likely making them resent us and school) but to work with them to identify the obstacle and help them remove it.

THE ADOLESCENT IN A FAST-CHANGING WORLD

One thing about our adolescents today is that they have access to any information they would like and likely know more about some topics than we do. Here are some ways to address this:

- Stay connected with them. Have conversations; use television programs, social media, memes, etc., as jumping-off points to discuss topics like teen pregnancy, drugs and alcohol, pornography, and mental health.
- Listen to their ideas more than we talk—conversations are not lectures.
- Continue to talk about consent with adolescents of any gender. We build on the relationship established in the first and second planes.

- If we see signs of depression and anxiety, seek out information both for ourselves and for ways to support them.
- Establish emotional and sleep hygiene in our homes. Maybe have a time once a week when they can process what is going on for them emotionally. Have mobile phones out of the bedroom at night. Allow enough time on weekends for them to follow their natural sleep rhythms.
- Let them know that practical life at home still matters, too. Cooking for the family. Taking care of their space and the communal spaces. Washing the car. Taking care of pets. Babysitting younger children in the family. Being in charge of the family vegetable patch. All of these tasks help our adolescents be part of the family and take on responsibilities, and they counter the rise in self-centeredness, the effects of the digital age and a competitive world, and the adolescent's feeling that they cannot make a difference.
- Support valorization. Even in a fast-changing world, our adolescents need to feel like they belong, they add meaning, and they matter.

Valorization may not be able to prevent all mental health issues arising at this volatile time. But if adolescents feel like they belong and have their needs met (as much as possible), they can thrive and prepare themselves for adulthood. If we implement the suggestions above, we are doing as much for their mental health as we can. We need to be vigilant for indicators, as it's best to get help as soon as possible. We can seek out the help and support we need (including for ourselves) and continue to focus on our relationship with our adolescent.

The most delightful part is seeing these adolescents grow into themselves. They are exploring who they are, and they want to talk about big issues and to make a difference in the world. The conversations are fascinating. Their goals for the future are not often about money. They want to love what they do.

Toward the end of high school, they start to explore what they might like to do next. Rather than taking over this exploration, we continue to be their guide, allowing them the space to do the research, complete the application forms, and prepare any essays or portfolios, miss the deadlines, ask for an extension, take a gap year. We could have a weekly meeting with them to keep them on track, yet we can also step back, removing the training wheels one more time.

Then, before we know it, our adolescent finishes high school, turns 18, and possibly prepares to leave home.

We have a fourth-plane child.

MATURITY:
THE FOURTH PLANE OF DEVELOPMENT

The fourth plane goes from ages 18 to 24, and Dr. Montessori referred to this plane's work as developing spiritual and moral independence.

Similar to the second plane of development, this is a more stable period, and the young adult uses their reasoning, logical mind. They are busy exploring areas of interest in work and study at a deep level. Their brains are nearly completely formed.

They know largely who they are and can be their own person. They will see if the values they received from their family are also their values. They may reject them now and readopt them later.

Dr. Montessori said that "the adult is a result of a child," meaning that if everything necessary has been done in the first three planes of development, the fourth plane takes care of itself. We come full circle and see before us everything that was sown in the preceding years.

Young adults primarily want to give back to society, for example, through volunteer work or the Peace Corps. They may enter university and/or join the workforce.

In *From Childhood to Adolescence*, Dr. Montessori outlined her views on higher education. She was discouraged that many universities were, and still are, offering top-down education to their students, unlike in the Middle Ages, when philosophical and political debate was encouraged. Universities are an opportunity to take a deep dive into a field of interest and learn how to study. We want to keep the student active and engaged. Yet debate is also not enough.

According to Dr. Montessori, we want the young adult to get beyond the four walls of the university (just as we encouraged the child from 6 to 12 years old to go out into the community to find answers to their questions). She advised there's no rush to complete the studies as quickly as possible; it is also important to take a job (e.g., as a tutor, an artist, a waiter, or as an intern in broadcasting, journalism, or diplomacy), learn to be in society with people of different ages, and master economic independence. This also helps them to adapt to the culture of their society.

Our role in the fourth plane

The young adult is now completely independent of us. They will still call us for help, and we will still give them our care and attention, but they are now discovering how to be a part of society in an unprepared environment. The scaffold has been removed.

Remember that Dr. Montessori said that childhood goes up to 24 years old. The prefrontal cortex is nearly fully developed, but there are likely to still be moments in this period when they will lack judgment and rational thought in their decision-making.

To help them in this fourth plane:

- Set up their finances so they are independent. They may be able to get a student loan, they may work, or we may choose to give them a monthly allowance. They will be responsible for ensuring that there is enough money each month to buy their groceries, pay their rent and bills, and have money for going out with their friends.
- Support their decision to move out of home where possible. They will be more independent when they are away from us. Some may even need to be a few hours away so we cannot drop by to rescue them.
- Be a facilitator. Check in on them; arrange visits where possible; sit next to them or be available when they are setting up bank accounts, completing application forms, arranging for mobile phones, or signing rental contracts. We can be their guide, but they make the phone calls, do the research, and complete any paperwork, just like a second-plane child arranges an outing.

If they still live at home:

- Discuss how they can contribute as an adult member of the household.
- Make a roster together to show who will be responsible for buying the groceries, cooking the family meals, and washing up during the week.
- Look for ways to replicate the experience of being responsible for arranging their whole week. If they weren't living at home, they would be learning to live with other students, interacting with others in a community of different ages, as well as cooking, washing their clothes, and cleaning for themselves.
- Encourage them to arrange their own financial responsibilities for things like mobile phones, insurance, and student loans.

We will want to hold on to them. This is another time for letting go. It's not called "empty-nest syndrome" for nothing. We have loved being their guide. Now we release them to the world to see where they fly.

May they fly far and wide. And know that our door is always open to them.

Note: The transition from the prepared environment to the unprepared environment generally goes quite smoothly with a little guidance from us. However, for those young adults who are neurodivergent (e.g., have ADHD or sensory processing issues or are autistic or twice exceptional), we may want to remove the scaffold more slowly. How they have been able to manage in the prepared environment can be very different from how they handle themselves in the unprepared environment without us there to manage difficult situations for them, help them with unexpected changes to schedules, or assist with the unpredictability of living with others. Raising these children with Montessori at home may have masked the full range of how their diagnosis presents. Go slowly. Be gentle. Pop in often. Or consider a gap year to build any lagging skills.

FURTHER READING

- *From Childhood to Adolescence* by Dr. Maria Montessori

THE PATH TO PEACE

Our hope is that these young adults embrace the principles and values we have offered them. May their upbringing serve them in unfolding into their full potential.

May they be capable, have creative minds and compassionate hearts, with a strong sense of who they are and a desire to serve.

We as the adult are not untouched. We have learned to see through another's eyes, we have acquired infinite patience, and we now know the power of unconditional love.

Where once we may have interfered, now we hold back. Where once we may have ignored, now we reach forward to connect.

Let's keep spreading this promise for peace and humankind. Be gentle with ourselves, with our fellow Earth travelers, and with our environment.

> "I beg the dear all-powerful children to unite with me for the building of peace in Man and in the World."
>
> —inscription on Dr. Montessori's grave in Noordwijk aan Zee, the Netherlands

APPENDICES

ACTIVITIES APPENDIX

Any ages given are only suggestions. Follow your child's unique development and interests. Refer to the online appendix "Starter Kits" for a useful list of items to use for these activities. As much as possible, they will be things we already have in our home. Montessori is not about buying more things but using what we have, buying secondhand, or—where possible—repurposing something else.

PRACTICAL LIFE ACTIVITIES

Practical life activities are a wonderful way to support our child's innate drive to function independently as a person of their time, place, and culture. Activities around care of self and our home and environment introduce our child to lots of vocabulary, involve gross- and fine-motor movements, and help our child build discipline and their executive functioning skills. They provide opportunities for our child to notice, create, maintain, and restore order; to master tasks through repetition as many of these tasks are done on a regular basis; and to involve our child in real, purposeful work.

Care of self	**This involves the child's activities around caring for themselves, maintaining hygiene, and caring for their belongings. Many self-care skills require the use of their hands and develop the child's fine-motor skills. They also contribute significantly to the child's sense of self. Children want to be shown and helped to care for themselves.**
Dressing and undressing	Our child dresses and undresses multiple times a day, putting on and taking off sweaters and jackets, shirts, trousers, dresses, underpants, socks, and shoes. Each of these involves different movements and requires different skills. Some items need to be pulled, others need to be pushed; our child might need to shrug out of one item or sit to take their legs out of the other. Different items have different closures or fastenings like zippers, buttons, buckles, and laces. We can help our child learn how to dress and undress by focusing on one skill at a time. If our child is learning how to button, we can offer more clothes that provide opportunities to practice. As they master each skill, we can add another.
Brushing teeth	We can show them how to unscrew and replace the cap of the toothpaste tube, how to squeeze the tube, the quantity of toothpaste to put on their toothbrush, how to wet the toothbrush and turn off the tap, how to brush their teeth, how to brush their tongue (if we do that in our culture), and how to rinse their mouth and their toothbrush.
Taking a shower or bath	We can emphasize the key areas to wash. We can show them how much soap to apply, how much to scrub, and how to rinse. We can show them how to run a bath and how much bubble bath to add, how to dry their body, and where to hang their wet towel.
Caring for hair	We can isolate, demonstrate, and help our children with the specific steps of hair care, such as detangling, combing, brushing, braiding, unbraiding, moisturizing, oiling, packing, and styling.
Washing hands	We can show them how to scrub their fingers, in between the fingers, the palms, the backs of the hands, under the fingernails. We can show them how much soap to apply, how to rinse, how long to scrub. We can teach our values around preserving water while washing our hands. We can show them how to apply hand lotion. We can share key times for washing hands, like when we come in from outside, before and after meals, after using the restroom, after blowing or picking our nose, after touching an animal or a dirty item.
Caring for fingernails	From around age 4, our children might be interested in cutting their nails. We can show them how to use nail clippers and how to dispose of the nail trimmings. We can show them how to apply nail polish if they are interested, and an older child may wish to learn to give a manicure and pedicure.
Blowing their nose	We can show them the quantity of tissue to use, how much force to blow with, how to dispose of the tissue when done, and to wash their hands when finished. We can demonstrate by blowing our own nose while facing the child or in front of a mirror and then let the child blow their own nose.

Wiping or washing after peeing or pooping	We can demonstrate how much paper to use, how to wipe from front to back, wiping until the tissue is clean, and washing our hands afterward. Some religions restrict the use of a specific hand, and we can share this with our child if it applies.
Caring for clothes	We can show them how to check their clothing when they take it off to decide if it is dirty or can be reworn. They can learn to sort their laundry by color, texture, category, and fabric type and how to handwash clothes, load the washing machine, and run it. They also can learn to fold their clothes, put them on a hanger, and iron them. We can show them how to iron in a safe way, on a low temperature. As they get older, they can be shown any special care for specific fabrics or colors like the selection of water temperature and the amount of soap or bleach to use. They can also be shown how to sew on a button or mend a tear. (For more on sewing, see page 259.)
Caring for shoes	Children can be shown how to brush off sand and dirt from their shoes, how to scrub flip-flops or sneakers, how to polish and care for leather shoes, and how to air their shoes.
Caring for minor injuries	Children can be shown how to wash or clean a minor injury and apply a Band-Aid.
Personal hygiene	As the child moves toward puberty, we can show them how to care for themselves. How to shave; how to use sanitary pads, period panties, or tampons; how to use deodorant; how to wash and clean themselves; how to wash stains. This preparation can empower our children as they make the transition to adolescence.
Preparing things for school	We can show them how to organize their things, fill up their water bottle, make their own lunch, arrange clothes for the next day, and gather any additional items for sports or music lessons. Older children can make lists. We can also show them how to pack for a trip.
Caring for others	They can learn how to assist others with their self-care activities.
Caring for pets	Our child can learn to brush fur, wash the water bowl and food dish, put out food and fresh water, change kitty litter, bathe the pet, and take the pet for walks.
Going out/ returning home	Children can be shown how to climb into and out of the car, buckle their seat belt, take things out of the car, and put away their shoes and jacket (if their shoes are dirty, they can brush the dirt off).
Care of Self Starter Kit	*Find this online at workman.com/montessori*
Care of the environment	**These are activities to maintain our surroundings, and this can include the indoors and the outdoors. The tools used and the ways that we care for our environment will differ from place to place and culture to culture. These activities support the development of gross-motor skills and the child's sense of order, invite deep concentration, and help the child develop a sense of responsibility and stewardship for their environment/their community/the world.**
Maintaining our spaces	• Arranging—closets, shoes, belongings, bookshelves, table surfaces, rooms, play spaces, and toys. • Beautifying the environment—they can learn how to cut and arrange flowers, open and close curtains or windows to let in light and air, and make decorations to beautify the space. • Caring for plants—watering plants, dusting or washing leaves, cutting off dry leaves, and, for older children, transplanting. • Working outside—raking leaves; working in the garden planting flowers, vegetables, and herbs; composting; clearing snow. • Picking up the mail from the mailbox. • Woodworking—hammering nails, cutting wood, and sanding or planing wood.

Cleaning our spaces	• Dusting—surfaces and shelves using a cloth or duster; removing cobwebs. • Wiping—spills and surfaces. • Sweeping and vacuuming—we can show them how to sweep or vacuum different floors or surfaces. One simple activity used to give practice in sweeping is having dry petals or pieces of torn paper in a box or basket. The child can sprinkle them over a space and be shown how to sweep them together into a pile. A spot can be marked with tape or chalk to indicate where to make a pile. They can then sweep it into a dustpan and pour it back into the box or basket and repeat. • Mopping—we can show them how to handle and rinse the mop. • Polishing—wood, mirrors, and metal surfaces. • Scrubbing/washing—windows, cars, tables, furniture, walls, toilets, sinks, bathtubs/showers, surfaces, containers, toys, clothes, napkins, and rags. Children can also be shown how to hang fabric items to dry. An older child can be shown how to take down curtains for washing and how to put them back up.
Care of the Environment Starter Kit	*Find this online at workman.com/montessori*
Preparing food	**Activities in the kitchen build our child's independence while helping them develop gross- and fine-motor skills, language, and confidence, and learn concepts in the areas of mathematics, geography, science, agriculture, and history. We can explore states of matter and different ways of combining ingredients, and we can follow our food from garden to table, all while connecting with our children. We can share stories about the source of an ingredient or recipe and travel around the world with our taste buds. We can introduce our child to our own family's cultural food traditions.**
Beginner-level activities	• Rinsing—fruits and vegetables, nuts and grains, utensils. • Drying—fruits and vegetables, dishes, utensils. • Arranging—setting the table, arranging utensils and ingredients in preparation for cooking or baking. • Sorting—groceries, grains, fruits, vegetables. These can be transferred into bags or containers for storage. • Helping at the grocery store—making a shopping list, pushing the cart, fetching items, greeting the cashier, helping to pay. • Handing us things as we prepare food—ingredients, utensils. • Tearing and plucking—salad greens, herbs, the stalk from a fruit or vegetable, perhaps feathers from a chicken if doing that ourselves is part of our culture. • Peeling/shelling using their hands—fruits like bananas or tangerines, nuts, eggs. • Chopping—fruits, vegetables. • Slicing soft items using (butter) knives and slicers—eggs, bananas, strawberries, cheese, kiwis. • Measuring and pouring—grains, flour, oil, water. For example, from a bigger container to a smaller one; from a pitcher to a cup; into multiple containers when we want the amounts to be equal; using a funnel when pouring from a container with a bigger opening into one with a smaller opening. Our child can also measure using cups, teaspoons, and tablespoons. • Scooping and transferring—using their hands, tongs, spoons, forks, or a small scoop to transfer ingredients from containers to mixing bowls and using a special tool to scoop melon balls. • Spreading and brushing—butter, peanut butter, and jam on bread; tomato sauce on pizza dough; an egg wash on pastry dough. • Squeezing and juicing using a hand juicer—oranges, lemons. • Sieving and draining. • Mashing—bananas, avocados. • Stirring and mixing.

Intermediate activities	• Washing vegetables. We can show them what to use in washing and how to wash. Some people use water, some salt and water, some vinegar and water. For an older child, this can lead to conversations about disinfectants, combining a solid and a liquid vs. combining liquids, and the effect of a solution.
	• Peeling/shelling using tools, such as a vegetable peeler for carrots, cucumbers, and potatoes and a nutcracker for nuts.
	• Slicing, chopping, and cutting softer vegetables like tomatoes, okra, peppers, and leafy vegetables using a knife.
	• Measuring by weight using scales and by volume using a calibrated container or pitcher and also setting temperatures for baking.
	• Washing grains and beans.
	• Serving meals, including placing serving plates on the table.
	• Drying dishes. A younger child may need a surface to lay the dish towel on at first and can then move on to being able to hold a dish in one hand and dry it with the other.
	• Arranging salads, pizza toppings, and food platters.
	• Sorting. This can involve more fine-motor skills like picking out sand/small stones from rice or beans.
	• Grating carrots, zucchini, apples, cheese, coconut, okras, nutmeg, and cinnamon.
	• Smelling and tasting as they cook or prepare dishes.
	• Pounding yams with salt crystals, garlic, ginger, and spices.
	• Juicing using an electric juicer; extracting juices or milk from leaves, seeds, and nuts.
	• Churning cream into butter.
	• Lighting a match, lighting a burner, turning off a burner.
	• Using a microwave if our family uses one.
	• Pitting and deseeding fruits—pitting cherries, tweezing pomegranates, hulling strawberries.
	• Cracking eggs, walnuts, and coconuts.
	• Reading and following advanced recipes.
Snack preparation ideas	• *Sandwiches.* Children can choose the meat, vegetables, and/or spreads and cut the sandwiches into halves, quarters, or a fun shape. An older child can make wraps. We may want to have a shelf in the fridge where sandwich fixings are in easy reach.
	• *Crackers, bagels, chips, breads, fruits, or vegetables with spreads or dips, such as peanut butter, jam, or hummus.* Nonperishables can be stored in airtight, easy-to-open containers where the child can get them. An older child can learn how to make their own spreads— by grinding roasted peanuts to make peanut butter, churning cream to make butter, or caramelizing fruits to make jam—or dips like guacamole.
	• *Salads.* Vegetables and fruits can be chopped and combined in different ways to make salads. An older child might explore salads from different geographical locations and also different salad dressings, such as those made with oil, lemon juice or vinegar, and salt, and yogurt-based dressings.
	• *Cereal.* The child can scoop cereal into a bowl/cup and pour milk from a pitcher over the top. They can scoop yogurt into a bowl and garnish it with granola and fruit. Older children could layer and arrange cereal and yogurt in different ways in a glass bowl/cup and pour directly from a larger milk carton/container.
	• *Eggs, boiled and sliced or quartered.* An older child might enjoy making stuffed eggs. They can also fry eggs or make French toast. Pancake batter can be prepared by the child and cooked on an electric skillet.
	• *Juices, lemonade, and smoothies.* Juice citrus, chop up fruit for the blender or juicer. They can experiment with different flavor combinations.

Cooking meals	Introduce any meals we cook in our home to our child. One-pot meals, soups, and stews can be good places to start.
Cooking on the stovetop	We can start with items that are relatively easy and can cook on low heat, such as scrambled eggs, omelets, pancakes, or French toast. We can orient the child by showing them the ideal distance from the pan to stand and how to handle the pan when it's hot. We can gradually move to cooking over medium heat—sautéing things like onions, tomatoes, and minced meat. When we can trust the child and know they can handle more, we can then introduce more complex cooking tasks. An adult should be present or close by when a child under 12 is cooking on a stove.
Lighting a match	Lighting a match can be isolated as an activity using tea light candles. We can teach the child to strike away from themselves, hold the match horizontally, and blow it out as soon as possible. We can have a small jar of sand to place the used matches into. We can build up to using a match to light a stove.
Cleaning up	• Clearing and washing up after preparing food • Clearing and cleaning the table after meals • Scraping dishes • Washing and wiping dishes, containers, and utensils • Loading and running a dishwasher • Arranging ingredients and other items on a rack or shelf after use or cleaning • Sweeping and mopping the floor • Sweeping, wiping, or scrubbing the work surface/table • Wiping the stove or oven
Baking	Baking invites the child to be precise with measurements and ingredients, and to read and follow a recipe's specific sequence. It requires that our child concentrate over an extended period of time. Baking can also introduce a variety of sensorial experiences: tastes, shapes, textures, temperatures, scents, and colors. Reading the recipe provides practice in reading and enriches the child's vocabulary. The measurements involve math and introduce the child to fractions, counting, volume, and equivalence. Older children can be challenged to halve, double, or triple a recipe, thus requiring them to use division or multiplication and making their operation skills more practical. Baking also allows the child to experience the science of combining. They can explore time and temperature. Baking naturally encourages discipline and exactness. An extra spoonful of salt can make a significant difference to a batch of cookies. These experiences hold important lessons for the child. Baking, like other food preparation activities, also provides an opportunity to develop self-control. Perhaps baked goods can be had at the next mealtime, or we can sometimes bake for others.
Some baking skills to build	• Measuring and pouring ingredients • Sifting dry ingredients • Breaking eggs, whisking eggs, separating the white from the yolk • Mixing dough, making pastry dough, rolling out dough • Using cutters—cookie cutters, pizza cutter, pastry cutter • Brushing pastry dough with an egg wash • Crimping pastry and piecrust edges • Decorating cookies and cakes • Putting baked goods into the oven and taking them out

Baking ideas	Cookies, bread, pastries, muffins, pies, granola, falafel, pizza, crackers, etc.
Baking Starter Kit	*Find this online at workman.com/montessori*
Considerations for cooking and baking	• Prepare the environment. Decide whether the child will sit or stand to cook/bake.
	• Think about each step of the process and what is needed: Where will the whisk go when the child is done whisking? Where will the banana peels go? Set up a place for everything so that the child experiences order and the process does not get messier than necessary.
	• For a younger child, the ingredients can all be premeasured and arranged in order of use.
	• We can prepare a visual recipe for a child who is not able to read. This does not have to be fancy and can be hand drawn. There are also commercially available visual recipe books. A child who is able to read can tell us each step of the recipe while we do the actions and they assist us; then we build up to them doing more themselves.
	• We can show the child how to set the oven temperature as well as how to put things into and take things out of the oven.
	• We can tell them the name of the dish we are making and introduce them to the ingredients and utensils we will be using.
	• We can describe our actions and give the names for the processes, like marinating, boiling, frying, grilling, mixing, grinding, and blending. With older children, we can get even more specific: simmering, sautéing, shallow frying, or deep-frying instead of just frying.
	• They can help us measure, and we can give them the vocabulary for the measurements: cup, tablespoon, teaspoon, half, quarter. They can add the ingredients. We can mention the names as they do to reinforce the vocabulary and include the names of utensils being used.
	• They can taste the food, and we can talk about the taste—sweet, salty, savory, spicy, peppery. We can introduce them to different spices, textures, temperatures.
	• They can scoop, spoon, pour, and stir.
	• Over time, they can take on more responsibility until they are able to complete the entire cooking process independently.
	• We can take the opportunity to share how to store or preserve the food, then how to warm it up.
Food Preparation Starter Kit	*Find this online at workman.com/montessori*
Safety in the kitchen	We talk to our child about safety in the kitchen before we begin. When demonstrating how we use tools, we can talk about the risks—germs, cuts, burns, fires—as well as what to do in case of an accident. We can talk about washing our hands before meals; being careful not to dip utensils back into mixing bowls or pots after tasting; putting up our hair; keeping surfaces, utensils, and ingredients clean; keeping food at the right temperature; keeping raw food away from prepared food; keeping paper and fabric away from stove burners; concentrating when working with sharp objects or heat; and turning off the burner before leaving the room. We can assess our environment to determine potential risks and remove them.
Botany in the kitchen	Planting and harvesting are ways that we can enrich our cooking and food preparation with our children. We can have a full vegetable garden or some pots growing herbs and spices on a window ledge. If we do have a garden, herbs like curry, basil, and parsley; alliums like chives, garlic, and onions; and vegetables like carrots, tomatoes, peppers, radishes, lettuce, spinach, and native vegetables in season are great to grow with children. Tubers like potatoes and ginger can be grown in buckets or sacks. Research how to grow fruits and vegetables from food scraps. The children can care for the plants as they grow, weed them, harvest them, and explore different ways to prepare them, both locally and around the world. Herbs can be dried and ground for storage. They can be used to make scent pouches and be given as gifts to neighbors.

Numbers and literacy in the kitchen	When setting the table, the child figures out how many people will be eating, placing a plate and cutlery for each person. This is an activity around one-to-one correspondence—"one plate for me, one plate for Grandma"—an important step for number sense and numeracy. They can fold and place napkins for each person—an unconscious lesson in geometry. A square can be folded into a rectangle or triangle or smaller square, or it can even be rolled into a cylinder. They can place name cards for each person, an opportunity to read and maybe write and design each card. A child who is unable to write for themselves can sound out the names while an older child or adult writes it for them.

Science in the kitchen	• States of matter, such as liquid (water, milk) and solid (grains, fruits).
	• Ice water vs. room-temperature water vs. boiled water. When watching water boil, we can draw our child's attention to the changes—the rising temperature, the gases forming, and the condensation that occurs when the lid is on the pot.
	• Raw eggs vs. boiled eggs vs. fried eggs.
	• Raw rice vs. boiled rice and other grains.
	• Batter vs. cake.
	• The effect of yeast on dough.
	• The difference in rising when the dough is left in a warm place vs. when it's left in a cold place.
	• Mold and fungus on old food.
	• The consequences of handling bread with dirty hands.
	• How different items like fruits and utensils float or sink.
	• Volume when measuring and pouring using different containers.
	• The different reactions possible with milk—curdled milk or yogurt, ghee, buttermilk, cream, butter.
	• How different ingredients dissolve in water or over heat.
	• The different types of nutrients—protein, carbohydrates, fat—and what they do for the body.
	• Balanced meals.
	• Food sources for essential minerals/elements.
	• Body systems like digestive and muscular.
	• Vertebrates and invertebrates—fish and chicken vs. snails and calamari.
	• Alternative lifestyles like vegetarian and vegan.
	• Where animals live, parts of their bodies, unique characteristics (like ruminants having a four-compartment stomach and being able to digest cellulose), body covering, how they take care of their young.

MOVEMENT

Movement is such an important part of life. Everything we do—walking, touching, talking, eating—involves movement. Even when we are not moving, we are consciously or unconsciously controlling or inhibiting our movements. Children in the first plane are in a sensitive period for movement and are acquiring, refining, and learning to control movement. As they do this, they also develop their personality and will. It is through their will that they become able to control their movement and develop discipline and character. There is a correlation between movement and cognitive development. Our goal is to help our children develop coordinated movement connected to their mind.

Movement for the 3- to 6-year-old child	Dr. Montessori described the 3- to 6-year-old child as a conscious worker. They move in a conscious, coordinated way and have developed basic gross-motor skills (for movements that use big muscles, like walking, running, and throwing) and fine-motor skills (for movements that use small muscles in the hands, like writing, threading, and cutting). Now they are in the process of refining their movement—improving, fleshing out, adding details, perfecting—through their activities.
Gross-motor skills	Gross-motor skills include body awareness, bilateral integration, and the ability to cross the midline. These are usually developed in the first subplane and then refined from the ages of 3 to 6.
Body awareness	Body awareness is the understanding of one's body in relation to a space, thereby improving coordination and reducing accidents. We can provide our child with opportunities to crawl around the floor or through tunnels and obstacle courses; push vehicles or toys; roll and play on the floor; jump; carry heavy things like groceries, trash bags, library books, logs, or buckets of water; push and pull a wagon or wheelbarrow; or climb a jungle gym, ladder, or trees.
Bilateral integration and crossing the midline	Bilateral integration is the ability to use both sides of the body in a coordinated way and is a significant part of the refining of movement. Bilateral integration reflects communication between the left and right sides of the brain. It is required for walking, running, climbing, dressing, and many other gross-motor activities.
	Crossing the midline is any action that involves moving our eyes, hands, or feet from one side of the body to the other side, like crossing arms or reaching for something on the right side of one's body with the left hand.
	A lot of practical life activities encourage bilateral integration and crossing the midline. For example, kneading dough, pouring from a pitcher, carrying heavy objects like watering cans, sweeping and mopping, woodworking activities, threading activities, sewing, working with clay, cutting strips of paper with scissors, baking, and tying shoelaces. Additionally, gross-motor-skill activities like climbing stairs or play equipment, skipping, doing jumping jacks, jumping from log to log, hopping on one leg, using monkey bars, engaging in movement games with rhymes, playing with silk streamers, bouncing balls, and playing hand and clapping games all also support bilateral interactions and crossing the midline.
Refining movement	One of the ways that the child from 3 to 6 refines their movement is by perfecting their balance and control of their body. They not only want to walk, they want to walk on a straight or curved line, run, climb, slide, jump, hop, pedal, somersault, cartwheel, do a handstand, stand really still, carry things, stack things, and be able to complete movements that require a higher level of control. They want to gain mastery of their body and balance. We can support this by first providing space, freedom, and opportunities for both free play and purposeful movement in our indoor and outdoor environment.
Movement in the outdoors	We can prepare an outdoor environment with things like logs, blocks, or rocks to carry, roll, push, stack, climb, and jump on and from. We can also create opportunities for purposeful activities that require big movements like sweeping or raking leaves, packing them into a wheelbarrow, pushing them into a pile, and jumping on the pile. Indoors, they can use large cushions to build forts, stacking them, arranging them in different ways, and jumping from them.
	Our child wants to be able to control and stop their bodies. Ledges, fallen trees, and balance beams are invitations to balance. Stumps are invitations to jump, lift, roll, carry, stack, climb, or squat by to observe the little ecosystems hidden in the dirt around them.
	If we have a garden, the child can run after butterflies, bend to pick flowers, harvest some produce, pull out weeds, or carry a heavy watering can or hose to water the plants. We can have a soft grass lawn, a soft rug, or padded foam surface for cartwheels and somersaults. If we don't have these at home, we can make visiting a park or playground a part of our daily or at least weekly routine.

Movement in daily life	Our children can pick up the mail, wash cars, or ride their bicycles to run errands with us. All of Junnifa's children learned how to ride their bikes by 3 years old. They started with balance bikes at 18 months or 2 years old and transitioned very easily to regular bikes around 3 years old without needing training wheels. Older children can also start with balance bikes, which can make it easier for them to learn to ride a regular bike.
Other movement activities	The following invite control and refinement of gross-motor movements and also really interest and engage the child at this stage of development.

- Walking with a bell without having it chime; walking with an egg or a ball on a spoon without dropping it; walking with a cup full of water without spilling it; or walking with a beanbag, book, or other item balanced on their head without dropping it. We can invite them to walk slowly at first and then attempt to go faster while still maintaining this control.

- Walking in a specific way, such as heel to toe while on a line or balance beam.

- Walking on lines indoors or outdoors—a straight line, a curved line, a zigzag line, a line that goes through tight corners—or on shapes made with chalk, tape, or even paint.

- Music activities that invite moving in different ways: walking, running, galloping, skipping.

- Rhythmic activities in which different movements are assigned to different songs. (We can use the CD *Walking on the Line & Rhythmic Activities on the Line* with music by Sanford Jones or make a playlist with songs of different tempos.)

- Reciting rhymes and singing songs that involve accompanying movements, like "If You're Happy and You Know It," "The Ants Go Marching," the "Hokey Pokey," "Head, Shoulders, Knees, and Toes," "Ten Little Monkeys," "The Goldfish (Let's Go Swimming)" by Laurie Berkner, etc. We usually do these with younger children, but older children would benefit from them, too.

- Command games like Simon says; move, freeze; duck, duck, goose; and hide-and-seek.

- Action-card activities where the child can choose a card and do the action.

- Moving like different animals—galloping like a horse, jumping like a frog, spinning like a spider, flapping their arms like a bird or butterfly flaps its wings.

- Moving around our home quietly or without bumping into furniture. We can set up obstacle courses to make this interesting. And they could practice:

  ◦ Walking, standing up from a chair, and sitting down without making a sound

  ◦ Lifting, moving, and putting down an object or piece of furniture without making a sound

  ◦ Closing doors, jars, boxes, and lids without making a sound

- Playing ball—catch, throw, throw into a container/box, kick, etc.

- Pushing the shopping cart in the grocery store and having to turn at corners and navigate past other customers

Gross-Motor Skills Starter Kit	***Find this online at workman.com/montessori***

Movement for the 6- to 12-year-old child	All of the activities for the 3- to 6-year-old child can be enjoyed by older children, too, and will also help improve any gross-motor challenges. The 6- to 12-year-old child is very strong. They have a lot of energy, and they know it. They want to exert themselves and push themselves to see how far they can go. They are also very social and enjoy working in groups. This is a key period for social and moral development, so this is a great time to introduce group sports and activities. They will enjoy: races (individual and relay), tennis, soccer, swimming, basketball, baseball, cricket, hockey, badminton, gymnastics, jumping rope, scouting (usually involves hiking/other physical activities).

In competitive sports situations, we can support them in developing the right attitude toward winning and losing. We can encourage them to focus on doing their best and improving as they can. We can choose groups with positive approaches to competition where collaboration and support are encouraged.

We can observe to see what our child is interested in and has talent for and then provide opportunities for them to build skills in this area. If they are not sure, we can expose them to different opportunities and see which one they become interested in. |
Fine-motor development	Dr. Montessori said that the hands are the instruments of intelligence. The work and creations of our hands tell the stories of culture and time. They are what we use to manipulate, work on, and improve our environment. Most occupations, from chef to teacher, artist to doctor, coder to tailor, involve the use of our hands. It is our hands that have helped create and preserve history and therefore helped each generation learn from the last. Dr. Montessori believed that cognitive development can be limited if it is not supported by the hands. Fine-motor-skill development includes hand-eye coordination, hand strength, manual dexterity, and the pincer grip.
Practical life activities	All of the practical life activities discussed earlier support the development of fine-motor skills. Buttoning, unbuttoning, tying, lacing, zipping, and unzipping strengthen hand-eye coordination, the pincer grip, and manual dexterity. Opening and closing different containers, mixing, peeling, and chopping support hand strength and manual dexterity. Peeling eggs, plucking stalks or leaves, and sorting seeds promote the development of the pincer grip.
Open and close activities	We can also set up a specific open and close activity by gathering six to eight small containers with different kinds of closures. There can be boxes, containers with flip caps, bottles with screw caps, snap purses, coin purses, and drawstring purses. We can show the child how to line up the lid on the top and then how to close it, to lift and open and operate the latch or closure, etc. It is also fun to put a bead, button, or other small object to find in each of the containers, and the child can extend the activity by taking out the objects and matching them to their containers. They can also be responsible for opening and closing windows, cupboards, and doors.
Locks and keys	Turning keys in locks. We can start with one key and one padlock. Putting the key into the lock requires hand-eye coordination; twisting and unlocking uses manual dexterity; and locking builds hand strength. We can then add one or two locks and keys to distinguish which key goes with which lock. We can also add a variety of locks, e.g., a twist lock, one with number codes, etc.
Screwing and unscrewing nuts and bolts	They can start with large nuts and bolts and then progress to smaller ones and then to using tools.
Pouring, spooning, and cutting to support manual dexterity	We can set up specific transferring activities with two containers holding things to pour or transfer. This could be beads, pom-poms, seeds, sand, or colored water. For pouring, it is better to start with dry objects like beans that are easy to pick or clean up and then progress to sand and then to liquids. We can contain the activity in a deep tray, encourage the child to work somewhere that we don't mind spills, and put out only as much as we are okay with potentially spilling all over the floor.

Using a hole/ shape punch or perforator	Strengthens the hand and improves manual dexterity. The punched-out shapes can be glued onto another piece of paper to make art. Picking up the shape and using a brush to apply the glue both support the development of the pincer grip.
Using scissors	Scissors can be used to cut paper, blades of grass, fabric, ribbons, yarn, play dough, or paper straws. The paper, fabric, and yarn can be used for mixed-media art. The straws can be threaded onto yarn or ribbons to make bracelets or necklaces. This supports hand strength, manual dexterity, hand-eye coordination, and threading. Our child can progress through cutting skills; they can start by cutting narrow strips (around $\frac{1}{2}$ inch/1 cm wide and 4 inches/10 cm long) that require just snips, then they can cut along lines on a thicker cutting strip (around $\frac{3}{4}$ inch/2 cm wide and 4 inches/10 cm long)—straight, curved, zigzag—and proceed to cutting out shapes, spirals, symmetrical designs, drawings, and then intricate designs.
Poking/prick pen	The children can trace the outline of a shape (or we can prepare shapes); and they can poke them out using an awl, toothpick, or skewer, following the line. It is easier to use thicker paper and place it on felt to poke. They can learn shapes, continents, animals, and vehicles. The poked-out shape can be glued to another piece of paper and assembled to make a book, chart, or map that can be used to review the vocabulary.
Folding	Supports the pincer grip, dexterity, and hand strength. Children can fold cloth or paper. Napkins are a great place to start. They can fold the squares into smaller squares or triangles. They can also fold socks and proceed to tucking socks in to make a ball. They can proceed to folding paper, which requires more accuracy and refinement. A piece of square paper can be folded just like a napkin into smaller squares or triangles. The children can proceed to folding different kinds of clothes and then to simple origami and more complicated folds.
Doing puzzles	Knobbed puzzles support the pincer grip, but jigsaw and layered puzzles are also good for hand-eye coordination and spatial awareness.
Tracing	In the classroom, we use various metal shapes from a circle to more complicated polygons for children to trace around. At home, we can find objects with different shapes, such as a plate or box, for children to trace around with their finger first and then with a pencil. They learn how to follow a contour and use a firm touch. It prepares their hand to apply sufficient pressure when using a writing instrument.
Threading	Supports hand-eye coordination, manual dexterity, and the pincer grip. The child can start with large flat beads with big holes; then proceed to large solid-shaped beads—cylinders, spheres, cubes—then tiny beads. Pipe cleaners and dowels are great to start with because they are stiff, and then we can progress to rope or yarn. The rope or yarn being used to thread should be stiff at the starting point. Purchased activities usually have addressed this, but if we're setting up the activity at home, we can use tape to stiffen the thread. The knot on the end should be big enough to not let the bead pass through, or use one bead in making the knot. As the child gets better at threading, they can also learn to thread needles.
Using clothespins	Uses the pincer grip and builds their hand strength. They can use a clothespin to hang up clothes after washing, or we can put clothespins in a container and the child can affix them around the rim of the container or to a piece of cardboard or plastic. We can also have a line that they can affix things to, e.g., their art or cut-out felt cloth. The clothespins can be big to start with and gradually get smaller and smaller. A fun DIY is to use paint chips from a hardware store with a matching colored clothespin.
Stickers	Working with stickers, peeling them and sticking them, first anywhere on the paper and then on specifically designated spots, supports the development of the pincer grip, hand-eye coordination, and manual dexterity.
Arts and crafts activities and handwork	Scribbling, drawing, painting, collage, and modeling with play dough and different kinds of clay all support the development of fine-motor skills. Children can also trace stencils of shapes, letters, and patterns. (See page 258 for examples.) Handwork is also wonderful for fine-motor development including sewing, woodworking, modeling, knitting, and crocheting. (See page 259 for lots of handwork ideas.)

Other fine-motor-skill activities	• Latch board; busy board, box, or van.
	• Dressing frame—practicing zippers, buttons, buckles, etc.
	• Lacing model (we can also just use a shoe that is not being worn).
	• Tying bows—on doll clothes, with shoelaces or fabric belts.
	• Braiding rag doll, using three laces or ribbons attached to a surface.

LANGUAGE

Language is the basis of the human tendency for communication. It is how we convey information, express our feelings, ask for help, and listen to others. It is how we can keep safe, learn, share what we learn, and build relationships and culture. An environment rich in language will help our child develop their vocabulary and ability to express themselves.

LANGUAGE HELPS OUR CHILD:

• Order, classify, and categorize the world around them.

• Express themselves with exactness and precision when they have the vocabulary.

• Orient themselves by knowing the names of things and places.

• Abstract and share what they know, express what they imagine, and paint vivid pictures out loud—Dr. Montessori called language the "abstraction of intelligence."

• Give and receive directions and enhance the lessons and demonstrations we share with them.

• Comprehend the vastness of the universe in a story and explore big ideas in books; find information in encyclopedias; and explore people, places, and cultures far away.

The child from ages 0 to 6 years old is in the sensitive period for language. After the acquisition of language (between 0 and 3 years old), the 3- to 6-year-old is ready to refine their language. They do this by building their vocabulary. There is unlimited potential for the amount of vocabulary the child can acquire at this stage. They also refine their articulation, pronunciation, syntax, and grammar and become able to communicate not only through speech but also through written language.

From around 4 to 5 years old, they begin to really understand the power of language and the effect of their words on others. This is a good time to consciously begin to help them develop empathy.

The 6- to 12-year-old child uses language to express themselves with more precise and specific vocabulary; to debate or argue their view; to write down their ideas and document their experiences; and to use language in artistic ways such as through story (written and oral) and poetry.

Spoken language	**We can help our child build the ability to express themselves clearly, logically, and articulately. The ability to express themselves will build self-confidence, which will stay with them. Spoken language is also the foundation for written language.**
Conversations with us	Conversations are a great way to connect with our children, learn about their interests and experiences, and build strong bonds while also supporting their development. We can tell them about our day and what is going on in the world; have discussions about our thoughts and their thoughts and encounters; and answer their questions. They can learn to introduce themselves and members of their family to others and talk about their ideas and identity and those of others. We can listen and ask probing questions that require thought and expression and take the conversation further. Objects, books, art, pictures, magazines, and things seen from the window or in stores can be great initiators of conversations in which they can describe, introduce, and explain.
Conversations with others	These could include weekly phone or Zoom calls with grandparents or family friends. Resist the temptation to answer for children when they are asked questions.

Question games	Question games are used in a Montessori classroom to help the children organize their thoughts and add details to their stories. They can also be used at home. When our child tells us about an event or occurrence, we can help them add details and develop the story by asking What? Who? Where? When? Why? With whom? We then end by summarizing the information they have provided. We don't have to ask all the questions. We can observe when the child is still sharing excitedly and notice when they are losing interest; then we can summarize and move on.
Use rich language	When conversing, we can use rich and specific language. Don't be afraid to use big words as long as they are being used correctly and in context. Instead of saying "Do you need me right now?" we can say, "Do you need me urgently?"; instead of saying "Show me how you did it," we can say "Show me your technique"; instead of "hungry," try "famished"; instead of "thirsty," we could say "parched," and so on.
Sharing stories	Children love hearing our stories. These stories can provide opportunities for connection and new vocabulary. Bedtime, car rides, and long waits in the doctor's office are all opportunities to share stories. We can tell stories about ourselves or people in our lives, places we have visited, or world events or share fond memories or funny experiences. We can practice telling these stories with expression and interest. They do not have to be too long. We can start with shorter stories for younger children and keep the story within 10 minutes even for older children. We can be very descriptive and speak slowly so that our child can paint a mental picture as we tell the story. When we are done, our child might ask questions or express their thoughts. Or they may not, and that is fine, too. These stories are simply for them to digest and enjoy.

PERSONAL STORIES WE CAN TELL OUR CHILD:

- The day they were born
- Our favorite birthday gifts as a child
- The first time we went on a trip

Our child will learn that they can tell their own stories both from their experience and their imagination. Simone enjoyed writing these down for her children, and they still enjoy looking at them together, years later.

Reading books	Reading to our children also supports the development of language, especially when we choose books with relatable stories and also those that expand our child's horizons. The books can be fiction, but especially for children under 6, we can choose books that are realistic. That way, our child gets to hear familiar-sounding dialogue and descriptions of things they may have experienced or might one day experience. They hear and gain new vocabulary, and they see how stories can be shared with words and pictures. As the reader, we can use different voices, tones, pitches, and expressions to reflect the emotions and characters. We can start with short stories for younger children and move on to longer stories for older children. Folktales, fairy tales, and fantasy can be introduced when the child is old enough to distinguish between reality and fantasy, usually when they're over 5 years old.

When we read, we can introduce the names of the author and illustrator. We can also model how to handle the book with care. If the child wants some time to observe the illustrations and notice details, give them time to do so.

Reading and reciting poetry	Like books, poetry introduces our child to another form that language can take, a form that they would not usually hear in everyday conversation. It also introduces them to new vocabulary, styles, and syntax. Many poems include rhymes and are fun to read as well as compose. Listening to poetry can also inspire the child to create their own poetry. When choosing poetry to introduce to children, we can choose a variety of lengths, styles, and content. The excitement with which we present poetry to our children will rub off on them. Some examples:

- *A Family of Poems* by Caroline Kennedy
- *Joyful Noise: Poems for Two Voices* by Paul Fleischman
- *Malaika: A Poetry Collection for Children and Those Who Love Them* by Dike-Ogu Chukwumerije

Grammar and syntax	With time, children become more aware of grammar and syntax, but they might initially make mistakes with things like tenses and plurals. Rather than correcting them, we can model using the words correctly in our reply and, with older children, share any applicable rules at a later time. For example, "We use *an* when a word starts with a vowel: an owl, an orange." These errors usually resolve over time. If our child always answers questions with a single word, we can practice with them to incorporate the question or subject into their response. For example, to the question, "Where did you go?" instead of saying, "Outside," they can say, "I went outside."
Introducing nomenclature/ vocabulary	We can support the development of spoken language also by introducing nomenclature: the names of people, things, places, specific shapes, parts of an object. We can do this using the three-period lesson (see below). We can give names of real objects, replicas, and also things shown in pictures.
The three-period lesson to introduce nomenclature/ vocabulary	This is a technique used to introduce nomenclature (vocabulary) to children. It usually begins with a sensory experience. It could be the child looking at, touching, tasting, smelling, or listening to an object. When they have gained sensory knowledge, we give them language to attach to it. There are three stages to the three-period lesson. 1. *Association.* This is the connecting of sensory perception with the name. In this part of the lesson, we give the noun (the name of the object) with no article attached. For instance, "turmeric." The word is pronounced distinctly. 2. *Recognition.* This is when the child is given the opportunity to practice recognizing the object and connecting it with its name. It can be done by asking a question or making a request. For instance, "Please get me the turmeric," "Can you show me the turmeric?" "Please put the turmeric in the basket," or "Point to the turmeric." This stage reinforces the name and is where we spend the most time. We can see which words the child has mastered and which they are still learning. 3. *Remembrance or recollection.* This is when the child is required to remember the name of the object. This is done by asking "What is this?" and pointing. We do this when we have observed that they know the name in the second period above.
Command games	Giving the precise names of actions and playing command games where we give the child commands and they act on them can provide a lot of fun and laughter. We can start with one-word commands (e.g., blink, clap, jump, glide) and then give one-step sentence commands (e.g., touch your nose, reach up high) and then progress to more descriptive and elaborate commands, adding adjectives, adverbs, and multiple steps to the command (e.g., stand on your toes and reach high for the sun—now jump quickly!).
Rhyming and other games	We can play rhyming games where we choose a word and each person takes a turn calling out rhyming words. With older children, we can also play games where we choose a category and they take turns coming up with words that fall into that category. It can be animals, vehicles, places, or things found in a kitchen or a garden. We can add a challenge by having each person find a word that starts with the next letter of the alphabet or the last letter of the previous person's word. For children who have been introduced to parts of speech, we can do this with adjectives, prepositions, or adverbs.
Spoken language— skills for our older child	The older child can be supported to further develop their spoken language. We can practice with them and also model for them how to present an idea, argue a point, defend a stance, debate respectfully, or get information by formulating the correct questions.

| Writing | In the Montessori classroom, we introduce writing before reading as it is easier to sound out words to write them than to sound them out and then to synthesize them to read them. Our child will learn to read and write at school, but there are activities we can do at home to support them. Remember, we follow the child. Every child will develop on their own timeline. We do these activities with our child because they show an interest and enjoy them, not because we want to teach them to read early. Observe your child. If they begin to recognize their name; spot letters on signs, in books, and on labels; or ask what certain letters spell, they are ready for these activities. |

In Montessori, the primary purpose of writing is to document and communicate one's thoughts. It's quite exciting for a child to learn that if they write it down, someone else can read and understand their idea. To prepare our child for writing, we can:

- Prepare their minds by helping them develop their thoughts, vocabulary, and expression through spoken language (page 243).

- Prepare their hands for writing, which comes with practicing their fine-motor skills (page 241).

- Introduce them to the mechanics of words and writing.

Introducing the alphabet

When introducing the alphabet in Montessori, we start with the sounds of the letter, e.g., "cuh," rather than the names, e.g., the letter "c." This gives the child the ability to sound out many words they come across.

The sound game

To introduce letters, we can start with the sound game (with children from around 2.5 years). This is similar to playing "I spy," except we ask them to look for something starting with a sound; for example, "buh." This is one activity that we encourage playing at home to give the child lots of practice listening for the sounds they will need for writing and reading.

This is a game that helps the child realize that words are made up of individual sounds and also helps them learn to isolate the sounds in a word, which will be important when they start to write words.

According to *Montessori Read & Write* by Lynne Lawrence, there are six stages of the sound game.

1. (around 2.5 years) Take one object that the child already knows the name of, like a cup, and isolate it on a table or in our hands. "I can see something on this table that begins with 'cuh,'" or "I spy with my little eye something that begins with 'cuh'"; because there is only one object and the child knows the name "cup," they will make the connection. We can play this game over and over with many different objects until we can tell that they have grasped the idea. It can be made more difficult once they master single letters to add phonograms like "tr" for "tree" or "traffic light."

2. (around 2.5 to 3 years) Play the sound game with two or more objects with distinct first sounds like a cup and a pen. The game now involves the child discriminating to make a choice between the options. It might help to keep track of the sounds that our child identifies easily.

3. We can expand the child's area of exploration to a section of the room, the whole room, in the car, or outdoors. We can invite the child to find objects that start with a specific sound. When they find several examples with the same sound, like cup, can, and corn if playing in a kitchen, we can repeat the game with another sound.

4. (between 3.5 and 4.5 years old) The child identifies objects that begin with a specific sound and end with a specific sound. "I spy something that begins with 'cuh' and ends with 'tuh.'" We can play this first at level two, where we isolate some objects that they can choose from, and then at level three, where the span of exploration is increased.

5. Invite the child to identify all the sounds in the words they have previously analyzed. They can identify the first, middle, and last sounds. They can do it without necessarily seeing or finding the objects.

6. We invite the child to think of words that begin with a specific sound, contain a specific sound, and end with a specific sound. We can also go beyond the limits of the room or environment. We can also invite them to think of words within a specific category. "Can you think of an animal that starts with the sound 'sss'?" "Can you think of any of your friends whose name starts with the sound 'sss'?" It might help to include an example in our question: "I'm thinking of a name that starts with the sound 'sss,' like Sophie. Can you think of any other names that start with the sound 'sss'?"

The activities for spoken expression can be enhanced with some emphasis on sounds. We can choose poetry that highlights a specific sound or play rhyming games that focus on a specific sound.

Letters	When the child can recognize the sounds of letters, we can then introduce the written alphabet. Ideally, we've already created an environment that is text rich: framed quotes around our home, the child's name over their door, time spent reading the signs in our neighborhood, and reading books at home.

Ideally, we introduce the lowercase letters first, using the three-period lesson (see page 245).

We can give our child a lot of experience with the letters to reinforce their ability to identify the letter symbols. They can color in an outline of the letter, do seed collages of the letter, do letter hunts in the house. We can write the letter on Post-it Notes or cards and place them around the house for the child to find, or they can look on labels, pictures, and signs around the house. They can check in books or old magazines—they can circle or underline the letter—and point it out on signs around our neighborhood. |
| Activities to support letter recognition | • *Alphabet books.* We can provide alphabet stamps and a blank booklet in which the child can stamp the letter and draw, stamp, or paste pictures of an object that start with that sound.

• *Alphabet collection books.* We can provide a blank booklet for each letter and have the child fill each booklet with items that begin with each letter.

• *Sandpaper letters/letter rubbings.* Sandpaper letters are often used in Montessori classrooms and can be purchased or cut out of sandpaper found at a hardware store. The child can trace the letters with their fingers to get a sense of their shape. They can also create rubbings by laying a plain piece of paper over the sandpaper letter and rubbing the side of a crayon over it.

• *Knock-knock game.* We can play this game once our child can recognize letters. We can write three to five letters or sounds on individual cards. We can turn the cards face down. Then our child knocks, picks a card, and thinks of a word that begins with the sound. For example: "Knock knock." "Who's there?" "T!" "T who?" "T turtle!" |
| Building words | Once we observe that our child knows several sounds, including some vowels, they can begin to build words. (Junnifa usually introduces s, m, a, t, v, b, e, c, and f first.)

It is ideal to have a movable alphabet for word building: individual letters that can be placed to make words. This enables our child to write before they have complete control over their pencil. We can purchase simple plastic letters or letter magnets, or make our own letters on little cards. Our child can start building words within a category (like *pets*) and ideally, words that can be spelled phonetically. The child can increase the complexity of the words as they progress. If our child wants to build long, nonphonetic words before they seem ready, that's okay; the spelling will probably be wrong, but we don't need to correct them. The focus is on the sounds and allowing our child to express their thoughts.

When our child has mastered the basic sounds, we can then introduce digraphs (or phonograms) in the same way. These are one sound made by more than one letter; for example, ch, sh, th, ph, ae, ai, oi, and oy. |
| Writing | Lots of fine-motor-skill work, including tracing, working with clay, and cutting with scissors, prepares our child's hand for writing. Our child will also have seen us write their descriptions under their artwork, make shopping lists, and make notes in our notebook or journal. When our child is ready, at around 3.5 to 5 years old, we can provide a variety of materials to support the development of writing. (See the online appendix for a writing Starter Kit.) Ideally, our child will begin by practicing drawing letters on a chalkboard, which is easy to erase and allows for lots of trial and error. (Sand trays, sticks in the sandbox, or mud outside are also great for this.) Our child can start with letters and sounds and then move on to words. When the child is ready, they can transition to writing on paper with a pencil.

We can collaborate with them as necessary. For example, when they are writing a thank-you note, they can dictate what they want to say while we write it out. They can then decorate it, sign their name, put a stamp on the envelope, or contribute as much as they can. Another idea: Our child can dictate a story to us that we can write out, then read back to them.

As the child starts to write in sentences, they will need to learn how to space their words. We can show them how to use a finger to leave a space after each word. We can also show them how to use a line guide or rule lines to keep their writing straight. |

| Activities to support writing for our younger child | YOUNGER CHILDREN WILL ENJOY WRITING: |

YOUNGER CHILDREN WILL ENJOY WRITING:

- Labels for items around the house
- Lists—names of things, shopping lists, party plans
- Thank-you notes
- Directions
- Short stories
- Recipes
- Names on maps
- Answers to the question game introduced on page 244
- Commands for the command games on page 245
- Collaborative notes or sentences where we start a thought and they complete it

THEY'LL ALSO ENJOY MAKING DIFFERENT BOOKS:

- Alphabet books
- Counting books
- Collections of nouns by categories
- Collections of verbs
- Storybooks
- Recipe books
- Comic books
- Magazines—they can make these around their interests, like a favorite animal or book series

Activities to support writing for our older child

For older children, writing is a way to share their ideas and document their experiences and discoveries. We can support their writing by encouraging them to be creative, curious, and playful with words and language outside of the work they do in school. We can:

- Provide them with a thesaurus to use in finding synonyms or a dictionary to gain a deeper understanding of the meaning of words.
- Provide them with examples of a range of writing styles, help them analyze the difference in styles, and encourage them to create their own writing styles.
- Encourage them to write more elaborate and formal letters to friends, family, favorite authors, or even government officials.
- Provide them with different styles of poetry and encourage them to write their own.
- Provide them with a notebook and encourage them to keep a journal. They can start with the basics: the day of the week, the date, what time they woke up, meals they ate, the weather, some details about what they did and whom they saw, what time they went to bed. As they get older, they can add more details, ideas, and thoughts. They may also enjoy keeping a travel journal on vacations.
- Encourage creative writing by asking them to come up with stories. We can prompt them to develop characters, settings, plots, problems to be resolved, and twists.
- Introduce a word-collector book in which they write new and interesting words they encounter.
- Offer blank comic strip paper to write and draw their own comic strip.

Hand preference

We may wonder if our child is left- or right-handed. In Montessori, we offer to the midline and allow the child to work with both sides of the brain/body. We allow them to develop hand preference in their own time.

Writing skills for our older child	• Punctuation—we can introduce them to the different punctuation marks and their uses.

- Editing—we can guide them on how to edit their work and help them understand the importance of editing. It is helpful to have a simple editing checklist with which they can check their writing.

  ◦ Check that all sentences start with a capital letter and end with a period.

  ◦ Check that all the proper nouns—names and places-names—start with a capital letter.

  ◦ Check that items in lists are separated by commas.

- Grammar—we can invite them to be descriptive in their writing by using adjectives, adverbs, and precise vocabulary to add details and interest.

- Poetry—they can try different forms such as a couplet, quatrain, haiku, limerick, or cinquain.

- Writing a biography—this is a fun exercise that can be done for people, animals, and even inanimate objects. The child can use the following pattern:

  ◦ First name

  ◦ Last name

  ◦ Three adjectives

  ◦ Child of . . .

  ◦ Who loves . . .

  • Who fears . . .

  • Who needs . . .

  • Who gives . . .

  • Who would like to be . . .

  • Is a resident of . . .

- ABC—the child comes up with a word or line for each letter. They can challenge themselves to make each line rhyme or every two lines rhyme like a couplet.

- Researching—they can learn how to conduct research and write reports, how to summarize, quote, and how to cite references.

- Word studies—these will also expand the child's vocabulary and improve their writing. They can study and make games around affixes (prefixes and suffixes), homonyms, homophones, homographs, synonyms, and antonyms.

Writing Starter Kit	*Find this online at workman.com/montessori*

Reading	**Reading opens up the world (even the universe!) to children. Through reading, our child can travel through time and space, visit faraway places, meet people of different cultures, and learn about diverse topics and experiences. We want to support our children so they not only learn to read but also come to love and enjoy it.**

Reading together	We can start reading to our children when they are in the womb and continue to read to them even when they are able to read to themselves. They will absorb the pleasure we feel when we read to them and always reference that feeling when they read.

When we read to our children, we can:

- Point to the words as we read.

- Act out what we read.

- Use tone, emphasis, and inflection to add interest.

- Discuss the illustrations.

- Point out the page numbers and keep track as we read.

Reading together builds the child's vocabulary and familiarizes them with many words. This helps when they are starting to read for themselves and have to decode words; they will be able to decode faster or guess more accurately because they have heard a lot of words in context.

Create a reading environment	In addition to reading to our child, we can model a love for books by reading ourselves and also surrounding ourselves with books. We can also ensure that the child has access to rich, quality books. We want books that interest them, expand their experiences, stretch their imaginations, help them make sense of their lives, and encourage them to experience and understand the lives of other people whose circumstances may be different from their own. We can visit libraries and bookstores with our child and choose quality books. We can build reading into our lifestyle and family culture.
Path to independent reading	The journey to independent reading is the same as the journey to independence in other areas. It starts with dependence on the adult. We read to our child from birth until they are ready for the second stage. The second stage is collaborative, also known as guided reading. This is when they read with us. The youngest child can point to the pictures as we read. An older child might say the last word in each sentence or read the words that they recognize as we read the rest. Gradually, they read more, with us there providing support as needed. This stage requires patience and observation to know when to help and provide the word the child might be struggling with and when to wait patiently and let them try to figure it out. Some books might allow us to read one page and the child to read the next. When our child first starts trying to read, they might just recite from memory books that they have heard often. This is not a bad thing and is a normal part of the process. We should not discourage them. The third stage is independent reading, when the child is reading by themselves. The other two stages continue even when our child is able to read independently. We continue to read to them and read with them. They will go through different levels of books, tackling more challenging ones as they are able.
Reading simple words	When our child starts reading simple words (usually as they practice their writing), we can provide things for them to practice with, such as: • A small collection of items with phonetic names with labels to match to them. • Simple labels to read and use to label items around the house, on their bodies, or in a book (pen, fan, red, cup, sink, flag, shirt, socks, etc.). • Phonetic command labels to read and act out, like jump. These can increase in complexity as the child becomes more proficient. • Little notes for them to find and read. We want them to see writing and reading primarily as a way to communicate. • Phonetic flash cards that have pictures with sounds or those that have pictures with words to match.
Phonograms	When the child has mastered phonetic reading, we can start to introduce words that include phonograms (for example, "ch," "sh"), using similar activities.

Books to read

WHEN OFFERING BOOKS:

- We want to offer our child books that they can be successful with.

- We can choose books that have simple text with related illustrations that help the child predict or remember if they're struggling.

- The text should reflect their everyday, familiar vocabulary.

- Books with one or two sentences that have repetitive or predictive text on each page are ideal for this stage.

- The youngest reader can start with phonetic readers.

- They will enjoy books that they have heard many times.

- We can choose books based on their interests.

- Counting, alphabet, and song books are great options for a beginning reader.

- We can use the Goldilocks analogy. We want books that are not too easy and not too hard. We want them to be just right. A child will be able to read 95 percent of words on each page of a "just right" book.

- We can introduce guided reading. This is when we collaborate in reading. We sit beside them and help with the challenging words or read alternate pages.

- When trying new books, we can read to them first and then have them read to us. We can have them point to the words as they read and do the same when we read. The illustrations can clue them in when they are unsure.

- When we notice them guessing, we can encourage them to read each word, pointing to it as they go. Gradually, they will become more proficient and fluent. While building proficiency and fluency, they might enjoy reading to their siblings, dolls, or grandparents.

OLDER CHILDREN WHO KNOW HOW TO READ CAN EXTEND THEIR READING BY EXPLORING:

- Different genres

- Longer books

- Book series

- Historical books with different language structure

- Biographies

Puzzle words

As the child is practicing phonetic words, we can also start to introduce sight or puzzle words like *through* or *because*. These are words that do not sound how they look, and many of the ones we introduce to the child are used frequently and learned through repetition. Children who are frequently read to will see these often and will find them easier to remember.

Be patient

The process of reading is unique for each child. It requires us to be patient and enjoy the journey with our child. They will eventually learn to read. If we suspect any signs of a learning challenge, we can visit a specialist to have them assessed.

Teaching respect for books	When reading to children, we can consciously model treating the book with respect: lifting it up and putting it down carefully, flipping the pages consciously from the top or bottom corners instead of pushing the page or wrinkling it, putting the book back on the shelf when we're done with it instead of leaving it out or dropping it on the floor.

As the child gets older and starts to handle books independently, we can:

- Talk about the importance of books and treating them carefully.
- Teach them about the components of a book, including the dust jacket or cover, spine, and endpapers.
- Show them how to take it from the shelf and put it back with the spine showing so it is easy to locate.
- Show them how to use a bookmark to remember their page.
- Repeat any lesson when we see the need for it.

SENSORIAL DEVELOPMENT

Children need and seek out sensory experiences. We can provide them with these in purposeful ways. Many of the practical life activities we have discussed provide sensorial experiences.

We can help the child acquire ways to classify and categorize the sensorial impressions they receive. We allow them to explore specific sensorial qualities and then give them the specific language for these impressions, such as big, small, bigger, smaller, biggest, smallest. In the period from ages 3 to 6, the child refines their sensory perceptions. With practice, they become able to discriminate and distinguish; they observe and make judgments about similarities and differences. At first, they may grade the objects by trial and error. With practice, they'll be able to discriminate through careful use of their senses. There are specific materials for this in the Montessori classroom, but we do not need them at home; we can find opportunities for our child to refine their senses in our home environment.

Three-period lesson

They can learn the names of the sensorial impressions using the three-period lesson technique (see page 245) or from absorbing through use in daily life.

Sensorial experiences

VISUAL

- Size: height, width, length, thickness
- Shape
- Color: primary (red, blue, and yellow), secondary (orange, purple, green), tertiary colors, white, brown, black, gray, pink, and shades from lightest to darkest

AUDITORY

- Pitch
- Timbre (tone quality)
- Sound

OLFACTORY

- Scent (e.g., different spices or citrus smells)

GUSTATORY

- Sweet
- Bitter
- Salty
- Sour
- Umami

TACTILE

- Texture: rough, smooth
- Thermal: hot, warm, cold
- Barometric/Weight: heavy, light

Refining and classifying sensorial experiences	• Identifying objects by their characteristics:

- Identifying objects by their characteristics:
  - ◦ Listening game: "I have three objects that make three different sounds." The objects might be, e.g., a piece of paper being crumpled or torn, a spoon being tapped on the table, and a hammer hitting a piece of wood. Then the child identifies the objects based on the sound. We also can do this for color (e.g., identifying fruits by their colors) or even taste (e.g., identifying citrus fruits by sweet, sour, bitter).
  - ◦ Stereognostic game: This game involves the stereognostic sense, the sense of touch when we can identify an object without looking at it. Place several items that feel different in a bag; the child puts their hand in and tries to identify an object before pulling it out; they can also pull out an object requested by another child. Suggest variations where the objects are paired or arranged by a theme.
- Sorting items by their characteristics.
- Matching items with similar characteristics.
- Matching things that go together. This can be real objects, like lids to their containers, or pictures of items like a pen and paper or a paintbrush and paint.
- Grading items by their qualities, e.g., shortest to tallest or quietest to loudest.
- Matching at a distance; e.g., we show them a yellow tile, and they cross the room to find the matching yellow tile.
- Treasure hunts/finding items with similar qualities. We could say, "Go outside and find as many things as you can that are red or this long."
- Patterning: color, shapes, sounds, textures.
- Sequencing: pictures in a story, ingredients for cooking or baking.
- Finding comparatives (e.g., hotter and colder) and superlatives (e.g., hottest and coldest).
- We can add challenge by using a blindfold to do the previous activities.
- Labeling items by their qualities, including comparatives and superlatives.
- Measuring items and comparing, such as by:
  - ◦ Measuring the length or height of furniture, people, or distances with a ruler or tape measure.
  - ◦ Measuring weights—of food items, people, books—using a scale. The child can guess which items are closest to each other in weight and measure to check.
  - ◦ Tracking the daily temperature.
- Older children can:
  - ◦ Find the average, mean, mode, or median for a group of items (we might need to look these up ourselves!).
  - ◦ Calculate the area of rooms.
  - ◦ Collect data—favorites, ages, heights—and analyze or graph them.

Sorting, matching, and grading

- Some things that we can sort, match, and grade include beads, buttons, blocks, toys, grains, seeds, clothes, shoes, socks, utensils, fruits, vegetables, leaves, flowers, cutlery, paper, pictures, paper clips, hair accessories, rubber bands, nuts and bolts, and locks and keys. In Montessori classrooms, we don't use sensory bins because we find so many opportunities for exploring the senses with objects already around us.

| Other sensorial experiences | • Following the sound. Children close their eyes, we make a sound—maybe clap or ring a bell—and they have to point to the direction where the sound is coming from. |

• Following the sound. Children close their eyes, we make a sound—maybe clap or ring a bell—and they have to point to the direction where the sound is coming from.

• Taking a listening walk to try to identify what sounds they hear, like a bird cooing, a leaf rustling, or the wind blowing.

• Going on a nature treasure hunt for objects, colors, or shapes.

• Finding as many items of a certain color that they can in our home and grading them from lightest to darkest.

• Playing "I spy" with colors, shapes, or sizes. This can also be done on the bus or in a car.

• Going on treasure hunts in the home. We can challenge them to find all the squares they can, all the curved lines, all the cubes, any rough surfaces, any smooth surfaces.

• Picking an item and having the child describe it with as many sensorial attributes as they can and as many descriptive adjectives as they can.

• Teaching them the names of different materials, textures, smells, senses, tastes, colors, shapes, weights, and temperatures.

• Identifying a song by listening to someone humming the tune.

• Finding similar sounds, smells, and tastes. "This sound is similar to _____."

• Exploring colors by doing some color-mixing activities with primary colors, secondary colors, and tertiary colors. The child can also do some tinting and shading to further explore grading of colors. Mixing colors of handmade play dough is also a beautiful way to discover that yellow and red make orange.

• Nesting boxes or bowls to stack or nest in order. They can be hidden around the room, and the child finds the next size and brings it to us.

• Searching for items while blindfolded.

• Listening to music.

• Learning to play instruments, which tunes the ears to different pitches and timbres.

• Filling glasses with water up to different heights and tapping with a spoon to observe the different sounds.

• Collecting an even number of spice containers or jars and filling up pairs with the same item (e.g., salt, sand, beans, rice, coins). The containers should not be transparent and can be wrapped if necessary. Then they are mixed up and the child tries to find each pair by shaking the jars.

We can find time to prepare some of these activities for our child, but many can happen during the normal course of practical life. For example, when we do laundry, we can ask our child to sort the clothes by color, fabric, texture, or type.

GEOGRAPHY, HISTORY, AND NATURAL SCIENCES

Our children love to learn about the world around them, past, present, and future. We can learn about our local area and follow any of our child's interests. If it's possible for our family, traveling is a great way to give our children the world. We can travel with them and also share our travel experiences with them through stories, souvenirs, and books.

These subject areas can be taken is so many directions but here are a few ideas to get started:

Earth and globe	· Learn about hemispheres.
	· Study compasses and learn the cardinal directions (north, south, east, west).
	· Explore Earth by studying and making maps. We can get map puzzles for the individual continents, especially our own continent.
	· Trace map pieces or stencils and cut or poke them out.
	· Draw the continents, countries, or states and label them with their names. Older children can add additional details, like the capital city.
	· Explore oceans, seas, lakes, and rivers.
	· Study flags, make a flag book, or make a map and color each country as its flag.
	· Research—people, food, landmarks, clothing, languages, architecture, animals, biomes, flora, fauna, art, music, and religions. Children, animals, and food are often good places to start.
	· Further the research by:
	◦ Cooking meals from the places
	◦ Making models of the places, people, and things
	◦ Sewing clothes or making paper dolls
Landforms	· Learn about the different kinds of landforms (islands, lakes, peninsulas, gulfs, isthmuses, straits, capes, bays).
	· Make models in a sandpit or by using clay, paint, sand, or paper.
	· Bake a cake or cookies in the shape of a landform. Color half of the batter or dough to represent water.
	· Make booklets or charts. Younger children can illustrate and label them with names, while older children can add a description or definition.
	· Find landforms on the globe and on the maps of different continents and countries.
	· Identify the biggest examples of each landform in our own city, state, and country, and on our continent and other continents.
Astronomy	· Solar system—read books, make and hang mobiles, do puzzles, make models.
	· Learn, identify in the night sky, and draw constellations.
	· Space—explore inventions and technologies developed for space exploration, such as spacesuits, rovers, telescopes, satellites, and the International Space Station; black holes; astronauts.
	· Rocks—research asteroids, meteoroids, meteorites, comets, moon rocks, impact craters.
	· Moon—moon phases, surface features, moon exploration, moon buggies.
Weather	· Seasons
	· Clouds
	· Rainbows

History	• Tell stories about the child's life.
	• Make a timeline of their life.
	• Make a family tree.
	• Help them research people and topics of interest.
	• Explore music, art, and dance around the world.
	• Study various beliefs around the world.
	• Discuss how people have met their fundamental needs (for nourishment, clothing, housing, transportation, defense) through time.
	• Explore interdependencies by coming up with a list of all the people who might have been involved in the production of their favorite piece of clothing or something they ate.
Botany and gardening	**We can engage our children in planting and growing seeds from fruits (e.g., it is fun to watch an avocado grow); plants from leaf cuttings; vegetables (potatoes, celery, carrots, yams) and alliums (onions, garlic) from scraps; herbs; bulbs. They will also love to build a terrarium. Below are other botany and gardening activities to explore with our child.**
Caring for plants	They will enjoy watering and misting; weeding; cleaning and washing leaves; cutting dead leaves and pruning; making and applying manure; crushing eggshells and adding to the compost; collecting scraps for the compost.
Observing and learning about parts and types of plants	• Look at plants and weeds to learn about their parts and their relationships: leaves, roots, stems, flowers, seeds.
	• Examine and learn the names of the parts of a leaf, root, stem, flower, and seed. Notice if all plants have all of the parts.
	• Draw plants in a nature journal or press samples in a leaf press.
	• Identify plants by leaves, flowers, bark.
	• Classify types of leaf by shape—such as cordate (heart-shaped) or flabellate (fan-shaped)—and arrangement. Can learn tree names and do a hunt to find examples.
	• Dissect a plant.
	• Make a chart or booklet of the plant parts.
	• Explore seed dispersal.
	• Dig up plants with similar leaves and see if they have similar roots.
Preserving plants	• Press flowers in a press.
	• Use petals to make scented water or perfume.
	• Sew petals or dry herbs into pouches to make sachets.
	• Create a nature table, jar or box.
Studying plant needs and characteristics	• Plant beans in different conditions—with and without water, light, soil, warmth.
	• Grow potatoes in the dark.
	• Explore plant experiment books.
	• Choose a plant to observe through the seasons. Write down observations about leaf color, shedding, flowering, fruiting, and animals feeding on it.

Researching plants	• Study specific plants or specimens—describe them, draw them, document changes to them over time, look up and write down interesting information about them.
	• Learn about seasonal plants.
	• Focus on regional plants by biome or geographic area.
Botany Starter Kit	*Find this online at workman.com/montessori*
Zoology	• Visiting an aquarium
	• Setting up a bird feeder
	• Finding tadpoles and frogs
	• Using a bug viewer
	• Going on insect/spider hunts (we can use an identification chart if we live somewhere with dangerous insects or spiders)
	• Raising chickens
	• Finding butterfly eggs and watching their life cycle
	• Building models of animals and insects
	• Using binoculars for bird-watching and on nature walks
	• Studying anatomical models and books
	• Exploring the differences and similarities between animal bodies and human bodies
	• Studying any animals of interest
Examples of some science experiments	• Sink and float experiments
	• Magnetic and nonmagnetic objects
	• Density of liquids—water, oil, and honey arranging themselves
	• Viscosity and fluidity—which liquid moves faster?
	• Different ways of combining—water and salt/sugar, water and sand/chalk, water and alkaseltzer, milk, and vinegar
	• Effect of heat on different materials—ice, wax, butter, etc.
	• Making crystals
	• Gravity—working out what will drop first: paper or a rock or another object
	• Condensation and evaporation—observing how condensation builds up when a lid is placed on a saucepan, or what happens when a container is left outside overnight
	• Making different weather instruments
Science Starter Kit	*Find this online at workman.com/montessori*

ART AND CREATIVITY

Open-ended art activities and projects are ideal for younger children, and we focus on the process over the product. We can be conscious of the way we give feedback about our child's art (refer to page 96 about giving feedback). We can model creating and enjoying art. Art can be a lovely way to spend time with our child. Think of how to display and store our child's creations—on the wall, strung on ropes with clothespins, in albums, portfolios, or photo books featuring pictures of each year's work.

Drawing	• Drawing, scribbling, open-ended drawing.
	• Drawing with different materials—oil or chalk pastels, charcoal, crayon, pencil.
	• Stencil tracing or drawing—shapes, animals, vehicles, nature; there are probably stencils for any subject that interests the child. We can also print out any outline onto sturdy paper and cut it out to make a stencil.
	• Guided drawing, using step-by-step drawing books. Some children enjoy these.
	• Drawing still lifes, self-portraits, and portraits of humans or animals. It can be helpful to draw from a picture of the person or thing at first, instead of using a mirror or live subject, as the subject is then stationary for them to draw.
	• Zentangling—making doodles, drawings, and patterns from dots, lines, and curves.
	• Symmetry drawing.
	• Shadow or silhouette drawing: We can put an object or person in front of a light source or window and outline the shadow or silhouette.
Painting	• Exploring colors—primary, secondary, tertiary.
	• Mixing colors, including tints and shades.
	• Painting by numbers or letters.
	• Painting on paper or canvas, at a table or easel.
	• Painting with different media—watercolors, tempera paint, and acrylic paints. These can be explored on different kinds and colors of papers.
	• Abstract painting.
	• Painting an object, scene, or person.
	• Marble painting; coffee filter–paper painting.
Collage	• Use paper, leaves, fabric, seeds, feathers, googly eyes, glitter, sequins, pom-poms.
	• Collect pictures and combine them to make Picasso-style collage art or mixed-media art.
	• Add letters cut out from the newspaper.
Beading	• Explore using paper beads or clay beads or make their own beads out of paper, clay, or felt.
	• Make different things with beads: bracelets and necklaces, earrings, bags, and bowls.
Printing	• Make prints with a leaf, a sponge, an onion, fruit, found items, or a shape carved into a potato.
	• Make fingerprint and hand art.
Rubbing	• Use a crayon to rub the imprint of a coin or leaf onto paper.
	• Make texture art by finding different textures around the house and rubbing them side by side on the same piece of paper. Can use the same or a different crayon color.
Mixed media	• Combine various media.
3D and other crafting	• Build models using papier-mâché or salt dough.
	• Make recycled art using toilet paper rolls, milk or juice boxes, plastic bottles, bottle caps, fabric scraps, food containers, lids, paper, and foil.
	• Make recycled paper.
	• Create nature art and mandalas using leaves, petals, flowers, rocks, and twigs.
Folding and cutting	• Do origami.
	• Try kirigami (a variation of origami in which the paper is cut as well as folded).

Art and artist appreciation	• Explore various artists' styles and try to replicate them. We can put up postcards of one artist's work weekly, biweekly, or monthly.
	• Collect examples of different styles from different artists; they can explore and try to create their own art in that style.
	• Visit local markets and galleries to see the work of local artisans.
	• Collect art for our home to appreciate and support Indigenous artists, emerging artists, and local artists.
	• Explore the intersection of art with history, geography, math.
	• Go to art galleries with a sketchbook; do a treasure hunt.
Performance art	We can offer various opportunities for performance art: puppet theaters using sock puppets, finger puppets, shadow puppets, and origami puppets; plays; debates; dances; poetry and spoken word performances; and comedy.
Art Starter Kit	*Find this online at workman.com/montessori*
Handwork	**Finger knitting, crochet, knitting, beading, needlework, sewing, embroidery, woodworking, sculpting with wire, weaving, soap carving, papier-mâché, and so on. Ideally, we can start with those that we enjoy ourselves or maybe learn alongside our children. Handwork is wonderful for their fine-motor-skill development, concentration, and creativity. It can also be very relaxing; they may choose to make something for a cause, like knitting squares for charity, and it can be a social activity when done in a group.**
Sewing	Sewing is a great activity for children from ages 3 to 12 years old. It supports the development of concentration and independence. It also supports the development of all the facets of fine-motor skills and is a practical skill that will serve the child throughout life. Sewing skills can be introduced gradually and scaffolded as the child acquires each skill. Here are some suggestions for developing sewing skills:
	• Threading a shoelace through perforated holes. The perforated holes can be on a piece of cardboard. Choose a shoelace with a narrow tip to fit through the holes or look for sewing cards.
	• A tapestry needle can be used to sew lines on cardboard. Holes can be poked or perforated or marks made so the child knows where the needle goes. We can start with a diagonal line, then a shape, and then the child might enjoy making simple paper purses. We can introduce running stitches and whipstitches.
	• We can show them how to sew on a button. This can be done on a strip of felt and made into a bracelet with a button closure (also great for buttoning and unbuttoning practice). They can also sew buttons onto any fabric. They can start with two-holed buttons, then move on to four-holed buttons and other kinds of buttons. When they have mastered sewing on buttons, they can sew buttons on a bag or cloth to decorate it.
	• The child can go on to improve their running stitches and whipstitches and learn other kinds of stitches.
	• Felt is an ideal fabric for beginning projects. Children can make wallets, softies, finger puppets, bookmarks, key chains, and many other items.
	• As their skills improve, they can start to sew with cotton and other fabrics. They can make pillows, bags, stuffed animals, doll clothes and accessories, and beanbags. Buttons can be used to make eyes or as decoration.
	• An older child may be interested in learning to use a sewing machine.

Knitting and crochet	Knitting and crochet support hand-eye coordination, manual dexterity, the development of the pincer grip, and creativity. Finger knitting can be introduced to 3- to 4-year-olds. They can use their fingers or a knitting fork, also called a lucet. Knitting with two needles can be introduced at around 4.5 to 6 years old. We prefer to introduce knitting before crochet to allow children to persevere to first master the challenge of knitting. Crochet can then be introduced to make dishcloths, doilies, necklaces, and then more complicated projects like amigurumi (small, stuffed yarn creatures).
Weaving	Weaving is great for hand-eye coordination and building concentration because it usually involves a repeating pattern, and to follow and repeat specific processes requires some alertness and focus while also being relaxing. There are so many different kinds of weaving that can be introduced to children at different stages: PAPER WEAVING • They can make simple squares or rectangles that can become place mats. • An older child can make baskets. YARN WEAVING • They can use straws to make a basket. • They can learn about and use sticks to weave an ojo de dios, a weaving on two crossed sticks. A younger child can start with two sticks and increase the number of sticks and patterns with proficiency. LOOM WEAVING • There are many different kinds of looms—vertical, horizontal, rectangular, circular. • We can purchase a loom, or an older child can make their own with cardboard, pieces of wood and some nails, or even an old picture frame. • They can learn how to weave different items. • It might be interesting to research weaving and looms around the world or through time.
Woodworking	Woodworking builds hand-eye coordination, strengthens hands, and builds manual dexterity and the pincer grip. Here are some woodworking ideas: • A young child can start with hammering nails. • They can also use tools like screwdrivers and wrenches. • Sanding wood also strengthens the hands. • The child can work on simple projects and then progress to more complicated ones like building miniature furniture or designing their own houses. • They can make yarn or rubber-band art, which involves hammering nails in a specific shape and then using yarn or bands to connect them. • A lot of geometry concepts—shapes, angles, diagonals, vertices—can be further explored through woodworking.
Woodworking Starter Kit	*Find this online at workman.com/montessori*
Modeling	There are many different modeling media, including play dough, clay, plasticine, modeling clay, beeswax, papier-mâché, and wire. All of these build hand strength, manual dexterity, and other aspects of fine-motor skills. Children will enjoy making their own play dough. (Find our favorite recipe in the online appendix.) Start with using their hands, then explore using different tools. First engage in open-ended exploration and then try to make or replicate specific models. Do wet and needle felting.

Handwork ideas for 6- to 12-year-olds

Older children can work on specific projects and can use handwork to express or explore what they know about topics of interest. They can build models of civilizations they have studied, make drawings or knitted items to reflect geometric concepts, or explore the art and handicrafts of different people around the world. They can also try higher levels of the handwork described earlier, like cross-stitch, embroidery, and other needlework as an extension of sewing; candle making and sculpting as an extension of modeling; and building furniture and other items as an extension of woodworking.

MEMORY

The memory supports every area of learning, and we can offer our child activities to build their memory by:

- Giving them multistep directions to act on
- Creating distance games to extend matching by attributes (e.g., the matching games mentioned in the sensorial section on page 252)
- Telling them a story and having them retell the story to us
- Asking them to memorize rhymes, poems, songs, passages, or religious scriptures (if applicable)
- Arranging some things on the table for the child to look at and then going to another room or closing their eyes and trying to list as many as they can remember
- Observing a picture together, like an illustration in a picture book, then closing the book or turning the picture face down and trying to remember as many things as we can from the picture
- Arranging some items on the table, asking the child to close their eyes, taking away one item, then asking them to open their eyes and see if they tell us which one was removed
- Playing memory games
- Doing spot-the-difference activities

MUSIC

Music is a form of expression and another language. We can expose our children to different kinds of music and give them opportunities to build skills around music.

Music appreciation

- Have a music player and a collection of different genres of music, including classical, that they can explore.
- Have an old record player and records to listen to.
- Make playlists for the family.
- Attend concerts and other events where we can enjoy music.
- Introduce any special music related to our family's culture.

Researching and studying music

- Read books about composers.
- Study composers.
- Introduce our child to the rich art of music. Attend concerts, listen to music at bedtime or on Sunday mornings while having breakfast, or play records on Sunday evenings.
- Learn to read music or practice solfège, i.e., do, re, mi, fa, so, la, ti, do.
- Explore instruments: of the orchestra, from around the world, and from musical categories.

Playing music	• Learn to play an instrument.
	• Use percussion instruments to explore rhythms.
	• Learn about different tempos and volume.
Dance and movement	• Free movement and expression
	• Ballet, modern dance, break dancing, etc.
Singing	• Traditional children's songs
	• Songs from our culture/religion/other
	• Songs that we hear on the radio
	• Songs with actions for younger children

MATH AND NUMERACY

Dr. Montessori believed that humans, including children, have a mathematical mind that notices differences and relationships between things. It pays attention to details and notices patterns and sequences. It is how we are able to plan our day, anticipate our bill at the grocery store, and know how far to reach when we want to pick up something. This mind is the foundation for mathematics, which is an abstraction of these relationships. To support our child's development with math, we can first support the use and development of the mathematical mind and can also help our child understand and build proficiency with math concepts.

Provide opportunities to observe	This might include watching the sun rise, watching birds build a nest, tracking a plant's growth over time, or watching shadows change shape throughout the day. Our children might spontaneously wonder about the process and ask questions, or we can seed their curiosity by wondering aloud and inviting them to think and wonder along. "I wonder what happens to the sun when we can't see it." "I wonder how long the shadow will be in an hour."

These opportunities to wonder invite the child to use their mathematical mind, to think logically, to try to figure it out. The goal is not necessarily to find the answer but to inspire curiosity. If the child is interested, we can guide them in researching and gathering more information about the questions.

Provide opportunities to estimate and make judgments	• All through food preparation, the child is estimating: Do I have enough water to fill my measuring cup? How much flour do I need to scoop to fill up the remaining space in the cup?
	• When playing, they will also estimate, for example, to figure out how far away to stand when they throw a ball into a basket, how much force to apply, and in what direction to throw.
	• Working with puzzles, as they figure out which piece fits in which space, they are estimating area and perimeter.
	• When preparing and serving a snack or lunch for multiple people, they might estimate how many pieces are needed in total and how much to give to each person.
	• When watering plants, they estimate how much water each plant needs, depending on the size of the pot or the plant.
	• In daily life, there are also opportunities for estimating, like how many cookies, erasers, or buttons it would take to fill up a certain container.

Patterning and sequencing	• Stringing beads
	• Pattern blocks
	• Playing clapping games
	• Sequencing pictures from a story
	• Finding differences between two similar pictures
Sorting, matching, and grading	• See activities for this in the sensorial area on page 252. All the sensorial work is a preparation for math.
Problem-solving	• Taking apart an object, such as a pen, a flashlight, or an old electronic item, to figure out how it works
	• Finding solutions to simple problems: wedging unstable furniture, finding something the right height to climb to reach something they need
	• Figuring out what size of paper they need for a project or for making a book
Counting and number sense	• Counting
	◦ While climbing stairs, how many cars drive past us, while skipping, etc.
	◦ Rote counting forward and backward. Note that knowing their numbers is different from counting. A child may be able to rattle off 1, 2, 3 . . . [know how to rote count] but not know how many things are in front of them [understand quantity]. By practicing counting, they will consolidate both skills, too.
	◦ Count the number of Legos or blocks used to build something—they can see how it gets taller as they add a piece.
	• Command activities including numbers
	◦ For example, clap ten times, blink five times, gather four erasers, find six flowers.
	◦ Pick a certain number of items from the shelves when shopping.
	◦ See how many of a given object they can find in our home—pillows, scissors, blue boxes, etc.
Number identification	• Hang number charts.
	• Identify numbers in books, on signs and mailboxes, in house addresses, in pictures.
	• Do number treasure hunts.
	• Memorize our address and phone number.
	• Order numbers.
	• Lay out number flash cards and put them in order.
	• Answer questions like what number comes after 4 and before 6. We don't do this to test them but to have fun. If they don't know or they get it wrong, we can make a mental note to practice counting from 1 to 10 at another time.
Counting and making associations with symbols	• Number cards with items to count and match them to items like toothpicks, matchsticks, rocks, buttons, and beads.
	• Differentiate odd from even numbers.
	• Invite an older child to count the money and pay in the grocery store.
	• Recite and sing counting rhymes and songs; read counting books; count items in illustrations.
	• Use a calendar to encourage counting. Each day the child can count up from the first day of the month to the day's date.

Writing numbers	• Young children around 3.5 to 4 years old can practice writing the numbers 1 through 9. They can learn this before learning to write the alphabet or concurrently.
	• They can write on chalkboards or in sand trays, with a stick in the dirt, with paint, with a pencil on paper.
	• When they master writing these numbers, they can combine them to form teens and other numbers.
	• Making calendars is a good way to practice writing numbers purposefully. Children can make a calendar each month and cross off the days as they pass; older children can write something interesting about each day. This is also a nice way to track improvements in their writing skills.
	• They can make counting books and illustrate them with drawings or stickers.
	• 4.5- to 5-year-olds can work on 1 through 100.
	• 5- to 6-year-olds can work on 1 through 1,000.
	• A number roll is fun to make. This is a series of strips of paper around 1 inch (3 cm) wide and 12 inches (30 cm) long on which the child writes numbers vertically, beginning at 1 and working on it a few strips a day, then attaching the strips together. The strip grows longer and longer until they reach their final number, usually 100.
Working with the decimal system (around 4.5 to 5.5 years old)	• Naturally introduce the idea of zero. Point out when something is empty. Talk about how there are zero cookies left in the box or zero words left to read of the book.
	• Play the zero game: Tell the child to do something a number of times and then eventually zero times. "Jump two times. Jump five times. Jump zero times." We might have to model a few times before they get it.
	• Read books about zero, like *Zero the Hero* or *Zero Is the Leaves on the Tree*.
	• Introduce the numbers 1, 10, 100, and 1,000. Point out how many zeros each has. In a Montessori classroom, golden beads are used for these lessons, but there are also other commercial materials available for exploring this concept.
	• Introduce all the members of the units, tens, hundreds, and thousands. Each of them has only nine members or possibilities:
	◦ 1, 2, 3, 4, 5, 6, 7, 8, 9 (units)
	◦ 10, 20, 30, 40, 50, 60, 70, 80, 90 (tens)
	◦ 100, 200, 300, 400, 500, 600, 700, 800, 900 (hundreds)
	◦ 1,000, 2,000, 3,000, 4,000, 5,000, 6,000, 7,000, 8,000, 9,000 (thousands)
	• Play "bring me" games where we request a number and the child brings it to us:
	◦ We can start with requesting from only one category: "Give me five units."
	◦ We can increase the challenge by asking for two categories and then three categories.
	◦ We can show how to combine categories and name them; for example, 6 tens and 4 units makes 64.
	◦ When the child has mastered this and also how to write, we can dictate numbers to them and then they can write the numbers.
	• Write a number and have them read it out to us.

Introduce operations (around 5 to 6 years old)	• Addition is putting together.
	• Subtraction is taking away.
	• Multiplication is putting the same quantity together several times.
	• Division is sharing equally.
	• It is best to introduce these concepts in concrete ways:
	◦ If I gave you two cookies and Biendu gave you three more, how many cookies would you have all together?
	◦ If you had seven balloons and you gave Metu one, how many would you have left?
	◦ If five of us each put three marbles in a jar, how many marbles would we have put in all together?
	◦ There are twelve chocolates in a box and there are four of us; how many chocolates would each of us get?
	• Snack preparation provides a lot of opportunities to explore operations.
Math facts	• We can provide opportunities to practice memorizing basic facts like times tables. Children can use Legos, rocks, or buttons initially and then recite the times table from memory. Play games to reinforce math facts. Lay cards face down. Two people pick cards and then try to say the sum, difference, product, or quotient.
	• Ideas for memorizing math facts:
	◦ Color by facts—the child does a sum to work out what color to make that area of the picture.
	◦ Chains of knowledge—these are paper chains that we or our child can make. On each link of paper, there is a math fact based on one number, such as 2 × 2 = 4. Each subsequent paper link has a math fact related to 4.
	• Multiples paper—circling all the multiples of 9, etc.
Fractions	• Sharing—an egg, a pizza, a piece of fruit, a cake, a cookie, a pack of juice.
	• Folding—napkins, paper.
	• Baking provides a lot of opportunities to explore fractions. The child can use measuring cups and spoons to explore the relationship between whole numbers and fractions. They can halve, quarter, or double a recipe.
Geometry	• Learn the names of various shapes—2D and solids. We can start with *triangle* and get more specific—*scalene triangle*, *isosceles triangle*—as the child gets older.
	• Make a model with straws and yarn, cardboard, or toothpicks.
	• Make a chart or book of shapes.
	• Hunt for the shapes in your home—a can or cup in the kitchen for a cylinder, a plate for a circle, a ruler for a rectangle. An older child can write a list or make a book. They can also use this for data to graph/analyze. Compare how many examples they found for each shape.
	• Use stencils of various shapes to trace and make patterns.
	• Draw or paint shapes.
	• Explore shapes and their relationships with Magformers, Magna-Tiles, blocks, etc.
	• Play with tangram sets.
	• Draw by using shapes.

Telling time	• Introduce the parts of an analog clock.

Telling time

- Introduce the parts of an analog clock.
- Show how the clock is laid out: twelve numbers with the 12 point also being the 0 or o'clock point.
- Help the child draw a clock or make a clock with moving parts of paper or straws or sticks.
- Introduce the hour or *o'clock*. We can explain that whenever the long hand is on 12, it is *o'clock*. We look to see what number the short hand is pointing to and call it first and add *o'clock*.
- Introduce *half past*, which is when the long hand is pointing to 6. We look at what number the short hand is pointing to, then say "half past" before that number.
- Introduce *quarter to* and *quarter past*.
- Read books about telling the time.
- Make a timeline of the child's day.
- Make a book about the child's day, indicating what they do at different times.
- Discuss concepts of time, like yesterday, tomorrow, and next week. These can be introduced at any age. For a while, children will use words like *yesterday* for any time in the past and *tomorrow* for any time in the future. We don't need to correct them, but we can respond with the correct usage for them to absorb: "Yes, we saw them at the park 2 weeks ago." We can use it correctly, and over time it will correct itself.

CONNECTING WITH AND FEEDING EARTH

Montessori children are connecting to the world and universe around them through exploration with their hands and minds. Through cosmic education, they learn that all living things have a purpose and deserve respect. They are appreciating and caring for nature (including the flora and fauna) and their community. They are becoming social citizens of the world. They are learning to think globally and act locally. And they are coming to realize that we and the world around us are all interconnected.

We may get to witness moments when, for example, they carefully collect eggs from a chicken, carry a worm on the road to safety, make a habitat for insects, write a letter to the local government about starting a neighborhood vegetable garden, or make a sign for a rally for the climate.

We can introduce our family to ideas like regeneration. This is how we look for ways to leave the Earth and our community better than we found it. It's looking beyond green alternatives, which still consume resources, and even beyond climate-neutral solutions for which there is a net effect of zero on the planet. It includes but goes further than reusing (repurposing items, from cardboard to clothing), reducing (learning to use less resources), and recycling (allowing resources to be made into a new item). It's about working to benefit Earth and heal the damage to natural systems.

We could explore permaculture in our home or community; collect rainwater; use a compost bin or worm farm; preserve, protect, and restore our local habitats; grow pollinating gardens to encourage bee communities; join a community garden; bake our own bread, make our own jam, and preserve fruits and vegetables; be involved in a beach cleanup; improve the soil quality in our schoolyards; help our school become a zero-waste school; campaign to stop the use of plastics in the community; or join people in our community or global community who are making a difference.

Bigger projects in the family could involve producing our own energy and improving our home design to need less heating and cooling. We might also work with our school community to connect with schools in other parts of the world to share experiences, ideas, and solutions.

Rather than making these efforts top-down, we can solicit ideas from our children. What are they interested in? Can they be involved in the research? Then we can make a plan together to effect change.

THE GREAT LESSONS

The Great Lessons are fables developed by Dr. Montessori to spark the 6- to 12-year-old child's imagination about the universe and to connect the different aspects of the cosmos.

There are 5 great stories

- the beginnings/creation of the universe (Geography and Science)
- the coming of life to earth (Botany and Zoology)
- the coming of man (History)
- the history of language
- the history of math

These stories give context to the child's learn and stoke an appreciation for man's conquests and creations through time.

Refer to the online appendix "Introduction to the Great Lessons" for more.

OPEN-ENDED CREATIVE PLAY

Children enjoy open-ended play that allows them to explore reality in different ways. We can support this interest. Various materials can be available to allow these creative explorations like building, counting, and making up their own stories. Some examples would be:

- Farm and animals
- Dollhouse
- Kitchen
- Airport or garage and vehicles
- Train tracks
- Blocks—unit blocks, Keva or Kapla planks, logs, architectural blocks
- Marble runs
- Building sets with connectors and rods.
- Lego
- Magna-Tiles

BOARD AND CARD GAMES

We can also build a selection of games for our family to use. Here are some of our favorites:

CLASSIC BOARD GAMES

- Chutes and Ladders
- Chess
- Scrabble
- Monopoly
- Candy Land

COOPERATIVE GAMES

- Max (the Cat)
- A Walk in the Woods
- Orchard

LITERACY GAMES

- Shopping List
- Match and Spell
- Alphabet Lotto
- Bananagrams

MATH GAMES

- Yahtzee
- Ligretto
- Rummikub

LETTER TO PARENTS, CAREGIVERS, AND LOVED ONES
FROM YOUR CHILD

To my lovely parents, grandparents, caregivers, and loved ones:

I appreciate your love. I see you always doing your best to love and raise me, and so I want to share some ideas from my perspective.

Please accept me for who I am. I know that you have dreams you'd like me to fulfill and that that you may feel the pressures from what other people might think, but it's safe to let go of these worries. You don't need to keep asking me what I'm going to do when I grow up. All I need is for you to support me to be and become the best version of myself.

Trust that I am developing on my own timeline, with my own interests, and learning in my unique way. Be patient with me and try not to nag me, scold me, or get frustrated with me. You can collaborate with me as I figure things out. I need your love and understanding.

I am really not trying to give you a hard time, so please don't take my misbehaviors personally. I am doing the best I can in this moment. I am probably trying to tell you what I need, but I don't know how. Help me to regulate myself, and once I'm calm, I can make a repair if needed.

As much as possible, please do not interrupt me when I'm concentrating. You can tell I am concentrating when I show intense interest in something. My face might be focused, my breathing might be smooth, and I might even have my mouth open or my tongue sticking out. It may not be what you would choose me to be interested in, but please let me finish. I'd be happy to tell you why I enjoy it.

Make time to connect with me each day. I may not want to answer all your questions as soon as I walk through the door. But if you wait, there will be time to talk, maybe while we are in the car, washing the dishes together, folding laundry, eating a meal, or throwing a ball. Or come listen to some music I'm playing for 5 minutes; or talk about animé; or this week's football results. You can also tell me about your day.

Allow me the space to rest and have quiet, too. I'm not being lazy. I need to decompress from all the input around me.

It is so much easier for me to learn from what you do than from what you say. So be aware I'm always watching you. Use your phone mindfully and put it away during meals, look into my eyes and listen with your whole body, and apologize when you get it wrong and do better next time.

I love you as you are. Be yourself when my friends are around. You don't need to act cool. If there are snacks, we'll be sure to hang out at the kitchen table. Then give us space to also hang out by ourselves.

I'll say it again, do not nag me. If something is bothering you, let's discuss it and make a plan together at a neutral time. We can make agreements, and I'll do my best to stick to them. We can review them regularly and see which ones might need adjusting.

If I push back on something, I'm usually trying to work out who I am or my thoughts on it. Give me space to explore this. You don't need to worry.

I don't need you to do my homework. I don't need you to solve my problems. I might complain about them. Just listen. Maybe ask if I need any help with planning. Otherwise, let me feel the consequences myself.

Focus on my strengths instead of what is not going right. I need to feel loved, accepted, and seen.

Allow me to make mistakes. But step in when I am doing something that hurts me, someone else, or the environment. It's nice to know you'll keep me safe, even if I don't seem happy about it at the time.

Keep me close and give me space. I want you to be interested in me, but you don't need to know everything in my mind.

Observe and seek to understand me. Assume the best in me (not the worst in me). Look for joy and moments when I'm engaged and can be myself.

I'm going to be happy. I'm going to be sad. Love me through it all, and let's journey on this road of life together.

I love you right back. xoxo

THE DECALOGUE OF MONTESSORI

We leave you with the Decalogue of Montessori, a helpful summary of the work of the preparation of the adult. The oldest version of the Decalogue of Montessori was found in a 1957 "Around the Child" publication by the Association of Montessorians in Calcutta. It was described as "compiled from Dr. Montessori's lectures," so not written by Dr. Montessori herself, but an overview of her ideas that we can use to check ourselves and our progress. It may be something to hang on a wall in our home as a reminder.

1. Never touch the child unless invited by [them] (in some form or the other).

2. Never speak ill of [them] in [their] presence or in [their] absence.

3. Concentrate on developing and strengthening what is good in [them]. Take meticulous and constant care of the environment. Teach proper use of things and show the place where they are kept.

4. The adult is to be active when helping the child to establish relation with the environment, and remain outwardly passive but inwardly active when this relation has been established.

5. The adult must always be ready to answer the call of the child who stands in need of [them] and always listen and respond to the child who appeals to [them].

6. The adult must respect the child who makes a mistake without correcting directly. But [they] must stop any misuses of the environment and any action which endangers the child or the other members of the community.

7. The adult must respect the child who takes rest and watches others working and not disturb [them], neither call or force [them] to other forms of activity.

8. The adult must help those who are in search of activity without finding it.

9. The adult must, therefore, be untiring in repeating presentations to the child who refused them earlier, in teaching the child who has not yet learned, in helping the child who needs it to overcome the imperfections in animating the environment, with [their] care, with [their] purposeful silence, with [their] mild words, and [their] loving presence. [They] must make [their] presence felt to the child who searches and hide from the child who has found.

10. The adult must always treat the child with the best of good manners and, in general, offer [them] the best [they have] in [themselves] and at [their] disposal.

GRATITUDE AND APPRECIATION FROM JUNNIFA

Grateful to my savior, Jesus Christ, for the grace to do all that I have been called to do.

My dear husband, for your patience and support. Writing and my passion for Montessori often leaves you with so little of me, but you are always there, steadfast and supportive. I love and appreciate you. To my children, Solu, Metu, Biendu, and Nalu, for being my biggest inspirations and teachers. My lab specimens and big pieces of my heart. Thank you for giving me purpose and for sharing me so graciously with work. I love you more than words could ever express.

My dad, my first love, who was looking forward to this book and always asking for updates. Daddy, your pride in my work spurred me on. I'm so sad you won't be here to touch and bless this book. I hope you are resting peacefully. My mum, my strong and consistent support. Helping me with every aspect of my life from the first day until now. I wouldn't be the woman I am without your help, and I wouldn't have been able to come so far on this Montessori journey or to write this book without you. Thank you, Mummy.

Manma, for supporting in all the ways you know and can. I love you and hope that you fly far, knowing that you'll always have a base to come back to. My brother, Udo, whose home was my writing retreat. Thank you so much for sharing your beautiful home with or without notice. Mandela and Fortune, who inspired me with their dedication to WheelZup, and Genti and Jamie and Debbie.

Sophie Ohuabunwa, my very able partner in work. Thank you for being my sounding board. For reading through this book and especially for all the times you had to be away from your family to work on this book with me. You have been such a gift to me, and I hope you know how much I appreciate you. Bidemi Adetutu and Pamela Chukwu for holding the fort in my elementary class as I worked on the book. The entire staff of Fruitful Orchard Montessori: Thank you for supporting me over the last two years as I worked on this book and also for partnering with me to build the dream. Fruitful Orchard parents and children, thank you for trusting me and for walking this journey with me. I don't take it for granted, and I feel so grateful for what we are creating together . . . now and for the future!

Mrs. Bola Kalejaiye, you are a key piece of my Montessori journey. God brought you into my life to keep me on this path. Thank you for inspiring me with your understanding and dedication to Montessori and the child. My trainers, Patty Wallner, Sylvia Dorantes, and Carol Hicks, who gave me keys to deeper knowledge of the child. Thank you! All my Montessori inspirations: There are too many of them to list, but I'll say Zoe Paul; Jennifer Turney McLaughlin and Pilar Bewley; and Regina Sokolowski to represent each level. Thank you!

Pastor Deborah Life Alegbemi, thank you for the constant and consistent prayers and spiritual support. I appreciate you. My friends Ijeoma Okoli, Lucy Agwunobi, Lilian Ibeh, and Paulette Ibeka, who inspired and encouraged me. Thank you for bearing with me and supporting me in spite of my unavailability.

To our publishers Workman and our amazing editor, Maisie Tivnan. Thank you, Maisie, for your grace, patience, and dedication. For having tough conversations with so much kindness that they don't feel tough. For believing in us and midwifing us through the birth of another book. Thank you, Analucia, for all your work on different aspects of the book. Thank you, Ilana, Cindy, Rebecca, Moira, and Chloe, for all your work promoting and selling the book. Thank you, Allison, for all your work in spreading the book around the world. And to everyone else at Workman/Hachette who works in big and small ways, maybe behind the scenes, to make our work successful. We are so grateful!

Thank you to Galen for laying out our book so beautifully and just knowing intuitively what we want. It has been such a delight to work with you on both books. Thank you to Naomi Wilkinson, our illustrator, for your beautiful drawings that perfectly illuminate our words. Thank you to Hiyoko Imai for the original book design. Your simple, timeless, and beautiful design has become a signature that has helped make these books all they are, and we are so grateful!

To my dear friend Sveta, thank you for living Montessori with your amazing family and for sharing your story with us. Thank you to Yuliya: You have been generous to me in many ways on this journey; I am grateful. Thank you to Jasmine, Nusaibah, and Joshuaa for sharing your stories and contributing to the book.

Finally, I want to thank my amazing partner in birthing these books, Simone. It has truly been a joy to go on this journey with you. You are a gift to me, to Montessori, and to the world. I'm not sure I could have done this with anyone else, and I am so grateful. Thank you, Simone, for being you: for your patience, flexibility, thoroughness, humor, experience, and most especially for your heart. You, Emma, and Oliver have inspired me in so many ways. Thank you!

I hope this book helps everyone who reads it enjoy the gifts they have been given!

"Children are a gift from God"—Psalms 127:3

GRATITUDE AND APPRECIATION FROM SIMONE

THE WORKMAN PUBLISHING TEAM—Maisie, you are a wonder. This book has become the book it is thanks to your keen eye, your patience and understanding, your kindness, and let's not forget your ruthless editing skills. Cindy, Ilana, Rebecca, Moira, and Chloe, thank you for being such fun and always so helpful. We could not have asked for a sweeter marketing, PR, and publicity team. Analucia, we appreciate your support whenever it was needed. To dear Allison, thank you for helping this book find its way into many more countries. And to the rest of the team: You have all helped spread Montessori into so many more homes than we ever possibly imagined. Thank you so much!

OUR DESIGNERS—To our ultra-talented illustrator, Naomi Wilkinson, thank you for bringing life to our words. We appreciate the care you have taken, and the beautiful illustrations add so much to the book. Galen, we love your design work and the fact that that you know even better than us how we want each page to look. And a big thank you to Hiyoko Imai for the gorgeous book design. It makes the book so beautiful and easy to read. We love it so much.

OUR CONTRIBUTORS—To Joshuaa, Nusaibah, Jasmine, Sveta, and Yuliya, who opened up their doors and shared their stories in the book; we appreciate you so much. As well as Mira and Angela, for contributing your expertise on the Montessori research.

EXTRA HELPERS—Terry Millie, Andy Lulka, Regina Lulka, and Tammy Oesting, thank you for guiding us as you read chapters for us. And to Kathy Porto Chang, Ksenya Kolpaktchi, Sophie Chamberlin, and Ruben Dahm for your helpful feedback to help make the book the best it could be.

MY FAMILY AND FRIENDS—To Mum, Dad, Jackie, Tania, Oliver, Emma, Luke, Blue, and all the family, thank you for all your love and support. To Debbie, Rachel, Agnes, Frans, Birgit, Monika, Floris, Carly, and Rich, I appreciate all the fun we've had together to fuel the writing and the endless times you had to hear about this book.

MONTESSORI MENTORS—To Ferne van Zyl for lighting the spark; to Judi Orion for sharing her love of the child; to Heidi Phillipart-Alcock who welcomed the whole family to Amsterdam; to An Morisson and Annabel Needs for being the best guides to my children and showing the way; and most recently to Vikki Taylor, Alison Awes, and Jenny Marie Höglund for giving me a deep dive into the 3- to 6-year-old child, 6- to 12-year-old child, and adolescent. I have also learned so much from my Montessori Everywhere friends—Dr. Ayize Sabater, Seemi Abdullah, Andy Lulka, Tammy Oesting, Barbara Isaacs, Wendelien Bellinger, Sue Pritzker, D. Ann Williams, Ochuko Prudence Daniels, and Gabriel Salomão—and so many others, like Kim Anh Nguyễn Anderson, Pamela Green, Jeanne-Marie Paynel, Britt Hawthorne, and Trisha Moquino.

FAMILIES AT JACARANDA TREE MONTESSORI—I am humbled to have been working with so many families here in Amsterdam since 2008. I learn from you all every day. Together we are growing, developing, and deepening our practice. Thank you for being such a special community.

YOU, DEAR READER—Thank you for picking up this book, putting our words into action, and bringing Montessori into your home. We love changing the world one family at a time and hope you find the same joy that we have in adopting the Montessori principles in your family.

Last but not least, **MY DEAR JUNNIFA**—Thank you so much for being on this journey with me. You and your family inspire me and fill me with hope, and I love seeing you shine so brightly. This book has been such a pleasure to birth together.

"Acknowledging the good that you already have in your life is the foundation for all abundance."

—Eckhart Tolle

INDEX

BRING THE MAGIC OF MONTESSORI HOME

THE
MONTESSORI
TODDLER

A PARENT'S GUIDE TO RAISING
A CURIOUS AND RESPONSIBLE HUMAN BEING

SIMONE DAVIES

ILLUSTRATED BY
HIYOKO IMAI

WORKMAN PUBLISHING | NEW YORK

Workman
Workman Publishing
Hachette Book Group, Inc.
1290 Avenue of the Americas
New York, NY 10104
workman.com

Workman is an imprint of Workman Publishing, a division of Hachette Book Group, Inc.
The Workman name and logo are registered trademarks of Hachette Book Group, Inc.

Design and illustrations by Hiyoko Imai
Author photo by Rubianca Han Simmelsgaard
Editing assistance by Alexis Wilson Briggs, alphaomegaconsulting.nl

The publisher is not responsible for websites (or their content) that are not owned by
the publisher.

Workman books may be purchased in bulk for business, educational, or promotional use.
For information, please contact your local bookseller or the Hachette Book Group Special
Markets Department at special.markets@hbgusa.com.

Feelings and Needs chart reprinted with permission by Yoram Mosenzon, connecting2life.net

themontessorinotebook.com
hiyokoimai.com

First Edition February 2019

Printed in China on responsibly sourced paper

10 9 8 7 6 5 4 3 2 1

This book is for Oliver and Emma.
I feel honored to be your mother.
You inspire me every day.

CONTENTS

INTRODUCTION

1

LET'S CHANGE
THE WAY WE SEE TODDLERS

Toddlers are misunderstood humans. People see toddlers as difficult. There are not many good examples of how to be with toddlers in a loving, patient, supportive way.

They start to walk, they start to explore, they're only just learning to communicate with words, and they don't have a whole lot of impulse control. They can't sit still easily in cafes and restaurants, they see an open space and start running, they have tantrums (often at the most inconvenient times and in the most inconvenient places), and they touch anything that looks interesting.

They get called "the terrible twos." They do not listen. They keep throwing everything. They won't sleep/eat/use the toilet.

When my children were small, it didn't feel right to get their cooperation with threats, bribes, and time-outs, yet it was difficult to find alternatives.

I heard a radio interview when my first child was very young. The guest talked about the negative effects of using time-outs as a punishment—it alienated the child when they needed support and made the child upset with the adult rather than helping the child make amends. I listened attentively for the guest to tell parents what to do instead, but the radio interview ended there. It's been my mission since then to find my own answers.

I entered a Montessori school for the first time as a new parent and instantly fell in love. The environment was so carefully prepared and inviting. The teachers were approachable and spoke to our baby (and us) with respect. We put our names on the waiting list for the school and joined the parent-toddler classes.

I learned so much about the Montessori approach in these classes and about toddlers. Toddlers thrive in an environment that challenges them; they seek to be understood, and they take in the world around them like sponges. I realized that I related easily to toddlers—I could see their perspective, and the way they learned fascinated me. I was lucky to start working as Ferne van Zyl's assistant in this classroom.

I did my Montessori training with the Association Montessori Internationale in 2004, and when life took us from Sydney to Amsterdam, I was surprised there weren't any Montessori parent-child classes in our new city. So I soon started my own school—Jacaranda Tree Montessori—where I lead parent-child classes, helping families see their toddler in a new way and helping them incorporate the Montessori approach in their homes.

I continue to love learning from the nearly one thousand toddlers and parents I've seen over the many years running these classes. I've participated in Positive Discipline teacher training and learned Nonviolent Communication. I continue to read innumerable books and articles, speak to teachers and parents, and listen to radio programs and podcasts. And I've learned from my own children, who have grown from toddlers to teenagers.

I want to share with you what I have learned. I want to translate the wisdom of Montessori into simple language that is easy to understand and that you can apply in your own home. By picking up this book, you have taken a step in your own journey toward finding another way to be with your toddler, whether or not your child will attend a Montessori school.

You will get the tools to work together with your child, to lead them, and to support them, especially when they are having a hard time. You'll learn how to set up your home to get rid of the chaos and to bring some calm to your family's life. To set up a "yes" space for your child to freely explore. And you'll discover how to create Montessori activities at home that are just right for toddlers.

This will not happen in one day. And you are not trying to re-create a Montessori classroom. You can start small—work with what you already have, put away some of the toys you already have so that you can rotate them, start to really observe the children as they follow their interests—and gradually you'll find yourself incorporating more and more Montessori ideas into your home and daily life.

I hope to show you that there is another, more peaceful way to be with your toddler. To help you plant the seeds to raise a curious and responsible human being. To work on a relationship with your child that you will continue to build upon for years. To put Dr. Montessori's philosophies into practice every day.

It's time for us to learn how to see through our toddler's eyes.

WHY I LOVE TODDLERS

Most Montessori teachers have a favorite age to work with. For me it is working with my toddler friends. People are often confused by this preference. Toddlers can be hard work, they are emotional, and they do not always listen to us.

I want to paint a new picture of the toddler.

Toddlers live in the present moment. Walking down the street with a toddler can be a delight. While we make lists in our heads of the errands we need to run and what we need to cook for dinner, they remain present and spot the weeds growing up from a crack in the pavement.

When we spend time with a toddler, they show us how to be present. They are focused on the here and now.

Toddlers pick things up effortlessly. Dr. Montessori observed that children under 6 years old take in everything without effort, just as a sponge soaks up water. She referred to this as the *absorbent mind*.

We don't have to sit down with a 1-year-old and teach them grammar or sentence structure. By the age of 3 they already have an amazing vocabulary and are learning how to construct simple sentences (and, for some, complicated paragraphs). Compare this with learning a language as an adult—it takes a lot of effort and work.

Toddlers are enormously capable. Often it is not until we have our own child that we realize how enormously capable they are from such a young age. As they approach 18 months old, they might start to notice that we are heading to Grandma's house well before we are there by recognizing things along the route. When they see an elephant in a book, they'll run over to find a toy elephant in a basket.

When we set up our homes to make them more accessible to our young children, they take on tasks with eagerness, capability, and delight. They wipe up spills, fetch a diaper for the baby, put their trash in the wastebasket, help us make food, and like to dress themselves.

One day a repairman came to fix something in our home. I'll never forget the look on his face when my daughter (then just under 2 years old) walked past him on the way to the bedroom, changed her clothes, put some wet clothes in the hamper, and walked off to play. Clearly he was surprised to see how much she was capable of doing for herself.

Toddlers are innocent. I don't think any toddler has a mean bone in their body. If they see someone playing with a toy, they may simply think, *I'd like to play with that toy right now* and take it from the other child. They may do something to get a reaction (*Let's drop this cup and see my parent's reaction*) or be frustrated that something did not go their way.

But they are not mean-spirited, spiteful, or vengeful. They are simply impulsive, following their every urge.

Toddlers do not hold grudges. Picture a toddler who wants to stay at the park when it's time to leave. They melt down. The tantrum may even last half an hour. But once they calm down (sometimes with help), they go back to being their cheerful, curious selves—unlike adults, who can wake up on the wrong side of the bed and be cranky all day.

Toddlers are also amazingly forgiving. Sometimes we do the wrong thing—we lose our temper, we forget a promise we made, or we just feel a bit out of sorts. When we apologize to our toddler, we are modeling how to make amends with someone, and they are quite likely to give us a big hug or surprise us with an especially kind word. When we have that solid base with our children, they look after us, just as we look after them.

Toddlers are authentic. I love spending time with toddlers because they are direct and honest. Their authenticity is infectious. They say what they mean. They wear their hearts on their sleeves.

Everyone who has spent time with a toddler knows they will point to someone on the bus and say loudly, "That person has no hair." We may sink down in our seat while our child shows no signs of embarrassment.

That same directness makes them very easy to be around. There are no mind games being played, no underlying motives, no politics at play.

They know how to be themselves. They don't doubt themselves. They do not judge others. We would do well to learn from them.

Note: When I refer to toddlers, I'm talking about children from around 1 to 3 years old.

WHAT WE NEED TO KNOW
ABOUT TODDLERS

Toddlers need to say "no." One of the most important developmental phases a toddler passes through is the "crisis of self-affirmation." Between 18 months and 3 years, children realize that their identity is separate from their parents' and they begin to desire more autonomy. At the same time they begin to say "no," they begin to use the personal pronoun *I*.

This movement toward independence does not come easily. Some days they will push us away, wanting to do everything by themselves; other days they will refuse to do anything at all or will cling to us.

Toddlers need to move. Just as an animal does not like to be caged, our toddlers will not sit still for long. They want to keep mastering movement. Once standing, they move on to climbing and walking. Once walking, they want to run and to move heavy objects— the heavier the better. There is even a name for the desire to challenge themselves to the highest level by, for example, carrying big objects or moving heavy bags and furniture: *maximum effort*.

Toddlers need to explore and discover the world around them. The Montessori approach recommends that we accept this, set up our spaces for our child to safely explore, get them involved in daily life activities that involve all their senses, and allow them to explore the outdoors. Let them dig in the dirt, take off their shoes in the grass, splash in the water, and run in the rain.

Toddlers need freedom. This freedom will help them grow to be curious learners, to experience things for themselves, to make discoveries, and to feel they have control over themselves.

Toddlers need limits. These limits will keep them safe, teach them to respect others and their environment, and help them become responsible human beings. Limits also help the adult step in before a boundary has been crossed to avoid the all-too-familiar shouting, anger, and blame. The Montessori approach is neither permissive nor bossy. Instead, it teaches parents to be calm leaders for our children.

Toddlers need order and consistency. Toddlers prefer things to be exactly the same every day—the same routine, things in the same place, and the same rules. It helps them understand, make sense of their world, and know what to expect.

When limits are not consistent, toddlers will keep testing them to see what we decide today. If they find it works to nag or melt down, they will try again. This is called *intermittent reinforcement*.

If we understand this need, we can have more patience, more understanding. And when we aren't able to provide the same thing every day, we will be able to anticipate that they may need additional support. We won't think they are being silly; we'll be able to see from their perspective that it's not the way they were hoping it would be. We can offer them help to calm down and, once they're calm, help them find a solution.

Toddlers are not giving us a hard time. They are having a hard time. I love this idea (attributed to educator Jean Rosenberg in the *New York Times* article "Seeing Tantrums as Distress, Not Defiance"). When we realize their difficult behavior is actually a cry for help, we can ask ourselves, *How can I be of help right now?* We move from feeling attacked to searching for a way to be supportive.

Toddlers are impulsive. Their prefrontal cortex (the part of the brain that houses our self-control and decision-making centers) is still developing (and will be for another twenty years). This means we may need to guide them if they are climbing on the table again or grabbing something out of someone's hands, and be patient if they become emotional. I like to say, "We need to be their prefrontal cortex."

Toddlers need time to process what we are saying. Instead of repeatedly telling our child to put on their shoes, we can count to ten in our head to allow them time to process our request. Often, by the time we get to eight, we'll see them start to respond.

Toddlers need to communicate. Our children try to communicate with us in many ways. Babies gurgle and we can gurgle back; young toddlers will babble and we can show an interest in what they are saying; older toddlers love asking and answering questions; and we can give rich language, even to these young children, to absorb like a sponge.

Toddlers love mastery. Toddlers love to repeat skills until they master them. Observe them and notice what they are working to master. Usually it is something hard enough to be challenging but not so difficult that they give up. They'll repeat and repeat the process until they perfect it. Once they've mastered it, they move on.

Toddlers like to contribute and be part of the family. They seem to be more interested in the objects their parents use than they are in their toys. They really like to work alongside us as we prepare food, do the laundry, get ready for visitors, and the like. When we allow more time, set things up for success, and lower our expectations of the outcome, we teach our young child a lot about being a contributing member of the family. These are things that they will build on as they become schoolchildren and teenagers.

PARENTING
THE MONTESSORI TODDLER

When I first came to Montessori, I confess, my interest might have been considered superficial. I was attracted to the Montessori environments and activities. And I wanted to provide beautiful, engaging materials and spaces for my own children. I was not wrong. It's the easiest place to start.

Years later, I see that Montessori really is a way of life. Even more than the activities or the spaces, Montessori has influenced the way I am with my children, the children who come to my classes, and the children I come in contact with in my daily life. It's about encouraging a child's curiosity, learning to really see and accept a child as they are, without judgment, and remaining connected with the child, even when we need to stop them from doing something they really want to do.

It's not difficult to apply Montessori practices at home, but it may be quite different from the way we were parented and the way others around us parent.

In a Montessori approach, we see the child as their own person on their own unique path. We support them as their guide and gentle leader. They aren't something to be molded into what we see as their potential or to make up for our own experiences or unfulfilled desires as a child.

As a gardener, we plant seeds, provide the right conditions, and give enough food, water, and light. We observe the seeds and adjust our care if needed. And we let them grow. This is how we can parent our children, too. This is the Montessori way. We are planting the seeds that are our toddlers, providing the right conditions for them, adjusting when needed, and watching them grow. The direction their lives take will be of their own making.

> "[T]he educators [including parents] behave as do good gardeners and cultivators toward their plants."
>
> —Dr. Maria Montessori, *The Formation of Man*

TODDLERS ARE BRILLIANT

What seems to be a lack of flexibility ("I can't eat breakfast without my favorite spoon!") IS ACTUALLY an expression of their strong sense of order.

What looks like a battle of wills IS ACTUALLY your toddler learning that things don't always go their way.

What looks like repeating the same annoying game over and over IS ACTUALLY the child trying to gain mastery.

What appears to be an explosive tantrum IS ACTUALLY the toddler saying, "I love you so much, I feel safe to release everything that I've been holding on to all day."

What seems to be intentionally going slowly to wind us up IS ACTUALLY them exploring everything in their path.

What can be super embarrassing to hear a toddler say in public IS ACTUALLY the child's inability to lie, a model of honesty.

What seems like another night of interrupted sleep IS ACTUALLY chubby little arms giving you a big squeeze in the middle of the night to express their pure love for you.

GETTING THE MOST
OUT OF THIS BOOK

You can read this book from cover to cover. Or just open it at a page that interests you and find something practical that you can use today.

Sometimes figuring out where to start can be overwhelming. To help make it more manageable, I've included key questions at the end of each chapter to help you begin to incorporate Montessori into your home and daily life. There are boxes and lists throughout the book for easy reference. You will also find a useful chart in the appendix titled "Instead of This, Say That." You may wish to copy it and hang it somewhere as a reminder.

In addition to all of the Montessori wisdom, I also draw on many of the resources (books, podcasts, training courses) I have discovered over the years that complement the Montessori approach and help me be a kind and clear guide for the toddlers in my classes and for my own children.

Use this book as inspiration. In the end, the goal is not to do every single activity, or have a completely clutter-free space, or be a perfect parent; it is learning how to see and support our toddlers. To have fun being with them. To help them when they are having a hard time. And to remember to smile when we start taking it all too seriously. It's a journey, not a destination.

INTRODUCTION TO MONTESSORI

2

A BRIEF HISTORY OF MONTESSORI

Dr. Maria Montessori was one of the first female doctors in Italy in the late 1800s. She worked at a clinic in Rome, tending to the poor and their children. She not only treated her patients' health but also provided them with care and clothing.

In an asylum in Rome, she observed children with emotional and mental disabilities who were sensorially deprived in their environment. In one case, she noticed that they were picking up crumbs—not to eat, but to stimulate their sense of touch. She proposed that education, not medicine, was the answer for these children.

Dr. Montessori did not begin with any preconceived methodology. Instead, she applied the same objective and scientific observation practices from her medical training to see what engaged the children, to understand how they learned and how she could facilitate their learning.

She immersed herself in educational philosophy, psychology, and anthropology, experimenting with and refining educational materials for these children. Eventually, the majority of the children passed state examinations with marks higher than children without disabilities. Dr. Montessori was hailed as a miracle worker.

She was soon able to test her ideas in the Italian educational system when she was invited to set up a place in the slums of Rome to care for young children while their parents worked. This was the first Casa dei Bambini—House of Children—which opened in January 1907.

It was not long before her work drew interest and spread internationally. Montessori schools and training programs are now on every continent except Antarctica. In the United States alone, there are more than 4,500 Montessori schools, and there are 20,000 worldwide. Where I live in Amsterdam, there are more than 20 Montessori schools for a population of around 800,000 catering to children from infancy to 18 years old. Larry Page and Sergey Brin (founders of Google), Jeff Bezos (founder of Amazon), Jacqueline Kennedy Onassis (former first lady), and Gabriel García Márquez (Nobel Prize–winning novelist) all attended Montessori schools.

Dr. Montessori continued to work in education and develop her ideas for children of all ages as she moved around the world—including living in India in exile during World War II—until her death in 1952 in the Netherlands. She called her work "an education for life"—i.e., not just for the classroom, but for our daily lives.

TRADITIONAL EDUCATION vs MONTESSORI EDUCATION

In traditional education, the teacher generally stands at the front of the classroom, decides what the children need to learn, and teaches the children what they need to know: a top-down approach.

It is also a one-size-fits-all approach. The teacher decides that everyone is ready to learn, for example, the letter *a* on the same day.

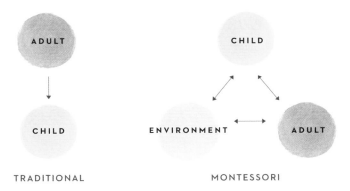

In Montessori education there is a dynamic relationship between the child, the adult, and the learning environment. The child is in charge of their own learning, supported by the adult and the environment.

The materials are laid out on shelves in a sequential order from easiest to hardest. Each child works at their own pace through the materials, following their interest in that moment. The teacher will observe the child and when it seems that the child has mastered the material, the teacher will then give them a lesson with the next material.

In the diagram of Montessori education above, the arrows are pointing in both directions. The environment and child interact with each other. The environment attracts the child and the child learns from the materials in the environment. The adult and environment are also affecting each other. The adult prepares the environment, observes, and makes adjustments where necessary to meet the child's needs. And the adult and child have a dynamic relationship, based on mutual respect for each other. The adult will observe the child and step in to give only as much assistance as necessary before stepping out of the way for the child to continue their self-mastery.

In her writing, Dr. Montessori reiterates that the objective of Montessori education is **not to fill a child with facts, but to cultivate their own natural desire to learn**.

These principles do not just apply in the classroom—they inform the way we are with our children in the home. We support our children to make discoveries for themselves, we give them freedom and limits, and we enable success by setting up our homes so they can take part in our daily lives.

SOME MONTESSORI PRINCIPLES

1. Prepared environment

I run eight classes a week at Jacaranda Tree Montessori. Much of my "work" is done before the children arrive. I prepare the environment with a lot of care and attention.

- I set up activities that are just the right level for the children—challenging to master but not so difficult that they will give up.
- I make sure the children have the tools they need to succeed—I look for trays they can carry, cloths at the ready to wipe up spills, a supply of art materials so they can practice and repeat, child-sized implements like spreaders for putting toppings onto crackers, and the smallest of glasses for drinking.
- I sit on the floor to see what it looks like from their height. I place artwork for them to enjoy low on the walls and plants for them to look after on the floor or on low tables.
- I prepare the space so it is simple and beautiful. I remove any clutter, I set out a few, well-chosen activities, and I make sure that activities are complete and not missing any parts so the children can work with them independently.

This never feels like "cleaning the classroom." The purpose of this preparation is to make things as attractive to them as possible and to allow the children freedom to explore and learn.

A prepared environment can be any space that we set up for our children: a classroom, our home, a holiday rental, an outside space.

2. Natural desire to learn

Dr. Montessori recognized that children have an intrinsic motivation to learn. Babies learn to grasp for an object, they learn to stand by trying again and again and again, and they master walking—all by themselves, within a supportive environment. The same applies to learning to talk, learning to read and write, learning mathematics, and learning about the world around them.

The discoveries children make for themselves—particularly within a *prepared environment*—build wonder in the child and a love of learning. They do not need to be directed to explore the environment.

In a Montessori classroom, the ages of the children are mixed. Younger children can learn from observing older children, and older children can consolidate their learning by helping the younger ones.

A toddler's work is play. They are intrinsically curious learners—if we allow them to be.

3. Hands-on, concrete learning

> "We may put it like this: the child's intelligence can develop to a certain level without the help of the hand. But if it develops with his hand, then the level it reaches is higher, and the child's character is stronger."
>
> —Dr. Maria Montessori, *The Absorbent Mind*

The hand takes in information in a concrete way to pass on to the brain. It's one thing to hear or watch something, but we learn on a deeper level when we integrate our listening or watching with using our hands. We move from passively learning to actively learning.

The materials in a Montessori classroom are so beautifully prepared and attractive that the child is drawn to them to make discoveries for themselves, **with their hands**.

We give toddlers tactile learning experiences. They hold an object as we name it, we offer a variety of beautiful art materials for them to explore, we provide interesting fastenings to open and close (from Velcro to zippers to buttons), and they help us prepare food in the kitchen—digging their fingers into the dough or using a butter knife to cut a banana.

Another example of hands-on learning is the math materials found in a Montessori classroom for 3-to-6-year-olds. A small golden bead represents 1. A string of 10 beads represents 10. A mat of 10 rows of 10 beads represents 100. A stack of 10 mats represents 1,000.

Using these materials, a young child can then do addition. For the sum 1,234 + 6,432, the child can go and get one 1,000 block, 2 mats for 100, 3 strings for 30, and 4 single beads. They can then do the same for 6,432. It is then very clear when they start adding that there are now 7 of the 1,000 blocks, 6 of the 100 mats, and so on. The child can concretely see and hold in their hands these values, unlike the abstract way in which most children learn addition on a piece of paper.

As the child moves into the upper elementary grades, they will be able to draw on this concrete base to move to abstraction. They will not need the materials, yet they are always available to them should they wish to revisit them.

4. Sensitive periods

When a child shows a particular interest in one area—for example, movement, language, math, reading—it is known as a *sensitive period*. This describes a moment when the child is particularly attuned to learning a certain skill or concept and it happens with ease and without effort.

We can watch our children to see what sensitive periods they are in and provide appropriate activities to encourage those interests.

When the toddler starts to mimic us—parroting certain words—we know they are in a sensitive period for language, and we can focus on giving the child new and familiar vocabulary for them to practice.

If a toddler is interested in climbing on the table, they are likely in a sensitive period for movement and need to practice those skills. Instead of allowing them to climb on furniture, we can create an obstacle course with pillows, blankets, things to balance on, and things to climb.

The table on the following page provides some examples of how we can feed our child's interest when they are in a sensitive period.

Note: Some people are worried that if they miss a sensitive period—for example, for reading—then the child will have problems learning to read. They will learn to read, but it will take more conscious effort, similar to an adult learning a foreign language.

SENSITIVE PERIODS FOR TODDLERS

The exact timing of these sensitive periods is unique to each child.

LANGUAGE	A sensitive period for spoken language. They watch our mouth, they babble, they start parroting what we say, and soon afterward, there is a language explosion. An interest in writing may begin from 3.5+ years; reading from 4.5+ years. • Use rich language. • Name everything with its proper name. • Read books. • Have conversations with the toddler—allow pauses for them to react. • Follow the child's interests.
ORDER	Toddlers love order. Dr. Montessori observed a child out walking with her mother, who became very upset when her mother took off her coat. The child was upset because the "order" (how things were) changed and, when the mother replaced the coat, the child calmed down. • Use routines so the child knows what to expect next. • Have "a place for everything and everything in its place." • Provide understanding if the child is upset when something doesn't happen the same way every day.
TINY DETAIL	From 18 months to 3 years, the child is attracted to the smallest objects and the minutest detail. • Provide exquisite details in the home: art, flowers, handmade crafts. • Sit on the ground at their height to see what they can see from their perspective—make it attractive. • We can remove imperfect items.
MOVEMENT ACQUISITION	The young toddler acquires gross- and fine-motor movement—they learn to walk and to use their hands. The older toddler refines these skills and begins to develop more coordination. • Offer different opportunities for them to practice gross- and fine-motor movements. • Allow time for movement.
SENSORIAL EXPLORATION	Toddlers are fascinated by color, taste, smells, touch, and sounds through exploration of the environment. The older toddler begins to classify and organize these impressions. • Give access to a rich indoor and outdoor environment to be explored with all the senses. • Provide time to explore freely. • Make discoveries together.
MANNERS AND COURTESIES	The sensitive period for manners starts around 2.5 years. Before this, the adult can model manners and courtesies for young toddlers, who will absorb them. • Trust in the child that these manners and courtesies will gradually develop without haranguing the child to use them. • Model manners and courtesies in the home, in daily life, and with strangers.

5. Unconscious absorbent mind

From birth until about the age of 6, children take in information effortlessly. Dr. Montessori referred to this as the *absorbent mind*. From birth to the age of 3, they do this completely *unconsciously*.

The ease with which a toddler learns gives us opportunities as well as responsibilities.

Opportunities because they absorb with such ease the language around them (building a rich vocabulary and understanding), how we handle furniture and objects (ideally with care), how we treat others (ideally with respect and kindness), where we put things (creating order), and the beauty of the environment around them.

Responsibilities because, as Dr. Montessori points out, a sponge can absorb dirty water as easily as it can clean water. A child will pick up negative experiences as easily as positive experiences. They can even pick up our feelings and attitudes, for example, when we drop something and get frustrated with ourselves (as opposed to forgiving ourselves) or if we have a fixed mind-set that we are bad at drawing (as opposed to a growth mind-set where we might show that we can always keep improving our skills).

We can therefore be mindful, as much as possible, to be positive role models for our young children, to provide beauty, and to offer kindness for them to absorb.

6. Freedom and limits

I've heard people say, "Aren't Montessori schools really hands-off and the children can do whatever they like?" And I've heard others say, "Aren't Montessori schools really strict and the children are allowed to use materials only in certain ways?"

Montessori actually falls in the middle, somewhere between permissiveness and autocracy/dictatorship.

At school or at home, we can have a few rules for children to live by to learn respect and responsibility for themselves, others, and the environment around them. Within these limits, children have freedom of choice, of movement, and of will.

In a Montessori school, the children have the freedom to choose what they would like to work on (as long as it is available), the freedom to rest or to observe another child (as long as they are not disturbing another child), and the freedom to move around the classroom (as long as they respect the people around them). Within these limits, we follow the child and trust they will develop on their own unique timeline.

At home, we can give them freedom to choose what they want to wear (as long as it's appropriate for the season), the freedom to make their own snack (as long as they sit down to eat), and the freedom to express themselves (as long as they do not hurt others or objects in the home).

Some people worry, *How will they ever learn that there are some things they have to do?* or *Won't they become spoiled if we focus on them all the time?* I am not suggesting that we give our children license to do whatever they want. As parents we can be clear about what is expected and follow through with loving limits when necessary. We will step in if they are hurting someone or themselves, or we will gently help them leave the park if they are having trouble leaving themselves. And while we are learning to see from their perspective, we are also showing them how to have mutual respect and care for others (including us, as their parents) and the environment.

We give them freedom within limits.

7. Independence and responsibility

"Help me to help myself."

In Montessori, children learn to become remarkably independent. We don't do this so that children will grow up as fast as possible. (Let children be children.) We do this because children love it.

Children want to be able to do more, to contribute, to be a part of the family/classroom/society. We see satisfaction on their face when they pull on their own shoe, put something back where it belongs, or help a friend. Peace washes over them when they can do it for themselves, when they do not have to fight someone putting their T-shirt over their head for them or plopping them into the bath without warning.

Through independence the child learns **how to be responsible** for caring for themselves, others, and the environment.

They learn how to handle fragile things with care. They learn how to offer help to a friend. They learn how to take care of their belongings. They learn how to make amends when they have hurt someone. They learn how to look after the plants, the classroom, and the environment around them.

Even toddlers.

8. Individual development

Each child is on their own unique developmental timeline.

Montessori respects not only each child's unique timeline but also the fact that each child has different energy levels and is able to focus at different moments. Children have different modalities for learning—visual, aural, tactile, or a combination.

Some children like to repeat and repeat until they master a skill. Other children will learn mostly through observing others. Some children need to move more than others.

Montessori respects how different children learn, and supports their individual development.

9. Respect

A Montessori teacher will have such respect for the child that they will treat them the same way they would an adult. We can see this in the way they speak to the child, the way they ask permission if they need to touch them (for example, "Would it be okay for me to lift you up?"), and the way they allow the child to develop in their own way.

This does not mean that the adult is not in charge. They will set a limit when needed. Not passive. Not aggressive. But in a respectfully assertive way.

10. Observation

Observation is the basis of the Montessori approach. As part of my Montessori training, we observed babies and young children for 250+ hours. We were training ourselves to unlearn the desire to analyze, jump to conclusions, have biases, and form preconceptions about a child or a situation.

Observing simply means watching like a camera on the wall. Being factual, and recording only what we see: the children's movements, their language, their posture, their actions.

Observing shows us exactly where the child is right now. It helps us see what they are interested in, what they are working to master, when there is a developmental change, and, on occasion, when to step in to set a limit or to provide a little help before stepping out again.

TO PRACTICE

1. Do we see our child displaying any of the sensitive periods? What are they showing interest in right now?
2. Do we see examples in our child of:
   - the absorbent mind?
   - their natural desire to learn?
3. How do we feel about top-down learning (a traditional learning approach) versus an approach where the child is engaged in their own learning?

In the following chapters, I will show how to incorporate these Montessori principles into daily life:

- Observing our children to see what interests they have that they can explore and make discoveries about for themselves
- Providing time for language, movement, and being together
- Setting up our home so they can be successful
- Including them in daily life
- Encouraging their curiosity
- Setting a few ground/house rules so children know the limits
- Being our children's guide—because they don't need a boss or a servant
- Letting them blossom into the unique beings they are—instead of molding them

Let's put this into practice with our toddlers.

MONTESSORI ACTIVITIES FOR TODDLERS

3

MONTESSORI ACTIVITIES FOR THE WHOLE CHILD

Often the easiest way to begin with Montessori at home is to start with activities.

Montessori activities are based on developing the whole child. We begin by looking at the child to see what their needs are. We then set up activities to meet those needs.

Toddlers' needs consist of using their hands in various ways (working on their grasp, the ability to reach across the middle of their body, hand-to-hand transfer, carrying objects, using two hands together); practicing gross-motor movement; self-expression; and communication.

Montessori activities for toddlers fall into five main areas:

1. eye-hand coordination
2. music and movement
3. practical life (activities of daily life)
4. arts and crafts
5. language

There is a list of Montessori activities for toddlers in the appendix of this book. Ages are given as an indication only. Be sure to follow the child and see which activities keep their attention, removing those that are too hard or too easy.

WHAT MAKES AN ACTIVITY MONTESSORI?

Montessori activities usually **target one skill**. For example, putting a ball into a box through a small hole allows the child to master this one skill. This differs from many traditional plastic toys that target multiple skills at the same time, with one part for pushing, one part where a ball drops, another part that makes a noise, and so on.

We also prefer to use **natural materials**. Toddlers explore with all their senses. Natural materials like wood are lovely to touch and generally safe for putting in their mouths, and the weight of the object is more likely to be directly related to its size. Although they are sometimes more expensive, wooden toys are often more durable and can be found secondhand and then passed on once the child has finished with them. Storing activities in containers made of natural materials, like woven baskets, incorporates handmade elements and beauty into the space, too.

Many Montessori activities have **a beginning, middle, and end**. The child may begin with a small part of the sequence and, as they develop, will be able to complete the full *work cycle*, including replacing the activity on the shelf. They experience peace while they are practicing the activity—and satisfaction once they complete it. For example, when arranging flowers, at first a child may show interest only in pouring water and using the sponge to wipe it up. Gradually they will learn all the steps and complete the work cycle, filling small vases with water, arranging all the flowers, putting away the materials at the end, and cleaning up any water that was spilled.

Montessori activities are **complete**. Completing an activity is important for their sense of mastery. A child can become frustrated if, for example, a piece of a puzzle is missing. If any pieces are missing, we remove the whole activity.

Activities are often organized in individual **trays and baskets**. Within each tray or basket is everything the child needs to complete the task by themselves. For example, if the activity involves water, we may want to include a sponge or hand mitt to clean up any spills.

Children gain mastery of an activity through **repetition**. The activity should be exactly at their level—challenging enough that it is not too easy yet not so difficult that they give up. I love seeing a row of clothespins along the top of a painting on the drying rack—a sign that a child has been busy working to master pinning up their paintings to dry.

They may focus on and repeat just one part of the activity. For example, they may practice squeezing a sponge or filling a jug with water from a tap. We observe and allow them to repeat and repeat the section they are trying to master. They will eventually add steps to the process or move on to another activity.

A child has the **freedom to choose** an activity. Our spaces are set up to encourage this freedom of choice by displaying a limited number of activities that they are working to master.

> "The task of teaching becomes easy, since we do not need to choose what we shall teach, but should place all before him for the satisfaction of his mental appetite. He must have absolute freedom of choice, and then he requires nothing but repeated experiences which will become increasingly marked by interest and serious attention, during his acquisition of some desired knowledge."
>
> —Dr. Maria Montessori, *To Educate the Human Potential*

HOW TO SHOW THE CHILD AN ACTIVITY

In Montessori teacher training, we learn to show children how to do each activity in the classroom by giving them "a presentation." In a presentation, each activity is broken into little steps, from taking the tray to the table, to presenting the activity step by step, to returning the tray to the shelf. We practice the presentation for each activity over and over. Then, if the child needs help in class, we know the activity so well from practicing that we can improvise and step in to give them just as much help as they need.

We can use the same approach at home. We can set up an activity, do it ourselves first, break the activity into little steps, and practice to see how our child might manage.

Let them choose the activity they are interested in and try it for as long as they can without interfering. Even if they drop something, we can sit on our hands to see if they will react and pick it up themselves. When we see that they are struggling and getting frustrated, we can step in and say, "Watch," and then show them, slowly, for example, how to turn the lid of the jar. Then we can step back again to see how they manage.

Here are some tips for showing an activity to the child:

- Make precise, slow hand movements so the child can observe clearly. For example, break down all the tiny steps we take to open a button, and slowly show them each one.
- Avoid talking as we demonstrate—otherwise the child won't know whether to look at us while we talk or watch our hands.
- Try to show them the same way each time to make it easier for them to pick up any steps they may be missing.
- Handle the objects in a way that the child can manage, for example, using two hands to carry a tray, a glass, and so on.
- If they don't want us to help, they may be open to a verbal cue, like "Push, push." Or we can let them keep trying by themselves until they master the task. Or they may walk away and try again at another time.

S LOW	I first heard the acronym *SHOW* from my Montessori friend Jeanne-Marie Paynel. It is a useful reminder to adults to use slow hands and omit words when we are showing our children something new.
H ANDS	
O MIT	This helps the child pick things up more easily. Our movements are slow and easy to follow. If we explain with words at the same time, our toddler isn't sure whether to listen to us or watch us— so we stay quiet so they can focus on our movements without words.
W ORDS	

GENERAL PRINCIPLES TO KEEP IN MIND

1. Let the child lead

Follow the child's pace and interests. Let them take the time to choose for themselves rather than suggesting or leading the play. Let them pick from activities they are working to master—nothing too easy or too difficult. Something challenging but not so hard that they give up.

2. Let them work with the activity as long as they like

As the child is mastering an activity, we do not want to rush them to finish—even if a sibling is waiting. Once they have finished the activity, ask if they would like to do it again. This encourages repetition and gives them the chance to repeat, practice, master the activity, and increase their concentration.

Ideally, we don't interrupt our child's deep focus. A simple comment from us can distract them from whatever they are working to master, and they may abandon the activity completely. Wait until they look to us for feedback, step in to offer help when they are frustrated, or see that they have finished before we make a request like coming to the table to eat dinner.

3. Avoid quizzing the child

We may not realize we are doing it, but we are constantly quizzing our children. "What color is this?" "How many apples am I holding?" "Can you show Grandma how you can walk?"

I did it too when my son was small. Often I'd ask him to demonstrate some new skill or perform some new trick on cue. Maybe to show off in some way. Or maybe to push him to learn a little faster.

Now I see that this prompting is a kind of test for a child. And there is generally only one correct answer, so if the answer they give is wrong, we have no other option than to say, "No, that flower is yellow, not blue." Not exactly great for building a child's confidence.

Instead we can continue to name things, ask questions to arouse curiosity, and use observation to see what the child has mastered and what they are still practicing.

Now, the only time I will quiz a child is if I am 100 percent sure they know the answer and will be excited to tell me. For example, if they have been identifying blue objects all by themselves, I could point to something blue and ask, "What color is this?" They will be delighted to shriek, "Blue!" This usually starts when they are about 3 years old.

4. Put the activity away when finished

When the child is finished with an activity, we can encourage them to return it to its place on the shelf. This routine emphasizes that there is a beginning, middle, and end to a task.

And putting things back in their special place on the shelf gives order and calm to the space.

With young toddlers, we can first model where things belong and introduce putting things back as the last part of the activity. We can then start to work together with our child to bring things back to the shelf—they might carry one part and we carry the other. Then we can scaffold onto this base by encouraging them to put it back by themselves, for example, tapping the shelf where it belongs. Gradually we will see them put things away more and more by themselves.

They may not do this every day, just as we do not feel like cooking every day. Instead of insisting that they do, we could say, "You want me to do it? Okay, I'll carry this one and you carry that one."

Even older children may need some help breaking the task into manageable parts. "Let's first put the blocks back, and then we'll work on the books."

If they have moved on to the next activity, I do not generally break their concentration. Instead I put away the activity myself, modeling for the child what to do the next time. They may not actually see us do it, but they may see us from the corner of their eye or unconsciously absorb what we are doing.

5. Model, model, model

Our child learns a lot from observing us and other people around them. So we can think how a young child could be successful and model that—for example, push in our chair with two hands, avoid sitting on a low table or shelf, and carry just one thing at a time.

6. Allow any use of the materials, but stop when they're used inappropriately

A child will explore activities in different ways (and often in ways we weren't expecting). We do not want to limit their creativity by stepping in to correct them. If they are not harming the materials, themselves, or someone else, then there is no need to interrupt them. We could perhaps make a mental note to show them its purpose at another time. For example, if a child is using a watering can to fill a bucket, we could show them at another neutral moment how to use the watering can to water some plants.

However, if the child is using the objects inappropriately, we may gently step in. For example, "I can't let you bang that glass on the window." We could then show them that the glasses are for drinking or show them an activity that allows them to use that skill, for example, banging a drum or doing a small hammer-and-nail activity.

7. Modify to meet their level

We may be able to modify an activity to make it easier or more difficult. For example, if our child is struggling with putting shapes into a shape sorter, we can keep the easier shapes (like a cylinder) and remove the more difficult shapes. Then we can build up slowly, adding in a few more shapes as our child gains more skill.

Sometimes for a younger child, when there are fewer items in a set, the child's concentration increases. For example, in my classroom we usually have five to eight animals in our wooden barn, which gets used all the time. We can make more items available as the child grows.

8. Arrange the activities on shelves from easiest to hardest

By putting the activities on the shelf in increasing difficulty from left to right, we help the child move from easier to more difficult activities. If they find an activity too difficult, they can move back to the earlier activity.

9. Use what is available

There is no need to buy all the materials featured in this book. They are meant only to give an idea of the types of activities that will interest toddlers. Similar ones can be made from things we already have lying around the house.

Here are some examples:

- If our child is interested in how coins go into a slot, rather than buying a coin box, cut a narrow slot into a shoe box and offer some large buttons for the child to put through the hole.
- If our child is interested in threading, they can thread dried penne pasta onto a shoe lace with a large knot at the end.
- If our child is interested in opening and closing, collect old jars and rinse them out so our child can practice taking the lids on and off. Use old wallets or purses with different clasps. Hide some fun things inside for them to discover.

10. Be careful with small parts and sharp objects

Montessori activities often involve objects with small parts, or may involve knives or scissors. These activities should always be supervised. We don't need to hover—yet we keep observing in a calm way to make sure they are using the items in a safe way.

HOW TO SET UP
AN ACTIVITY

Toddlers generally choose what to play with according to what looks interesting to them in the moment.

So, instead of simply placing an activity on the shelf, I recommend taking a couple of minutes to set it up in a way that makes it even more engaging for our child.

1. **Display it on a shelf.** Rather than storing activities in a toy box, it is much easier for a toddler to see what is available when we set a few things out on a shelf.

2. **Make it attractive.** Putting an activity into a basket or tray can make it more appealing to a child. If the child does not seem interested in the activity anymore, sometimes changing the tray can make it more appealing.

3. **Show what belongs together.** A tray or basket keeps all the necessary items together. For example, with a play-dough tray we can include a container of play dough; implements they can use to mold, cut, and make patterns; and a mat to protect the table.

4. **Prepare everything so our child can help themselves.** In a painting area, we can have the apron hanging on a hook off one side of the easel and a damp cloth hanging off the other side at the ready for spills, to wipe their hands, or to clean the easel at the end. There could be a basket of fresh paper so they can help themselves and a folding clothesline with clothespins so they can hang their paintings to dry by themselves. Younger children will need some help with these steps, but gradually they will be able to take on more and more themselves.

5. **Undo the activity.** A completed activity is less attractive to a toddler than one that has been left undone. Disassemble the activity before returning it to the shelf. Place the pieces in a bowl to the left (say, puzzle pieces) and the activity to the right (the empty puzzle base). Tracking the movement from left to right is indirect preparation for reading.

HOW TO SET UP
AN ACTIVITY

EXAMPLES

ELEMENTS

- tray
- undone
- left to right
- easiest to hardest along shelf
- at child's height
- beautiful to attract child's interest
- challenging to child—not too easy, not too difficult
- everything at the ready
- items the child can manage themselves

Nº1 **WATERCOLOR**

On a tray:
- watercolor brush
- small jar with small amount of water
- watercolor tablet (begin with one color if you can find the colors separately, so the colors aren't mixed together)

Also provide:
- an underlay to protect the table
- watercolor paper (a little thicker than regular paper)
- a cloth for small spills

Nº2 **SETTING TABLE**

We can show our child how to set the table, providing the following:
- a real glass, small enough for a toddler to manage
- bowl or plate
- small fork, spoon (knife if your child is using one)

Also provide:
- a place mat with markings for fork, spoon, knife, bowl, and glass

TYPES OF ACTIVITIES

01 / EYE-HAND COORDINATION

Toddlers are constantly refining their grasp and practicing working with two hands together. Look for new ways to challenge these movements.

Threading activities

Threading allows our child to refine their grasp, eye-hand coordination, and dexterity, and provides practice working with two hands together.

- Up to 12 months, a baby will be able to remove large rings from a peg and start to replace them.
- Young toddlers can begin to sequence these rings in order from largest to smallest.
- There is also a version with three colored pegs (red, yellow, and blue) and three corresponding colored rings. At first the child is interested in putting the rings onto any peg. Eventually, they start to put a red ring on, say, the blue peg, stop, look for the red peg, and move the red ring to the red peg, matching the color.
- We can then offer ways for the child to thread a ring horizontally—instead of a vertical peg, we can make it horizontal. This introduces a movement called *crossing the midline*, where the child makes a movement with one hand from one side of their body to the other side across their midline.
- Then we move from threading to bead stringing. A good intermediary step is to first offer the child some beads and a wooden stick around 12 inches (30 cm) long.
- Next we can offer a shoelace with some beads. Look for threading sets where the shoelace has a wooden end on it around 1.5 inches (3–4 cm) long, which makes it easier for younger toddlers.
- Then we move on to stringing large beads onto a regular shoelace . . .
- . . . and then stringing smaller beads onto a thin shoelace.

Posting activities

With posting activities the child learns to release an object into a container and begins to understand object permanence (i.e., when something goes away, it can come back).

- Up to 12 months—a baby enjoys putting balls into a box or banging a ball through a hole with a hammer.
- Around 12 months—the young toddler moves on to pushing shapes through holes, starting with a cylinder. Then they can move on to more complex shapes such as a cube, triangular prism, and so on.
- With increasing dexterity the child can start inserting a large coin (or poker chip) into a narrow slot. In our class, inserting coins into a coin box with a key is one of the children's favorite activities.

Opening and closing activities

Another way to work a child's hands is to provide opportunities for them to open and close various containers.

- Use old purses with clasps, empty jars, containers with press stud fasteners, wallets with zippers, and so on. I hide different objects inside for the child to find—a small toy baby, a die, a spinning top, a key ring with the ring removed, etc.
- Find lockboxes where the child can open and close various locks (including a padlock with a key) to reveal small items hidden inside.

Pegboard and elastic bands; nuts and bolts

These activities are great ways to refine the child's fine-motor development.

- The child improves their coordination by stretching elastic bands over a pegboard.
- The child can screw a nut onto the bolt with one hand holding the bolt and the other turning the nut, allowing both hands to work together.
- Offer various sizes of nuts and bolts so the child can organize them by size.

Sorting

Starting around 18 months, toddlers become interested in sorting objects by color, type, and size. Supply a group of objects (or even better, find them with the child at the beach, in the forest, or in the garden). Place them in a large bowl to sort into smaller bowls. A container with compartments would also be perfect for a sorting activity. Some examples of good sorting objects:

- buttons in two or three different colors/sizes/shapes
- shells, two or three different kinds
- nuts in their shells, two or three different kinds

Stereognostic bags

Around 2.5 years, the child will be interested in figuring out what an object is simply by feeling it. Then begins the fun with stereognostic bags, more simply known as mystery bags. (*Stereognosis* is the ability to know an object by feeling around it.)

Find a bag (ideally one that is difficult to peek inside) and put a variety of objects inside. The child can put their hand in and guess what they feel, or we can name an item for them to feel for in the bag.

- Place inside the bag random objects *or* objects around a theme *or* paired objects with two of the same of each item.
- Choose objects that are distinctively shaped, like keys or spoons, rather than items like animals that are harder to distinguish.

Puzzles

Babies and young toddlers like pulling apart puzzles. Knob puzzles where the puzzle pieces fit into a designated shape are perfect for this age. By the time our child is around 18 months, they may be able to fit some simple shapes into the puzzle base.

- The young toddler can start with simple three-to-five-piece puzzles with large knobs. Even if the child is unable to put the pieces back, they are refining their fine-motor development. In this case, I would step in to model putting the pieces back so they can repeat the process of taking them out.
- From about 18 months, the child can move on to nine-piece puzzles with smaller knobs or no knobs.

- Jigsaw puzzles are the next step. Some look like a traditional puzzle with all the pieces the same size. Other puzzles are in the shape of an object—for example, the shape of a tree. The difficulty will depend on the number of pieces.

Note: Young children do not complete a jigsaw puzzle in the same way as an adult. Adults often find the corners and edges first. Children, on the other hand, tend to tackle the puzzle spatially, seeing which shapes fit together. When they are first starting to work on jigsaw puzzles, we can have a turn first to show them or give them two pieces at a time that fit together. They will gradually do more and more by themselves until they have mastered it.

02 / MUSIC AND MOVEMENT

Music

All humans need to move, and all cultures have a long history of singing and dancing. We don't have to be able to sing or play music well for children to enjoy music in the home. If we enjoy it, they will too. Making sounds with instruments, mimicking the rhythm our child makes, copying the movements they are making, or playing start-and-stop games are just as fun as singing along to a song.

Examples of musical instruments that are suitable for toddlers:

- Instruments to shake, such as maracas, tambourines, gourds, and shakers
- Instruments to strike with a mallet, such as a xylophone, drum, or tone block
- Instruments that you blow into, such as a harmonica or recorder
- Music boxes where we turn a handle to make a tune

Listening to music is its own activity. Even though they are a bit old-fashioned, a CD player or an old iPod (one that stores only music) allows a child to select music for themselves. We can even have a mat that they can unroll as a dancing mat.

Many children move instinctively when music comes on. A family may have traditional or cultural dances that they enjoy performing or watching. Spontaneous singing with actions is also fun, like singing along to "The Wheels on the Bus" or "Head, Shoulders, Knees, and Toes."

It is also lovely to take young children to concerts—many concert halls welcome young children or have special performances for children where they can look at the instruments at the end.

Movement

We can provide many movement opportunities for our children:

- running
- jumping
- skipping
- hopping
- brachiating (swinging like a monkey)
- biking
- climbing
- sliding
- balancing
- kicking and throwing balls

If possible, we can head outdoors for movement in the backyard, nearby forest, playground, town square, beach, mountain, river, or lake—even if the weather is not great. "There is no such thing as bad weather, just bad clothing," as the Scandinavians like to say. Living in the Netherlands, we put on our wet-weather clothes and cycle on.

We can also think about how to incorporate movement inside our home, space permitting. In my classroom we have a climbing wall. The young children start to pull up on the lower holds; as they get to around 2 years old, they climb with some support from an adult, and it is not long before they are able to hold their own weight and climb independently. Every muscle of their bodies is hard at work.

Children also like to hide, so think about creating spaces with blankets and chairs, hammocks, and tents. Overgrown gardens make fun hiding spots, too.

03 / PRACTICAL LIFE

ACTIVITIES OF DAILY LIFE AROUND THE HOME

Most parents notice that toddlers love to help around the home, participating in activities that have to do with looking after ourselves and our environment. These activities might be chores to us, but young children love them. And I should mention that they are great for calming active children.

Dr. Montessori discovered quickly that the children in her school wanted to help care for the classroom, themselves, their classmates, and the environment. So she introduced child-sized tools to help them succeed.

These activities are great for learning a sequence, like retrieving and putting on an apron all the way through washing and drying the dishes.

The task will go more slowly and require supervision when the child helps. We'll need to lower our expectations about the final product—the banana slices may be a bit mashed and the beans may have some ends that were missed. However, once they have mastered the skills, our child will become more and more independent. My children have grown up baking and cooking. Now that they are teenagers, they bake a lot and sometimes offer to cook dinner as well.

Here are some ways children can help around the home:

- **Plant care**—watering the plants, dusting the leaves, planting seeds, arranging flowers in small vases (using a small funnel and small pitcher to fill the vase with water)
- **Food preparation**—washing vegetables, beating eggs, scooping their own cereal out of a small container and adding milk from a small jug
- **Snack time**—helping themselves to food from an accessible snack area (which we restock daily with the help of our child, putting out only as much as we are happy for them to eat), peeling and slicing fruit, spreading topping on crackers, squeezing orange juice, pouring water to drink from a small jug
- **Mealtimes**—setting and clearing the table, washing dishes
- **Baking**—taking turns, measuring ingredients, helping to add ingredients, stirring
- **Cleaning**—sweeping, dusting, wiping spills, cleaning windows, polishing mirrors
- **Caring for pets**—feeding the pet, helping to walk the dog, filling up a water bowl

- **Learning to care for themselves**—blowing nose, brushing hair and teeth, washing hands
- **Dressing themselves**—taking socks on and off, fastening Velcro shoes, putting on a T-shirt, pulling trousers up and down, putting on a coat (see page 140 to learn the coat flip), practicing opening and closing zippers/snaps/buttons/shoelaces
- **Helping with the laundry**—bringing dirty clothes to the laundry basket, putting clothes in and taking them out of the washing machine, adding soap, sorting the clean clothes
- **Getting ready for overnight visitors**—making the beds, putting out a clean towel for the guests, putting away toys
- **Trips to the supermarket**—making a list with pictures, getting things from the shelves, helping to push the shopping cart, passing things to us to put on the checkout counter, carrying bags of groceries, putting groceries away at home
- **Volunteer work**—It's never too early to set the example of helping others. When my children were young, one of our weekly outings was to a local nursing home where we would visit the same residents each week. Seeing a young toddler and baby was the highlight of their week, and it taught my children at an early age that it feels lovely to help others.

Tips for practical life activities at home

Most of all, remember that it is meant to be fun. Stop before becoming overwhelmed. And keep practicing!

- Put out only as much as we want to clean up, be it water, dish soap, or a travel-sized bottle of shampoo.
- Have cleaning supplies at the ready: a hand mitt on the table to wipe up small spills, a child-sized broom and mop for larger spills.
- When children are younger than 2 years old, activities will likely have only 1 or 2 steps. As they gain mastery, add more steps (for example, put on an apron, wipe up at the end, take wet cloths to the laundry, and so on).
- Focus on the process, not the result. When the child helps, the task will take longer and the result may not look perfect, but the child is learning to master these skills and will become a lifelong helper at home.
- Look for ways the child can help. When they are younger, keep it simple (an 18-month-old can help carry the T-shirt while we carry the pants to the laundry basket and/or rinse some salad leaves for dinner); as they get to 2+ years, they can help out with even more.

- Look for baskets, trays, and simple caddies to arrange items for them to help, for example, to keep all the window-cleaning items together at the ready.
- We don't have to spend a lot of money. Keep it budget friendly by creating activities with things around the home. And look out for a few nice things like a wooden broom or a larger item like a learning tower to add to a list for birthdays and other special occasions.

Benefits of practical life activities at home

Beyond the simple pleasure young children take from these practical life activities, they are valuable in more ways than one:

- The child is learning to take responsibility in the home.
- We are working together to create, practice, and master the activities.
- Collaboration creates connection.
- These skills require repetition to gain mastery, which is great for building concentration.
- Our child enjoys feeling like a part of the family and being able to contribute.
- These activities involve sequences. As our child's concentration grows, we can increase the number of steps in the activity.
- These activities involve a lot of movement, great for refining fine-motor and gross-motor skills (for example, pouring water without spilling, using a sponge).
- There are many language opportunities around these activities: talking about what we're doing together and giving vocabulary for kitchen implements, food, tools for cleaning, and so on.
- The child learns new skills, independence, and a feeling of self-reliance.

I always say it is good to start young to lay a strong foundation while they are willing. These practical life skills help children learn to care for themselves, care for others (pets, for example), and care for their environment.

SOME AT-HOME PRACTICAL LIFE ACTIVITIES BY AGE

Wondering how to include your child around the home? Here are some ideas for various ages.

You can see how we scaffold their skills with these simple one-step activities for children from 12 to 18 months. Then, in addition to these activities, we offer activities of increasing difficulty for children from 18 months to 3 years. The child from 3 to 4 years old can begin longer, more complex tasks, in addition to those activities from earlier age groups.

12 to 18 months

KITCHEN
- Pour glass of water or milk using small jug—use small amount of liquid to avoid large spills
- Add milk to cereal
- Scoop cereal into bowl
- Wipe up spills with hand mitt
- Take plate to kitchen
- Drink from a glass

BATHROOM
- Brush hair
- Brush teeth with assistance
- Wash hands
- Pack away bath toys
- Fetch and hang up towel

BEDROOM
- Fetch diaper/underwear
- Put dirty clothes in laundry basket
- Open curtains
- Choose between two options for clothing
- Get dressed with assistance
- Take off socks

OTHER
- Help put toys away
- Fetch shoes
- Help the parent (for example, "Can you bring me the watering can, please?")
- Turn light switch on/off

18 months to 3 years

KITCHEN

- Prepare a snack/sandwich
- Peel and slice a banana
- Peel a mandarin orange
- Peel and cut an apple with assistance
- Wash fruits and vegetables
- Make orange juice
- Set the table/clear the table
- Wipe the table
- Sweep the floor—use a dustpan and brush
- Make coffee for parent (push buttons on coffee machine/fetch cup and saucer)

BATHROOM

- Blow nose
- Brush teeth
- Wash body—use small travel-sized soap bottles to minimize waste
- Clean face

BEDROOM

- Help to make bed by pulling up cover
- Choose clothes
- Get dressed with little help

OTHER

- Arrange flowers in small vases
- Pack and carry bag/backpack
- Put on coat
- Put on shoes with Velcro closure
- Water plants
- Put toys into baskets and return them to shelf
- Clean windows
- Load/unload washing machine and dryer
- Sort socks and clothing by color
- Fetch products in supermarket/push cart/help unpack groceries
- Dust
- Put leash on dog and brush dog

3 to 4 years

KITCHEN

- Unload dishwasher
- Measure and mix ingredients for baking
- Scrub and peel vegetables, such as potatoes and carrots
- Assist with cooking (for example, making lasagna)

BATHROOM

- Use toilet/flush toilet/close toilet seat
- Place wet clothing in laundry area
- Wipe with assistance after using toilet
- Wash hair—use travel-sized bottles to minimize waste

BEDROOM

- Make bed—pull up duvet
- Pack clothes into drawers/closet

OTHER

- Feed pets
- Help with recycling
- Fold laundry
- Fold socks
- Vacuum
- Open car door with remote

04 / ARTS AND CRAFTS

Dr. Montessori was asked if the Montessori environment produced good artists. Her response: "I don't know if we produce good artists. But we do produce a child with an eye that sees, a soul that feels, and a hand that obeys." For toddlers, arts and crafts activities are about self-expression, movement, and experiencing different materials. **The process takes precedence over the product.**

Types of arts and crafts activities:

- For young toddlers, we start with drawing. Look for crayons or pencils that glide easily on the paper. Chunky pencils are generally easier for a young toddler to grip, and produce more color than a regular color pencil. Crayons made of natural materials like beeswax or soy are lovely to draw with.

- We can then add a watercolor activity. I like to start with one or two colors at first. If we add more colors, everything tends to turn brown. The tray can contain a very small jar for holding water (little jam jars from hotels are the perfect size), a watercolor brush, and a dish with the watercolor tablet/s. We can have a piece of paper on an underlay (to protect the table), more paper if they would like to repeat, and a cloth at the ready for spills.

- We can introduce using scissors (with supervision) from around 18 months. For the cutting work, use real scissors with rounded ends that cut well, and show the child how to use them appropriately. We can show them we sit down at the table to use them and hold the handles, not the blades. Offer small strips of paper, which will be easier to snip. The pieces can then be collected into a small envelope and closed with a sticker.

- Around 18 months, a gluing activity can be great fun and help them refine their movements by using a small brush with a pot of glue (or a glue stick) to apply glue to the back of the shape and stick it onto the paper.

- Paint and chalk are also fun for toddlers. For younger toddlers, we may wish to only put out paint when we are able to supervise. Again, have wet cloths at the ready for wiping hands, the floor, or the board.

- Clay, play dough, and kinetic sand are lovely creative mediums for toddlers. We can add some simple tools like a rolling pin, cookie cutters, a blunt knife, or shaping tools to manipulate the material in many ways. I love making play dough with them, too. (See page 234 for my favorite recipe for homemade play dough.)

- Around 2.5 years, we can offer simple sewing activities. The sewing box can contain a needle case with a blunt darning needle, some thread, and a 4" x 4" (10 cm x 10 cm) cardboard square with holes punched along the diagonal.
- Short visits to museums help cultivate an appreciation of art. At the museum, we can look for colors, textures, and animals. We can play simple games, like selecting a postcard from the museum shop and then looking for the painting in the gallery.

Tips for arts and crafts

1. Try not to be prescriptive. Rather than showing a child what to make with the art materials, we show them how to use the materials and leave the experimentation up to them. For this reason, Montessori teachers prefer not to use coloring books because of the suggestion that children need to stay within the lines. Similarly we try not to limit children to using only green for grass and blue for sky. They can be creative in their choices.

2. Give feedback. In Montessori, rather than tell the child their artwork is "good" we like to leave it up to the child to decide if they like what they have made.

Instead we can give feedback and encouragement. We can describe what we see; for example, "I see you made a line over here in yellow." This can be more meaningful than saying, "Good job." Then the child really knows what we appreciate when we are looking at their work.

Also, because toddlers are mostly still just making movements of self-expression, we can ask, "Would you like to tell me about your painting?" rather than "What is it?" It may not be a picture of anything in particular but may simply be an expression of the movements in their body.

3. Use good-quality materials. I always recommend quality over quantity, which is particularly important when working with art materials. I would rather buy a few good-quality pencils than have many cheaper ones that break easily and do not have rich colors.

4. Show by example. When showing our child how to use art materials, it is often better to draw squiggles or loose lines than draw a picture. If we show them a perfect-looking flower and they can only scribble, some children will not try at all.

And although it is fun and highly recommended to create together, side by side, it's better to take our own piece of paper than to draw on our child's paper. We do not know the child's intention for the work. Think of it as a fellow student's picture in an art class. Would we draw a little love heart on their self-portrait?

The best example of all is to hang beautiful artwork from artists on the walls of our home and at child height, too, for the whole family to appreciate.

05 / LANGUAGE

"There is a 'sensitive period' for naming things . . . and if adults respond to the hunger for words in an appropriate way, they can give their children a richness and precision of language that will last a lifetime."

—Dr. Silvana Montanaro, *Understanding the Human Being*

We have an amazing opportunity to expose our toddlers to beautiful, rich language that they will absorb with ease. Just as a child can learn the names of different fruits (bananas, apples, grapes, and so on), they can learn the names of different vehicles, from front-end loader to mobile crane, or different birds, from flamingo to toucan. Have fun with it. Likely we will discover limitations in our own vocabulary when we don't know the name of a specific bird, tree, or truck. Then we can look up the names with our child to find out.

Vocabulary baskets (also known as nomenclature materials)

To help toddlers grow their desire to learn words, we can put together vocabulary baskets for them to explore. These baskets have objects classified by theme: items from the kitchen; Australian animals; tools; or musical instruments. This makes it easy for our child to learn new words in a group of familiar objects.

- The first type of vocabulary basket contains **real objects** that the child can touch, feel, and explore as we name them, such as three to five fruits or vegetables.

- The next level is **replica objects**. Because we can't have real elephants in our classrooms or homes, we use replicas to present more vocabulary objects. Again the child can hold the object in their hand as we name it—a very tactile, hands-on approach to learning language.

- The child is then ready to learn that a 3D object is the same as a 2D picture. We can make **matching identical cards** with pictures of the objects on them so the child can match the object to a picture that is exactly the same. It's nice to take photos of the objects and print them so the image is the same size as the object—toddlers love to place the matching object on top to "hide" the picture underneath.

- Once a child is matching pictures that are exactly the same as the objects, they will start **matching similar cards**. We can make a card with a picture of a garbage truck that looks similar to it but isn't exactly the same. They then have to really abstract

(continued on page 48)

HOW TO WORK WITH
LANGUAGE MATERIALS

GIVING A THREE-PERIOD LESSON

PERIOD ONE
name the objects

The primary objective of vocabulary baskets is for the toddler to learn the word for something. We name each object as we look at it, turn it around, feel it, and explore it. We give just the name of the object, for example, *giraffe*, instead of a full description of a giraffe with a long neck and so on.

PERIOD TWO
play games

We can play games to see which objects they can identify. "Can you find me the whisk?" They show us the whisk, and we say, "You found the whisk." And we mix them up.

When working with the cards, we can play several games:
- Lay the cards down one by one and have the child find the object that matches.
- Ask the child to choose an object, and one by one show them the cards until they spot the matching card.
- Fan the cards with the pictures hidden from them and ask them to pick a card; then they can look for the matching object.

If they choose the wrong object to go with the card, make a mental note of which object names they are mixing up. We do not correct them and say "no." I might say something like, "Ah, you wanted to put the violin on the cello." At a later time we can go back to period one and present the names again.

PERIOD THREE
testing

With children over 3 years old, when we know they have mastered the name of an object, we can ask, "What is this?" The child is delighted they know the answer and are very pleased with themselves as they name the object. When they are younger than 3 years old, we do not do the third period, because they are often preverbal or may make a mistake, which undermines their confidence. Wait until our child absolutely knows the names of the objects before doing this step.

the essence of a garbage truck, rather than simply matching the size, color, or shape. This step can often be done by matching pictures in books to objects in our home. Our child may pick up a toy cockatoo and run over to their bookshelf to show us a picture of a cockatoo in their favorite book.

- The final step for toddlers is **vocabulary cards**. We can offer cards with pictures of objects around a theme—vehicles, gardening tools—to help children learn names.

Books

We can choose lovely books to share with our children, and we can read aloud often. Children under 6 years old base their understanding of the world on what they see around them. Therefore, they love books that reflect things they know from their daily life: books about going shopping, visiting grandparents, getting dressed, city life, the seasons, and colors. One of the favorites from our classroom is *Sunshine* by Jan Ormerod, a book without words that tells the story of a little girl waking up and getting ready to leave the house.

Don't be surprised if children read a book about a witch and think that witches are real and scary. The Montessori philosophy is to wait until they are over 6 years old to introduce fantasy (especially scary fantasy), when they begin to understand the difference between reality and fantasy.

What to look for in books:

- **Realistic pictures**. This is what children see in their daily lives and can immediately and more easily relate to—rather than having a bear driving a car, look for pictures of people behind the wheel.
- **Beautiful images.** Children will absorb the beauty of the artwork in the book, so look for gorgeous illustrations.
- **Number of words.** For young toddlers we may have single words or simple sentences on a page. This will build to longer sentences on a page for older toddlers. Older toddlers also enjoy rhyming books. And don't forget poetry books.
- **Different types of pages.** Start with board books; move on to paper pages as the child learns how to handle books. Lift-the-flap books are also fun for toddlers and teach children to be careful as they open the flaps.
- **Books we enjoy.** Children pick up a love of reading from adults, so choose books you will want to read many times, knowing that a toddler will often shout, "Again! Again!"
- **Books that reflect diversity.** Find books that reflect families, races, nationalities, and belief systems that are different from our own.

We show children how to handle books, just as we would show them how to carry a glass. We can slow our movements to turn the page carefully and replace the book with care on the shelf when finished.

Occasionally we may want to have a book in our collection that is not based in reality. Then I would point it out in a fun way. "Do bears really go to the library? Noooo. How interesting. This is pretend. Let's take a look at what happens."

Conversations with our child

Describe the world around us

The adults in the environment are a child's primary source of language, so we can use any moment during our day to describe what we are doing. This could be anything from walking outside to getting dressed in the morning to cooking dinner. Use rich language, giving the proper words for the things we find, like the names of dogs, vegetables, food, vehicles, trees, and birds.

Self-expression

Even a young toddler can have a conversation. Conversations help children learn that what they say is important and encourage language development. We can stop what we are doing, look them in the eye, let them take as long as they need, and—hard as it is— try not to finish their sentences.

If our child says "ba-ba" for ball, we can show we have listened by including the real word in a sentence. For example, "Yes, you threw the ball into the garden."

We can ask simple questions to help them expand their story. Or if the child is preverbal and we are not sure what they want to tell us, we can ask them to show us.

Moments of silence

Don't forget to include moments of silence in the day. It is difficult to filter out background noise, and it's not ideal for language acquisition. In addition, we adults like to give our children feedback on everything they do. But it is also okay to remain silent sometimes and allow our child to evaluate for themselves what they have done.

Children understand more than baby talk and simple instructions. They want to be included in the communications of our daily life.

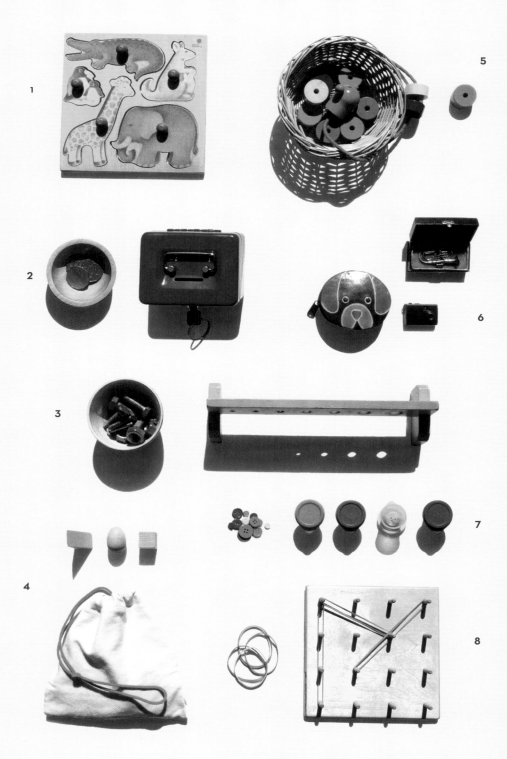

01 / EYE-HAND COORDINATION

Nº1 PEG PUZZLE
This peg puzzle has five pieces, which is perfect for a young toddler. The size of the knob is small to help refine their grasp. From around 18 months.

Nº2 POSTING
The child works on refining their posting skills to fit a coin through a small slot. This is one of the favorite activities in our class for children starting around 16 months.

Nº3 NUTS AND BOLTS
This set is great for organizing the nuts and bolts from smallest to largest and practicing putting the nut on the bolt. The child begins with placing the bolts in the correct holes. Older toddlers will love to master the nuts. From around 2 years.

Nº4 MYSTERY BAGS
These mystery bags are for learning what an object is, using only the sense of touch. We can hide objects around a theme, paired objects, or—most difficult—random objects from around the home. From 2.5 years.

Nº5 THREADING
Threading activities are great for the child to practice working with two hands together. We can vary the size of the beads and the thickness of the thread, depending on their ability. From 16 months.

Nº6 OPENING AND CLOSING
Children love to find small objects inside old purses, jars with lids, or containers with different openings such as zippers, press studs, and clasps. From 18 months.

Nº7 SORTING
Sorting by type, size, and color is interesting to toddlers. Sorting small buttons by color is for children from 2 years.

Nº8 PEGBOARD AND ELASTICS
I love watching toddlers develop their eye-hand coordination with this activity. They learn to stretch elastic bands over the pegs, which takes great concentration. Older children also use this activity to make some fun patterns. From around 2 years.

1

2   3   4

5   6

7   8

02 / MUSIC AND MOVEMENT

N°1 STRIKING

Making sounds by striking/banging an instrument is perfect for both young and older toddlers. Think of triangles, drums, tone blocks, and xylophones. With a younger toddler, assist if needed (for example, hold the triangle while they strike it). For any age toddler.

N°2 SHAKING

Instruments that make sound by shaking are the easiest instruments to begin with. I love the variety of maracas available, from egg shaped to the more traditional kind. Look out for rainmakers, which make soothing sounds as the beads fall or are shaken. For any age toddler.

N°3 MUSIC BOX

Turning a handle to make music is enjoyable for toddlers. Younger toddlers may need some assistance at first, perhaps with the adult holding the music box while they turn it. Seek out large, solid versions for younger toddlers. Older toddlers will enjoy the challenge of turning a smaller music maker (as pictured on opposite page). For any age toddler.

N°4 BLOWING

Simple instruments like a harmonica or recorder are fun for toddlers. They can experiment with rhythm, speed, and volume, and perhaps a variety of notes. For an older toddler.

N°5 BALANCE BIKE

Once the child is tall enough, a balance bike without pedals can be a great alternative to a traditional tricycle. Riding on two wheels, they push themselves along with their feet. Then gradually they begin to take their feet off the ground while they coast, getting used to the feeling of balancing—a useful step before they learn to ride a bike. With time and at their own pace, they often transition easily to a regular bike without training wheels. From around 2 years.

N°6 OUTSIDE

Heading out into nature, making nature collections, and crafting with treasures from our walks are just a few of the ways to enjoy the outside with young children. Go outside often—just add some weatherproof clothing if needed! For any age toddler.

N°7 BALLS

Taking a variety of balls outside encourages kicking, rolling, coordination, strength, and, of course, fun. For toddlers, it is generally best to use balls outside, so that they have enough space to play. For any age toddler.

N°8 SLIDE

This is a Pikler slide, which could be used inside the home. The height of the slide can be adjusted as the child grows. They can also enjoy climbing up the slide as much as sliding down. Or look for a slide on a playground, preferably one they can manage independently. For any age toddler.

03 / PRACTICAL LIFE

Nº1 CARE OF SELF

There are many opportunities for our child to learn how to look after themselves as we gradually scaffold their skills so they can do more and more for themselves. They love to master these tasks, including brushing their hair and their teeth, blowing their nose, and washing their hands. From 15 months.

Nº2 FOOD PREPARATION

Toddlers love to make their own snack or help with meal preparation. Look for tools that are suited to small hands so they can succeed. At first the child will need some assistance. For example, first we can show them how to peel the apple. Then we can hold the apple on a board while they peel from top to bottom, putting the peel into a bowl to take to the compost bin afterward. We show them how to place their hands safely on the apple cutter. We can slice the apple across the middle so the child can easily push the apple cutter through the fruit. Apple cutting from 2 years.

Nº3 TABLE SETTING

Use a low cupboard to provide toddlers access to their bowl, cutlery, and glass so they can set the table following a marked place mat as a guide.

Nº4 BAKING

Toddlers can help to add ingredients that we have measured, mix ingredients with a wooden spoon, knead dough, use cookie cutters, and decorate baked goods. And yes, they also can help us with tasting the finished product. From 12 months.

Nº5 WINDOW CLEANING

It is amazing how toddlers are able to manage squeezing a spray bottle to clean the windows—the repeated movement is great for their hand strength. Then they can wipe the windows from top to bottom with a squeegee and use a cloth to dry them. We can use water or add some vinegar to make the windows sparkle. From 18 months.

Nº6 FLOWER ARRANGING

Flower arranging is a multistep process that allows the toddler to refine their fine-motor skills and practice carrying and pouring water with control—all while adding beauty to the home. First, they can fill a very small jug with water from the tap and place it on a tray to catch any water that might spill. Using a small funnel, they can pour the water into the vase. Then they can place a flower in the vase and place the vase on a doily (which is a nice extra step, good for developing concentration). Have a sponge at the ready for small spills. From 18 months.

Nº7 CLEANING

Having small cleaning tools at the ready—for example, a broom, a mop, a dustpan and brush, hand mitts, and sponges—allows the toddler to learn to care for the home. Most toddlers love to help sweep, mop, and dust. This small dustpan and brush are useful for sweeping up crumbs and provide great practice for working with two hands together. From 12 months.

1

2

3

4

5

6

7

04 / ARTS AND CRAFTS

N°1 WATERCOLOR PAINTING

Watercolors are perfect for toddlers who want to paint—even a young toddler can have success, without as much potential for mess as markers or paint. Start with just one color. Look for single watercolor tablets, pop out one color from a watercolor palette, or cut the palette into single colors if possible. The child can practice wetting the brush, getting paint onto the brush, and making marks on the paper. They are not learning how to draw at this age—they are learning how to use the materials and how to express their movements on paper. From 18 months.

N°2 SEWING

Start with a simple sewing card, a blunt darning needle, and thread that is doubled and knotted at the end. We can show them how to push the needle into the hole, turn the card over, and pull the needle out the other side. Then the needle goes into the next hole, the card is turned over, and again the needle is pulled through, making a stitch. When the card is complete, cut the thread with scissors to remove the needle and make a knot. From 2 years.

N°3 SCISSORS

First the child learns how to hold the scissors safely while sitting at the table. At first, they use two hands to open and close the scissors. Then we can introduce cutting, starting with a sturdy piece of card cut into thin strips. Hold the strip for them to snip. The pieces can be collected into a bowl and then placed into a small envelope and sealed with a sticker. Repeat. As their hand strength develops, they will be able to hold the scissors in one hand and hold the strip for themselves. Around 2 years.

N°4 SCRIBBLING

My favorite scribbling materials for toddlers are soft chunky pencils and beeswax crayon blocks. We can change the paper size, color, and material from time to time to offer variety. Again, they are learning how to use the materials rather than learning to draw. From 12 months.

N°5 CHALK AND ERASER

Offer chunky chalk that fits easily in the child's hands, and provide a large surface, such as a big chalkboard or the sidewalk. A large surface allows movement of the whole arm as they practice using the chalk and cleaning with the eraser. From 12 months.

N°6 GLUING

Affixing small shapes onto paper with a glue brush and a small pot of glue helps refine movements. (Alternatively, offer a glue stick.) The glue can be brushed onto the back of the shape, then turned over and stuck onto the paper. From 18 months.

N°7 CLAY/PLAY DOUGH/KINETIC SAND

Working clay with their hands and using simple tools encourages the child's hand strength and creativity. The clay can be rolled flat, made into a log, cut into small pieces, rolled into a ball, or molded in infinite ways. I love to switch out the clay for play dough or kinetic sand from time to time to provide a variety of sensorial experiences. From 16 months.

1

2

3

4

5

05 / LANGUAGE

N°1 REPLICA OBJECTS
To learn new vocabulary, we can offer realistic replicas around a theme like cooking implements, African animals, or musical instruments. The child can touch and feel around the object while they hear its name—another example of learning with concrete materials. For any age toddler.

N°2 CARDS
As the child gets older, we can extend opportunities to build vocabulary by offering cards with pictures around a theme. That way we are not limited by the replicas or objects we can find. Featured here are artworks by Vincent van Gogh. From 18 months.

N°3 BOOKS
Reading with our toddlers is a joy when we find books we both love. Look for books about seasons, daily life, animals, colors, shapes, vehicles, nature, and our child's favorite topics. For older toddlers, we can add books filled with details to explore or counting books. For any age toddler.

N°4 REAL OBJECTS
The most direct way for the child to learn vocabulary is from objects in their daily life. Just as they learn the names of fruit, we can name flowers in our home and at the market, trees and birds we see in the park, and items around the house. Shown here are some garden peas and a set of cards, where the child learns that a three-dimensional object can be represented by a two-dimensional image. From 12 months. With cards from 14 months.

N°5 OBJECTS WITH CARDS (IDENTICAL AND SIMILAR)
We can draw or photograph an object to make a set of identical cards. Once the child is able to match objects with cards that are identical, we can increase the difficulty by using images that are similar to the objects but not exactly the same. The object may be a dump truck, and we would offer them a picture of any dump truck (of a different model, color, size). This helps them understand the essence of a dump truck. With cards from 14 months.

AN EXTRA NOTE ON THE OUTDOORS AND NATURE

> "Let the children be free; encourage them; let them run outside when it is raining; let them remove their shoes when they find a puddle of water; and, when the grass of the meadows is damp with dew, let them run on it and trample it with their bare feet; let them rest peacefully when a tree invites them to sleep beneath its shade; let them shout and laugh when the sun wakes them in the morning as it wakes every living creature that divides its day between waking and sleeping."
>
> —Dr. Maria Montessori, *The Discovery of the Child*

I love how even in the early 1900s, Dr. Montessori had such a holistic idea of children and their development, including the importance of the outdoors and nature. Nature has the ability to calm us, to connect us with beauty, and to reconnect us to the earth and environment.

Young children are sensorial learners. The quote from Dr. Montessori above embodies how rich their experiences can be. Even now as an adult, the memories of walking barefoot in the grass from my own childhood are still so strong.

If we live in the city, we can plan adventures in nature every few months. It might be for an afternoon at the seaside or spending a few nights away in a tent or cabin.

Here are some ways to include Montessori activities outdoors and in nature:

1. **Seasonal activities.** Depending on the season we could take a basket to the local park or a nearby forest to collect leaves, acorns, shells, sticks, rocks, stones, and pinecones. Fruit picking varies by season, too.

2. **Grow vegetables.** It isn't necessary to have a garden to grow vegetables at home. Set up a potting station with some soil, a scoop, and some seeds. Have a watering can at the ready. Composting—adding food waste to a compost bin or worm farm—helps our children learn about the food cycle and returning nutrients to the soil.

3. **Movement opportunities.** Climb trees; balance along walls, tree stumps, or logs; hang from branches; swing from a tire; ride a balance bike; kick a ball; jump with a jump rope; chase each other; run fast; and walk slowly.

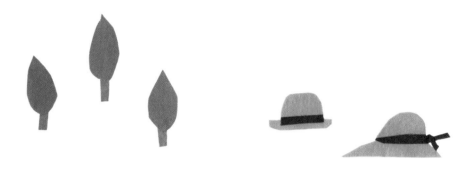

4. **Notice the beauty of the outdoors together.** Watch insects at work, droplets on leaves, the colors of the sunset, the vistas from the mountains, the stillness or the ripples on a lake, the movement of the ocean, or the wind in the trees, or simply take in the gloriousness of the flowers and bees in a neighbor's garden. Grab a magnifying glass to explore close up, touch with our hands, listen to the movement of the trees and grass, and smell the rain or flowers.

5. **Find moments of quiet.** Find a place to sit and watch the clouds, to sit in silence, or just to breathe.

6. **Make treasure hunts.** Make a list of pictures and work together to find all the items on the list. It could be in the garden, at the park, in the forest, or any outdoor place.

7. **Build a hut, cubby house, or obstacle course, and invite over some friends.**

8. **Make outdoor art.** Use mud, water, leaves, flowers, soil, seeds, grass, and any other natural treasures that you find. Lay them into patterns, make them into shapes, or work together to make a face or an animal.

9. **Make a musical wall.** In the garden, hang old pots and pans, bells, and any other objects that make some sound when banged. Find some sticks to make some music.

10. **All-weather exploration.** There is no such thing as bad weather, just bad clothing. So get some great all-weather clothing and shoes (for the adult and the child) and stomp in those puddles, make a snowman, or put on a hat and sunscreen and explore the beach. Get out each and every day.

Bonus: **Anything to do with water**—spraying the windows, filling a bucket and painting bricks with a brush, running through a sprinkler, making rivers with sand and water, or using a water pump at the playground.

WHAT ABOUT NON-MONTESSORI TOYS?

There is a difference between a Montessori classroom and a Montessori home. Although we would not include these toys in a Montessori classroom, we may choose to include a few well-selected toys for open-ended play at home. If we are new to the Montessori approach, we can start with the toys we already have in our homes—keep out our child's favorites, donate the ones that are no longer being used, and put some toys into storage that we will rotate later.

Here are some ideas:

- Duplo/Lego
- wooden blocks
- construction vehicles, emergency vehicles, farm vehicles
- barn and farm animals
- Playmobil sets based on daily life (rather than fantasy, like princesses or pirates)
- a wooden marble run
- loose parts collected from nature adventures
- construction sets
- train sets
- board games

There is room for such open-ended play in the home—the child explores the materials in many creative ways, makes discoveries for themselves, and plays out imaginative scenarios from their daily lives. Yet they aren't a replacement for the Montessori activities we have discussed in this chapter, which give a toddler such satisfaction from mastery and meet so many of a young child's developmental needs.

If a child starts attending a Montessori preschool program, I'd advise against replicating the Montessori materials at home so that they will stay engaged at school. Instead we can continue Montessori at home by including the child in daily life and making sure they have time for unstructured play, opportunities to create, time outdoors, and time for rest. They will continue to practice skills through practical life, arts and crafts, movement and music, and books.

TO PRACTICE

1. Can we provide eye-hand coordination activities to challenge our child's fine-motor skills?
2. Can we provide rich music and movement opportunities?
3. Can we include our child in daily life (practical life activities)?
   food preparation / self-care / care of the environment
4. What arts and crafts possibilities are available?
5. How can we support a rich language environment at home?
   objects / books / conversation

In this chapter, we have seen how observing our children's interests and abilities and providing them with beautiful and engaging activities can help develop the whole child.

We can use items we already have in the home, and Montessori activities don't need to be fully integrated from the first day. Instead we can try a few things to shift toward a Montessori approach at home, observe our child more, build our own confidence, and keep following the child.

And, let's not forget the simplest things, the things that will create memories with our children:

- Let's savor the laughter and giggles.
- Let's invite our children to share in the daily activities of the home.
- Let's enjoy the puddles when it rains.
- Let's collect autumn leaves and hang them in the window.
- Let's build tents indoors.
- Let's leave our children to explore a moment longer.
- Let's comb the beach for shells, in any season.
- Let's cuddle our loved ones an extra time or two.
- Let's enjoy the crispness of the air as we cycle through the city.

SETTING UP
THE HOME

4

SETTING UP MONTESSORI-STYLE SPACES

Walk into a Montessori classroom for the first time, and it is immediately apparent that the space has been beautifully arranged with the children's needs in mind.

The same principles are easy to apply in the home. We aren't aiming to have a perfect home, but we can be intentional in setting up our spaces.

Not every space has to be child-sized. After all, there are different-sized people with different needs in our home. However, it is possible to have a space in each area of our home that is set up for our child to enjoy and feel comfortable in, too.

Eight tips for setting up your home

1. **Child-sized.** Find furniture that the child can manage without help. Look for chairs and tables that are the right height to allow their feet to sit flat on the floor; cut the legs of the furniture a bit if necessary.
2. **Beauty in the space.** Display art and plants at the child's height for them to enjoy.
3. **Independence.** Have activities and materials set up in trays and baskets so they have everything they need at the ready; look for ways to make it easy for the child to help themselves.
4. **Attractive activities.** Have age-appropriate activities beautifully arranged on shelves—rather than in toy boxes—that are inviting to them.
5. **Less is more.** Displaying only a few activities helps the child's concentration; display only the ones they are working to master, so they don't feel overwhelmed.
6. **A place for everything and everything in its place.** Toddlers have a particularly strong sense of order. When we have a place for everything and everything is in its place, it helps them learn where things belong (and where to put them away).
7. **See the space through their eyes.** Get down to the child's height in each space to see what it looks like from their perspective. We may see some tempting wires or some clutter under the shelves, or it may feel overwhelming.
8. **Store and rotate.** Create storage that ideally is out of children's sight and easy on the eye—think floor-to-ceiling cupboards that blend into the wall color, an attic space, or containers that can be stacked in a storage area or behind a couch. Store most of the child's activities, and rotate the activities on their shelves when they are looking for new challenges.

ROOM BY ROOM

Let's look at the different areas of our home and see how these principles can be applied. (For a resource list, see page 226.)

These are only ideas and are not prescriptive. Adapt them to suit. Limitations of space or light give us opportunities to be creative.

Entrance

- Low hooks at the child's height where they can hang up their (child-sized) backpack/bag, jacket, hat, and raincoat
- Basket or shelf for shoes
- Basket for seasonal items such as mittens, scarves, woolen hats, sunglasses, and so on
- Low mirror with a small table or shelf for things like tissues, hair clips, and sunscreen
- Low chair or bench where they can sit to put on their shoes and take them off

Note: If we have more than one child, we may choose to have one basket per child.

Living room

- Low two- or three-tier shelves for activities. If we have more than one child, we can use lower shelves for the younger child's activities and higher shelves for older children's activities. Be sure the higher shelves are out of reach of the younger sibling, or use containers that the younger child cannot manage to open. For reference, the shelves in my classroom are 40" long by 12" deep by 15" high (120 cm by 30 cm by 40 cm).
- Small table and chair, preferably by a window—cut the legs down if needed so the child can put their feet flat on the floor. For example, the chair seat height would be around 8 inches (20 cm) and the table height around 14 inches (35 cm).
- Easy-to-roll floor mats (around 27 inches by 20 inches, or 70 cm by 50 cm) stored in a basket and used to mark a space for their activity.

Kitchen

- Low shelf, cupboard, trolley, or drawer with a small number of child-sized plates, cutlery, glasses, and place mats
  - Use real glasses, plates, and cutlery—children will learn to carry these items with care if they are aware that the items may break. We can remind them that glass is fragile and to use two hands (rather than saying, "Don't drop the glass").

- Stepladder or learning tower or kitchen helper so the child can reach the kitchen counter to help (alternatively, bring food preparation items to the dining table or a low table)

- Child-sized cleaning materials
  - broom, mop, small dustpan, and brush
  - hand mitts (cloths where the hand fits inside; easy for a child to use to wipe up spills)
  - sponges cut to fit their hands
  - dust cloth
  - child-sized aprons

- Child-sized kitchen implements for food preparation
  - apple cutter and corer
  - metal juicer with arm to pull down, orange squeezer or electric juicer to squeeze orange juice
  - little spreaders that toddlers can use easily to spread their favorite topping onto small crackers (stored in a container)

- Cutting implements
  - start with nonserrated butter knives for cutting soft items such as bananas
  - offer a crinkle cutter for firmer fruits and vegetables
  - increase difficulty as the child's skills build, for example, sharper knives may be introduced with a cutting guide as they become preschoolers (with supervision)

- Water source so the child can help themselves to a drink—a water dispenser that they can reach, a low sink, or a little water in a small jug on a tray (with a sponge or cloth at the ready for spills)

- Easy-to-open containers with nutritious snacks—put out only as much food as we are happy for them to eat between meals. If they choose to eat it right after breakfast, the snacks are done for the day.

- Measuring cups and spoons, a scale, and mixing spoons for baking

- Spray bottle and squeegee for cleaning windows

- Small watering can, if there are indoor plants

Note about safety: Keep sharp knives out of reach and show the child how to use them when they are ready; be available to supervise.

Eating area	• For snack time, children could use their low table and chair, and encourage them to keep food at the table (don't let them walk around with food).
	• At mealtimes, I like to sit together as a family at the kitchen/dining table. Look for a chair the child is able to climb in and out of independently, like a Stokke chair or one similar to it.
	• Have a child-sized jug on the table at mealtimes with a small amount of water or milk so children can help themselves—fill with only as much as we are prepared to clean up.
	• Have hand mitts or sponges at the ready for spills.
	• A small basket can be used to carry items from the kitchen to set the table. If we are setting the dining table for the meal, we may need a stepstool for our child to be able to reach the table.
	• A place mat with a guide where to place the plate, cutlery, and glass can be useful for a toddler. One of the parents in my classes had the great idea to photograph her child's favorite set, print it on letter-sized paper, and laminate it—a perfect guide for the child to use when setting the table.
	• Some (handpicked) flowers on the table make mealtimes a special occasion every day.
Bedroom	• Floor mattress or toddler bed that the child can climb in and out of by themselves
	• If space allows, a small shelf with a few activities for them to quietly play with when they wake
	• Book basket or shelf
	• Full-length mirror—helps the child see their full body schema, and aids dressing
	• A small wardrobe with shelves, drawers, or hanging space that the child can reach. Or use a basket with limited choices of seasonally appropriate clothing to choose from each day. Store out-of-season clothing out of reach to avoid potential battles.
	• Ensure the room is completely childproof—cover electrical sockets, remove any loose wires, put curtain cords (which present a choking hazard) out of reach, and install child locks on windows.

Bathroom	• A changing area. Once they are standing, children wearing diapers often don't like to be laid down to be changed. Instead, we can change them standing up in the bathroom to introduce them to the idea that this is where they will use the toilet. We can also start to offer the potty or toilet as part of the changing routine (more on toileting in chapter 7). • Low step to help them to reach the bathroom sink and to climb into the bath • Small bar of soap or a soap pump they can manage by themselves to wash hands • Toothbrush, toothpaste, hairbrush within the child's reach • Mirror at the child's height or accessible to them • Basket for dirty/wet clothing (or in the laundry area) • Low hook or towel rack for the child to have access to their towel • Small travel-sized bottles for body wash, shampoo, and conditioner that the child can learn to use. Refill them each day with a small amount if they like to squeeze bottles.
Arts and crafts area	• Access to art materials—for example, a small set of drawers with pencils, paper, glue, stamps, and collage items • As the child gets older, we can include access to scissors, tape, and a stapler. • Choose fewer but higher-quality art materials. • For toddlers, activities can be set out on trays with everything at the ready—for example, one tray for drawing and one tray for gluing. • Around 3 years, the child will start to enjoy collecting things they will need. Then we may have a tray they can use to select art materials by themselves from a display. • Make putting things away easy: a place for artwork to dry; a place for scraps of paper that can be reused; a place for recycling. • Toddlers are mostly interested in the process, not the product, so here are some ideas for finished artwork: - Use office "in-trays" for things they want to keep or come back to; once the trays are full, glue a selection of favorites in a scrapbook. - Keep a record of artwork that is too bulky to keep by photographing it. - Reuse the artwork as gift paper. - Encourage children to work on both sides of the paper. - Make a gallery to feature some of the child's artwork. For example, have frames where the work is rotated, a string or wire where work is hung up, or magnets on the fridge.

Cozy place for reading	• Have a forward-facing bookshelf or ledge so the child can easily see the cover of the books. Or use a book basket.
	• Display only a few books and change the selection as needed.
	• Provide a beanbag, cushions, low chair, or cozy floor mat.
	• Near the window gives lovely light to read by.
	• Make a cozy space in an old wardrobe by removing the wardrobe doors, or have a pup tent to crawl into.
Outside	• Create opportunities for movement activities: running; jumping; skipping; hopping; brachiating (swinging like a monkey); sliding; dancing; swinging on a rope, an old tire, or a regular swing
	• Gardening—small rakes, trowels, garden forks, wheelbarrow
	• A small vegetable garden they can help care for. If we are able to grow vegetables in a raised garden bed, in pots on a balcony, or inside, they will also learn to appreciate their food by seeing where it comes from and how long it takes to grow and nurture.
	• A place to sit or lie quietly to watch the clouds
	• Water—a bucket of water and a paintbrush to "paint" the bricks or concrete pavers, spray bottles to wash windows, a water table, a water pump
	• Sand pit
	• Labyrinth with small rocks to make a path
	• Place by the door where they can put on outside shoes or brush off their shoes to come inside
	• Baskets and jars for making (seasonal) nature collections
	• Digging in dirt, making mud, reconnecting with the earth
	• Huts or tunnels made from willow branches
	• Create secret paths for the child to explore

There are many sources of inspiration for our outside spaces. I love seeing "natural playscapes" where natural elements are incorporated into the design. For example, a slide built into a slope in the yard, or paths made from natural rocks or found materials. For inspiration, look up Rusty Keeler, who creates such natural playscapes for children.

Note: If there is no outside space at home, look to provide such possibilities at a nearby playground, woods, beach, lake, or mountains.

AT-HOME STARTER SET FOR MONTESSORI TODDLERS

Here are eight basic pieces of equipment to introduce Montessori at home at very little expense.

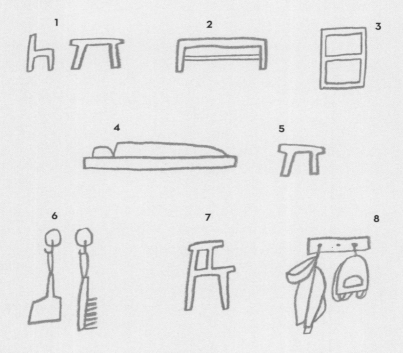

1. small table and chair **2.** low shelf **3.** bookshelf/book box **4.** low bed/floor mattress child can get into themselves **5.** low stool for reaching sink, toilet, and so on **6.** low hooks with cleaning equipment **7.** stepladder/learning tower for helping in the kitchen **8.** low hooks for coat and bag by the entrance

GENERAL PRINCIPLES
TO KEEP IN MIND

Tackling the clutter

Some may be thinking, *I could never keep such a tidy house. We have too many things.*

The first step is to reduce the number of toys, books, and arts and crafts materials, and the general mess that accumulates in our homes. Place into a box the activities and toys our child is not using very often or things they are finding too difficult. This box can be stored for now; we can rotate and reintroduce these activities when our child needs a new challenge. Place into a second box items that are for younger children, activities that they do not use anymore or are too easy. Find a new home for them or keep them aside for a younger sibling.

Keep out just the few things the child is using a lot. It's about continually finding the right number of activities to keep the toddler engaged without holding on to ones that no longer capture their interest.

This will be an ongoing process that will eventually include our child, developing ideas about reusing, recycling, charity, and taking care of our toys with the idea that they can be passed along when we are ready for something new.

Toddlers do not let go of items easily. Get them used to the idea that the items are going into a box for charity or for another family. Offer them one last turn to play with an item; they can put it into the box when they are all finished. They can then help you carry it out of the house to deliver it. And if the box can't be delivered straight away, remove it from view so the child doesn't have to repeat the parting process.

For those interested in adopting an even more minimalist approach at home, I recommend looking up Marie Kondo, the author of *The Life-Changing Magic of Tidying Up*. She recommends keeping only those things in our homes that bring us joy or are useful. Imagine applying the same principle to our child's activities and clothing. And always saying "thank you" to the things we no longer need or use before letting them go.

Making it cozy

Getting rid of clutter does not mean that our home should be without character. We can place cushions, blankets, plants, and artwork at the child's height. Choose natural materials for baskets and carpets to add warmth.

Our homes are adapted to the country and time we live in. With varied family origins, we may display treasures or furniture from these other cultures, in addition to incorporating their rituals and traditions.

I love adding handmade elements like paper bunting, hand-knitted or hand-sewn items, or other crafts that we have created together. These details make a home distinctive and special, something that our child will absorb and cherish.

Vintage items can also make a home unique and full of personality without feeling overly cluttered.

All these elements make a house a home, with the goal of making the space feel calm, warm, and accessible to our child.

Setting up our home to save us work

Raising toddlers can be a lot of work, and we can get pretty tired. So we can also set up our homes to make things easier for them and, consequently, for ourselves.

Arrange things so children can manage more independently and successfully. Have things they need at their height, so that they're easily accessible. Remove items that are not suitable for them to touch. Keep adjusting and improving, particularly as the child grows.

Susan Stephenson, an experienced Montessori teacher, shared this story with me. She would note each time a child asked for help in her class and then set up a way the child would be able to help themselves the next time. So if the child asked for a tissue, a tissue box could be placed at the child's height; if they pulled out all the tissues, a small basket could hold a few tissues carefully folded, ready for use.

Remember, we want our homes to be "yes" spaces that are safe for our toddlers to explore. When we find ourselves saying "no"—for example, when our child is touching something dangerous or banging on glass—we can look for ways to set up the space to remove the temptation. We can cover an electrical outlet that is proving tempting, move furniture to block places we don't want them to explore, use child safety locks on a cupboard we don't want opened, or put a fragile glass cabinet into storage until our child is a little older.

If we can't make the whole home safe, we can at least make one area a "yes" space where our child can play freely, perhaps with a baby gate across the door. (We still want them to be able to move a lot, so avoid playpens, which will limit their movement.)

Sharing spaces

If we have more than one child, here are some extra things to consider:

- Set up spaces for different ages
  - Use lower shelves for activities for the younger child or for any age; use higher shelves for activities with smaller parts more suitable for the older children.
  - Store small parts in containers that are difficult for younger children to open.
  - Establish a place or two where each child can go to be by themselves. This can be as simple as making a hiding place with two chairs and a blanket. We can even hang a sign on the outside that says "Private" and point to it when their sibling comes close. We can tell them, "It says private. It looks like they want to be alone right now. Let's find something else to do."
  - If a younger sibling is interfering, try to simplify the activity so they are able to participate.

- Sharing toys
  - Come up with a plan for how toys and activities will be shared. (See chapter 7 for more information on sharing.)

- Sharing a room
  - Personalize each child's area with, for example, a shelf above their bed with personal items, photos, and collections.
  - Provide privacy if needed, perhaps using a curtain to divide the room.
  - Make clear agreements about using the space, like when to turn the lights off.
  - Set up the space so each child can be alone somewhere.

Small spaces

It's easy to think that it would be easier to apply these principles if we had a larger home. However, it is possible—and perhaps even essential—to use these ideas if our home is smaller. We want to make the best use of the limited space available, which otherwise becomes easily cluttered and overwhelming. I see limitations like small spaces as opportunities for creativity.

Here are some ideas to help:

- Use bunk beds/high beds, or store beds away during the day using Japanese-style futon mattresses.
- Buy multifunctional furniture or get rid of some furniture to create space to play.
- Look for light-framed, less bulky furniture and use a neutral palette to give a feeling of more space.
- Keep fewer things on display at a time to keep the space from feeling cluttered.
- Use space on the walls (such as pegboards to hang craft materials) or underused spaces for storage (under beds, for example), or disguise cabinets for storage near the ceiling (perhaps by painting them the same color as the wall).

THE IMPORTANCE OF THE HOME ENVIRONMENT

These ideas should help inspire us to reduce the chaos and create more engaging spaces for our child.

Other benefits include:

- Encouraging the child to take part in daily life
- Aiding their independence
- Providing peaceful, nurturing, and creative spaces for the whole family
- Helping build the child's concentration with less clutter and fewer, more focused activities
- Allowing the child to absorb and appreciate beauty
- Beginning to show them how to be responsible for their things
- Helping them absorb the culture(s) in which they live

Setting up our home can help to create some calm in our life with our child. I hope these ideas serve as inspiration to make a few changes today. We can always continue to work on our homes, gradually making things even more accessible, more attractive, and more engaging for our child.

TO PRACTICE

1. Can we provide
    - child-sized furniture?
    - beauty, for example, with plants and art?
    - ways for our child to be independent?
    - attractive activities?
    - less clutter?
    - a place for everything and everything in its place?
    - storage?
2. Can we see the space through our child's eyes?
3. Can we make a space in each room of our home for our child?

HOME TOUR

Austria

Now it's time to be inspired by the home of Anna, from Eltern vom Mars.

Let's take a look at Anna's Montessori home in Austria. Everything is set out at the child's height, and the space is simple and beautiful. The child has everything in its place and at the ready. The simple color palette is so calming. Can we please move in?

SELF-CARE AREA

This small self-care area is simple and attractive. Here the child can blow their nose, wipe their face, or brush their hair. A low stool holds two baskets, one with tissues and the other with a hairbrush. A small basket underneath is for dirty tissues. The mirror hung vertically allows the child to see their full body and is perfect for a quick check as they leave the house.

ARTS AND CRAFTS AREA

This arts and crafts area is set up for an older toddler. The open shelves are inviting and accessible, and the use of trays and containers makes it easy to see what is available.

The pencils on the top shelf look attractive, set up by color in simple DIY glass jars with a sticker for each color.

Small pots contain beads and thread for threading activities; materials like washi tape, a hole punch, and scissors are at the ready; marker pens are displayed in a see-through container; and paintbrushes and watercolor are also available.

A plant softens the space, and a music player is available for the child to independently select music.

A small table and chair are next to this shelf where the child can use these materials (not pictured).

KITCHEN

A low drawer in the kitchen allows the child to help themselves to food preparation tools.

Cutlery is held in jars, and baskets hold a rolling pin, whisk, and peeler. Also available are a small grater, juicer, egg slicer, and apple cutter/corer.

OUTSIDE

A paved area has been transformed into a beautiful
outdoor space to explore.

We can see a broom and gardening tools hung
on hooks at the ready, alongside a watering can and
bucket. Potted plants are fun to water, and vertical space
has been used for more plants.

When the weather allows, this area is also used for
working with other activities, simply using a small
breakfast tray or sitting at a table and chair.

RAISING A CURIOUS CHILD
WHO FEELS SEEN AND HEARD

5

ENCOURAGING CURIOSITY
IN OUR CHILD

As we discussed in chapter 2, Montessori teachers do not believe a child is a vessel to be filled with facts. The child genuinely loves learning, making discoveries for themselves, and coming up with creative solutions.

As parents we can also encourage curiosity in our children at home with five ingredients.

FIVE INGREDIENTS FOR CURIOSITY

1. Trust in the child

Dr. Montessori encourages us to trust that the child wants to learn and grow—and that the child intrinsically knows what they need to be working on to develop as they should. This means that if we provide them with a rich environment to explore, we don't need to force them to learn or be worried if they are developing "differently" from their peers.

We can trust that they are developing along their unique path, in their unique way, on their unique timeline.

We can also trust them to learn the limits of their bodies for themselves. Toddlers are curious learners who want to explore the world around them. There may be accidents along the way that we cannot prevent (and maybe that we should allow to happen). After all, that is how they learn. And we will be there if they want to be held. "Ow. Was that a shock? It's hard to see you hurt yourself. I'm so glad your body is made to heal itself. Isn't it amazing?"

Are we constantly worrying about how our child is developing or whether they will hurt themselves? Can we practice setting aside those worries about the future and enjoy where they are today, on their unique journey?

2. A rich learning environment

For a child to develop curiosity in the world around them and a desire to learn, we must provide a rich learning environment and time to explore it.

This rich learning environment does not have to be filled with expensive materials. Explorations in nature can be totally free, dropping a chain or string into a cardboard tube can cost nothing, and sorting out some dried beans can cost very little.

What we learned in chapter 3 about activities was to keep observing our child and offer them opportunities to practice what they are mastering right now.

What does our child's environment look like—the physical, the social, even the adults around them? Does it provide them with rich opportunities for exploration?

3. Time

For children to develop and follow their urge to discover, explore, and wonder, they need time. Time that is unscheduled. Time that is not rushed. Even times when they feel bored.

Allow time to explore. Allow time for movement. Allow time for language and conversation. Allow time for building connections. Allow time for wonder and curiosity.

Whether we work or are with our child full-time, let's think creatively about our days and weeks. Can we change things to carve out 15 to 30 minutes of unscheduled time every day? Perhaps an hour or two on the weekend? What commitments can we let go of?

4. A safe and secure base

As a parent we can provide physical and emotional safety and security. We keep our child physically safe from electrical outlets, busy roads, and other dangers. We childproof our homes, or at least one area of it, so that our child can freely explore.

Emotionally we can give them safety, too. We can accept them for who they are. And they can trust us to be there for them even when they are having a hard time.

This safety and sense of security allow the child the freedom to be curious in the world.

Are there ways to show our child that we are there for them, even (and particularly) when they are having a hard time? Are we able to look them in the eye and acknowledge the big feelings they are having about things that seem small to us?

5. Fostering a sense of wonder

We can ask our child questions about the world we see, invite them to explore with all their senses, and get out into nature as often as possible.

Are we modeling wonder for our child? Do we allow them to explore with all their senses? Do we use nature to inspire a sense of wonder in our child?

SEVEN PRINCIPLES FOR CURIOUS HUMANS

When we ensure these five ingredients are available to our child, they have a strong base from which to become curious about the world around them and develop the ability to think and do things for themselves.

With a foundation of the five basic ingredients, we can apply seven principles to help them become curious human beings.

1. Follow the child—let them lead.

2. Encourage hands-on learning—let them explore.

3. Include the child in daily life—let them be included.

4. Go slow—let them set their own pace.

5. Help me to help myself—let them be independent and responsible.

6. Encourage creativity—let them wonder.

7. Observe—let them show us.

Let's take each one in turn to explore how they can help us bring Montessori into our daily lives.

1. Follow the child

> "It is the child's way of learning. This is the path he follows. He learns everything without knowing he is learning it . . . treading always in the paths of joy and love."
>
> —Dr. Maria Montessori, *The Absorbent Mind*

We have already talked about how important it is to let the child lead, to not interrupt when the child is focusing deeply on something (as much as possible, at least), and to follow their interests. But I don't think it can be repeated too many times. This is the root of the Montessori approach.

This may mean that we choose to go for a walk and let the child lead. We stop and go at their pace.

It may mean that we talk about lighthouses a lot, go and visit lighthouses, read books about lighthouses, and make a model lighthouse with our child if that is their current area of interest.

It may mean getting things ready in the evening if our child is not a morning person.

Following the child means following their unique timeline, seeing where they are today, and not imposing our idea of what they should be learning when.

Let me be clear. **Following the child is not permissiveness, allowing them to do whatever they like.** We will set limits when needed, ensuring the safety and care of themselves, their environment, and others.

But it is not being directive either. When we hear ourselves giving commands, giving lessons, or giving too much information, may we remember, *Ah, yes. How can I find a way to step back and let them lead?*

We do have to do things, though, we often think. *We have to get dressed; we have to get to day care; we have to have dinner; we have to have a bath.* We will still make these things happen, but in a way that allows us to "follow the child." We can learn to work with our child rather than doing something to them like bribing, threatening, or punishing them. We will look into ways we can set limits and cultivate cooperation with our toddler in chapter 6.

2. Encourage hands-on learning

Toddlers learn best when they touch things, smell things, hear things, taste things, and see things. To raise curious learners, look for ways to provide hands-on, firsthand experiences for them.

When they start to ask questions, instead of simply giving them the answer, we can say, "I don't know. Let's find out together." Then we might be able to do a small experiment or explore together, like getting out a magnifying glass to let them take a closer look. Or, we may visit the zoo, go to the library to find some books, or ask a neighbor who knows more about the topic.

Our toddlers are learning that if they don't know something, they can be resourceful and find it out, often in a hands-on, concrete way.

At home, they will explore their environment by touching and feeling things. Instead of saying, "No, don't touch," we can observe the skill they are practicing and look for a way to redirect it toward an activity that is more appropriate. If they are taking the books off the bookshelf, we can put them back so they can practice it again and again. Or, if we don't feel like playing that game, we can think of other things they can empty, like a collection of scarves in a basket. When we find them exploring our wallet and taking out all our cards and cash, we can prepare some other containers in a basket for them to open and close and find things inside. In our classroom we even have an old wallet with some of my old loyalty cards and library cards.

Again, nature is a great place for hands-on and sensorial learning, from the wind or sun on their face, to the sand or soil in their fingers, to the sound of the waves or the crunch of the leaves, to the smell of the sea or the leaves in the woods.

3. Include the child in daily life

Toddlers are curious about what we are up to. They want to be a significant member of the family. They are not just trying to drive us crazy by clinging to our leg.

In chapter 3, we looked at many practical day-to-day activities in which we can include our toddlers.

Maybe we get them to help with food preparation. We can invite them by saying, "We are getting dinner ready. Which part would you like to do?" They can hand us things, or we can get a stepladder for them to join us in the kitchen, have an apron on a hook that they can wear, get them to wash their hands, have them tear some lettuce for the salad, have them rinse the leaves. Let them wander off if they lose interest.

Rather than thinking, *I have to do the laundry,* we can think of it as an activity to do together. I remember when my son was a toddler, I would hold him up so he could reach the buttons for the washing machine. He would often help me unload the items and then play around with the clothespins as I hung up the clothes. (There could be a low clothesline where children can hang clothes, too). We were lucky to be living in Australia at the time, where we had space for an outdoor clothesline. My daughter would lie on a little mat and kick around and watch us as we all chatted. Some days it nearly looked like domestic bliss. Most days it looked a bit more like organized chaos, but it was a lot of fun.

Having young children involved does mean that it's messier and slower. But we are making connections and memories that will last a lifetime. Those of us struggling with fitting this into our days and weeks with work and life commitments can start with moments when we do have time. This might mean setting aside an hour or two each weekend when you stay home and do laundry together, or a baking project, or care for the plants and garden. Recognize that on weekdays, we may not have the time or patience to let our children help cook, but they can be involved in setting the table, pouring their own drink at dinner, and taking their plate to the counter after the meal. We can start with the things we enjoy the most and would love to do with our children.

For more ideas, revisit the list of "practical life activities" in chapter 3 or the activities list in the appendix.

4. Go slow

> "Be fast when it makes sense to be fast, and be slow when slowness is called for. Seek to live at what musicians call the tempo giusto—the right speed."
>
> —Carl Honoré, *In Praise of Slow*

With toddlers, the "tempo giusto" will often be a lot slower than we are used to. Toddlers do not like to rush (except if they see a large open space, and then they will need to run).

Stop and look at the cracks on the pavement together, and enjoy the process rather than the product. Going slowly gives our child time to explore and be curious. And we would do well to learn from them. They remind us to slow down and be present. We can let go of making mental checklists and worrying about the past or future, too.

If we want their cooperation, we are well advised to go slowly. This means practicing not saying, "We're late again!" every morning. We will stress them out. They will resist. We will be even later. (Some ideas on how not to be late are on page 142.)

If we live more slowly, then in those occasional times when we need to rush—for example, to catch a bus or because we missed our morning alarm—our child will be a lot more accommodating. When rushed every day, our child may tune out our requests when we really need their help.

5. Help me to help myself

"Help me to help myself" is an expression often used in Montessori. It means:

- setting up things for our child to be successful by themselves
- **stepping in as little as possible and as much as is necessary**, then stepping back for our child to continue to try
- allowing time to practice
- showing our acceptance and support

How to teach our child skills

Break the task into **small steps** and show them **very slowly**. Toddlers will pick it up faster if we **don't talk** at the same time we're showing them. Simply say, "Look!" and demonstrate with slow, clear movements.

Scaffold skills

I love how Montessori materials in a classroom build on each other as the child works through them from simple to more complex, each skill building on the next.

We can apply the same principle to teaching our child to do things themselves at home. We scaffold skills as the child gains competence and maturity. The skills will become more difficult or have more steps or require them to follow multistep instructions.

For example, first we can show them how to put their foot in their shoe. Next we can show them how to pull the Velcro to tighten the shoes. Once they master that, they can learn to push down on the Velcro to fasten them. Then we invite them to put on their shoes all by themselves.

Allow time

When we allow enough time in our daily routine, we can help children help themselves. For example, we can let them get dressed at their own pace. That doesn't mean allowing unlimited time, but it might mean allowing ten to fifteen minutes while we sit on the floor with a cup of tea nearby, so we can relax and enjoy the process of helping our child learn to get dressed.

We can also practice on a rainy day, for example, letting our toddler take off their socks and put them back on, and take them off and put them back on.

These daily activities can provide moments of connection and opportunities for learning, when our child learns to do things for themselves and becomes confident in their own abilities.

If we start to feel frustrated when it is taking too long, rather than getting irritated, we can acknowledge that this time we are going to help them, and try again tomorrow.

Be friendly about mistakes

> "Nothing can take away initiative as fast as when we redo something that they did."
>
> —Jean K. Miller/Marianne White Dunlap,
> *The Power of Conscious Parenting*

Mistakes are simply opportunities to learn. Our children will make mistakes, break and spill things, and even hurt someone sometimes. Or when they offer to help, they may not do the task as well as we would have done it ourselves.

Instead of punishing, lecturing, or correcting them, try this:

1. If they get the name of something wrong, we can make a mental note that they don't know it yet. We can teach it again at another (neutral) time. They will be more open to learning it later than they will if we correct them. In Montessori we have a phrase for this: **"Teach by teaching, not by correcting."**

2. If they break or spill things, we can have supplies at the ready for them to help clean it up.

3. We can support them while they make it up to someone they have hurt.

4. We can model not taking ourselves too seriously when we make mistakes and show them that we apologize. "I'm sorry. What I should have said is . . ." or "What I should have done is . . ."

Offering help

Rather than rushing in to help our toddler, we wait to see how much they can manage themselves. If they are stuck or the task is difficult or new, we can offer help.

"Would you like me or someone else to help you do that?"
"Would you like to see how I do it?"
"Have you tried . . . ?"

Then we help only if they want it.

6. Encourage creativity

> "The more experience a child has with real purposeful activity and solving problems, the more useful, creative, and effective her imagination will become."
>
> —Susan Stephenson, *The Joyful Child*

There is a common misconception that the Montessori approach does not support and encourage children's creativity and imagination. Reasons cited include the fact that Montessori materials are for a specific purpose rather than being more open-ended, that we do not have a pretend-play corner in our classrooms, and that we do not encourage fantasy in children under 6 years old (rather, we focus on the concrete world around them).

Imagination is different from fantasy

Fantasy means making up something that does not exist in reality. Children under 6 don't easily perceive the difference between something that is made up and something that is real. In a research study, "Do Monsters Dream? Young Children's Understanding of the Fantasy/Reality Distinction" by Tanya Sharon and Jacqueline D. Woolley, young children were shown fantastical and natural pictures of animals. The 3-year-olds had difficulty distinguishing real from fantastical scenes.

We may witness this when a child is scared by something in books or other media, from dragons and monsters to images they see on the news. It can feel very real to them.

Imagination, on the other hand, is used when our mind takes the information we have collected and comes up with creative possibilities. In Montessori, we lay the foundation for our child in the first years in reality, planting the seeds for their life as creative and imaginative citizens of the world. To establish a strong foundation, we can provide our children with hands-on experiences in the real world in the early years. Around 2.5+ years, we will see our child begin with pretend play. This is a sign that they are processing what they see around them (imagination). They play families, bake us cookies, and pretend to be the schoolteacher. They are being creative without becoming overwhelmed by the idea of dragons, monsters, or other things they can't see or experience directly (fantasy).

When providing materials for such play, we can keep the items less prescriptive—scarves and other objects can be used in many ways, whereas a firefighter's suit can be used in only one way.

The focus on reality won't limit their creativity; it will enhance it. We can see the groundwork flourish in adolescence when the imagination becomes particularly strong and they start to come up with creative solutions to our world problems and for social change.

What about artistic creativity?

As we discussed in chapter 4, we can provide a rich and inviting area for artistic creativity. We can:

- Set up beautiful materials at our child's height.
- Create invitations for creativity—beautiful trays with age-appropriate materials to explore.
- Make beauty part of our home, including art and plants, which they will absorb and be inspired by.
- Choose quality over quantity when it comes to the materials.

In addition, there are key principles that we can practice to support our child's development of their artistic creativity. We can:

- Invite open-ended use of materials (use fewer art kits and coloring books, which are more prescriptive).
- Prepare ourselves to encourage creativity—allow time and be open to allowing mess and exploration; prepare a space that is okay to get dirty; relax, join in, and create together.
- Ask, not tell. Rather than instructing our child, we can encourage exploration.
- Allow boredom. When we have unscheduled time in our day to sit without anything planned (and without technology to entertain us), our child has a chance to be bored. Their mind can wander and daydream, they can come up with new ideas, and they can make new connections. When the mind is bored, it seeks stimulation and becomes increasingly creative.
- Look at the process, not the result. Focus on our child's effort by describing their effort. "You made big circles." "I see you mixed these two colors."
- Show our child that there are no mistakes in this work. We can experiment and learn when things don't turn out the way we expected.

Most of all we can have fun inspiring, exploring, and creating with our child.

7. Observation

Often Montessori teachers will tell parents, "Just observe your child." *Observe what about my child? Why? And how?*

Observing is seeing or perceiving without any judgment or analysis. It means being just like a video camera, which objectively records the situation and doesn't analyze what is being seen.

For example, a Montessori teacher might make the following observation about a student: "John releases the pencil from his right hand. It falls to the ground. He looks out the window. He transfers his weight from the left foot to the right foot. He bends his knees. He picks up the pencil using his thumb and index finger of the right hand."

By observing, we are scientifically recording what we see rather than rushing to react or making any assumptions. **With the information, we can respond rather than react.**

We see more details, we notice when something changes, and we practice taking the judgment away from what we see. It allows us to see the child with fresh eyes every day.

What to do with these observations?

These observations will help in many ways.

We learn to see that our child is developing in their own unique way. We are able to follow their interests and keep them curious about the world around them.

We may hold back before stepping in, seeing opportunities instead of limiting their curiosity and creativity. And we also see those occasions when we need to step in calmly to keep them safe.

When we observe over a period of time, we will begin to observe subtle differences about our child that we might otherwise miss.

We can also identify factors in the environment or with the adults that help or hinder independence, movement, communication, or other areas of development.

Observing helps us support our children to be the curious learners they are. Observing enables us to look at our child clearly and without judgment or a preconceived idea of what they are capable of.

SOME THINGS WE CAN OBSERVE

FINE-MOTOR SKILLS

- How they grasp and hold objects
- Which fingers and which hand they use
- The grip they use on a paintbrush or pencil
- Which fine-motor skill activities and skills they are practicing, such as using their pincer grip, threading, and so on

GROSS-MOTOR SKILLS

- How they come to stand or sit
- How they walk—distance of legs or arm movements
- Balance
- The gross-motor skills they are practicing
- Whether they choose activities that use gross-motor skills
- Whether the environment helps or hinders their movement

COMMUNICATION

- Sounds/words they make to communicate
- Smiling
- Crying—intensity, duration
- Other body language
- How they express themselves
- Eye contact during conversations
- Language used
- How they are responded to when they communicate

COGNITIVE DEVELOPMENT

- What they are interested in
- What they are practicing and learning to master, and the activities they can complete
- How long they play with an activity

SOCIAL DEVELOPMENT

- Interactions with others—peers and adults
- Whether they observe others
- How they ask for help
- How they provide assistance to others

EMOTIONAL DEVELOPMENT

- When the child cries, smiles, and laughs
- How they get comforted or comfort themselves
- How they respond to strangers
- How they deal with moments of separation
- How they manage when things do not go their way

EATING

- What they eat and how much
- Whether they are passive or active eaters—being fed or feeding themselves

SLEEPING

- Any sleep patterns
- How they fall asleep
- Quality of sleep
- Position during sleep
- How they transition to waking

INDEPENDENCE

- Signs of independence
- Relationship to adults

CLOTHING

- Whether the clothing helps or hinders movement and independence
- Whether they try to put on and take off their own clothing
- Whether they express preferences for their clothing

SELF-OBSERVATION

- Record our communication—what we say and how we interact with our child
- If anything comes up for us as we observe our child
- How we respond if our child does not eat or sleep
- What we say when our child does something we like or don't like

INGREDIENTS AND PRINCIPLES FOR ENCOURAGING CURIOSITY

1.   Trust in the child

2.   A rich learning environment

3.   Time

4.   A safe and secure base

5.   Fostering a sense of wonder

1.   Follow the child

2.   Encourage hands-on learning

3.   Include the child in daily life

4.   Go slow

5.   Help me to help myself

6.   Encourage creativity

7.   Observation

ACCEPTING OUR CHILD
FOR WHO THEY ARE

Toddlers want to feel significant, they want to feel like they belong, and they want to be accepted for who they are. If we understand this, we can move away from doing battle with them or being triggered by them, and move toward being able to guide, support, and lead them.

GIVE TODDLERS SIGNIFICANCE, BELONGING, AND ACCEPTANCE FOR WHO THEY ARE

Seeing the world through our toddler's eyes helps us **see their perspective**. This is similar to empathizing with, or having compassion for, our child. Whichever we choose, we recognize that everyone is right in their own eyes.

If our child grabs a toy out of another child's hands, they are not trying to be naughty. If we look at it from their perspective, we can see they simply want to play with that toy *right now*. Then we can observe them, see if they need any help, or be ready to step in if needed.

We may think our child is being destructive because they are pulling the soil from the potted plants, but when we look from their perspective, we can understand that they are seeing something in their environment at their height that needs to be explored *right now*. We can observe them and decide if we need to step in to remove the plant or perhaps cover the soil.

Instead of thinking that our child is trying to wind us up by poking out their tongue at us and then laughing, we can look from their perspective. They are testing out a new sound, seeing our reaction, and figuring out cause and effect. Again, let's observe and see if they stop all by themselves. Or we may come up with something else that is okay and say something like "I don't like it when you poke your tongue out at me, but we can go and tumble on the carpet over here."

When we stop to observe and remove the judgment, it opens us up to be able to see our child and accept them for who they are.

When we ask, "How can I get my child to be less shy/concentrate more/be more interested in art/be more active?" and so on, we are not accepting them for who they are. Instead, we can work to show our child we love them just as they are, where they are right now. Really, that is what anyone wants.

Significance. Belonging. Acceptance for who we are.

BE THEIR TRANSLATOR

When we can see things from our child's perspective, we can also be their translator when needed, as though we're looking up what they are trying to say in a dictionary.

"Are you trying to tell me . . . ?" is a useful phrase for translating the toddler's needs into words.

When they throw their food on the floor, we can say, "Are you trying to tell me you're all finished?"

We can also use this for an older child who is calling people names or acting inappropriately. "It sounds like you are pretty angry right now. Are you trying to say you don't like it when they touch your things?"

And we could translate for our partner or the child's grandparent if we notice they are getting upset. "It sounds like it is important to your mother/grandfather to sit at the table to eat, and you really want to walk around with your food."

SOMETIMES

OUR JOB IS TO

BE OUR CHILD'S

TRANSLATOR

ALLOW ALL FEELINGS, BUT NOT ALL BEHAVIOR

We might think, *If I accept them for who they are, see things from their perspective, and allow all their feelings, do I have to accept all their behavior?*

This is absolutely not the case. We step in if necessary to stop any inappropriate behavior. As the adult, we often need to act as our toddler's prefrontal cortex (the rational part of their brain), which is still developing. We can step in to keep them safe. To keep others safe. To keep ourselves safe. To show them they can disagree with others in a respectful way. To show them how to show up and be responsible human beings.

Examples:

"It's okay to disagree, but I can't let you hurt your brother/sister. You sit on this side of me, and you sit on the other."

"I can't let you hurt me/I can't let you speak to me that way/I cannot let you hurt yourself. But I see something important is going on, and I am trying to understand."

GIVE OUR CHILD FEEDBACK

—INSTEAD OF PRAISE

Montessori teachers like to help children build their own sense of self, learn how to accept themselves for who they are, and learn what feels good in the way they treat others.

Since the 1970s and '80s, there has been a big push for parents to praise their child to build the child's self-esteem. So we hear parents saying, "good job," "good boy," "good girl." In Dutch, they even have a phrase: "*goed zo*." We say it in response to everything. We praise children for their paintings, for flushing the toilet, we applaud them, and we declare every physical feat a triumph.

These types of praise are extrinsic motivators that do not come from within the child themselves.

Alfie Kohn wrote a useful article, "Five Reasons to Stop Saying 'Good Job!'" in which he points out that:

- Praise can actually be used to manipulate children when we use it as a bargaining tool to motivate them.
- It can create praise junkies.
- Praise can actually take the joy away, with children looking to us for reassurance rather than experiencing delight at what they have achieved.
- Children can become less motivated when they do something for praise, because it removes the meaning for themselves.
- Praise can lower achievement—when an activity is tied to the pressure to perform, the child's interest or pleasure in the activity goes down, or they take fewer risks.

Montessori teachers believe instead that a child will learn to behave if we help to develop their intrinsic motivation—their internal radar that tells them that something is right (or wrong) and recognizes what helps (or hurts) themselves or someone else.

What we can say instead . . .

It can be surprising at first how often we find ourselves saying "good job." When we start to be conscious of it, we can choose to change it. When looking for alternatives, the best guide is to think about what we would say to another adult when **giving them feedback**.

Here are some ideas that I first learned from the book *How to Talk So Kids Will Listen and Listen So Kids Will Talk* by Adele Faber and Elaine Mazlish. What I love about these suggestions is that they let the child know more specifically what we appreciate and give the child vocabulary that is so much richer than simply "good job."

1. Describe what we see

Focus on the process rather than the product and describe what our child has done. Give feedback by using positive and factual descriptions of the child's actions and accomplishments.

"You took your plate to the kitchen."
"You look really pleased with yourself."
"You got dressed all by yourself."
"You put the blocks in the basket and put them back on the shelf."
"You used blue and red paint. I see a swirl over here."

2. Sum it up with a word

"You packed your bag and are ready to go to the beach. Now, that's what I call *independence*!"
"You helped your grandma with her bag. Now, that's what I call being *thoughtful*."
"You wiped up the water on the floor with the mop without me asking. That's what I call being *resourceful*."

3. Describe how we feel

"I am so excited for you."
"It's a pleasure to walk into the living room when everything has been put away."

ROLES AND LABELS

Another part of accepting a child for who they are means seeing them without any preconceived judgments or ideas about them.

As the adults in their lives, we need to be careful about labeling our children.

We likely have someone in our life who has been labeled "the clown," "the shy one," "the naughty one." Even positive labels can be difficult to always live up to (e.g., "the clever one," "the athletic one").

These labels can last a lifetime—something the child never grows out of.

Instead, we can give them **another view of themselves**. Recall stories with them of times when they have been successful in difficult areas. Let them overhear us tell someone how they worked hard to overcome an obstacle. For example, we can say, "I liked watching you carry that glass so carefully to the table with two hands," to a child who might otherwise be labeled clumsy.

Labels are commonly used with siblings, too. Once a new baby is born into the family, a young child suddenly becomes the "big brother/sister." It is a huge responsibility to have to behave all the time and show their sibling how to be a "big kid." Instead of always leaving the eldest in charge, for example, while we are in the bathroom, we can **get children to look after each other**, regardless of their age. We can make sure that younger children also take on age-appropriate responsibilities rather than leaving everything to the eldest.

Let's see our toddler and accept them for who they are. In moments of celebration. And when they are having a hard time. Every day.

Allowing our child to be curious and giving them a sense of significance, belonging, and acceptance provides a **solid foundation of connection and trust** with our child— something we will need to cultivate cooperation and when we have to set limits with them.

Without connection, we get very little cooperation; without trust, setting limits becomes difficult.

TO PRACTICE

1. How can we allow our child to be more curious?
   - Does our child feel we trust them?
   - Is there a rich learning environment?
   - Do we allow time to let them explore and to go at their own pace?
   - Is it physically and psychologically safe for them?
   - How can we foster a sense of wonder?
2. Practice observing our child for ten to fifteen minutes a day.
   - Be curious
   - Be objective
   - Avoid analysis
3. How can we give our child a sense of significance and belonging, and let them know we accept them for who they are?
   - See from their perspective
   - Translate for them
   - Give them feedback rather than praise
   - Avoid roles and labels

NURTURING COOPERATION AND RESPONSIBILITY IN OUR CHILD

6

PART ONE

CULTIVATING COOPERATION

WHEN YOUR CHILD WON'T LISTEN TO YOU

Cultivating cooperation in a toddler is a tricky thing. Toddlers are naturally curious, they are impulsive, and they are servants to their will. Common ways of trying to get cooperation from toddlers include threats, bribes, punishment, and constant repetition.

We find ourselves thinking, *Why won't they listen to me?*

> "If you've told a child a thousand times, and the child still has not learned, then it is not the child who is the slow learner."
>
> —Walter B. Barbe

WHY THE MONTESSORI APPROACH DOES NOT USE THREATS, BRIBES, OR PUNISHMENTS

The word *discipline* comes from the Latin word *disciplina*, meaning "teaching; learning." So we should consider **what we are teaching our children and what our children are learning** from the way we discipline them.

Threats, bribes, and punishments are extrinsic motivations. The child may cooperate to avoid a punishment or to get a sticker or some ice cream. But that kind of discipline rarely has a long-term effect. It is a quick fix, if it works at all. It can also be a distraction from the issue at hand.

I once got a detention at school for writing a mean note about the teacher (in my defense she was scary, but I should never have called her a dragon). Of course, the teacher found the note. I was so upset about getting a detention that I told everyone in the class that the teacher was mean. Did the punishment work? Not at all. Instead of being sorry that I had wronged the teacher, I felt that the teacher was the one who had done something wrong.

When we threaten a child with punishment like a time-out, we begin to erode the trust between parent and child. Two things can happen. They can become scared of the adult and cooperate out of fear, or they find a way to do what they want sneakily, without their parent finding out.

Similarly, threats and bribes may get the child to cooperate, but not because the child wants to help us. They simply want to avoid the negative consequences (punishment) or take advantage of the positive ones (rewards). Threats and bribes may need to get bigger and more elaborate as the child grows. If they have learned to do something only so they'll get a sticker, the "price" of their cooperation will rise.

These methods of getting our toddler to cooperate are exhausting. They place all the responsibility on us, the adult. We are thinking, *How am I going to get my child to get dressed/eat/wash their hands?* We end up nagging, and the child stops listening to us altogether.

There is an another approach.

Each time we are challenged by our child, we can see it as a teaching opportunity for us and a learning opportunity for them.

Let's add to our toolbox for cultivating cooperation and look for ways to work with our child to get them to cooperate (without losing our cool).

And let's ask ourselves, *How can I support my child right now?*

Cultivating cooperation involves:

- problem solving with our toddler
- involving the child
- talking in a way that helps them listen
- managing our expectations
- a little bonus

Note: We'll need a foundation of connection and trust with our toddler to get their cooperation. So when everything seems like a battle, it's good to go back and review the ideas from the last chapter.

PROBLEM SOLVING
WITH OUR TODDLERS

I like to start by finding a way to work with the child so they feel like they have some control over the situation. Even though they are small, toddlers want to be involved in how things happen.

The child is not in charge, but they can have input into how to solve problems. We can ask, **"How can we solve the problem?"** and then come up with solutions together.

We might be coming up with most of the ideas, but the toddler is learning the process. Don't underestimate them. Sometimes they will come up with great ideas (often much more creative than ours).

- "You want to stay at the park and I'm ready to leave. I wonder how we can solve the problem."

- "You'd like to finish that puzzle and then you'll put on your shirt? Okay, I'll go and get dressed and come back to see if you'd like some help."

- "Two kids and one toy. I wonder how you'll work that out."

Even a preverbal child can help. For example, if a crawling sibling has taken one of their toys, they might come up with the idea to bring their sibling another toy to play with.

If it's a bigger problem, we can write a list of solutions. Include even silly ideas if they come up. Then we can review the list together and find solutions that everyone can live with. We can select one to try and set a time to come back to see if it is working or needs to be adjusted a little. This process may not be quite so formal with a toddler, but they are learning a practice that we can build on as they get older.

In addition, the toddler is more likely to take ownership of the planned solution and follow through. It's also a great skill for solving problems with others. (This is an idea to come back to when we talk about siblings in chapter 7.)

When we get our toddlers involved in solving problems, we may even find we are more relaxed. We get to share a little of the responsibility. We remain open and curious about how it might happen in a way we may not expect, without forcing it.

Making a checklist with our child

One way to solve problems with toddlers is to make a simple checklist with them (especially one with pictures).

If they resist getting dressed in the morning, we can make a morning routine chart of all the steps they need to do to get ready. If bedtime is difficult, the list will include all the things they need to do before bed, including drinking some water and using the toilet.

We can draw pictures of each step or take photos of them and print them out. If they want to change the order each day, we can make sticky notes for each step or laminate some pictures with Velcro on the back.

Then we can check the chart to see what we need to do next. That way it's the chart doing the work, not us. "Can you see what is next on the list?" or "The checklist says we brush our teeth next."

When they are involved in making and using the checklist, they take ownership of the solution.

GOOD MORNING CHECKLIST

MAKE BED

EAT BREAKFAST

GET DRESSED

BRUSH HAIR

BRUSH TEETH

SHOES/COAT ON

GOOD NIGHT CHECKLIST

EAT DINNER

BATH

PAJAMAS ON

BRUSH TEETH

DRINK WATER

USE TOILET/CHANGE DIAPER

STORY TIME

CUDDLES

SLEEP TIME

WAYS TO INVOLVE OUR CHILD

Give age-appropriate choices

We can offer our toddler choices to encourage cooperation. Not big decisions like where they will go to school, but age-appropriate choices, like which color T-shirt they would like to wear (out of two seasonally appropriate options); or when they are heading to the bath, we can offer them the option of jumping like a kangaroo or walking on all fours sideways like a crab.

This gives the toddler a sense of control over the situation and involves them in the process.

Note: Some toddlers do not like choices. Just as with any of these suggestions, use the ones that work for the child and leave the rest.

Give them information

Rather than issuing commands—"Put the orange peel in the bin, please"—we can give information instead: "The orange peel goes in the bin." Then they can figure out for themselves that they need to take it to the bin. It becomes something they choose to do rather than another order from the adult.

Use one word

Sometimes we use too many words to give instructions to our children. "We are going to the park. We'll need to get our shoes. Our shoes protect our feet. It's good to put them on. Where are your shoes? Did you put them on yet?" And on and on it goes.

Try using just one word. "Shoes." Again the child needs to figure out what they need to do on their own, giving them some control in the situation.

We are also modeling respectful communication to our children. And they will pick this up. One day my family was leaving the house, and we were all putting on our coats and shoes by the front door—a pretty tight spot. My son (around 7 at the time) said to me, "Mum. Laces." I looked down, and indeed I was standing on his shoelace. He could have rolled his eyes at me and said, "Mummmm, do you have to stand on my laces?" or worse.

It's another reminder that what we *do* speaks louder than what we *tell* them.

Get their agreement

Getting our child on board and letting them feel like they're part of the process will help with gaining their cooperation. If we know that our child has trouble leaving the house or the playground, we can let them know we'll be leaving in five minutes. We can then **check to make sure they heard and make a plan with them**. They may not understand exactly how long five minutes is, but they learn the concept over time.

We could say, "I see you are working on this puzzle, and we are leaving in five minutes. I'm worried you might not have time to finish it before we leave. Do you want to put it somewhere safe to keep working on it when we get back, or do you want to put it away and do it later?"

At the playground, we could say, "We have five minutes before we leave the playground. What would you like to have one last turn on?"

I don't love using an alarm to remind a child (used a lot, this could become an extrinsic motivator). However, used from time to time it can be an effective way to get their agreement, especially if they are involved in helping to set the timer. And, just like a checklist, it's the timer that tells them the time is up, not us.

HOW WE CAN TALK
TO HELP THEM LISTEN

Use positive language

Instead of telling a child *what not to do*, we can tell them with positive language *what they can do* instead. Rather than, "No running" (what they should not do), we can say, "We walk inside" (what we would like them to do).

Instead of, "No, don't climb," we can say, "You can keep your feet on the floor or you can go outside to climb."

If we tell our toddler, "Stop yelling!" we may also be raising our voice. First, they will mirror us and shout back; second, they will hear precisely what we don't want them to do. Instead we could say (perhaps in a whisper), "Let's use our quiet voices."

Speak with a respectful tone and attitude

Our tone of voice is a way to show our toddlers that we respect them. A whiny tone, an insecure voice, a strict voice, or a threatening tone can distort the best of intentions and does not show our child we value them and want to work with them.

If we can remember, it is helpful to check in with our voice and whether we are coming from a calm place in our heart. (See chapter 8 for ways to calm ourselves down.) We can even use a whisper now and then. Our toddler's ears are sure to prick up.

Ask them for help

Toddlers want to be involved, so if we would like our child to come inside, we might be able to ask for their help in carrying the keys or a heavy bag. At the supermarket, we can get them to help by making a visual shopping list, which they can be in charge of (we can cut out pictures from a food magazine together or draw simple pictures); let them take the items off the shelf; or put them on the conveyer belt at the register.

Say "yes"

If we are saying "no" a hundred times a day, our child will gradually begin to ignore it altogether. It is best to reserve "no" for times when their safety is a concern.

Instead of saying "no" to set a limit, we can generally find an alternative way to express what we want to say by actually agreeing with them and saying "yes."

Say a toddler wants another cracker but they haven't finished their first one. We could say in a gentle tone, "Yes, you can have another cracker . . . when you have finished this one." Or maybe if there are none left, "Yes, you can have more . . . when we go to the store. Let's write it on our shopping list."

It takes some time to break this habit. It can be useful to note down all the times we say "no" and then brainstorm (perhaps with a friend) some more positive ways to respond next time.

Use humor

Children respond well to humor, and it is a lighthearted way to encourage cooperation.

Sometimes when I've been helping a child get dressed and they are resisting, I pretend to put their shoe on my foot. The child laughs and tells me, "No, Simone, it goes on my foot." And they put it on.

Humor is particularly useful when we are on the verge of losing our temper. Something as simple as singing a silly song can relieve some tension for us and coax a smile from them. It's a simple way to start fresh.

If our child is going through a "no" phase, adjust our language

It is easy to know when a toddler is in this phase. Ask them if they need to use the toilet, if they will get dressed, if they want chocolate, and they'll just say "no."

During the "no" phase, we may want to adjust our language to tell them what is happening, rather than asking them. We might say, "It's time to eat/have a bath/leave the park." This can still be done with respect, using a gentle voice and kind words, but as their leader.

Show them

Sometimes we might need to actually get up to show them what they need to do rather than repeating ourselves from the other side of the room. If they are still not sure what to do with the orange peel, we could go over to the bin and physically touch or point to it, saying, "It goes in here." Show them.

Actions speak louder than words.

MANAGING EXPECTATIONS

Have age-appropriate expectations and be prepared

We cannot expect our toddler to behave in the way we like all of the time. Sitting quietly in a doctor's waiting room or in a cafe or on a train can be very difficult. Remember that they have a strong will to explore, move, and communicate, and are very impulsive. This is not meant to excuse their behavior. However, it does mean we can prepare ourselves.

First, we may need to adjust our expectations—we may not get to read a magazine, check our phone, or make a phone call. In a cafe or restaurant, be prepared to take them for a little walk when they start to get agitated or loud, perhaps to see the chef at work or look at the fish tank together. Waiting for a plane, we can stand at the window of the airport and watch all the action happening outside to prepare the plane for departure.

Second, be prepared. Don't forget to pack plenty of water, food, a few favorite books, and a little zippered pouch with a few favorite toys—a couple of small vehicles, a bottle with a coin to drop in, some shells, and so on. If there are any delays wherever we may be, we will be prepared to support our child and help them cooperate.

Try to wait until they have finished their task before making a request

If a toddler is busy working on a puzzle and we ask them to get ready to leave, they often won't respond. We may think, *They never listen to me!*

When I put myself in a similar situation—perhaps someone interrupts me while I am right in the middle of answering an email—it can be irritating. I just want to finish what I am doing, and then I can give 100 percent of my attention.

So if we want our child to come eat their lunch or to remind them to use the toilet, whenever possible, we can try to wait until they have finished what they are working on and then ask them before they start the next thing.

Allow time for processing

It can take a toddler (and older children, too) a while to process what we say.

Maybe we ask them to put on their pajamas and get no response. We can try counting slowly to ten in our head. Not aloud. This is for our benefit, to help us wait for them to process what we have said.

By the time I get up to three or four, I would definitely have repeated myself already, and by seven, I would have asked another time. By the time I get to eight or nine, often I find that the child is starting to respond.

It's not that they aren't listening; they are just processing what we said.

Keep a daily rhythm

Do not underestimate how much a toddler likes having the same rhythm every day. We can use that to manage expectations: wake up, get dressed, eat breakfast, leave the house, lunchtime, nap time, dinnertime, bath time, get ready for bed. It does not have to be on a fixed schedule, but the more regular the routine, the less resistance we will get. (See chapter 7 for more on daily rhythm.)

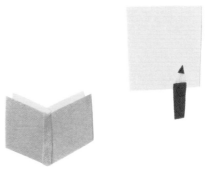

BONUS

Write a note

Most toddlers can't read yet, but notes can still be very powerful. We can write a note that says "No climbing" and place it on the table. Then we can point to the note and say, "It says, 'No climbing.'" If it is written down, it gives a certain weight and authority to the message. It is the sign setting the rule rather than the adult having to repeat the rule. And it is always consistent.

We can use a note in the kitchen if the oven is at the toddler's height. When we turn on the oven, we can show our child that we are putting up a note saying "HOT" to remind them the oven is on and dangerous to touch.

Notes are very effective, even with prereaders. But use them in moderation. If notes are stuck everywhere, they will definitely lose their effectiveness.

Another way to use notes is to keep a notebook. If our child is upset about leaving or something is not going their way, we can write it down in a notebook and perhaps draw a picture. This acknowledges to the child that we have heard them. Sometimes that is all they need.

IDEAS FOR
CULTIVATING COOPERATION

PROBLEM SOLVING WITH OUR TODDLER

- Ask, "How can we solve the problem?"
- Make a checklist.

INVOLVE THE CHILD

- Give age-appropriate choices.
- Give them information.
- Use one word.
- Get their agreement.

TALK IN A WAY THAT HELPS THEM LISTEN

- Use positive language.
- Speak with a respectful tone and attitude.
- Ask them for help.
- Say "yes."
- Use humor.
- If our child is going through a "no" phase, adjust our language.
- Show them.

MANAGE EXPECTATIONS

- Have age-appropriate expectations and be prepared.
- Try to wait until they have finished before making a request.
- Allow time for processing.
- Keep a daily rhythm.

BONUS

- Write a note.

SETTING LIMITS

HELPING OUR CHILD TAKE RESPONSIBILITY

Cooperation can be cultivated without resorting to threats, bribes, and punishments. But if our child is still not cooperating, then it's time to learn about setting limits.

This is the most difficult part of caring for a toddler in a Montessori way. We want to give them as much freedom as possible to explore so they remain curious, but within limits to keep them safe, to teach them to respect others, and to establish our own boundaries.

In the Netherlands, I notice that the Dutch people (generally speaking, of course) seem to do this very naturally. I don't see many Dutch parents or caregivers getting into a battle with their toddler or having exchanges that end up with the adult shouting at them. From time to time, I see a young child crying on the back of their parent's bike, yet the parent remains calm, continuing where they need to go, and offering some comforting words to the child.

I'm going to show how to do the same, to set limits in a respectful way for both the child and the rest of the family.

It will take some practice. We are basically learning a new language. It can be easier to learn if we are able to get support from other people raising their children in a similar way so we can learn from one another and discuss tricky moments. And when we get it wrong, we can remind one another that we are doing our best and use it as an opportunity to apologize to our child.

IT'S OKAY TO SET LIMITS

When my children were small, I thought my job was simply to make them happy. To be honest, that's the easy part. As parents we are here to help them deal with *all* life will throw at them: to be there to celebrate with them, to help them deal with moments of disappointment and grief—the good and the bad.

Sometimes we need to set limits. To keep them safe. To show them how to be respectful. To step in when they are not making a positive choice. To help them grow into responsible human beings.

Setting limits can feel difficult. Our child may not be happy with the limit being set. Yet when we set a limit in a supportive and loving way, they learn to trust that we have their best interests in mind, and the connection with our child can even grow stronger.

Difficult times make us grow. Difficult times make our children grow. And how amazing that our children know that we love them even when they are having a tantrum, pulling our hair, or refusing to get dressed.

BE CLEAR ON THE LIMITS

SET GROUND/HOUSE RULES

Children, toddlers especially, need order. They need to know what to expect. They need to know that things are consistent and predictable. That their parents will keep them safe and secure. That they will get the same answer whether their parent had a full night's sleep or the baby woke them every hour on the hour.

It's a good idea to have a few rules that are important to the family. Too many rules and it will be like a dictatorship. But it's helpful to have a few simple and clear rules aimed at keeping everyone safe and living more peacefully with others—just as we have some agreed-upon rules and laws for living together in the larger society.

How many of us already have some ground rules in our home? Maybe stuck on the fridge? Maybe a list of family values framed on the living room wall? Or maybe simply discussed between the adults of the household?

When I ask this question in my parent workshops, I find that most participants don't have any ground rules at all. That means we are mostly just winging it—making it up on the spot. This can be difficult to keep track of, for us and definitely for our toddler. Imagine if they changed the rules for traffic lights and some days the red light meant "stop" and on other days it meant "go." No wonder toddlers get mixed messages when we change our minds.

Here are some ideas for rules that we could use at home, adjusting for what works for each family:

Examples of ground/house rules

- **We are kind to each other.** This means that even if we disagree, we will not hurt each other physically or tease each other; it teaches children to respect themselves and each other.

- **We sit at the (dining) table to eat.** This is a practical rule that prevents food from going everywhere in the house. It also reminds people that eating is a social occasion and that we don't play and eat at the same time.

- **We contribute to the household.** No matter what our age, we help around the house, and our help is valued.

- **We engage in rough play by mutual consent.** This is a mouthful for young children, but they understand its meaning. If someone says "Stop," they are saying that they are not having fun anymore and the game needs to stop.

These ground/house rules provide a foundation that we can always return to. We may need to revise them as our children grow. Not in the middle of an argument, though. Do it at a neutral (ideally, planned) moment.

FOLLOW THROUGH WITH KIND AND CLEAR ACTION

"If you say it, mean it. If you mean it, follow through with kind and firm action."

—Jane Nelsen, *Positive Discipline: The First Three Years*

If, despite our best efforts to work with our child, our child refuses to cooperate, then we take **kind and clear action**.

Let's say they do not want to have their diaper changed, they are throwing their food, or they won't leave the playground. Then we **acknowledge their feelings**. But we take action. We are the leader—a respectful leader.

We touch gently if we need to handle them. We pick them up if we need to, giving a short explanation as we go. We change their diaper. We help them bring their plate to the kitchen. We leave the park. We are setting clear, loving limits for our child.

Make it logical and age appropriate

The consequence should be directly related to the behavior. Young toddlers cannot follow the logic where there is no direct relationship. It doesn't make sense to them that if they don't listen, they won't be able to go to the park or have ice cream later.

I once was on an airplane and heard a father say to his son, "If you don't behave, we will turn the plane around and go home." That's a threat that is going to be very difficult to follow through on.

Also, no stickers—seriously. That is just a bribe.

Instead, find a logical consequence. Let's say they are throwing the ball inside, and we have asked them to stop. A logical consequence would be for us to put the ball away and let our child try again later.

Let me share an example from when my children were a little older but one that gives a clear example of logical consequences and following through.

My children were around 7 and 8 years old and sitting in the *bakfiets* (a bike here in the Netherlands where there is a box in front with enough room for up to 4 children to sit). They were irritated with each other and encroaching on each other's personal space. They started stomping on each other's feet, and it was hard for me to concentrate on cycling, so I asked them to stop. When they continued, I quietly pulled my bike over to the side of the road and asked them to get out. We were going to walk until they were ready to sit in the bike calmly.

It was hard to follow through with kind and clear action. My children were pretty angry at first, but I kept an even tone. "Yes, you sound upset that we had to get out of the bike." Gradually they calmed down. After walking for a bit, I asked if they were ready to try again. I don't remember them ever stomping on each other's feet in the *bakfiets* again.

Express the limit clearly

I feel most comfortable setting limits with language like "I can't let you . . ." or "I'm going to . . ." It's clear. It takes ownership of our role as the parent. And it is respectful to both child and parent. We can also make sure they hear us by going to them and getting down to their level.

- "I can't let you take that toy out of their hands. I'm using my gentle hands to take your hands away."
- "I can't let you hit that child. I'm going to separate you."

- "I'm going to put a pillow here to protect you from hurting yourself."
- "I'm going to put you down. If you need to bite, you can bite on this apple."

No need to explain the limit every time

Once the child knows the limit, we don't need to explain it at length every time.

Let's say that our child throws food at every mealtime. We find ourselves having the same conversation over and over—how we can't let them throw food, that food is for eating, and so on. We do not need to get into a negotiation or give them lots of chances.

If the behavior continues, it's a reminder to talk less and move to kind and clear action. We can say, "It looks like you are all finished. Your plate goes in the kitchen." (See page 146 for tips on food throwing.)

Set limits for safety

If our toddler is doing something dangerous, we must step in and take them out of danger. This is the one time I say "no." This helps to get their attention when there is danger.

Some things I consider dangerous: touching something hot, going near an electrical outlet, running onto the road, getting too far ahead in the street unattended, climbing near a window.

Pick them up, say, "No, I can't let you touch that," and remove them from the area.

We may need to continue to repeat this if they keep going back. In that case I would look to see if I could change the environment to remove or hide the danger. Place a box over the power outlet, move a couch in front of wires, or move a glass cabinet to a room with a door that locks.

If they laugh

It is difficult if they laugh when we set a limit. I would still continue to follow through with kind and clear action. They may be used to getting a reaction from us. Instead, stay calm and say, for example, "You want to have fun right now, but I can't let you hurt your brother."

ACKNOWLEDGE NEGATIVE FEELINGS

They will probably be unhappy about a limit being set, so we acknowledge their feelings and see things from their perspective.

Guess their feeling

I have learned from Nonviolent Communication to guess what a child might be feeling rather than simply naming it.

- It looks like you . . .
- Are you telling me . . . ?
- Are you feeling . . . ?
- It seems like . . .
- I'm guessing you might feel . . .

Ask them if they are disappointed, make guesses about how they feel ("Are you telling me you're upset we are leaving the park?"), or describe how they look ("You look really angry right now").

You may guess the wrong feeling, but that's okay. They will just shout back something like, "I'm not!" or "I'm just disappointed." You have still helped them clarify their feelings.

Sportscasting

We can also use the sportscasting technique that I first heard about from Janet Lansbury, author of *No Bad Kids* and *Elevating Child Care*. Just as a sportscaster gives commentary about a football game, we can describe what is happening in a factual way (just as we do in observation). This can give us some emotional distance during this difficult moment, allow us to observe and name what we see, and stop us from jumping in to solve the problem.

"You are holding on to the swing. Your hands are holding tight. I'm using my gentle hands to help you let go. I'm holding you close to me as we leave the park."

Let the big feelings out

We can also acknowledge their feelings when things don't go their way, like when they want to wear something that isn't available or appropriate. Let them rage, hold them if they'll let us or keep them safe if they won't, and offer them a hug once they have calmed down.

Let them release the full range of emotions. Allow even ugly feelings. Show them we are able to love them at their worst. Once they are calm, we'll be able to help them make amends if needed.

Tip
—

I've noticed that once toddlers have processed their feelings and are calm, they often take a deep breath or release a big sigh. We can look for this kind of physical sign to show they are completely calm again.

DEALING WITH TANTRUMS

When a toddler has a tantrum, they are communicating that something did not go their way. They are having a hard time. They may have done something wrong, but right now, the first thing to do is **help them calm down**.

I love the analogy used in the book *The Whole-Brain Child* by Daniel Siegel and Tina Payne Bryson—when a child is upset, he "flips his lid." This means that the upstairs part of the brain—the cerebral cortex, the part of the brain that makes rational decisions and allows for self-control—is not available to the child.

Therefore, all the reasoning in the world or explanations will fall on deaf ears. We need to first help them close the lid by giving them support to calm down.

We can offer them a cuddle; we don't assume that they want one. Some children like to be cuddled to help them calm down. Some children will push us away. If they push us away, we make sure they are safe and we can offer them a cuddle when they are calm.

We are saying it's okay for them to melt down. Rather than trying to get the tantrum to stop as soon as possible, allow them to express all their feelings safely until they are calm, and show that we are there to help if they need us. And, once they are calm, we can help them make amends if needed.

That's it.

It may happen in the street, in the supermarket, in the park. That's okay. Move them out of the way (if you can). Give them the time they need to calm down. We try to stay calm as well and refrain from trying to speed it up or distract them. **Let them get it out.**

When my son was around 2 years old, he had a tantrum that lasted about 45 minutes because he did not want to get dressed. He raged, he was angry, then he was sad, then he was embarrassed. He went through the full range of emotions. Gradually his cries slowed. He took a deep breath. "I'm ready to get dressed now." I stayed calm and our connection was maintained (and maybe even strengthened, because he knew I would love him even when he was upset).

If I had needed to leave quickly that day, I would have helped him get dressed using my hands as gently as possible and calmly applying the sportscasting technique mentioned earlier: "Are you having a hard time getting dressed? You can dress yourself, or I can help you. I see I'll need to help you. Yes, you are pulling your arm away. You don't want to put it in. I'm gently putting your T-shirt over your head. You are trying to push it off. Thanks for telling me that this is difficult."

Should I ignore a tantrum?

I have heard people suggest that it is better to ignore a tantrum completely. The idea is that helping children or giving attention to behavior we do not like or want means we are encouraging them.

I don't agree.

Imagine if I had a bad flight and told my friend that my luggage was lost, I was disappointed with the airline, and I hadn't gotten any help at all. If my friend ignored me and walked out of the room, I'd think they didn't care about me. I'd be angry with them because I had just wanted them to listen, help me calm down, or maybe ask if I'd like some space.

Ignoring the tantrum directs our child's feelings at us instead of at the problem that upset them. It creates a conflict just when they need connection.

Calm and kind acceptance encourages them to express their feelings. Over time, they will find healthier forms of expression, but they will not be scared to share their feelings with us because they will know that we are capable of being kind and calm even when they have feelings that are big and scary.

Setting up a calm space

In *Positive Discipline: The First Three Years*, Jane Nelsen talks about setting up a calm space for an older toddler around 3 years old, a place with some of their favorite things where they can go anytime they need to calm down. This is different from a time-out because the child can decide to go there and how long they would like to stay, and it is never used as a threat.

Instead, if we see them getting worked up, we can suggest it to them. "Would you like to go to your calm place to calm down?" or "Shall we go to your calm place together?" If they refuse and we want to calm ourselves down, we could say, "I think I'll go to the calm place myself." If they come out and are still fired up, we can kindly and calmly suggest that they might like to go back until they are feeling calmer.

The aim of this step is *not* to say that we accept their behavior. It's to help them first calm down.

RECONNECTING ONCE THEY ARE CALM

Once they are calm, they will be able to talk about what happened. We can offer a hug or wait for them to ask for one. We can then acknowledge their feelings and see things from their perspective. "Wow, was that difficult for you? You really didn't seem to like that. You looked furious."

HELPING THEM MAKE AMENDS

"When everyone has calmed down, any damage should be addressed. Thrown items can be picked up, torn papers gathered and discarded, or pillows stacked back on the bed or sofa. Adults may offer to help a child with these tasks. It may also be appropriate to help your child repair additional damage, such as a broken toy . . . a very real way to learn about making things right."

—Jane Nelsen, *Positive Discipline: The First Three Years*

Once our child has calmed down, we can help them make amends. This teaches them to take responsibility for their actions and is a very important step. Restorative justice ("How can we make this better?") is preferable to punishment (taking something away).

Yes, accept all their feelings (even the ugly ones) and help them calm down. Then once they are calm, we help them take responsibility for their behavior.

If we do this too soon before our toddler has calmed down, they will resist and will not want to make it better. That's why it is best to make sure they are calm first. Then they are really learning how to make it up to someone.

DEALING WITH TANTRUMS

UNDERSTAND TRIGGERS AND AVOID THEM IF POSSIBLE

- Frustration
- Anger or rage when things don't go their way
- Wanting to be in control
- Trouble communicating as their language may still be limited

HELP YOUR CHILD CALM DOWN

- Offer a cuddle—rub their back, hold them, sing to them as they go through the range of emotions, from anger to intense frustration to sadness and sometimes regret.
- If they push you away, make sure they are safe and not harming themselves, something, or someone. Stand nearby and keep offering help. "I'm here if you need some help calming down. Or we can have a cuddle when you are ready."
- If they are throwing toys at their sibling or trying to hit you, remove them so that everyone is safe. "I can't let you hit me. My safety is important to me. Would you like to hit these pillows instead?"

OLDER CHILDREN

- For a child over 3 years old, you can set up a "calm place" to use when they are upset, such as a tent with pillows and their favorite things or a corner with some trains.
- You can ask them if they would like to go to their calm place. If they come back still in a rage, we can gently tell them that they look like they still need to calm down and can come back when they are ready.

MAKING AMENDS—DON'T SKIP THIS STEP

Once they are calm, I help them make amends. For example, if they drew on the walls, they can help clean up; if they broke their brother's toy, they can help to fix it.

In this way, they learn to take responsibility when things go wrong.

How to make amends

If our child hit someone and they are calm again, we can help them see if the other child is okay, get a tissue for the other child, ask if they want to apologize, or some combination.

I often use an example from when my children were older to show how children can learn to make amends on their own over time. My daughter had a friend come to our house for a sleepover. My son was feeling a little left out and set the alarm in their room to go off at 4:00 a.m. When I heard them in the morning, my daughter and her friend were furious because the alarm had woken them up in the middle of the night. I stepped in to offer a little guidance, acknowledging both my son's feelings of being left out as well as the girls' anger at having been woken. In the end, they worked out that he would make them breakfast, and he was very pleased with himself as he cooked them French toast. Needless to say, when the same friend came for another sleepover, I asked him if he would wake them again. He was quick to say he wouldn't, and it hasn't happened again.

Modeling making amends

If they are still young, we can model it for them. "Let's go and see if our friend is okay." "I'm sorry my child hurt you. Are you feeling okay?" Modeling is more effective than forcing them to apologize if they don't mean it, having them mutter "Sorry" under their breath, or having them say it in a sarcastic tone.

We can model apologizing when we forget things, if we let people down, or if we bump into someone accidentally. We can model making amends to our child when we have regrets about how we have handled a conflict with them. As they grow, our child will learn to genuinely apologize.

For me, helping children to **take responsibility** when they have done something wrong is the most difficult part. Yet this is one of the most essential parts of helping these seeds grow into respectful human beings.

TIPS FOR SETTING LIMITS

Set limits early

It is difficult to be respectful to our children when we allow them to go beyond our limits. When we give too much. When we try to be accommodating and let them have too much freedom. We end up losing our temper and getting angry.

If we start to get uncomfortable about something our child is doing, we can step in early to set a kind and clear limit without losing our patience or shouting.

Or perhaps at first we feel okay with something they are doing but then notice we are starting to get irritated. It's not too late. We can say, "I'm sorry. I thought I was okay with you throwing the sand. I've changed my mind. I can't let you throw the sand." (If they become upset, see page 125 for tips on acknowledging negative feelings and dealing with tantrums.)

If we are getting upset

Remember that we are our child's guide. We cannot be a very good guide or leader when we get upset ourselves. They are looking to us for direction. If we are feeling upset by a difficult situation, it is likely that our toddler has a problem and is **making it our problem**. Our job is to support them while they are having a hard time. We do not need to fix it for them.

- When we are working really hard to get our child to eat dinner, they have made it our problem.
- When we are working really hard to get our child to get dressed, they have made it our problem.
- When we are working really hard to get our child to leave the playground, they have made it our problem.

Let them work it out—with our support.

- Provide nutritious meals for our child, but let them control how much they eat.
- Use a checklist to help set up a system with our child to get dressed, but take them out in their pajamas if they do not want to cooperate.
- Let them know we are leaving the playground in five minutes. Don't change the plan and stop to talk to another parent. Keep leaving the playground, helping them if needed.

Consistency

One last note on consistency. Toddlers are trying to make sense of the world around them. They will test limits to see if they are the same every day (often more than once a day). It really helps them when we know our limits. They learn that when we say "no," we mean "no." We are reliable, we are trustworthy, and we have their best interests in mind.

If we say "no" but then change our mind because they keep nagging and nagging, they will quickly learn that this works. This is what psychologists call *intermittent reinforcement*. If they get a different response one time, they will keep trying.

If we are not sure, we can say, "I'm not sure" or "Let's see."

Note: We can question why we say "no" in the first place. If we end up giving them the ice cream after they have nagged, perhaps we could have just said "yes" at the beginning and avoided being inconsistent.

TO PRACTICE

1. How can we cultivate cooperation with our child?
   - Is there a way to solve the problem with them?
   - Is there a way to give them a choice?
   - Is there a different way in which we could speak?
   - Do we need to manage our expectations or theirs?
   - Can we write a note?
2. When we set limits, are we kind and clear?
   - Do we have clear house/ground rules?
   - Is the child learning something?
3. Do we acknowledge their negative feelings to help them process their emotions?
4. Do we help them make amends once they have calmed down?

Children need parents who will show them they love them by:

- accepting them 100 percent for who they are
- giving them freedom to explore and be curious
- working with them to cultivate cooperation
- setting limits so that they are safe and learn to become respectful and responsible human beings

Let's be our child's guide. They don't need a boss or a servant.

> "The liberty of the child ought to have as its limits the collective interest of the community in which he moves; its form is expressed in what we call manners and good behaviour. It is our duty then to protect the child from doing anything which may offend or hurt others, and to check the behaviour which is unbecoming or impolite. But as regards all else, every action that has a useful purpose, whatever it may be and in whatever forms it shows itself, ought not only to be permitted, but it ought to be kept under observation; that is the essential point."
>
> —Dr. Maria Montessori, *The Discovery of the Child*

A HANDY CHECKLIST FOR LIMITS

IS THERE CLARITY?

- Have a few house rules.
- Be consistent with the limits.

IS THERE LOVE IN OUR LIMITS?

- Get down to their level.
- Use a clear and loving voice.
- Manage our own anger first.
- Give respect and understanding if they are sad or frustrated.
- Be there to hold them or keep them safe if they lose control.

IS THERE REASON BEHIND THE LIMIT?

- Is it connected to their safety or respect for others, their environment, or themselves?
- "Because I said so" is not a good enough reason.

IS THE LIMIT APPROPRIATE FOR THE CHILD'S AGE AND ABILITY?

- Limits can be revised as our child grows.

DOES IT INVITE CHILDREN TO FIND SOLUTIONS?

- Sometimes the best ideas are found by children themselves.

PUTTING IT INTO PRACTICE

7

PART ONE

DAILY CARE

I believe that we can take many of the daily struggles of life with a toddler and possibly even transform them into peaceful moments of connection. Did I mention I was an idealist?

DAILY RHYTHM

Toddlers thrive on regular rhythm. They like the predictability of knowing what is happening now and what is coming next. It provides them with a feeling of safety and security.

It does not have to be a fixed schedule kept to the exact minute. Rather, it can be valuable to have our rhythm follow the same pattern every day. The child is then able to predict what is coming next, which will minimize those difficult moments of transition. The rhythm follows the child's energy and interests. From time to time, it may well be different. We can then know ahead that this may be difficult for them and prepare ourselves (and our child) accordingly.

Moments of care = moments of connection

We spend a lot of our day caring for our toddler—helping them get dressed, eating meals together, changing diapers or helping them use the potty, and giving them a bath. Rather than seeing these daily care activities as something we need to get through quickly, we can see them as moments of connection with our child.

These can be times to smile, make eye contact, talk to them about what is happening, listen as they communicate (even if they do not yet have words), take turns in a conversation, show respectful ways to touch, and have hugs.

They present many opportunities to simply live together. And live together simply.

An example of a daily rhythm for a toddler

- Wake up
- Play in bedroom
- Cuddle with parent(s), read books
- Use potty/change diaper
- Breakfast
- Get dressed, wash face, and brush teeth
- Play at home/morning outing/visit market/leave for day care (if applicable)
- Lunch
- Use potty/change diaper
- Nap time/rest time
- Use potty/change diaper
- Play at home/afternoon outing
- Afternoon snack
- Get picked up from day care (if applicable)
- Play at home
- Dinner
- Bath
- Use potty/change diaper
- Story time
- Bedtime

RITUALS

Rituals in our family's life can be used to mark moments and establish memories.

At special moments during the year we may wish to make some rituals around events such as:

- birthdays
- holidays
- seasons—seasonal crafts, food, outings
- annual vacations
- regular weekly rituals like going to the park on Friday afternoons or making a special Sunday morning breakfast

Over time these rituals become familiar to our child, something to look forward to, and are often the things our children will remember the most from their childhood. Just as toddlers enjoy the predictability of daily rhythms, they love knowing what to expect around these events.

If the parents come from different backgrounds, cultures, and nationalities, it's an opportunity to come up with a unique way to celebrate these origins and create special new family traditions of our own.

Rituals may be created around the food we eat, the songs we sing, the people with whom we celebrate, or the things we make, like seasonal displays in our home.

In a Montessori school, we create a special celebration for each child's birthday. The child walks around a representation of the sun the same number of times as the number of years since their birth. This is a concrete way to show the passing of time and our relationship on earth to the sun.

As a child, I always knew exactly what food would be prepared for our backyard birthday parties and the party games we would play. Summer meant loads of mangoes and cherries, wearing swimsuits all day, and running around barefoot in the grass (and getting bindi-eyes—those horrible prickly weeds that grow in Australian grass—in my feet). I'm feeling surprisingly nostalgic now, even for the bindi-eyes.

At the end of the year here in Amsterdam, our family has many traditions. On the first of December, we make a homemade Advent calendar in which I hide little slips of paper with something fun to do each day, like going for a nighttime walk to see the festive lights, baking cookies, or making a craft. On December 5, we celebrate Sinterklaas with the Dutch tradition of writing poems and making surprises for each other. Later in the month during Hanukkah, we light some candles and sing "Maoz Tzur." And on Christmas Day, we exchange some presents and have a family meal. We keep each of these pretty low-key, inexpensive, and not too elaborate. The emphasis is on being together, rather than every moment having to be picture perfect.

 For an in-depth look at some beautiful family rituals and traditions, I recommend reading *The Creative Family* by Amanda Blake Soule.

GETTING DRESSED AND LEAVING THE HOUSE

Getting dressed and leaving the house no longer have to be battles. Instead, we can apply the principles of guiding the child and finding ways to work with them, rather than threatening or bribing them.

Again, getting dressed can be used as a moment of connection—even if we are a parent who works outside the home.

Type of clothing

As our toddlers start trying to do things for themselves—"Me do it!"—look for easy clothing they can manage themselves or with little assistance.

Good choices:

- shorts and trousers with elastic waists that they can pull up without having to undo a zipper and/or button
- T-shirts with large openings for their head (or a press stud on the shoulder to open it wider)
- shoes with Velcro openings or buckles—easier than laces—or slip-on shoes

Avoid:

- long dresses, which can be difficult for toddlers to manage and restrict their movement
- overalls, which are difficult for the child to put on independently
- skinny jeans or other tight and restrictive clothing

A place for everything and everything in its place

As we explored in chapter 4, we can set up our homes in ways to make things easier for everyone. When we have a place for everything, then everything is (mostly) in its place and easy to find. We are less likely to be frantically searching for a missing glove or shoe.

For example, in the hallway, it is helpful to have:

- hooks for hanging coats and scarves
- a basket for gloves and hats
- a place for storing shoes
- a place to sit while putting on and removing shoes

With this preparation, the area is attractive and functional for getting out the door (and for when we get home, too). We'll have less "Where is the other shoe?" and more "Would you like to wear your black shoes or your blue shoes today?" Instead of a chaotic departure, it can be an opportunity to work together and create connection.

Learning to do it themselves

Don't forget that we can also take the time to teach children the skills for getting dressed when we are not in a hurry to leave the house. Toddlers love to be able to do things themselves. For example, we can teach them the Montessori coat flip so they can learn to put on their own coat.

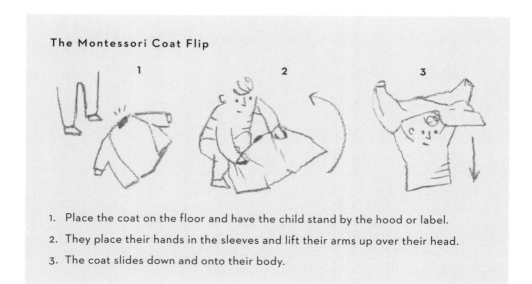

The Montessori Coat Flip

1. Place the coat on the floor and have the child stand by the hood or label.
2. They place their hands in the sleeves and lift their arms up over their head.
3. The coat slides down and onto their body.

Scaffolding skills

Younger toddlers may need some help to get dressed. This is an opportunity to scaffold skills. They will learn how to dress if we break it down into small steps, each one building on the other, and over time will manage more and more of the process themselves.

Always observe to see how much help they need. Let them first try a step by themselves. Sit on our hands if we need to—it is so satisfying for them if they manage it successfully. We might put the T-shirt over their head and see if they can wiggle their arms into the sleeves.

When they are starting to get frustrated, we can offer some help. Step in to help a little and then step back to see how they manage. If they are stuck putting on their shoes, we may try holding the back of their shoe down while they put in their foot, and then see if they can succeed from there.

If they push us away completely, we can say, "Okay, just let me know if you need any help. I'm right here."

As our toddler gets older, they may be able to manage more and more steps independently. We might be able to get dressed at the same time in the same room. Or eventually we may find that we are able to leave the room and pop back to check on them now and again.

Slow down. Allow time. Connect.

How long does it take everyone in the house to get dressed when we don't need to leave the house? Maybe fifteen minutes? Twenty-five minutes? We can allow the same amount of time when we need to leave the house to get to school, work, or someplace else.

If we find it difficult to sit and watch a toddler get dressed at toddler pace, we can find a way to make the process enjoyable, like bringing in a cup of tea or coffee (keep hot drinks out of their reach) or putting on some relaxing or upbeat music.

When they don't want to get dressed

Be prepared for times when they won't want to dress themselves. It can be frustrating to see our child refuse to put their own shoe on when it seemed just yesterday they were pleased to have accomplished it on their own. Remember, we don't want to cook dinner every day either. Be prepared to help, perhaps offering, "Would you like some help with your shoe today?"

Remember that toddlers are in the process of becoming independent from us—some days they will want us to help and sometimes they will want to do it themselves. It's what I like to call *the crisis of independence.*

If it is an ongoing problem, we can go back and review the ideas on working with our child to encourage cooperation in chapter 6. Here are some ideas that would be useful for getting dressed:

- waiting until they have finished their activity
- allowing them time to process our requests
- offering them choices of clothing
- using humor
- keeping our expectations age appropriate
- using a checklist

Note: If they don't want to have their diaper changed, it may be because they don't like to lie on their backs while it's happening. It can feel like a very vulnerable position. Although it is more convenient for us if they lie down, with some practice we can sit on a low stool to change them while the child stands between our knees. For bowel movements, we can get the child to lean forward and hold onto the edge of the bathtub or a low stool while we clean their bottom.

When we need to leave

Even though we can allow children time to go slowly, we don't have to be saints and allow unlimited amounts of time. If we run out of time, we can say something like, "You really want to get dressed by yourself, and it is time to leave. I'm going to help you put the last things on." Know our boundaries and set a limit when needed.

Use our gentle hands and sportscast to help acknowledge any resistance they are giving. "I am putting on your T-shirt. Yes, you are pulling away. Are you trying to tell me you don't like it when it goes over your head? Now I'm going to help you with your left arm . . ."

You can also go stand by the front door. Instead of saying, "I'm leaving without you," we could say calmly and clearly, "I'm not leaving without you. I'm putting on my shoes now and will be by the front door."

EATING

Mealtimes are another moment for connection—for our toddlers to learn that meals are social occasions, as well as times for nourishing our bodies.

There can be a lot of stress around mealtimes. As parents, we want to make sure our toddlers eat enough to stay healthy and maybe so they will not wake up hungry at nighttime. We may have gotten into the habit of letting them walk around with a snack or feeding them as they play so we know they have eaten. Sometimes it's the other way around, and we are worried our toddler is eating too much.

A Montessori approach to eating is quite different. We create a beautiful setting, maybe with a few flowers on the table. The child can help us prepare the meal and set the table (with help at first), and as often as possible, we sit down together for a family meal.

The adult's role

We are laying the foundations for our child's relationship with food and for good eating habits. The adult decides where, when, and what the child will eat. Rather than the parent feeding the toddler, we set things up so the child can successfully feed themselves and choose how much they want to eat at their own pace. No flying airplanes, bribes with dessert, or using the television or iPad to distract them.

Setting a rule like sitting at the table for meals helps our children learn the following:

- meals are social occasions and a time for connection
- sitting at the table is safer than walking around with food in their mouth
- we do one thing at a time (eat or play, not both)
- food stays at the table

As we discussed in chapter 4, we can set up our kitchen so the child can be independent, as well as be involved in the meal preparation. Children often have more interest in food when they are involved with preparing the meal, and they can learn to get a drink when needed if they can reach a water source by themselves.

Where—a place to eat

I know that children often eat early in the evening and that our evening schedules can feel rushed when combining work and children. However, we are the best model for them to learn manners and to learn that mealtimes are social occasions. So it can be great to sit down to have meals together with our child. If we do not want to eat a full meal so early, we could have something small, like a bowl of soup.

Personally I like eating main meals at the family dining/kitchen table. So it is useful to find a seat that the child can get in and out of independently rather than high chairs with straps and a tray table in front, which keeps them farther from the table and requires our assistance.

We can also have a low table where the child sits on a low chair with their feet flat on the floor. I like to use this at snack time, sitting on a low chair or a floor cushion to join them. I know some people use this for all meals. It's up to each family.

I would not expect toddlers to sit at the table until everyone finishes their meal. In our house, when they were all finished, they would take their plate to the kitchen and go play. As they got older, they would gradually stay longer at the table to enjoy the conversation.

If they walk away from the table with food or a fork in their hand, we can say: "I'll keep the food/fork at the table. It's okay for you to go." I say this a lot in my classes when children are learning to sit at our snack table. If they want to keep eating, they sit back down with the food. If not, I model clearing things away to show that by leaving, they are choosing to be all finished.

When—time to eat

Keeping with the daily rhythm discussed earlier, I like to offer meals at regular times during the day—rather than having the kitchen open at all hours. Three meals a day (breakfast, lunch, dinner) and a small snack in the morning and/or afternoon. This gives time for their bodies to digest food and helps them refrain from filling up too much on snack foods.

What—type of foods to eat

As the adult, we can decide what food we would like our family to eat. If we want to offer a choice, we could offer the child two options that we find acceptable. They are not yet capable of making good food choices completely by themselves but will learn about these choices by the food we offer and the conversations we have.

From 12 months, a toddler no longer needs a bottle to drink and can take regular milk in a glass at mealtimes. Start with a small amount in a small glass, filled only as full as we are prepared to clean up. Over time, they will master the skill and have no need for a sippy cup or bottle. We may also be offering breastfeeding, usually at regular moments in the day.

My children were allowed some sugar now and then, applying an "everything in moderation" approach. They still eat sugar occasionally but are remarkably self-disciplined. Again this is a personal decision—just be consistent.

How much—the child's choice

Fortunately, the days of being told to finish everything on our plates are long gone. We want our children to learn to listen to their bodies to understand when they are full. Rather than filling up a toddler's plate (which can feel overwhelming or end up on the floor), we can start with a small amount of food and let them serve themselves more if they would like.

Leave the child in charge. Trust that they are taking enough. Children at this age generally will not starve themselves. They will take as much as they need if we remove our control around food and trust them to listen to their bodies.

If our child is not a big eater, we will often observe that their appetite fluctuates. Sometimes they don't seem to finish anything on their plate, yet during growth spurts, they may eat three meals a day, plus snacks, and still be hungry. Their bodies know exactly what they need.

A young toddler can also learn to use cutlery to feed themselves. A fork is easier to use than a spoon at the beginning. We can show them how to pierce a piece of food with the fork, and leave it in front of them so they can bring it to their own mouth. Then they will take over more and more steps themselves. For learning to use a spoon, we can provide thicker offerings like oatmeal until they gain more mastery.

Food battles

If we find ourselves needing to hand-feed our child, bribe them, or distract them with books or TV to get them to eat, then they are making mealtimes our problem. It's time to reestablish good eating habits.

We can explain simply to our child that we have changed our mind about mealtimes. We can tell them that we want to enjoy our food together and it is important that they learn to listen to their own body to decide how much they will eat for themselves.

Start at breakfast time. Offer a nutritious breakfast, and then sit down with them and eat breakfast, too, talking about anything (except food!). If they do not eat anything, simply ask if they are finished (no lecturing) and help them bring their plate to the kitchen. We could say, "You listened to your body, and it said it was all done."

If they come back asking for food, we can be understanding but clear that the meal is all finished and there will be more food at the next meal.

Repeat at lunchtime and dinner. It's a good idea to avoid snacks for a few days so they don't fill up on them while we are trying to improve mealtimes. If they have not eaten very much, likely by the end of the day they will be hungry and eat some food at dinner. Include some of their favorite foods, but don't make different food if they demand it. They are also learning to eat what the family is eating.

Continue this for one week and keep a diary of what the child eats. Write it down, stick the list on the fridge, and be unattached to the outcome. Don't make a big deal about food or mention it much at all. Have confidence. It may take only a few days before the food battles have been replaced by a child who sits at the table and feeds themselves.

Note: Make sure the child doesn't have any medical reasons for refusing to eat or have other food-related issues. If there is no improvement in eating after a week or if you have any concerns, consult a doctor. There may also be a change in the child's bowel movements as their digestion adjusts.

Throwing food

Toddlers like to explore the world around them. Throwing food off their plate can be an experiment to see what happens when it falls. Usually they start throwing their food when they have had enough to eat: **They are telling us they are all finished**. We can ask them, "Are you telling me you are all finished?" We can show them a sign with both our hands out, palms up. "You can say 'all finished' like this. All finished. Now let's take our plates to the kitchen. Let me know if you need some help."

If they are not finished eating but continue to throw their food, we can be **kind and clear** and tell them that we will help them take the plate to the kitchen. Again not with a threatening tone, simply setting a clear limit. Generally food throwing is a phase. Remain calm and (yes) consistent. It will pass.

Similarly if they were spilling their water on purpose, I would take their glass away. "I'm going to put the glass over here. Let me know when you would like to use the glass for drinking." If they asked for it but then poured it on the table again, I would calmly remove it for the rest of the meal.

SLEEPING

We can apply Montessori principles when it comes to sleeping—whether we choose to have our child in their own room, in their own bed in our room, or co-sleeping in a family bed. In our Montessori training, they recommended having the child in their own room, but sleeping is a very personal choice, so find an arrangement that works best for the family.

Around 12 to 16 months, a toddler will generally move to one nap time in the middle of the day and then sleep at night from ten to twelve hours. If our child is getting more or less than this, we will know if our child is getting enough sleep if they generally wake happy and are pretty happy during the day.

Where to sleep

A toddler's sleeping place should be truly restful. Make the sleeping area safe and free from too many distractions and visual clutter. Look for a way for the child to be able to get into and out of bed independently. By around 14 months, they could move into a toddler bed with a low side that they are able to climb into independently, or use a floor mattress.

We may wish to use a night-light. In Sarah Ockwell-Smith's article "One Simple Way to Improve Your Baby or Child's Sleep Today!" she advises avoiding white- and blue-based lights and looking for red-based light, which does not affect melatonin production.

We can have a drink at the ready if children are thirsty in the night.

We also may choose a family bed or allow our children to come in during the night. It is up to each family.

Just be clear on what is okay. If we are complaining about a toddler's sleep, it's likely that a part of the sleeping arrangement is not working for us, and we may need to make a change.

Getting to sleep

I have shared a lot about the importance of giving the child just as much help as they need. We support them, step in to help, and step back again. The same goes for sleep.

Establish a clear, regular bedtime sequence. Allow around an hour to have a bath, brush teeth, read some books, and talk about all the things that happened that day. Then give only as much help as they need to fall asleep.

Some children have a good relationship with sleep from birth and will simply put themselves to bed when they are tired (often on a floor mattress, from birth)—the holy grail. These children often have clear sleep associations from birth, and consistent bedtime sequences. They go to bed drowsy but awake, do not have sleep crutches, and feed separately from falling asleep.

Some toddlers may be happy to read books and fall asleep by themselves, whereas others may need to cry at bedtime. If we know they have eaten well, have a dry diaper, and have had a good play, then their crying is saying they are ready to sleep. But I would not recommend leaving them to cry it out alone.

A nice, gentle technique to help them fall asleep by themselves is to place a chair by their bed. Once the bedtime sequence is finished, sit in the chair quietly (maybe read a book). If they are crying, rub their back occasionally and say something soothing, rather than picking them up. We can lay them back down if they stand up and not engage in conversation or too much eye contact.

Once they have learned to fall asleep like this, we can move our chair farther away from the bed and repeat for a few nights. Every few nights the chair moves closer to the door, and after about two weeks, we can sit in the chair outside the door where they can still see us. After a couple of nights, the child usually no longer needs us to sit with them.

If they are sick or teething, they may need some additional support from us. These things can disrupt their sleeping pattern, and we will need to reestablish it once they are feeling better.

Sleep crutches and night waking

We all drift in and out of light sleep during the night, move around a little, and then resettle. Generally we resettle so quickly, we don't remember waking. If the conditions change, however—for example, if our pillow has fallen off the bed—we will wake up, look around until we find it, and then need to get back to sleep.

The same is true with babies and toddlers. If they fall asleep while being rocked or fed, they will wake up from light sleep during their nap or night sleep and look for the adult, unable to resettle until the same conditions are established. We become their sleep crutch.

I got into a crazy cycle with my firstborn. I rocked him to sleep for months, he often fed to sleep, and he'd wake often at night looking for the breast. I'd feed him again, his tummy would hurt (in hindsight, I realize that he probably hadn't had time to digest his food), and he'd wake again.

I learned my lesson. With my second child, we kept a clear daily rhythm from birth. Eat, play, sleep. It was much clearer for us (and her) when it was time to rest. She lay in bed drowsy but awake before falling asleep, loved sleeping in her bed, and needed very little help at all to sleep (though she wouldn't sleep while out and about—probably too much to see).

Learn from my mistakes and remove sleep crutches.

If the child is waking to be fed at night and we want to remove the sleep crutch of feeding to sleep, we can look for ways to feed less during the night. Watering down the milk gradually in a bottle is an option. I know one breastfeeding mother who fell asleep by accident on the couch one night. Asleep in the other room, their child didn't wake up. So she slept on the couch in the living room for a week and their child stopped waking to feed.

If they are waking at night to request a cuddle or a drink, to have their cover adjusted, or to find their favorite soft toys, I would discuss those things during the day, at a neutral time. "You know how you woke up last night and couldn't get back to sleep without your covers over you? Let's think of a way that you can take care of it yourself in the night. Do you have any ideas? Perhaps we can put the cover across the bed and tuck it in extra tight, or practice pulling up the covers."

If a child is continuing to have sleep difficulties that **affect the well-being of the child or the family**, please see a sleep specialist.

BRUSHING TEETH

There are no official Montessori guidelines for brushing teeth, but it is a commonly asked question when children do not like brushing their teeth.

We come back to having a respectful relationship with the toddler. We are working with our children, where they are today. We let them lead. They choose whether to brush their teeth before, during, or after their bath. They come with us to the store to select the toothbrush they want. But we are clear that teeth brushing is not optional.

Again, we set things up for the child to be independent so they can help themselves. For a toddler, that might mean helping them at the end to "finish off" and make sure their teeth are clean. When we assist, we do so gently and respectfully. It must feel pretty strange for someone to poke a toothbrush in our mouth if we are a toddler.

We could brush our teeth alongside our child to help give them a concrete understanding of caring for our teeth. We can sing, "This is the way we brush our teeth, brush our teeth, brush our teeth. This is the way we brush our teeth every night and morning." Not to distract them, just to make it a light moment in our day.

If our child detects that we are trying to distract them, they may feel like we are tricking them rather than getting their cooperation and may resist even more. Just as stickers work for a while as a reward, distraction works only up to a point before they tire of that "trick" and you need to work even harder to keep them on task.

If we have tried working with them and they are still avoiding brushing their teeth, we can say calmly with confidence and handling them very gently, "Now I'm going to help you brush your teeth. We are going back to the bathroom. I'm opening your mouth . . ." We are being kind and clear.

DEALING WITH CHANGES

TOILETING

The period when a toddler learns how to use the toilet does not have to be dreaded. After all, it is a completely natural part of being a human. Our children pick up our attitudes toward dirty diapers from infancy, and if we are screwing up our face, they will learn that it is a dirty thing instead of a normal bodily process.

I love this analogy from a fellow Montessori teacher. When a baby pulls themselves up to standing, falls down, stands up again, and then falls down, over and over until they master it, we think it is cute. When our child is learning to use the bathroom and they pee on the floor or poop in their pants, they are also practicing until they master it—except there is pee and poop.

So with open minds, I would love to help make this process a little less stressful.

Scaffolding skills

The child will slowly build skills around using the toilet, starting with being able to manage their own clothing. At first they practice pulling their shorts or trousers up and down, and then later their underwear.

We can offer a potty/toilet when we change their diaper, never forcing them, but making it part of the daily rhythm. "Would you like to sit on the potty/toilet?" "Now that you're finished on the potty, I'm going to put your diaper back on."

Using cloth diapers can also help the child feel wet when they have peed, increasing their body awareness.

Signs of readiness—Let the child lead

The most important thing is to follow our child. It is not a competition.

I'm not including any ages here, but rather, signs that the child may be ready:

- pulling at their diaper when it is wet or soiled
- squatting or going to a private place while they poop
- telling us they have peed or pooped
- resisting having their diaper changed (sometimes)
- taking off their diaper

Set up the bathroom with our child

Have a potty or a small toilet seat on the toilet. If they are using the toilet, we will need a step that the child can manage themselves and as a place to rest their feet to feel secure while sitting on the toilet.

We can also have a place in the bathroom for soiled clothes and a pile of clean underwear. A pile of cleaning rags for puddles is useful, too.

Having everything at the ready and being prepared will help us remain relaxed and not rushing about, looking for things. If they don't make it to the potty/toilet, we can calmly say, "Ah. I see you are wet. We have everything we need right here. Let's get dry."

Keep it normal

Involve the child in the process. Buy some underwear together, as well as a potty. We can also find training pants that hold a little bit of pee to help when they are trying to get to the toilet in time.

As we are scaffolding skills, we can start by letting them wear just their underpants when we are at home so there is less to have to take on and off, and less to wash. They are learning what it feels like to be wet and may even stand to watch the pee run down their leg. That's the first step. Increasing body awareness.

Next we can help them go to the bathroom to change. Montessori teachers generally say, "You have wet clothes. Let's go change," rather than, "You had an accident."

Offer the potty/toilet regularly at first. If we ask a toddler if they need to go to the toilet, they usually answer "no." It's a common response for a toddler who is developing autonomy. Instead, we can wait until they aren't in the middle of an activity and simply say, "It's time to go to the potty," leading them to the bathroom.

After some weeks, they generally will begin to have more awareness of their body and sometimes tell us that they need to go to the toilet. We will also observe that they are able to hold it in for longer periods at a time. Eventually they won't need reminders at all.

Dry at night

We can move to underpants at nap time and night at the same time or when we notice they can hold for longer periods and wake with a dry diaper/underwear.

Place a thick towel across the child's sheets and tuck it in, or use a bed protector; either can easily be removed during the night if needed.

Holding it in

Sometimes a child becomes scared of pooping. It may have hurt once to poop, someone may have had a reaction that made them scared to poop on the toilet, or we may not know why. Check with a doctor if you believe there is a medical issue.

If all appears healthy, help the child relax by being calm and supportive. We can tell them, "The poop will come out when it is ready. It may take a week, it may take two weeks, but it knows when to come. Our bodies are very clever." Then try not to talk about it too much. Rub their tummy if their abdomen hurts.

If they usually go somewhere private to poop, gradually invite the child to move to the bathroom to poop in private. Then we can start to invite them to sit on the potty with their diaper on. Gradually they will feel safe on the potty/toilet without the diaper/underwear on. Again, we are simply supporting them and scaffolding skills.

If they refuse to use the toilet

We don't force a child to use the toilet. This is their body. We can't rush it or do this for them. We can only support them and find ways to work with them.

We can make sure we aren't interrupting them to take them to the bathroom. We can keep offering the potty/toilet and trust that they will learn to use them. We accept them for who they are and where they are in this process.

Peeing on the floor intentionally

Sometimes a toddler who knows how to use the toilet will suddenly start to pee on the floor intentionally. Observe them. Often they are telling us through their behavior that they are unhappy about something in their world, for example, a sibling who has started crawling and taking more of their space.

They want us to see them, and we can look from a place of curiosity, in order to understand them. We can acknowledge their feelings but set a clear limit about the behavior. "You're upset about something? I can't let you pee on the floor. But I want to work it out with you." We can go back to creating connection, finding ways to work with them, and do some problem solving together with them. (See chapters 5 and 6.)

SAYING GOODBYE TO PACIFIERS

When applying the Montessori approach, pacifiers aren't used much or are phased out within the first year. If a young toddler still uses a pacifier, phasing them out does not have to be a difficult process.

Even though the child is young, we can let them know that we are going to make a change.

The first step is to start using the pacifier only for sleeping. When our child wakes, we can put it in a box by the bed out of reach, so our child (or even the adult) will not be tempted to use it.

If our child asks for the pacifier at other times, we can try to observe why they feel the need to suck and address the root cause. Maybe they need something engaging to do with their hands or a toy to play with, maybe they are seeking connection and we can offer a cuddle, or maybe they need help to calm down or to relax their nervous system.

Here are some ideas that may help:

- sucking yogurt through a straw
- blowing bubbles
- holding tightly on to a book or soft toy
- using a bottle with a straw
- blowing water through a straw to make bubbles
- a brisk towel rub after a bath
- deep-pressure bear hugs
- kneading dough
- squeezing bath toys
- a slow, firm back rub

We can then make a plan with our toddler to get rid of the pacifier at bedtime, too. One popular choice is to give it to a friend with a new baby.

It generally takes a few days for the child to learn to fall asleep without it, during which they may need a little—just enough—extra support. Be careful not to add any new sleeping crutches into the routine. (For children who find this difficult in the middle of the night, see the section on sleeping, beginning on page 147.)

SIBLINGS

Often parents tell me that these ideas would be simple to carry out if they had only one child. Having more than one child makes it difficult for parents to find time to observe each child, meet their individual needs, and deal with arguments among siblings. Not to mention that having a new baby in the home, or an older sibling bossing them around, can be disruptive to a toddler.

The new baby

In their book *Siblings Without Rivalry*, Adele Faber and Elaine Mazlish open with a story that illustrates the effect a new sibling can have on a child's life.

Imagine that our partner comes home one day and says that they love us so much, they are going to get another partner, in addition to us. The new partner is going to sleep in our old bed and use our clothes, and we are going to share everything with them. I think many of us would be furious and feel very jealous. So it's not surprising that a new addition to the family can have a huge effect on some children.

We can do a lot to prepare our toddler before the baby arrives. We can talk to our child about what life with a new baby might look like. Especially helpful are books with realistic pictures showing parents looking after the baby while still spending time with the other children in the home. We can let them talk and sing to the baby in the belly and begin to build a connection. We can let them help prepare the baby's space. And we can make a point of enjoying our last days together in our current family configuration. (The memory of going to the park with my son the day before my daughter was born is one I'll always cherish.)

When it's time to introduce our toddler to the new baby (if our toddler has not been present at the birth), we can put down the baby before they enter the room so our attention is solely on them. This can be easier for the toddler than walking in to see us holding the new baby in our arms.

Try to keep the early weeks at home simple and, if possible, have extra hands to help. We can ask others to help with the newborn for some of the time, so we can have time to be alone with our toddler.

Some toddlers like to be involved in caring for the new baby—fetching a clean diaper or getting soap for the baby's bath. Some won't be interested, and that's okay, too.

We can keep a basket of books and some favorite toys on hand while we feed, so we can feed the baby and connect with our toddler at the same time.

When the toddler is playing and the baby is awake, it can be fun to talk to the baby about what the toddler is doing. The baby will benefit from our conversation, and the toddler will like being the topic of discussion.

(For ideas on how to set up the home with more than one child, see page 75.)

When the toddler gets upset about the new baby

Our toddler may say they hate the new baby. They may be emotional or difficult or intentionally destructive at this disruptive time in their life.

This behavior is simply their way of telling us they are having a hard time. Instead of saying, "You don't really hate the baby," and denying their feelings, remember that they need us to see things from their perspective, to be understanding and to offer them connection.

We can allow all the angry feelings. We can ask, "Is it annoying you that they are touching the one thing you are playing with?" and listen to them. Really allow them to let it out.

But we don't have to allow all behavior. For example, if they are hitting the baby, here are some things we can do:

- Step in immediately and remove their hands gently. "I can't let you hit the baby. We are gentle with the baby."
- We can translate for the baby. "The baby is crying. They are saying that's too much."
- We can show them a safer way to interact. "Let's show the baby this soft toy instead."

Make special time with each child

We can find creative ways to spend regular one-on-one time with our toddler: a trip to the supermarket, a walk down the road to a cafe for a snack, or a visit to the playground for ten minutes on the swing.

Then, when they want something from us and we're not available, we can write it down in a notebook and talk about it during our special time together.

Stay neutral

Siblings like to draw us into their disputes to take sides. My favorite advice (which I need to remind myself of at times) is to stay neutral and not take sides in these conflicts.

Our role is to **support both children**, keep them safe if needed, and help mediate so that both parties take responsibility. We see things from both perspectives and give them just as much help as they need.

Yes, even with a toddler. There was a time when my children were young (2 years old and 9 months old) and both wanted the same toy truck. It's tempting to solve the problem for them—find another toy, distract one of them, try to get them to share. However, I simply said, "One truck and two children. Now, that's a problem." Then my son took off the back part of the truck and gave it to his sister, keeping the front wheels for himself. He thought of something far more creative than I would have come up with.

Parent as if we have a big family

In his book *Thriving!* parenting educator Michael Grose suggests that we raise siblings as if we have a large family with four or more children. Parents of large families can't solve every argument and entertain every child. Parents are the leaders of the family. They lay the foundations of the family's values and oversee the running of the ship.

When to step in

Generally when children fight, we rush in and ask, "Who did it?" The children immediately try to defend themselves or blame their sibling: "They started it!"

Here are alternative ways to step in if siblings are fighting.

1. Be visible

During minor arguments, we can let them see that we are in the room and then leave again. Think of this as an important experience in conflict resolution. They know that we have seen them arguing, but we are confident they can work it out themselves.

2. Observe

When arguing heats up, we can stay and observe. They will feel our presence without our having to say anything.

3. Remind them of the house/ground rules

We may need to remind them of a rule. For example, if it sounds like rough play is going too far, we can check in with them. We can say, "Rough play by mutual consent" or "Do you need to say stop? You don't sound like you are having fun anymore."

4. Provide some support

When they can't work it out themselves, we can give them support to help them solve the conflict:

- Listen to both sides (without judgment).
- Acknowledge how both parties feel, and show that we understand and can see things from both of their perspectives.
- Describe the problem.
- Express interest in hearing how they work it out.
- Move away to let them find a solution.

An example:

"You two sound mad at each other." (Acknowledge their feelings.)

"So Sara, you want to keep holding the puppy. And you, Billy, want to have a turn too." (Reflect each child's point of view.)

"That's a tough one: two children and one puppy." (Describe the problem.)

"I have confidence that you two can work out a solution that's fair to each of you . . . and fair to the puppy." (Move away.)

5. Separate children so they can calm down

When we start to feel uncomfortable with the level of fighting, we can step in to separate them. "I see two angry children. I can't let you hurt each other. You go over here, and you go over there until everyone is calm."

Even with preverbal children, it's the same process.

6. Problem solve

Once the fighting has calmed down, we can do some problem solving together. As we discussed in chapter 6:

- Everyone brainstorms ideas of how to solve the problem (with younger toddlers, we might come up with most of the ideas).
- We decide upon a solution that everyone can live with.
- We follow up to see if the solution is working or needs to be adjusted.

Foster gratitude for, and positive interactions with, siblings

Generally, the more we foster positive interactions between our children, the closer they become. We can create situations for them to enjoy each other's company, regardless of whether there is a large age gap.

At neutral times, we can discuss the positive side of having siblings or ask our children what they like about having a sibling.

Even if they aren't close friends, we can expect them to treat each other with respect.

Treating each child individually

Just as counting out an equal number of peas at every meal is nearly impossible, so is trying to parent our children equally. Instead, we can strive to parent our children **individually, based on their needs**.

There will be times when one child needs more one-on-one time from us, perhaps around their birthday or when passing through a developmental change. Each sibling learns that we will be available when they need our help.

If the children demand our attention at the same time, we can say, "As soon as I have finished here, I will come help you." And if two children want to speak at the same time, we can let them know that we are available to listen to both of them, although not at the same time. "First I'll finish listening to you [Child A], and then I really want to hear what you [Child B] have to say."

We can also avoid comparing siblings. It is easy to make offhand comments like "Look at your brother eating his dinner."

Children themselves may try to compete with their siblings. Again, we can bring the focus back to the individual, rather than making it about their sibling. For example, if one child says that their sibling has more cheese, we can say, "Did you want more cheese?" thereby treating each child individually.

Labels

For more on avoiding labels and accepting each sibling for who they are, see chapter 5.

PART THREE

USEFUL SKILLS FOR
OUR TODDLERS TO LEARN

SHARING

When our child was a baby, they may have easily handed things to us or, when something was taken out of their hand, they may have simply turned around to find something else to play with.

This willingness to share changes when they become a toddler, as they develop a heightened sense of "I," and want to practice something until mastery. Suddenly, around 14 to 16 months, we may see them pull their activity close to them, push away another child who is watching them at work, or shout "No!" to an innocent toddler walking by.

Before 2.5 years, toddlers are mostly interested in parallel play—playing on their own alongside another child—rather than sharing their toys and playing together. So we may need to adjust our expectations that a toddler will be able to share their toys. (If they have older siblings or play regularly with others in day care, they may learn to share a little earlier.)

Share by taking turns

Instead of asking the child to share their activity with someone else, in Montessori schools the ground rule is that we share by taking turns. We have only one of each activity; a child can work as long as they like with it (to allow repetition, concentration, and mastery); and children learn to wait their turn, a useful skill.

We can have the same rule in our home and provide support if needed:

- Observe to see if they are happy to allow another child to watch or join in the activity. We can see a lot from their body language, and give only as much help as they need. Allow them to resolve low-level disputes as much as possible by themselves.

- Help them use words if someone wants their toy. "My turn. It will be available soon." They can put their hands on their hips for emphasis.

- Help the child who is having trouble waiting. "Do you want a turn right now? It will be available soon."

- If a child is being physical, we can step in to be a bodyguard, maybe by using a gentle hand or placing our body between the children. "I can't let you push them. Are you telling them that you were playing with that?"

Around 2.5 years, they may become interested in playing with another child for a while. They may need some guidance, for example, to help them with some words or to learn from situations that come up. "It looks like Peter wants to play by himself now. Let's come back later and you can have a turn then."

At the playground or in public places

It can be difficult in public places where different families have different rules.

If someone is waiting for our child to finish on the swing, we can say to the other child, "It looks like you'd like a turn. You can have a turn when our child is all finished. The swing will be available very soon." Then they (and their parent) know that we see they would like a turn and they will be next.

To our child, we could say, "I see another child is waiting to use the swing. Let's count to ten and then we'll give them a turn." Rather than staying with the activity until our child is completely finished, we are modeling grace and courtesy toward others.

Sharing with visitors

When visitors are coming over, we can ask our children if there are any toys they would like to put away in a cupboard. Then we can check that they are happy for the visitors to play with everything else. We are helping them prepare themselves and have a say in what their friends can play with.

LEARNING HOW TO INTERRUPT AN ADULT

Although Montessori is a child-led approach to education, a young child can learn to wait and interrupt conversations in a respectful way.

My children's first Montessori teacher told the children that if she was in the middle of giving a lesson to another child and they had something they needed to tell her, they should put their hand on her shoulder. This would tell her that they had something important to say. Then, as soon as there was an appropriate place to pause in the lesson, she would stop and see what the child needed.

This principle can be used in the home, too. If we are on a phone call or talking to someone and our toddler has something to say, we can tap our shoulder to remind them to put their hand there. They place their hand there, and as soon as we can, we ask them what they wanted to say.

It takes practice, but it really works. A hand on our shoulder, with our hand on theirs, gives them the message, "What you have to tell me is important. I'll be right with you."

SKILLS FOR INTROVERTED TODDLERS

Parents of more introverted children may be worried that their child is not as confident or outgoing as other children. Or they may recognize that their child is an introvert, but worry that they don't have the skills to manage in a world that expects a child to maneuver confidently through social situations.

In her book *Quiet: The Power of Introverts in a World That Can't Stop Talking*, Susan Cain argues that introverts are undervalued for their empathy and their ability to listen. As parents of introverts, we can help support them without trying to change them.

First of all **accept them for who they are**. Jump back to chapter 5 for a refresher on these principles. Avoid using labels like *shy*. These can become crutches, excusing a child from awkward situations ("They're just shy"). Instead, we can help them learn how to manage these situations ("Do you want some more time to warm up/join in?"). And try not to compare them to siblings or other children by saying things like, "Look how well they play with the others."

Then, from this place of acceptance, we can **see things from their perspective and offer understanding. Acknowledge their feelings**. We can listen to them or hold them if needed. "Are you feeling worried about going to Grandma's house/the birthday party/the supermarket?" Allow them to feel safe.

It can help to **prepare them in advance** for situations that might make them nervous by giving them an idea of what to expect.

If our child takes some **time to warm up** in social situations, allow them to stand by us and observe the scene until they are ready to join in. We don't need to give them any special attention or make it a big deal. We can carry on our adult conversation; the child will drift off once they are ready.

Over time, we can help our child **build skills** that will empower them, so that they don't feel like they cannot handle certain situations.

Such skill building could include:

- Role playing. For example, they can practice saying "hello" to the adult at the door and "happy birthday" to the child having the party.

- Showing them how to excuse themselves to have a break, if they are finding a social situation overwhelming. For example, "I'm just going to have some quiet time."

- Practicing in less confrontational situations, such as handing over the money in a shop or ordering a drink in a cafe. We will be there to support them if needed. "Would you be able to say that a little louder? It looks like the waiter can't hear you."

- Practicing easy phrases they can use to be assertive. For example, "Stop. I don't like that."

- Showing them how to use their body language, such as putting their hands on their hips if someone has done something they don't like.

Finally, we can help them **gain confidence** by celebrating the skills they do have and by learning how to care for themselves, others, and the environment.

On the other hand, if our child is very confident and loves to run up to other children and hug them, we can translate for the child who does not seem to be enjoying their attention. "It looks like they are pulling away. Maybe we should check to see if they feel like being hugged." Our child may take it personally that the other child isn't as excited as they are; we can model how to accept other children the way they are.

As adults, it is also useful to remember to check in with any child before we handle them, particularly if they are not our child. We can check with them before we give them a hug ("Would you like a hug?" rather than "Give me a hug!"), tell a young toddler we are going to pick them up and get their consent before handling them, and ask if they'd like help before we do something for them. We respect that the child has a say about if, when, and how they will be handled.

A HITTING/BITING/PUSHING/
THROWING PHASE

Toddlers are learning how to communicate. Sometimes they use words or sounds. Sometimes they use body language. And sometimes they hit, bite, or push us or other children. It is another way of communicating. It isn't desirable, but it is a phase we can support and help them through.

First, let me say that if our child is hitting, biting, or pushing other children, we should be prepared to shadow our child in social situations and be ready to step in to keep other children safe. We don't have to be anxious—our child will pick up on it—but we can stay close or sit on the ground next to them to support them. We can step in gently or place a hand between the children if needed. We can acknowledge their feelings while stopping the behavior and separating the children.

We may also want to limit outings that are likely to make our child uncomfortable and trigger this behavior (lots of children, a noisy environment, etc.), at least for a time.

Observing the behavior

A Montessori teacher's answer to almost everything is to first observe. We are looking to see what kind of situations seem to cause the behavior. Here are some questions we can ask:

- **Time.** What time does the behavior happen? Is our child hungry or tired?
- **Changes.** Are they teething? Are there any changes at home, such as a new baby or a new house?
- **Activity.** What are they doing/playing with at the time of being triggered?
- **Other children.** How many children are around? Are the children the same age, younger, or older?
- **Emotion being expressed.** Just before it happens, how do they look? Playful? Frustrated? Confused?
- **Environment.** Look at the environment where it happens. Is it busy? Is it very colorful or otherwise too stimulating? Is there a lot of clutter? Is there a lot of children's artwork around the room, which is possibly too much sensory input? Or is it peaceful and serene?
- **Adults.** How do we respond? Do we bring additional anxiety to the situation?

Preventing the behavior

By observing, we may see patterns to their behavior and identify ways we can support our child. Here are some examples:

- **Hungry.** Just before mealtime, give them something hard to snack on before they get too hungry (good for relaxing their nervous system).
- **Teething.** Offer a variety of (cold) teething toys.
- **Needing to explore.** Allow them to explore toys with their mouth.
- **Overstimulating environment.** Reduce the amount of stimulation to make it calmer.
- **Too much noise.** Remove them when we notice that things are becoming too loud.
- **Transitions.** Is the structure of the day predictable enough? Are transitions difficult for them? Allow enough time for them to finish what they are doing. Make sure they get enough free, unstructured play.
- **Protective of their activity.** Model words they can use. They can put their hands on their hips and say, "I'm using this now. It will be available soon."
- **Sensitive to their personal space.** Help them avoid situations where they are cornered or do not have enough personal space.
- **Misguided playfulness.** Some children may bite to be playful or show love, perhaps misunderstanding games such as blowing raspberries on their tummies. Show them other ways to be affectionate, such as cuddles or mutual rough play.
- **Learning social interaction.** If they push another child, they may be wanting to say, "Can we play?" Give them words.
- **Problem with their hearing and eyesight.** A problem with either can feel disorienting for a child, and they may react by being aggressive.
- **Need to relax their nervous system.** Refer to page 155 for ideas on relaxing their nervous system, such as big bear hugs.

Children are very sensitive to our emotions, so we can try to stay confident and not show signs of worry when we are around other children. Our child may sense our anxiety, which will add to their discomfort.

See them every day with fresh eyes and a blank slate. This too will pass.

What to do if they hit/bite/push?

We can be clear that we allow all feelings—toddlers have a lot they need to express—but they cannot hit, bite, or push others. Acknowledge their feelings and remove them from the situation. Once they are calm, we can help them make amends, check that the other child is okay, offer them a tissue if they are crying, or model apologizing.

Here are a couple of examples:

"You look angry. I can't let you bite me. I'm putting you down." We can make sure they are safe while they calm down. Then we can get them to help check that we are okay. "Shall we see if I am hurt? Let's see. Yes, it's a bit red here." If we have allowed enough time for them to become completely calm, they will often want to rub it or give us a kiss.

"You didn't like them touching your hair? I cannot let you hit them. Let's go over here where it is quiet to calm down." Then, once they have had time to calm down, we can help them see if the other child is okay. Or model apologizing. "I'm so sorry that my child hit you. I think he was frustrated, but it's not okay for him to hit you. Are you okay?"

We can help our child explain the problem—for example, that they were playing with the toy the other child took.

Hitting, biting, and pushing phases may require a lot of patience and repetition. We need to remember not to take their behavior personally and be their calm guide during this difficult phase.

What if they laugh after hitting, biting, or pushing?

Children are generally testing a limit by laughing after they hit, bite, or push. They are looking for clear leadership, clarity about what is okay and what is not. We can continue to step in to stop the behavior—calmly and clearly—rather than telling them to stop laughing.

However, if the laughing causes a reaction in us, we can tell them how it makes us feel and find a place to calm down if needed. "It upsets me when you hit me. It's important for me to feel safe. I'm going to make a cup of tea to calm down. I'll be back when I'm feeling better."

And throwing?

Again, this is usually a phase. They want to touch and explore everything around them.

- Look to see if there are any patterns to the behavior.
- Take preventive measures by moving things that they are pushing off tables, placing them on the ground or out of reach. We may need to remove wooden toys that will hurt if thrown for this period.
- Provide opportunities to do lots of throwing at the park or with soft items in the house (socks are excellent for this).
- Be kind, clear, and consistent about what they can throw. "I can't let you throw that inside, but you can throw these little bean bags."

BUILDING CONCENTRATION

"The essential thing is for the task to arouse such interest that it engages the child's whole personality."

—Dr. Maria Montessori, *The Absorbent Mind*

Concentration is not just a matter of being busy. It means engaging all the senses. To help a toddler build their concentration, we start by observing them to see what they are interested in and learning to master. Then we give them time, possibility, and a prepared environment, and let them repeat the activity and allow them to deepen their concentration.

Tips for building concentration

1. Try to avoid interrupting

Sometimes we comment too much on what the child is doing. We name the puzzle pieces, the colors, and so on. Trust the child. Remain silent when they are working on something. Respond if they look to us.

There are many other moments when we can talk and offer rich language possibilities: when we are out exploring the world together, while preparing and eating meals, and during moments of care, such as bathing. Not when they are in a moment of concentration.

2. Watch what they repeat

Are they opening and closing drawers? Taking objects in and out of baskets? Sorting clothing? Picking up small objects? Collecting rocks? Cleaning the floor? Preparing food? This repetition shows us what they are interested in.

Allow this repetition. Ask them if they would like to repeat it when they have finished. Provide similar opportunities with increasing difficulty.

3. Less is more

Have only a few activities available. Anything that is too easy or too difficult can be put into a storage box and rotated onto the shelves at another time. We will see that children can focus more easily when there is less available. And we can see clearly which activities are no longer being used or which are being thrown—a good sign that we can put them away and bring out another choice.

4. Help as much as is needed and as little as necessary

If we observe that our child is having difficulty, we can wait to see if they can manage themselves. When they are about to give up, we can step in to just give a little bit of help, then step back to see how they get on. This may help them get further with the activity and allow them to continue concentrating. For example, we may be able to help them with turning a key, then step back to see if they can open the box.

5. Have a work area

A floor mat or small table can help a child focus on the activity they have chosen. When they select an activity, there is a small moment when we could help them take it to the mat or table.

However, if they are already working at the shelf, I would not interrupt their concentration. Our interference may be enough to break their concentration completely, and they might walk away from the activity.

DEALING WITH FRUSTRATION

It is common to want to jump in to help our child if they are frustrated. Dr. Montessori used to have some rosary beads she would patiently count to hold herself back from stepping in too quickly.

The child's struggle is important. The child will enjoy mastering activities that are hard enough to provide a challenge, but not so difficult that they'll give up easily. We can wait until they are about to give up and, as before, step in to give a small amount of assistance before stepping back again.

Types of help we can give our child:

- Showing them. "Would you like me to show you?" "Would you like a little help?" Then we could show them slowly (without words) how to, for example, turn a puzzle piece around until it fits.
- Giving a verbal cue. "Have you tried turning it?"

Sometimes they will refuse all help, and their frustration will turn into anger. It's okay for the child to express that, too. They will try again another time.

When we support them in these ways, we recognize that frustration is a part of learning.

WHEN OUR CHILD IS CLINGY

Some children don't want to play by themselves. They won't let us leave the room, even to use the toilet. And the more space we want, the more clingy they get. There can be many reasons why they are clingy:

- The child's temperament. Some children prefer the safety of their parent's company.
- A trip, a change in routine, sickness, a change in work situation, new child care. These big changes can make the child feel cautious.
- Our attention is elsewhere. For example, we're cooking dinner or writing an email.
- They can't manage independently because they lack the skills or access to what they need, or they're reliant on an adult to do things for them.

It is normal for toddlers to need supervision, and they won't be able to play by themselves for hours. It's also important to enjoy time together. But if our child is constantly attached to our leg or wants to be picked up all the time, we can help them play alone for longer periods.

- First, we can play together. Then we can play a little less and watch more. Let them lead the play. Over time, we can sit a little farther away while we watch them.
- Give them our undivided attention and then leave for a moment, telling them that we are going to the kitchen to put the kettle on, going to put laundry in the washer, or something similar. Come straight back. Then pop out again to make the cup of tea or do another little job and come straight back. This gets them used to us going away and coming back.
- When they want to stay with us, don't feel irritated but make it a little bit boring. For example, we can chat with the other parents at a birthday party while they stand with us. If they feel ready, they may go join the other children all by themselves.

Do it together

Include them in daily life. We will find that with age, they will start to play more independently, but in the meantime, we can enjoy that they want to spend time with us.

- Use a stepladder so they can help in the kitchen.
- Let them press the buttons on the washing machine.
- Give them the socks to make into pairs while we do laundry, and so on.
- Our child may say "Mommy do it"—give a little help and step back to see if they can manage the rest themselves. Stay close at first so they still feel safe and secure.

Understand our child

- See things from our child's perspective and acknowledge their feelings. Instead of saying, "Don't worry, it will be okay," we can provide understanding: "Are you feeling scared about this?" This doesn't mean we have to solve the problem; it just lets them know we understand.
- Fill their emotional bucket. Starting the day with a long cuddle and reading books can fill our child's emotional tank before the day gets busy. And when they start to get whiny, rather than looking for more space, we can offer them a cuddle to help them rebalance.
- Our child's "love language" may be touch or spending time together. This child will enjoy a lot of contact with us to feel loved. (See *The Five Love Languages* by Gary Chapman for more on this.)
- An introverted child may find groups overwhelming. They may need to stay with us at first, or we may want to make our visit shorter to accommodate our child's needs.

Make them feel safe

- If we are going somewhere new, give them a little tour when they arrive so they feel oriented.
- Always tell them where we are going rather than sneaking out. "I'm just going to the toilet. I'll be back in two minutes." Our child may cry, but over time they'll begin to trust that we'll come back when we say we will.
- It can help to arrive a little early to parties or group activities. It can be daunting for some children to walk into a room already full of busy children.

I like to think of our child's excursions like petals on a flower, with us at the center. They will make small excursions first, crawling to the other side of the room and coming back; walking farther away as they grow in independence and then coming back; then going off to school and coming back; and one day biking themselves to high school and coming back at the end of the day to check in with us.

If they are clingy, we can help them feel safe enough to explore, maybe just a little before they check in; they will gradually explore longer and go farther, and then they'll be back again soon to check in with us. Even though my children are now teenagers, I am still an important check-in point for them before they head off again to explore further.

SCREEN TIME

In a Montessori approach, we want to offer our toddler many hands-on and firsthand experiences of their world. Screens don't provide such rich sensorial learning.

The website Screen-Free Parenting offers a lot of useful research on screens, including this:

- Young children do not learn language from a screen—they learn language best from a personal relationship with another human.
- Screens can negatively affect children's sleep and attention levels.
- There is concern about physical health—children could spend screen time being active and/or outdoors.

What to do instead

To remove temptation, put screens out of sight and out of reach. We can also be conscious of our own use of screens while our children are around.

If they are bored in a cafe, take them for a walk to see the kitchen staff at work, or bring some books to read and an activity to do together.

Rather than using a screen to help calm our child if they are upset, use the ideas from chapter 6 and they will learn to identify their feelings, learn to calm down, and learn from the difficult times.

My personal experience with screens

My children had very little exposure to screens and electronic toys when they were young. The television was not left on in the background, and we brought along things like books to read when we were out in cafes. From time to time, they saw some carefully selected television programs or short films.

In my children's Montessori school, once the children were 6+ years, there were 2 computers for 30 children, and they would book time if they wanted to research something.

Around the same time, we chose to allow a limited amount of screen time at home. We carefully chose which programs or games they were watching or using, and there was always supervision. This also gave them an idea of what their friends were talking about at school.

For those worried that their child will be left behind, I've found that my children are still very competent on computers. For example, they can build a website, write presentations, and code some simple games with introductory coding programs.

 For more ideas about the "whys" and "hows" of limiting screens, I recommend the book *Toxic Childhood: How the Modern World Is Damaging Our Children and What We Can Do About It,* by Sue Palmer. It is very realistic and proactive about how to deal with things like technology with our children.

BILINGUALISM

Because toddlers have an *absorbent mind* and are in a *sensitive period* for language acquisition, it is a wonderful time to expose them to more than one language. They will take in additional languages with little effort, although it does take some effort from the adult to provide language in a consistent way.

If there is more than one language in the home, we can use the *One Person, One Language (OPOL)* approach. Each parent chooses their mother tongue when speaking with the child, while the family uses one agreed-upon "family language."

Here is an example:

A family who lived across the road from me had a child. One parent spoke Italian with the child, the other spoke German with the child, and the parents spoke English with each other. The child also went to a bilingual day care where they were exposed to Dutch and English. The child learned to ask for an apple in Italian with one parent and in German with the other, and if she ever saw me in the street, we would speak in English. (She now goes to a Dutch school where she studies in Dutch, continues to speak Italian and German at home, and speaks less English but has relatively high comprehension.)

We can also use an approach called *Domains of Use*. This is where we have agreed-upon times or places when we use certain languages. For example, on the weekends the family chooses to speak English; out of the home they choose to speak the local language; and at home they speak the parents' mother tongues.

Look at the literacy goals for each of the child's languages. If the goal is to have the child be able to eventually study in a language, they need to spend around 30 percent of the week with that language. Calculate the hours the child is awake and see if it is necessary to increase their exposure in any language. For example, have a teenager read and play with our child in that language, a babysitter who speaks that language, or play groups in that language. Be creative.

Some parents worry that their child will have a language delay if they are being raised to be bilingual. When they have more than one language, the research shows that they should not have any learning delay. For comparison, a 1.5-year-old who is monolingual may have ten words; the bilingual child may have five words in one language and five words in another. So it can appear that their language level is lower, even though they can say ten words in total, too.

The research also does not support parents abandoning their mother tongue to encourage their children to pick up the local language. The mother tongue needs to be strong for any other languages to be acquired. What we can do is increase their exposure to the local language to ensure there is enough input.

I recommend *A Parents' and Teachers' Guide to Bilingualism* by Colin Baker for anyone with questions about bilingualism or learning more than one language.

TO PRACTICE

1. How can we increase connection during daily care?
2. How can we support our child's eating/sleeping/toileting?
   Can we let go of our anxiety in these areas?
3. Can we keep neutral in conflicts with siblings?
4. How can we build skills with our child
   - around sharing?
   - to interrupt an adult?
   - if they are an introverted child?
   - if they hit/bite/push/throw?
   - to build concentration?
   - to deal with frustration?
   - when they are clingy?

When we apply Montessori principles at home in this way, we are learning to be the child's guide. We are kind and clear when needed. We help them scaffold the skills they will need. And we cultivate connection with our child every day.

BEING THE ADULT

8

PREPARATION OF THE ADULT

Dr. Montessori was well aware of the work we need to do on ourselves. She called this *preparation of the adult*. How can we be the best model for our children? How can we stay calm with an unpredictable toddler in the home? What might we be bringing to the situation? What unresolved issues are showing up here?

We are not aiming to be perfect parents. When I tried to be (or appeared to be) a perfect parent, I was stressed and disconnected from my family, busy worrying about everything. Rather, we are aiming to have fun and feel relaxed with our families, starting from where we are today. Maybe some of these ideas can help us to parent from a calmer place—a place where we can support and guide our toddler.

We cannot change our partner, only how we react to them. The same is true with our children. Who knew that parenting would become an almost spiritual journey?

And what a journey it is. Sometimes I wish I had known all of this before I became a parent. Yet, we know only what we know. So I think of how I've grown up alongside my children—that they see me trying and getting it wrong and trying again and getting a bit better, constantly learning and growing.

What I have learned may not work for every family. I don't want to tell other people how to live. Instead, I'd like to share some of my practices that have helped me as a parent and Montessori teacher, including apologizing and "doing it over" when I get it wrong.

PHYSICAL SELF-CARE

We do best when we keep our bodies, our minds, and our souls strong and healthy. To nurture our families, we must also nurture ourselves.

We need good food. Some movement (perhaps biking around town or chasing our toddler in the park). Time outside every day. Maybe long baths in the evening when no one can disturb us. We can always look for new ways to add fun or peace to our day.

We can acknowledge the guilt we may feel about putting ourselves first. And let it go. Reframe it instead as being a great example for our children to look after themselves.

If we are feeling tired or burned out, we can get help. Pushing past our limit is not a sustainable long-term option. The help could be a babysitter, a grandparent, a friend who will swap with us, a partner. Our toddler will learn that there are other special people in their life whom we trust and with whom they will be safe. So it's a win-win.

If we are feeling depressed, we should absolutely get help from a doctor, even if it is just to see what options are available. I remember turning up at the doctor when both my children were still under 2, worried I might be depressed. It helped to have someone to talk to and to care for me when I was so busy looking after others. If the depression is concerning, a doctor will help to figure out the next steps.

CULTIVATE A LEARNING MIND-SET

We don't undertake any paid job without some training, and we expect that our child's schoolteachers will continue their professional development. So, as a parent, we can keep learning, too. (By reading this book, you are already cultivating a learning mind-set about raising your child.)

In addition, we can:

- Learn more about our child's unique development.
- Research things that are different about our child and get the support we need.
- Find a training like a positive discipline training or a course in nonviolent communication.
- Explore many and varied books and resources. (See my recommendations on pages 218 and 219.) Perhaps try listening to podcasts and audiobooks.
- Read and learn things that have nothing to do with raising children. We need to have our own rich life as well.
- Learn to follow our intuition. Our thinking brain is so strong these days, so switching it off and listening to our intuition—that calm voice inside—is another skill we can practice.

START AND END THE DAY RIGHT

My morning and evening rituals probably have the biggest effect on how I show up as a parent. It's not strict, but it's fairly consistent most days. It helps me be intentional about how I live each day, rather than reacting to what life throws at me. If I can get in good "alignment" at the beginning of the day, it sets me up for the rest of the day.

Even when my children were toddlers, I would try to wake up half an hour before anyone else in the house so I could have some quiet time for myself.

If we can't be awake before the rest of the family, consider how we can create a morning routine that we love that includes them. This might be morning snuggles, reading books, having breakfast together, putting on some happy music, or making a cup of coffee or tea to drink while we are all getting ready for our day.

When I wake up before the rest of the family, I use the time in the following ways:

- I lie in my bed to meditate—it's impossible to be bad at it. Some days I notice my mind is super active, and other days I manage to focus on my breath for longer. This practice really helps me be less reactive during the day. And on those scattered days, I can come back to that drop of peace I was able to find in the morning.

- I spend five minutes writing:
  - things I am grateful for and appreciate.
  - a few things that would make the day amazing (things I actually have control over and that can be as simple as having a cup of coffee or sitting outside on the steps).
  - my intention for the day (for example, to choose ease, to listen to others, or to focus on love and connection).

- With any time that is remaining, I start to get dressed before I hear the sound of lovely children's feet.

If I am interrupted before I am finished, I try to think of it as a reminder of how lucky I am to have a lovely family and to hear the sounds of them coming to join me.

At the end of the day, I take a bath and read a book. I write down three amazing things that happened and an intention for the next day.

We may not think we have time, but it is possible if we make it a priority. I do this before I read the news or check social media. It makes a big difference in how I can be my best self.

We can set aside some time to think through what morning and night rituals serve us best. Just as we look after our families, we will benefit from looking after our own well-being in the same way.

PRACTICE PRESENCE

It's difficult to stay present when we are trying to be all things to all people and being pulled in lots of directions as adults with lots of commitments, including as parents.

Here are some ways to practice being present:

- **Focus on doing one task at a time.** I know I'm not really listening to my children about their day if I have my back to them while I am preparing something in the kitchen. It works better for all of us if I tell them that I'd love to hear what they have to say as soon as I am finished. Or stop what I am doing, listen, and then finish what I am doing.
- **Use a notebook.** I always have a few notebooks to write down things I think of when I am playing a board game with the children or running one of my classes. It's written down for when I can look at it at a later time. I "process" the notes later, leaving my mind free to be present.
- **Use technology consciously.** I love technology. Yet we rarely switch off from it. So I often hide my phone in my bedroom so that I don't pick it up to check it as I pass by or as soon as it beeps. Anytime I pick up my phone for one task, I inevitably start looking at some other app.
- **Calm the mind.** It's not only technology. It's also our mind. It's really hard to stay in the here and now. We continually play back moments from the past and make plans for the future. We can make ourselves crazy.

Right now, here, in the present moment, there is nothing to worry about. Hold this book and just breathe in. Then breathe out. For that short moment there was nothing to think about. Being present. Still. I love it when my mind quiets like that.

Imagine if we could spend more time in that peaceful space. With practice we can.

The more we can practice making space for these moments, the easier it is for us to slow down, to observe our child, to see things from their perspective. The more time we spend finding a calm space inside ourselves, the easier it will be for us to return to that space when we need to be a calm leader for our child while they are having a hard time.

And guess who is great at being in the present moment to help us practice? Our toddlers.

Remember how they squeal with excitement at the sound of an airplane. How they find flowers to pick in the most unexpected of places. How they wriggle their toes in the grass at the park.

Follow them and learn.

OBSERVATION

As discussed in chapter 5, observation is a tool Montessori teachers use a lot. We discussed how we can make factual observations at home, too, to allow us to let go of judgment, bias, and other analysis.

I include it again here because observation can help us:

- remove our judgment of the situation, which stops us from being triggered by our child's behavior, and allows us to respond rather than react. (Instead of "They are always dropping their bowl on the floor," we observe, "The bowl dropped onto the floor.")

- really see our child objectively with fresh eyes

- be more present and notice more details about our child and the world around us

- connect with our child as we see things from their perspective and gain a greater understanding of them

If we are feeling wound up, we can grab a notebook and observe. If we have our hands full, we can try to observe without writing it down. Stay away from analysis, and enjoy the present moment observing our child.

FILL OUR EMOTIONAL BUCKET
AND OUR CHILD'S

We all have an emotional bucket. Our emotional bucket is full when we feel safe, secure, loved, and accepted. It needs to be continuously refilled. When we neglect our emotional buckets, we become more reactive.

We are responsible for filling our own buckets, for finding ways to look after ourselves, and for making sure we are receiving the help and support we need. Our partners are not the only ones who can help here. With a little creativity, we can come up with lots of ways to fill our bucket.

Some ideas:

- make a cup of tea or coffee
- play some music
- have a Skype conversation with grandparents
- go outside
- invite friends around for a meal
- bake something
- arrange a night out (by ourselves, with our partner, with friends)
- do a babysitting swap with a friend

When our bucket is full, it is easier to fill our child's bucket. The easiest way to fill a child's bucket is with connection—making them feel the belonging, significance, and acceptance we discussed in chapter 5. We can spend some time reading books with them, have a snuggle in our pajamas, laugh. This fills our child's emotional bucket (and our own) and helps them be more receptive and less reactive throughout the day.

SLOW DOWN

Going slowly is a tool we can use in our daily life to live with more ease with a toddler, older children, and our family.

We speed through our days, often worried we'll miss out on something. Yet, I know how much more I get out of every day when I slow down and use all my senses: smell the rain in the air before a storm, feel the wind on my cheeks as I cycle through the city, taste and enjoy every bite of food rather than eating on the run, and so on.

We will have to figure out what is really important to us and what will have to wait or not happen at all.

For me, going slowly means things like:

- sitting down for a cup of tea when I get home from class rather than immediately starting on the innumerable tasks waiting for me
- putting on some music to make the moment richer
- cooking wholesome food and enjoying the cooking process, remembering to savor the tastes as I eat
- not putting too many things in my calendar so I don't have to rush from one thing to the next

- saying "no" to a lot, so I can say "yes" to more time with my family and friends and, sometimes, the couch
- being selective about what I work on, choosing only things I enjoy and that will have the most impact
- reading every night
- a weekend of travel to new places and in nature to recharge, and taking in more of an impression than having to see everything—the simpler the better

Toddlers will appreciate our slower pace, making it easier for them to absorb all that is around them.

Here are some examples:

- When dressing, first allow them to try; then step in to show them when they need help, using slow, precise movements.
- Slow down when we show our child how to carry a basket or a tray—use two hands so they can be successful themselves when they try.
- Slowly move chairs using two hands.
- When singing together, sing slowly and do the actions slowly as well. This allows time for our child to process and perhaps join us in singing or doing the actions.
- If we ask our child to do something, like sitting down to eat, count to ten in our head before repeating to allow time for the child to process our request.
- Go slowly when we are encouraging our child's curiosity, too (see chapter 5)—going at their pace, rushing less, and saving more time for play and exploration.

For more ideas, I enjoyed the book *In Praise of Slow* by Carl Honoré. It's not at all scientific, just one person's attempt to try out different genres from the slow movement philosophy. Spoiler alert! The final chapter is my favorite. It concludes that it is ideal to go slowly most of the time so when we do need to hurry, our children will be more accommodating.

One last thing. Unless our child is in immediate danger, there is generally enough time to at least count to three in our head before reacting to any situation. Pretend to be Dr. Montessori counting rosary beads before rushing in to help. Go slowly.

It will allow us to **respond rather than react**.

BE THE CHILD'S GUIDE

When my son was 1 year old, I read the book *How to Talk So Kids Will Listen and Listen So Kids Will Talk*. (I've referred to it throughout this book, if that is any indication of what an effect it had, and continues to have, on me.)

The biggest takeaway for me was realizing that my role as a parent is not to rush in to solve every problem for my children. Rather, we can be there to support them, be their sounding board, or be their safe place to release whatever frustrations they have had in their day.

This is an enormous shift. And a huge weight off my shoulders. We are the children's guide, planting the seeds but letting them grow. We are their rock in the background, helping only as much as is necessary but as little as possible.

A guide:

- gives space for the child to work it out for themselves
- is available when needed
- is respectful, kind, and clear
- will help a child take responsibility when needed
- will provide a safe, rich environment to explore
- listens
- responds rather than reacts

We don't need to be a boss giving them orders, directing them, or teaching them everything they need to learn. And we don't need to be their servant doing everything for them.

We can simply be their guide.

USE OUR HOME AS A HELPER

Just as a Montessori teacher uses the classroom environment as the second teacher (see chapter 2), we can set up our homes to help us as well. We've discussed how to do this in detail in chapter 4, but I'd like to return to some of those ideas here to illustrate how the changes we make to support our child can support us as well.

When we are feeling tired, we can look for ways that our home can do more of the work for us. Here are a few examples:

- If we find that our child is overly reliant on us, then we can look for ways to add independence into our daily rhythm.

- Every time we do something for our toddler that they can do themselves, we can make a small change so they can do it successfully by themselves—eventually taking away some of the burden on us. For example, we can add a scoop to a container so they can serve their own cereal at breakfast time. If they pull all the tissues onto the floor, we can look for a way to put out a few at a time on a dish and keep the box out of reach. The options are limited only by our imagination.

- If we find that we are saying "no" a lot, we can look for ways to change the environment.

- If we find that we are spending a lot of time tidying up, we can look for ways to reduce the number of toys available. We can make more thoughtful selections, observe what our child is no longer interested in, or find ways to support scaffolding the skills necessary for our child to clean up after themselves.

BE HONEST

Our children learn more from watching us than from us telling them how to behave. So we want to model honesty with our children. We want them to learn that being truthful is an important value in our home. No white lies.

I'd say most people think they are honest. Yet, little white lies are common:

- "Tell them I'm on the phone." (When we don't want to speak to someone.)
- "What do I think of your haircut? It looks great." (When we don't think that at all.)
- "I don't have any money on me." (To a person asking for money on the street.)

Instead we could say:

- To an unwanted call, "I'm tired right now. Can I call you back tomorrow?/Can you send me an email?"
- About someone's new haircut, "You look really happy with it."
- To a person on the street, "Not today—good luck" or "Can I buy you some fruit in the shop?"

It is actually really hard to be kind and truthful. It's something to strive to model.

TAKE RESPONSIBILITY FOR OUR LIFE AND CHOICES

There are many things that are difficult or challenging about life that we cannot change. But we can acknowledge it when some of life's headaches are a result of choices we've made.

If we choose to live in a house with a garden, it will require maintenance. Or if we choose to live in a cosmopolitan city, it means rents are high. Or if we want a nontraditional education for our children, it may cost money. We don't have to change these choices. Indeed, we are lucky to be able to make choices about these things at all. We can own these choices and the resulting responsibilities.

We can also model accepting responsibility for our choices to our children, commenting out loud when we run into a frustrating problem. "The train is late again! I'm grateful to live in a city with public transportation, but I'm not feeling very patient today. Next time we could leave earlier." We can observe ourselves neutrally and, with some distance, calm down and adjust our perspective.

We can take all the shoulds out of our life and do only the things we want to do. "I should iron these shirts." "I should cook the children's dinner." "I should call her back." "I should pay more attention to my children." This may seem like I'm advising against cooking dinner or paying attention to our children. Rather, I'm saying we cook dinner because we want to provide a nutritious home-cooked dinner for our children. Own that choice. I'm saying we pay attention to our children because we want them to grow up feeling secure and accepted. Own that, too.

Every time we say "should," we can think about whether it's important to us. Otherwise we can be creative and change it. And for the things we cannot change, we can see these as opportunities to be creative. If we work full-time, we can apply these ideas on the weekends, during mealtimes and bath times, and on our morning drop-off. If we cannot afford a school that offers the perfect setting, we can find one that complements our family values. And if we can't find that, we can keep applying the principles from this book to our daily life.

We can figure out what is important and preserve it. When we take ownership of our life and our choices, we are steering the ship that is our life rather than pulling the ropes senselessly against the storm.

LEARN FROM OUR MISTAKES

When we make a mistake, it is easy to blame someone or something else. For example, our toddler drove us crazy so we lost our temper, or the map was not clear so we went the wrong way. Just as we take ownership of our choices, we need to own our mistakes as well. There are days we are not going to have as much patience. When we get things wrong. When we do something that means we let our child down, our partner down, ourselves down.

Making mistakes means that we have an opportunity to apologize. And to think about what we could have done instead. I can always say to my child (or anyone, for that matter), "I'm so sorry. I should not have . . . What I could have said/done is . . ." This sets a far stronger example for our child than blaming someone else. They see that we can learn from our mistakes, and it shows that we are always trying to make kinder choices. And that no one, not even their parent, is perfect.

CELEBRATE WHERE WE ARE

We can be so busy trying to improve things that we forget to reflect on the present. I know that I forget to acknowledge and accept where I am right now while I am striving to learn more and be a better model for my child.

We often forget to say to ourselves, *We are enough. We are doing our best.*

I like to imagine that we are all full glasses of water. Rather than looking to others to fill our glass—our partner, our children, our work—we are full just as we are.

That gives me a huge sense of relief. It doesn't mean that I will stop learning and stop improving, but I feel okay with who I am today. That means I feel like I can be more to those in my life, including my children.

I also like to think of our toddlers as full glasses. They are doing the best they can in their little bodies where they are today. We can support them without being frustrated by them or angry with them.

SELF-AWARENESS

To parent in this way takes an increasing amount of self-awareness. In our Montessori training, this is part of self-observation.

We need to **recognize when our limits are about to be tested** and find a way to assert our limits—with kindness and clarity. If we let a situation build up, and we get irritated, it is almost impossible to calmly step in and provide clear guidance.

It's okay to have limits. It is part of being aware of ourselves and our needs, and balancing them with the needs of our children and others in our family. (See chapter 9 on working together with others.)

When we **find ourselves being triggered**, we can observe ourselves. Are we taking on our child's problem? Is it bringing up something that we don't like about ourselves?

We can step back to take a look objectively or write it down so we can figure it out later, when we are calm. We can give ourselves compassion and see which of our needs are not being met (for example, need for connection or to be cared for), and brainstorm ways to meet those needs.

Then we can move back to being the guide, the confident leader, the rock our child needs us to be.

KEEP PRACTICING

All the ideas in this book will take practice. Being this way with our child is like learning a new language and takes a whole lot of practice. I'm still practicing, and my children are becoming young adults, and I've been working as a Montessori teacher for years.

But it does get easier and more natural every day.

> "The child developing harmoniously and the adult improving himself at his side make a very exciting and attractive picture ... This is the treasure we need today—helping the child become independent of us and make his way by himself and receiving in return his gifts of hope and light."
>
> —Dr. Maria Montessori, *Education and Peace*

TO PRACTICE

1. What brings us into alignment during the day? Are we happy? Are our needs being met?
2. Can we be more present? Slower?
3. Can we shift from being our child's boss or servant to being their guide?
4. Can we use our home to save us some work?
5. Are we blaming others for our life situation? Can we take responsibility for our choices? Or change them?
6. Can we celebrate where we are today?

WORKING
TOGETHER

9

WHAT ABOUT EVERYONE ELSE?

We don't parent alone. There are many ways of being in a family—married, partners, single parent, living with grandparents, opposite or same-sex parents, divorced, from different cultural backgrounds, and so on. The number and types of family constellations will only grow as our society evolves.

No matter what our family constellation, we live in the context of the people around us as well—an extended family. These may or may not be blood relatives but could also include friends, friends from parenting groups, school friends, or the people in the local shop where we purchase our groceries. These are the people in the life of our family.

Many questions come up when we are parenting alone, with a partner, and with extended family.

- Maybe we have read this book and would love our "family" to also try some of the ideas mentioned here. How do we get them on board?
- What are our family values, anyway?
- Do we listen and speak to our family as we do to our toddler?
- Where do an adult's feelings stand in this child-driven approach?
- What if our toddler prefers one parent?
- What about a grandparent or caregiver? How can they apply this approach?
- What if we are separated from our partner? How will it affect our child? And how can it remain a positive experience for the child?

These are important questions. Here are some thoughts that align with the Montessori approach to get us started.

PARENTS ARE PEOPLE, TOO

It is easy to end up making life all about the children. We put our own needs on hold or feel guilty if we do something for ourselves.

We are all people, deserving of having our needs met. Following the child does not mean ignoring ourselves. Work together with our child. Be assertive if we need to be.

We allow our children a lot of freedom. But we can express our needs, too—for example, wanting some peace in the evening while our child rests in bed. (You may wish to refer to the table of feelings and needs on page 232.)

Make time for the adult relationship. Our partner, if we have one, is a person, too. And that relationship is very important. Without it, we might not have become a parent in the first place. However, we often forget to prioritize it.

I love the example I once heard about a French family with four children. When the parent who was working outside the home returned to the house each evening, the parents would sit down and have a glass of wine, check in, and connect with each other for about ten minutes rather than rushing to prepare dinner and into the usual evening routine. The parents did not jump up to rush to their children's rescue during this time. Their children learned that this was their parents' special time. They were showing their children that their relationship was important.

And that their parents are people, too.

PREFERRING ONE PARENT

Toddlers and children may go through phases of favoring one parent. They want only this parent to bathe them, read to them, dress them, or tuck them into bed.

If this continues, it can be upsetting and alienating for the other parent.

There is no one-size-fits-all approach to this situation, but here are some things to consider.

Is the child looking for a reaction? I think in many of these cases, the toddler is looking for clarity and is testing limits. We don't need to react or give in to their demands. If they push away one parent, that parent can gently acknowledge the toddler's feelings. "You wanted someone else to help you. And I'm helping you today." Remain calm, gentle, and confident.

Look for changes at home. If one parent has been traveling a lot, or there is a change at home like a new baby or moving to a different house, this can be the way the child expresses themselves; it's one thing they can try to control when everything else is out of their control. It does not mean that we need to change caregivers to meet their demands. But they may need some extra understanding and cuddles, and for us to see things from their perspective.

THE KEY TO WORKING TOGETHER AS A FAMILY

I believe the key to working together as a family is to recognize that each one of us has needs and to be creative in finding ways to make sure everyone's needs are met. It won't be easy, but it's possible. Or at least we can start the conversation.

Working with our child

The adult is in charge, but the child can definitely have input into how to solve problems. "You really want to keep playing outside, and I'm ready to go in. **How can we solve the problem?**" We can do this even with preverbal children. Revisit chapter 6 for specific suggestions.

Working with our partner

I truly think that, with some flexibility and understanding, everyone's needs can be met.

Let's take a regular weekend afternoon as an example. It is time to go to the supermarket, the children would like to go to the playground, our partner would like a nap, and we would like to meet a friend for a coffee.

Rather than bribing the children by saying, "We'll go to the park if you are good," we can choose to plan something for everyone that is **not conditional**. Perhaps we can go to the supermarket without the children and then take them to the playground while our partner naps. Or we order the groceries online and our friend comes to visit us at home while the children play and our partner naps. Any combination or other solution is possible.

Working with others

Our toddlers will have other people to care for them other than us. They may have a grandparent or babysitter look after them, or they may go to day care or school.

They will learn that there are other people in the world whom their parents trust with their care. They will learn to trust others. And they will learn a lot from other people's knowledge of the world. The child's world will be enriched by these interactions.

When we find someone we trust with the care of our toddler, our child will sense it. The best advice I received from my children's Montessori preschool teacher was to give them a big positive, yet short, goodbye. "Have a lot of fun and I'll see you after story time." I think I said the same thing every day. It reassured me, and it reassured them. When they ran out of class, I'd welcome them with a hug if they wanted it and say, "It's so lovely to see you." I did not need to tell them how much I missed them—that is a lot for a toddler to carry.

What they do need is the message that their parent trusts this person, so they trust them, too.

They also need to trust us in this process, so we should let them know if we are leaving and be okay with the fact that this may cause them some sadness. This is easier for the child than disappearing without telling them, having them suddenly notice we aren't there, and not being able to understand where we have gone or when we are coming back.

GETTING FAMILY ON BOARD

It is impossible to change someone else: not our children, our partner, or our family. We want them to take on these Montessori ideas. Yet we cannot force this upon them.

Do not despair.

We can start with ourselves. I often think the best thing we can do is to keep practicing. Often people will notice that we are parenting differently, and then ask for more information. "I see that you did not shout at your child when he was upset in the playground. Can you tell me more?" We are models not only for our children, but for others around us. Some will be curious and ask. But not everyone. That's okay, too.

Find different ways to share the information. Pass along a short article. Share a story about someone who is following a similar approach. Find a radio program or podcast episode that touches on one aspect that might resonate. Pass on this book. Forward a newsletter. Watch an online workshop with them. Get them to come to an in-person workshop at a Montessori school. Have conversations. Drip. Drip. Drip. Slow and steady information, easy to digest, in small doses, at a pace they are open to trying.

Watch how we talk with our family. Often we want our family to speak to our child in a gentle way, without correcting them, limiting criticism, and encouraging them. Then we end up talking to, and listening to, our family in exactly the way we are trying not to with our child. We correct them if they say the wrong thing. We get frustrated at their impatience. We end up talking over them and not showing them respect.

Acknowledge our family's feelings and translate for them. No one is right and no one is wrong. Just as we have learned to see from our child's perspective, we can also learn to see from the perspective of members of our family.

We may not like the way they talk or interact with our child, but we can always translate for them.

"It sounds like Grandad does not want you to climb on the couch."
"It sounds like your mother does not want you to throw your food."
"You two are having a hard time with each other. Let me know if you want me to help."

We can use the same idea on the playground, with neighbors, or with relatives with whom we may not agree. We can translate for them, too.

Go for agreement on the big family values. With enough wisdom, we can have conversations in which our family can find points of agreement. For example, we may find that we all want the best for the child. That we want them to grow up to be respectful and responsible. That we want them to be curious but that we all have our own limits.

Within this big picture, our toddler will learn that **each person in their family has their own unique approach**. Indeed, they will learn naturally who to go to when they want to be silly, who to go to when not everything is right in their world, and so on.

What a lucky child to have so many people caring for them. Even if we are not in contact with our immediate family, they can receive a lot of care from the village around us.

GRANDPARENTS
AND CAREGIVERS

If you are a grandparent or caregiver, this section is for you. You can apply any of the techniques mentioned in this book.

At first this approach may seem very different from the one you are used to and that may have served you well with your own children. Here are a few easy ways to start. If you like this approach, you can learn more about it by reading more of this book.

1. **Watch the child.** Take your cues from them. What are they interested in? Is it okay for them to explore freely? How can you let them explore while making sure they are safe?

2. **See if they can work it out themselves.** Whether it is trying to feed or dress themselves or struggling with a toy, give them a little time to see if they can figure it out themselves. The joy on their face when they manage is priceless.

3. **What do you enjoy that you may be able to share with them?** Sharing your interests can help the child have rich experiences. Do you play an instrument? Have some beautiful handcraft materials they can explore? Enjoy playing a sport that you could simplify to show them?

4. **Explore outside.** If you are worried about them breaking something or keeping them entertained, head outside to a park, playground, or walking trail, or simply walk to the local shops. Let them show you everything they see—you can name what they show you—and talk about it.

5. **Give feedback about what you see.** Rather than simply praising them by saying, "Good job," let them know what you saw. "I saw you swinging all by yourself." "You ran all the way to the top of the hill and rolled down. That looked like fun." We are trying to allow them to judge for themselves rather than to look for external approval.

6. **Give your presence, not your presents.** Gift giving can be fun. It can show your love. But what shows your love even more than another toy is your time. If you really want to buy a gift, consider buying tickets for the zoo so you can visit together, a book you can enjoy on the couch, or a gift card for their parents to have a meal while you babysit. Having less stuff means we can stay on this planet longer together. We want to show our children how to care for their environment, as well as for themselves and others.

7. **What values do you share with their parents?** This common ground is a good place to start. It will show some consistency for the toddler who likes order. Some of your rules may be different, which the toddler will learn. As long as the big picture is the same, the child will feel safe and secure in their relationship with both you and their parents.

8. **Can you give the parents a sense of belonging, significance, and acceptance?** Usually differences of opinion within the extended family (caregivers included) indicate a longing for acceptance. Even adults have an inner child wanting to be loved and accepted for who we are. Showing the child's parents that you understand their perspective can go a long way toward creating space for the differences.

WHEN THERE IS CONFLICT IN THE FAMILY

To help us communicate our concerns and hear the concerns of the other member(s) of the family, try this active listening exercise. All that is needed is to ask the other party if they have twenty minutes. This technique is adapted from Dr. Scilla Elworthy's keynote address at the 2017 Montessori Congress.

For the first five minutes, the other person can talk about whatever is bothering them. Listen, hear what they say, and notice the feelings that are coming up for them.

For the following five minutes, we tell them what we heard them say and what we think they were feeling. They can let us know if we misunderstood anything.

Then we switch roles. Now we can talk for five minutes about anything that is bothering us, while they listen.

In the last five minutes, they let us know what we said and any feelings they noticed coming up for us. We can also let them know if they didn't understand anything correctly.

If it feels like the conflict would benefit from another session, we may want to repeat the process for another twenty minutes.

We will start to see the other person and their needs and how we are all human and just want to get our needs met.

Tip 1

Try to avoid language that blames the other person. For example, say, "It's important for me to be respected" rather than "You don't respect me." Use "I" statements, make observations, and identify feelings and needs.

Tip 2

Make requests, not demands, of others. There are always many ways to solve a problem if we are creative, so be open to other solutions, too.

You can find a table of feelings and needs in the appendix (see page 232).

DIVORCE DOES NOT HAVE TO BE A DIRTY WORD

When parents decide to separate, it is possible to transition to an amicable family arrangement where the child simply has two parents living in different homes. Ideally, a co-parenting arrangement can be reached where parents have shared responsibility and both have time with the child.

Even in the 1900s, Dr. Montessori acknowledged that both parents played an important role for the child, as long as there is no psychological or physical reason for a child not to have contact with one of the parents. The child's safety is the first priority.

There is still a stigma around separation and divorce. It is sad when a relationship between parents ends. But it does not have to be negative. In fact, if both parents are happier as a result, it can be a more positive experience for the child who, even at a young age, can sense the atmosphere in the house when there is fighting, disagreement, and disharmony.

Stability is important for the child at this time. Have a regular schedule with each parent so the child knows what to expect. We have discussed how toddlers have a strong sense of order. Make it a priority.

Be honest with the child in an age-appropriate way. Don't assume they are too young to know what is going on. On the other hand, they don't need to know all the details. Be factual and keep them involved and updated as the situation evolves.

Being kind about the other parent in the child's company is critical. The parents' commitment to speaking kindly to and about each other when the child is present is paramount. Sometimes it will be very difficult, in which case we can physically step away from the conflict and discuss the matter later. We can talk to our friends, our family, or a counselor about difficulties we are having with the other parent, but not to the child. It is not fair to put the child in the middle.

Remember, we are both still the child's parents, their family; we're just not living together.

TO PRACTICE

1. Are our needs being met? If not, brainstorm ways to meet our needs.

2. Is there a way that everyone in the family can have their needs met? Be creative.

3. What ideas would help to get family on board?

4. Are there any conflicts that need to be resolved? Try the exercise from the section "When there is conflict in the family" (see page 200).

WHAT'S NEXT

10

GETTING READY
FOR PRESCHOOL/SCHOOL

Here are a few tips for those families who will be getting ready for preschool or school soon, particularly if the child will be going to a Montessori school.

The first thing is to **practice skills of independence**. For example, we can look for ways to support putting on their own jacket, being able to get their shoes on and off by themselves, and learning to wipe their nose.

Next is to **practice separation**. Particularly if there has not been another caregiver helping with the toddler, we will want to practice this skill just as we would any other skill. We can start with having someone come to our house to read and play together. Once the child is comfortable with them, we could make a short trip to run errands (being sure to tell them as we are leaving, even if our child is sad about it). They will learn that we come back. We can build up to longer periods apart until they are used to being away from us for the same amount of time as they will be at school.

Finally, something they will do throughout their lives is **practicing social skills**. At the playground, we can help translate for them so they learn to use their words, guide them to stand up for themselves if needed, and model care of others. This will provide them with the support they need to be ready to learn how to get along with, and care for, others in their new school.

Montessori materials at home

When our child starts school, it's best not to have the same Montessori materials at home. There are several reasons for this:

- They may be spending up to six hours a day at school and will be much more engaged with using and learning from the materials if they are found only in their classroom.

- We do not want to present the materials in a way that is different from how they learn at school—this may be confusing for them.

- They also need time for unstructured playtime, time outside, being involved in our daily lives, and simply catching up with friends.

The one Montessori activity from the classroom that my children's Montessori teacher said was okay to do at home was to play "I spy with my little eye something beginning with . . ." The only difference from regular "I spy" is that this game uses the phonetic sound of the letter rather than its name. For example, *buh* is used instead of *b* for a ball, *tr* instead of *t* for a tree.

THE COMING YEARS

Dr. Montessori developed an overview of a child's development from the age of 0 to 24 years based on her scientific observations. She called this the *four planes of development*.

It may be a surprise that she considered us children until the age of 24. Now brain research shows that the prefrontal cortex of the brain—the area for rational decision making and controlling social behavior—keeps developing until our early twenties. More than a hundred years later, brain research is backing up what Dr. Montessori observed.

In each plane of development, with each plane being six years in length, Dr. Montessori recognized similarities in a child's physical, psychological, and behavioral development.

Let's see what lies ahead after the toddler years.

Infancy (0 to 6 years): the first plane of development

The purpose of these first six years is for the child to gain physical and biological independence from their parent. With such enormous changes taking place during this time, it is generally a very volatile period.

The child goes through significant physical change in this period—growing from a baby entirely dependent on an adult into a child able to walk, talk, and eat by themselves.

Moving toward independence also means sometimes wanting to be close to the parent and other times pushing us away or wanting to do everything for themselves—a kind of crisis of independence. The child also does a lot of testing to make sense of the world around them.

The absorbent mind is also active during this whole period, with children from birth to 6 years being able to absorb all the information around them like a sponge. In the first three years of this cycle (0–3 years) the child absorbs this information completely unconsciously and without effort—i.e., with an *unconscious absorbent mind*. In the second three years (3–6 years) the child becomes a conscious learner, the *conscious absorbent mind*.

What does this mean in practice? The child moves from simply accepting and adapting to the world around him (0–3 years) to a child asking *why* and *how* (3–6 years). They want to understand all that they have taken in during the first three years. They also become fascinated by other cultures and enjoy maps of the world, flags, and landforms. They may also show interest in reading, writing, and mathematics using concrete learning materials.

They are sensorial learners in this plane, even in the womb. From 0 to 3 they are using all their senses to explore the world around them. From 3 to 6 they begin to classify these sensations, for example, big and small, hard and soft, rough and smooth, or loud and quiet.

They are based in reality in this period—they understand most easily the world they see around them and are fascinated with seeing how things work. Imaginative play may be seen from around 2.5+ years as they make sense of the world around them, for example, playing store or families.

This period is also when the child lays down their personality. Their experience in these early years will greatly shape who they are in their adult years.

We are indeed planting the seeds . . .

Childhood (6 to 12 years): the second plane of development

Where the first-plane child was working on physical and biological independence, the second-plane child is working on their mental independence. They are driven to know everything and to explore the reason behind things, no longer simply absorbing the information.

They are beginning to develop independent thought about the world around them and developing their moral sense. They start to explore the gray areas. "Is it right or wrong?" "Is it fair or unfair?"

They explore the world with their imagination—able to understand history and to project ideas into the future. This is also a collaborative age where they love to work in groups around large tables or on the floor.

There is not so much rapid growth in this period, so it might be nice for parents to hear that this is a more stable period and the child is less volatile. The foundation is already laid in the first six years when we set clear limits; in the second plane, our child understands the limits and does not need to challenge them every time.

The stem is growing tall and strong . . .

Adolescence (12 to 18 years): the third plane of development

The adolescent period has much in common with the first plane, so for parents who think that toddlers and teenagers are similar, Dr. Montessori would agree.

Again this is a period of enormous physical and psychological change as children move through puberty. And where the infant was becoming physically independent from their parent, the teenager is working on social independence and moving away from their families. There is a struggle between sometimes wanting to be part of the family and other times wanting to be independent—another crisis of independence, this time of a social variety.

Teenagers love sharing ideas and their ideals with others, particularly ways in which they would change the world (including developing social policy). Interestingly, Dr. Montessori observed that they are not actually as academic in this period, at a time when traditional schools generally become more academic.

Instead, Dr. Montessori proposed an *Erdkinder*, or farm school, as the perfect learning environment for a teenager. There they could learn by working the land, selling their goods at market, and figuring out their place in a social group. There are Montessori high schools in cities, known as "urban compromises." They try to apply similar principles in a city setting.

I want to add a personal note here to say that puberty and teenagers do not have to be scary. I found that having two teenagers in the house was a pleasure, and they were lovely people to spend time with.

Leaves and blossoms unfurl, nearing maturity . . .

Maturity (18 to 24 years): the fourth plane of development

Dr. Montessori said that if everything has been done in the first three planes of development, the fourth plane takes care of itself. She referred to this plane's work as developing spiritual and moral independence.

These young adults primarily want to give back to society, for example, through volunteer work or the Peace Corps. They may enter college and join the workforce.

Similar to the second plane of development, this is a more stable period, and the young adult has a reasoning, logical mind. They are busy exploring areas of interest in work and study at a deep level.

And their brains are nearly completely formed.

The plant is fully grown, still requiring our care and attention, but now completely independent of us.

FOUR PLANES OF DEVELOPMENT

FIRST PLANE	SECOND PLANE	THIRD PLANE	FOURTH PLANE
0–6 years	6–12 years	12–18 years	18–24 years
We are planting the seeds.	The stem is growing tall and strong.	Leaves and blossoms unfurl, nearing maturity.	The plant is fully grown.

FIRST PLANE

- physical and biological independence
- absorbent mind
- concrete understanding of the world
- sensorial learner
- children work in parallel with small amounts of collaboration
- rapid growth and change

SECOND PLANE

- mental independence
- developing moral sense (right and wrong) and exploring how things work and relate
- moves from concrete to abstract learning
- mode of learning through imagination
- collaborates in small groups
- less growth, more stable period

THIRD PLANE

- social independence
- developing social policy (how they would change the world)
- sharing ideas and ideals with others
- enormous physical and psychological change (similarities to the first plane)

FOURTH PLANE

- spiritual and moral independence
- gives back to society
- reasoning, logical mind
- more stable period (similarities to the second plane)

IT'S TIME FOR A CHANGE IN EDUCATION

When we become parents, we begin to realize how the current education system is failing our children. We see an educational system that was built for the Industrial Revolution to train factory workers, where children sit in rows and memorize facts to pass tests.

You may be reading this book because you want to raise your children to be able to think for themselves, research to find answers to their questions, think creatively, be able to problem solve, work with others, and have meaning in their work.

People like Sir Ken Robinson, an educational and creativity expert, are constantly asking us to question the education system. To see that traditional schools kill creativity. To see that we need a revolution in the way our children learn.

I was just like you. I had a toddler and a baby, and I looked at the schooling options ahead. I was idealistic. I didn't want my children to learn just so they would pass tests. I walked into the Montessori classroom and saw there could be another way to learn.

IT'S TIME FOR PEACE

"You have very truly remarked that if we are to teach real peace in this world, and if we are to carry on a real war against war, we shall have to begin with children and if they will grow up in their natural innocence, we won't have to struggle, we won't have to pass fruitless idle resolutions, but we shall go from love to love and peace to peace, until at last all the corners of the world are covered with that peace and love for which, consciously or unconsciously, the whole world is hungering."

—Mahatma Gandhi, *Towards New Education*

It's time to take this information to the next level. I want to ask you to help me with my not-so-surreptitious plan to spread some peace and positivity in the world.

Often we feel helpless and like there is nothing we can do about all the violence in the world around us. But there is something we can do. We can learn to understand our toddlers better.

Once we can apply these principles with our toddlers, we can start spreading peace around us with our partners and our families, at school, in the supermarket, with friends, with strangers, and—most importantly—with people who see the world differently.

Let's apply the perspective-taking skills we have learned in this book. Let's sit in conversation, listen to each other, and really see each other.

We may have different approaches to raising our children and make different educational choices. We may have differences of sex, race, ethnicity, politics, sexuality, religion, and more. All our underlying beliefs and value systems may be different.

I truly believe that who is right is not important. What is important is for us to give significance to others, to give them belonging, and to accept them for who they are, just as we have learned to do with our toddlers. Our toddlers are enough, we are enough, and so is every living thing.

To come to peace in this world is to celebrate our differences, seek the commonalities, address others' fears, find peaceful ways to live together, and recognize that **we are more alike than we are different**. After all, we are all human.

So where can we start? With understanding our toddlers better. And planting the seeds to raise beautiful, curious, and responsible human beings.

Dr. Montessori died on May 6, 1952, in Noordwijk aan Zee, in the Netherlands. The inscription on her tomb says

> "I beg the dear all-powerful children to unite with me for the building of peace in Man and in the World."

TO PRACTICE

1. How can we prepare ourselves and our child as they grow from toddler to preschooler and beyond?

2. How can we apply the perspective-taking skills learned in this book to our relationships with:
   - our toddler?
   - our partner?
   - our family and friends?
   - neighbors?
   - strangers?
   - people who see the world differently?

REAL STORIES

HOME TOURS AND QUOTES
FROM MONTESSORI FAMILIES

AUSTRALIA

Kylie, Aaron, Caspar, Otis, and Otto

How We Montessori

"No matter how much you read, I always recommend parents attend a Montessori parent-child class and experience Montessori in person."

"He is still very hands-on with his learning. I love to observe him in his element. He loves to bake sweets, and he gets so much enjoyment from cooking for his family. He loves getting messy with his art, and he loves being around his family. He is still very snuggly, and we love to curl up together with a good book."

"The thing that resonates the most about the Montessori approach is the way parents are taught to observe and follow the child. That each child learns at their own pace. This is magic."

MONGOLIA

Enerel, Bayanaa, Nimo, and Odi

Mininimoo

"I felt like my eyes were opened like never before when I saw the word *Montessori*. I could not sleep that day; I searched about it for the whole night and started preparing Montessori activities for my son the next day."

"I think teaching about discipline is much more important than the activities. Parents should set an example. We, as parents, also gain discipline throughout the process. And learn from the child. This takes a great amount of effort, but we get so much joy when the child is interested and learning."

"Even though my home and our Montessori room is small, I like to make it appear bigger, living in a small apartment. I try to squeeze everything in together and I make fewer items available at a given time. Always make a space for the child to explore. And I would suggest to try to always make a place cozy and comfortable."

CANADA

Beth, Anthony, and Quentin

Our Montessori Life

"Our absolute favorite thing to do is to be in nature with our boys, introducing them to all the natural world has to offer. So much natural learning happens when outside."

"We looked for a way to help our child meet his needs, on a holistic, individual level. Of course Montessori was the perfect and gentle answer."

"Above all, Montessori has at its center peace education. It is a pedagogy that has at its foundation the teaching of peace for the next generations. No other pedagogy or learning system has this. It's why I love Montessori so much."

"Montessori at home is about honoring and respecting the child. Can your child make their own food? Can they get their own clothes out of the closet? Do they have access to water or do you have to get them a drink? Most importantly, how do you speak to your children and the other members of your family?"

USA

Amy, James, Charlotte, and Simon

Midwest Montessori

"My favorite thing to do with my toddlers is observe them. Once I have prepared their environment, I absolutely love just sitting back and watching them at work. Through this, I have a glimpse into their minds, and it so fascinates me. Aside from watching them, I love spending time with them outdoors (either in nature or on the streets or in parks), reading books, listening and making music, and all things practical life."

"There is such care and detail placed upon creating an optimum environment for children to grow. This includes the preparation of the adult, which may be the most difficult part, particularly for a parent. We honor our children when we prepare ourselves and their home this way. The rest is up to them."

"We often think of toddlers as rambunctious, but if we take time to slow down, give them space, and observe, I have seen that young children can become deeply concentrated in their work."

MY FAMILY

Simone, Oliver, and Emma

Australia and the Netherlands

"View the world from the child's perspective. When we see the world through their eyes, we gain so much understanding and respect. And this will help you guide and support the child."

"I wanted my children to love learning, not to just pass tests. When we walked into a Montessori preschool, I was so touched. The thought that had been put into the activities laid out on the shelves. Everything was so beautiful. I wanted to start exploring everything myself, so I knew it was the right environment for my children."

"I'm constantly inspired as my own understanding of the Montessori philosophy deepens. It's like layers of an onion and you can just keep peeling back layer after layer. You can look at Montessori as just an approach to learning at school. But I love how Montessori can also be a way of life."

MY CLASSROOM

Jacaranda Tree Montessori

Amsterdam, the Netherlands

"Every week I welcome over 100 children with their parents and carers to learn in a Montessori environment, offering classes for babies, toddlers, and preschoolers."

"The children love to explore the environment, set up exactly for their age with everything accessible for them. The adults learn to observe the children, ask questions, and meet like-minded families. I love seeing both the children and the adults undergoing enormous transformation through coming to class."

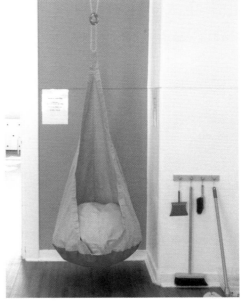

FURTHER READING

BOOKS AND LECTURES BY DR. MONTESSORI

The Absorbent Mind, Maria Montessori, Holt Paperbacks, 1995

The Child in the Family, Maria Montessori, ABC-CLIO, 1989

Education for a New World, Maria Montessori, ABC-CLIO, 1989

The Formation of Man, Maria Montessori, Association Montessori Internationale, 2007

The Secret of Childhood, Maria Montessori, Fides Publishers, 1966

The Discovery of the Child, Maria Montessori, Ballantine Books, 1986

Maria Montessori Speaks to Parents, Maria Montessori, Montessori-Pierson Publishing Company, 2017

The 1946 London Lectures, Maria Montessori, Montessori-Pierson Publishing Company, 2012

BOOKS ABOUT THE MONTESSORI APPROACH

The Joyful Child: Montessori, Global Wisdom for Birth to Three, Susan Mayclin Stephenson, Michael Olaf Montessori Company, 2013

Child of the World: Montessori, Global Education for Age 3-12+, Susan Mayclin Stephenson, Michael Olaf Montessori Company, 2013

Understanding the Human Being, Silvana Quattrocchi Montanaro M.D., Nienhuis Montessori, 1991

How to Raise an Amazing Child: The Montessori Way to Bring Up Caring, Confident Children, Tim Seldin, Dorling Kindersley, 2007

Maria Montessori: Her Life and Work, E. M. Standing, Plume, 1998

Montessori Madness, Trevor Eissler, Sevenoff, 2009

Montessori from the Start, Paula Polk Lillard and Lynn Lillard Jessen, Schocken, 2003

BOOKS ABOUT PARENTING

Positive Discipline: The First Three Years, Jane Nelsen, Ed. D., Three Rivers Press, 2007

How to Talk So Kids Will Listen and Listen So Kids Will Talk, Adele Faber and Elaine Mazlish, Piccadilly Press, 2013

Siblings Without Rivalry, Adele Faber and Elaine Mazlish, W. W. Norton & Company, 2012

The Whole-Brain Child: 12 Proven Strategies to Nurture Your Child's Developing Mind, Daniel J. Siegel, MD, and Tina Payne Bryson, MD, Delacorte, 2012

Unconditional Parenting: Moving from Rewards and Punishments to Love and Reason, Alfie Kohn, Atria Books, 2006

The Sleep Lady's Good Night, Sleep Tight, Kim West, Vanguard Press, 2010

Thriving!: Raising Confident Kids with Confidence, Character and Resilience, Michael Grose, Bantam, 2010

Toxic Childhood: How the Modern World Is Damaging Our Children and What We Can Do About It, Sue Palmer, Orion, 2006

The Creative Family Manifesto: How to Encourage Imagination and Nurture Family Connections, Amanda Soule, Roost Books, 2008

A Parents' and Teachers' Guide to Bilingualism, Colin Baker, Multilingual Matters, 2014

BOOKS ON PERSONAL DEVELOPMENT

Nonviolent Communication, Marshall B. Rosenberg, Phd, Puddledancer Press, 2003

Mindset: How We Can Learn to Fulfill Our Potential, Carol S. Dweck, Ballantine Books, 2007

Quiet: The Power of Introverts in a World That Can't Stop Talking, Susan Cain, Penguin Books, 2012

In Praise of Slow: How a Worldwide Movement Is Challenging the Cult of Speed, Carl Honoré, Orion, 2005

The Five Love Languages, Gary Chapman, Northfield Publishing, 2004

OTHER RESOURCES

"Seeing Tantrums as Distress, Not Defiance," Jenny Anderson, the *New York Times*, October 30, 2011

"Lexical Development in Bilingual Infants and Toddlers: Comparison to Monolingual Norms," Barbara Pearson et al., *Language Learning* 43, no. 1 (March 1993), 93–120

Sarah Ockwell-Smith, https://sarahockwell-smith.com/2015/03/19/one-simple-way-to-improve-your-baby-or-child-sleep/

Yoram Mosenzon, Connecting2Life, www.connecting2life.net/

Screen-Free Parenting, www.screenfreeparenting.com

Scilla Elworthy, www.scillaelworthy.com

Sir Ken Robinson, www.sirkenrobinson.com

Rusty Keeler, www.earthplay.net

THANK-YOUS

I have so much gratitude and appreciation for . . .

HIYOKO—I could not have asked for a more amazing illustrator for this project. I never could have dreamed that this book could be so beautiful. I would send an idea to Hiyoko to include in the book and it always came back exactly as I meant and even better than I expected. Her aesthetic, care, and generosity are of the highest quality. Thank you, Hiyoko, for translating my words into this beautifully illustrated and designed book.

ALEXIS—What a pleasure and honor to have Alexis and her brain working on this book with me. I asked Alexis to help me with a bit of copy editing. It turned into her giving me feedback on every word in this book. Her light and sensitive touch made the manuscript even better.

THE TEAM AT WORKMAN PUBLISHING—I'm still reeling in happiness that Workman has taken on this book to help me with my not-so-surreptitious plan to spread some peace and positivity around the world. Special thanks to Page for finding this book and bringing it to Workman; to Maisie for all your hours of work, staying forever positive, being an amazing editor, and listening to all my requests; to Rebecca, Lathea, Moira, and Cindy for getting the word out in fun and creative ways; to Galen for all his book layout skills and for appeasing the many design requests; to Kristina for getting this book into more and more countries; to Sun for the super organizational skills; and to the rest of the team at Workman working behind the scenes.

EXTRA HELPERS—Dyana, Kevin, and Niina were so kind as to be early readers and gave generous feedback on the book. Lucy and Tania also read through it to dot the "i's" and cross the "t's." Yoram generously contributed the feelings and needs table in the appendix. And Maddie jumped in to do some invaluable quote research, too. For the Montessori quotes, I was inundated with help from my Montessori friends who had fun tracking down all the sources for Dr. Montessori's wisdom. Thank you all for your invaluable help to make this book the best it could possibly be.

FAMILIES FOR SHARING THEIR HOMES—I am constantly surprised by the generosity and kindness of others. When I reached out to the families whose homes and children are featured in this book, they unhesitatingly offered to share their photos and lives with us. I hope you find their stories and photos pure inspiration for bringing Montessori into your own home. Thank you to Anna, Kylie, Enerel, Beth, and Amy for sharing the beauty, the joy, and the calm that Montessori has brought to your families.

MY INSPIRATION—I am eternally grateful for being introduced to Montessori by these three wise ladies—Ferne Van Zyl, An Morison, and Annabel Needs. I was lucky enough to attend classes with my children and work with Ferne, getting an amazing introduction to Montessori. Ferne shared her love for Montessori with me and showed me how to see things from the child's perspective. An and Annabel were my children's first Montessori teachers. It was from attending an open day at Castlecrag Montessori School in Sydney, Australia, that I was first touched by the beauty of a Montessori classroom, the respect of Montessori teachers, and the care with which everything is prepared for the children. Thank you for inspiring me to follow in your footsteps.

MY MONTESSORI TRAINER—Judi Orion shared her love of babies and toddlers with us and her wealth of experience during our AMI Assistants to Infancy training. I soaked up every word of our training and found the training so thorough in preparing us for all the work we do with children. A fundamental part of the training that I learned from Judi was the power of observation—learning to see the child with fresh eyes every day and accepting them for who they are. Thank you Judi for showing me how to see in a new way.

MONTESSORI FRIENDS—I have had the pleasure of learning from many Montessori friends both in person and online. These include Heidi Phillipart-Alcock, Jeanne-Marie Paynel, the lovely folk in the AMI head office, Eve Hermann and family, Pamela Green and Andy Lulka, and all the Montessori community from the Montessori congresses to our online

Montessori communities. Thank you for sharing your wisdom and helping me to keep growing and learning every day.

FAMILIES AT JACARANDA TREE MONTESSORI—I feel very grateful to work with such amazing families who come to my classes at Jacaranda Tree Montessori here in Amsterdam. Every week I greet more than 100 children and their mamas, papas, carers, grandparents, and others. I am learning from these families every day.

MY MUM + DAD + SISTERS—and all my extended family. We are a funny, random bunch. So different from each other in many ways, but so similar in others. My parents have always supported me, even when I say, "I think I'm going to be a Montessori teacher" or "move 16,633 kilometers away." I love chatting with them all on Sunday mornings and catching up on each other's news. Thank you for giving me both roots and wings.

LUKE—for dreaming about having kids while wandering through the market in London that day and for making it a reality. For working the night shift and waking up to look after Oliver and Emma while I did my Montessori training. For living in the UK, Australia, and the Netherlands. For all I have learned through 17 years of marriage, through separating amicably, and through our ongoing co-parenting journey. I would not have wanted to do it with anyone else. Thank you for being my intellectual sparring partner.

MY WORK BUDDY—When we work for ourselves, it can be hard to find the support we need. And then one day there was Debbie. She is not just my weekly work buddy. She listened to me go through a huge transition, we went on work retreats in cabins, had nature adventures with our children, and her family are the best people to share Sint "surprises" with. Then we wrote our books side by side at the cafe, celebrating and supporting each other. She is always there with a listening ear and just the right words. Thank you for Thursday afternoon work sessions and more.

MY FRIENDS—I have friends here in Amsterdam who hear all the nitty gritty as we catch up over coffee, stroll around a museum, or see a film. I have old friends whom I speak to less often but pick up exactly where we leave off and seem to be flowing in the same path even if we aren't in the same city. Thank you Rachel, Agi, Michelle, Birgit, Emily, Becci, Narelle, Emmy, Claire, Monika, and many others for all the fun to fuel my work.

KICKSTARTER BACKERS—I am indebted to all the people who backed this book in its early Kickstarter days, and for trusting me and helping to get this project off the ground and into homes all around the world.

ALL THE THINGS—for everything around me, from the cups of tea, to the nature visits, to cycling on my bike to class, to my bath, to yoga in the living room, to cozy spots where I've perched with my laptop to write this book (cafes, sitting outside, my bed, my kitchen table, my desk, the couch, a train through France, a plane to Stockholm, an apartment in Lyon), to my camera for capturing the beauty around me, to the internet for allowing me to connect with so many people, to the inspiring podcasts, to ALL the books, to Amsterdam which I now call home. I have so much I am grateful for.

TO YOU—for joining me in this work to spread peace in the world, one family at a time. Thank you, thank you, thank you.

MY OWN CHILDREN—Lastly, I want to thank the most important people in my life, Oliver and Emma. They are my favorite people to spend time with. They have taught me so much about being a parent, and I have loved growing up alongside them. Their support, patience, and understanding for my work means so much to me. Thank you from the bottom of my heart both for being you and for putting up with me talking nonstop about this project. Thank you for the pure love that fills my heart to write this book.

APPENDIX

INSTEAD OF THIS, SAY THAT

TO...	INSTEAD OF THIS...	SAY THAT...
See through our child's eyes	Denying: "Don't worry about it. It's just a bump."	See the situation from their perspective/ acknowledge their feelings: "Was that a shock? A bump can hurt."
	Judging: "You are always taking toys from other children."	Translate for them: "It sounds like you would like to have a turn when they are all finished."
	Blaming, lecturing: "You shouldn't have ..." "What you should do is ..."	Seek to understand by guessing how they feel: "Are you telling me...?" "It looks like you..." "Are you feeling...?" "It seems like..."
Build independence	Telling them what not to do: "Don't drop the glass!"	Tell them how to have success: "Use two hands."
	Avoid always taking the lead: "Let's go take a look at the puzzles."	Follow the child: Say nothing (wait to see what they choose).
Help our child	Taking over and doing it for them: "Let me do it for you ..."	Step in as little as possible and as much as necessary: "Would you like me/someone to help you?" "Would you like to see how I do it?" "Have you tried...?"
Help our child love learning	Correcting: "No, it's an elephant."	Teach by teaching: "Ah. You wanted to show me the rhinoceros." (Then make a note to teach them *elephant* at another time.)
Cultivate curiosity	Giving the answers to all questions: "The sky is blue because ..."	Encourage them to find out: "I don't know. Let's find out together."
Help our child assess for themselves, i.e., cultivate intrinsic motivation	Praising: "Good job!" "Good boy/girl!"	1. Give feedback, describe effort: "You put all the trucks in the basket." 2. Sum it up with a word: "Now, that's what I call being resourceful." 3. Describe how we feel: "It's a pleasure to walk into a tidy room."
Share	Forcing them to share: "Give them a turn now."	Allow them to finish and share by taking turns: "It looks like they are playing with it right now. It will be available soon."
Accept our child for who they are	Dismissing their angry/big feelings: "It's just a spoon. Don't be silly."	Acknowledge and allow all feelings: "It looks like you are upset that your favorite spoon isn't available."
Remind them of a house/ground rule	Shouting: "No fighting!"	Have a few house rules: "I can't let you hurt them. Use your words to tell them what you would like."
Cultivate cooperation	Saying no: "Don't touch the baby!"	Use positive language: "We are gentle with the baby."

TO...	INSTEAD OF THIS...	SAY THAT...
	Getting involved in the problem: "You are driving me crazy. Why don't you get dressed? We need to leave!"	Find ways to solve the problem: "How can we find a way to solve the problem? Let's make a checklist of all the things we need to do to leave in the morning."
	Getting frustrated: "Why don't you listen to me? It's bath time!"	Find ways to involve the child: "Would you like to hop to the bath like a rabbit or walk sideways on all fours like a crab?"
	Nagging, shouting: "How many times do I have to ask you to put your shoes on?"	Use one word: "Shoes."
	Repeating ourselves: "Don't go near the oven again!"	Write a note: "The sign says, 'It's hot.'"
	Accusing: "Why don't you ever put away your toys when you are finished?"	Show them: "It goes here" (while tapping the shelf).
Help our child be responsible	Threatening, punishing, bribing, or giving a time-out: "If you do that again, I'll..." "If you come now, I'll give you a sticker." "Go to time-out to think about what you have done!"	Help them calm down and then make amends: "You look upset. Would you like a cuddle?" "Would you like to go to your calm place to calm down?" THEN "Our friend is crying. How can we make it up to them?"
Communicate limits	Avoiding conflict, being very strict, or setting a bad example: "They are too young to know what they are doing." "If you bite me again, I'll bite you and let you see if you like it."	Set a kind and clear limit: "I can't let you hit/throw/bite me. I'm going to put you down. If you need to bite, you can bite on this apple."
Avoid sibling rivalry	Comparing siblings: "Why don't you eat your peas like your sister/brother?"	Treat each child uniquely: "It sounds like you would like some more."
	Putting the eldest in charge: "You are a big brother/sister now. You should know better."	Give all siblings responsibility: "Can you both look after each other while I visit the bathroom?"
Be neutral in sibling disputes	Trying to decide who is right and wrong: "What happened here?"	Leave them to solve the problem: "I see two kids who want the same toy. I know you can come up with a solution that both of you are happy with."
Avoid using roles and labels	Putting a child in a role or using labels: "They are the shy one/the clever one."	Give them another view of themselves: "I noticed that you asked for help all by yourself."
Communicate with family/other caregivers	Getting angry with a family member: "Why are you shouting at them?"	Translate for them: "It sounds like Mom/Dad would like you to..."
Model grace and courtesy	Blaming others: "You should have told me earlier."	Take responsibility: "What I should have done is..." "What I should have said is..."

WHERE TO FIND MONTESSORI MATERIALS AND FURNITURE

Sources for materials and furniture will vary from country to country. However, here are some suggestions of places to get started.

I like to recommend first looking locally where possible to support local businesses and to reduce our footprint by minimizing shipping costs.

A few things from somewhere like Ikea can be useful for basics, and we can customize them to add our own unique touch. They have some suitable low shelving, tables and chairs, arts and crafts materials, book ledges, and items for the hallway, kitchen, and bathroom.

1. Activities

To find a wide selection of wooden puzzles; sorting, stacking, posting, and threading activities; and musical instruments, look in wooden-toy shops or secondhand stores.

Coin boxes can be found at stationery shops or specialty lock shops.

Another activity that is easy to set up at home is a basket full of purses with hidden treasures inside. I love finding these purses at flea markets and thrift stores. Some favorite hidden treasures to look for are small spinning tops, miniature animals, a small toy baby, and trinkets found on key chains (with the key chain removed). (As these items are often small and possible choking hazards, always offer with supervision.)

I also love Schleich plastic animals; they are a bit expensive but great for gifts. They're available at wooden-toy shops or online.

2. Craft Supplies

For small scissors; painting supplies; chunky, good-quality pencils; and watercolor paints, look in an art supply shop. There we can also find paper and paintbrushes in various sizes.

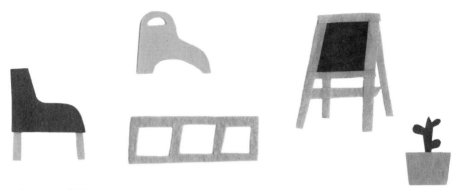

3. Baskets and Trays

Baskets and trays are perfect for organizing the activities on our shelves at home. We can look in storage supply shops, thrift shops, or department stores. Muji stores also have some lovely options.

4. Snack Area

Be on the hunt for a kitchen or housewares store that stocks glasses that are the right size for small hands while being durable and chip resistant. Look for glass, not plastic. We show the child how to use real objects around the home. If they are aware that the items may break, they learn to carry these items with care. Drinking from a glass tastes better, is a more sustainable choice, and doesn't tip over as easily when our child is learning to pour a drink for themselves. I use the smallest size of Duralex glasses in my classroom.

We can find nice enamel bowls in housewares shops or small metal bowls at Ikea, as well as cute tin boxes for crackers in antiques stores or at Ikea.

5. Cleaning

We can also include small cleaning items in our kitchen area, such as a mop, broom, or dustpan with brush. These are generally available at toy shops or online. Hand mitts (made of terry cloth to fit over the hand) are useful to have at the ready; look in department stores. I have found some great toddler-sized aprons on Etsy by searching "Montessori aprons."

6. Furniture

We may be able to find a workshop where they can make us a small table, chair, and low shelves. I also like to look at secondhand shops. The shelves in our class are 47 inches long by 12 inches deep by 16 inches high (120 cm by 30 cm by 40 cm).

ABOUT MONTESSORI SCHOOLS

What to look for in a Montessori school

Because the name *Montessori* was never copyrighted, there is a wide range of so-called Montessori schools, and it can be difficult to know which are genuinely applying the principles and theories of Dr. Montessori.

Here are ten things to look for:

1. The school promotes hands-on understanding of the world with tangible materials. The children make discoveries for themselves through touching, exploring, and working with beautiful, solid materials.

2. The materials are set out on shelves at the children's level. The activities are beautiful, attractively presented on trays or in baskets, with no missing parts.

3. There are mixed age groups: 3-to-6-year-olds, 6-to-9-year-olds, and 9-to-12-year-olds. The older children can model for, and help, the younger children.

4. The work time is unstructured. The children are free to choose what they work on and free to work uninterrupted for (ideally) three-hour periods.

5. The children are happy and independent.

6. There is little or no testing. The teacher knows which activities each child has mastered, so there is little need to test a child.

7. The teacher has completed a recognized Montessori training program. I particularly like Association Montessori Internationale, because this is the training organization Dr. Montessori's family set up to maintain the integrity of their courses.

8. The teacher talks respectfully to the children as a guide, encouraging them to be resourceful about finding answers to their questions: "I don't know. Let's find out!"

9. Natural learning is emphasized over traditional learning. Rather than the teacher standing at the front of the class telling the children what they need to know, the children are free to explore and make discoveries for themselves in a natural way.

10. The school treats each child as a unique individual, while looking at all aspects of their development (social, emotional, physical, cognitive, and linguistic).

What does a typical day at a Montessori school look like?

It can be difficult for parents to understand how there can be thirty children in a Montessori class, all working on different lessons and on different subjects simultaneously. I often get asked, "How can the teacher manage all this?"

Here's an impression of how it works in practice.

Before the day starts, the Montessori teacher has prepared the classroom. Activities line the shelves at the children's height in the various subject areas, with meticulously arranged materials that scaffold onto each other, building skills upon skills upon skills. During the class, the teacher observes the children, sees what each child is learning and mastering, and offers the next lesson to a child when they are ready.

If we walk into a Montessori classroom, we might see one child working on their math skills, another child doing a language activity, and an additional pair of children completing a project together. The idea is that the child can choose for themselves what they would like to work on.

In a Montessori classroom, less time is spent on "crowd control," such as getting everyone to sit and listen to a lesson or visiting the bathroom as a group. This gives the teacher more time to focus on observing and helping the children.

Because the children in the classroom are in mixed-age groups, older children can help younger children. When they explain something to another child, they consolidate their own learning. The younger children also learn from observing older children.

We might be concerned that, with all this freedom, our child might avoid an area of learning. If this happens, the Montessori teacher will observe whether the child is not yet ready, and they can offer them activities that may be more accessible and attractive to them, showing them in a different way that follows their interests.

Is Montessori suitable for every child?

We often wonder if Montessori is suitable for all children or only for children who can plan well, are very independent, or can sit quietly to work.

1. Does Montessori work for different learning types?

I've found that Montessori is suitable for all children. The materials offer opportunities to learn visually, aurally, kinesthetically (through touch), and verbally, so they appeal to children who learn in different ways.

Some children learn by observing, others by doing. Children do not have to be "busy" all the time—they are welcome to observe others doing an activity. Sometimes, they will have learned so much through observation that by the time they try the same activity themselves, they are already close to mastering it. Another child may learn more by doing the activity themselves, repeating and repeating it until they master it. Both children can thrive in this environment, despite their different learning styles.

2. Does our child have to be able to plan?

Planning their day is something Montessori children learn how to do over time. In younger age groups, children follow their natural rhythm and interests. As they get older, they gradually build their planning skills in small steps.

Some children may need more guidance than others. A trained Montessori teacher should be able to guide children who need more assistance with organizing their work.

3. What if our child needs to move a lot?

A Montessori approach can be ideal for children who need to move. When we enter a Montessori classroom, it can often seem surprisingly quiet. The children appear focused on their activities without the teacher having to yell at them to calm down.

However, we also notice that the children are free to move around the classroom, observe others, and go to the toilet when necessary. In addition, a lot of movement is built into the activities themselves, so Montessori can be perfect for a child who needs to move.

4. Does Montessori match our parenting approach at home?

Montessori is suitable for all children, but some may find the limits of the classroom too constraining, and others may find the freedoms of the classroom too permissive.

I believe that Montessori works best when the child experiences a similar approach at home, where parents respect the child but also set clear limits—and the child learns to stay within them.

How does a child transition to a traditional school after being at Montessori?

Parents are often concerned that their child may need to switch to a traditional school at some stage in the future.

It is natural to think, *How will my child adjust to having to listen to the teacher giving the same lesson to everyone? To follow the teacher's timeline, rather than my child's? To sit still during class?*

Children generally transition well from Montessori schools to other schools. They are usually very independent, respectful, and sensitive to the other children—skills that are useful as they move to a new school.

I've heard a child say about the transition, "It's easy. You just have to do what the teacher tells you."

In another case, a child had been in Montessori schools until high school. The biggest challenges she faced were:
1. Asking the teacher if she could use the toilet
2. Not being able to look up information during tests if she didn't know the answer, because she was used to finding out the solution herself

Another family found it amusing that the children in the new school always put up their hands to ask the teacher if something was on the test. The Montessori children were used to learning because they loved to do so, not because they were being tested.

FEELINGS AND NEEDS

I have learned a lot from the Nonviolent Communication courses run by Yoram Mosenzon from connecting2life.net. I asked him if I could include his feelings and needs tables in this book, and he kindly agreed.

PLEASANT (EXPANSION)

FEELINGS · SENSATIONS · EMOTIONS

UNPLEASA (CONSTRICTIC

CALM

relaxed
serene
tranquil
peaceful
quiet
at ease
comfortable

trusting
relieved
centered
content
fulfilled
satisfied
mellow

LIVELY

excited
enthusiastic
eager
energetic
passionate
vibrant
anticipation

blissful
ecstatic
radiant
thrilled
astonished
amazed
optimistic

CONFUSED

torn
lost
hesitant
baffled
perplexed
puzzled

BODY SENSATIONS

pain
tense
shaky
breathless
squeezed

shrink
sick
weak
empty
choked

WORRIED

concerned
stressed
nervous
anxious
edgy
unquiet

HAPPY

amused
animated
delighted

glad
joyful
pleased

COMPASSION

tender
warm
openhearted
loving
affection
friendly
sympathetic
touched

FEAR

afraid
scared
suspicious
panicked
paralyzed
terrified
apprehensive

UNCOMFORTABLE

troubled
unsettled
restless
uncertain
disquiet
agitated

disturbed
cranky
shocked
surprised
alert
uneasy

EMBARRASSE

ashamed
shy

CURIOUS

fascinated
interested
involved

engaged
inspired

SAD

heavy hearted
disappointed
discouraged
melancholy
depressed
gloomy

pity
longing
despair
helpless
hopeless
nostalgic

BORED

disconnected
alienated
apathetic
cold
numb
withdrawn
impatient

GRATEFUL

appreciative
thankful
moved
encouraged

VULNERABLE

fragile
insecure
reserved
sensitive

REFRESHED

rested
enlivened
restored
reactivated
clearheaded

ANGRY

upset
furious
rage
resentful

JEALOUS

envious

PAIN

hurt
heartbroken
lonely
miserable
suffer
grief

agony
devastated
regretful
remorseful
guilt
turmoil

CONFIDENT

empowered
open
proud
safe
hopeful

HATE

dislike
hostile
aversion
bitter
disgusted
scorn

FATIGUE

overwhelmed
burnout
exhausted
sleepy
tired

ANNOYED

irritated
frustrated
impatient

displeased
exasperated
unsatisfied

NONVIOLENT COMMUNICATION

How to use these tables: When we have a thought, we can use the "Feelings/Sensations/ Emotions" table to pinpoint what we are actually feeling. Once we've identified the feeling, we can use the table of "Universal Basic Needs" to see which underlying need is not being met, for example, to be seen or heard. Then, we are able to be more compassionate with ourselves and communicate more effectively with others about our feelings. We can also turn this compassion to others and try to understand their feelings and needs.

UNIVERSAL BASIC NEEDS

PHYSICAL WELL-BEING

air
nourishment (food, water)
light
warmth
rest / sleep
movement / physical exercise
health
touch
sexual expression
shelter / security /
protection / safety /
protection from pain /
emotional safety /
preservation
comfort

HARMONY

peace
beauty
order
calm / relaxation /
equanimity / tranquility
stability / balance
ease
communion / wholeness
completion / digestion /
integration
predictability / familiarity
equality / justice / fairness

CONNECTION

love
belonging
closeness
intimacy
empathy / compassion
appreciation
acceptance
recognition
reassurance
affection
openness
trust
communication
sharing / exchange
giving / receiving
attention
tenderness / softness
sensitivity / kindness
respect
seeing (see / be seen)
hearing (hear / be heard)
understanding
(understand / be understood)
consideration / care / that my
needs matter
inclusion / participation
support / help / nurturing
cooperation / collaboration
community / companionship /
partnership / fellowship
mutuality / reciprocity
consistency / continuity

MEANING

purpose
contribution / enrich life
centeredness
hope / faith
clarity
to know (be in reality)
learning
awareness / consciousness
inspiration / creativity
challenge / stimulation
growth / evolution / progress
empowerment / power /
having inner strength /
competence / capacity
self-value / self-confidence /
self-esteem / dignity
efficacy / effectiveness
liberation / transformation
to matter / take part in /
have my place in the world
spirituality
interdependence
simplicity
celebration / mourning

FREEDOM

choice / acting out of my
own spirituality
autonomy
independence
space / time

HONESTY

self-expression
authenticity
integrity
transparency
realness / truth

PLAY

liveliness / alive / vitality
flow
passion
spontaneity
fun
humor / laugh / lightness
discovery / adventure
variety / diversity

Note: The words in this list are not "pseudo feelings," like when we say we are feeling "attacked." Pseudo feelings often imply the person receiving our message is at fault. So stick to words on this list that have been carefully selected so that we will be heard.

PLAY-DOUGH RECIPE

To make the best play dough, you usually have to cook it, which gets very messy. This recipe uses boiling water instead. We just stir the ingredients, add the boiling water, mix for a few minutes until it's cool, then knead. Voilà, we've got lovely play dough.

INGREDIENTS (makes about a cup [240 ml] of play dough)

Regular Play Dough
1 cup (125 g) flour
2 tablespoons cream of tartar
½ cup (150 g) salt
¾ to 1 cup (175 to 250 ml) boiling water
1 tablespoon cooking oil
Food coloring or cinnamon, spirulina powder, or other natural coloring

Chocolate Mud Play Dough
1¼ cups (150 g) flour
½ cup (50 g) cocoa
1 teaspoon cream of tartar
¼ cup (75 g) salt
¾ to 1 cup (175 to 250 ml) boiling water
2 tablespoons cooking oil

INSTRUCTIONS

1. The children can mix the dry ingredients together in a medium bowl.

2. Add the boiling water, food coloring, and oil to dry ingredients and mix until it pulls away from the edges of the bowl. (This is a step for the adult.)

3. Once the mixture is cool enough (this takes a few minutes), have the children knead it until it's smooth.

4. Store in sealed container for up to 6 months. Does not need to be refrigerated.

LIST OF MONTESSORI ACTIVITIES FOR TODDLERS

AGE	ACTIVITY NAME	DESCRIPTION/MATERIALS	AREA OF DEVELOPMENT
All ages	Music/dance/ movement/singing	• Playing musical instruments • Listening to beautiful music (preferably not as background music but as the focus) • Dancing and moving to explore and stretch the body • Singing	• Music and movement
All ages	Books	• Collection of books with realistic images that relate to the life a young child is living • One picture per page for infant, *then* one picture with one word, *then* a picture with a sentence, *then* build to simple stories, and *then* more complex stories • Arranged so that children can see their covers and access them easily, perhaps in a small basket for a few books or on a small bookshelf • Start with board books and move on to hardcover and paperback	• Language
All ages	Rhythmic language	• Poetry, songs, rhyming ditties • Simple and not too long • Fairly realistic • Finger and body movements that go along with them. Examples: action rhymes, finger rhymes, haiku, pat-a-cake	• Language
All ages	Self-expression	• Moments during the day when the child wants to share something with the adult • For a nonverbal child, it can be sounds, expressions, or poking out their tongue. • A verbal child will use words, then phrases and sentences. • The adult needs to get down to the child's eye level, maintain eye contact (if culturally appropriate), and be present. • We can restate what they have said. • Through body language and speech, the adult lets the child know that we are very interested in what they are sharing.	• Language
12 months	Scribbling	• Block crayon or chunky pencil (like Stabilo 3 in 1) • Paper—different sizes, colors, textures • Underlay to protect entire table, or a place mat	• Art/self-expression

12 months	Easel-chalk	• Chalkboard—examples:
		  1. on the other side of a painting easel;
		  2. very large piece of plywood with chalkboard paint, wall mounted low to ground; and/or
		  3. small chalkboard that sits on a shelf
		• Chalk—start with white and gradually introduce colors and different types of chalk
		• Small eraser
			• Art/self-expression

Able to stand unaided	Easel-paint	• Easel • Paper that completely covers surface of easel • Start with one color of thick paint in a cup and gradually introduce other colors one by one. Can use two or more colors for an older child. • Chunky paintbrush with short handle • Painting smock/apron • Cup hook to hang smock/apron • Paper rolled in bin • Wet cloth to wipe up spills	• Art/self-expression

AGE	ACTIVITY NAME	DESCRIPTION/MATERIALS	AREA OF DEVELOPMENT
12+ months	Base with rings of dimensional gradation	• Base with spindle and four or five rings of varying gradation, ideally alternating colors • Bottom ring should not be bigger than child's hand span.	• Activities for eye-hand coordination
12+ months	Nuts and bolts	• One- or two-shaped bolts with a corresponding nut of the same shape • Have the nut on the bolt to start	• Activities for eye-hand coordination
12+ months	Opening and closing	• Basket with two or three common household objects for opening and closing, for example, a decorative box, tin, purse with snap fastener, makeup containers, toothbrush holder	• Activities for eye-hand coordination
12+ months	Vocabulary objects	• Three to six real or replica objects from the same category • Examples: fruits, vegetables, clothing, zoo animals, farm animals, pets, insects, mammals, birds, vertebrates, invertebrates, and so on	• Aids language development • Expands vocabulary
12+ months	Peg box	• Wooden box with six holes along back and an inset tray area for placing pegs removed from holes	• Refinement of eye-hand coordination and grasp
12+ months	Cubes on a vertical dowel	• Base with three cubes on dowel—keep cubes in basket or on dowel • Preparation for bead stringing	• Refinement of eye-hand coordination and grasp
12–14+ months	Puzzles	• Collection of knobbed puzzles progressing through greater and greater degrees of difficulty • Subject matter depicted on puzzle needs to be realistic and appealing, for example, animals or construction vehicles.	• Refinement of eye-hand coordination and pincer grasp • Develops the ability to recognize a background shape
Around 13+ months	Locks and keys	• Lock with the key strongly attached to a string	• Activities for eye-hand coordination
Once a child can walk	Table wiping	• Tray or basket with a sponge/drying mitt • Replacement sponges/mitts	• Care of environment
14+ months	Objects with identical cards for matching	• Classified sets of objects that have matching cards • Pictures that are identical to objects—in size and color, if possible—where the object can be put on top so that it covers the picture completely	• Aids language development • Helps a child move from 3D object to a 2D representation
14+ months	Objects with similar cards for matching	• Classified sets of objects that have matching cards • Similar pictures of the objects, perhaps different in color, size, or other	• Aids language development • With similar cards, allows the child to extract the essence of the object
14+ months	Wooden box with sliding lid	• Box with sliding lid, object inside, changed regularly	• Refinement of eye-hand coordination and grasp
14+ months	Box with bins	• Wooden box with three bins that open out • Three different objects, placed in each bin	• Refinement of eye-hand coordination and grasp • To exercise the wrist motion

AGE	ACTIVITY NAME	DESCRIPTION/MATERIALS	AREA OF DEVELOPMENT
14+ months	Posting activities	• Boxes for posting different shapes and sizes • Basic set with a single shape, for example, one lid with a circle, one with a square, one with a triangle, and one with a rectangle • Make it more challenging—for example, two shapes cut out of one lid—and then even more challenging—for example, with four shapes	• Refinement of eye-hand coordination and grasp • Introduction to, and naming of, geometric solids
14+ months, walking steadily	Watering plants	• Tray (to protect shelf) • Small watering can • Small container with small piece of dish sponge • Plant	• Care of environment
14+ months	Undressing, dressing, and storing clothes	• Putting on and taking off their own coat, shoes, and clothing and hanging them on a hook or putting the items in a basket	• Care of self
14+ months	Handwashing at sink	• Bar of soap or liquid soap • Towel	• Care of self
14+ months	Wiping nose	• Tissues—can be cut in half and folded • Mirror • Small trash can with swinging lid • Show them how you wipe your own nose; then allow them to wipe their nose.	• Care of self
14+ months	Brushing teeth	• Bathroom sink • Place to store toothbrush • Toothbrush • Toothpaste • Allow child to start brushing their teeth; then, offer to finish for them.	• Care of self
14+ months	Dressing frame: Velcro	• Wooden frame, two pieces of fabric fastened with Velcro • To practice opening and closing Velcro	• Care of self
14–16 months	Climbing	• For example, dome climbers, poles, climbing wall, obstacle courses, trees	• Activities for gross-motor movement
14–16 months	Pushing/pulling	• For example, a wheelbarrow for pushing and a wagon for pulling	• Activities for gross-motor movement
14–16 months	Brachiating—swinging by arms like a monkey	• For example, monkey bars, rings	• Activities for gross-motor movement
14–16 months	Sliding	• Ideally with large platform at top and wide enough for them to manage independently	• Activities for gross-motor movement
14–16 months	Running	• For example, running tracks with arrows; a basket of balls sits at each end of the track and the child carries a ball from basket to basket	• Activities for gross-motor movement
14–16 months	Jumping	• For example, jumping over a line flat on the floor; once child is jumping with both feet, you can introduce something with elevation	• Activities for gross-motor movement
14–16 months	Riding	• For example, a balance bike or low trike propelled by pushing feet on floor; then from 2.5 years, you can introduce pedal tricycles	• Activities for gross-motor movement

AGE	ACTIVITY NAME	DESCRIPTION/MATERIALS	AREA OF DEVELOPMENT
14–16 months	Balancing	• Balance beam, for example, a plank of wood on top of some books or bricks • Initially walking sideways while holding on to wall/beam in front of them; then walking forward on beam holding on to wall with one hand; then one foot on beam, one foot on ground (and then alternate feet so other foot is on beam and so forth); then can alter height or move beam away from wall; can also crawl on a wide balance beam	• Activities for gross-motor movement
14–16 months	Swinging	• Ideally, low to ground so child can get on and off by themselves and push themselves. Child can lie over seat and push with feet or sit on seat, back up, then lift feet and go.	• Activities for gross-motor movement
14–16 months	Other movement possibilities	• Platform on semicircular base (aka therapy top or balance board)—very good for building balance, understanding feedback given by the body, and coordinating movement • Y-shaped tunnels made of natural elements like willow branches or similar • Labyrinths from box hedge • Sand pits • Ball or tire swing • Gardening and composting • Cave made out of natural elements, for example, sticks, willow, or similar • Running water	• Activities for gross-motor movement
14–16 months	Discs on horizontal dowel	• Straight, horizontal metal dowel on a wooden base with one to three discs	• Refinement of eye-hand coordination and grasp • To cross the midline • To work on wrist movements
14–16+ months	Discs on serpentine dowel	• Serpentine dowel made of metal on a wooden base with one to three discs	• Refinement of eye-hand coordination and grasp • To cross the midline • To work on wrist movements
Around 15–16+ months	Washing leaves	• Little (leaf-shaped) dish with sponge cut to size inside dish • Tray to protect shelf from water	• Care of environment
Around 15–18+ months	Latches	• Collection of latches attached to different furniture or doorways in a room, for example, latch with chain, hook latch, and bar latch	• Refinement of eye-hand coordination and grasp
Around 15–18+ months	Hair brushing	• Mirror plus hairbrush • Tray to carry hairbrush and a dish with hair clips and bands	• Care of self
Around 15–18+ months	Three pegs with small rings	• Wooden square base with three pegs in primary colors • Three rings of each color	• Refinement of eye-hand coordination and grasp

AGE	ACTIVITY NAME	DESCRIPTION/MATERIALS	AREA OF DEVELOPMENT
Around 16 to 18+ months	Clay	• Plastic mat or special table with canvas covering for clay work • Lump of real mud clay (white/terra-cotta) wrapped in a damp cloth in a container or white DAS clay or play dough or kinetic sand • Tools to sculpt and cut with	• Art/self-expression
16–18+ months	Sweeping	• Broom • A sweeping guide (or a circle drawn in chalk on the ground) can be used to show where to collect the dirt • Dustpan and brush	• Care of environment
16–18+ months	Dusting	• Dusting cloth	• Care of environment
16–18+ months	Mopping	• Child-sized mop or flat mop with washcloth attached • Hang mop on cleaning stand	• Care of environment
16–18+ months	Dusting plants	• Handmade plant duster made of wool • Container to hold duster	• Care of environment
16–18+ months	Dressing frame: zipper	• Wooden frame, two pieces of fabric fastened with a zipper • The fabric does not come apart—the zipper is attached at the bottom. • Metal ring can be placed on the zipper pull. • Practice using a zipper	• Care of self
16–18+ months	Bead stringing	• Piece of plastic tubing used as thread—easier to use initially because it allows the child to push a bit of thread through the bead • Five or six wooden beads—can build to more beads • More challenging: thicker string, bigger beads, a shoelace with small beads	• Refinement of eye-hand coordination and grasp • Two hands working together
18+ months	Flower arranging	• Collection of different vases • Doilies • Flowers—cut to length to be used • Tray with a lip • Small jug • Small funnel • Sponge • The child can pour water into the vase using the funnel, place the flower in the vase, and arrange the vase on a table or shelf with the doily underneath.	• Care of environment
18+ months	Hanging up cloths	• Wet items of laundry—napkins, hand mitts, washcloths, aprons • Clothesline • Clothespins	• Care of environment
18+ months	Collecting debris and placing it on the compost pile/ in the compost bin	• Debris • Child-sized rake, dustpan, and brush • Wheelbarrow • Compost pile/compost bin	• Care of environment • Outdoor environment

AGE	ACTIVITY NAME	DESCRIPTION/MATERIALS	AREA OF DEVELOPMENT
18+ months	Germinating seeds	• Seeds—Use a small glass jar with a picture of the type of plant on the outside. Choose seeds that will germinate quickly (peas, beans, corn, radishes, pumpkins, sunflowers). • Small pots made of clay, newspaper, or peat • Small gardening hand tools, including trowel and rake • Apron • Small tray with a little dish • Small gardening tray and jug on windowsill or near light source • Dirt from outside or, if necessary, a bag of dirt	• Care of environment
18+ months	Other activities to take care of the outdoor environment	• Sweeping • Raking • Digging • Scrubbing tiles, tables, and benches • Watering plants • Picking and caring for flowers • Planting a flower/vegetable/herb garden that then requires ongoing care	• Care of environment
18+ months (able to carry a jug)	Handwashing at table	• Small basin for washing hands • Jug • Soap dish with small piece of soap • Apron • Washcloth for drying hands • Mitt to dry table • Discard bucket for the dirty water • Suitable for child wanting to repeat handwashing at sink	• Care of self
18+ months	Cleaning shoes	• Mat • Brush with handle, or nail brush	• Care of self
18+ months	Setting table	• Help set table with a basket for cutlery • Help lay tablecloth • Help fold napkins • Help make warm washcloths	• Food preparation
18+ months	Help to clear table	• Wipe face with warm washcloth • Bring plate and cutlery to kitchen	• Food preparation
18+ months	Preparing crackers	• Small spreaders • Small container of butter, nut spread, hummus, or similar • Small box of crackers • Child spreads a small amount of spread onto cracker and sits to eat. • Can prepare standing or sitting	• Food preparation
18+ months	Squeezing orange juice	• Citrus press or squeezer—look for one that the child can use independently • Jug to collect juice • Glass for drinking • Child can squeeze orange and bring peel to (compost) bin or trash can	• Food preparation
18+ months	Cutting banana	• Banana prepared by cutting a slit at the top so child can peel off skin, strip by strip • Chopping board • Butter knife/nonserrated knife to cut banana • Child can bring peel to (compost) bin or trash can • Child can place in bowl to serve on table	• Food preparation

AGE	ACTIVITY NAME	DESCRIPTION/MATERIALS	AREA OF DEVELOPMENT
18+ months	Peeling and cutting apple	• Peeler • Apple cutter/corer • Cutting board • Child can peel apple by laying it on the board and peeling from top to bottom. • The apple cutter is pushed from top to bottom to divide the apple into eight segments and to remove the core. • Child can place in bowl to serve on table.	• Food preparation
18+ months	Pour a glass of water	• Access to a tap/small jug/water dispenser • Glass • Have a sponge and hand mitt ready for spills	• Food preparation
18+ months	Watercolor painting	• Tray • Watercolor tablet • Small jar with water • Brush • Cloth to wipe up spills • Underlay • Paper • Show child how to wet brush, put paint on brush, paint onto paper.	• Art/self-expression
18+ months	Sorting objects	• Dish with three sections and two different kinds of the same item, such as shells, nuts, seed pods, geometric shapes—four of each kind	• Works with refinement of tactile sense • Aids in classifying abilities
18+ months	Vocabulary cards	• Sets of classified cards that relate to the child's life • Start with simple classifications	• Aids language development • To increase vocabulary
18–22+ months	Dressing frame: buttons	• Wooden frame, two pieces of fabric attached with three large buttons • Vertical buttonhole • To practice buttoning	• Care of self
18–22+ months	Dressing frame: snap fasteners	• Wooden frame, two pieces of fabric with snap fasteners	• Care of self
18–22+ months	Table washing	• Tray with bowl, soap, brush, and sponge for scrubbing table	• Care of environment
18 months– 2+ years	Mirror polishing	• Little container of nontoxic mirror polish • Rectangular sponge as an applicator • Finger mitt • Underlay to place items on	• Care of environment
18 months– 2+ years	Wood polishing	• Container that is easy for the child to handle • Bottle of nontoxic polish, such as beeswax • Small dish • Finger mitt • Items to polish	• Care of environment
18 months– 2+ years	Gluing	• Gluing box with space for brush, glue pot with small amount of glue, up to six large shapes, and paper to glue onto	• Refinement of eye-hand coordination and grasp • To teach the practical skill of gluing • Refine movement of fingers • Art/self-expression

AGE	ACTIVITY NAME	DESCRIPTION/MATERIALS	AREA OF DEVELOPMENT
Around 2+ years	Washing dishes	• Table with two tubs • Dish brush with small handle, or small sponge • Travel-sized bottle of dishwashing detergent with small amount of liquid • Jug—plastic and transparent; can put mark on jug to show desired water level • Apron • Drying mitt • Hand-drying cloth	• Food preparation
Around 2+ years	Drying dishes	• Lay the drying cloth on the table, place bowl or glass on cloth; fold cloth into the bowl or glass; press; unfold.	• Food preparation
Around 2+ years	Cleaning windows	• Spray bottle with 1 cup (240 ml) of water (vinegar optional) • Small squeegee • Piece of chamois or cloth	• Care of environment
Around 2+ years	Washing cloths	• Table with two tubs • Small scrub board • Bar of soap • Soap dish • Jug • Two plastic baskets on either side of table on floor • Apron • Drying mitt • Hand-drying cloth	• Care of environment
Around 2+ years	Use of scissors	• Pair of small scissors in a case • Handmade envelopes • Narrow strips of index card, slim enough to allow the child to cut across the strip in one snip	• Refinement of eye-hand coordination and grasp • To learn practical skill of cutting • To develop precise hand movements

Around 2+ years	Classified stereognostic bags (mystery bags)	• Attractive bag with five to eight related, unrelated, or paired objects
		• Bag you can't easily look into, so child feels around the object
		• Examples:
		  1. Cooking implements—child-sized spreader, cookie cutter, sieve, bamboo whisk, spatula
		  2. Bag of items from another country, such as a bag made out of a kimono containing Japanese items
		  3. Hair items
		  4. Gardening tools
			• To aid in the development of the stereognostic sense
			• To increase vocabulary

Around 2 years— the child needs some spoken language	Questioning exercise	• Conversations that can occur throughout the day, such as while folding laundry or preparing food • Example: "Do you remember when we planted the basil and then it started growing?" "Where did we plant the basil seeds?" "What did we use to pick the basil?" • Done very naturally and conversationally	• To use vocabulary they are developing • To broaden child's thinking, help them abstract information from their experiences, and verbalize it • Builds self-confidence • Allows the adult to model language usage

AGE	ACTIVITY NAME	DESCRIPTION/MATERIALS	AREA OF DEVELOPMENT
2+ years	Sewing	• In a basket or box - Scissors - Thread - Needle case with blunt tapestry or embroidery needle - First sewing card consists of a punched diagonal line on a square card; progress to holes in square and circle shapes; then to embroidery or sewing buttons.	• Refinement of eye-hand coordination and grasp • To learn the practical skill of sewing • To practice precision and exactness
2+ years	Grading sizes of nuts and bolts	• Wooden board with various-sized holes • Nuts and bolts that fit into the holes in a container	• Eye-hand coordination
2+ years	Stretching elastic bands on a grid board	• Using a geoboard to stretch elastics—can create patterns or keep it open-ended	• Eye-hand coordination
2.5 years	Polishing shoes	• Container to hold 1. shoe polish (small amount) 2. finger mitt for applying polish 3. soft-bristled brush • Underlay that covers the whole table • Shoe horn, if outdoor shoes are worn	• Care of self
2.5+ years	Dressing frame: buckles	• Wooden frame, two pieces of leather fastened with three or four buckles • To practice buckles	• Care of self
2.5+ years	Helping with baking	• Help measure ingredients • Stir ingredients • Sweep and clean up after baking	• Food preparation
3+ years	Help unpack dishwasher	• Assist in emptying the dishwasher	• Daily life
3+ years	Help with recycling	• Sort recycling and bring it to container	• Daily life
3+ years	Make bed (pulling up a duvet)	• Make their own bed—duvet only	• Daily life
3+ years	Use toilet independently	• Have a step stool and a smaller toilet seat available or use a potty	• Daily life
3+ years	Assisting with more advanced cooking	• For example, helping to make lasagna	• Food preparation
3+ years	Feeding pets	• A small amount of fish food can be placed in an egg cup. • Getting water for dog • Giving food to cat, hamster, or other pet	• Daily life
3+ years	Help with folding laundry and socks	• Take part in the clothes-washing process • Invite child to sort items by person or color, pair socks, learn basic folding skills, and so on.	• Daily life
3+ years	Helping to get ready for visitors	• Making beds • Clearing spaces, picking up toys, and so on • Preparing meal	• Daily life
3+ years	First board games	• Orchard by HABA • Shopping list and other games by Orchard Toys • Simple card games, such as Snap • Games can be simplified, depending on the age of the child.	• Turn taking • Understanding simple rules • Fun

AGE	ACTIVITY NAME	DESCRIPTION/MATERIALS	AREA OF DEVELOPMENT
3+ years	More difficult sewing, arts and crafts materials	• Cards with more complicated shapes, like a heart • Sewing buttons • Sewing embroidery patterns • Sewing a cushion • Art projects with more than one step	• Art/self-expression
3+ years	Exploration of world around us	• For example, nature collections, birds, animals, plants, and trees	• Botany • Cultural studies • Life sciences
3+ years	More refined threading, sorting	• Shoelace with small beads • Piece of wool with small pieces of straw, using an embroidery needle	• Eye-hand coordination • Refining the grasp
3+ years	Composition puzzles—twelve or more pieces	• More difficult puzzles, including layered puzzles, composition puzzles, and puzzles with more pieces	• Refinement of eye-hand coordination and pincer grasp • Develops the ability to recognize a background shape
3+ years	Hammering shapes in corkboard	• Corkboard • Wooden shapes • Small nails and hammer	• Eye-hand coordination
3+ years	Pinprick work	• Shape drawn on paper to prick • Felt underlay • Pricking pen • The child follows along the line until the shape can be removed.	• Refinement of eye-hand coordination and grasp
3+ years	I spy	• If showing interest in sounds of letters, use phonetic sounds of letters.	• Language development • Prereading skills
3+ years	Calendar	• Make your own or buy a simple calendar in which the child can change the day, month, and weather. • Can add more details as the child gets older	• Time
3+ years	Lots of free play and outdoor play	• Allow time every day for the child to be outdoors and to have unstructured time to play.	• Daily life • Outdoor environment • Fun
3+ years	WEDGiTS	• WEDGiTS can be purchased; they allow building in sequence, and various patterns can be made.	• This is not a Montessori activity but would be suitable for the home environment.
3+ years	Well-selected building materials	• For example, Lego, Magna-Tiles, wooden blocks	• These are not Montessori activities but would be suitable for the home environment.
3+ years	Marble run	• There are beautiful wooden marble runs that children can build themselves.	• This is not a Montessori activity but would be suitable for the home environment.

INDEX

THE
MONTESSORI
BABY

THE
MONTESSORI
BABY

A PARENT'S GUIDE TO NURTURING YOUR BABY WITH
LOVE, RESPECT, AND UNDERSTANDING

SIMONE DAVIES AND **JUNNIFA UZODIKE**

WORKMAN PUBLISHING | NEW YORK

Workman
Workman Publishing
Hachette Book Group, Inc.
1290 Avenue of the Americas
New York, NY 10104
workman.com

Workman is an imprint of Workman Publishing, a division of Hachette Book Group, Inc.
The Workman name and logo are registered trademarks of Hachette Book Group, Inc.

Design by Galen Smith and Hiyoko Imai

The publisher is not responsible for websites (or their content) that are not owned by
the publisher.

Workman books may be purchased in bulk for business, educational, or promotional use.
For information, please contact your local bookseller or the Hachette Book Group Special
Markets Department at special.markets@hbgusa.com.

First Edition March 2021

Printed in China on responsibly sourced paper

10 9 8 7 6 5 4 3 2 1

To every baby,
may you be guided to develop your unique potential.
You are a gift.
—Simone

For Solu, Metu, and Biendu, my Montessori babies:
Thank you for teaching and inspiring me daily.
You are my greatest blessings.
—Junnifa

CONTENTS

ONLINE RESOURCES

GO TO WORKMAN.COM/MONTESSORI FOR:

Junnifa's observations of Solu—birth to 15 weeks

Psychomotor development timeline

How to make a topponcino

How to make Montessori mobiles

How to make a patchwork ball

How to make rings on a peg or dowel

How to make rattles

How to make an object permanence box

How to make a ball tracker

INTRODUCTION

1

IT'S TIME TO CHANGE
THE WAY WE SEE BABIES

For a long time, people believed that babies were unable to understand what was going on around them. They thought babies couldn't "do much." "They just eat and sleep and cry a lot," people would say. Babies were treated as fragile. We were told we needed to wrap them up to protect them.

Then we discovered that babies are in fact learning so much in the early months, and we began to overparent them. We pushed them to learn faster and earlier. We compared our new baby to other babies, afraid that our baby wasn't developing fast enough.

We were told that we needed to buy the best gadgets for our baby: the best educational toys, the best clothing to cover every part of their body, a support for while they sleep, a device to help them sit up sooner, a bed that rocks them to sleep, monitors of every kind, and apps to track everything.

Let's stop.

Let's bring into focus this new life we have brought into the world. Let's look to our baby to see what their unique needs are; what they want to learn; and how we can support them in a more mindful, slower way.

> *What if we handled babies with respect and learned to ask their permission before handling them?*

> *What if we observed our baby first, rather than rushing to fix things?*

> *What if we saw babies as strong and capable, discovering the world around them like explorers, seeing everything for the first time?*

> *What if we realized that babies are already taking in everything from birth (even from in utero) with all their senses?*

What if changing diapers, feeding, and bedtime became moments of connection instead of chores to be rushed through?

What if we slowed down to make time for language and for conversation, even with a newborn baby?

What if we made time for babies to lie on a simple mat to stretch and learn about their bodies?

What if we didn't prop them up into positions that they are not yet ready for, like putting them up to sit or holding their hands to allow them to walk before their muscles are ready?

What if we recognized that a baby has points of reference—their hands, our voices, the places we feed them, and the rhythm of our days—that help orient them?

What if we let go of everything we are told we need to buy, and instead provide a simple, beautiful space for our baby?

What if we learned to see that every baby is a unique soul, and that we are here to be their guide on this planet, to support them to grow into the best version of themselves, without pressure from us, and without feeling abandoned?

What if we lie in the woods, on the beach, in the park, and in the mountains, and exposed them to the awe and wonder of nature?

OUR MONTESSORI STORIES

When Simone's first baby was born, she remembers feeling deeply moved by the ability to create new life. She did the best she could with the information she had, but all became a lot clearer when she found the Montessori approach when her son was around 18 months old. And, like many parents, she wished she had learned these principles earlier.

With her second baby, Simone applied everything she had learned about Montessori as best she could. Since then she completed her Montessori training (over 15 years ago); her little babies are now young adults, and she's been helping families apply the Montessori principles with their own babies through her parent–baby Montessori classes at Jacaranda Tree Montessori in Amsterdam.

Junnifa was working as a strategy manager for an automotive company in Kentucky, when she serendipitously discovered Montessori. She had accompanied her mother, a teacher, on a visit to a Montessori school and was so moved by what she observed that she decided to take a 6-week introduction to Montessori course to learn more.

Junnifa completed the AMI 0–3 diploma training one week before the birth of her first child. She implemented what she learned and was amazed by the positive effects it had on her parenting and on her child. She started her blog, nduoma.com, to share her experiences. Hungry for more, she continued to expand her knowledge of child development. She completed the AMI diploma courses for the 3–6 and 6–12 age groups as well as the Resources for Infant Educarers (RIE) training.

Junnifa now runs her own Montessori school called Fruitful Orchard Montessori School in Abuja, Nigeria, where she lives with her husband and three young children. Junnifa sits on the executive board for the Association Montessori International (AMI), the organization founded by Dr. Montessori to preserve and propagate her work.

The birth of this book came about effortlessly. Junnifa was visiting Amsterdam from Nigeria for some AMI board meetings and came over to Simone's for some home-cooked food. We were just planning to catch up but within an hour we realized we both wanted to write a book about Montessori for babies. By the time Junnifa departed just a few hours later, we had eaten some tasty food and drafted the outline for the book you are holding today.

Every parent and child can benefit from the Montessori approach from the first weeks, the first days, the first hours—and even while our baby is in utero.

Babies are natural learners from birth, not empty vessels to be filled. They are observing everything. They communicate with gurgles and different cries. They never stop moving.

As Dr. Maria Montessori wrote in her book *The Absorbent Mind*:

> "[A baby] is by no means passive. While undoubtedly receiving impressions, he is an active seeker in his world. He himself is looking for impressions."

May we all learn from this book how to apply Montessori in our homes from birth, how to respond to our babies' cries, how to know which activities they are looking for, how to set up our homes—and how to do the work we need to do as parents to raise secure babies who are ready to explore the world around them with confidence and respect for themselves, others, and the Earth.

WHY WE LOVE BABIES

It's true that babies demand a lot of time, they wake us during the night, they leave us exhausted, and sometimes they cry inconsolably for hours. So why do we love babies?

Babies remind us of how innocent we are when we come into this world. When we see a newborn baby, we can't help but see how every person started life in this way, without any judgment, without any fears, without any baggage. Just as themselves.

Babies give us hope for the future. The birth of a new child and our hope for their new life lead us to hope for a better world for them. That they will love learning, that they will learn to care for humanity and the Earth, and that there will be no violence or war.

Babies are seeing the world for the first time. We love observing a baby take in the world around them. The way they look and explore everything for the first time. Our faces, a leaf, the sun peeking through a branch. It reminds us to look again with fresh eyes at the world around us with wonder.

Babies don't give up easily. We can sit and watch a baby stretch for their toes and try to bring them to their mouth again and again until they finally reach them. A baby will bat at a ball on a string until they master accurate movements. Babies learn to persevere if we give them the chance.

Babies say what they need. A baby doesn't think, "Is this a good time to ask?" They use their cries to tell us that they have a dirty diaper, that they are hungry or tired, or that they are all done with whatever they are playing with. We might be able to distract them for some time, but they will keep insisting until their needs are met. This directness is a handy skill to have.

Babies smell so good. Ha! But it's so true. Why do babies smell so good? There is nothing better than the smell of a freshly bathed baby.

Babies are new human life. It is a powerful experience to create another human life, and research shows that we are wired to look after babies. And we ask ourselves, "How can something so small be so perfectly created?"

WHAT WE NEED TO KNOW ABOUT BABIES

In past generations, most people grew up with a lot of babies around. We shared homes with parents and grandparents, and cousins, nieces, and nephews would be in and out of each other's homes, with older children looking after the babies of the extended family.

Simone was the youngest child in her family. The first baby she spent a lot of time with, other than while babysitting, was her son.

She read some books, attended some birth and prenatal yoga classes, but she felt largely unprepared for looking after her son. It was trial and error. Getting him to sleep was not easy (a complicated sequence of rocking him and singing), but luckily feeding went well. Simone prided herself on taking him wherever she went, even in the very early days. She cooked food while he napped and played with him nonstop when he was awake.
She didn't want him to cry, so if nothing else would work, she would feed him again.

Looking back she understands that she made a lot of extra work for herself. She hadn't yet learned to observe her son's natural rhythm, let him explore on his own, and trust that he didn't need an adult to entertain him full-time.

Here's what she wished she had known.

Babies are absorbing everything. Babies are exhibiting what Dr. Montessori identified as *the absorbent mind*. Babies may not be able to focus more than 12 inches (30 cm) in front of their face, but they are already taking in as much visual information as they can. They also absorb the smells, the space around them (for example, if it is light/dark, cluttered/calm, warm/cold), and the feeling of touch on their bodies. They hear the sounds of our daily life, our voices, music, and moments of silence. They taste their fingers, the milk, and anything that goes into their mouths.

We can have conversations with babies. Here we don't mean just speaking to a baby. We mean speaking *with* a baby and waiting for their response—even with newborns. The conversation needn't be verbal. We can lay our baby on our forearms with their head cradled in our hands, face-to-face. We can poke out our tongue. Wait. Watch. They try to open their mouth. Their tongue comes out. We respond by poking out our tongue. And so it continues.

Babies need time to move and explore. A baby needs time to lie on a mat on the ground and stretch their whole body. Even newborns can lie on a mat, a mirror beside them, as they start to see what it's like to move their limbs and interact with the world around them, and notice how things respond to their efforts. We can support them by giving them as little help as possible and as much as necessary.

Babies need to be treated gently, but they are not fragile. We need to be sensitive to their transition from the womb to the outside world (a period of symbiosis) and handle them gently with a respectful touch. And at the same time, we don't need to wrap them up and over-coddle them. They can have their hands, feet, and head uncovered (if the home is warm enough), so they can have free movement. Their neck and head will get stronger in the first weeks and won't need extra support after too long.

Babies are building trust in their environment, their caregivers, and themselves. During the first 9 months—sometimes referred to as extero-gestation or the external pregnancy—the baby is still adjusting to being in their new environment. They are working on building trust in their environment and in themselves and learning to rely on their parents (and any other caregivers).

In the first year, babies move from dependence, to collaboration, to independence. At birth a baby relies on the adults for their food, shelter, clothing, diapering, and to transport them from place to place (dependence). As they grow, we invite the baby to take part in the process—asking them to raise their arms while dressing, explaining what we are doing as we prepare meals, giving them time to touch and explore the things around them (collaboration). Before the end of the first year, a baby is taking steps toward independence—sometimes actual physical steps, as well as voluntarily choosing a toy and making it work, calling out or making a sign to express themselves, bringing food to their own mouth to eat, confident of their place in the world (independence).

Babies thrive from a secure attachment. When we lay the foundation of a strong and secure attachment, the baby feels safe to explore, to move toward independence over time. They learn to rely on us, to trust us, that we will respond to them and give any help or support (if needed). "Secure attachment" in attachment theory is where one's needs for closeness and food are usually consistently met as a baby. Attachment creates the deep emotional connection between baby and primary caregiver(s), a bond that endures over time.

Babies will cry to communicate their needs. Some people are able to tell why their baby is crying. Sometimes the cries will all sound the same. We can become a detective. We ask them, "What are you telling me?" as we observe them. We respond, rather than react. We don't simply pick them up and start bouncing them to stop them crying. Because first we need to see *what they are telling us.*

Babies don't need so much stuff. The principle of *less is more* applies to babies. Some loving arms, a place to stretch, a place to sleep, adequate nutrition for their belly, and a warm and cozy home to explore. These are the things a baby needs. We do suggest some Montessori activities in this book, but we could buy nothing at all and still practice Montessori at home. Montessori is less about the stuff and more about looking at our baby, accepting them for who they are, seeing how we can meet their needs, and supporting them to independence, which will continue throughout toddlerhood, childhood, and adolescence.

Babies gain security from points of reference. As they discover the world around them, they will come to look to *points of reference*. These are things in their daily life that help them to orient themselves. These can be their hands, our voices, the space where they lie to sleep, where they feed, and the daily rhythm (doing things in the same way each and every day). Such predictability provides reassurance to the baby.

Babies know a lot that we don't know. When we look into a baby's eyes, there is a lot of mystery waiting to be discovered. They are saying to us, "If you want to learn about me, watch me." Observation becomes a form of respect—we observe our baby before responding and learn to understand them better.

HOW TO READ THIS BOOK

This book has answers to the questions we get asked every day about raising babies in a Montessori way. It can be read from cover to cover. Or picked up and opened to any page for some inspiration.

The book covers what we need to know about babies, how we can set up our homes for them to feel secure and welcome (we don't need much), how to observe our baby to see what they are practicing in the moment, and how we can support their development. It addresses all the practical questions about eating and sleeping (and the Montessori floor bed) and explores all the ways to build a respectful bond with our baby.

Don't overlook the chapters on the work we adults can do to prepare ourselves for parenting in a Montessori way (like letting go of our own desires for who our children will become) and how we will work with others in our baby's lives (from grandparents to caregivers to partners) who are so important in parenting our babies. And we won't leave you hanging—we'll also cover what is coming next as our babies become young toddlers, and a little about what to expect from Dr. Montessori's observation of children from right at birth through 24 years old.

There are handy checklists throughout the book for easy reference, observation exercises, and at the end of each chapter there are practical suggestions on how to get started. In the appendices, there is also a comprehensive list of activities by age and a month-by-month guide to refer back to often. (We've also provided some DIY instructions for some Montessori mobiles and activities, which can be found online at workman.com/montessori.) And in chapter 9 (page 236), there is one of our favorite pages in the book—a note from our baby to visiting grandparents, friends, and caregivers, which can be copied and hung somewhere visible.

The principles in this book are based on our Montessori training with the Association Montessori Internationale and on our experience working with families and raising our own children. All of this is derived from what Dr. Montessori has written about infancy, as well as her collaborations with her students Adele Costa Gnocchi and Grazia Honegger Fresco, who have been largely responsible for developing Montessori's vision of the youngest children—this includes creating the Assistants to Infancy training (by Costa Gnocchi) and the Montessori Birth Center in Rome (where Honegger Fresco was honorary president up to her passing in 2020). Dr. Silvana Montanaro was also a contributor to this work, and we draw on many supportive principles from Emmi Pikler's work, the RIE approach, and the principles of respectful parenting.

We wrote this book to speak for the babies in utero, those just born, or rolling, or sitting, or crawling, or taking their first steps. They want us to know that they are all unique souls, born into our homes for us to care for them in a way that they will feel secure, respected, and loved. That we will help them grow from a baby dependent on us for all their needs, to a baby who is able to collaborate and communicate with us, and by the end of the first year, moving toward increasing independence as a curious child ready to explore the world even more.

We can give our baby the message: "You are capable and respected. We want to be present for you, we seek to understand you and your needs, and we will do our best to be patient." We can learn how to handle our babies with love and respect and to support them to build their trust in themselves and their surroundings (including us).

Every baby is unique. No baby has walked or talked in the same way, fallen asleep in exactly the same way, or fed at the same time as every other baby.

May this book allow you to observe the joy of your growing baby. Observe the smallest ways in which they are developing and changing every day, hour, and minute. May they never lose that joy and wonder.

Here's to learning more about our Montessori babies.

WHAT BABIES ARE REALLY TELLING US

Instead of thinking they don't understand

They want us to tell them what is going on and treat them with respect

Instead of nonsense baby talk

They want real connection and conversation where we take turns

Instead of being picked up quickly from behind to have a diaper changed (or hearing that it stinks)

They want to be able to see us, be asked if they are ready to be picked up, and have time to respond

Instead of the latest gadgets

They want a simple, beautiful, inviting space to explore

Instead of distracting them when they are crying

They want us to pause, observe, ask what they need, then respond

Instead of allowing anyone to touch or kiss them

They want us to ask them first

Instead of being overstimulated

They want to have one or two things to interact with

Instead of interrupting them when they are playing

They want us to wait until they are finished concentrating

Instead of putting them into a sitting or standing position before they are ready

They want us to follow their unique development and let them master this for themselves

Instead of rushing through eating, bathing, and changing diapers

They want to use these activities as moments for connection with us

Instead of sitting in front of a screen

They want to interact with the real world

Instead of rushing through our busy days

They want us to handle them gently, mindfully, and slowly

MONTESSORI
PRINCIPLES
FOR BABIES

2

WHAT?
MONTESSORI EDUCATION FOR BABIES?

You may be encountering Montessori for the first time, you may know of Montessori but perhaps did not know it could be applied at home or specifically to babies, or you may already know about Montessori and babies. This section can be an introduction for beginners or a refresher for those already familiar, as it will provide an overview of Montessori education and how it applies specifically to babies.

This education that we speak about in Montessori does not just happen in a classroom and is not limited to the traditional notion of an instructor teaching a child. Instead, it involves everything that we do with children and everything that they experience from the very beginning.

Montessori is a philosophy that looks to support the natural development of each child to their maximum potential. It views education as a tool to aid this process and believes such learning can start from birth. This means that it can be applied to babies, too.

> "The first hour of education is the hour after birth. From the moment the senses of the newborn child begin to receive impressions from nature, nature educates them. It takes great strength to be able to wait patiently for them to mature."
>
> —Johann Heinrich Pestalozzi

A BRIEF HISTORY OF MONTESSORI

Dr. Maria Montessori was an Italian medical doctor and scientist with a background in anthropology. Montessori education grew out of her work with children with learning differences. Dr. Montessori believed that the children needed to nourish their minds in addition to their bodies. She recognized that they needed more stimulation, so she incorporated materials and techniques developed by French physicians Jean-Marc-Gaspard Itard and Edouard Seguin. After working with the children for a while, she registered them for a statewide exam. The results were inspiring. The children did very well, exceeding expectations, and she began to wonder if her newfound method could work for other children.

An opportunity came for her to try out her ideas on children without learning differences, when the developers of a housing project in San Lorenzo invited Dr. Montessori to build classrooms for the children who would be living there. She called these classrooms *Casa dei Bambini*, meaning "children's house."

Dr. Montessori observed the children in the children's house much like a scientist conducting an experiment. She made modifications based on her observations and was astonished by her findings. She discovered that there were many misconceptions about children and that, given the right environment, they flourished in ways that had not been previously thought possible. They were capable, careful, kind, unselfish, and able to teach themselves if there was a rich learning environment to explore. People visited the San Lorenzo children's house from around the world to study her program and take her training. They then went home to start their own schools and programs.

Her trainings were often taken by young mothers who would come with their babies. Dr. Montessori observed these babies and noticed that they were more conscious and capable than most people believed them to be. This piqued her interest. She continued to observe these babies and wrote about her ideas. She later collaborated with prenatal clinic workers and went on to start a birth center, an infant school, and training programs for "Assistants to Infancy" in Rome.

Dr. Montessori came to believe that education should begin from the moment of birth.

WHAT IS MONTESSORI?

Montessori is different from the top-down learning of traditional education, where the teacher stands at the front of the classroom and tells children what they need to learn. Instead, Montessori sees every child (and baby) as unique, with their unique way of learning, unique interests, and unique timeline.

The Montessori educator sets up the classroom as a rich learning environment. The child has the freedom to choose an activity they wish to work on (either by themselves or with another child or in groups), and the teacher will observe to see who needs help or who needs a new lesson. With mixed ages, the older children will be modeling for the younger children and are able to help them. In doing so, the older children reinforce their own learning. And the younger children naturally learn so much by observing the older children.

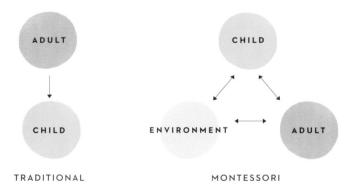

Observing a Montessori classroom for the first time, it's hard to believe that no one is telling the children what to do and that they are self-motivated to master new skills and acquire new knowledge.

Similarly, in our homes and with our babies, we can set up beautiful spaces with inviting objects and activities for our babies to explore, we can observe when they need help, and we can allow them to make discoveries for themselves.

SOME IMPORTANT MONTESSORI PRINCIPLES

The Montessori philosophy is based on some foundational principles, which include an understanding of our child's nature, characteristics, and needs. Understanding these principles is key in applying Montessori to our babies.

1. Absorbent mind

The absorbent mind is a special state of mind that children possess from birth until around the age of 6. It allows them to learn easily and pick up the characteristics and cultural elements of their immediate environment. They do this unconsciously and without effort. They see and hear things around them, they take them in, and then one day, without having made any effort, they replicate what they have taken in. It is the absorbent mind that makes it easy for children to learn language spoken in their environment. It is why children pick up the same gestures as the people they spend time with, or easily learn to dance when surrounded by dancers. Every aspect of the environment—tangible (like language) or intangible (like our attitudes)—is absorbed by our youngest children.

There is a common experiment in elementary school where children place a plant or celery stalk in a cup of water with some food coloring in it. The children observe the leaves and petals as they change color. This is exactly how the absorbent mind of the child works—it absorbs the characteristics of the environment, and these characteristics then become an inseparable part of the child.

The absorbent mind is a great tool, but like most great tools, its benefits depend on its use. It is an enormous opportunity, as well as an enormous responsibility.

"He absorbs the life going on about him and becomes one with it."

—Dr. Maria Montessori, *The Absorbent Mind*

Knowing this is a great gift to us as parents. We can model the behaviors and attitudes we want our child to adopt, surround our child with beauty and nature, speak to them using rich language, and give them rich experiences, knowing that even from birth, they are absorbing all of these things, which become an indelible part of them.

2. Human tendencies

Humans are born with natural instincts or inclinations. These human tendencies guide our behaviors, perceptions, and reactions to our experiences.

When we understand what might be driving our babies' behavior—their standard human tendencies—we are better able to perceive and interpret their needs and respond appropriately.

Some human tendencies that are evident in infancy are:

Orientation

This is the desire to know where we are, to familiarize ourselves with our surroundings, and to have an idea of what is happening around us. As adults, when we go to a new place, we often try to orient ourselves with familiar landmarks. We might also find a person familiar with the place who can guide or direct us. This need is also present in babies. They too have a need to be familiar with their surroundings and what is happening around them. We can help them by providing familiar markers or connections.

When the baby is first born, the earth is a brand-new environment without "points of reference." But the mother's voice and heartbeat—both of which the baby would have heard in the womb—are familiar landmarks, or points of reference, that can help them orient to their new surroundings. The baby's hands are another familiar landmark. They have touched their face and moved their limbs while in utero, so they can find comfort in these familiar friends. We often unknowingly take away these references when we put gloves on the baby's hands or dress or wrap our baby in a way that restricts access to their hands or to free movement.

Soon, a hanging mobile, a picture in the baby's room, furniture, or designated places for different activities can all serve as points of reference for the baby. The baby will continue to add new ones as they grow, but a caregiver's presence and voice will continue to serve as landmarks for the baby through infancy.

Order

As human beings, we desire consistency. It is the same for babies. Order and consistency are what help them to orient themselves and to feel secure. In our baby's surroundings, there needs to be a place for everything, and things needs to be in their place. The baby's days and activities need to be predictable. We can help them by creating orderly environments and developing routines and cues that will help them anticipate where they are or what comes next. We can make a place for everything— starting with a place for feeding, a place for sleeping, a place for physical care, and a place for movement and playing. We can go further and have a fixed place for objects in the environment.

Communication

Communication is how we share our feelings, experiences, thoughts, and needs. Humans are able to communicate from birth. Babies communicate with their gestures, body language, cries (yes, they are letting us know they need something), babbles, and, eventually, with their words. In the same way, they pay attention to, absorb, and gradually begin to understand our communication with them. From the very beginning, we are programmed for two-way communication.

Therefore, we can communicate with our baby by talking to them, smiling, gesturing appropriately, and also being conscious of our body language. Even the way we touch the baby is a form of communication and a message to them. We can also pay attention, listen, and look to understand the baby's communication to us, and in so doing we can meet their needs.

Exploration and Activity

Humans are explorers. We interact with our surroundings to understand and master them. Babies look at things, taste them, smell them, touch them, move them around, bang them, throw them, and generally explore. This is how they come to understand how things work. We need to allow opportunities for this exploration. We can provide the baby with things to explore, give them time to explore, and make the environment safe for exploration.

Solving Problems

We humans are problem solvers who need to use our mathematical mind. We often unknowingly rob babies of the opportunities to meet this need. You might wonder how a baby could solve problems. It can be as simple as reaching out for a toy rather than having it placed in their hand. Or using their senses of smell and sight to find the nipple of their mother or bottle instead of having it put in their mouth for them. Or crawling the distance to get a ball versus having the ball brought to them. Or figuring out how to free their hand when it is stuck under them. These little opportunities allow the baby to figure out distance, consider options, and solve problems, thus meeting the human tendency of a mathematical mind. We can support this tendency in the baby by allowing opportunities for free play and exploration.

Repetition

Watch a baby who is learning to sit, stand, or walk. Often, the baby pulls up to a stand, sits or kneels, and then stands right back up. They do this repeatedly if they are not interrupted. Repetition is a human tendency that allows us to master skills. When we observe babies repeating an action, instead of assuming they are struggling, need help, or might be bored, we can allow the opportunity and time for repetition.

Abstract Images and Imagination

Abstraction is the ability to see beyond the concrete, to interpret and generalize. It means envisioning ideas, concepts, or things that are not physically present. From a very early age, we are able to see things that are not right in front of us and imagine solutions to our needs. The baby learns they have a mother or father even when that parent is absent. They look for things that are not present.

This need and ability to imagine also helps us solve our problems and meet our own needs. To imagine and abstract requires a knowledge and understanding of reality. The baby is able to understand what a cup is and what it is used for because they have seen one, used one, or seen another person use one. A baby of 7 months who has used a cup before will try to drink from another object shaped like a cup. From very early on, we will observe babies using remote controls as phones.

While this tendency becomes stronger and more apparent as the baby becomes older, it is present from birth. So babies too need many hands-on experiences, because their ability to imagine and abstract is built on this.

3. Sensitive periods

A sensitive period is a moment of time when the baby develops an irresistible attraction or interest in something. It could be an action/skill or a particular aspect of the environment. We can usually tell when the baby is in a sensitive period because they show intense repeated interest in that area. Sensitive periods are like spotlights that focus the baby's absorbent mind on certain aspects of their surroundings.

There is a sensitive period for movement, from rolling over to crawling and walking. There are also sensitive periods for language, introduction of solids, and small objects. Each of these sensitive periods allows the baby to gain new skills and grow more independent.

Some of the sensitive periods in infancy are:

Order: Babies are in a sensitive period for order. They seem to crave order in tangible and intangible ways. A baby who is always placed on the left side of their bed might notice and react negatively when placed on the right side. We can help the baby by preparing an orderly environment where everything has a place. We can also be as consistent as possible in our processes and routines when caring for the baby. Just as with helping them get oriented (see page 16), we provide landmarks or points of reference to help the child absorb the order. These points of reference could be auditory (a sound or a song) or even olfactory (a scent that tells the child it is time for bed or another that signals time for food).

Movement: From birth, children are in a sensitive period for movement. In the first year of life, they pass through and master many stages of movement. They learn to reach, grasp, roll, crawl, sit, stand, and walk, along with many stages in between these ones. There is a lot of practice that is required to progress through each stage of movement. We can help the baby maximize this period by preparing a safe environment where they can move and also allow time and opportunity to move.

Language: This is another sensitive period present from birth. It is associated with the human tendency for communication. Because of our need to communicate, from birth the spotlight is on language so that the baby can acquire the skills needed for communication. If we observe a baby of even 3 months when an adult is talking to them, we will see how they focus on the sound and watch the movement of the adult's lips. They work hard to make their own sounds and create language. Most of this work is not seen in the beginning, but it is happening.

We can help by talking to the baby from the very beginning and using rich, beautiful language. We don't need to dumb down sentences or use imaginary words. Instead, we use the most beautiful words we can, name objects that the baby encounters, talk to them about what is happening around them, and also listen and acknowledge when they communicate using sound and babbles.

From the beginning of the baby's life, we can get into the habit of conversing with our baby. When we pick them up in the morning we can say, "Good morning, sunshine! Did you sleep well?" Wait for a response. It might be a smile or a slight movement, and you can respond accordingly: "Yes you did. Today we are going to take a walk to the park, but first, let's change your diaper. May I pick you up?"

Eating solids: This includes the introduction of solids and learning about their bodies. There is a time when the baby starts to show interest in food, reaching for our food and literally drooling. This is also usually around the time when the baby's teeth are coming in. This is the ideal time to gently begin the process of introducing solids.

Assimilation of images and small objects: During the period from birth to age 3, children seem to be very interested in details and small objects. They enjoy looking at images and will stare intently for extended periods. We can provide images for the babies at their level and give them time to enjoy them. When we notice our baby staring at something, if we are carrying them and moving, stop and give them time to take it in. We will notice when they lose interest. Take slow walks and just allow them to look. As they get older, they may also enjoy looking at book illustrations that have rich details.

4. Observation

Now that we know the nature of the baby's mind, their needs and tendencies, and how the sensitive periods work, we can only put this knowledge into use in our parenting by observing.

When we observe the baby, we will start to see these characteristics at work and catch glimpses of what might be going on inside the baby. Observation is really the key to implementing Montessori with our baby. It is what helps us get to know our individual baby and respond appropriately.

Observation allows us to:

- **Understand and follow the baby's development:** When we observe the baby, we can notice subtle changes in their abilities and provide an environment and activities that offer the right challenge. It is through observation that we can tell if the baby's human tendencies are being served. Are they able to explore freely? Are they getting opportunities for repetition?

- **Notice the baby's efforts and abilities:** See how the baby interacts with the environment: How are they using their senses to interact with the environment? Observing with their eyes? Tasting? Touching? Testing? Trying to modify? Are their actions intentional? What might be their intention?

- **Identify sensitive periods:** Where is the baby's interest and activity focused right now? What are they constantly returning to, repeating, or concentrating on?

- **Recognize and remove obstacles to the baby's development:** What are the obstacles to their movement, communication, and activity? What might be interfering with their independence?

- **Know when to help and what kind of help to offer:** For example, if the baby is trying to crawl, but their clothing is restricting their movement, we can choose alternate clothing or gently help them remove a foot from the hem of their clothing.

Junnifa discovered the power of observation with her first baby.

During her son's first 3 months, he would nap on her bed. He usually slept for about 2 to 2.5 hours. Around 3 months, she decided to move him to his floor bed in his room (we explain the floor bed in detail later on page 59). She would hold him in her arms until he fell asleep and then lay him down. She thought naps would be a good way to transition him to his room, and then they would gradually move to night sleeping in his bed. However, when she would put him down for his nap, he would wake up around 40 minutes later. This was much shorter than his usual 2 hours, so she immediately thought the floor bed was not working. She talked to one of her Montessori mentors, Pilar Bewley, who asked Junnifa what she had noticed when observing her son. Junnifa realized that she hadn't been observing him at all.

So when she put him down for a nap in her room the next day, she stayed and observed. She noticed he slept around 40 minutes and then he woke up, lifted his head, looked around, and then went right back to sleep and slept for a little more than 2 hours in total. The next day, she did the same but in his room. She put him down, and right around 40 minutes, he woke up just like the day before, lifted his head, and looked around, and she noticed a change on his face. He did not recognize where he was. He was disoriented! He started to cry, she picked him up. . . . She had figured out the problem.

Over the next couple of days, Junnifa and her son spent more time in his room when he was awake. She now knew that he woke up around the 40-minute mark during his nap, so she would stay close so that when he looked around, he would see her—his landmark—and he would go back to sleep. She also put a picture of their family on his headboard and gradually started watching from a distance. He would wake up, look around, stare at the picture for a little while, and go back to sleep. Junnifa stopped checking after a few days, and he would only make a sound when he woke up after about 2 hours. Observation helps us understand our baby's behaviors, needs, and tendencies, and how to respond to them.

(continued on page 24)

SOME THINGS WE CAN OBSERVE

MOVEMENT

- Physical response to visual or auditory stimuli
- Reflexive movements; intentional movements

FINE-MOTOR SKILLS

- How they grasp and hold objects
- Which fingers and which hand they use
- What grip they use on a rattle or spoon
- What fine-motor skills they are practicing, such as using their pincer grip or fingers against palm

GROSS-MOTOR SKILLS

- How they come to stand or sit
- How they walk—distance of legs or arm movements
- Balance
- Whether they choose gross-motor activities
- Whether the environment helps or hinders their movement

COMMUNICATION

- Sounds they make to communicate
- Smiling
- Crying—intensity, volume, duration
- Body language
- How they express themselves
- Eye contact during conversations
- Language used
- How we respond to their communication

COGNITIVE DEVELOPMENT

- What they are interested in
- What they are practicing and learning to master
- The activities they can complete
- How long they stay with an activity
- Times they repeat an activity or explore in another way

SOCIAL DEVELOPMENT

- Interactions with others—siblings, other babies/children, and adults
- Whether they observe others
- How they ask for help
- Whether they initiate interactions
- How others respond to their attempts
- How they respond to people they don't know

EMOTIONAL DEVELOPMENT

- When the baby cries, smiles, and laughs
- How they are best comforted or comfort themselves
- How they respond to strangers
- How they deal with moments of separation
- How they manage when things do not go their way

FEEDING

- Breast or bottle, including amount or length of time feeding
- What they eat and how much
- How is/was schedule established
- Who is feeding the baby
- How the baby detaches from feeding
- Whether they are passive or active eaters—being fed or feeding themselves
- Whether self-feeding is encouraged or taught
- If eating solids, what foods they are offered and how often
- Response of adults to feeding attempts, communication attempts, body positions

SLEEPING

- Sleep/wake rhythm
- Night schedule
- How they fall asleep
- Quality of sleep
- Position during sleep
- How they transition to waking—length of time, temperament upon waking

INDEPENDENCE

- Symbiotic relationship with mother and other family members
- Whether there are aids or hindrances to the growth of independence

CLOTHING

- Whether the clothing helps or hinders movement and independence
- Whether they try to put on or take off their own clothing
- Whether they express preferences for their clothing

SELF-OBSERVATION

- Record our communication—what we say and how we interact with our baby
- What comes up for us as we observe our baby
- How do we respond if our baby does not eat or sleep
- What we say when our baby does something we like or don't like

(continued from page 21)

We can observe on-the-go and informally. Whenever we spend time with our babies, we can watch them with a desire to truly see and understand. We can also set out time to routinely formally observe and write what we see, like a scientist studying their movements, their sounds; the things they focus on; how they eat, sleep, play; and any social interactions.

Observation leads to an even deeper understanding and love for the baby, and a respect for their abilities.

- When we are actively observing, we can try to be as invisible as possible so that we are seeing the baby's actions independent of our presence.
- When we notice that the baby is focused on something, even something as simple as looking at their own hands or playing with their feet, it is important to not interrupt. When we observe, we start to recognize the baby's amazing capabilities, and it can be tempting to praise or acknowledge in that moment, but as much as possible, we should remember to enjoy observing and not interfere with or break the baby's focus.

5. Prepared environment

Dr. Montessori called the spaces we create for learning "the prepared environment." When we look at our baby's needs, we can set out exactly what they need for their development, and we can adjust them as our baby grows. This can be indoor physical spaces, outdoors in nature, and even the people in our baby's life. A rich place for learning, where they feel safe and secure to explore.

> "The period of infancy is undoubtedly the richest. It should be utilized by education in every possible and conceivable way. The waste of this period of life can never be compensated. Instead of ignoring the early years, it is our duty to cultivate them with the utmost care."
>
> —Dr. Alexis Carrel (quoted by Dr. Montessori in *The Absorbent Mind*)

TO PRACTICE

- Are we being thoughtful about what our baby will absorb?
- Have we noticed any examples of our baby reflecting back what they see or experience?
- What familiar points of reference are we providing to help our baby orient?
- Are we slowing down and allowing our baby time and opportunity to take in the details of the environment?
- Are we making time to get to know our baby better by observing them?
- Can we begin to look at our spaces—our prepared environment—to see what we are offering our baby?

FROM CONCEPTION TO THE FIRST 6 WEEKS

3

We know that there will be a range of families who will be coming to this book. In the past, Montessori has held a fairly traditional view, centering the mother as the primary caregiver. Of course, this traditional arrangement does not reflect many of today's families. Raising our babies the Montessori way is possible no matter who takes on the role of primary caregiver and in families with equal co-parents. The same goes for mothers who choose not to or cannot breastfeed, adoptive parents who were not present for gestation or the early weeks or months of a baby's life, and for parents who return to work outside the home not long after the baby is born. The promise of this book is to give everyone the tools to adapt the Montessori principles and apply them in ways that work for their individual family constellations.

We encourage all new parents to read the following sections, whether they are carrying the baby or not, as there are helpful things to learn about the baby in utero and about the birth mother's experience.

CONCEPTION:
PREPARING THE BABY'S FIRST ENVIRONMENT

In utero is our baby's first *prepared environment*. Even before we conceive, we can give a lot of thought to the physical and emotional environment in which we welcome our baby.

Physically, we want our bodies to be strong. We can spend time learning about how to care for our body to get ready to carry a baby (for a birth mother), how to make healthy sperm (for a birth father), and how to get emotionally ready to welcome the baby (including for adoptive parents or parents who are not carrying their child).

We can also prepare our emotional environment, adding the ingredients of love and acceptance so our baby arrives knowing that they are welcomed and loved. When a baby is unplanned, the work of the adult is to come to a place of acceptance during the pregnancy so that the baby feels wanted and loved. We can say to the baby we are conceiving or that has been conceived, "You are so wanted. You are so loved."

Part of preparing our environment to welcome our baby is getting to know what is involved in caring for and raising a baby. Parenting is a challenging 24/7 job for 18-plus years of life. At the same time, it is also beautiful to bond with a child and help them grow into the best version of themselves. We can read books. Even better, we can spend time (preferably full days) in someone's home helping to look after their baby to see what it involves.

If we have a partner, we can begin conversations before conception and during pregnancy about our hopes and dreams for our family and, even more important, the values and vision for our family. Who will care for the baby, and how? Why are we bringing a baby into this world?

We can also examine our expectations and prepare ourselves (as much as possible) for change. We may be used to being in full control of our lives. We may need to consider that there are things we may need to forgo—at least for a little while. We may need to work on ourselves to build a space for inner peace, which we can tap into on those days when things get a little chaotic.

We can slow down and turn inwards. If we are trying to conceive, we may need to make space in our lives. We can consider making some changes (scheduling less, finding more space in the day, doing some breathing or meditation, finding time for quiet reflection) to allow our body, our minds, and our hearts to slow down to be ready for conception. Ready for our baby.

DURING PREGNANCY:
THE BABY'S FIRST ENVIRONMENT

How can a baby grow so perfectly? How can the cells divide, each knowing exactly what it needs to do? Pregnancy and birth are likely the most complex and naturally intelligent processes our body is capable of.

Along with wisdom gained in our Montessori training which covers conception and pregnancy, one of our favorite sources for this topic is Pamela Green—a Montessori educator, birth doula, and assistant midwife for over 30 years. (A doula provides guidance and support to mother and baby during birth.) Her expertise and knowledge informs much of what we share here.

Even in utero, our baby's life is already unfolding, and we can learn so much from them and about them. Here are ten things we can do during pregnancy to get to know our baby and prepare for the transition to parenthood.

1. Acknowledge that our baby is already taking in so much.

There is already so much our baby is absorbing in utero through their developing senses. They are not passive. They are taking in their first environment.

The table on the following page outlines some of this development, "What baby is already taking in while in utero."

2. Connect with and welcome our baby

We can talk with our baby, sing to them, massage them by rubbing our belly, and build a connection when they are in utero. Our voices, the music, our touch, our movement, and the rhythms of our bodies will all become important points of reference for our baby out of the womb. These connections create a safe, loving, and accepting emotional environment in utero, making our baby feel welcome. We can play an instrument, play some favorite music, dance, read to them, and notice any ways our baby responds.

If we have a partner, they can connect with the baby by touching and massaging the belly, talking, and singing to the baby. If there are other siblings or family members, they can regularly connect with the baby through touch, talking, and telling stories, jokes, or songs. We can notice if the baby responds differently to the resonances of our voices.

If we have other children, it can be easy to forget we are pregnant, because we are busy attending to everyone's needs. We can make time to check in during the day to listen to our baby, get the other children involved, and perhaps make a special time in the evenings for extra connection.

Prenatal yoga can be helpful to take time out of our week to turn inward, slow down, and connect.

And as the birth nears, we can dance to welcome the baby with the whole family or celebrate our baby's impending arrival with rituals or celebrations with dear friends.

For those interested, look for prenatal singing groups following the work of Marie-Louise Aucher. These can be for the mother and their partner, too. There are many physiological benefits in addition to connecting with the baby through our voice and resonance. The singing can also be helpful during labor (ancient wisdom connects the opening of the throat to the opening of the cervix), and singing can continue after birth too as a way to connect with our baby.

WHAT BABY IS ALREADY TAKING IN WHILE IN UTERO

TACTILE SENSE

- At 5.5 weeks, the embryo is sensitive around the mouth and nose.
- By 12 weeks, the entire body is able to feel (with the exception of the top and back of the head, which are not extremely sensitive until after birth).

VESTIBULAR SENSE (I.E., SENSE OF BALANCE AND MOTION)

- By 10 weeks in utero, the baby moves parts of the body in response to internal stimulation.

SENSE OF SMELL

- At 28 weeks, the fetus can smell, e.g., the food the mother has eaten.

SENSE OF TASTE

- Taste sensations are experienced in utero via the amniotic fluid. Some researchers say babies can taste what we eat from around 21 weeks.

VISION

- From 32 weeks, electrical impulses can pass along the baby's optic nerve allowing some vision in utero, e.g., light vs. dark.
- A baby's vision is very primitive at birth. They can focus to 12 inches (30 cm), which is the distance from the mother when they are held for feeding, and cannot yet track visually.

HEARING

- By 23 weeks, they can hear sounds (our voices, singing, music, etc.) outside their mother's body.
- From 30 weeks in utero to a few months after birth, hearing cells can be damaged by prolonged loud noise.

3. Learn to observe our baby in utero

We can observe how our baby responds to stimuli in their first environment. For example, when our hands are on our belly, we can pause and see what movement the baby makes. We may feel them responding to our touch, moving toward our hand, or increasing activity. Sometimes they move away from voices and touch that they do not recognize. We may notice patterns to their sleep-and-wake rhythms in utero.

This is going to be our work once they are born, to observe them and meet their needs accordingly, and we can begin this process now. We can be open and curious. We may choose to use a journal to note down our observations.

4. Provide a healthy in utero environment

Just as we are careful to prepare the home environment after birth, we can think about the environment we are creating in utero.

Are we getting enough good nutrition and rest so that the baby can grow and thrive? Are we looking after ourselves to maintain our own optimal health—our diet, exercise, rest?

When we are pregnant, our baby will also absorb our emotions—the highs and the lows. It's not always possible to prevent large emotional swings—life happens. Yet, as much as possible, a stable and predictable emotional environment in the adult(s) will help our baby thrive and grow.

It's so important to look after ourselves, let caregivers look after us, and be okay with sometimes having to cancel a social engagement when we need to rest. Are we able to receive care from others (a partner, friend, or professional like a chiropractor, osteopath, midwife, or doula)?

If there are lots of highs and lows, look for extra support from professionals. Some people find it useful to work with someone—for example, their doctor or a psychologist—before and after the birth to attend to their mental health as they go through this enormous transition.

5. Prepare for our baby's first environment outside the womb

Nesting starts, and we begin to set up the physical spaces in our home to welcome the baby—a time to create a warm, simple, loving space for them, without getting drawn into the commercialization of having a baby. Babies do not need a lot.

We can prepare as many things as possible before the baby is born, while we have more time. Junnifa had boxes sorted by month with clothing and some simple activities that she had made or purchased. Then, when she was tired after birth and busy with the new baby, it was easy to pull out the box as the baby grew and have some things at the ready. For example, items for the parent (such as nursing pads in the early months), activities for our baby at different ages, clothing in different sizes, and other supplies like bowls and cutlery for eating (around 6 months).

6. Choose our parenting community and support network

We can surround ourselves with people who support us and want to be part of our parenting community. Some Montessori playgroups and schools offer classes for expecting families, and they can be a great way to find like-minded families.

We will likely still receive unsolicited advice from strangers, friends, and family; however, we can prepare ourselves and respond with kindness when we are clear on our own choices.

During pregnancy is also the time to build our support network for the birth. Who do we want as part of our birth team? Who will make us feel safe and supported? We might consider having a doula to support us through the birth—some offer pro-bono work to lower-income families.

We may wish to attend breastfeeding groups to learn from other women who are breastfeeding their babies, and also to establish a network and find specialists if we need support after the birth.

And who can help us arrange meals and take care of laundry and cleaning after the baby is born? It's a good idea to organize this ahead of time in case we get overwhelmed or are too tired to arrange things after the birth.

7. Explore our birthing options

During pregnancy we have time to explore our birthing options. And though our options may vary depending on our location or circumstances, it is important to know that we have choices. Seek them out. Use them.

We can look at the kind of environment we choose to give birth in, both the physical and emotional.

The physical space might be at home, at a birthing center, or in a hospital. We look to see if the space will support the kind of birth we want. Some may want a birthing pool available. Others want room for a birthing ball. Can we make the space feel like home? Is there space to move? How much freedom of choice is there?

The emotional environment will be created by those around us during the birth process—including whichever support partners we choose.

How we give birth is a personal choice. We cannot manage all the outcomes, yet we can feel empowered to set up the birth environment—where and with whom—as we choose.

Once these choices are made, we don't hand over our birth. We remain active participants, looking at what we want, realizing the things that are important to us—for example, choosing our own positions—and understanding what our options are through the whole process. We need to be able to ask for what we want and to have someone know what these choices are, in case we need an advocate for us during the birth (if we are not able to ask for these choices ourselves).

8. Take the time to explore our stories around birth and parenting

In her Preparation for Birth classes, doula and Montessori educator Pamela Green discusses allowing space for families to explore their ideas about birth and parenting. Many of these will be generational stories inherited from our own family or society. Some of these stories will come with fear or anxiety, others with acceptance. It's important to investigate these stories.

We may wish to talk with our mother to learn more about her experience. For those with parents who are no longer living, this work can be done by exploring what we have been told about our birth.

BOOK RECOMMENDATION

Ina May Gaskin's books, *Ina May's Guide to Childbirth* and *Spiritual Midwifery*, give so many examples of positive birthing experiences and an understanding that pain in birth is the only time we experience "good pain," pain that will bring our babies into the world. Listening to and reading these birth stories show us that a positive birthing experience is possible.

We can explore our ideas through art like working with clay, drawing, belly casting, or painting. We can make mandalas, write letters, light candles.

There is also the choice to rewrite the negative stories we have heard and internalized and turn them into strong, positive ones. When we feel relaxed approaching the birth, our baby will experience this, too.

9. Transition to being a parent

Growing a baby takes energy and love. It is a special time when, if possible, we can try to slow down and enjoy. Pregnancy is a transition period. A time to transition to parenthood. Or, if you are already a parent, a time to transition into a larger family. We don't need to become "all about the baby," but we can take time to get to know our baby while they grow in utero and include them in our daily life.

We can educate ourselves on the physiological changes. Understanding the changes that are happening to ourselves and our baby during pregnancy and birth can fill out the picture as we transition into parenting and learn about our baby and our new relationship.

10. Make additional preparations

We can physically prepare for birth. There are options like hypnotherapy and active birthing. In our Montessori training, they advocate for RAT (respiratory autogenic training), a special breathing technique to manage the pain during birth. The mother learns to link the breath to relaxation and practices during pregnancy until it becomes automatic. Some describe the birth using RAT as pain-free.

If possible, take a first-aid training class for children and babies before the baby comes. It can give us valuable information and help us feel confident in the event of any emergency. When we feel prepared, we can give a feeling of safety and security to our baby. And there will be more time to do this during pregnancy than when the baby is born.

And the rest of the work is on ourselves—to heal from our past, to connect to our baby, and to prepare to welcome our baby with so much love, respect, and acceptance. That is our wish for every baby in the world.

THE BIRTH

Birth is often seen as a painful, scary medical procedure to be done in a hospital. But when we hear that it can be a beautiful and connecting process, one where we will meet our baby, we are able to look forward to the birth and let it unfold.

While the suggestions that follow are about making choices to have the birth experience we want, it can often be very difficult to make this a reality. Obstacles include health insurance restrictions, lack of coverage and high out-of-pocket expenses, and limited access to birthing centers or home birth expertise, just to name a few. When possible, we can look for a doctor or midwife who will support us in having the kind of birth we choose. And if it doesn't work out or isn't possible, we can remember that we are doing our best and that delivering a healthy baby is the ultimate goal.

The physical environment will play an important role in the birthing process. To feel safe, the mother generally wants privacy, familiarity, some warmth, and a place where she can introspect. We can look at creating a sacred place for birth—lights dim, a quiet space in which to focus inward, perhaps with soft music. If not birthing at home, we can bring some items to the birth center or hospital to create a familiar space. And there may be a birthing ball, a birth pool, and other materials to help during the birth. The birth environment will be unique for each person, a place where they have a feeling of trust and safety and where there is freedom (of choice and movement).

Mother and baby work together, the baby moving down, rotating, and descending as an active participant. When a mother is left to herself and given freedom, she may move, make sounds, sing, find her own rhythm, and breathe at her own pace. If a mother has practiced relaxation or hypnotherapy in the prenatal period, these tools can help her go deeper into herself. The mother turns inward with every contraction, in a process of surrendering and acceptance. Getting closer to welcoming the baby.

The birthing mother can be very aware of her surroundings. Even sitting with her eyes closed, she can notice anyone coming into the room, lights turning on, or people speaking. So we aim not to disturb her, moving and talking quietly, keeping the lighting and temperature consistent. And if there is an interruption, it can cause the labor to slow or stop completely.

Partners, family members, and birth attendants (midwives, obstetricians, doulas) make up part of the birth environment and can hold space for the mother and baby. This means they are available, present, observing, but in a non-intrusive way, not interrupting the process. If they need to step in to assist, they do so gently, quietly, swiftly, and then retreat.

Pamela Green, birth doula and Montessori educator, describes it like a dance. The attendant moves in a synchronized way with the laboring mother, gently does their work, then moves away. An experienced birth attendant will focus on the mother more than measurements. They look for cues like how high the baby is and how it lowers, and focus on how to get the baby into good alignment, not just focusing on dilation.

When the baby crowns, the mother and partner can bring their hands to feel the baby's head. A mother can be allowed to receive the baby and bring them up to her chest. Interestingly, most times the mother will bring the baby to the left side of her chest, bringing the baby closest to their mother's rhythmic heartbeat, which is so familiar to them from in utero. The baby is transitioning from their inner life within the womb to being out in the world.

Ideally, the baby is on their parent's chest, skin-to-skin, until the cord stops pulsating. If left alone, the umbilical cord eventually narrows to a point where it can then be cut.

There is wonder, bliss, joy, and relief in the mother's face. And the baby is a perfectly formed human being, with their own character and personality. If present, the partner joins them as a new family unit, and once all is stable they can be left to be alone together.

When this connection time has taken place, the birth attendants can be called back over to weigh the baby and take measurements. These attendants are the baby's first social contact outside of their family. They can do this in a positive, loving, and respectful way by getting the baby's permission before handling them. They can come close to the baby's face to make eye contact, tell them what is about to happen, and if the baby is not ready, they can wait.

Once weighed and returned to the parents, the baby left skin-to-skin can make their way to the breast for the first attachment. This can happen in the first hour or two. A midwife or nurse can support this first attachment if needed.

Perhaps we are wondering if this special experience can be created in a hospital environment. It's absolutely possible when we are able to choose our collaborative care team. Many hospitals now allow rooming in, partners staying in the room overnight, and other choices around the birth.

JUNNIFA SHARES LESSONS FROM HER BIRTHS

My three births were very different but each beautiful in their own way.

My first son was born in a birthing tub at a wonderful birth center, after about 6 hours of labor and 2 minutes of pushing. He was born into water and *en caul*, which means his sac was intact.

SOME THINGS THAT STOOD OUT TO ME:

- I remember being very conscious of the work my baby was doing during the labor. It was our first collaboration. I was very in tune with his movements and moved in response. He worked hard to gain his independence from my womb, and I was his helper. This knowledge made a difference for my labor, as I was following his lead and conscious that he was working even harder than I was.
- I had a midwife that I trusted and who trusted me. I still hear her voice saying to me "just relax, your body knows what to do."
- My husband and mum—my two strongest pillars of support—were there with me through every step, and that made a big difference.

My second son was born in the hospital after a few hours of laboring in the birth center. I had always heard that the second labor would be shorter than the first one, and so when it became much longer, I worried that something was wrong.

My mum was also not around, and I had left my older son in the care of extended family members. So I was very conscious of wanting to get back to him. The labor process was beautiful again, but I could feel a stall and so we decided to transfer to the hospital. Something about the drive must have helped, because as soon as I got to the hospital, I felt he was finally ready to come out.

I remember the significant change from the birth center to the hospital. The lights were bright, the nurses and doctors were very loud, and when I told them the baby was ready to come, one nurse roughly checked me and told me I was hurting/tearing myself by attempting to push. It was such a different experience from the calm and trusting feel of the birth center with my midwives, but I remembered my midwife from my first birth, who told me my body knew what to do. I insisted that my baby was coming, and he was out about 2 minutes later. I refused the post-birth injections to the chagrin and criticism of the doctor. When they came to check on the baby and me a little while later, they expressed surprise at how alert and strong we both were.

My third child was born in a regular bathtub. It was my shortest labor and fastest birth. She literally popped out.

MY LESSONS FROM THIS BIRTH:

- Trust our body and our instincts.
- Make care arrangements for our other children that allow us to truly relax and labor for as long as needed.
- Find caregivers (midwives/doctors) who share our values and mutual trust.
- Make sure our pillars of support are present.
- Contrary to popular belief, sometimes the labor for a second or third child is much longer than the labor for the first or previous child. Knowing and accepting this can make a difference in our endurance.
- Sometimes, a drive or a walk around the block can change things up for our labor and trigger transition.

I had been worried after the experience of having to transfer to a hospital with my second child. I prayed and prayed and prayed for a quick labor because again I wanted to get home quickly to my two other children, who were both under 3 years old. I remember driving to a shop to make some purchases. I walked out of the shop and saw a big double rainbow. I don't know why it had such an effect on me, but I cried and told my boys that the baby would be coming today. I was not ready, but I just knew. I went home and put the baby's clothes in the washer, got everyone ready for bed, and we laid down as it rained heavily outside.

I remember thinking that this would be the last time that I would go to bed with two children.

A few hours later, I woke up and messaged my midwife that it was time. She seemed doubtful and told me some things to do, but I told her the baby was coming soon and that I was heading to her.

I got there and lay down for a little bit and then felt the need to throw up and use the bathroom. My daughter popped out 40 minutes after I arrived.

MY TAKEAWAYS WERE AS BEFORE:

- Our baby actually does most of the work, observes, pays attention, and listens.
- Trust our body and our instincts.

All of my births were vaginal, and I had no tears. I moved around while laboring and also labored partly in water. I was very active during all of my pregnancies and tried to eat healthy and stay happy.

I wish you births as beautiful as mine or better.

Some additional notes on birth

We may have preferences for the birth, and we can make them clear to others who may need to represent us during labor. At the same time, know that things can change, and the safe delivery of the baby is the most important thing in the end.

In a vaginal birth, know that:

- our bodies are made to birth children.
- we can work with the naturally occurring hormones, like oxytocin, which allow our bodies to transform during labor.
- we can move if we want to, eat if we can, relax in any way that works for us.
- no two births are the same—what helps for one person or even for our first birth may be different in following births.
- in the first stage, we can picture the cervix opening and thinning to make way for the baby to enter the world.
- in the second stage, we can visualize the baby moving down and out.
- we can be surrounded by people who will encourage us, massage us, feed us, and make us feel comfortable.

Sometimes babies are delivered by caesarean birth—this can be a choice or a necessity. When it's a necessity, there can be a grieving of sorts for some mothers who wished for a different delivery. It's important to let these feelings come up. And also be happy for the safe delivery of our baby into the world. With a caesarean birth, extra assistance may be required to help with lifting things during these first weeks, because there is likely to be additional pain related to the surgery.

Babies born by caesarean have not passed through the vaginal tract, which usually would help remove fluid from their lungs, as well as receive important natural bacteria for their immunity. Some midwives will help get some of these important bacteria from the mother through a process called "seeding" and apply the bacteria to the baby at the time of birth.

BOOK RECOMMENDATION

Mindful Birthing: Training the Mind, Body, and Heart for Childbirth and Beyond by Nancy Bardacke

SYMBIOSIS—THE FIRST 6 TO 8 WEEKS WITH OUR BABY

"The newborn is most utterly sensitive, misunderstood and treated too hurriedly.

His most profound needs are not acknowledged.

The first days of his life are the most important."

—Adele Costa Gnocchi, *Quaderno Montessori*, volume 39, 1993

In Montessori, the first 6 to 8 weeks of the baby's life are called **symbiosis**, which means "a life together." This is such a beautiful way to see these early days, welcoming our new baby into our home, getting to know and adapt to them, and them to us.

In science, mutually beneficial symbiosis is when two organisms live in a way that benefits both parties. For example, coral and algae have a mutually beneficial symbiotic relationship—the coral provides algae with shelter, and the algae gives coral reefs their colors and supplies both organisms with nutrients.

Applying this to these first weeks of the baby's life, the parent–baby relationship is **mutually beneficial**—when the baby is nursing, the baby receives the perfect food, and the feeding helps contract the womb. Holding the baby can help replace the feeling of emptiness that can be experienced after the birth. A father, partner, or other caregiver can be involved by protecting and caring for this new family unit—they become like the gatekeeper, taking calls and messages, offering practical support like getting supplies, providing physical care such as bathing the baby or allowing the mother to sleep, as well as bonding with mother and baby. We are becoming a family.

We have time to **bond** with the newborn through feeding, singing, bathing, gentle touching, and caring for them.

The baby develops **trust** through close contact with us, being held, and having their needs met.

By simplifying the environment and activities for these first weeks, we are reminded to slow down. To connect. To establish a relationship with our new baby. To get to know what they are telling us. To be together and talk—about who we are, where they are, and what is happening. To be looked after. Many cultures have rituals for the first 40 days after birth, and we can create our own.

The strong attachment built during these first months gives a solid foundation for the months (and years ahead). After the first months, the baby is ready to start experiencing more from the world around them, including being introduced to extended family and friends.

> "Developing the right type of attachment during the symbiotic period
> paves the way for natural detachment, and psychological birth happens."
>
> Dr. Silvana Montanaro, *Understanding the Human Being*

It's important to find ways in which the mother (and co-parent) can be supported at this time. It is different for every family, but there can be an enormous emotional and physical impact after the birth. Sometimes the love we expect to feel is not immediately present—there can be baby blues or some post-partum depression. Even with a smooth birth and easy connection, there is less time to sleep, clean, or even shower with a newborn in the home. This blurriness is both the beauty and the struggle of this time. If one is able to do so, thinking ahead to have family, friends, or a paid helper to assist and support can be invaluable.

Tips for the Symbiotic Period

1. The home environment

- During the symbiotic period with our newborn, the baby is making an important transition from being in utero (where life was largely consistent in terms of warmth, food, and ambient lighting) to being outside the womb (where life is more unpredictable and noisier, and often colder and brighter).

- In the first days, if possible, it can help to keep the home a little warmer than usual and the lighting a little dimmer. We can also be aware of limiting the stimulation for the newborn, perhaps receiving fewer guests and allowing time to connect and learn about the new baby in our lives.

- A thin, quilted pillow, called a *topponcino*, is a favorite for many parents. The topponcino can be used starting at the birth and through the first few months at home during the symbiotic period to ease this transition period for the baby. It's a little longer than the baby and a little wider, made of natural fabric, in which baby can be held or laid down upon. The topponcino can become a point of reference for the baby and gives a soft layer of protection. The baby finds security and a familiar scent—their scent and the scent of their parents, siblings, and family—in this thin cushion. It prevents overstimulation when handled by family and friends, and it allows the baby to be transferred from arms to bed without triggering their startle reflex. Parents using the topponcino say they take it everywhere. Instructions for making your own topponcino are included online at workman.com/montessori, or you can find them available for sale online.

Topponcino

- If there are older siblings in the home, it may not always be possible to create a calm, quiet environment during the symbiotic period. However, the baby will be learning about their siblings, adjusting to the rhythms of the house, and finding their place in this home.

2. The adult(s)

- We can begin to observe our baby and their early rhythms.
- We learn to feed our baby and to help them transition to sleep.
- We can sing and dance with baby—our voice and movement will be familiar to our baby from in the womb.
- We can create a special bathing time.
- We should allow time for breastfeeding—this is a way of communicating with our baby with our full body (not while scrolling on our phone) and a time to rest.
- We can allow time for skin-to-skin moments with both parents—it's calming for baby and parent; promotes the parent–baby bond; regulates baby's heart rate, breathing, and temperature; it can stimulate an interest in feeding; and can help build immunity.
- We can share our wonder of the world around us.
- We can find ways for our partner (if we have one) to develop their own bond with baby. Partners have their own unique way of being with the baby and are another special and familiar person for the baby to connect with. The way they move and talk, bathe, and sing may soothe our baby in a new way, and even may have a different way of holding our baby over their shoulder, providing relief to baby's belly.
- We can receive care from others, such as cooking, cleaning, and washing, so we can provide care for the baby and take time to rest. For some, it may be family and friends. Without extended family around, we may have to be creative to make this happen, and it's a good idea to arrange this ahead of time before the baby arrives and

we become overwhelmed or too tired to ask. We can get an organized friend to make up a roster for meals, request gift vouchers for food service as birth gifts, have meals in the freezer before the baby arrives, and we may be able to afford someone to come clean every couple of weeks, or think about arranging a babysitter or neighbor who may be able to look after an older child while we rest. Some countries have home visitors in the first week or two to support the family—and where this is not available, we are making it happen by building this support network ourselves.

- Keep things simple—keep visitors and appointments to a minimum.
- We can journal our experiences, for ourselves and our baby. Symbiosis also allows time to process any trauma from the birth experience or feelings of loss from not being pregnant anymore that may come up.
- For some, the natural feelings of love for their baby take longer to form. There are also the baby blues a few days after birth and the possibility of post-partum depression. Please seek help from a doctor if needed and accept support from others. It is not a weakness. It is the kindest thing we can do for our baby.
- For adoptive parents, the symbiotic period may come later, when the baby is welcomed into the home. It is possible to consciously create this special connection by blocking out 6 to 8 weeks. To become a family. To build trust and bond. To learn about the new baby, and again for them to get to know us.
- If the baby is adopted, it may be possible to ask the birth mother for any points of reference from in utero (i.e., music played during pregnancy, or to voice messages to the baby).

3. The newborn

A newborn has many memories—tactile, auditory, visual (though limited)—from prenatal life. We can offer experiences in the first weeks that are familiar to our newborn, to help them orient and to continue to stimulate their senses. Here are some ideas in the symbiotic period to help them adjust from in utero to the external environment.

Tactile experiences

- We can keep baby's hands free as much as possible, because their hands will come to their mouth area, just as they did in the womb.
- The baby is sensitive to every touch on their body—these are completely new sensations. So we handle them with the lightest touch, with the most efficient movements, and we slow everything down so the baby can learn these new processes, like having their diaper changed, having a bath, and getting dressed.
- Clothing should be very soft, made of natural fibers, without hard fastenings, and not needing to be pulled over the baby's head. If you can manage it, cloth diapers are soft

against the baby's skin, better for the environment, and will allow them to feel the natural wetness when they poop or pee (feeling these natural body sensations will be useful later when toileting). If we use disposable diapers, we can allow the baby plenty of time to go diaperless while lying on a soft blanket or towel.

- We can use a topponcino (see page 42) as a point of reference and to soften the stimulation to the baby.

- During our baby's short waking periods, we can give them time to be held and time to stretch on a movement mat. A movement mat is a thin mattress for the baby to lie on, around 1" high and large enough for the baby to stretch their limbs in all directions (see page 57 for more on setting up a movement area). When outdoors, we can take a padded blanket to provide a place for movement on the go.

- Gentle baby massage can be comforting and connecting.

Auditory experiences

- The baby has auditory points of reference from the womb—the main one is our voice(s), which they have heard throughout pregnancy. We can continue to talk to and sing to them.

- The maternal heartbeat and digestive sounds will be familiar—we can re-create them by allowing the baby to lie on our belly.

- Bird sounds can be appealing to a newborn.

- Playing music—either from a music box or soft, recorded music (especially music that was played in utero).

Visual experiences

- A newborn baby can see a distance of about 12 inches (30 cm). We can hold the baby close to allow them to focus on our face. Human faces fascinate babies—in research studies, babies begin to make sucking motions when presented with facial features.

- If the baby is facing a light source, a hand between the light source and the baby will look dark, and the fingers can move very slowly. A baby will observe this for a very long time, until they avert their gaze and show that they are done.

- Mobiles also provide visual experiences. The mobiles should be lightweight and move with the natural air currents in the room. There is a beautiful series of Montessori mobiles that we'll explore later in this book, going from a black and white mobile to simple colored mobiles to ones beginning to represent dancers or things that fly. (For more on mobiles, see page 134.) These are not placed over their sleeping area, but where they can explore them during awake times.

- The baby will begin to observe any siblings in their environment, not in focus at first, but soon tracking their movements. Their siblings become points of interest for them from the first days, and they will be fascinated by them, sometimes for long periods.

Many newborns do not want to be put down. They are very attached and love to be kept close. Symbiosis is the time for snuggling and comfort and being close. At the same time, we can also begin to offer our baby the chance to spend some time on their movement mat, especially when they become more wakeful after the first 2 weeks.

We can use the topponcino to transfer the baby from our arms to the movement area, keeping the topponcino underneath them. We can also start by lying down with the baby on our belly in the movement area. Then we can try the next time to move them from our belly to the movement mat next to us. They will still be able to see, smell, and hear us. If they are uncomfortable, we can lay a hand on them, look into their eyes, provide our sweet words or song. And over time, they will feel more comfortable lying down on their movement mat with us a little farther away. This same method applies to helping our baby get used to lying down in their sleeping area. (See page 59.)

TO PRACTICE

1. What steps will we take to prepare ourselves for birth?
   - physical preparation, e.g., nutrition, rest, etc.
   - arrange support from others
   - read about positive birth experiences
   - make a birth plan with alternatives for different outcomes

2. What can we prepare for the symbiotic period (the first 6 to 8 weeks)?
   - how can we transition baby from in utero to the external environment?
   - how can we adjust the home (e.g., temperature, lighting, etc.)?
   - how can we adjust ourselves (e.g., handling baby gently, slowly)?
   - how can we support their senses at birth (tactile, auditory, and visual)?
   - how can we allow time to learn about our new baby, and them about us?

THE VOICE OF THE NEWBORN:
AN INTERVIEW WITH KARIN SLABAUGH

In memory of Grazia Honegger Fresco (September 30, 2020)

Since 1992, Karin has been an early childhood educator. She now specializes in the care of newborns based on the work of the very first Montessorians trained in the 1950s. She has observed newborns for more than 500 hours, studying their behavioral language, their communications, and their incredible sensitivity, which is observable in how they respond to their caregiver and environment.

What does Dr. Montessori's principle "education from birth" mean?

It means removing obstacles from natural development and allowing children to self-regulate and self-develop from the moment of their birth.

Will you talk to us about your love of newborns?

The newborn is the purest form of human life that exists. A newborn begins learning at birth—even before, actually. At birth a baby is completely unconditioned, because learning is basically experiencing and creating habitual responses to what life's sensations are offering. So right after birth, as soon as the senses begin to take it all in, all of these new stimuli of the world outside the mother, newborns respond to all of this. Whether they feel trust or love, or whether they feel fear or terror, all of these experiences are recorded and "learned."

You talk of a newborn baby's ability to look into a person's eyes.

In the 1960s American developmental psychologist Robert Fantz demonstrated that newborn infants not only could see but also had clear-cut visual preferences. Visual ability is what makes it possible for the newborn to find the breast, which is his source for survival, by finding the dark circle of the areola. The black pupils and contrasting whites of the eyes on the mother's face are another visual target that give a newborn an important point of reference that his limited visual ability can capture. Babies at birth are programmed to look for their mother's eyes. This is how they make the first bond.

Can you describe for us the "first alert state" you have observed in newborns right after birth?

During my research, I have observed maybe 100 newborns in the hours after birth. When a baby has had an unmedicated birth, and if the environment is not too bright and the baby is allowed to spend his first hours in mother's arms, he often is very alert. To be in this position, on her body, skin-to-skin, warmed by her body heat, smelling her colostrum, listening to the sounds of her heartbeat and her voice, looking into her eyes, held and contained by her embrace, he can begin to take in the reality of being on the outside. In this position, though he is no longer on the inside, he is in similar conditions. After he gets his bearings, he may begin to open his mouth and thrust his tongue and turn his head, all reflexes that will help him find and attach to the breast for the first time.

Can you describe what you have felt when looking into the eyes of many newborns?

During the second hour after birth, many of these babies were very much alert and wide-eyed in the incubator, and I would place myself within 12 inches (30 cm) of their face to allow them to be able to see me. They were looking for their mother's face, of course. It was sad for me to be there in place of their mother. But I would describe it as a privilege to have "met" eyes with so many tiny people, and with whom I felt such a deep connection simply from the act of staring at each other.

Can you give new parents some ideas for how they can treat children with respect and dignity from birth?

The first thing that comes to mind about respecting a newborn is to respect the process that the newborn has to go through to find his or her individual rhythms. As he has never eaten before or slept before outside the womb, he needs a period of time to establish his own rhythms that are going to come out from the inside of his being. So we have to be very careful not to impose a rhythm for this person, or else we completely interrupt and prevent this person from finding a natural rhythm on his own.

So what we can do as parents, from birth, is to really focus on what it means to observe another person in order to understand what he or she is communicating. Newborns communicate with their body language and they communicate with their vocalizations, so they have a large repertoire of communications that we can learn to read, learn to understand. But it's a very different language, and like learning any new language, it takes effort and time. It is not just the language of crying—even more so, it is the language of behavior. It's a bit like a cat or a dog who has a bark or a meow. That is their vocal language, but they have a lot of behaviors—they go sit by the door, they get really happy in their whole body. They look sad and depressed when they want to go outside for a walk and they know we are not taking them out. So there is a lot of communication that we can read in a newborn's expressions and movements that doesn't come from crying, but comes from how his autonomic nervous system is responding to the various stimuli. Their body language tells us how they feel, what they need, even what their preferences are, and this is the language that we have to learn in order to respect a newborn.

Treating a newborn with dignity, now that's a very interesting question. Would you like to be handled by others, say, during a hospital stay, as if you weren't there, moved about and touched without being addressed, without being told what was happening? Dignity is offered simply by taking into consideration what the other person is needing or feeling, and acting accordingly. How often do we really take into consideration the real and urgent needs of the newborn to be able to process all of the new stimuli and feel safe throughout this transitional period of adaptation, being newly outside the womb, a reality that is 100 percent different from the world in which he lived during his entire life?

Could you describe how we can do our best to change a newborn's diaper without him crying?

Crying is simply an expression of fear, discomfort, or physiological dysregulation. A newborn has a high level of sensitivity to sensorial input such as the temperature of the air, movement that happens too quickly, or the sensations from the clothing that is touching him. The newborn skin is very sensitive. What we have to do is to take into consideration this person's high sensitivity to stimuli. Now, of course, over time there is an adaptation, so throughout the course of the days and weeks and months all of these actions and feelings become normal. So if you pay careful attention from the beginning—from the very beginning—to do all of these things in a way that, in your best attempts, does not provoke crying, does not cause an expression of dislike for the experience, then you are conditioning him (creating a learned response) of understanding that these things happen regularly and they are not uncomfortable.

Many parents make the mistake of working really rapidly through a diaper change so it is over very quickly, and also so the crying is over quickly, and then they can soothe the baby. But that is a very different thing from attempting to act in a way so that you don't even provoke the upset feelings.

As for some practical advice, just slow down, more than you can even imagine is necessary. This is the key: to move through everything you do with a newborn at 5 percent of your normal speed. Don't allow yourself to get stressed and feed off of the crying baby's anxiety, rather, offer a calm energy that he can feed off of. This is what is called co-regulation. Talk to him about what will happen before it happens. Before picking him up, talk to him about how you are going to pick him up. Before each action, pause and look into his eyes, at a distance of 12 inches (30 cm), to see how he is doing, what he is thinking. If you want to see what this looks like, at the very beginning of Bernard Martino's documentary, *Loczy: A Place to Grow* (available on the internet), there is a scene where the caregiver prepares a newborn for a bath. This gives you an idea of what this level of sensitivity to the newborn person looks like.

Birth is the first experience that is very much a shock to the newborn's senses, coming out of the mother's body and coming into the world. It can provoke a response of crying and does most of the time, but it doesn't have to. This is what Frédérick Leboyer was able to show the world in his books and the film *Birth Without Violence*. His films show births where babies come into the world with wide-open eyes, curious about where they are, looking around in the dim light, and they often do not cry.

So if a baby at birth can come into the world without sensations that are disturbing to him and that make him cry, then every event, every diaper change, everything you do with the newborn, if you consider his basic needs, the urgent needs of this person, those things that should not be ignored, then you can have a very different outcome. What does a newborn need for the level of light in the room in the moments after his birth? What does a one-day-old-baby need for the amount of noise around him? What does a newborn need on his third day, concerning the level of stimulation from a diaper change, with his clothing being taken off for the fifteenth time? What does the newborn need? That is the question at the root of this.

SETTING UP
THE HOME

4

SETTING UP MONTESSORI-STYLE SPACES

Never underestimate how much we can use our homes to create an inviting, cozy, attractive, and engaging space for our baby.

Montessori educators use the classroom as a "second teacher." We get the classroom to do a lot of the work. We take the time to prepare activities in a way where the children can see what is available; the whole space is prepared with such love and care, and the children respond by treating it with respect; and there is beauty in the space, with living plants and artwork placed at the child's height. Dr. Montessori called her first classroom *Casa de Bambini*—"children's house." The classroom can make the child feel like they belong and are important.

We don't have to completely transform our homes to look like Montessori classrooms, but we can create intentional spaces in each area of the home to make our baby feel special, to welcome them, and to give them a sense of security as each space becomes a point of reference for them.

This can be achieved in even the smallest of homes. Small or difficult spaces are opportunities for creativity.

BABIES DO NOT NEED THAT MUCH

There is a general idea that we need a lot of of furniture, clothing, toys, and supplies for a new baby. We can buy fancy feeding cushions, cribs with matching chests of drawers, a changing table, a baby bath, and more. Then we need a stroller that collapses, one we can push while jogging, and maybe one for traveling too.

One of our favorite things about the Montessori approach is that it aligns with the idea of *less is more*. Buy only what we need, keep things simple and beautiful, and perhaps put the extra money toward a higher quality, or more natural, version. These special things can be used by any future children in the family or donated or passed on to another family. And they are much more sustainable for the environment.

Tips for setting up your home

1. **Baby-sized.** Look for small furniture that the baby will learn to use by themselves—like a low bed to crawl in and out of (see pages 59 and 64). By the time our baby learns to sit, we can have a low table and chair where they can eat, play with their activities, and pull up on. We want the baby's legs to reach the ground with their feet flat on the floor, so we can trim the legs of the table and chairs if they are too high.

2. **Beauty in the space.** Display art, photos of the family, and plants at a low height for the baby to enjoy. (Make sure the plants are safe for curious babies who want to put them in their mouths or move them to where the baby can see them but not reach them.)

3. **Independence.** To help our baby move from dependency to increasing independence in the first year, we can set up simple activities on a low shelf or in a low basket so the baby can learn to choose for themselves. Older babies will be able to roll, wriggle, or crawl to fetch things they want to use, and we can look for ways to make it easy for them to help themselves.

4. **Attractive activities.** We can create inviting, age-appropriate activities for each stage of our baby's development, beautifully arranged on shelves, rather than in toy boxes.

5. **Less is more.** Displaying only a few activities helps develop the baby's concentration. Display only the ones the baby is working to master, so they don't feel overwhelmed.

6. **A place for everything and everything in its place.** When we have a place for everything and everything is in its place, the baby learns where things belong (and eventually, as toddlers, where to put them away).

7. **See the space through their eyes.** Get down to the baby's height in each space to see what it looks like from their perspective. Remove messy wires and clutter.

8. **Store and rotate.** Create storage that ideally is out of sight or easy on the eye—think floor-to-ceiling cupboards that blend in with the wall or containers that can be stacked in a storage area or behind a couch. Keep out a few activities, store the rest, and rotate them when the baby is looking for new challenges.

CREATE "YES" SPACES

In Montessori classrooms, we like to remove obstacles to the child's development. When we set up our home, we can do the same. What we create are "yes" spaces where our baby is free to explore safely, we are okay with everything they can touch and reach, and the chance of us having to say "no" is limited. (The term "yes" spaces originates from Janet Lansbury, a RIE—Resources for Infant Educarer—educator and author.)

People love to come to Simone's classroom with their babies because they know that the space has been carefully prepared so the babies can explore freely with little danger to them. Everything is set up with the babies in mind—low furniture they can pull up on; open spaces for them to practice rolling, scooting, and crawling; no wires to reach; no loose cords to look out for; and only objects that are safe for them to put in their mouth.

In our homes, we can:

- remove anything we do not want our baby to reach—this may mean storing it for some time or moving it to a space the baby cannot access
- lie on the floor to see what the baby can see and reach
- make the space inviting to explore with a few simple activities on a low shelf, including baskets of objects that are fun to investigate
- if we cannot make every space a "yes" space, we can make one large area of the home a "yes" space for the baby, where they can move freely. We may need to be creative, for example, using our furniture to create a safe boundary for this area or having a gated-off area
- if we need to gate off an area, avoid brightly colored plastic room separators and look for subtle options which will feel light in the space

We want to allow the baby (from birth) free movement and unobstructed vision. So we prefer not to use baby boxes, playpens, or cribs in our homes—these contain the baby's movement, and the bars do not give a clear view of the whole space from the baby's perspective. We even prefer not to use a high chair. Controversial, we know. These containers have been developed for our convenience, not the child's.

Simone's Montessori trainer, Judi Orion, said that the only time we might want to use a playpen is for the adult to stand in if we are ironing (meant quite literally!). If we need to use the bathroom, place the baby in their "yes" space, where we know they will be safe and have space to explore.

AT-HOME STARTER SET FOR MONTESSORI BABIES

1. A topponcino (a thin, quilted cushion) **2.** A *cestina* (also known as a "Moses basket") for sleeping (newborn to 3 months) **3.** A low mattress for sleeping **4.** Floor mat for movement **5.** A long horizontal mirror in the movement area **6.** A place to hang a mobile **7.** A low shelf to display simple activities **8.** A changing mat—have just the changing pad and store when not in use **9.** A low table for eating food (once baby can sit)

Because we value giving freedom to our baby, we need to ensure that the home is safe for our baby. Household chemicals are securely locked and out of our baby's reach; cords from curtains are tied and out of reach; electrical wires are hidden by plastic tubing that can be adhered to the wall; furniture such as shelving is secured to the walls; and window locks are installed. If there are stairs, we may wish to have baby gates across the opening so that the baby only practices on the stairs with supervision.

> "Remember that a supportive environment is sometimes distinguished more by what objects are left out, than by what are included."
>
> —Susan Stephenson, *The Joyful Child*

OBSERVE, STORE, AND ROTATE

One of the secrets to the success of our intentionally created spaces is to limit the number of activities available for our baby to the ones they are working to master. We can display a limited number—about six of their favorites—on a low shelf in their movement area. It's easier for our baby to choose from a smaller selection, the activities will be just the right challenge for them, and there will be less for us to tidy up.

Then we observe. When we notice that they are no longer interested in an activity or it appears to be too easy or difficult for them, we can store it for another time and bring out a different activity.

Storing mobiles can be a little more difficult because they get easily tangled. One idea is to display them on the wall on small hooks when they are not being used. They make an attractive wall display too. We can then hang the mobile the baby is interested in on a mobile hanger above their movement area.

We'll look more at which activities to choose in chapter 6. For now, remember to observe, store, and rotate.

ROOM BY ROOM

Entrance
- Low hooks in the entrance where we can hang the baby's coat, hat, bag, etc. As our baby grows, they will have naturally absorbed that this is where these things belong.
- A basket for the baby's shoes once they are walking.

Living room

Movement area
- A movement mat, where the baby can stretch and move their limbs, reach for their toes, observe a mobile, and look at themselves in a low mirror (see page 45). This is a great alternative to a bouncer chair, which limits the baby's free movement and exploration. Avoid propping them up with pillows, which which may limit them from moving freely.
- Once the baby is crawling, the movement mat can be removed to allow free movement and the movement area becomes the whole room (always check for safety).
- A low mirror hung horizontally to support development of the full visual body schema (i.e., learning what parts make up their body and how they look as a whole).
- A place to hang a mobile—this could be from the wall, attached to furniture, or hanging off a wooden frame suspended over the baby.
- A basket containing up to five or six board books.
- When baby is getting ready to pull up, we can provide sturdy furniture to pull up on and cruise along, for example, a heavy ottoman or coffee table, or even a horizontal bar on the wall with a mirror behind where they will be delighted to practice pulling up and cruising while seeing themselves in the mirror.
- We can hang art low on the wall. They enjoy gazing at familiar scenes and objects, so attractive pictures of plants, animals, or photos of the family are always favorites. Vintage pictures from old books placed in a frame can also be a beautiful choice.

- As our baby gets older, the low table and chair (see Kitchen section below) may be placed in the movement area for pulling up on, for activities, and for eating. As our baby gets close to walking, don't be surprised if the chair becomes a support that they stand behind and push along.

- There is a trend to buy colorful foam squares to cover harder surfaces, and we question whether this is necessary. These foam squares can become tripping hazards as our baby begins to pull up onto their feet, and the colors can add a lot of visual noise to the space. Instead, the movement mat provides a soft surface for our baby to explore when they are not yet crawling. Once our baby is on the move and trying to put themselves into a sitting position unassisted, they may get fewer bumps than we would expect. And remember that when there are bumps, they are learning about the limits of their bodies. Babies relearn how to navigate physical space with every new stage of development—it is the natural process.

Kitchen

- We can set up a low cupboard or drawer to store the baby's plates, bowls, cutlery, and glasses. They will learn where their things can be found before they begin to walk.

- Before the baby is walking, we can keep a basket of items such as a whisk, a wooden spoon, a metal spoon, or a small pot and lid, where the baby can sit and explore while we are working in the kitchen.

Eating area

- Once the baby is sitting, a low table can be used for eating food. Cut down the legs of a low table and chair so that the baby has their feet flat on the floor. We can add a vase with a flower to make eating time a special occasion.

- The low table and chair could be used for snacks and also for mealtimes if that works for the family.

- Simone likes to include the baby at the family table at mealtimes to introduce them to the social aspects of eating. A tray-less high chair with baby attachment (or similar) allows the baby to share mealtimes with the family and is a good alternative to a traditional high chair because the baby will soon be able to climb up into it independently and there is no tray distancing them from the table.

Bedroom   *Sleeping area*

- A floor bed—a mattress about 6 inches (15 cm) thick that is placed on the ground. Low frames are also possible to find, like ones for futon mattresses, or ones with raised edges that prevent the baby from rolling out but is low enough for a crawling baby to climb out of by themselves. See more about floor beds on page 64.

- For a newborn, the cestina (Moses basket) can be placed on the low mattress from birth—the baby learns this is the place for sleeping, a point of reference. The cestina may be used for the first few months or until the baby grows out of it.

- In order to keep the space calm for sleeping, it's not recommended to hang a mobile over the sleeping area.

- If the baby sometimes rolls off the mattress, have a soft surface on the ground next to the mattress. (Check that the space complies with SIDS guidelines outlined on page 63.) *Note:* We have observed babies move to the edge of the floor mattress in their sleep, feel the edge of the mattress, and move away from the edge, just as adults unconsciously do during sleep.

- SIDS guidelines currently recommend that the baby sleep in the parent's bedroom. Some people have an area in the baby's bedroom for daytime naps, which can assist with the eventual transition into this space for night sleeping.

- Some families may choose to co-sleep—either in the parents' bed or in a co-sleeping attachment. If possible, a family bed that is close to the ground will allow the baby to learn to crawl out safely as they grow. (Look into additional SIDS risks when co-sleeping.)

Note: Not all families feel comfortable using a floor bed. If this is the case, then we recommend moving the baby into a toddler bed as soon as they are able to climb in and out of it independently (at about 12 to 15 months old). We can begin with daytime naps to orient the baby to their new sleeping place. And we can sit next to them until they fall asleep for the first few days to help with orientation and then begin to move out of their room.

Quiet play area/movement area

- A low shelf with a few quiet activities or a basket of board books— once our baby is wriggling and crawling they can explore these upon waking.

- If space allows, a movement area could also be set up in the bedroom. (See page 57 for more on setting up a movement area.)

Changing area

- A place for changing diapers—a changing pad/cushion can be placed on the ground (if the adult has no back problems) then stored when not in use; or it can be placed at the height of the adult's hips on a table or set of drawers. (Always have one hand on a baby when they are at a raised height.)
- Have all the things for diapering at the ready, for example, a basket with clean diapers, wipes/cloth wipes, any creams, a place for dirty diapers.
- A low dressing stool can be useful once the baby is sitting steadily (from about 9 months). The height of the stool is very low so the baby can have their feet flat on the floor. This allows the baby to have a clear place for dressing; enables collaboration during dressing; and, as they become more independent, it will allow them to have more success when putting on pants and underwear and when dressing themselves. A wooden stool will be sturdier and easier to use than plastic.
- By the time a baby is standing, they may resist lying down on a mat to be changed—then we can change them in the bathroom while they stand up and we sit on a low stool (space allowing).

Feeding area

- A place for feeding—if space allows, a comfortable adult chair is ideal for feeding in the night. This allows the baby to remain largely undisturbed. Have a glass of water, tissues, etc., on hand for the nursing mother.
- We can also choose to lie on the floor bed to feed.

A note on decoration

- Decorations can be simple and attractive.
- We can hang a couple of realistic pictures at the child's height, for example, of animals, nature, and familiar people. A Montessori principle is to have artwork that depicts real things our baby sees and experiences in their daily life. It will be some time before they will be able to imagine things that are not in front of them.

- Homemade elements like bunting or something meaningful to the family can also be hung to add some cozy, personal touches.
- It's possible to have something bolder like patterned wallpaper and still create a cozy space—we then may wish to have a more neutral shelf or furniture to create calm and make it easy for the activities to stand out and be attractive for the baby to explore.

Bathroom

- While it will be some months before the baby is using this space independently, we can already set things up for how they will be used as they grow, for example, their toothbrush in a special place and a mirror where they can see their face as it is cleaned.
- Around 12 months, some babies show an interest in using the potty, and we can offer this when we change their diaper or training pants (cotton underpants with extra padding to catch a little pee). Other children will be much older. Always follow the child. The toileting area will be added to as they become a toddler (see page 69).
- Some people do elimination communication with their baby from the first few days (using a baby's cues to know when to offer them a potty) and would want to include a potty earlier in the bathroom for the baby to use.

Outside

- A soft blanket or picnic blanket for the baby to lie on when we are at the park, the beach, the forest, or anywhere outdoors. Babies love to lie under the trees and watch the shadows change and the movement of the leaves and branches.
- Many babies enjoy going for walks outside in a baby carrier or stroller. We can talk to them about what we see and enjoy quiet moments listening to the world around us. In the early months (up to around 3 months old), we will have our baby facing us as we walk so they can see where we are and we can talk with them. Soon, we can face them away from us so they can experience more of the world around them. With a stroller, we can stop and come stand next to them when they are looking for us.
- A sitting baby can enjoy the swings at the playground (or at home if space allows).
- Once a baby can pull up to standing, it won't be long before they can push a wagon (which can be used inside or outside). Avoid jumpers or baby walkers where the baby is placed in an upright position, putting pressure on their hips. Wait until they can pull up and push the wagon by themselves.

At first, these changes to our home might seem quite unattainable. We might ask, "Won't my baby pull everything out now that they have everything accessible to them?" Yes, they probably will at first. And then they will lose interest, or we can show them what they can play with instead. We make sure to babyproof cupboards that have dangerous chemicals or objects. For the rest, it is a matter of trust. They will find some things that are not meant for them, but that is their job—to explore the world around them.

So as much as possible we create "yes" spaces and babyproof unsafe things, and then the baby will learn by experimenting that it hurts when fingers get closed in drawers, and we will be there with loving arms to soothe them if needed.

TO OBSERVE

- Does our baby look relaxed in the space? Bored? Overstimulated?

- Lie down next to our baby to look from their perspective. What do we see? How can we make the space interesting to them without it being too "busy"?

- Can our baby see us? Being able to have us in their eye line can make a baby more secure to explore on their own.

- Do we need to adjust the space as our baby grows? Are they moving off the movement mat? Maybe it is time to remove it? Can they pull themselves to standing? Does the mirror need to be changed from horizontal to vertical?

- Are there any obstacles to their development that we can remove (e.g., that limit their freedom of movement)? A playpen? A crib?

- Does any activity need to be changed? We can store those that are not being used and rotate them again when we see our baby looking for something new.

From these observations, is there something new we learned about our baby?
Is there anything we would like to change as a result? Something in the environment?
Another way we can support them? Obstacles we can be removing? Including our
own intervention? Observe joy!

SIDS GUIDELINES FOR SLEEP

These are the current SIDS guidelines from the American Academy of Pediatrics (AAP).

1. Baby should sleep on their back for every sleep.

2. Baby should sleep on a firm surface.

3. It is recommended that babies sleep in the parents' room, close to the parents' bed, but on a separate surface designed for infants, ideally for the first year of life, but at least for the first 6 months.

4. Keep soft objects and loose bedding away from the infant's sleep area.

5. Consider offering a pacifier at nap time and bedtime—studies have reported it reduces the risk of SIDS.

6. Avoid overheating and head coverings for infants.

7. Avoid the use of commercial devices that are inconsistent with safe sleep recommendations. Examples include, but are not limited to, wedges and positioners and other devices placed in the adult bed for the purpose of positioning or separating the infant from others in the bed.

8. Do not use home cardiorespiratory monitors as a strategy to reduce the risk of SIDS.

9. There is no evidence that swaddling reduces the risk of SIDS.

FLOOR BED QUESTIONS

Won't my baby roll out of the floor bed?

- If the floor bed is new for our baby, they may indeed roll off the floor bed. Luckily, the bed is close to the ground, so there is little chance that our baby will be hurt. If the floor bed is used from birth when our newborn isn't moving that much, they will learn the limits of the mattress as they grow.

- After a couple of times, our baby will learn to unconsciously feel for the edge of the bed—they are learning about their body, their environment (the edge of their bed), and their strength (how gentle they need to be to stay on the bed versus falling off).

- We can also lay a soft blanket on the floor if we have hard floors—make sure it is not loose or easily tangled as it could be a SIDS hazard.

- If our baby has just learned to roll, we may want to roll up a towel and place it lengthwise underneath the mattress along the edge that is not against the wall.

- Some people use a mattress frame that is high enough to stop our baby from rolling out but low enough that they will be able to climb or slither out on waking.

Won't they get out of bed to play in the night?

- They may crawl out of bed during the night when they are wakeful. That is one advantage of the floor bed. They can play with some activities, then crawl back to bed when they are done (or sometimes they happen to fall back to sleep on the floor of their room). Keep the room babyproof and offer quiet activities for them to explore.

How will I get my baby, who crawls/walks, to stay in a floor bed?

- A baby who has always had the floor bed as their point of reference will be clear that this is the place where they rest and often even crawl to their bed when they are ready to sleep.

- If the floor bed is new to them and they are already crawling or walking, we can help by introducing the floor bed for them to explore. Then at sleep time, when we see their tired signs, we can lay them in their bed. We can sit next to them, perhaps with a gentle hand on them, and enjoy relaxing with them as they learn their new place to sleep. After a few days, we will be able to move farther from their mattress, and eventually we won't need to sit with them for them to stay in bed.

- Over time, they will enjoy being able to choose to get up to play and not need to call out to us, and we will trust them. It's hard to believe that they will choose to sleep. But remember all the Montessori families who have experienced just that.

We live in a warm climate— what about bugs in their bed?	• Light-colored flooring in the sleeping area (or a light-colored rug) will make it easy to see any bugs. Also, keep the room clean and close the door when the sleep area is not in use. • The floor bed has the advantage in warmer climates of being cooler for our baby because it is close to the ground.
We live in a cool climate— won't they get cold on the floor?	• Block any drafts coming under the door with a draft snake or a rolled-up towel. • Have a woolen underlay under the sheet. • Dress the baby in warmer pajamas with socks (this allows them to have freedom of movement in their feet). • Use a warm sleep sack until it becomes a tripping hazard once the baby is crawling or walking.
Do you need a frame around the mattress?	• It's a personal preference. • A frame can look nice and a low lip around the mattress can help to keep the baby from rolling out. A frame can also keep the mattress off the floor to provide air circulation. • Putting a mattress directly on the floor is also okay.
What size should the floor bed be?	• It can be a crib-sized mattress or larger. • If there is space, many families enjoy a larger floor bed so they can lie down with the baby to nurse or soothe.

TIPS FOR TRICKY SITUATIONS

When there are older siblings

One of the most common questions about setting up a Montessori-style home is how to use the space with children of different ages. In this case, we are working to meet the needs of all the children in the home in these (sometimes small) areas.

1. **Use higher shelves for older siblings.** We can look for shelving that is three shelves high—the lower shelves can be for the baby to use or can hold activities with large parts that are safe for all ages; and the higher shelves can be used for activities with smaller parts for the older children.

2. **Look for containers for small parts that the baby cannot open.** We can use things like a screw-top jar or a container with a tightly closed lid to hold small nails for hammering; small blocks like LEGOs for building; and other small parts, like little pegs, that are used by the older siblings.

3. **Make a space where each child can go to be by themselves if they wish.** An older child may get very frustrated with a crawling baby who seems intent on destroying the building structure they have created. Even the baby may wish to be left in peace instead of being dragged around by an older sibling or dealing with a sibling who keeps interfering and taking over what they are playing with.

   It might be that building materials are brought to the dining or kitchen table, out of the baby's reach; a blanket can be placed over the back of some chairs with a sign that says "Private," and we can show the baby the sign and tell them, "It says *Private*." Or we can create an area for the baby using some low shelves or a floor rug to mark their area and have a separate area for older children.

It's not going to be argument-free. Think of it as giving the children many opportunities to practice problem-solving and finding ways to meet everyone's needs. And we can continue to adjust our spaces as our children grow and find ways to make it work even better for everyone.

Small spaces

It's almost more important in smaller spaces to have a place for everything and everything in its place. Otherwise the space quickly becomes cluttered and uninviting to our baby.

If space is tight, we have the opportunity to be creative.

- We could roll up the sleeping mattress each morning to create more space.
- There could be space high on the walls that we could use to mount some storage (paint it the same color as the walls and it's barely visible).
- Some of the furniture might be unnecessary and could be taken out of the space, at least for now—for example, a desk or couch that is used infrequently.
- Look for light-framed and light-colored furniture that can give the appearance of more space.
- We can arrange a toy swap with friends. In some places, it may be possible to rent toys for a monthly fee rather than buying things that need to be stored.
- And clever storage will also play a big role in a small space, keeping out only the things the baby is using right now.

Getting rid of the clutter

When we start with setting up our homes Montessori-style from birth, we have the advantage of not having a lot of extra toys and baby stuff before we get started.

We may still have quite a lot of our own things that we could streamline to make space for a calmer, less cluttered home to welcome the baby.

It can be a good idea to see what we no longer need and remove it to create more space for curious babies, who are natural explorers. And to be conscious of what we bring into our homes for the baby.

BOOK RECOMMENDATION

There is good reason Marie Kondo's decluttering method has become so popular: It works. She encourages us to only keep those things that spark joy or are useful. And for those things we are going to let go of, we can say "thank you" for the joy we felt when we received them. To read more, we recommend her book *The Life-Changing Magic of Tidying Up.*

WHAT'S NEXT:
PREPARING THE HOME FOR A YOUNG TODDLER

It won't be long before our baby becomes a young toddler on the move. Here are some ideas for setting up the home for young toddlers so we can be ready for what is coming next.

Kitchen

The young toddler loves to be involved in what is going on in the kitchen. They will want to be able to see what is being prepared and to help in simple ways, so a stepladder or learning tower can be useful once they can stand steadily.

They will start to be able to carry a plate, glass, and cutlery to their snack table, so have these in a low drawer or cupboard. We can also set up an area where they can help themselves to a glass of water (a water dispenser or jug with a small amount of water, a cloth at the ready, and a small glass) and a simple snack (look for containers that they can open themselves).

Bedroom

The young toddler may want more space to explore and move in the bedroom when awake. If an adult chair was being used for feeding, this may need to be removed to create more space. We can make sure the activities on the low shelf are becoming more difficult, to challenge them. Again, choose quieter activities for the bedroom area.

As the young toddler is likely to be pulling up, standing, and even climbing, make the space as safe as possible. Think about having window locks installed if necessary, ensure bookshelves are attached to the walls, and remove any items we don't want them to reach (toddlers can be remarkably resourceful).

Living room

The horizontal mirror will likely no longer be used in the movement area and could be reused in the entrance area and hung in a vertical orientation (perfect for checking themselves before leaving the house). Similarly, if the movement mat has not already been removed, it can be cleared away to make space for more exploration and movement.

Young toddlers love to climb—if space allows, a climbing frame like a Pikler triangle with slide will get a lot of use. For smaller spaces, it's possible to find versions which fold up for storage, or can be hung high on a wall out of the way when not in use. Alternatives like wooden stepping stones, a balance beam, or rocker are also wonderful opportunities for toddlers to practice their movements. A wagon for pushing is popular for young toddlers learning to walk.

Keep updating the activities provided for them to master and rotate ones from the storage area when new challenges are needed.

Reading books becomes a favorite activity for many young toddlers. Think about creating a cozy book corner with front-facing bookshelves displaying a small selection of books and have cushions, a bean bag, or comfortable low chair to read in. We can rotate books when needed with others from a bookshelf or storage area to keep it interesting without being overwhelming to a young child.

Bathroom

Young toddlers want to be able to wash their own hands, reach their own toothbrush, and possibly climb into the bath by themselves. Having a low step stool at the ready will be very useful.

Some young toddlers may show interest in toileting—then it's time for a potty (or a step to reach the toilet), a place for wet clothing, dry underwear, and cloths for cleaning up at the ready.

Entrance

Now is the time—if not already—to get the entrance ready with some low hooks for a bag, coat, hat, etc. A basket down low for shoes and another for items like scarves and gloves will be helpful for toddlers who like to know where things belong so they can be found easily.

The mirror from the movement area can be relocated to the entrance area, hung vertically. A small table with tissues and sunscreen can be handy for last-minute leaving-the-house checks.

Outside

The young toddler is becoming more and more active. Once they are standing and walking, a whole world opens up for them to explore. We can begin to provide opportunities for running, cycling (e.g., a small tricycle they can push with their legs by themselves), jumping, hanging from their arms, sliding, and swinging.

Simply exploring a garden or going for a walk in the forest will be rich experiences for young toddlers. Look out for rocks, shells, feathers, and other things to find in nature to start a nature collection. And they may start to show an interest in working in the garden and helping to pick homegrown vegetables, giving water to the plants, and raking up leaves.

BENEFITS OF SETTING UP
A MONTESSORI-STYLE HOME

We're always surprised at how setting up our homes in this way creates a lighter, calmer space for the family. In addition, setting up our home in this way:

1. Provides a sense of security for the baby by offering consistent points of reference in the home
2. Allows the baby to absorb beauty and feel that we care for our home
3. Gives a clear place for everything and everything in its place—beautifully arranged with everything needed at the ready (also in the adult spaces)
4. Enables the baby to absorb aspects of their culture through artwork, ceramics, and other cultural elements found in the home
5. Allows the home to become an aid to move from dependence, to collaboration, to independence
6. Helps the baby learn their effect on the world by using spaces set up where they can move their body, explore spaces, and try out different activities
7. Gives a sense of belonging to the baby, being included in all areas of the home and family life

By being intentional in creating these spaces for our baby, we have laid the foundation for the coming months and years. There is one last thing about setting up our homes—the work is never finished. Our babies become toddlers, and our toddlers become children and then teenagers. Yet there is now a strong base in place from birth that can be adjusted easily as our child grows.

TO PRACTICE

- Can our baby use their spaces in an independent way as much as possible (e.g., a movement mat instead of a bouncer chair)?
- Are our spaces beautiful and clutter-free for our baby to experience?
- Can we place attractive activities in a way that our baby can see what is available and begin to learn to choose for themselves?
- Do we have a consistent place for feeding, changing, bathing, and sleeping?
- Have we created sufficient storage so we can rotate activities and store items that are not being used?
- Have we laid down on the floor next to our baby to see what the space feels and looks like from their perspective?

**ENVIRONMENT
0 TO 5 MONTHS**

1. Floor bed
2. Center for changing and clothes storage
3. Receptacle for rubbish or dirty clothes
4. Shelves
5. Adult chair
6. Movement mat with mirror
7. Mobile

**ENVIRONMENT
5 TO 9 MONTHS**

1. Floor bed
2. Center for changing and clothes storage
3. Receptacle for rubbish or dirty clothes
4. Shelves
5. Adult chair
6. Movement mat with mirror
7. Ottoman
8. Weaning table and chair
9. Bar on wall

ENVIRONMENT
9 TO 12 MONTHS

1. Floor bed
2. Center for changing and clothes storage
3. Receptacle for rubbish or dirty clothes
4. Shelves

5. Adult chair
6. Ottoman
7. Weaning table and chair
8. Bar on wall
9. Basket of balls

These rooms are based on illustrations by Gianna Gobbi in the AMI Assistants to Infancy training.

A MONTESSORI HOME FROM THE
BABY'S PERSPECTIVE, BY ZACH, 16 MONTHS OLD

We see here how the home setup has aided his development and joy in exploration from birth. Enjoy this "interview." (imagined and transcribed by his mother, Pilar Bewley, Mainly Montessori)

Welcome! Come on in. . . . I'm Zach, and this is my home. I was born in my parents' bedroom upstairs and have spent my entire life—a whopping 16 months—living here. I love what my parents have done with the place, and I want to share my favorite spots with you.

Let's begin in the kitchen. When I started being strong enough to open the drawers on my own, my mom had to do some rearranging. She moved all the chemicals to the bathroom (the only cabinet in the house with a childproof lock). She put her glass containers in a higher drawer so I wouldn't accidentally break one while playing with other containers, and she moved the silverware (except the sharp knives) down to a low drawer so I could have access to it. Other than that, she left everything else as it was. A few times I tried investigating the delicate items she had in some of the drawers, but she would come over and tell me, "No, those are not for you." She would then show me which drawers I could play with. Now I know! I got my fingers caught in the heavy drawers a couple of times, but now I'm really skilled at closing them.

Next to the kitchen is the little wooden cupboard where I keep my toys. My mom found it at a swap meet, and I love it because it's the perfect size for me! We keep my cars in one basket on the floor and my balls in another. Mommy says baskets are great, and I agree! I especially like to dump everything out of them and then put things back (or walk away and leave a giant mess behind, depending on my mood).

Next to my toys is my weaning table. This is where I had my first meal with a bowl and a spoon! When I first used the table, at 4 months of age, I needed help sitting up. Now all mom has to say is "It's time to eat!" and I run to my table, pull out my chair, and sit down on my own! Sometimes I share my weaning table with my friend James. We have so much fun eating lunch together! My dad and my aunt Debbie made the weaning table from plywood he had lying around in the basement. They also built my Learning Tower [a Montessori stepstool], which we move into the kitchen when I need to wash my hands or help with the cooking. I hope one day I can be as crafty as they are.

I have breakfast and dinner with Mom and Dad at the dining room table. I have a Tripp-Trapp chair that was a present from my grandparents, aunt, uncle, and cousins. I love knowing that my entire family has contributed to my independence. I am learning to climb in and out of the chair on my own, and it's so nice to share meals with Mom and Dad. We always light a candle and use real china, silverware, and glasses. I love feeding myself, which can get a little messy, but it's also a lot of fun. I've broken a couple of glasses and plates, but now I have a lot of respect for them and am so careful that I am now in charge of taking the plates and silverware to the table when it's time for dinner!

Careful with those steps. You might want to hold on to the low railing my dad installed so I could go up and down them on my own. This way, I can get to the bathroom when I have to use the potty. Here's my little toilet. I have another one upstairs. Here are my underwear and my books. Mom and I spend a lot of time here, reading books, singing songs, and waiting for me to do my business. When I pee or poop, I proudly empty my potty into the toilet on my own, while my mom flinches and tries to pretend like she's not dying to help me.

Oh, look, right outside the bathroom is the dogs' water bowl. I used to make a giant mess every time I walked by—I couldn't resist turning over the bowl and spilling the water everywhere! I'm much more mature now; I notice when it's empty and take it to my mom so she can fill it up. She didn't understand me the first time I took it to her and said "agua." She told me, "No, there's no water in the bowl right now." Moms can be so dense! I persisted, and eventually she understood and got really excited at my new "level of awareness," which is what she called it when she told Daddy. Call it whatever you want, Mom, but someone had to give the dogs water!

Let's go upstairs. Mind the gate at the bottom of the stairs, which nowadays is only used for keeping the dogs downstairs. We still use the one at the top of the stairs when Mom has to take a shower and I am hanging out upstairs.

Here's my bedroom. I slept on a floor bed for many months. It was a crib mattress placed on the floor, and I really enjoyed the freedom it gave me to explore my room after my nap or if I wasn't feeling sleepy. Unfortunately, I am a big-time roller, and in the winter I would roll out of bed and get very cold sleeping on the wood floor. My parents found the perfect solution: this neat bed from IKEA! Instead of using slats to raise the mattress off the floor (like the original design intended), my dad came up with the idea of putting the mattress on the floor so that there would be a low wall surrounding it. There's a little entry/exit built into one end of the bed's frame, but I'm also really good at climbing in and out of the side of the bed (I landed on my face the first few times I tried this, but now I'm a real pro). Next to the bed is my stool and my laundry hamper. Mom says I'm a wiggle worm; she tries to get me to sit down to get dressed, but I often end up running around the room half-naked. However, I do love to put my dirty clothes into the hamper!

In the upstairs bathroom, I have a stool to reach the counter so I can brush my teeth, and I also have another potty like the one downstairs. In my parents' room, I have a few toys on a shelf, which I mostly use only when Mommy is getting dressed. This was my movement area when I was younger; I had my mobiles, mirror, and a bar for pulling up and cruising. We'll soon turn it into a climbing wall so I can give Mom more heart attacks and start bouldering!

Well, that's it, folks! I hope you've enjoyed the tour of our Montessori home. Thanks for visiting, come back soon!

HOME TOUR

Let's take a look around the home of Nicole, founder of the site The Kavanaugh Report. There are four children in the family, and we can see how the space is set up to meet the needs of, and include, the youngest member of the family.

Pictured here with a DIY black and white mobile, inspired by the Munari mobile, and the topponcino.

BEDROOM

The bedroom area is calm and relaxed. A mattress on the floor serves as the floor bed, a sheepskin with a wooden mobile hanger as a movement area, and low shelves can display simple activities. Botanical artwork is down low for the baby to enjoy when awake, and an adult feeding chair is in the corner so the baby can be fed in their room during the night. The space is baby-proofed so it is safe for baby to explore upon waking.

MOVEMENT AREA

A soft carpet is used as a movement mat where the baby can have free movement, stretch, and explore their body and the things around them. A mirror allows them to see themselves, take in their body schema (how their body is made up) and also allows the baby to see their siblings busy alongside them. There is a bar on the wall when the baby is ready to pull up to stand and cruise.

A low shelf with some objects to explore is at the ready— an object impermanence box with a ball, grasping beads, a palmar grasp cylinder, a basket of objects, and some simple board books.

A plant and wall hanging soften the space to make it feel cozy and inviting.

FEEDING AREA

A low table and chair provide a baby-sized space for their first meals and snacks. A tray with a small glass and pitcher of water is at the ready, along with some flowers and a cloth placemat showing how we prepare even the baby's feeding area with love and care.

The table height is about 12 inches (30cm) and the chair seat height is about 5 inches (13cm), so their feet can reach the ground.

FAMILY ROOM

This photo shows the baby being included in the family's life. The baby has the space to do their explorations—lying on a sheepskin with a grasping object to investigate—while also tracking their siblings and parents going about their play. In the background, we see a bookshelf with books from the older children and a large puzzle on a mat next to the baby, nearby enough to see but out of reach for safety.

CHANGING AREA

The baby's clothes are easy to see and, once wriggling,
the baby can make their way over to indicate which one
they would like. This also establishes a sense of order
once they are dressing more independently, as they
learn where their clothes are stored. We do not need
so many clothes and can rotate these seasonally and as
the child grows.

On the top of the low shelf is a changing pad for diaper
changes, which can also be placed on the floor as the
baby gets bigger. Once they are standing, we can change
their diaper as they stand (for example, with us sitting on
a low stool). It takes some practice, but babies might feel
more vulnerable lying on their back. Standing confers a
sense of agency, and lying down makes the baby more
passive, being acted upon. It involves them, and often
leads to less resistance to diaper changing.

PARENTING THE MONTESSORI BABY

5

TRUST

Like many parents, Junnifa spent a lot of time thinking of and researching the best gifts for her son's first birthday. Her wish list included wooden stacking blocks, a tricycle, and musical instruments. Then one day, while observing her almost-1-year-old, she realized that the best gifts for the first year cannot be bought; they are not material, but psychological. They are the basic trusts. These gifts are made even more special because they can only be given in the first year and only under the right conditions.

The two basic trusts are the *trust in the environment* and the *trust in self.*

Basic Trust in the Environment: This first basic trust is usually acquired by the end of the second month of life, which also marks the end of a very important time in the baby's growth, the period of adaptation to their new world. During this time, the mother and the baby depend on each other to meet both physical and psychological needs—this is the period of symbiosis we discussed in chapter 3. This stage lays the foundation for the child's personality and their view of the world and life. A child who has basic trust in the environment will approach life with optimism, security, and trust in the world as a good place where they can thrive.

Basic Trust in Self: This second basic trust is usually acquired by the ninth month, which marks the end of exterogestation, or the external pregnancy. The child will have spent as much time outside the womb as they spent inside. The basic trust in self lays the foundation for confidence and strong self-esteem. The child who has basic trust in self will approach challenges with confidence in their abilities. They will not be discouraged by failures. They will be curious and approach the world with an exploratory attitude.

We can give our baby this gift by helping the child develop independence and providing opportunities for movement, exploration, and communication.

Each time the baby succeeds, a deposit is made in their basic trust in self. It is important that we do not interrupt our baby or try to "help" our baby too much, for example, by putting the bell or ribbon of their tactile mobile in their hands. In addition to creating themselves and building their basic trust in themselves, the baby is also building their ability to concentrate. This process should be respected.

We can prepare an environment that will enable the baby to acquire basic trust in self. We can also continue to observe the baby to notice changes and then adjust the environment to balance challenge with their ability to succeed. We also continue to model the behaviors and social expectations for them and provide the baby with feedback for their actions. We talk to the baby, sing to the baby, and, even more important, listen to and converse with the baby. The parent observes the child for verbal and nonverbal cues of hunger, care, sleep, etc., while responding and providing language. Gradually, the baby improves their ability to communicate. It may be a word, or a sign, or a gesture, like bringing over their bib when they are hungry. They know they can communicate and make their needs known—another deposit in their basic trust in self.

And then one day, before they turn a year old, we will be together and our baby will smile at us and walk or crawl away. They look back at us now and then but continue to move away with purpose. They go out of sight and we wait for them to come back, but they don't. We go to check and we find them. They are sitting down and exploring their shelf or sitting at their table and having a snack. Maybe they are drinking from their glass or in their reading corner, flipping through a book that they have chosen by themselves.

And then we realize that they have received the best gifts for the first year. They trust the environment and themselves. They are optimistic and know that the world is a good place, and they trust in their abilities—so they are not afraid to explore independently. The foundations for a good life of happiness, lifelong learning, and exploration have been laid.

And while the role of the parents remains paramount, any informed caregiver of our baby can support us in giving of the two gifts of basic trust.

ACCEPTANCE

Imagine the feeling of visiting a place and before you get there, a message comes from your hosts telling you how much they are looking forward to having you. And when you arrive, you find them waiting excitedly and you see that they have beautifully prepared the home for you. Wouldn't it make such a difference for your stay?

We can welcome our babies in this way, and in so doing, we send them a message of acceptance that will stay with them for the rest of their lives and lay a foundation for all future relationships and transitions. We can send this message of acceptance through our interactions with our babies, and this can start from the moment of conception. When we rub our bellies while pregnant, spend time talking to the baby in utero, call the baby by name, read books, and sing to the baby, we send the message that we accept them and are looking forward to welcoming them. Being happy and as relaxed as possible during pregnancy helps keep our hormones balanced and also sends the message of acceptance versus stress and unhappiness.

This message of acceptance can continue to be sent after birth by the way we prepare ourselves and our environment for the baby. The time spent holding the baby, the way we look at them, touch them, love on them, and give our undivided attention during caregiving are all ways that we continue to send the message. They can sense that we waited for them and are happy to receive them.

This message sent and reinforced during pregnancy and after birth tells the baby that they are wanted and that they have come to a safe place. Dr. Silvana Montanaro, one of Dr. Montessori's infancy collaborators, believed that this message stayed with the child through life and gave them an optimistic view of the world that allowed them to adapt positively.

RESPECT

Respect is not a word that many people associate with babies or children in general, but Dr. Montessori believed that "Children are human beings to whom respect is due, superior to us by reason of their innocence and of the greater possibilities of their future." (*Dr. Montessori's Own Handbook*)

Montessori parenting is based on respect. Respect for the child as they are, and for the innumerable possibilities of their future.

There are many ways to show our babies respect starting from birth.

Respect our baby's body: The first interaction the baby has with the world is often through touch, and this continues to be the predominant interaction during the first year. Babies are touched a lot by their caregivers. We touch them when we feed them, change them, and hold them. This provides many opportunities to show the baby respect.

We can start by asking permission before handling our baby, picking them up, or handing them to someone else, especially a stranger. We might say, "Hello, baby, may

I pick you up?" When we ask a baby if we can touch or carry them, we can usually tell if they accept or reject. We can stretch our hands toward them, make our request, and wait. There is usually a change in their gesture or body. If they smile or move in our direction, we take it as a "yes" and pick them up. Then we can say, "Thank you," or otherwise acknowledge their acceptance verbally. If they frown, look away, or just shrink back, we can say, "No worries, maybe next time." In this way, we tell the baby from the beginning that they own their body and have a choice in how it is handled.

When carrying the baby, we do not yank or forcefully carry them. Instead, we carry them as gently and gracefully as we can. Our hands can teach the baby peace or violence. Gentle, slow, deliberate hands communicate respect and teach peace.

Physical care, including diaper changes and baths, provides lots of opportunities for respect.

Thank our baby: We thank adults for many things but often don't have the same courtesy when dealing with children. When we get into the habit with our babies, it will stay. And guess what? They are absorbing it and will adopt it too.

"Thank you for letting me hold you."

"Thank you for being here and spending time with me."

"Thank you for napping and giving me a break."

Trust our baby and their abilities: We can trust them to control their bodies, and we do not put them in positions that we feel they are not ready for. We can trust them to make choices about how to move and interact with the environment we create for them. We can trust them to problem-solve and we do not always rush in to help or provide a solution to their struggles.

When we respect the baby's abilities, we invite collaboration at every stage. It can be waiting for our newborn to find the nipple; saying something to our 3-month-old and waiting for their acknowledgment; putting the fork in the avocado for our 7-month-old and waiting for them to pick it up and bring it to their mouth; or holding out the arm of their shirt and waiting for our 9-month-old to put in their hand. All these small gestures tell the baby that we trust their ability. The gestures also support the baby's development of functional independence. We offer as little help as possible and as much as necessary, observing before intervening and allowing the baby to solve problems.

Observation is a form of respect: When we observe our children before responding or to understand them, we are effectively saying to them, "You know something I don't. Show me. Help me understand more about you."

Respect their individuality: Each child is unique, different in their timelines, personality, and expressions. Simone has two children and Junnifa has three—and we marvel at how different they each are from their siblings. Even if you provide the exact same environment and treat them the same, each child will be their own unique self. When we accept this from the beginning, we are able to accept and respect each child for the unique individual they are. It can be so hard not to compare or have expectations of one child based on another. Instead, we can observe our babies to understand and support their uniqueness. One unexpected way in which our children's personalities can differ is with sleep. We might have a baby who winds down easily and just goes to sleep or one who just doesn't want to miss a thing and so fights sleep with all their might. Even this aspect of individuality can be respected. We respect it by first accepting that this is how our baby is, and then finding ways to help them thrive in their individuality.

Consider the baby's needs: We want to always have the baby's tendencies and sensitive periods in mind and try to understand which of these might be motivating the baby's actions. (For more on sensitive periods, see page 18.)

Follow our baby's rhythms: Each baby is different and will have to find their own rhythm. We can respect this by providing situations that make it possible for them to do so and to allow time in our busy days to prioritize this. This includes rhythms around food, sleep, diapering, and the day in general. From birth, we can notice the baby's cues, build routines around them, and stay consistent.

Encourage our baby's activity: In her book *Child in the Family*, Dr. Montessori invites us to "respect all reasonable forms of activity in which the child engages and try to understand it." But how does one determine what is reasonable, and how do we try to understand it?

If an activity is safe, we can consider it reasonable and then we can stop to observe. This is how we can try to understand it. If we observe our baby touching something, watching something, moving in a certain way, and generally exploring, we respect their activity by not interfering or intervening.

Often babies can struggle but not necessarily need help. When we observe, we will learn to tell when they are asking for help, and then we can offer just the right amount of assistance. With babies, when we watch them play or try to reach for something, they might make little sounds indicating their effort and maybe a little bit of a struggle. As parents, our first instinct is usually to step in and help. Instead, we can first take a moment to observe, and often, when we hold ourselves back, we are rewarded by the evident joy when they succeed without our interference. And they are, too.

Knowing that all of the baby's activities are the work that they do to develop themselves, we respect their effort and protect their concentration by not interrupting. Sometimes even our words of acknowledgment can be an interruption. We respect our baby's exploration by sitting back when they are active, observing to understand and support them better.

"Never help a child with a task at which he feels he can succeed."

"Every unnecessary help is an obstacle to the child's development."

—Dr. Maria Montessori

ALTERNATIVES TO PRAISE

Praising our babies can be a hard habit to break or avoid. Often when our children do something, we feel the need to acknowledge it in some way. Many times our instinct is to acknowledge by praising, but when we do this, we teach the baby to look to us for how to feel about their efforts.

In Montessori we are wanting to build a child's intrinsic sense of self rather than having them look for or get used to external praise and validation. Instead of praise, saying "Good job," or clapping, we could try the following alternatives with our babies:

1. Don't do anything. This allows the baby to enjoy the moment in their own way.
2. Sportscast—say what we saw the baby doing: "You put the ball in the hole."
3. Describe what you observe about the baby's feelings: "You look content/excited!"
4. Acknowledge our baby's effort: "You worked on that for a long time" or "You did it."
5. Give a gentle smile.
6. Offer encouragement: "I knew you could do it."
7. You could talk about what comes next: "I see you are done. Shall we go get ready to nap?"
8. Or talk about how it feels: "I'm so excited for you. You did it."

Respect the baby's pace (slow down): Respecting the baby's abilities also means understanding that it takes children a little longer to process and figure out things, so we give them "tarry time" to process and try. When we say something to our baby, it can take 8 to 10 seconds for them to process it, so we can build this time into our interactions and wait for their response.

It also takes longer to involve a baby in dressing, feeding, and other moments of daily life. Yet, we often save time when we involve them, because they may not become upset so easily, and we are laying the foundation for them to develop concentration, focus, skills of independence, and to explore the world around them.

Respect the baby's choices: When we respect the baby, we give true choices as often as possible and respect what the baby chooses. We do not impose our thoughts or emotions and instead listen to hear and understand them. This can start from as early as 3 months with our babies. We can offer two shirts and see which one they gesture or smile toward. We can offer two books and see which one they choose. We put two rattles within reach and let them choose which one and how to use it. For an older baby, they will select an object from a selection of 3–5 items in a basket. Offering a choice is a form of respect, and then we respect the baby's choices.

This helps us already practice for the choices our baby will make as they become a toddler, preschooler, school-aged child, and beyond. We won't give them the choice of which country we might live in or which school they attend, but we will give them age-appropriate choices.

> "Now we must learn how to care for the newborn child. We must welcome him with love and respect."
>
> —Dr. Maria Montessori

HAVING KIND AND CLEAR BOUNDARIES

"Freedom within limits" is how we help our Montessori children develop self-discipline, and, like other ideas, we start with this at birth. We try as much as possible to give the baby freedom within the limits of safety and their abilities.

Offering our baby choices, giving time and opportunity for movement and activity, and letting them feed themselves are some of the ways that we give our baby freedom. "Freedom" can be a difficult word to understand, as we are often used to it meaning "freedom from" something, like rules or having to work. In a Montessori context, we give the baby/child "freedom to" do something—like freedom to choose, to move, and to express themselves. It's not a license to do whatever they like—it's freedom within the rules of our family and society.

So with all of these, we also set limits or boundaries. Here are some of the ways that we set boundaries with babies:

Limit the options or choices: When preparing the baby's environment, we consciously only include the items that are safe for them to use. When we offer choices, we limit them to options that we have approved and that are acceptable to us.

Keep them safe or give safe alternatives: Babies are still getting to understand the world. They do this by exploring, and sometimes they will explore beyond the safe areas of the home or space or do things that are unsafe. In these situations, we can stop unsafe behavior and redirect unacceptable actions. For example, if a baby crawls to an electrical outlet, we tell them it is unsafe and carry them to a safe part of the room. A baby who is throwing inappropriate objects can be redirected to a basket of balls or objects more appropriate for throwing.

Respond to the need or message being communicated: The baby's behavior is usually their way of communicating something. It might be a need or a message. A baby who is throwing objects might be communicating a need for more gross-motor movement, and a baby who is throwing food might simply be communicating that they are full or not interested in the meal. Our response would be based on our observation and interpretation.

Modify the environment or a process: If our baby often pours the water out of their cup while they're not drinking, we can modify our process by keeping the cup by our side until it is time for the baby to drink, or pouring just enough for one drink and taking the cup back once the baby is done. If our baby keeps going back to an electrical outlet, we can make sure it is protected or maybe move a piece of furniture in front of it. In this way, we set limits using the environment.

Be prepared to repeat ourselves: We have only a few limits because we will need to repeat ourselves many times until our baby's will is developed enough to stop themselves, for example, from touching something they want to explore. Their prefrontal cortex, which is responsible for inhibiting themselves, is in the earliest stages of development and will be developing into their early twenties. So we need to be their prefrontal cortex.

Teach them what to do, rather than tell them what we don't want them to do:
Remembering that babies are new here and just figuring out how things work, we can
see ourselves as their guides, here to help them and show them how things work. With
this in mind, when the baby goes beyond our boundaries or limits we can see this as an
opportunity to teach them appropriate and acceptable behavior. This understanding can
make a difference to how we respond. If we are teaching the baby what is acceptable, we
might say. "The water stays in the cup. Put the cup down here," instead of "Don't pour
the water," or "Why do you keep pouring the water?"

We might model like this: "I see you are done. Let me show you where the cup goes."
Modeling is so important in helping the baby figure out the boundaries.

A NOTE ON POSITIVE LANGUAGE

This is a great time for us to practice saying things in a more positive way. Children
tune out when they constantly hear "don't" and "no" all the time. So we tell them what
we want them to do: "Let's keep your feet on the ground" rather than "Don't climb
on the table." In addition, it's simpler for them to process our request. When we
hear someone say, "Don't put your hands on your head," first we think of our head
and then need to work out where to put our hands instead.

Start now, and by the time they are toddlers and we are seeking their cooperation
more and more, it will be automatic.

ENCOURAGING CONCENTRATION

Babies can concentrate. Given free time and a prepared, orderly space, they can concentrate from birth. So we create the following conditions that support concentration starting from birth.

1. Ensure our baby is sleeping enough

Babies from 1 to 12 months old need 14 to 15 hours of sleep. We can guard our baby's sleep. Watch for signs that they are tired, and help them wind down and sleep. Once asleep, avoid waking them up. Without enough sleep, it is hard for babies to focus, even if the environment is well prepared.

2. Keep our baby hydrated and well nourished

Once babies are eating solid food, they need balanced meals that include carbohydrates, protein, fat, fruits, and vegetables. They do not need processed foods and sugars. Even as adults, we find it hard to concentrate when we are hungry or have had too much sugar. We can also teach our baby, as soon as possible, how to get water when they are thirsty. A baby as young as 7 or 8 months old can crawl to a small cup of water or a bottle with a straw.

3. Prepare an orderly environment

Order on the outside leads to order on the inside. Babies need order. This means an uncluttered environment, a place for everything and everything in its place. Order makes it possible for the baby to make a choice. It also makes it possible to focus. If we have hoarding tendencies, we can try to limit our clutter to one room or storage area that the baby doesn't spend time in.

4. Allow the baby to experience peace and quiet

What is the noise level of our home? Are there times of the day when the baby can experience silence and peace? A time when no one is talking on the phone, the radio is not on, and neither is the TV. When pots are not clanging, and everything is quiet and still. Can you imagine it? These can be the best times for concentration. Junnifa tries to make sure her family has many times like this daily, when the only sounds they can hear are the whir of the unavoidable fan for the Nigerian heat and the baby's voice as they hum while they explore. Even an hour of this daily is good for the soul (of both adult and baby).

5. Limit passive entertainment

We don't need to constantly entertain the baby. It becomes exhausting for the adult and can be detrimental for the baby. Babies learn through active experience and by doing instead of being entertained. So we provide an environment that encourages our baby to engage themselves. This can start at birth. Toys that entertain also affect concentration. These are the toys that sing, flash, beep, talk, and do all sorts of things at the press of a button. This kind of entertainment leads to passivity and takes away that sense of wonder and accomplishment that comes from direct discovery. Magda Gerber, founder of the RIE approach, described it well when she said that we want passive toys and active children, not active toys, which lead to passive children.

6. Avoid screens before age 2 and have little or no screens after age 2

You can try this experiment. Put on a cartoon or a typical children's television program. Take out a stopwatch and count how many scene and color changes happen in 3 minutes. The real world moves much more slowly. Children can get used to this stimulating pace and will struggle to slow down and focus. This passive entertainment is often very noisy.

Our babies are sensorial learners best suited to learning through their mouths and hands, so we can turn off screens and let them discover this beautiful world we live in.

7. Choose simple and developmentally appropriate toys and materials

For babies, many of the skills they concentrate on building are ones that require no materials at all. Some examples include when a baby first discovers their hands and stares at them for extended periods of time, or when they are learning to turn over and can sometimes try more than 30 times in a row. The majority of a baby's explorations fall in this category and require nothing but space and uninterrupted time. Mobiles and very simple toys that the baby can explore in different ways also support the development of concentration.

8. Observe

In all things Montessori, observation is important. We observe to make sure the baby gets enough rest, to make sure they are not hungry or dehydrated, to see when they are overstimulated, to identify their interest, to identify their developmental stage and support it, and, most importantly, to recognize moments of concentration and respect them.

9. Avoid interrupting

Once we have recognized concentration, *we do not interrupt.* Not to help, not to congratulate, not to correct. We can simply smile to ourselves, enjoy their achievements and process, and watch from a distance. During their development, concentration is fragile. It is easily broken, and when the baby experiences this a few times, they can stop trying to concentrate. It is so beautiful to watch a baby completely absorbed and engaged in something.

FREEDOM OF MOVEMENT

One significant way to give freedom to a baby from birth is by giving freedom of movement. We have already talked about it a lot in this book, but it cannot be overemphasized. There are many benefits, including the development of strong gross- and fine-motor skills, increased body awareness, confidence, determination, and an early start to learning problem-solving, among other things.

The following are some of the ways we allow freedom of movement for our baby:

Offer food and wait for baby to accept and take it. If breastfeeding, from birth, the baby can be placed on the tummy and chest and, if we wait, they will find and move toward the breast by themselves.

Avoid swaddling. Babies move their limbs freely in the womb, so we allow them to have freedom to do so from birth. We all have a startle reflex in the beginning because we are no longer constricted by the womb, but we will gradually work it out. If necessary, we can swaddle loosely so that the baby feels covered or cocooned but still has some freedom of movement.

Avoid containers or restrictive devices like bouncers, exersaucers, or similar items.
There are times like when we are cooking or busy and need to have the baby close by.
In these moments we can wear our babies, use a blanket on the floor, or even use a small
bath in the kitchen. If we do find it necessary to use a container, minimize the time the
baby spends in it.

Allow free time for movement. Put the baby down on the floor on a blanket or mat
or on the bed. They can be put on their back and on their belly. Observation will tell
us if the baby is okay. Prepare a movement area where they can freely and safely explore.
We can also set up temporary movement areas as needed so that the baby can always
be around us in different parts of the house.

**Try not to prop our baby into sitting, standing, or other positions that they cannot
get into by themselves.** When not being held, they can either lie on their backs or on
their stomachs. They will come to sit up, pull themselves to standing, and walk when
their own bodies can manage this.

Avoid putting toys into their hands. Instead, we can hold or put the toy close enough
that they can reach it with some effort, but not too far away that they get frustrated.

Choose movement-friendly clothes. These are comfortable and not too big or too tight.
They have minimal fastenings and decorations, which can make the baby uncomfortable
if lying down, slithering, or crawling. Leave the feet and knees exposed as much as possible.

Remember that each baby will develop at their own pace. The goal is not to make a
baby move faster. Whenever they do move, they will do so with control and confidence.

A SECURE ATTACHMENT

Dr. Montessori saw life as a series of attachments and separations, like pregnancy
(attachment) and birth (separation), or breastfeeding (attachment) and weaning
(separation), right through to a teenager needing their family as a base (attachment)
but gradually spending more time with friends (separation).

Attachment

A secure attachment is the optimum kind of attachment that the baby can develop with
their caregiver. It is an innate human need, which babies seek to achieve from birth.

SOME TIPS FOR FORMING SECURE ATTACHMENTS

CONNECTED PREGNANCY LAYS THE FOUNDATION

Even in the womb, the baby receives messages of acceptance. When the mother is happy, relaxed, and makes efforts to connect with the baby (rubbing her stomach, talking to baby, responding to baby's kicks, etc.), messages of acceptance are transmitted, and this lays the foundation for a secure attachment.

RESPONSIVE PARENTING BUILDS TRUST

Contrary to some beliefs, we will not spoil our baby by responding to their needs. Instead, we will be helping them form a secure attachment. From birth, our baby will communicate their needs to us using their vocalizations, facial expressions, and other body language. It is important to spend time with the baby and observe to understand what they are trying to communicate, and then respond appropriately and as quickly as possible. This helps the baby acquire a basic trust in their environment. This is the feeling of security and the knowledge that their needs will be met in this place. It allows the baby to go from self-preservation to attachment.

RESPECTFUL AND CONSISTENT CAREGIVING FOSTERS SECURITY

A large portion of the baby's first year is spent receiving care in the form of feeding or diapering. These times provide a great opportunity to connect with our baby and in doing so, support their formation of a secure attachment. Feeding the baby on demand, notifying them before we pick them up or handle them, and handling them respectfully when we dress and undress them are some ways that we can help form a secure attachment. We can also be consistent with other caregivers such as babysitters or day care workers, having limited, consistent, and well-selected people to care for them.

SPENDING TIME TOGETHER CREATES A BOND

Spending time with the baby and being truly present creates a special bond. Nursing provides a special opportunity for bonding, and while breastfeeding is ideal, bonding doesn't necessarily require that the baby feed at the breast. Skin-to-skin touch, eye contact, holding the baby, observing, and responding to the baby all foster a bond.

There is a great deal of research that supports the notion that a secure attachment sets the foundation for the baby's overall well-being and emotional, intellectual, and social development. A securely attached baby is joyful, curious, and interested in exploring their environment. They will deal with separations more positively and will grow up to be happy, empathetic, creative, resilient, and better able to self-regulate and learn. They will also have a positive sense of themselves and be able to form and maintain more positive relationships throughout their lives.

Separation

It is up to us as parents to observe signs that we can allow our baby more distance to explore safely from this secure base. We can allow them to stretch and move on a mat as we observe; to attempt to reach for things to explore; to slither and crawl away, and come back; and to make little expeditions, then longer ones as they become confident babies and toddlers.

WHEN OUR BABY CRIES

Our baby's cry can trigger strong reactions in us. This is natural and one of nature's ways of protecting our babies. Other things, like our emotional state and our childhood experiences, can affect the way we react to our baby's cry. It is important to move beyond an instinctive reaction to a calm, respectful response. How can we do this?

Take a moment to calm down. Our baby's cry can trigger our freeze, fight, or flight mode. This is not a rational mode, so it is important to take a moment to take our brains out of that mode before responding. It can be a deep breath and a reminder to ourselves to calm down. If the baby is not in danger, we might even step into another room, a bathroom, or a closet and shut the door for a minute or until we feel calm enough.

Next, we can acknowledge our baby. Even before we get to them, we can calmly say, "I hear you, Solu. I am on my way." When we get to them, we can assess and respond. Sometimes our presence is enough to calm the baby down. Sometimes we have to pick the baby up and hold them. Tell them we are going to pick them up and then pick them up and hold them close. Our words are important, and we can choose them carefully. If we know why our baby is crying, we might say, for example, "You bumped your head and it hurt." When we say things like "You're okay" or "Stop crying," we can inadvertently negate, brush away, or ignore the baby's feelings. Instead, allow the feelings and let the baby know that we hear them, we recognize their feelings, and we are there. In this way, we accept and respect their emotions.

It is important to try to understand our baby's cry. Our baby's cries are their way of communicating with us. In the beginning, our baby's cry is uniform, but by the second or third month, it becomes differentiated.

These cries are usually trying to communicate a need, whether it is hunger, tiredness, or discomfort.

We can try to understand and respond appropriately. There are often other signals that our baby gives us before they even start to cry. We might miss them in the beginning, but as we start to observe, we start to see these cues and can anticipate our baby's needs and, in doing so, help them to communicate without needing to cry.

CHECKLIST FOR WHEN OUR BABY CRIES

- Calm ourselves down.
- Acknowledge baby's cry.
- Observe if they need help.
- If needed, comfort with our presence and by holding them.
- Allow our baby's feelings and name them.
- Respond to their need.

BEING THEIR GUIDE

Modeling: Montessori parents, like Montessori teachers, can be our child's guide. This means that we are neither their boss nor their servant. As guides, when we prepare the physical environment for them, we can guide them and model to them how to engage with it, but then we step back and allow them figure it out in their own way. It is a fine balance, and it requires some practice to find the line of allowing exploration and knowing when to intervene. We are not the boss, so we do not dictate how our babies will engage, but we are also not their servants, so we do not rush in to solve every problem. We give them the reassurance of our presence and availability but step back to allow them to figure things out. We offer just enough help when necessary but not too much.

We are always modeling how to engage with the environment and show up in the world. We drink and eat in the baby's presence to model how to use a cup and cutlery. They watch our movements, our conversations, and interactions, and they absorb them.

Knowing this reminds us to be mindful of our actions. To prepare ourselves to be the best version of ourselves. And to apologize and acknowledge when we aren't. "What I should have done is . . ." or "What I should have said is . . ."

When we acknowledge how we are feeling, we are modeling to our baby how to be authentic with feelings and emotions. Some days are hard, and it is okay to be sad or frustrated or tired. We can say that to our babies and then model to them how to find calm by finding it for ourselves (see chapter 8).

Removing obstacles: One of our roles as guide is that of an obstacle remover. We are responsible for identifying and removing obstacles to our children's optimal development. This requires observation and in many cases selflessness. Some of the obstacles actually make our adult lives easier but might be an obstacle for the baby's development. A pacifier might be helpful sometimes, but it can soon become an obstacle that can interfere with the baby's need to communicate and the process of acquiring the skills for communicating. Putting the baby in front of a television might give us a break for a while, but again, it interferes with the baby's optimum development and becomes an obstacle.

We have to be willing to remove the obstacles we identify. Disorder, noise, disproportionate furniture, and things that constrict the baby's movement are some obstacles.

We can also be an obstacle when we put pressure on them to do something like performing on cue. Simone remembers saying to her son, "Show Nanny and Poppy how you can clap/wave/point to the dog." She loved that her son rarely did what she was commanding him to do. So she stopped these "tests" and saw his refusal to perform as a reminder that babies will show their skills in their own time. They are their own person.

We can also be obstacles when we interfere and don't allow opportunities for independence, or when we react instead of observing and then responding.

Being their guide means:
- Giving space for our baby to work it out for themselves
- Being available when needed
- Being respectful, kind, and clear
- Trying not to change who they are
- Supporting them and helping them learn skills where needed
- Using gentle, slow hands and waiting for their response
- Setting limits by modifying the environment instead of having to limit the baby
- Giving as little help as possible and as much as necessary
- Listening and responding (pausing first before we act) rather than reacting (acting straight away without pausing to check ourselves or the situation)

FRAMING THEIR VIEW OF THE WORLD

In many ways, our babies see the world through our eyes in their early years. They come to define safe and unsafe, good and bad, and other qualities by watching us and listening to us. They reflect what they see and hear from us.

We can be intentional in the messages we pass on about different subjects. For example, when it comes to gender, we can be careful not to unconsciously assign qualities like strength, beauty, or specific interests to one gender over the other. Girls can be strong and boys can be caring. Boys may enjoy playing with dolls and girls may enjoy playing with vehicles. By the way we talk to our babies, the way we dress them, and the opportunities we offer them, we can frame the way they perceive gender and the roles they assign to each gender. Research has shown that there are actually very few differences in the first year between girls' brains and boys' brains. The differentiation begins around a child's first birthday. Some of the ways that we can give them a balanced view are by using gender-neutral pronouns when reading books, avoiding labels like "pretty" versus "handsome" and by seeing each child as capable regardless of gender.

This framing also applies to how we view or label our baby's abilities and character. When we say things like "You naughty baby," we might be joking or not mean it seriously, but it still sends a message. We can instead frame it differently: "I see you are struggling with . . ." In this way, we don't define our baby by a temporary situation. When we trust our babies and say things like "You can do it" or show them that we trust them by allowing them freedom and to struggle to work something out, we frame their view of themselves as capable.

A HANDY CHECKLIST
FOR FOSTERING CONNECTION
WITH OUR BABY

NURSING

- Skin-to-skin contact
- Eye contact
- Observing and responding to our baby's cues

TWO-WAY COMMUNICATION

- Let them know what we are doing
- Wait for their response
- Incorporate their response into our actions

GENTLE HANDS

- Be slow and deliberate when handling our baby
- Collaborate with our baby to dress, bathe, etc.

QUALITY TIME

- Take advantage of caregiving activities like feeding and changing to connect with our baby
- Make time to observe and understand them better
- Spend time just holding and enjoying our baby with no agenda

GOING SLOW

Babies, by nature of their abilities and speed, invite us to adopt a slower pace of life. To support them optimally, we in a sense have to move at their pace. Once our babies are slithering or crawling, instead of picking them up to go to a different room, we can tell them where we are going and invite them to come with us.

It takes longer to involve our baby in their care, to talk them through our actions, to wait for their response, and to do many of the other things we have talked about in this book so far.

We can view this time of slowing down with our baby as an inconvenience, or we can take advantage of it and slow down and enjoy this time. We might enjoy it so much that even when this stage passes, we find opportunities and ways to slow down in the midst of our regular lives.

Some of the ways we can slow down with our babies are:
- Using slow, gentle, and deliberate hands when handling them
- Speaking slowly and clearly so that they can hear each syllable
- Waiting for their response after we speak to them
- Letting them move by themselves and do things by themselves, regardless of how long it takes. We can take these moments to observe them and marvel.
- Stopping to observe before reacting when they struggle or fall, or when we are tempted to intervene
- Stopping for them to stare at things that catch their attention, regardless of how long it takes
- Taking slow walks that allow both baby and us to enjoy the sights, scents, and sounds of nature
- Doing nothing while baby naps. Not trying to catch up on laundry, not catching up on our emails, just sitting in the silence and enjoying it.
- Making some of the baby's materials by hand. There are so many options for materials available commercially, but there can be something soothing and special about making something for our baby by hand. We could sit next to our baby's movement mat while we are working, so they can see us while they do their own explorations.

- Putting on some music and dancing slowly with the baby in our arms or just dancing while baby watches
- Making time to read something daily. It could be something about our baby or just anything that interests us.
- Taking a nap or going to bed early

When Junnifa thinks back on the first years of her three children, one word comes to mind: *joy*. The pace of their family life was slow. Each baby had time and freedom to explore and develop, which led to joy, and a baby's joy is contagious. We hope you too get to experience this joy.

Our baby's first year can feel long and demand so much of us, because we are learning so much and doing so much to support another life. But in our experience and that of everyone we've asked, in retrospect, the time always seems to have flown by. We can find moments of connection and joy, and enjoy the journey.

TO PRACTICE

- How would we like to give our baby the gift of basic trust?
- Can we see our baby for who they are and accept them in their individuality?
- Can we see and treat our babies with respect?
- Can we be intentional in the words that we say to them?
- Can we find opportunities to connect with them?
- Can we enjoy them and enjoy the journey during this special and transient time?

MONTESSORI ACTIVITIES FOR BABIES

6

PART ONE

INTRODUCTION TO ACTIVITIES

HOW WE CAN SUPPORT OUR BABY'S DEVELOPMENT

For more than a century of observing babies, Montessori parents and educators have documented the ages and stages of development in children. We can use these stages as a guide as we observe our own baby's development—and prepare the environment with activities that support these developments.

WHY WE CHOOSE ACTIVITIES FOR OUR BABY

These Montessori activities will help our baby's brain development (by three years old, a child's brain will have reached 80 percent of it's adult volume—an enormous amount of change over a small amount of time). However, the purpose of these activities is not to make our babies "smarter" or to help them reach milestones before their peers. It is to treat them as the unique human they are, to support their developmental needs, to establish a secure attachment, and to help them transition from dependence, to collaboration, and then to independence.

The main areas of development that we can support during infancy are movement and language. Activities can support their intellectual and psychological development— our baby learns to make connections (e.g., "When I hit this with my foot, it moves"), their understanding of our language grows, their bodies are challenged, and they build confidence and trust in the world around them.

The activities presented in this chapter are organized by age, but these are just guidelines. Every baby will develop at their own pace, on their unique timeline, and that is okay. We want to support our baby on their own path—not try to speed up or slow down their individual process. If we are concerned about our baby's development, we can seek support. This is not a bad or shameful thing; this is giving them and us the tools that they need to thrive.

HOW TO CHOOSE ACTIVITIES FOR OUR BABY

1. Read about their current stage of development.

2. Observe our baby.

3. What are they developing/practicing/showing interest in right now?

4. What can we offer to support this?

When choosing activities for our babies, there are several things to consider:

Choose natural materials. Babies explore with their mouths, so the things they use will inevitably end up in our baby's mouth. Therefore it is important to choose materials that are safe to be tasted and chewed. Natural materials like wood, fabric, rubber, and stainless steel are usually safe. The texture and temperature of these materials also provide different sensory feedback. Metal is cold and smooth; wood is warmer and can feel different depending on the grain and finish. If the object is painted, check to make sure the paint is safe. We can also look for materials that are stained with natural/food-based dyes. Natural materials also last longer and can be enjoyed by multiple children.

Consider the size of the entire object as well as any components. The object should be a size that the baby will be able to manipulate. Check that all the components are securely attached and will not be choking hazards. A choke tester can be used to check the size of objects offered for children under 3 years. This is a cylinder that is 2.25 inches long by 1.25 inches wide (5.7 cm long by 3.2 cm wide), about the width of two fingers. A toilet paper tube can also be used to check for safety. If it can fit in the toilet paper roll, it is probably a choking hazard.

Choice of beautiful materials. In chapter 2 we talked about the baby's absorbent mind and how it takes in everything. With this in mind, we can offer beautiful materials or find ways to beautify less-than-lovely materials. Many things can be repurposed to make materials for the baby, e.g., empty water bottles, food boxes, and cans. We can improve the aesthetic value by using colorful tape on the edges, tying a ribbon around it, or covering it with nice paper.

Variation in qualities and functions. We can offer an array of activities that are different from one another. This can be variations in color, size, weight, texture, or shape. They can also vary in function, for example, some objects that make sounds and others that don't, some that bounce and others that don't, some that are elastic and change shape when manipulated and others that don't. Through our baby's explorations, they start to understand the properties of things and how they work.

Most of the materials we choose for babies are intuitive to use. We don't need to show them what to do. Our role is to set up their play environment, prepare the toys and materials, and make them available and accessible at the ideal time. When our baby is working on the skill that the material supports, they will naturally do what it calls for. This time of exploration is the time during our baby's day when they can be in complete control. They can choose if, how, when, and what to engage with. They can experience being in control and the effects of their actions and choices. It is important for our baby to experience this control as part of their daily life. This is how they build trust in themselves and their abilities—trust that they will carry with them into adulthood and rely on when they encounter challenges.

If we notice our baby struggling with how to use a material or not showing interest, it could be that they are not ready, so we might put the material away and try again a little while later. For babies, there is not really a right or wrong way to use an object. As long as it is safe, we allow their exploration and discovery.

One way that we can guide our baby's exploration without showing them directly is by ensuring the baby finds materials in their correct and complete state whenever they spend time in their movement area. So if we have a puzzle, for example, it would be in its regular place when the baby finds it. They might not put it back properly and that's okay, because that is not the goal at this stage. The goal is in the process of the baby touching and using their hands in different ways. This changes as they become toddlers, and at that time, we change the way we prepare the activity. Even though the baby might not complete the activity, they are absorbing how it should look when they first see it put together, and as they explore, they will find that they know exactly what to do.

One of the human tendencies is self-perfection. We want to push ourselves to do better and feel successful. This tendency is present even in babies. We all enjoy activities that are at the edge of our abilities. If it is too easy, we become bored, and if it is too hard, we become frustrated. The right material for our baby is just a little beyond their current ability so that it requires effort but is not hard enough to be discouraging. We can observe our babies as they use activities and see how they react. As much as possible, do not interfere or offer help even if it looks like the baby is struggling. As long as they are not frustrated, we should sit on our hands and observe. If we notice frustration, we observe to see what might be causing it. For an older baby, we might model and then observe again, or we might remove the material and try again later.

"The struggle is essential."

—Nichole Holtvluwer, Radicle Beginnings

Limiting the number of activities. Limiting the number of activities allows our baby to concentrate and not get overwhelmed. In the beginning, our baby's age can be a guide for the number of activities we can make available. We could have one activity out for a 1-month-old, two for a 2-month-old, etc. Ideally, we do not want more than five or six things available at a time in one place even for an older baby. As the baby reaches about 7 months old, the activities might not all be in one place. We might have four on one shelf in their play area, a basket in the kitchen, and maybe two activities in their room. We can store most of the activities and rotate a few out at a time. Every time an activity comes out of rotation, it feels new or like a long-lost friend.

Maintaining and restoring the environment. When our baby plays, they will usually move from one thing to the next, leaving behind a trail. We talk about order a lot, and with older children we usually show them how to put one thing back before getting another. We don't do this with our babies because they are not yet able to put things away, and we don't want to interrupt their concentration as they move from one thing to another. We can wait until the baby is done completely and then tell them we are going to restore the activities. They watch us as we do this and are absorbing this. When they start walking and are able to collaborate, we can invite them to put the things back together and show them how to do it. One day we will observe them starting to do it independently.

With older children, we also create order by putting the materials on trays that the child can carry to a table. For babies, this can be an obstacle because they are not able to carry the tray yet or might be more interested in the container than the activity.

Quality over quantity. There are so many possibilities for materials and toys that we can offer our babies. However, many of them are only enjoyed for a short period of time, and others are easily damaged. Instead, we can choose a few quality options over many not-so-great ones. We can invest in materials that can stand the test of time by considering:

- The materials they were made with. Natural materials often last longer.
- The construction. Babies bang, throw, and drop materials, so we want well-constructed objects that can withstand rough treatment.
- The flexibility of use. We want materials that our baby can continue to use in different ways even as they get older.

Quality doesn't have to mean expensive. We can find really lovely options in markets selling handmade items and also in secondhand shops, or we can make some of them ourselves.

"Each rattle, grasping toy, toy, puzzle, and other piece of material has been chosen for a specific purpose. It is up to the adult to watch carefully to see that the challenge is not too easy as to be boring, and not too difficult to cause frustration and giving up."

—Susan Stephenson, *The Joyful Child*

Our role is to prepare the environment, not to entertain

The foundation for independent play is laid during our baby's first year. The Montessori phrase "Help me to do it myself" applies to everything the baby does including entertaining themselves. "Help me to entertain myself." A parent of an older child of between 2 and 6 years old might ask, "How can I get my child to play alone?" While it's never too late to teach our child to be independent, starting when the child is a baby is the surest route.

It is important to understand our role in the baby's play. We are to gain knowledge about our baby's development, prepare the environment, link the baby to the environment, and allow freedom and time for the baby to explore. We avoid entertaining or initiating the baby's activity. What does it mean to link the baby to the environment? It means that we simply put them in the movement area or in the space where they have freedom to explore. We first study to know more about the baby's natural development so that we can prepare an environment that is suited to their needs. We then observe to find their rhythm and see when they are awake, alert, satisfied, and happy. This is when we put them in the movement area, which is already prepared for them. Once we have put them there, we gently withdraw ourselves and observe.

In Montessori, when we make an activity available to a baby, we say we "present it." The term highlights that we are giving or making available something special to our baby.

WHEN TO OFFER ACTIVITIES TO OUR BABY

1. They are alert.
2. They are full.
3. They are happy and comfortable.

What if the baby does nothing and is not interacting with the materials? This is perfectly okay. We often expect the baby's play to be noisy and busy. This is not always the case. Many times the baby's activity may be calm and not very obvious to the undiscerning eyes. If the baby is calm and happy, we don't need to interfere. Sometimes the baby's interest is on a different aspect of the environment than what we expected, for example, a container or an object close by or a sibling. We trust that they know what they need and we still do not interfere.

Junnifa remembers once observing an infant watching a mobile at a parent–baby class. The Montessori mobiles are designed to be moved by air currents, so they move very slowly. The baby was so calm and relaxed while watching the mobile's floating butterflies. The baby's parent was sitting alongside of them, watching. After some time, the parent must have felt that the baby was bored or not getting enough stimulation, so he started to blow the mobile to make it move faster. It was a well-intended gesture, but the mobile began to move too fast for the baby's eyes and neck. The baby soon looked away and started to cry. In a world that is so fast-paced, loud, and full of stimulation, many of us don't remember how to sit with stillness or enjoy moments of slowness, and we can unconsciously impose this on our children when we try to entertain them. Remember to observe them to see when they are ready for a change, rather than use our own feelings as an indication that it's time to move on.

As much as possible, we avoid placing toys in the baby's hands or rattling them above their faces to get their attention or entertain them. We place an item within view and within reach, leaving it up to them to choose to reach for it. This is practice for them in making choices and requires persistence and patience. When we allow these choices, we are allowing the baby to follow their own initiative and laying the foundation of intentional and purposeful actions.

When we focus on entertaining the baby, we make their concentration impossible. Often we entertain by talking or moving, and we can soon get tired and stop before the baby is done. When babies entertain themselves, they are in control of this aspect of their day and can choose what, how, and for how long they engage with each activity. We try not to interrupt or interfere, even to compliment or praise. Babies are amazing, and when we prepare the environment and observe, they will do amazing things. We have to learn to celebrate internally or maybe wait until we can tell a partner or friend or relative to recount and celebrate, or we can surreptitiously take a picture. But as much as possible, do not distract the baby. When we observe them, we will start to notice that they know when they have made an achievement, and they can acknowledge it in their own way. When we have a strong reaction, whether positive or negative, we inadvertently teach them to look to us instead of themselves for how they feel.

Babies enjoy stillness and quiet. We can protect this and help them continue to enjoy it by allowing them to sit with stillness and seek activity when they choose to.

The baby is the main actor in their play. They are their own entertainer. This means we avoid toys that talk or light up and make all kinds of sounds when buttons are pressed. We choose materials that come to life because of the baby's action. We also don't use the television as an entertainer.

If we keep these ideas in mind and help our baby learn to entertain themselves, we will lay the foundation for them to be able to do so as they get older. And there are many other moments when we can interact with, hug, and connect with our baby—what we like to call moments of connection—when we are changing the baby, feeding the baby, bathing them, and watching the world go by. These are not moments to rush through, but rather where we establish the foundation of our relationship (see page 102).

OUR ROLE IN OUR BABY'S PLAY

We study to understand the natural course of development.

We prepare an environment where our baby can be free to move and explore.

We identify ideal times to bring our baby to their movement area.

We observe our baby's play to understand them better.

We watch to see when they are tired, hungry, overstimulated, or soiled.

We foster concentration by not interrupting or interfering with their activity.

How to help if our baby is stuck or struggling

Let's say a baby is trying to turn over and we notice they are struggling to get their hand unstuck. If they are making an effort and struggling, observe but don't interfere. If they start to get frustrated, we might get closer, tell them what we see, and offer to help. We can then give just enough help, like helping to take out the hand but still leaving them to turn over themselves. We offer just enough help and never take away the baby's opportunity to succeed at something they set their mind to.

FURTHER NOTES ON ACTIVITIES FOR BABIES

1. Spontaneous exploration with objects

The materials we offer here are specific in supporting the development of gross- and fine-motor movement. In addition to these materials, we can allow opportunities for the baby's free exploration and open play. We call this heuristic-style play.

Usually, as the baby's mobility increases, they can move to examine things in the environment. We can allow this exploration and notice what holds our baby's attention the longest. Often the materials being explored are not necessarily toys. Junnifa remembers her son running his hand through a shaggy rug and trying to grasp the strands, and crawling after light reflections from the window. She also had a few blocks in a basket that her son enjoyed for a long time and four small plastic bottles that she filled with rice, colored water, and glitter or colored water, oil, and beans. He enjoyed shaking them and crawling after them. She also remembers him rotating one of the wheels of his toddler brother's tricycle, which was parked in a corner; touching the ruffles on a pillow; and exploring a spinning top and a music box controlled by a string that can be pulled. Her babies often enjoyed exploring the tray, basket, or container that held the materials more than the material itself. She would provide two or three animal replicas in a basket, choosing animals that they have in their environment, e.g., cow, chicken, dog, and peacock (a common sight in Nigeria!). Junnifa's babies enjoyed looking at these, moving them around, and exploring them with their mouths.

We can observe our child in silence in their exploration and—sometimes—use it as an opportunity to offer them language around the names of the objects, how they sound or feel, or the child's experience. And then leave them to explore again uninterrupted.

2. Dressing for movement

Removing obstacles is one of our roles as adults. One obstacle that is sometimes overlooked is clothing. The wrong kind of clothing can interfere with the baby's experience and thus development of movement.

In the first three months, when the baby spends time on the floor on either their back or tummy, consider the placement of buttons, zippers, and other accessories. Make sure they are not situated in such a way that they dig into the baby's body or they feel it in a *Princess and the Pea* way.

Choose clothes that are not too tight and allow for free movement of all limbs. The baby will involuntarily flail arms and kick legs, and we can select clothing that allows for these movements.

Swaddling can impede the baby's movements and interferes with the use of the Moro (startle) and fencing (neck) reflexes. If we do choose to swaddle, we can leave room for some movement of hands and legs.

When our baby starts to slither or crawl, they use their knees and toes for traction. At this stage, the baby has usually adapted to the temperature, and if it stays moderated, choosing clothing that allows movement becomes a priority. Shorts, onesies, or other clothes that keep the knees exposed are most suitable. Dresses and long shirts can trip the baby, especially when they are beginning to crawl.

Feet are better left exposed. They are used for a lot of transition positions, and shoes can interfere with both the baby's perception of the feet and their development. Remove their socks and allow the baby to dig in their toes as they scoot and crawl and get a better grip as they climb on the stairs, a Pikler triangle, and other obstacles. If necessary use nonskid socks or thin, flexible-soled shoes that allow feet to move. As cute as mini sneakers look, they are not helpful for a baby to move, crawl, or walk.

Hands are best left exposed, too. As tempting as it is to cover a newborn's hands to stop them from scratching their face, having their hands near their face is a tactile experience they had in utero. Keep them uncovered as much as possible.

PART TWO

LANGUAGE ACTIVITIES

Language refers to both verbal and nonverbal communication. We act on our human tendency to communicate by expressing ourselves and understanding others. Language is also connected to other human tendencies.

- It helps orient ourselves in both new and familiar environments.
- It helps us explore.
- It helps us adapt to our environment.

Let's think about these tendencies from our baby's perspective. From the time our baby is born, the sound of our voice lets them know someone familiar is close—it orients them, consoles them, and makes them feel safe. It invites them to look around and explore to find the source of the voice, and soon they start to replicate the sounds we make and become like us, adapting to their new environment.

At birth, we are wired to learn the languages we are exposed to.

Junnifa remembers being amazed by the process of developing language with each of her children. Her third child was immersed in two languages, and by age 2, she understood everything said to her in both languages and could speak in sentences.

To develop spoken language, the baby needs the ability to speak (functioning vocal chords), to hear the sounds we make (check their hearing often, especially if they have ear infections in the first year), a desire to speak (so we should respond to their efforts to communicate), and rich language (the input we provide). We need little or no materials to do this in the first year. One of the most important things we can do is to provide rich language for our baby and show our babies that we listen to them.

Our work to support our baby's development of language actually starts before they are born. The development of language starts in the womb. At about 23 weeks in utero, the fetus starts to hear sounds. It can hear the mother's breathing and voice, as well as other voices and sounds in the external environment. If we speak to the baby, sing, and even play music while they are in the womb, the baby recognizes these sounds at birth.

ACTIVITIES TO SUPPORT LANGUAGE
IN THE FIRST YEAR

- Speak to the baby from the womb using rich language instead of nonsense words like "goo goo ga ga."

- Speak clearly and correctly so that our baby hears the distinct sounds that form the words.

- Check their hearing and create an environment conducive to hearing.

- Remove obstacles to communication, e.g., pacifier, television, and background noise.

- Acknowledge and encourage every effort at communication, e.g., crying, cooing, blowing raspberries, babbling.

- Sing, tell rhymes, read poetry, play music.

- Read books with real themes and characters.

- Model conversation with eye contact, expression, and body language.

- Involve our baby in daily life and allow them to listen to conversations.

- Make it a habit to come down to our baby's level or lift them up to our level when talking to them.

- Speak gently and respectfully.

O TO 3 MONTHS

Speak to our baby

Our babies seem to be born with a special sensitivity to the human voice. Even from their first days, they will turn toward the sound of a familiar voice and are interested in other voices in their environment.

A significant portion of a baby's day is spent being held or handled. (By handling, we mean the interactions we have with the baby when feeding, bathing, and changing, or otherwise being with them.) These are wonderful opportunities to talk to the baby.

We can refer to them by name and talk them through our actions: "Metu, I'm going to pick you up. It's time for your bath. I'm washing your left leg and now your right one." We can also talk about their actions or reactions. "You smiled! You enjoyed that," or "You're pulling your ears, looks like you're sleepy." In this way, our baby starts to make connections between actions and words.

When we talk to our baby, we can make it a conversation. When we say something to them, we make sure we are making eye contact and then we wait for their response. It takes babies a little more time to process than adults. In the RIE philosophy, there is a concept called *tarry time*. It is a wait time that we give ourselves to allow the baby to process and respond. After we speak, we wait a little and observe for their response. They might make a sound or gesture and we can repeat it back to them or verbalize what we think they might be saying. We can poke out our tongue, and wait for them to make a movement with their mouth back. They are learning the art of conversation and that what they "say" matters to us.

> "When you speak to a baby . . . he will look directly at your mouth. When you speak to him, in the charming and affectionate way we all speak to babies, he will not understand what you are saying, but will feel emotion and be so thrilled that he will start to move his own mouth."
>
> —Dr. Maria Montessori

We can also point to items in the environment and name them for our baby. When Junnifa first came home with her babies, she gave them a tour of their home, showed them the rooms, and told them what happens in each one. She repeated this process often during their first year. We can give babies cues about their routines, share jokes, and just enjoy a conversation with them. It may seem like they don't understand, but the brain is making a lot of connections by figuring out how language works, how to form words, and how to repeat sounds. They are building their language bank and will eventually be able to express all they have accumulated. In Montessori, we use rich language and correct vocabulary even with babies, from their body parts to the breeds of dogs to the types of flowers we might see around us. We are limited only by our own knowledge.

If we want to raise a multilingual child, it can be preferable to have one person speak one language to the baby (instead of multiple languages). For example, one parent can be dedicated to speaking one language and the other person speaking another; or perhaps a grandparent or other caregiver might speak one language, while the parents speak another. Like with everything to do with babies, consistency is important. For more about bilingualism, see page 127.

We can start reading to our babies before they are born and continue after birth. The great thing about reading to the baby in the first few months is that it is not necessarily about the content but about hearing the phonemes (sounds) and the cadence of language. So we could choose a book that we want to read for ourselves and just read it aloud in the presence of the baby.

We can also choose simple books that have only pictures or minimal words and read by describing the pictures or illustrations. One fun idea is to make homemade books using familiar people or things. We can use a small album and put in photos of our family members or blank board books that we can fill with our own photos. We can look at the pictures together and tell the baby about each person. Many older children continue to enjoy looking through these books that they loved so much as babies.

It is important to check the baby's hearing soon after birth and continue to check it frequently, because colds and other infections can cause problems that affect hearing if not detected early. Many hospitals and birth centers offer hearing checks soon after birth. We can continue to check from time to time by calling out to the baby, clapping or ringing a bell from a distance, and checking for a response or reaction from the baby.

We can play beautiful music that our baby (and we) can enjoy. Dance with them, hold them, and sway them to the rhythm of a song. This supports our baby's development of language because identifying rhythms is part of learning language. Junnifa had some beautiful music boxes that she would play at different points during the day. One of them was transparent and you could see the mechanism moving inside, and her babies watched intently as they enjoyed the music. Another music box was controlled by pulling a string, and as it played, the string retracted and got shorter. Her babies also loved this and learned very early (around 6 to 7 months) how to pull the string and listen. Provide music in different forms. If we live in a place that has birds, we can open our windows in the morning or take the baby out to the garden and enjoy the music of the birds and the other sounds from nature. This is also an aid to the development of language and rhythm.

Babies need to experience and absorb conversation happening between others. So we can keep them with us or close by when we converse with our partner, friends, or their older siblings. Wearing them in a baby carrier or sling when we are out and about also allows them to observe and listen to these conversations.

Remove obstacles

Loud environments or a space with constant noise, like a room where the television is always turned on, can be hindrances to language. It makes it hard for the baby to clearly hear words spoken in the environment and can also overstimulate the brain. Even background music needs to be filtered out by the baby. So instead of having music on constantly in the background, it can be better to make a moment to listen to music with our baby.

Pacifiers can also be obstacles to the proper development of language. It is hard to coo, babble, or speak when you constantly have something in your mouth, especially at an age when you can't remove it yourself. In the beginning, the baby's main means of communication is crying, and it can be tempting to offer a pacifier, but apart from potentially impeding the baby's communication, it can also send a message that we don't want to hear what they have to say.

If we choose to use a pacifier, we can try to limit its use by placing it in a box in the sleeping area. And we can gradually remove the pacifier by the end of the first year. A pacifier is often offered for a baby that likes to suck—then we observe to see the moment that they are done, so that we can remove it and they can communicate with us with their sounds and cries.

Tips for choosing books in the first year

- Sturdy board books are best for hands that are still refining their grasp and their ability to turn the page. These books can also withstand being chewed on.

- Start with black-and-white images, then, around 4 to 6 weeks, move to colorful images on a white background, and then to images with more details.

- We can start with books with no words, then move to single words, then short sentences.

- Choose beautiful pictures—a baby absorbs the beauty we present to them, including in books.

- Choose books about things in daily life: animals, sounds, smells, the seasons, the senses, vehicles. In the first years until around 6 years old, children understand the world around them from what they see and experience—and a good deal of research suggests young children prefer realistic books. So we like to choose books based on things that a baby would understand from the world around them, i.e., reality rather than fantasy.

- In a similar vein, we can (mostly) avoid books where animals or toys are doing things a human would do, e.g., a teddy bear is driving a car or an elephant is on roller skates. We want to give our baby as accurate information as possible.

- When the baby is around 1 year old, they may enjoy lift-the-flap books (but may still tear the flaps by accident). Interestingly, research shows the flaps distract children so they learn a little less from such books—but they are fun.

- If the baby is interested in turning the pages or reading the book backward, follow their lead. This will not last forever. We are getting them interested in reading even if we never finish the book.

3 TO 6 MONTHS

As the baby matures (around 3 to 4 months), we will notice that they pay more attention to and even stare at our face and mouth when we are speaking. It's like they realize the sound they hear is made by the movement of our lips and they are trying to figure out how it works. Give them opportunities to do this by talking to them slowly and at a level where they can see our face.

Soon after, we will notice that they are not only interested in watching our mouths when we speak, but they also start to move their mouth and try to imitate our mouth movements. If we stick out our tongue or make fish lips or any exaggerated gestures to the baby, we will notice that they try to imitate it. Engage them by making these gestures and acknowledging their efforts with a smile or another gesture for them to imitate.

We continue to talk to our baby, but when we talk to them, we remember it is a conversation and not a monologue, so we pause and give them the opportunity to respond. Babies are very capable of responding vocally or with their gestures. Their responses become more noticeable around 3 to 4 months. When we observe a response, we can acknowledge it and incorporate it in our response back to the baby. We can repeat the sounds they make, or smile back at them, or say what we think they are trying to communicate. This tells them we are listening and also models conversations. It lets the baby know that we care about what they say and that they can always talk to us.

Repeating the sounds they make back to them is different from "baby talk" (like "goo goo ga ga"). When we talk to the baby in baby talk, we talk to them as if they don't understand anything else. Although we'll naturally use a singsong voice with babies—sometimes called "parentese"—we don't need to over-exaggerate this. Babies like the sing song tone and yet we still want to treat them with the same respect as a friend, a partner, or any other person.

Around this time, the baby also starts to produce vowel sounds—their first sound that is not crying. These sweet sounds called *cooing* (for their similarity to bird sounds) are delightful and can be acknowledged by the adult. Maintaining eye contact, we listen, and when the baby stops, we acknowledge by repeating the sound and talking back (e.g., "Ahhhh . . . I hear you. Ooo really? Tell me more") and then giving them a chance to talk. This encourages the baby's efforts at communicating and models the back-and-forth of conversation. Again, this is a conversation, not "baby talk." The baby's hearing should also continue to be checked periodically.

Around 4 to 5 months, a baby who is given freedom to produce sounds, acknowledged, and encouraged to communicate will also start what we think of as vocal gymnastics. They scream and test the limits of their voice. These sounds may become irritating to us, but they will pass. As much as possible, allow them to make these explorations rather than telling them to stop screaming.

They also "blow raspberries" (make sounds by fluttering the lips), blow spit bubbles, and make funny sounds. All of these are steps in their development of language and can be encouraged. This is how they work on regulating their voices and figure out tone, pitch, and volume. They are also practicing coordinating their diaphragm, mouth, tongue, and lips. We can encourage such attempts by blowing raspberries in response. This is fun and will usually elicit a lot of laughter and giggles, and it provides a wonderful opportunity for bonding. As before, it is important to continue to talk to the baby, sing, and read books to them.

Around 3 to 6 months, the baby may begin responding to specific pages in books. They may smile at a favorite page or try to imitate the faces on the page.

Around 5 to 6 months, the baby adds consonants to the vowel sounds and produces their first syllable. The first consonants are usually m, n, d, and p, so the baby might produce "mama," "nana," "dada," or "papa," much to the excitement of the parents. This reaction causes the baby to continue to repeat these sounds.

This can be a good time to introduce some sign language. Often babies understand so much more than they are able to express verbally, but they can use their developing motor skills to give simple signs to communicate. Babies are able to sign before they can speak, thanks to the early development of motor neurons that send signals to their hands. We can teach basics like "milk," "more," "eat," "done," and "sleep." We can say the words while also signing. Once they start signing these back after a couple of months, we can add a few more signs, and keep adding as our baby masters them.

BOOK RECOMMENDATION

If you are interested to learn more about baby signs, we recommend *Baby Sign Language Made Easy* by Lane Rebelo.

6 TO 9 MONTHS

From around the end of 6 months, the baby starts to understand words and can respond to requests like "Clap your hands," "Open your mouth," and "Say 'bye-bye.'" They know the names of family members and can react appropriately to statements like "Daddy is at the door" by looking or crawling toward the door. They also understand the different tones of voice and the word "no."

We can support them by continuing to talk to them and providing them with the correct names for things. We name things and sounds that they come across. For example, if they turn toward a ringing phone, say, "My phone is ringing"; if they look around at the sound of a dog barking, say, "Do you hear the dog barking?"; or when they are looking at a spoon we are holding, "That is a spoon . . . spoon. Spoon. Would you like to hold it?"

Singing provides opportunities to play with pitch, tone, speed, and volume. We can sing the same song with different voices, speeds, volumes, etc. And if we can play a musical instrument and sing, we can watch our baby open their mouth and sometimes match the sounds we make.

Babies up to around 7 months can reproduce sounds of any language although they favor the sounds of their parent language right from birth. These cooing and babbling sounds change around 7 to 8 months, when babies start to "purposefully babble" and try to practice the sound of their language (or languages). If we listen, we can hear some of the sounds. A lot of times they attempt to repeat sounds they hear. Again, all of this requires the baby's mouth to be free and the environment to be rich in language.

9 TO 12 MONTHS

By 9 months, babies understand many words even though they can't say them. They babble a lot and try to communicate more using signs and gestures. They appear to have a better understanding of object permanence. Research has shown that a 4-month-old can remembers that an object is there; what changes around 9 months is they become more capable of retrieving these "hidden objects." They will enjoy playing peekaboo games with us. Around this time, they also start to point with their index finger. We can name the objects as the baby points to them.

We continue to talk, sing, and read, and use clear and specific vocabulary. We can also play games with the baby by making sounds like shaking a rattle or clapping from different locations around the room and watching for them to turn or crawl in that direction.

Around this stage, the baby might start to get into things and explore cause and effect. Instead of saying "no" or "don't do that," we can practice positive language. For example, when our baby throws food while eating, we might say, "Food stays on our plate or goes in our mouth." If they seem to be done, we could say, "You seem to be done, I'll take the plate away." In Montessori we have a phrase to describe this: "teach by teaching instead of correcting." So instead of simply saying "no," we observe them trying out something in the moment, then wait to show them what to do instead at another time. We also try to tell them what to do instead of what not to do. This does not mean that we never say "no" to them. We just use it sparingly so that they know its importance.

12 MONTHS+

Around their first birthday, they may produce their first word, and shortly after they might know a few words, usually names of family members or requests, e.g. "water," "milk," "up!" etc. This is the product of a whole year of work! Remember that every child will learn to talk on their own schedule. The range for speaking their first word is wide (from 5 to 36 months) with the average first word spoken at 11.5 months.

Around this time, the young baby also starts to walk, which leaves their hands free to work. They can be included in practical aspects of the household, like cooking, cleaning, setting the table, and putting away groceries. Each of these activities provides opportunities for rich vocabulary, as the baby can learn the names of foods, fruits, vegetables, tools, utensils, processes, furniture, and also the particular vocabulary of their culture.

Materials like replicas (for example, model animals and tools) and eventually pictures can also be provided to introduce the baby to new words. Babies have an amazing ability to absorb language around this time, so we can introduce as many words as possible at this time. Talk, talk, talk. Sing, sing, sing. Read, read, read. Come down to the baby's level and listen when they speak.

LANGUAGE IN THE FIRST YEAR

- Speak to the baby from the womb.
- Speak clearly and correctly so that our baby hears the distinct sounds that form the words.
- Remove obstacles to communication (i.e., pacifier) and hearing (i.e., television); and check their hearing.
- Acknowledge and encourage their efforts at communication.
- Sing, tell rhymes, read poetry, play music.
- Read books with real themes and characters.
- Model conversation with eye contact, expression, and body language.
- Involve our baby in daily life and allow them to listen to conversations.
- Come down to our baby's level or lift them up to our level when talking to them.
- Speak gently and respectfully.

NEWBORN

- Will respond to soft or familiar sounds by listening; they will become still
- Will startle or blink in response to loud or unexpected sounds
- Expresses needs by crying
- Attempts to imitate facial gestures

MONTH 2

- Turns head toward sources of sound
- Focuses on caregiver while being fed
- Coos
- Frowns and smiles

MONTH 3

- Starts to make vowel sounds, e.g., aaaa
- Starts to show excitement
- Enjoys physical care routines like bathing
- Intently studies faces

MONTHS 4 TO 6

- Vocal gymnastics—spit bubbles, loud sounds
- Consonant sounds introduced in cooing to form simple syllables like "na," "ma," "ba"
- Coos have rhythm

MONTHS 7 TO 9

- Searches for and localizes faint sounds
- Understands "no"
- Can wave "bye-bye"
- Babbles tunefully in syllables and canonical babbling (where they duplicate the sounds, "ma ma," "ba ba")
- Turns to their name
- Can begin learning baby signs

MONTHS 9 TO 12

- Can play peekaboo
- Can respond to simple directions
- Can recognize several words
- Can recognize and point to body parts
- Can say some single-syllable words
- Can express wants and preferences without crying
- Can repeat baby signs
- Can point to alert us to interesting sights

OBSERVING THE DEVELOPMENT OF LANGUAGE

- How do they respond when they hear a familiar voice?

- How do they respond to an unfamiliar voice?

- Their cries: Do they sound different at different times? Can we differentiate them by cause?

- How do they respond to different sounds?

- What are they doing with their eyes and mouth when we speak to them?

- Observe the sounds they make. Are they vowel or consonant sounds?

- How are they making the sounds?

- How do they react to hearing their name?

- Are they making single sounds?

- Same sounds but strung together?

- Different sounds strung together?

- If we are also using baby signs, notice when they start responding and when they use the signs too.

- Notice how they respond when we read a book to them. Are there particular pages that hold their attention? What are they doing with their face or mouth while they look at the pages?

- Notice how they communicate pleasure or discomfort, with or without crying.

- Notice when they start to use words with intention.

From these observations, is there something new we learned about our baby? Is there anything we would like to change as a result? Something in the environment? Another way we can support them? Obstacles we can remove? Including our own intervention? Observe joy!

BILINGUALISM

Because babies have an absorbent mind and are in a sensitive period for language acquisition, infancy is a wonderful time to expose our baby to more than one language. They will take in additional languages with seemingly little extra effort.

If there is more than one language in the home, we can use the One Person, One Language (OPOL) approach. Each parent chooses their mother tongue when speaking with the baby, while the family uses one agreed-upon "family language."

We can also use an approach called Domains of Use. This is where we have agreed-upon times or places (temporal domains) when we use certain languages. For example, on the weekends the family chooses to speak English; out of the home they choose to speak the local language; and at home they speak the parents' mother tongues.

We need to spend around 30 percent of the week speaking any language that we hope our child will use as a literacy language. To increase our baby's exposure to any language, we might have a teenager read and play with them in that language, a caregiver who speaks that language, or play groups in that language. We can be creative.

Some parents worry that their child will have a language delay if they are being raised to be bilingual. When children have more than one language, the research shows that they should not have any learning delay. For comparison, a 1½-year-old who is monolingual may have ten words. The bilingual child may have five words in one language and five words in another. So it can appear that their language level is lower, even though they can say ten words in total too.

BOOK RECOMMENDATION

A Parents' and Teachers' Guide to Bilingualism, by Colin Baker is a book for anyone with questions about bilingualism or learning more than one language.

PART THREE

MOVEMENT ACTIVITIES

Movement is how humans explore and come into contact with their surroundings. Movement is also a means of self-expression, and it allows us to nourish ourselves, stay safe, and work to improve our environment. Movement in many ways is linked to our survival and progress, so we want to help our babies develop this skill to its full potential.

At birth, our babies already move. They move their heads, hands, and legs and stretch, but these movements are involuntary. They are not controlled or conscious choices. Many of the baby's movements at birth are linked to primitive reflexes. These are muscle reactions that automatically happen in response to stimulation. These reflexes are important because they signal that the baby's brain and nervous system are working. They also help the baby with different things needed for survival (e.g., feeding) until they can move voluntarily.

Babies need to train their muscles to move voluntarily. As the baby begins to move voluntarily, many of the reflexive movements that they are born with get integrated and disappear. (If movement does not develop naturally and optimally, some of these reflexes remain and can interfere with other areas of development later. It is helpful to know what some of these reflexes are so that we can check for their presence in the beginning and observe them as they get integrated and disappear, or notice if they remain. See page 271 for a list of infant primitive reflexes.)

The optimal movement for our baby to develop is voluntary and coordinated movement. This is movement that is initiated and directed by the baby. This is what we support with the activities we provide. We provide opportunities for the baby to train their muscles and control their bodies through repetitive movements.

The baby's role is to explore, initiate movement, enjoy challenging their body, and refine their coordination.

The adult's role is not to interfere with this exploration but to support it. We can set up a rich environment to support the baby at their current developmental level and provide some new challenges for them to reach for.

There are many different movement skills that our babies develop in the first year, each falling under the categories of gross-motor skills and fine-motor skills.

Gross-motor skills are the movement of our baby's body (including their arms and legs) in space: crawling, walking, waving arms, etc. These movements usually require large muscles. Gross-motor skills are necessary for their balance and coordination.

Fine-motor skills are the skills required for the movement of the hands, wrists, and lower arms. These are the unique rotations in these body parts that allow humans to grasp tools and work in a way that is different from (most) other animals. We can have a huge impact on the level of our baby's coordination and the development of the ability of their hands. Dr. Montessori referred to the hands as the instruments of human intelligence. She also said that whatever we want to give to the mind, we must give to the hands first. In essence, the hands and the baby's intellect are directly connected. When we help our baby develop their fine-motor skills, we are also supporting the development of their intelligence.

It is important to note that while we can support the development and quality of our baby's motor skills, there is a natural process to this development that every neurotypical baby follows. The process cannot be sped up, but it can be slowed down. Our goal is not speed, but rather to allow our babies to develop increasing control and coordination.

To understand this, let's have a quick science lesson. At birth, our baby has very limited gross- and fine-motor skills. Before the baby can control the muscles of a certain area, the axons in the nerves in those areas have to be covered with myelin, a fatty substance that insulates the axons, allowing messages to be able to be transmitted along the nerves. So as an area gets myelinated, the baby can gain control of that muscle. Myelination progresses from head to toe and from the chest out to the arms, hands, and then out to the fingers. The development of the baby's gross- and fine-motor skills follows the same progression.

So the baby gains control of their head before control of their torso, and has control of their torso before their feet, and they can move their arms before they can grasp with their fingers.

Kinesthetics is the ability to feel movements of the limbs and body. It is muscle sense. With repetition, the baby continues to feel the results and sensory experience over and over again. In the process, they incarnate these movements and also build dendrites and build dendrites for neuron to neuron connections, which helps their brain development.

The progression of myelin can be seen if we observe our baby closely—when we see them gaining increasing control of movement in their arms, hands, fingers, and legs. And we can prepare or modify the environment and provide activities to support the progression at each developmental stage as it arrives. By 12 to 14 months, all the axons are myelinized for movement, but the exact progress of their actual movements in each baby will depend on what their environment has to offer. A well-prepared environment where the baby has freedom to move and finds materials that encourage development and exploration will allow movement to progress optimally. We want to do more than allow movement—we want to encourage it.

Before we look at the activities, here is a guide to the ages and stages of the development of movement.

Remember: These are just general guidelines, and each baby will follow their own timeline, which might be plus or minus a few weeks or months.

Fine-motor skills can be seen developing in our baby as follows:

- **Reaching:** At around 3 to 4 months, our baby will have voluntary control of their arms.

- **Grasping:** At birth, our baby will have an involuntary reflex to grasp; at about 4 months they will be able to do it intentionally.

- **Raking:** At around 4 months, babies will scoop an object into their palm and then their fingers will wrap around it.

- **Thumb Opposition Grasping:** At 8 to 9 months, our baby will use four fingers with their thumbs. At 10 to 12 months, they will progress to the pincer grasp, first using two fingers and their thumb, then one finger and their thumb.

- **Releasing:** At 8 months, our baby will be able to voluntarily release an object into a small chosen space.

By preparing the environment and providing activities that support the baby's movement development, we also support the development of the following:

- **A "Can-Do" Attitude:** The baby will experience the feeling of being a conscious participant in their development of movement. Each successful acquisition builds the baby's confidence.

- **Self-Esteem:** In order to let children do these movements, the adult has to trust the baby. This trust becomes absorbed by the baby and helps them develop positive self-esteem. A safe, prepared environment makes it easier for the parent to trust the baby.

- **Body Schema Awareness:** Our baby will become aware of and get to know their body, its orientation, and the location of its parts.

- **Self-Awareness:** They will learn how their bodies work in relation to the environment. They will come to understand how to respond to their environment and become self-reliant.

ACTIVITIES TO SUPPORT THE DEVELOPMENT OF MOVEMENT

We do not need many things to support the baby's development of movement. The most important thing to have is knowledge of the natural process of development. This helps us to observe intelligently, prepare the environment, allow freedom, remove obstacles to movement, and notice early if there are delays or other concerns.

Remove obstacles

Removing obstacles is just as important as providing ways to support movement. We can:

- avoid dressing our baby in restrictive clothing (see page 113)
- avoid placing our baby in a playpen; instead, we can set up a "yes" space for them to explore
- avoid placing our baby in carriers such as strollers, car seats, bike seats, even baby carriers or slings for long periods of time
- avoid placing our baby in a "jumper," walker, or exersaucer; these devices put a lot of pressure on the baby's hips and limit the baby's control over their own movements
- avoid placing our baby in a position they cannot get into by themselves—e.g., sitting before they are able to on their own
- avoid holding our baby's hands above their head before they are ready to walk

0 TO 3 MONTHS

In the first month, our baby is adapting to this new world and orienting themselves. The best activity is just being held and snuggled by us, ideally at home or in an environment with very subdued stimuli, i.e., lights are not too bright; the space is quiet, with soft voices and maybe low music; temperature is regulated. This allows us to welcome and bond with the baby while allowing them to orient, feel safe, and build trust in their environment. This is important because if they feel safe, they are able to explore and engage with activities that we provide. We will notice when they start to feel oriented.

GRASPING AND DEVELOPMENT OF MOVEMENT

0 TO 3 MONTHS

Reflex grasp

Observe own hands

Grasp

3 TO 6 MONTHS

Intentional grasp

Manipulation

Clap hands

6 TO 9 MONTHS

Hand to hand

Release

Finger grasp

9 TO 12 MONTHS

Refined movement

Pincer grasp

They will be more relaxed, cry less, and start to look beyond us. Then we know that they are ready to spend more time on their movement mat.

Tip: We can use a topponcino when transitioning baby from arms to a mat or bed. This allows the temperature, feel, and smell to remain relatively consistent, so the baby is not disoriented or startled. Always lower the baby slowly and tell them what is happening.

Movement mat

By the second month, the baby could be spending a significant portion of their awake time on their movement mat. They can be placed on their back on a blanket and given the freedom to move.

If we haven't already done so, read about the movement area and how to set it up (see page 57). Many of the activities in this chapter can be presented or made available in the movement area.

Floor bed

A floor bed can support the baby's development of gross-motor skills because it allows and even encourages the baby to move. The floor bed is a Montessori alternative to a crib. It is very close to the ground and allows the baby to have a clear view of their surroundings. It can be used from birth, or the baby can be transitioned to the floor bed at around 3 months. Even families who co-sleep can use floor beds for naps and for part of the sleep cycle. Junnifa co-slept with her three babies but would put them on their floor beds at 7 p.m. and then bring them into bed with her when they woke up to feed at night. If we observe our newborn on their floor bed, we will notice that they move unconsciously. Often, we might find them in a different position from where we left them, but strangely enough, they typically don't fall off the floor bed. They move very slowly and seem to be aware of reaching the edge, and they will change direction or just stop themselves.

Grasping rattles

In the first 2 months, the baby has the grasping reflex that makes them wrap their fingers around anything that touches their palm. While breastfeeding or at other times, we can put our finger gently on their palm and they will wrap their fingers around it. We can offer them a small, light rattle or a narrow silk tube with batting inside. Remember that primitive reflexes become integrated with use, so this activity encourages use of this reflex while also bringing the baby's attention to their hand.

The visual mobiles

Visual mobiles are the main Montessori material used in the movement area for the first 3 months because they support so many of the baby's developmental needs during that time.

Montessori visual mobiles are a series of handmade mobiles that follow a specific sequence. They can be homemade or purchased and are made available to babies from the early weeks and rotated as the baby progresses in their development. The mobiles support a baby's development in several ways including:

Visual Sense: From birth, babies can begin to take in and explore their world with their eyes. While their vision is not yet acute at birth, it gradually improves, especially in a well-prepared environment. Visual mobiles provide an opportunity for the baby to both track (follow with their eyes) and focus on an object. They can also provide beauty and a point of reference for the baby. The development of vision also supports the development of both gross- and fine-motor skills.

Gross- and Fine-Motor Skills: In these early months, our baby is working on gaining control of their neck and arm muscles. As they watch the mobile, they will follow its movement initially with just their eyes and then with their head, turning from side to side, and then with their torso and entire bodies. Our baby will also eventually start reaching for the mobile. The movement is usually involuntary in the beginning, but they repeat it many times, building muscle strength and control.

Orientation and Adaptation: The mobiles are usually hung one at a time over the baby's movement mat, so they can provide a point of reference for the baby, as it is something familiar that they can recognize in the environment. The mobile is changed when they lose interest or when we notice progress that indicates the baby is ready for the next mobile. Ideally, the mobile could be changed within the baby's view. We can tell them we are going to change the mobile and then change it. Imagine coming to a room that you always visit and realizing that, without your knowledge, it has been changed. Imagine how disorienting that would feel. It is the same with babies—actually, even more than adults—so we try to make changes as respectfully as possible and in a way that does not disorient them.

Beauty: We have talked about the baby's absorbent mind and how the baby absorbs the things they see in the environment. The mobiles are beautiful, so they allow the baby to absorb beauty.

Below we describe four specific visual mobiles, but these can also serve as a guide for choosing or making other mobiles. Templates for the Munari, Gobbi, and dancer mobiles can be found at workman.com/montessori.

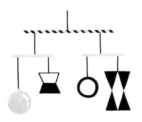

The black-and-white (Munari) mobile is usually the first mobile we present to the baby.

Research has shown that newborns prefer looking at high-contrast (black-and-white) geometric shapes. This is because the nerve cells in their brain that enable vision and their retina are not yet fully developed—studying the contrast helps them develop.

The Munari consists of black-and-white geometric shapes and a glass sphere that catches and reflects light and the other shapes. This mobile can hold the attention of a baby as young as a few days old for a long time. This mobile can be hung in the baby's movement area from birth, and they can start to enjoy it as soon as we feel they are ready. Junnifa felt her babies were ready around their second week.

The next visual mobile is called the **octahedron**. It is made of three octahedrons, usually in the three primary colors. The octahedrons are made using origami techniques or by cutting and folding paper into shapes. The shapes can be cut from red, blue, and yellow shiny paper (recycled gift bags work well). The reflective paper allows the mobile to catch and reflect light.

The third mobile is the **color gradation (Gobbi) mobile**, which is made of five same-sized spheres in progressively lighter shades of one color. The spheres are arranged in gradation. This helps the baby see the small color differences and can be fun to watch when put near a sunny window. Each ball casts a shadow on the next ball. Children love this mobile. It can be made by wrapping embroidery floss around spheres. We have also seen knitted, painted, and stained versions. By the time our baby is using the

mobile (around the end of their second month), we may observe them starting to bat at the mobile with their hands or arms.

The **stylized dancers mobile** is the final mobile in the Montessori visual mobile series. Like the other mobiles, it holds the baby's attention for a long time. It is made of stylized paper in gold or silver and a contrasting primary color cut in the shape of a person. The way they move makes them seem like dancers (hence the name).

The mobiles described here are specific to Montessori. But we can make or buy any mobiles for our baby, keeping these qualities in mind:

- Select simple, beautiful, and interesting mobiles.
- Choose light mobiles that move with the air current and do not require batteries or electricity.
- Visual mobiles are for visual stimulation and do not need to have music. It is easier to hone one sense when the focus is on that particular sense alone. In this case, the sight is the sense being stimulated.
- Look at the mobile from underneath. Remember, this is the baby's view. What are they seeing?
- Select mobiles that have either geometric shapes or real animals/items that they will encounter in real life. Avoid cartoon characters.
- Things that fly or float in the sky can also be lovely, for example, birds, butterflies, clouds, and aircraft.
- Choose bright, interesting colors.
- Mobiles should provide different views from different angles.
- Ensure the mobile does not have too many elements and is not overstimulating. Less is more. Ideally, mobiles for the first three months should have no more than five or six items.
- Ensure the mobile is not boring or understimulating.

Ideally, the mobile can be hung over our baby's movement mat, because this is where they will spend a lot of their waking time. The mobile gives them something to concentrate on. The baby can be laid on their back under the mobile. We hang it at least 8 to 12 inches (20–30 cm) above them when they are a newborn. This distance (which is also about the distance between our face and our baby's face when they are breastfeeding) is the distance that the baby can see at birth. Their range of vision gradually increases, and the distance can be increased as they grow and their vision develops.

We can avoid placing a mobile over the baby's bed, because this is their resting place. A mobile is for "work," that is, working on their visual development.

When we put our baby on the mat under the mobile, we can observe their interest and interaction with the mobile. If they are enjoying it, we remember not to interfere. We can read a book or get some rest nearby. If they are crying or upset, we might need to adjust the mobile to see what works. One of Junnifa's children did not like to have the mobile hanging directly above him and would cry whenever he was placed under it. After observing him, she moved the mobile just off to the side, and that made all the difference. He started to enjoy it. If our baby is visibly upset by the mobile, move the mobile away, reposition the mobile, or try another day.

Mobiles and other activities are best offered when the baby is full (not hungry) and alert (not sleepy). In the beginning, they might observe the mobile for a few minutes and then lose interest. This is normal. The time will gradually increase. We've observed babies watching their mobiles intently for more than 15 minutes. Remember the baby is building concentration, so we try not to interrupt or distract. We don't need to constantly talk either. We know they are done when they begin to look away from the mobile, no longer appear relaxed, or cry.

We can rotate three to five visual mobiles over the course of the baby's first few months, perhaps after 2 or 3 weeks or as we observe that the baby starts to get bored or loses interest in a material.

We may notice they no longer interact with the mobile or that the time of concentration consistently reduces, or they might show signs of being upset when put under the mobile. These signs suggest it is time to rotate it out. We can bring back a mobile after a couple weeks and find that the baby is delighted with it again and interacting with it in a different way.

We can also hang up beautiful art or other images on the wall, low enough that the baby can see them. We can stand a book with black-and-white and other high-contrast images within the baby's view during the early weeks.

A tree makes a very special mobile. The moving leaves and branches make the light and shadows dance, and the baby watches, mesmerized. Similarly, holding up our hand with light behind it or making shadows for our baby to focus on can be enriching, too.

"The training and sharpening of the senses has the obvious advantage of enlarging the field of perception and of offering an even more solid foundation for intellectual growth."

—Dr. Maria Montessori, *The Discovery of the Child*

OBSERVE 0 TO 3 MONTHS

- What do their eyes do while taking in the environment, like when they see a familiar face or hear a familiar voice?

- What is their reaction when their body first comes in contact with the bed or mat?

- Notice when they start to turn their head from side to side. Do they prefer looking in one direction? What happens to their hands and legs when they turn?

- Can they lift up their head? Are they on their backs or tummies when they do?

- How do they watch the mobile? Do their eyes track it continuously or do they only watch when it comes back into view? Does this change with time?

- Do they have a preferred component of the mobile? Is it the same every time?

- Apart from the mobile, what else in the environment do they look at?

- How is their hand? Is the palm open or closed most of the time?

- How do their arms and legs move? Often the movement will be of the whole limb, not yet bending at the wrist, elbow, ankle, or knee.

- What do they do when we call their name?

- When they are on their back, what are their hands and legs doing when they turn their head?

From these observations, is there something new we learned about our baby? Is there anything we would like to change as a result? Something in the environment? Another way we can support them? Obstacles we can be removing? Including our own intervention? Observe joy!

3 TO 6 MONTHS

From 0 to 3 months, we provided activities to stimulate our baby's visual and auditory senses. Starting around 3 months, we can offer more activities to develop their grasp and tactile sense.

In the pages that follow, we will begin to distinguish between activities for fine-motor skills and gross-motor skills, even though many materials support the development of both. Myelination (myelin is the substance that coats the axons in the nerves allowing increased motor control) follows two paths. One path starts at the head at birth and moves slowly down to the feet, making gross-motor movements possible. The other path starts at the chest and slowly moves outward toward the fingers. These two processes mean that our baby is usually developing aspects of gross-motor skills and fine-motor skills simultaneously. By the third month, myelination of axons is occurring in the shoulders, upper trunk, arms, and hands. The baby's vision is also better, so we start to see the beginning of voluntary fine-motor skills.

Fine-motor skills

Around the beginning of the third month, we will start observing our baby making a larger range of hand movements. If the baby has mobiles, we will notice their efforts to reach for them. This is a good time to introduce reaching and grasping materials, starting with tactile mobiles.

Grasping materials support the development of the baby's fine-motor skills, specifically reaching and grasping. We know that from birth children grasp involuntarily as a result of the grasping reflex. If we put our finger in a baby's palm, they will close their fingers around it. This is an unconscious action. They become very interested in their hands around the time when their vision becomes clear. If we observe the baby, we will notice when they become almost fascinated with their hands. They will look at them for extended periods of time. Around this time, they also gain control of their upper body and are working on getting better at directing their arms. We will observe that they start to reach for and bat at their visual mobiles. We don't interfere with this exploration of their hands but can then make grasping materials available by exchanging the visual mobile for a tactile one and providing a selection of rattles.

The best tactile materials are simple and beautiful. In choosing, we can:

- Consider the size. The materials should not be too big. Our fingers can be used as a reference for width and length. Some objects might be bigger, but they should have graspable parts that the baby can hold and manipulate. They should also not be small enough to be a choking hazard. A toilet paper roll can be used to check. If an object can go through it, it is probably a choking hazard.

- Consider the material. Our baby will almost definitely bring the grasping materials to their mouth. This is how babies initially explore. Therefore we can make sure we choose materials that are safe for putting in the mouth, e.g., wood, cloth, rubber, and metals such as silver or stainless steel. Offer a variety that gives the baby different feedback. For example, stainless steel feels cool in their hands and mouth, different from how wood or cloth would feel.

- Grasping mobiles or rattles that make a gentle sound like a wood clack or a gentle chime are nice because they provide the baby with feedback for their effort.

Tactile mobiles

Tactile mobiles are designed to be manipulated by babies. Unlike the visual mobiles, which are fragile and made just to be looked at, tactile mobiles can be touched, grasped, and even brought to the baby's mouth. The baby can use a tactile mobile independently. It is hung within our baby's sight and reach, and they can decide to interact with it. It is also good for repetition because our baby can continue batting and reaching and then stop when they want.

Like the visual mobiles, there are specific Montessori tactile mobiles and a suggested sequence. We can also consider the qualities of these mobiles and apply them when choosing or using non-Montessori mobiles. Even a rattle can be hung as a mobile. With the grasping mobiles, the baby will be reaching, grabbing, and pulling, so it is helpful to attach some elastic to one end so that the mobile can stretch when pulled. It should also be hung sturdily so that it does not pull off and fall on the baby.

Bell on a ribbon: Attach a bell about the size of the baby's grasp to a ribbon and add a little bit (about 4 inches) of elastic to the end of the ribbon. We can hang this above the baby. Initially, their flailing arms will bat it unintentionally and it will jingle. This auditory feedback is satisfying and will encourage our baby to repeat the motion with some intent. With practice, they will get more accurate with their reach. The sound from the bell might be one of the first impressions that gives the baby the message that they can affect their environment. We can imagine it—the baby lies there watching the mobile, hands moving, and they hear a ding. They might not initially register that they caused the sound, but then it happens again and again and they realize, "Every time my hand hits the mobile, it makes that sound. I am causing that sound!" It then becomes a conscious effort: "I want to make that sound again. I will move my hand in the same way and the sound continues." We can observe the quiet determination with which our baby works, never giving up. They will continue to try and will one day grasp the bell and bring it to their mouth. This is why the elastic is important. It stretches as the baby pulls. If the mobile is hung near the baby's feet, they can also kick at it.

Ring on a ribbon: This is a wooden or metal ring attached to an attractive ribbon that the baby can grasp and pull toward them. Unlike the bell, which provides the satisfaction of a sound if the baby hits it both voluntarily and involuntarily, the satisfaction of the ring is experienced when the baby pulls it and brings it to their mouth. This is more advanced because it requires the baby to reach and grasp using their palm and fingers and then bring the ring to their mouth.

Remember that our baby has a tendency for self-perfection and wants increasing challenges in line with their development. We can offer materials requiring increasing levels of effort to serve this tendency.

Other grasping materials

Rattles can only be independently enjoyed when the baby's grasp is somewhat developed and they can slither or turn. Before that stage, babies are prone to dropping rattles and cannot pick them back up by themselves.

As the baby's reach and grasp develop, we can provide different rattles and safe objects of different colors, shapes, textures, and weights that call for the hands to be used in different ways.

Rattles can be made of different materials that provide different tactile impressions. For example, metal will feel cooler and smoother than wood. Keep in mind that the baby is going to bring these rings to their mouth, so choose safe materials.

Junnifa offered her children wooden balls, a wooden egg with wool knitted over it, interlocking silver rings, and cylinders made with dowels that can be grasped. Interlocking circles are easy for babies to grasp. Silver interlocking rings fit nicely in their hands, and they enjoy teething on them. A nipple teething ball made of safe plastic is easy to hold and perfect for a baby to use to massage their sore gums, and a variety of rattles provide different ways for them to practice their grasp.

Gross-motor skills

Movement Area: Floor time continues to be the simplest and most important activity to support the development of gross-motor movement at this stage (3 to 6 months). Floor time can take place on the movement mat in the baby's movement area, with a mirror that allows the baby to observe their voluntary and involuntary movements. This time spent in a safe space without any obstacles to movement helps our baby strengthen their muscles and perfect the control needed for movement. It gives them complete freedom and control of their body and allows for involuntary movements. The mirror allows the baby to observe their actions and the resulting movements. Their hands and legs can move as much as they want because they are not restricted. If we are carrying our baby all the time or if they are always restricted in well-intended containers (bouncers, exersaucers, walkers, etc.), they do not get the opportunity to master control of different movements.

There is often a debate within Montessori, RIE, and other gentle-parenting circles about placing the baby on their tummy, i.e., tummy time. There are some people who prefer not to lay the baby on their tummy because the baby can't get into this position on their own. The two of us think that it is important for the baby to spend time on both their backs and tummies, as long as we start from birth and give the baby opportunities to spend time on both sides. We can make tummy time more enjoyable for our baby by using a mirror so the baby can see their reflection, or by laying the baby on our body or lying on the floor next to them. We can also add interest by doing tummy time in front of a mobile. This allows our baby to look at the mobile from a different perspective. Tummy time allows our baby to build the core strength needed for most gross-motor movements and is also recommended by the American Academy of Pediatrics. We can notice when our baby is uncomfortable and make changes or pick them up as necessary.

Kicking activities: We can provide activities that encourage the baby to observe their feet and work toward control of their leg movements. A simple way to do this is to hang a tactile mobile or a kicking ball above our baby's feet. A patchwork ball also works well and can be used later for them to crawl after. Interesting objects like a bell, button, or ribbon can also be sewn to the baby's socks. These will catch the baby's attention, and they will work to bring them to their mouth, thus building their coordination.

Note: Always be careful of choking hazards and use small bells with supervision.

Provide interesting things in the environment for the baby to move toward. We can set up a shelf for the baby with materials that are attractive and developmentally appropriate. It should be within view but at a distance from the movement mat so that the baby has to move to get to the materials. If we put toys in the baby's hand, there is little motivation for them to move. We encourage movement by putting a toy or something that attracts the baby a little distance away from them. We do this even before the baby can move. They will keep observing it and, one day, they will attempt to move toward it and slowly but surely will succeed. Different babies find different techniques for moving. Some will slither, others will roll. Each of these techniques requires effort and perseverance from our baby, and they are the beginning of building characteristics that will serve them through life.

Slow-Rolling Object: When our baby starts slithering, we can provide interesting balls or rattles that roll, but not too fast nor too far. These rolling objects encourage our baby to move and provide them with the satisfaction of achieving a goal, subconsciously teaching them that they are capable of doing things for themselves. They reach and reach and reach and then they grasp! These little successes are deposits in our baby's confidence bank. They are building a basic trust in themselves and their abilities. Junnifa's babies enjoyed a rain stick, which made beautiful sounds as it rolled.

OBSERVE 3 TO 6 MONTHS

- Continue to observe the suggestions from 0 to 3 months.

- Notice their shoulders. Can they lift them? When they do, what is their hand doing?

- How do their arms move? One at a time or both together?

- Watch for when they start turning from tummy to back and back to tummy. Which came first? Which do they do more often?

- Do they turn with intention, or is it spontaneous?

- Pay attention to where we leave them and where we find them. Have they moved? How did they move? In what direction?

- Do we notice any development in their movement? Are they moving faster? Do they use hands when they move? Are knees involved?

- When they move, do they have a destination or goal? Do they reach it? What do they do when they stop?

- Notice their hands when they grasp. What parts of the hands are being used? Fingers? Palm? Thumb?

- What do they do with the object once grasped?

- How is it released?

From these observations, is there something new we learned about our baby? Is there anything we would like to change as a result? Something in the environment? Another way we can support them? Obstacles we can be removing? Including our own intervention? Observe joy!

6 TO 9 MONTHS

At this stage, myelination is occuring in the lower trunk, thighs, and down to the leg. It has also moved to the fingers. Like with other stages, the best way to support this development is by giving our baby time to spend on the floor with freedom to move.

Gross-motor skills

During this stage, our baby will start to slither and will then gradually transition to crawling. They will enjoy a wider space to explore and get more efficient with their movement and cover longer distances. We might leave our baby in one end of the room and find them on the other end. If our baby has been using a floor bed, they might learn how to get off it and find us when they wake up. One of the great joys of parenting is the first time our child wakes up from a nap and doesn't think to cry, and instead climbs off from their floor bed, listens to hear where sounds are coming from, and sets off to find us. Just think of the trust our baby must have in themselves and in their ability!

TIPS

This is a good time to childproof our home by:

- Lifting up curtains so our baby can't pull themselves up on them
- Making sure wires are not exposed
- Securing furniture to the wall so it won't fall on the baby if they try to pull up or lean on it
- Covering electric sockets
- Securing cupboards that we don't want our baby to open

Baby-sized furniture and pull-up bar

We have observed that crawling, pulling up, and sitting often happen in quick succession. Once our baby starts crawling, a few changes can be made to the movement area in preparation for these other movements. If we have placed a mat or rug in their movement area, we might remove it now because it can become an obstacle.

A **child-sized shelf** can be added to the movement area. The baby can pull up on the shelf, lean against it to work, cruise along it, and hold on to it to practice lowering into a sit or kneel. The materials on the shelf also provide motivation for movement.

Solids are usually introduced around this time, and a **child-sized table and chair** can be placed in the space for that purpose. The table can also be an aid for movement. Soon after Junnifa started her baby on solids, she would announce when dinner was ready and her baby would crawl to the table, pull up, and climb into their chair. We could also provide a sturdy stool or small **ottoman** that our baby can pull up on and push around, using it as a support as they get to their chosen destinations. A heavy coffee table is also a good support. We could install a **bar along the mirror**, which they can pull up on and cruise on. We can attach the bar at chest height for our baby and 2 or 3 inches from the wall to allow their hand to wrap around it.

We can give our baby a **basket containing balls** of different shapes, sizes, weights, and textures. They can explore in different ways, and often the balls roll, inviting our baby to turn, crawl, and move in different ways that support the development of coordination. Manipulating the balls also supports fine-motor development.

Usually around this stage the baby can sit with support, and it will be tempting to prop them up in a sitting position. We encourage waiting until the baby can put themselves in a sitting position. When we put the baby sitting upright before they are ready, we can put strain on the baby's bones and muscles and take away their sense of achievement when they manage it themselves. Some babies may like sitting so much that it becomes their preferred position, and this discourages crawling or other important transition positions and movements. Junnifa learned this after her first two children. When her third child came along, she did not sit her up before she could do it on her own, and Junnifa noticed a significant difference. First, her daughter crawled before sitting. Sitting was a natural transition from being on all fours. She could also get both into and out of the sitting position and did not fall back like her older sons had done. They would fall backward and couldn't get back into a sitting position without help. Junnifa also noticed that both her sons slouched or bent a little forward when she put them in a sitting position, but her daughter had, and still has, a straighter sitting posture.

Fine-motor skills

The rattles, balls, and other objects that we present to our baby to encourage gross-motor movements can also support the development of fine-motor skills.

As the baby's hand movements become more precise, they will begin to transfer objects from one hand to the other and use their two hands together. Around 7 months, wrist flexion becomes possible and our baby begins to use their palm and thumb. Often when our baby gets to a material, they might grasp it, move it from one hand to the other, and otherwise explore it using their hands and mouths. They will eventually move to what is sometimes called a monkey grasp, where the thumb is almost side by side with the fingers instead of facing the forefinger when the baby is picking up an object. We continue to offer various objects of different shapes, sizes, weights, and textures for the baby's manipulation. We can offer some rattles and objects with thinner circumferences, like a thin bracelet, to strengthen the use of the thumb.

Once the baby starts sitting, their hands become free to use for exploration. We can start providing more opportunities for exploration, like **treasure or discovery baskets**. These can provide rich sensorial experiences, extended periods of concentration, and entertainment. They are baskets with three to six items for the baby to explore. The baskets can hold random objects, and the baby learns to choose which one to explore. The basket could also contain objects that belong to a category. For example, a wooden spoon, a metal whisk, and a rubber spatula are all items used in a kitchen. They are different shapes and made of different materials that will provide unique sensorial experiences for the baby. Each of the objects and the baby's interactions with them provide opportunities for the baby to use and improve their fine-motor skills.

Here are some examples of category-themed baskets:
- Fabric basket (different fabrics with different textures, e.g., cotton, linen, felt, satin, wool, tulle; ideally, they would be of the same color with the only difference being the texture)
- Kitchen items (wooden spoon, metal spoon, cup, whisk, etc.)
- Bathroom items (hairbrush, toothbrush, comb, washcloth, etc.)
- Color-themed baskets would contain different items of the same color. (The balls from the Gobbi mobile would be great here.) These baskets also support the development of gross-motor skills because they often invite the baby to slither or crawl.

These baskets can be kept in different areas of the house for the baby to use while spending time there. For example, we might have the kitchen-themed basket available for our baby to explore on a blanket or mat in a corner while we cook.

Tip: While they are exploring the treasure basket, we could use it as a language opportunity to name what they are exploring. Not all the time. It's lovely for them to simply concentrate on exploring. But from time to time.

A favorite with babies from this age is the **glitter drum**. It's a wooden rotating barrel that spins when the baby's hand strikes it to make it turn. The balls inside provide a soothing sound as additional feedback, too.

Introducing solids provides a practical opportunity for the baby to work with and develop their fine-motor skills. The baby gets to use child-sized cups and utensils, which they pick up and manipulate using their hands. They can also manipulate the food with their hands using different grasps, depending on the size and their ability. A meal containing sliced carrots and peas, for example, will involve a whole hand grasp as well as a pincer grip. Often the baby will transfer food from hand to hand. While we don't want the baby to view the food as a toy, we can give time and opportunity for the baby to purposefully use their hands while eating.

We can also use a mobile for a sitting baby. Even when the baby has more control of their hands, their coordination can still be limited. While sitting, they will get a different perspective from when they were lying down and trying to catch the mobile by reaching up. Now they are sitting, and they are reaching forward to grasp the mobile. This requires different skills. Trying to catch the balls provides opportunities for hand-eye coordination and refined control of movement. The *takane* (or patchwork) **kicking ball** is a great one to hang for a sitting baby.

During this time, children also get interested in items used in their environment and can be provided with opportunities to explore them. Empty water bottles with screw tops can encourage newly acquired fine-motor skills. Or exploring the baskets or trays that hold their toys, or perhaps a toy with wheels. Being able to move gives the baby freedom to follow their interests. As long as it is safe, we do not interfere with such exploration and instead observe to see what draws our baby's attention and then provide similar opportunities for exploration.

OBSERVE 6 TO 9 MONTHS

- Observe how our baby moves. Watch their chest and stomach and then their knees and feet. Notice how they work together.

- Observe how they manipulate objects. What is each hand doing? What are the fingers doing? What is the thumb doing?

- Observe for intention. Do they decide what they want to reach for on their shelf and then move toward it, or do they get to their shelf and then look around to decide?

- Notice how they react when they struggle with an activity.

- Notice the difference between struggle and frustration.

- Observe how they change direction when slithering or crawling.

- How do they transition from crawling to sitting and vice versa? From standing to sitting and vice versa?

- Observe how they climb onto and off their bed. Do they go forward or backward?

- Observe how they explore objects. Notice when they start to explore less with their mouths and more with their hands and eyes.

- When they pull up and are exploring while standing, where are they putting their weight?

- Notice their preferences. Do they have preferred areas of the home? Preferred objects?

- What is their cycle of activity? How do they start their exploration and what do they do when they are done? Notice gestures.

From these observations, is there something new we learned about our baby?
Is there anything we would like to change as a result? Something in the environment?
Another way we can support them? Obstacles we can be removing? Including our own
intervention? Observe joy!

9 TO 12 MONTHS

Nine months is an important point in the baby's development. It is often considered the end of the external pregnancy. In 9 months, our baby went from a fertilized egg to a fully formed human ready to be birthed. And in another 9 months, they go from helpless uncoordinated newborn to capable (more) coordinated human. By 9 months old, if we have provided the right environment and opportunities, our baby will have acquired a basic trust in their environment and in themselves. The signs of this are observable. We will see signs that they feel capable—capable of movement, communication, and some independence, such as feeding and entertaining themselves. They can make simple choices, communicate beyond crying, set and achieve small goals, and solve simple problems by themselves. Most important, they will begin to build and show their personality.

Gross-motor development

At around 9 months, our baby may begin crawling. After some weeks of pulling up to a stand and cruising along furniture, the baby may attempt to stand without support. It is important to allow this process and not step in too quickly to help. As they learn to sit and stand, children also learn how to fall. Initially they might fall backward and hit the back of their head. Hopefully this happens on their movement mat and there is some cushioning. If we try not to react with too much shock, often they will go back to playing. We have observed that after the second or third time they fall, babies will learn to hold up their heads, and this is a skill that will help them as they grow through toddlerhood and childhood. So we can allow this process when they practice pulling themselves up to stand, cruising along a low surface, and one day find that they are able to stand without support, perhaps as they attempt to work at their shelf.

The activities to support the development of gross-motor movement are the same as in the last stage. **Low furniture** that they can pull up on and cruise along is very important. We could also add a **walker wagon** as the baby gets more efficient with cruising. A walker wagon has a handle they can use to pull up on and then push the wagon around. (It is not a baby walker, where the baby is placed in a "saucer," which puts a lot of pressure on their hips and places them in a position they may not yet be ready for.) We can put the walker wagon within view of the baby once they start cruising along furniture. One day when they are ready, they will crawl to it, pull up, and start to walk with it. For a baby starting to walk, we may need to place some heavy books in the wagon to slow it down until they are steadier on their feet as it moves. Enjoy watching them climb in and out of the wagon part. We have seen children in our classes come to stand in a wagon and balance as if they were surfing. It's amazing how babies challenge their bodies if we allow them to.

A large stable **ball tracker** that the baby can pull up on, drop a ball into, bend down to retrieve, and repeat is another popular activity at this age. The cycle of standing, bending, and repeating provides a lot of muscle- and coordination-building opportunities. The baby also benefits from tracking the ball with their eyes and crossing the mid-line (when their right arm moves across to the left side of their body, or their left arm to their right side).

Babies really enjoy crawling up stairs around this stage. If we have stairs in our house, we might provide opportunities for our baby to crawl up them with supervision. Often they can climb up unassisted but might need extra time to explore or guidance through modeling to figure out how to climb down. Babies in this stage also enjoy climbing equipment that incorporates stairs or a Pikler triangle.

One of the favorite activities in Simone's baby class is a **basket of soft balls** of various sizes and textures. Since the balls are soft, the babies are able to grab them with one hand and roll them, catch them, and, best of all, crawl after them.

Around 12 months, just like they did with standing, our baby will start to let go of their support object while cruising and will attempt to walk unsupported. Allow this process to follow its natural course and one day, the child will be walking! This milestone can be reached around 9 months, and sometimes it's closer to 16 months or even later. Remember that each child is different. Some babies will take a step or two and fall down. Other babies will wait until they are completely steady and able to walk across the room.

One important thing to note is that it takes an enormous amount of neurological effort to walk or to talk. So what we often see is that one of these—either the movement or language acquisition—plateaus as the other takes off.

It is always exciting when we notice the baby is close to acquiring a new skill or reaching a new level of independence. It can be tempting to help or see how to speed up the process, but by doing this, we can interfere with the process and also take away the baby's joy in having achieved something by themselves. So instead we can sit back and observe—our role is to prepare the environment and remove any obstacles. And when they walk, we can say, "You look so pleased. You walked all by yourself!"

If we do want to walk with our baby before they are very stable, we can offer a finger and let them take the lead. If they are not able to, then they are probably not ready. Offering one finger and letting them lead is different from taking both their hands over their head

GROSS-MOTOR DEVELOPMENT

0 TO 3 MONTHS

On the back

Head up

Chest up

3 TO 6 MONTHS

Roll over

Sit

Slither

6 TO 9 MONTHS

Crawl

Pull up

Stand

9 TO 12 MONTHS

Cruise

Walk

WHAT TO DO WHEN OUR BABY FALLS

As the baby builds their coordination and learns to control their body, there will inevitably be many falls. They might fall back while sitting, while standing, or while cruising or climbing. It can be so hard as a parent to watch our little baby fall, and this might lead us to react strongly by shouting, looking terrified, or running toward the baby to quickly pick them up. Often our reaction has a stronger effect on the baby than the actual fall. Babies are close to the ground, so these falls are usually not as terrible as they may look or sound.

So first, what not to do:

Do not follow the baby around to catch them when they fall or prevent them from falling. By not preventing every fall, we allow children to encounter, assess, and solve problems. As they do this, they will learn to discern what they can and cannot do. They will learn the limits of their bodies and how to read their environment. They will develop a positive attitude to risk that they will take with them for the rest of their lives.

Do not shout, look horrified, or run toward the baby when they fall.

Instead, prepare the environment for safety. We could have a large rug in the space where the baby spends most of their time during the first year. This will reduce the impact of falls.

When they do fall, take a deep breath, pause, and try to respond calmly with the most relaxed facial expression we can muster. This allows us to see the baby's authentic reaction to the fall instead of their reaction to our fear or shock. Mirror neurons in our baby's brain can pick up the sense of danger or calmness, safety, and well-being from our expressions and mimic them.

Often, if we pause and react calmly, they will get up and just continue what they were doing. The pause allows this to happen. By reacting in this way, we are helping the baby regulate their emotions and comfort themselves not just physically but emotionally. They will learn to react graciously and calmly to setbacks and will take this with them into adulthood.

If the baby is crying, pick them up and talk to them calmly to console them. If we rush in to save them every time they fall and immediately pick them up, we give them the message that they always need someone to rescue them. We also take away the opportunity for the baby to try again, and this interferes with their cycle of activity. Learning to fall, get up, and move again is an important preparation for life.

A last note: We often heard our parents say, "Don't worry" or "It's okay." If the baby is very upset, instead of brushing away their feelings, we can ask them if it was a shock. This often calms them faster too.

and walking with them. In that case, the adult is mostly taking the baby's weight and putting them into a position they are not yet ready for. This is similar to a ballet dancer who goes into pointe shoes too early and hurts their feet. Be patient. They will walk when their body has developed and is ready.

Fine-motor development

The baby's grasp is becoming more refined. The thumb is working in opposition to the fingers, and the baby begins to be able to voluntarily release and to coordinate eye and hand movements. They are able to retrieve hidden objects, and they are starting to explore cause and effect.

Children at this stage enjoy materials like the **object permanence box**, where they can put objects, perhaps a ball, through a hole and wait for it to roll out. They could also put pegs in holes or straws in bottles. Initially, the holes are big, but they can gradually become smaller as the baby's coordination and fine-motor skills improve. Older babies are able to manipulate a poker chip–sized coin to fit into a narrow slot.

We can continue providing **different kinds (size, texture, material, etc.) of balls, rattles, spoons, and other objects**, which allow the baby to explore the capacities of their hands. At this stage, we can also introduce play dough, tissue paper to tear, squeezable bath toys, and other pliable materials that encourage the use of the thumb. We are building strength in their hands that they will later be using to cut things with scissors and hold a pencil. If the baby is more interested in eating the play dough, then we can say, "Look!" and show them how we flatten it on the table with our hands or squeeze it in our fists. If the baby continues to eat it, we can try again in a few weeks.

We continue to provide activities that allow the baby to **use their hands in different ways**, build their hand-eye coordination, and build cognition and problem-solving skills. As the baby's grip evolves, they will enjoy:

- Activities where an object fits in a precise space; some examples include a wooden egg or peg in a matching cup. Nesting toys also provide this opportunity to put things in a precise space and invite the use of the baby's developing grip and grasps.

- Putting things onto a holder, like threading a ring onto a horizontal or serpentine dowel. This can even be done with bracelets and a mug hanger. We can offer smaller rings as the baby becomes more proficient. A stacker with rings will also be fun for them to explore, first taking off the rings, then putting them back on—we can adjust the number of rings and add more as they become more proficient.

- Some simple one-piece or three-piece knobbed puzzles. Between 9 and 12 months, they will mostly be taking the pieces out, practicing their pincer grip in different ways (as well as exploring with their mouth). We can put the pieces back in for them to pull out again.

- Rings on three colored pegs. This activity allows the baby to thread and adds the opportunity to begin sorting by color.

- Drawers to open. As our babies become more stable on their feet, they will enjoy opening drawers and emptying them. This supports both gross- and fine-motor skills. We could choose a drawer in our home that is at our baby's level and put in a few items that we don't mind being dumped out. There are also commercially available materials that allow the baby to drop an object in the hole and pull out the drawer to take out the object. This activity provides an opportunity for our baby's hands to work together, each doing different things, for example, pulling open a drawer with one hand and retrieving an object with the other hand.

The **introduction of solids** will also be an opportunity for our baby to develop their fine-motor skills. In chapter 7 (see page 173), we'll provide more information about this, including introducing a fork and a glass.

Remember that it is through repetition that the baby masters and perfects movement.

OBSERVE 9 TO 12 MONTHS

- What is our baby's preferred way of moving around? Do they prefer cruising or crawling? Do they switch modes when they want to move faster?

- When they stand, how are their feet? Do they stand on tiptoes or flat-footed? Are their feet facing forward or facing outward? Notice when this changes.

- Do they move differently when wearing socks versus being barefoot? When their knees are exposed versus not?

- How do they react when they fall?

- Do they squat, and how?

- When they are trying to balance with their hands free, how high are their arms and how far apart are their feet?

- How has the use of their hands changed? When picking up an object, what is their thumb doing?

- Are they crossing the midline?

- Is their wrist moving?

- Do they drop to the floor from standing or do they lower themselves carefully?

- Do they crawl, cruise, or walk while holding objects? Are they holding objects with one hand or two?

- How do they, hold thin objects?

From these observations, is there something new we learned about our baby? Is there anything we would like to change as a result? Something in the environment? Another way we can support them? Obstacles we can be removing? Including our own intervention? Observe joy!

PART FOUR

OTHER ACTIVITIES

MUSIC

Music can support our baby's development of language and fine- and gross-motor skills.

When listening to music, our baby hears rhythm, which is important for understanding spoken language. Often we can observe our babies responding to the rhythm of music by moving their heads, hands, or feet. We can also hold them and move with them to the music. In these ways, music provides a sensorimotor experience even before the baby is mobile.

We can offer it as an independent activity for our baby to choose. When Junnifa's babies were around 8 or 9 months old, she placed a sticker on the play button of a small CD player that she had placed at their level, and they could crawl over to it and press play, pull up, and move with the music. This supports the development of coordination. When they were tired, they could just press the same button to pause. There are also CD players that are operated by pulling a string that would be ideal for a baby.

Instruments to explore: Babies will enjoy maracas or other shakers as activities for developing their grasp. Junnifa's babies enjoyed drumming on a tom-tom once they could sit and kneel, and blowing into a harmonica. These instruments can be used by themselves or as an accompaniment to music being listened to. When Simone's son was around 9 months old, she put on some music to listen to with him. He immediately crawled off to the other room with some determination. He came back with two maracas and, indeed, they usually played along to the music while shaking the maracas.

We would gently caution against having music playing nonstop. Not only is it extra stimuli for the baby to take in, but babies adapt to their conditions and might begin to view it as background noise and block it out instead of enjoying it.

THE OUTDOORS

From as early as the first month, the outdoors provides activities that support the baby's development of both movement and language, in addition to giving the baby fresh air and other health benefits.

Trees, leaves, and flowers are nature's own mobiles. We can lay the baby in a *cestina* (a Montessori Moses basket) under a tree in the early weeks. They can watch the leaves, insects, and birds.

They can be placed either on their back or tummy on a blanket in the grass. If possible, make sure the grass is safe and has not been sprayed with pesticides.

When the baby starts to reach and grasp, they might enjoy trying to grab leaves, blades of grass, twigs, rocks, etc. Nature provides many natural grasping materials.

Grass provides a great cushion for a baby that is learning to stand or walk and who will fall many times. It also provides a different experience from walking on tiles, wood, rugs, or other indoor flooring.

As the baby practices walking, it is helpful for them to experience movement on different surfaces and textures—paved, rocky and uneven, smooth, etc. The outdoors offers variety to our baby. We can bring their walker wagon outside or to the market for them to practice pushing it along as they walk on different surfaces.

There is also rich vocabulary outside to give the baby—names of trees, birds, dogs, vehicles, shops, items at the market, etc.

TO PRACTICE

- Can we have conversations with our baby?
- Can we observe to find the ideal times for our baby to spend time in their movement area and build it into their routine? Can we make time to observe them daily to see what our baby is working on?
- Can we provide activities that support them?
- Can we check and remove obstacles like restrictive clothing and unsafe objects?
- Can we trust in our baby's abilities and allow them freedom to move, explore, and discover?

MOVEMENT IN THE FIRST YEAR

- Prepare movement area where the baby can spend time—make it a "yes" space.
- Enlarge this space when the baby starts to slither, creep, and crawl.
- Provide opportunity and freedom to move.
- Remove obstacles to movement, like swaddles or props.
- Do not put the baby in containers (like playpens, and limit time in car seats, etc.).
- Dress the baby appropriately to allow for comfortable movement.
- Observe the baby and provide activities that support the development of movement.
- Provide appropriate simple toys that the baby can interact with.
- Do not interrupt or interfere with the baby's activity.
- Don't hurry or encourage any kind of movement before the baby comes to it on their own.
- Ensure the space is safe and childproof.
- Allow the baby time.

NEWBORN

- Gross-Motor Skills
  - Arms and legs are bent and usually symmetrical
  - Moro, fencing, walking reflexes
- Fine-Motor Skills
  - Grasping reflex
  - Hand is usually fisted

MONTH 2

- Gross-Motor Skills
  - Starts to gain head control: can turn neck left or right
  - Eyes start to follow dangling objects
  - Can tilt head back to look at something above
  - Holds head up when on tummy
- Fine-Motor Skills
  - Hand starts to open loosely when lying down
  - Grasp reflex still present
  - Can bring hands to midline
  - Reaching still largely ineffective

MONTH 3

- Gross-Motor Skills
  - Holds head and upper chest up when lying on tummy and also when tilted up on back
- Fine-Motor Skills
  - Hand starts to open loosely when lying down
  - Grasp reflex starts to disappear
  - Can bring hands to midline
  - Observes hands

MONTH 4

- Gross-Motor Skills
  - Holds head and upper chest up when lying on tummy and also when tilted up on back
  - Rolls from back to tummy
  - Slithers slowly
- Fine-Motor Skills
  - Efficient reaching
  - Palmar (squeeze) grasp with no thumb participation

MONTH 5

- Gross-Motor Skills
  - Rolls from tummy to back
  - Slithers slowly
  - Stepping reflex
    (when baby is held upright)
    disappears
- Fine-Motor Skills
  - Efficient reaching
  - Raking grasp fingers only

MONTH 6

- Gross-Motor Skills
  - Uses hands to slither faster
  - Begins to bear weight on feet
  - Can sit with support
- Fine-Motor Skills
  - Efficient reaching
  - Precise pincer with no thumb
    participation
  - Eyes and hands start to work together

MONTH 7

- Gross-Motor Skills
  - Begins to crawl
  - Pulls up to a stand while holding
    on to something
  - Begins to bend
- Fine-Motor Skills
  - Whole-hand grasp
  - Can transfer objects from one hand
    to the other
  - Can wave

MONTH 8

- Gross-Motor Skills
  - Cruising
  - Stepping reflex disappears
  - Begins to bear weight on feet
- Fine-Motor Skills
  - Monkey grasp with thumb and next
    two fingers but not yet opposite
    fingers

MONTH 9

- Gross-Motor Skills
  - Standing against a shelf
  - Stepping reflex is gone
  - Bears weight on feet
- Fine-Motor Skills
  - Inferior pincer—grasps with thumb
    and index finger
  - Points with index finger
  - Begins voluntary release

MONTH 10

- Gross-Motor Skills
  - Pulls up to a stand
    (maybe without support)
- Fine-Motor Skills
  - Precise pincer using tips of thumb and
    index finger
  - Throwing

MONTH 11

- Gross-Motor Skills
  - Takes uneven steps
- Fine-Motor Skills
  - Precise pincer
  - Throwing

MONTH 12

- Gross-Motor Skills
  - Walking
- Fine-Motor Skills
  - Smooth release for large objects

MOVEMENT ACTIVITIES

0 TO 3 MONTHS

Munari mobile

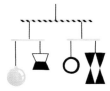

Octahedron mobile

Gobbi mobile

Rattle

Interlocking rings

Mirror

3 TO 6 MONTHS

Ring on ribbon/
Bell on ribbon

Ball with protrusions

Patchwork ball

Balls

Pop-up toy

Wooden book

6 TO 9 MONTHS

Glitter drum

Object permanence box

Wooden egg and cup

Basket of balls

Knobbed puzzle

Drawers

9 TO 12 MONTHS

Push balls with hands

Object permanence
box with drawer

Imbucare peg box

Walker wagon

Stacker

Cubes on dowel

PUTTING IT
INTO PRACTICE

7

DAILY LIFE

DAILY RHYTHM

Babies do not always show a daily regular rhythm, and it can be difficult to read their cues. Are they hungry again? Are they tired? If they didn't sleep well, should we try to get them to sleep again? It can get so confusing.

To avoid the confusion, remember that a usual cycle goes **wake, feed, play, sleep**. Using observation we can notice our baby's unique rhythm through this cycle and start to detect signs that our baby is transitioning from one part of the cycle to the next. We fall into a natural rhythm with our baby.

We can pay attention to signs that the baby is ready to feed (for example, opening their mouth or making certain faces or giving a warning cry); signs they are ready to play (for example, being alert, having burped, and becoming active); or signs they are ready to sleep (maybe starting to look away from an activity, touching their ears, getting restless, making jerky movements, or rubbing eyes).

It can be difficult to tell the differences between cries. If our baby starts becoming unsettled and we know they have already had a good feed and some awake time to play, then we can start to help them transition to sleep. Simone's son got into a crazy cycle of falling asleep while feeding, then waking soon after. He'd be crying, so Simone would end up feeding him again. It was all guesswork, and he wasn't super settled when he was awake. Simone learned from her mistakes and did things differently with her second child. Simone chose not to feed her daughter to sleep. Instead, her daughter would feed upon waking, then play a little, and then she was ready to go to sleep again. Simone observed to determine if she needed any help to fall asleep, for example, sitting next to her, a hand on her, or to pop in and check on her if she was happily chatting to herself.

- A newborn baby will wake from sleeping, feed upon waking, have some short cuddle time or stretch on a mat and diaper change (play), and be ready to sleep again.

- As they get a little older, they'll wake, then feed, have a little longer time to play and cuddle, before, again, a diaper change and sleep time.

- After a few months, we may find our baby wakes without desperately crying of hunger—they will then be able to play a little first, then back to the usual rhythm of wake, feed, play (plus a diaper change), and sleep.

While this is the general rhythm, through observation we can find our baby's specific rhythm and begin to predict and follow it. This is not a schedule—it is simply following our baby's rhythm to aid their orientation and sense of order.

Once we understand their rhythm, we can respect it as much as possible, for example, arranging to meet a friend after the baby wakes or planning for the baby to sleep in the car or stroller or carrier while we drop an older sibling off at school.

Things like growth spurts, teething, travel, and changes in the home or larger environment can affect the baby's rhythm. So we keep observing and make small adjustments if necessary. We don't need to make big changes at once—small modifications help the baby make such transitions more smoothly.

In our daily rhythm, we can also help our baby recognize transition times by having cues like a song, or saying the same thing every time, or having a regular process, for example, bath before bed or wiping their hands before meals. Again, they predict and come to know what to expect.

Similarly, if there is some predictability in the week—a weekly rhythm—this makes it easier for the baby to begin to follow what comes next, for example, with outings, bath times, time with sitters, etc. For those of us working, our baby will learn the rhythm of our week—when we are together as a family and when they are with other family members or a caregiver. As much as possible, we can coordinate with others so that their daily rhythm can be similar in all environments for some consistency for our baby. By the time they are a young toddler, this predictability becomes enormously important as they begin to develop a very strong sense of order and begin to know what comes next in the flow of their daily and weekly rhythms. There is an abundance of research to show that children who grow up in homes with regular routines and rituals are healthier and happier. For more information, we recommend reading *Montessori: The Science Behind the Genius* by Angeline Stoll Lillard.

RITUALS

It's never too early to introduce rituals for special moments throughout the year, or even the week. These rituals can include special elements that are unique to our family or culture.

- birthdays, holiday seasons—making crafts, preparing food, and going on special outings
- annual vacations
- regular weekly rituals such as going to the park on Friday afternoons or making a special Sunday morning breakfast

Our baby will absorb these rituals and, as they get older, look forward to celebrating them with us. It is an opportunity to create family rituals of our very own, for instance, incorporating different cultures into our family.

When there are older children in the family, the baby will enjoy being included in rituals that have already been established and they are sure, with time, to make their own contributions to these rituals too.

EATING

In the first year of the baby's life, the baby will move from being 100 percent reliant on the adult for feeding to taking over more and more steps for themselves. It's the process of moving from dependence, to collaboration, to the beginning of independence.

A baby of around 1 year old who can choose something from their plate, bring it to their mouth, chew and swallow it, and repeat, is a young child in control of their own food intake—they have learned to listen to signs from their body that tell them they are hungry or full and have acquired the physical coordination to feed themselves (albeit not with 100% accuracy). In addition to the independence, they are developing a healthy relationship with food.

Breastfeeding and bottle-feeding

Traditionally, the Montessori approach recommends breastfeeding when possible and that the mother be the primary one to offer milk to the baby, especially in the early weeks. But these days, we also welcome having the primary caregivers offer milk to the baby. This is to help the baby associate their primary caregivers with feeding. In day care, it's ideal to have the same caregiver feed the baby. However, once a baby is introduced to a bottle, feeding can be shared with a partner. Involving both parents in the feeding of the baby provides additional opportunities for bonding.

The production of colostrum in the first days after birth and breast milk thereafter is human biology at its finest: being able to produce the perfect food for the baby, which is (nearly always) available when the baby is hungry, is portable even when we are out of the home, and does not require any extra labor in the kitchen. Breast milk contains all the nutrition our baby needs, including important antibodies passed from mother to baby to help fight against any incoming illnesses.

There are also benefits for the mother: Breastfeeding helps shrink the uterus; studies show that it can lower the risk of breast and ovarian cancers, type 2 diabetes, and postpartum depression; and when there is a feeling of loss or emptiness after carrying the baby in the uterus, holding the baby for extended periods while breastfeeding can help.

Breastfeeding is considered more than simply food; it establishes a very important connection between mother and baby.

> "An infant suckling at his or her mother's breast is not simply receiving a meal, but is intensely engaged in a dynamic, bidirectional, biological dialogue. It is a process in which physical, biochemical, hormonal, and psychosocial exchange takes place."
>
> —Diane Wiessinger, Diana West, and Therea Pitman,
> *The Womanly Art of Breastfeeding*

When we nurse, we can use a relaxed position (reclined and nested in cushions for support). We can have full contact along the baby's belly and legs and some contact on their feet. This position allows the baby to lie with very little support and triggers their latching reflexes. Rather than bringing the nipple to the baby, we first adjust ourselves, then the baby, and then the breast if needed. For more information, look up "natural breastfeeding positions."

Some women may choose not to breastfeed. And for others, breastfeeding may not come easily. There can be problems with a baby latching on; or a tongue tie (when the tongue is held down in the floor of the mouth by a membrane) can make it difficult for the baby to attach; or the mother's milk production may be affected by her hormonal levels or she may have fewer breast ducts in the breast tissue. Early intervention by a specialist can be effective in many of these situations.

Mothers who work outside the home are often able to successfully continue to breastfeed by pumping milk while they are away from the baby. This puts an extra demand on the parent, but it allows all the benefits of breast milk to be passed on to the baby and to maintain breastfeeding when together.

Sometimes breastfeeding doesn't work out. If that happens, we may feel grief that we weren't able to offer our baby breast milk as we had hoped, that our bodies failed us, or that we let our baby down in some way. We can allow these feelings, perhaps find someone to help us process them, and do what we need to do for our baby to thrive. Regardless if we breastfeed or not, we can provide the care, connection, and nutrition for our baby by holding our baby while they feed, gazing into their eyes.

There are organizations that can match us to people with excess milk and supply breast milk for our baby. And there are now lots of formula products available that are as close as possible to breast milk. Whether we feed with breast or bottle, we can remember that holding our baby, looking into their eyes, and having a communication during feeding meets the needs of the baby and parent.

Tips for breastfeeding or bottle-feeding

- Make eye contact with the baby (rather than reading, talking on the phone, or watching a screen)—it is a built-in time for connection and rest with our baby.

- Observe our baby to learn about them in every way—what movements do they make with their hands, their head, their feet? What sounds do they make? What are they looking at? How do they respond to noises around them?

- Sit in a comfortable position with good posture because we will be sitting in this position for many hours in the first months after birth—keep shoulders relaxed and not hunched forward, and use extra pillows for support if needed, at least initially. Or use the reclining method as described on page 167.

- In the days just after birth, the baby may fall asleep while feeding and we can allow this. After these first days have passed, a slightly cool cloth can be used to help them stay awake until the feeding is finished. If they fall asleep while feeding, they will likely wake up again soon after, wanting to finish their feed, and it can feel like the baby is constantly feeding (affectionately referred to as "snacking").

How can we tell if the baby is hungry?

We will learn to observe the signs our baby makes if they are hungry. These could include:
- mouth gaping
- whimpering or squeaking
- body and mouth tensing
- breathing becoming faster
- starting to cry

How often will the baby feed?

A newborn feeds for around 30 to 40 minutes, 8 to 12 times a day. The baby will eventually become more efficient at feeding, so feeding times will become shorter.

After feeding, we can burp them, change their diaper, and give them cuddles and time to kick on the floor. Soon after, they will show signs of feeling tired, and it will be time to start a short sleep-time routine.

During the night, this rhythm will be simplified to feeding, burping, changing their diaper if needed, and then going right back to sleep. Keep the light dim or use a night-light. Note that night waking is quite normal in the first year—though not always to feed.

When we feed a newborn on demand, over time they will gradually establish their own rhythm with a few hours between feeds. They will go from dependence, to collaboration, to increasing independence. Not every cry means that they are hungry. They may be cold or experiencing some other discomfort so we can see if there is something else they may want before offering them the breast or bottle.

Burping

Burping helps to get rid of some of the air that babies tend to swallow during feeding. Burping the baby can be done over our shoulder, holding the back of their head and rubbing or patting gently on their back. Some babies burp more easily seated on our lap in a (very gentle) sandwich-type hold—one of our arms is placed vertically along their stomach with their chin resting on our hand, and our other arm running vertically along their back with their head resting on the hand.

Burping does not need to be rushed. We can use this moment to connect with our baby.

Some common problems while breastfeeding

Allergies. Allergic reactions often appear as diarrhea, sore bottoms, runny noses and eyes, rashes and eczema, or a crying, sleepless baby. Some babies have an intolerance to cow's milk protein and will present colic-like symptoms, wheezing, vomiting, diarrhea, constipation, a rash, eczema, or a stuffy nose. If breastfeeding, we can remove suspected sources of allergies from our diet to see if it helps—though keep in mind that it can take up to 21 days for all traces to leave our system. If bottle-feeding, we could try a different formula.

Biting during nursing. We do not have to stop if our baby bites us while nursing—though it might come as a shock! We can remove the baby from our breast by inserting a clean finger (usually the pinky) between the breast and baby's mouth to release the suction and their jaw. We can give a clear message that it hurts: "Ow. I'm taking you off the breast. Biting hurts me." When we continue to give this kind and clear message that biting hurts and we remove them, our baby learns not to bite us.

Nipple confusion. If we are hoping to exclusively breastfeed our baby, it is generally recommended to wait until the end of the first month to offer bottle-feeding to avoid nipple confusion (when the baby has difficulty switching between the breast and the bottle as they require different ways of sucking).

Introducing solid food: The Montessori approach

Around 6 months of age (and sometimes earlier), our baby will start to show increasing interest in solid food, watching intently as we eat or tracking the food from our plate to our mouth. At this age our baby's prenatal iron supply is depleting, they can usually sit (maybe with a little support), some teeth may be coming through, they can support their own head weight, and they start producing ptyalin (an enzyme that breaks down complex carbohydrates). These are signs our baby is getting ready to start eating some solid food. The current recommendation is to wait until our baby is 6 months old and showing signs of readiness before offering any solid food.

Introducing solids is an important milestone:

- Our baby is starting to see themselves as separate from their parent, and learns that food can come from another source.
- Early food experiences are explorations for the baby. Food from ages 6 months to 1 year is less about the intake of nutrition than the experience of food. We can remember this if we start to worry about how much (or how little) they are eating.
- We are helping them experience food in its natural form and learn more about it. For example, we can show them the fruit we are going to give them and let them feel its texture, smell it. Then they see it being prepared, and they get to taste it.
- They learn skills to feed themselves, and as young toddlers they will be involved in preparing food too.
- We expand their vocabulary around food—the food, the utensils, the actions we are doing.

> "Sitting at a table brings about a change in the child's ego and the start of a new human relationship that will recur throughout life. . . . He begins his separation with food which becomes the external agent of a much more important internal process; the building of a personal identity. The different food and the different way of receiving it is strictly correlated to detachment, independence and development of the ego."
>
> —Dr. Silvana Montanaro, *Understanding the Human Being*

We don't need to wean our baby onto bland baby food or rice cereal, or plain pureed vegetables or fruit. For our baby's first solid food, we can offer them a meal that includes all food types and is food that we would want to eat ourselves (rice with vegetables, a little cheese, some oil and seasoning).

Instead of spoon-feeding the baby, where they open their mouth to our rhythm, we can look for ways they can feed themselves at their own pace. It will be messy and it won't be quick, so we may need to prepare ourselves—but it encourages the baby to manage as independently as possible and follow their own rhythm.

Baby-led weaning aligns well with the Montessori approach to introducing solids. The food that is offered is cut into large pieces that a chubby-fisted 6-month-old can hold, bring to their mouth, and taste. Vegetables do not have to be pureed, but instead cooked until soft so that they fall apart in the baby's mouth. And small amounts are placed in front of the baby for them to pick up, bring to their mouth, and taste. This method is also great for refining their fine-motor skills.

Solid foods that are popular with young babies include:
- well-cooked sticks of carrot, broccoli, or other vegetable around 4 inches in length
- strips of toasted bread
- soft fruits first, building up to pieces of harder fruits that they can hold in their hand and nibble off small pieces
- whatever the family is eating, in a form they can manage themselves

CHOKING SAFETY

Babies have a gag reflex at this age. This is not a sign they are choking; this is a perfect reflex by the body to remove something going the wrong way. Choking signs to watch for are loss of color in face and the absence of sounds. If that happens, we can place the baby stomach-down along our arm horizontally with their chin in our hand. Strike between the shoulder blades with the heel of the opposite hand, and see if anything comes out. Repeat four more times. If the food has not dislodged, sandwich-hold the baby between our forearms (their chin and neck supported gently by our hands) to turn them onto their back for five breast compressions. Take a first aid course to practice this and learn of any updates to these protocols.

Where to eat

In Montessori we want to give our baby a sense of independence. So rather than using a high chair, we introduce a low table and chair called a *weaning table and chair*. The child can sit by themselves and get out of the chair when they are done, be an active participant in feeding, and feel more capable.

We can use this from the time the baby is able to sit steadily (around 6 to 8 months). The height of the table and chair allows them to reach their feet to the floor for stability. We can set the table with a small vase of flowers and can use a placemat for their meals to show where the bowl and cutlery goes. Sometimes the baby throws the placemat to the floor, so it's something we can keep introducing until they become less interested in removing it. This table can be used for all the baby's meals or only for snacks.

Our baby can join us at the family table in a tray-less high chair. This allows us to eat together rather than feed the baby separately. Our baby is learning that mealtimes are social occasions, and they can feel less pressure to eat when we aren't solely focused on them or rushing them to finish eating. Instead, they are learning cues from their own bodies about when they are hungry and when they are full, and they are taking part in the family meal.

Tools for eating

Rather controversially, in Montessori we like to use real plates, glasses, and metal cutlery rather than plastic ones. Not only are these choices more sustainable and made from more natural materials, but the food and drink generally taste better, and the baby can learn the logical consequence that plates and glasses will break if they fall. There are bowls and glasses that don't break too easily (for example, bamboo or enamel), that we can use when they are busy experimenting with letting things fall to the ground.

We can start first with a fork, which is easiest for the baby to coordinate. There are lovely videos online of babies feeding themselves with a fork from around 8 months. The parent spears one piece of food onto the fork and lays the fork on the plate in front of the baby with the handle pointing toward the baby. The baby chooses which hand to use to pick up the fork and brings the food to their mouth. Then the parent fills the fork again and waits until the baby is ready to continue.

It takes our baby more coordination to keep food on their spoon, so we can offer thicker foods to master at first, like oatmeal or thick yogurt.

As young babies are still refining their fine- and gross-motor coordination, we are available to assist them when needed, for example, offering a gentle hand to support the glass to their mouth and then giving less and less support as they develop, and only filling their glass with a small amount of water.

We don't need to use bottles or sippy cups for water. It might take a few days of wet clothes, but babies learn quickly. If we would like to use a water bottle for outside of the home, we can look for bottles with straws as the teats on sippy cups keep the tongue in the sucking part of the mouth.

With any of these tools, look for metal cutlery that is baby-sized, small enough to fit in their hand with a shorter handle. In Simone's classes, she uses cake forks with prongs that are not too sharp and small teaspoons. She uses the smallest Duralex glasses (which hold 3 oz/90 mL) or shot glasses as baby's first drinking cup. Small bowls with low sides make it easier for the babies to serve themselves and get the food out by themselves. Size does matter. In this case, often the smaller the better.

Learning to handle a fork and glass are the first practical life activities we introduce to our baby. Practical life activities are also known as activities in daily life. As a toddler and preschooler, these daily activities will include preparing, serving and cleaning up after meals as well as sweeping, cleaning windows, and taking care of plants and of themselves.

We can also offer them a cloth to wipe their hands and mouth before, during, and after meals. These are the first self-care activities they learn. A small mirror by their snack table can be useful for this.

It's not a perfect process, and we will have to clean up, but practice makes perfect. And we can involve them in the cleanup—an 8-month-old can wipe the table, albeit imperfectly. And when they are done, they can place their cutlery into a small basket that is sitting on their table.

More tips

1. **The adult is in charge of what their baby eats, where they eat, and eventually when they eat. How much they eat is up to the child.** Trust that they are learning to listen to their bodies. We do not have to force in one more spoon, pretend an airplane full of food is flying in their mouth, or distract them with a screen.

2. **In Montessori, breastfeeding and food aren't usually used to help calm a child or help the child fall asleep.** We are available to offer comfort to our child in other ways—cuddling, listening, wiping away tears, and with understanding.

3. **Role of the father or partner.** The father or partner can be involved in feeding from time to time as a way for them to feel involved and bond with baby. If breastfeeding, the mother can pump milk for their partner to offer in a bottle.

4. **Some adoptive mothers and non-gestational mothers can breastfeed their baby.** It is possible to begin lactating even if we have never been pregnant. Supplemental nursing systems are also available, which can be used to induce lactation. Even if no milk production is possible, holding the baby while feeding will help attachment and bonding with the adopted parents.

5. **If they throw food.** If a baby throws food, they are generally all done. When they are hungry, they sit to eat and may take in all they will eat in 5 to 10 minutes. If they then start to throw food, we can ask them, "Are you all done?" Then we can show them how we take the plate to the kitchen and offer to help them get down from the table. They will soon learn that food is for eating.

TO OBSERVE

Observe our baby to learn about them in every way while feeding and eating:

- What movements do they make with their hands, their head, their feet?
- What sounds do they make?
- What are they looking at?
- How do they respond to noises around them?
- When do they feed/eat? How long do they feed/eat for?
- Are they a passive or active eater?
- If nursing, how do they detach?
- How is food presented? What are they eating?
- How is self-feeding encouraged?
- How do we feel about the baby's feeding attempts? Are we bringing any fears to feeding/eating?

From these observations, is there something new we learned about our baby? Is there anything we would like to change as a result? Something in the environment? Another way we can support them? Obstacles we can be removing? Including our own intervention? Observe joy!

Weaning baby from the breast

Deciding when to stop nursing is a very personal decision.

Exclusive breastfeeding has been recommended by the WHO for the first 6 months of the baby's life (this means without giving extra water or solid food) and then with complementary feeding (giving nutrition from food in addition to breastfeeding) from 6 months to 24 months and beyond.

Some Montessori sources, like Dr. Montanaro's *Understanding the Human Being*, suggest weaning around 10 months, when the baby starts to have increasing independence and is beginning to separate more from the parents as they begin crawling and soon walking.

For others, there may be personal reasons for wanting to stop breastfeeding in the first year. If we are no longer enjoying it and beginning to resent it, stopping might be a better decision than continuing longer than we are comfortable with, as our attitudes will also be absorbed by the baby.

Whenever we choose to wean from breastfeeding, we can tell our baby that we will wean in a couple of weeks. That it has been a special time. And that we will enjoy the last weeks feeding together in this way. This gives closure to us and to the baby in a positive way, and acknowledges the special feeding relationship we enjoyed together.

BOOK RECOMMENDATIONS

For more information on breastfeeding, we recommend La Leche League International's *The Womanly Art of Breastfeeding* and *Breastfeeding Made Simple: Seven Natural Laws for Nursing Mothers* by Nancy Mohrbacher.

SLEEPING

The most common questions Simone receives in her parent–baby classes are about sleep: learning to settle the baby in a Montessori way, night waking, using a floor bed, and (mostly) how everyone can get more sleep.

The only problem is, what works for one baby doesn't work for another. Or for every family.

And what exhausted parent wants to even read the words "consistency," "sleep routine," or "make sure the room is dark," one more time?

So how can we give some practical advice on sleep that aligns with the Montessori approach and will be helpful to tired parents?

The best we can really offer is to go back to the principle of **observation**, which has guided us through every step of raising and working with newborns, babies, toddlers, and children.

Every child is unique. Let's look to our baby and observe like a scientist—how many minutes they took to fall asleep, what they ate, how and why they woke up, and more. Then, armed with information about our child, we can help them have a good relationship with sleep and make small adjustments when needed.

The Montessori principles that follow can work whether we have our baby in our bedroom, in their own room, or choose to co-sleep.

Remember that we are our child's guide. We cannot make them close their eyes and fall asleep. But we can nurture beautiful infant sleep by observing, responding, and preparing a safe and comfortable sleeping environment.

"A great deal of mental work goes on during sleeping and dreaming. All daily experiences must be integrated and all personal 'programs' must be reviewed on the basis of the new information received during the day."

—Dr. Silvana Montanaro, *The Joyful Child* by Susan Stephenson

We can apply the following Montessori principles to sleep.

1. Observe our baby and learn their sleep/wake rhythms

A baby has their own sleep rhythms. We can meet their needs for sleep by observing them to learn:

- when they show us they are ready to sleep (tired signs)
- how much (or little) help they need to fall asleep
- their activity during sleep (yes, they are active even while they sleep)
- how long they sleep for, and
- how they wake up

Because it can be difficult to always differentiate among the baby's cries, remember the rhythm—new babies wake, feed, play, then sleep. After a good feed, they enjoy some playtime—on a movement mat, perhaps watching a mobile, having some cuddles—with enough stimulation (but not too much). And then, by observing the baby, we will see their tired signs. These may be:

- jerky movements in their arms and legs
- rubbing their eyes or yawning
- other signs unique to our baby (we are always observing to learn our baby's signs)

When we see these tired signs, we can begin a slow sleep-time routine. A simple, short routine for each sleep time may include:

- telling the baby that we see they are getting tired and that we are going to bring them to bed
- waiting until they respond, for example, by raising their head
- using gentle hands to pick them up, change their diaper, and carry them to their bed
- singing to them, reading a short book, or doing another connecting activity
- laying them down on their back while they are awake, so they can sleep in their consistent sleeping place
- providing calm reassurance that we are there if they need us

Enjoy this process of observing them. It is much more relaxing to observe and assist them than to feel like we have to "put them to sleep." Remember, we are their guides. They generally know when they are tired; it is up to us to read their cues. Then they are the ones who will close their eyes and fall into sleep, with us as their guides to support them if needed.

Tip: Young infants will still be adjusting their circadian rhythms, so lots of sunlight and fresh air during the day help them begin to adjust to day and night over the first months.

TO OBSERVE

It can be helpful and even fascinating to make and review observation notes in a dedicated notebook like a scientist. We can note the following:

When they are getting tired:

- What signs do they have that show they are tired?
- Have their wake windows gotten longer?

While falling asleep:

- What are the movements they make with their arms and legs?
- Are their hands in fists or open?
- Do they make any cries or sounds?
- What are their facial expressions?
- Do they continue to move right up until the moment they fall asleep? Or do they fall asleep gradually?
- How much help do they need to fall asleep? Are they ready to move to the next stage, going from dependence, to collaboration, to increasing independence?

During sleep:

- What is the quality of their sleep— fitful, peaceful, etc.?
- How is their body positioned?

- Do they make any movements with their limbs or head?
- Can they resettle themselves from light sleep back to deep sleep? If not, why do they wake up? Are they looking for us to reestablish a condition from when they fell asleep?

Upon waking:

- How long does it take them to wake up?
- What is their temperament on waking?
- How do they communicate to let us know they are awake?
- What is their body position?

Wake/sleep patterns:

- How long are they awake between naps? How long are their naps?
- Is there a pattern developing? (how long they can stay awake or if they have a regular bedtime.)
- Are they affected by light entering the bedroom?

From these observations, is there something new we learned about our baby? Is there anything we would like to change as a result? Something in the environment? Another way we can support them? Obstacles we can be removing? Including our own intervention? Observe joy!

2. Give as much help as necessary, and as little as possible

When a child is learning to crawl or walk, we can set up a supportive environment and offer help when it is needed—as much help as necessary and as little as possible. Then we let our baby master these skills.

Similarly with sleep, we set up a safe environment and support them, giving just as much help as is needed and as little as possible. This might be sitting with them until they fall asleep, placing a hand on their belly, rubbing their back, or offering a soothing sound.

They may fuss a little as they transition to sleep—this is normal, and we can be there to perhaps place a hand on them and provide a few comforting words. If they have not settled after some time (say around 20 minutes), we can offer them a bit more milk or, if they are an older baby who is thirsty but not hungry, some water.

Sometimes the baby will not settle at all—we can still give them "rest time" by placing them in a baby carrier or taking them for a walk.

3. Move from dependence, to collaboration, to increasing independence

As we have mentioned more than once in this book, in the first year, the baby will move from dependence, to collaboration, to increasing independence. This also applies to sleeping.

In the early days, our baby depends on us noticing when they are tired, giving them a short sleep-time routine that they will come to recognize, and consistently putting them in the same place to sleep. We learn to observe our baby and then provide as much help as necessary and as little as possible (*dependence*).

This will create a foundational pattern from which the baby will gradually pull away in the first year. Some babies will crawl to their floor bed when they are tired. Others will need us to observe their tired signs, follow their sleep-time routine, and come to sit next to them until they sleep (*collaboration*).

Toward the end of the first year, babies sleeping in their own room may come to find us upon waking— indicating that we have supported them to build a good relationship with sleep (*increasing independence*).

If our baby becomes dependent on us to sleep, rocking them or feeding them to sleep, for example, become sleep crutches. When the baby gets into a light sleep during the night, they can find it difficult to resettle without this rocking or feeding. As an adult, if our pillow moves during the night, when we get into a light sleep, we will wake to find it and put it back, unable to sleep until we're comfortable again. Similarly, when a baby gets into a light sleep, they will wake to look around for the arms that were rocking them or breast they were sucking on.

If we are currently rocking them or feeding them to sleep, it's okay. But at some point this will need to change for them to fall asleep by themselves and stay asleep—when we and our baby are ready.

As the baby gets older, we can continue to observe them to see how much (or little) assistance they need to sleep. We may be able to sit farther away from them, then sit by the door, then leave them to sleep by themselves, gradually moving from dependence, to collaboration, to increasing independence.

4. A consistent sleeping area, ideally with a floor bed

As we discussed in chapter 3, having a consistent sleeping area is so important for the baby's points of reference.

We like to use a low mattress that is around 6 inches (15 cm) high on the floor for sleeping—a floor bed. This gives the baby the freedom to eventually crawl into and out of the bed independently, and they are able to see the whole room, without bars blocking their view of the space. It can be relaxing for the adult to be able to sit or lie next to our baby as they settle, rather than standing while leaning over into a crib.

At birth, we like to use a cestina (a Moses-style basket) for them to sleep in. It gives a feeling of security to be in a smaller bed. The cestina can be placed on top of their floor bed from birth to orient the baby to their sleeping place, a point of reference they will remember. Following SIDS guidelines, this may be in the parent's bedroom.

Cribs were designed to be convenient for adults, not babies. It can be difficult to drop these ideas that have always been used in the past. If we are uncomfortable with using a floor bed, we can transition the baby from a crib to a toddler bed at around 12 to 16 months, when they are able to climb in and out of bed by themselves. They will then get to experience the benefits of a floor bed before they are (likely) going through the "no" stage of development, which commonly happens around 2 years old.

Note: It's important that the room is thoroughly checked for babyproofing, because the baby will soon be able to wake, wriggle off the bed, and begin to explore the whole space. If we cannot make it safe for our baby to leave the bedroom independently, a baby gate may be put across the doorway so they are free to crawl out of their bed to play.

5. Allow free movement

We like to offer the baby as much opportunity for movement as possible—even in sleep. During Simone's Montessori training, she participated in 50 hours of newborn observation (from birth to 8 weeks). She couldn't believe how much there was to observe while a baby was sleeping. During sleep, their hands constantly move, their arms rise and lower, their legs kick and straighten, their head can move from side to side, and their mouth makes movements too.

We can look for sleep clothes that are soft on the baby's skin, with few labels or seams to irritate them, that will also allow free movement of their legs and feet. If it's cooler outside, consider using socks rather than all-in-one suits to allow the feet more movement.

Swaddling can limit the baby's free movement. However, swaddling can also provide comfort for some babies, giving them a feeling of safety like being back in the womb or to keep them from being startled by their Moro reflex. In these cases, the upper body might be swaddled, while the legs are left loose to allow for free movement.

Sleeping bags or sleep sacks have become popular in recent years as the American Academy of Pediatrics recommends no blankets until 12–18 months. Look for one that enables the baby to move freely while keeping in mind that it may limit their ability to crawl, stand, and walk upon waking.

6. Topponcino

A topponcino is a soft, quilted cushion that we can lay the baby on from their first days. We have mentioned that the toppocino is often used during the day to limit the stimulation the baby experiences when we hold them, or give them to someone else to hold. The toppocino has a familiar smell to it, a consistent warmth, and becomes one of the baby's points of reference.

It is useful for sleeping time too. Imagine we are holding our baby and they become sleepy. Without the topponcino, most babies do not like to be transitioned from our arms to their bed. Using the topponcino, we can lay them down in their bed or cestina (Moses basket) with their topponcino under them and they rarely startle. The temperature, scent, and cushioning remain the same.

Junnifa was so fond of the topponcino, she brought it everywhere—when they were visiting Grandma's house or if they were out for the day—and she used it for the first few months at sleep time, while she and her baby were co-sleeping. The topponcino became a point of reference for her babies when they eventually transitioned into their own beds.

Consider going pacifier-free

Most Montessori sources do not recommend the use of pacifiers. A young infant cannot easily put a pacifier back in by themselves in the night, and pacifiers can be overused by the adult when a baby is attempting to communicate their needs. So we may wish to go pacifier-free. See more on pacifiers on page 195.

WAKE WINDOWS AND NUMBER OF SLEEPS A DAY

While every baby is different, it can be useful to know how long on average a baby stays awake between sleeps so that we can keep an eye out for tired signs.

0–12 weeks	1–1.5 hours (many naps)
3–5 months	1.25–2 hours (3–4 naps a day)
5–6 months	2–3 hours (3–4 naps a day)
7–14 months	3–4 hours (2–3 naps a day)

*Source: TakingCaraBabies.com

Around 12 to 16 months they will start to stay awake all morning, with one nap a day in the middle of the day, and they are able to stay awake until bedtime.

Co-sleeping

Co-sleeping and Montessori can coexist.

Some families choose to co-sleep with their baby. Sleeping arrangements are a personal decision, and each family must decide what works for them. Even with co-sleeping, we can provide a consistent sleeping area for our baby.

Junnifa co-slept with her children for the first few months. She would put them to bed in their floor bed and then when she herself was ready to sleep, she would transfer them to her bed so she could feed them easily during the night. She would lay them on their floor bed for daytime naps, and once they were no longer breastfeeding, they transitioned to spending the whole night in their own bed. Junnifa felt that the co-sleeping arrangement was more for her than for her babies, and they peacefully transitioned to their own bed at their family's pace.

Whatever the sleep arrangements, we are always observing to see when the baby is ready to move to the next step from dependence, to collaboration, to increasing independence. And we can consider if it is our need or theirs we are meeting.

Note: Please refer to page 63 for SIDS guidelines.

THINGS THAT CAN HELP NURTURE BABY'S SLEEP

- observe our child's sleep/wake rhythm and how it changes
- note how much assistance we give them to sleep
- be consistent—do not try three things one night; if we make a change, keep it the same for a week and record it objectively in a notebook
- provide a safe, comfortable place for sleep
- have realistic expectations around sleep—most babies are not sleeping through the night in the first year
- note sleep crutches and remove them when we are ready
- nap when baby naps—take care of our sleep and well-being; do our chores when the baby is awake and allow them to observe, talk to them about what we are doing, and involve them

COMMON SLEEP QUESTIONS

The first answer we usually give when it comes to questions about sleep is, of course, to observe the baby. However, here are some more specific answers to the most frequently asked questions about sleep.

Why does my baby wake up at night?

- From 0 to 3 months, our baby will be waking at night to feed. Their bodies will still be adjusting their circadian rhythms, so lots of sunlight and fresh air during the day helps their bodies begin to adjust to day and night over the first months. When nursing at night, try to keep the lights dim and move the baby as little as possible, ideally feeding in the room where they are sleeping. After feeding, burp them, change the diaper if necessary, and put them right back to sleep.

- Are they teething or sick? They may need some extra comfort at this time. Once the tooth is through or they are better, we can try not to let this extra comfort become a new crutch, by helping them go back to how they slept before the teething or sickness.

- Do they have a wet or soiled diaper? Is there a noise? A crease in their sheets that is bothering them? Are they too hot/cold? Are they going through a lot of developmental changes that they are processing? Are they checking that we are still there?

- For an older baby who is feeding and growing well, we may wish to first offer some water in the night. Sometimes this is enough and they will go back to sleep. Many families find that the baby then becomes less interested in waking and will sleep for longer periods. We can also gradually offer less milk at night if the baby drinks from a bottle by diluting the milk with water at a proportion of 75/25, then 50/50, then 25/75, until they are drinking water.

- Is our baby smelling the mother's milk and waking up? We may wish to have them sleep in their own room if space allows.

- When in doubt, take notes—objective observations can be very helpful. What time do they wake? For crying, what is the intensity, duration? How do they respond to our efforts to soothe them? What do we do when baby wakes? Is this the same every night? If we bring them to our bed in the middle of the night, may this be a reason our baby wakes?

- Be consistent—we can make a plan (not in the middle of the night when we are tired and can't think) and respond in the same way to our child for at least seven nights before changing. New patterns take time.

How can I get my baby to resettle when they wake during their nap or during the night?

- Babies enter into light sleep at the end of their sleep cycle—often after around 40 to 45 minutes. They may stir or completely wake up. When this happens, they will look for any conditions that existed when they were asleep, for example, if they were sucking a pacifier, being rocked, or fed. So when we help them gradually learn to fall asleep in their bed, it will be easier for them to resettle. We give them as little help as possible and as much as necessary—maybe sitting next to them, or placing a hand on their belly, or saying some comforting words.

- We can use observation to help us understand why our baby is waking up. Revisit Junnifa's story in chapter 2 about observing her son when he was waking up 40 minutes into his nap. He was looking for her in his new space.

Is it okay to wake a sleeping baby?

- We like to follow their rhythms as much as possible. If they sleep late, they are likely tired. It requires some flexibility on the adult's behalf and some creativity. Try to make plans around your baby's naptimes. Or try to leave the house when they are getting sleepy so they can sleep in a carrier, stroller, or in the car.

Should I use a night-light?

- Most babies under 12 months old are not yet scared of the dark. So it can be preferable to keep the room completely dark if possible.

- We could use a night-light as we are getting them ready for sleep, or during night feeds.

- If using a night-light, look for a red-based night-light and avoid white- and blue-based ones, which can suppress melatonin and affect the baby's sleep.

What can I do about early waking?

- If they wake early, some babies will feed and go back to sleep. Many will already have had most of their sleep, so they will have difficulty going back to sleep.

- Check for any light coming in through their blinds or around the edges.

- Are they having long daytime sleeps? Is it possible to delay their first nap a little?

- Many sleep experts suggest an earlier bedtime can help, even though this may seem counterintuitive.

- Does baby associate coming into our bed with waking up early?

Why won't my baby settle?	• We can take them to their room, sit by their bed to observe them, and let them crawl and babble until they show tired signs (e.g., yawning, rubbing eyes). Then lay them in their bed. This can also work when they are overtired and become very busy. Let them explore until they are tired, then change their diaper and lay them on their bed. • It is fairly common for younger babies to have a period during the day when they won't be able to settle. If they haven't fallen asleep after around 20 minutes, we can take them for a walk in a carrier or stroller or have them in a carrier while we do some things around the house. If they don't fall asleep, at least they will have had some rest and will be ready to begin the next cycle of feed, play, sleep.
Help! My baby is going through a sleep regression.	• A sleep regression is when our baby was sleeping well and then it changes. At these times, our baby is going through some transitions. We don't love the word "regression," as these phases generally mean that our baby is making a "progression." Our baby's sleep is changing to something different. • At around 4 months they become more wakeful and alert, have increasing awareness, and may find it more difficult to fall asleep. • At around 8 months they are going through enormous developmental changes, now able to slither or crawl and sometimes pull up—they are busy with these newfound skills. • At around 12 months they have developed more gross-motor skills, like crawling and coming to a stand, and are gaining new understanding about object permanence (that when something goes away, they can bring it back with their own actions). These motor changes bring on a host of psychological ones. They can also be transitioning to one nap a day. • We may need to move back to some collaboration until it passes. Then remember to observe when our baby is ready to move back to increasing their independence. • Hang in there. Give it some time and try again.
Questions about using a floor bed	• See chapter 4, page 64

How can I move my baby out of our room?

- If our baby has been sleeping in our room and we are ready to move them into their own room, we can spend time with them in their room during the day for them to get used to the space.

- We can place them in their room for their daytime naps. Then they begin to have their night sleep in their room too.

- Be confident with the change. Bring them to their bed, explain, "This is your own bed," and have limited choices available—they can explore quietly in their room while we sit by their bed to observe until they are ready to sleep.

- Set up points of reference that are familiar to them, e.g., using a topponcino, a familiar picture of the family, a blanket.

- We may need to sit with them while they fall asleep. Once they have adjusted to their new space, little by little we won't need to be there anymore for them to fall asleep.

I'm stressed— my baby won't sleep.

- Consider offering the baby the opportunity to "rest" rather than "sleep." Then we can let go of the idea that they need to sleep; they will at least have some quiet time. The baby will not feel pressure from us to sleep. And often they do fall asleep.

- We can examine our own fears around their not sleeping. We may be worried they will be cranky or not in a good mood for some visitors. What are we bringing to the situation?

- Keep our sleep-time routines consistent for a week. Instead of trying something different every time, we can do our best to respond in the same way when baby wakes in the night.

- If we are feeling stressed or burned out, we can also get some support with sleeping from an early childhood nurse or sleep consultant.

- We also need to consider the adult's needs. If our baby's sleep is affecting the whole family, then we need to look at a way that everyone's sleep needs can be met.

BOOK RECOMMENDATION

For more information on sleep, we suggest *The Sleep Lady's Good Night, Sleep Tight* by Kim West.

PART TWO

PHYSICAL CARE

CLOTHING

Giving our baby freedom of movement is an important part of the Montessori approach. We can select clothing for them that is comfortable, soft against the skin, and allows for easy movement.

We can look for:
- clothing that is easy to get over the baby's head—look for tops that wrap (for example, kimono tops) or that have buttons on the shoulder to create a wider opening when dressing
- natural materials like organic cotton, silk, or wool
- clothing that is not too tight (which can restrict movement) nor too loose (which can create uncomfortable creases for them to lie on or get tangled in)
- a top that is separate from the trousers and without feet attached, which will enable the most freedom of movement
- socks to cover feet, if needed
- we can save party dresses, denim jeans, and baby sneakers for special occasions (if at all)

When dressing

Dressing our baby is a perfect opportunity for connection with them. We use gentle hands, tell them what we are planning to do, and wait for their reaction first before picking them up. We talk about the clothes we are going to put on, we ask for their assistance to raise their arm or leg, and we are careful yet confident when putting clothing over their head. And we move them as little as possible. The idea of using our gentle hands, which we talk about a lot in this chapter and in this book, Junnifa learned in her RIE training based on the work of Emmi Pikler.

We can also start offering choices—even with a young baby. For example, we can offer two T-shirts of different colors and observe to see which one the baby's gaze lingers on or which one they reach for. Over time they will be a more active participant, sliding an arm into their T-shirt sleeve, possibly managing to take off their socks by themselves, or pointing to the trousers they would like to wear.

Simone still remembers the shocked faces from parents in her class when she helped ready a baby for class while the mom visited the bathroom. Simone asked the baby if it was okay to take their coat off for them. There was no objection from the baby, so she told them she was going to undo the jacket first and sat the baby in such a way that they could see Simone as she carefully unzipped it. Then she asked the baby to help her take their left arm out of the jacket. While she was handling the baby, she asked, "Is that okay?" using as gentle hands as possible. She continued with the other arm until the coat was removed.

The other parents were surprised because it's so different from the way we unconsciously dress and undress our babies.

So let's slow down. Let's make it a special moment with our baby. Let's look into their eyes. And let's always be respectful and gentle with our touch.

DIAPERING

Rather than rushing through diapering, we can use this time for conversation and connection with our baby. And we we can show them respect.

When changing a diaper, we can:

- Watch our language and gestures, for example, not scrunching our nose or saying things like "You stinky baby" or reacting negatively. Instead, we can say, "I see your diaper is soiled" or "I see you pooped. Let's go change." Wait for the baby's response and then pick them up.
- Give the child some privacy when we change them, ideally a changing table or area.
- Communicate what we are doing while changing them: "I am going to take off your diaper." We wait again for a response from the baby and then begin to change them, talking through the process and collaborating with them as much as possible: "First this snap and now this one. I will help you lift up your leg."
- Describe bodily functions and parts with their correct names.

- Use gentle hands during diaper changes. Be careful and respectful in the way that we lift up their legs when changing them. If we pause and touch gently, we will find that they collaborate and actually lift their legs by themselves from very early on.

- Change the diaper in the same way and in the same place as much as possible each time—babies thrive on predictability.

- Once the baby is pulling up to standing, they may resist being laid down to be changed. We can understand how vulnerable this position must feel. Instead, we can sit on a low stool while they stay standing during the change. This takes some practice but reduces their resistance to being changed. For a bowel movement, we can have them lean forward to place their hands maybe on the side of the bathtub while we clean them.

- A general note, when cleaning them during diapering, it is more hygienic to wipe from front to back, especially for girls, to prevent infections.

Even in the first 12 months, we are laying the foundation for their later toilet independence. That doesn't mean that our baby will be using the potty or toilet by themselves yet, but:

- By using cloth diapers or thick underwear (sometimes called "training pants"), our baby will feel wet, have freedom of movement, and gain increasing awareness when they pee or poop. These days disposable diapers are so effective at keeping the baby feeling dry that the baby misses the feeling of wetness when they urinate, which they will need later when they learn to use the toilet independently.

- By using proper vocabulary when changing them, we are teaching them about how their body works and to not feel shame about their bodily functions.

When they refuse to get dressed or have a diaper changed

There are several things to consider if our baby is resisting getting dressed or getting a diaper change:

1. Are they telling us they are ready for the next step? For example, an older baby may want to take over more control in the process. A baby who is trying to wiggle away while having their diaper changed may want to stand to be changed or may show interest in the potty.

2. Involve them in the process, for example, giving them time to allow them to pull the shirt over their head, choosing the T-shirt from a limited selection, or, once they are walking, carrying the pants while we carry the rest.

3. Are we interrupting their play to get them dressed or change their diaper? Instead, we can allow them time to finish what they are doing and let them know that when they are finished we will change them.

4. Don't underestimate humor and singing silly songs—not as distraction but as a form of connection.

5. Seek to understand them and guess how they might feel: "Are you feeling frustrated?" or "You don't want to be touched?"

Sometimes they may not be willing to be dressed or changed, meanwhile we need them to be ready to leave the house. If this happens and we have done everything outlined above, we can be as gentle as possible getting them dressed or changing their diaper. "Sportscasting" can be useful at these times too—we describe aloud and in an objective way to the baby what is happening, just as a sportscaster might give a detailed account of a sports event.

Using as gentle hands as possible, we can tell them what we are going to do, pausing for them to process it, and seeking to understand. "I can see that you are pulling away from me. It's important for me to give you a clean diaper. Are you saying you don't like that? And I'm lifting you with my gentle hands. . . . That was a tough one, wasn't it?"

They see that we are respectful, gentle, and taking care of their physical needs as well. And by saying "I'm using my gentle hands," it's a reminder to use softness at all times, especially when there is resistance.

BATHING THE BABY

As with dressing and diapering our baby, when bathing the baby we want to be as gentle, calm, and confident as possible, and use it as a moment of connection. Most babies are very relaxed in the bath and enjoy it a lot.

With a newborn in particular, we want to limit any unexpected movements, make our movements as minimal and efficient as possible, and support their head at all times. In our Montessori training, we practiced bathing the baby with the same sequence of movements each time. This can make us more confident to find ways to handle the baby as gently as possible and with adequate support for the baby.

Make the temperature of the room where the baby will be bathed a little warmer, and run the bath to around 2 to 4 inches (5 to 10 cm) deep, with water at body temperature (check the temperature with your wrist to get the most accurate read). There is enough water in the bath so the baby can float, with our gentle hands for support. Have everything we'll need at the ready, including a towel open to receive the baby.

When bathing the baby, move slowly and use equal pressure on all body parts, including their genitals, to give the baby a full sense of their body schema (how their body is made up). Talk to the baby during the bath, smile, and make eye contact.

The WHO now recommends waiting at least 24 hours before baby's first bath. Also, our baby does not have to be bathed every day—instead maybe three times a week.

RECOMMENDED WATCHING

To see how gently we can bathe a baby, watch Thalasso Bain Bébé's videos online. There is also one with twins holding each other while being bathed.

TRAVELING IN THE CAR

Car seats limit both a baby's movement and what they can see around them. However, car seats are essential for safety, so we can be respectful, understanding, and use our gentle hands as we place the baby into the car seat.

Make sure the baby is not hungry and their diaper is clean before getting in the car. We can tell them that we are going to place them in the seat and allow them to collaborate as much as possible for their age, for example, asking them to give us their arm so we can pass it through the seatbelt.

Being confident also helps as the baby picks up any sense of unease we may have. If there is a period where our baby is not enjoying being in the car, we may start to become anxious before any car trips—anxiety that our baby will pick up on and share.

Once in their seat, we can have something for them to look at in the car, like a black-and-white picture board, something from nature hung up for them to look at, or a board book, which can be attached for them to pull at, teethe on, and look through. Music that we enjoy or classical music can be relaxing for some babies, and longer audio books become interesting when they are a little older.

BABY WEARING

Most babies feel secure and soothed by the movement in a baby carrier or sling, and they love being close enough to smell their special people. Using baby carriers gives us flexibility in places like public transportation, the supermarket, or around the house when we need both arms free. An unsettled baby can be worn close to our chest and have a rest even if they don't fall asleep. During symbiosis in particular, baby wearing can help the transition for the baby from womb to the outside world.

The variety of baby carriers has grown enormously, so look for one that gives you enough support for your back and can grow with your baby.

That said, we love giving babies an opportunity to move their bodies. So we can allow time for them to be on a mat on the floor as well. As our baby starts to crawl and take their first steps, also allow them to crawl and walk freely when outside, and keep the carrier for longer distances.

TEETHING

Some babies may never have trouble with teething. However, if you've ever had a baby that drools nonstop, starts night waking when they normally wouldn't, has poop that looks different, and sometimes has a red bottom, these are signs the baby is teething.

We can observe the baby and try to make them more comfortable with a natural teething gel or powder, have cloths on hand to wipe their chins, and perhaps have them wear a sweet bandana to catch the drool while it lasts. Some babies get a bit of relief from sucking on something cold, and so some natural teethers can be kept in the freezer.

Fortunately, once a tooth comes through, we can reestablish the baby's regular rhythms (until the next tooth is on its way).

We can also start to clean their newly emerged teeth with a soft cloth or toothbrush and some water.

USING A PACIFIER

Most Montessori educators do not encourage the use of a pacifier. If the baby has something in their mouth all the time, they cannot communicate their needs—all of baby's cries have meaning and shouldn't be stopped with a pacifier. And the youngest babies cannot put it in their mouth by themselves or take it out themselves.

Studies show that pacifiers may reduce the risk of SIDS. If using a pacifier helps an unsettled baby or it helps a baby to fall asleep instead of crying for a long time, then use it at these limited times. It can be useful to keep the pacifier in a box by the bed so that it isn't tempting to use during the day, when we feel like we want some quiet.

The earlier we are able to reduce use of and remove the pacifier, the easier it will be, before it becomes an attachment for the baby. Ideally, this would be in the first year.

We can explain that they are getting older and that we will help them to find a new way to calm themselves. Since sucking on a pacifier often helps to relax their nervous system, here are some other ways for them to relax:

- holding tightly onto a book or soft toy
- using a bottle with a straw
- getting a brisk towel rub after a bath
- getting deep-pressure bear hugs
- squeezing bath toys
- getting a slow, firm back rub

Usually the transition goes surprisingly easily, but understand that it may take some days for some babies. If we are clear on wanting to get rid of pacifiers, it can help to remove all of them from the house, because the more consistent we can be, the clearer it will be for our baby to understand the new way. It can also be helpful for our baby to see them being removed.

Some people ask if thumb- or finger-sucking is preferable to using a pacifier. This can be preferable because the baby is in control of putting their fingers or thumb in their mouth and how often they do it. And we can also observe to see when and why they suck and determine if we can meet this need in another way. For example, if we observe them sucking their thumb when they are bored, we can offer them something to manipulate with their hands.

SHARING

The concepts of sharing and toy ownership do not often present in babies until close to 12 to 16 months old. In the first year, a baby generally explores by playing with one thing and then releasing it to move on to the next object of exploration. If another young baby or child sees what they are playing with as interesting and takes it out of their hands, often a baby will turn around to find another object.

If there are older siblings who are often taking their things, a baby may learn to hold on tight and not let go. We can translate for them, explaining to their sibling, "It looks like the baby wants to finish playing with it first." This models to the baby that it's okay to finish playing with their toy and that eventually we'll share by taking turns.

If our baby is the one who is taking things from another child, it can be respectful to model that we ask before taking something. "Did you want to play with that? Let's ask the other baby if they are all done." If the other baby looks like they want to hold on to it for now, we can say to our baby, "It looks like they are playing with it right now. It will be available soon." Our baby will learn to watch and wait or to find something else to play with.

COLIC AND REFLUX

Colic is when a baby has "frequent, prolonged and intense crying or fussiness," and no reason for it can be found. Infant reflux "occurs when food backs up (refluxes) from a baby's stomach, causing the baby to spit up." (Mayo Clinic)

Both colic and reflux make for a very fussy baby. And most of the advice says that both will get better at around 3 to 4 months, once the baby's digestive system has matured a little more, so just hang in there. This is not very helpful for tired, stressed-out parents whose hearts are breaking seeing their child crying or in pain.

Like everything in Montessori, we suggest observing. We can write down what we have eaten if we are breastfeeding, the ingredients in our baby's formula, what time the crying occurs, how long the crying or symptoms last, if the baby is pulling up their legs or making uncomfortable faces, how they latch on when feeding, if they have a tongue tie or cleft lip and palate, whether they are overtired or overstimulated. We can look for any patterns and present them to our doctor or pediatrician.

We can also seek medical advice to see if there are any allergies, histamine sensitivities (in foods like strawberries), or a physical problem like an intestinal blockage, bacterial overgrowth, ulcers, or occasionally a narrow entry preventing food from entering the small intestine or the stomach pushing through the diaphragm. (Some research has also shown that birth trauma or a breach presentation may create colic symptoms.)

The good news is that many parents who follow their intuition that their baby's crying or pain is not normal are able to get to the root cause.

And, in the meantime, we can be be present for our baby, make them feel as comfortable as possible with body contact and time together. Often, a little pressure on the belly helps, we can lay them, belly side down, on our own body or give them supervised tummy time on a softer surface like a bed or carpet. We also need to look after ourselves and get support if we can—perhaps someone to take over for some time each day—because hearing a baby crying constantly is tiring and emotionally challenging for parents.

SCREEN TIME

The Montessori approach is for the child to experience the world around them in real life. For a baby, this is with their bodies, their hands, and their mouths. This experience cannot be replicated on a screen, so we do not offer screens to babies. And we can be mindful of our own use of screens and put them away as much as possible in front of the baby.

If the baby gets bored at a café, rather than using a screen, we can walk around to show them what is happening, look out the window at passing vehicles and people, and bring a small pouch with a few favorite things for them to explore. And rather than distracting a baby with a screen if they are upset, we can provide loving arms, calming words, and patience.

PART THREE

COMMON QUESTIONS

WHAT SHOULD WE DO WHEN BEHAVIORS CHANGE? (HITTING/THROWING/BITING/PUSHING)

Some babies show strong preferences from birth. Others seem to be pretty relaxed, aside from telling us when they need to eat or sleep—then, at around 9 to 12 months, we start to see them show preferences. They may hit us, throw things, bite, or even push us or another child. They may seem to become strong-willed, not changing their mind regardless of what we say or do.

With their limited communication skills, our baby is telling us something important. Instead of thinking of them as "naughty," we can ask ourselves, "Why would my baby be doing this?"

- If they hit us, are they telling us they don't like what is happening? That we took something away? How we are holding them?
- If they throw something, is the toy too hard or too easy for them? Are they experimenting with how things fall down? Learning about cause and effect? Are there ways for them to try this in a way that is not dangerous or disruptive?
- If they bite us, are they hungry? Has something upset them? Are they teething?
- If they push us or another child, can we translate for them? Can we say, "Are you trying to get past here?" or "Were you wanting to play with that toy right now?"

So we first seek to understand.

Then we translate or make a guess: "Are you telling me . . . ?"

Then we kindly and clearly let them know that we won't let them hurt us/themselves/ someone else/the environment. We may be able to find another way for them to meet their need, e.g., to hit a cushion. And, if necessary, we will remove them from the room or the situation and sit with them until they are calm.

Once they are calm, we can connect with them and model how to make amends if needed, for example, apologizing to a friend, offering a tissue or wet cloth if a child is hurt, or putting back things that have been thrown. As they become toddlers, they will learn to help us to repair any hurt feelings or mistakes.

Early tantrums

If our baby is crying uncontrollably, they won't be able to hear many of our words. We can offer a cuddle and our love. And stay nearby if they don't want to be touched. We first want to help them release whatever emotions need to come out, then help them calm down.

Once they are calm, we can give a short, age-appropriate explanation and tidy up with them and model apologizing if needed.

This also lays the foundation as our baby becomes a young toddler and they begin to exert their independence.

Tantrums and having a strong will are important phases of development, and we can be a supportive guide to help them through these—first giving them space to let out the feelings, then helping them calm down, and finally, helping them make amends if needed.

Observation

If this behavior continues, we can practice objective observation to see if there are any triggers causing the behavior. We can then use this information to limit these triggers. For example, we can note if the behavior happens before meals, in particular environments, around particular children, or if the space is very stimulating (which could be a trigger for sensitive children).

When there is difficult behavior, we can observe:

- **Time.** What time does the behavior happen? Is our baby hungry or tired?
- **Changes.** Are they teething? Are there any changes at home, such as a new house?
- **Activity.** What are they doing or playing with at the time of being triggered?
- **Other children.** How many children are around? Are the children the same age, younger, or older?

- **Emotion being expressed.** Just before it happens, how do they look? Playful? Frustrated? Confused?

- **Environment.** Look at the environment where the tantrums happen. Is it busy? Is it very colorful or otherwise too stimulating? Is there a lot of clutter? Is there a lot of children's artwork around the room, which is possibly too much sensory input? Or is it peaceful and serene?

- **Adults.** How do we, as adults, respond? Do we bring additional anxiety to the situation?

Preventing the Behavior

By observing, we may see patterns to their behavior and identify ways we can support our child. Here are some examples:

- **Just before mealtime.** Give them something hard like an apple they can bite into to snack on before they get too hungry (good for relaxing their nervous system).

- **Teething.** Offer a variety of (cold) teething toys.

- **Exploration.** Allow them to explore toys with their mouth.

- **Environment.** Reduce the amount of stimulation to make the surroundings calmer.

- **Noise.** Remove the baby when we start to notice that things are becoming too loud for them.

- **Sensitive to their personal space.** Help them avoid situations where they are cornered or do not have enough personal space.

- **Playful.** Some babies may bite to be playful or show love, perhaps misunderstanding games such as blowing raspberries on their tummies. Show them other ways to be affectionate, such as cuddles or mutual rough play.

- **Learning social interactions.** If they push another child, they may be wanting to say, "Can we play?" Model words that they will learn over time.

- **Check their hearing and eyesight.** A problem with either can feel disorienting for a baby, and they may react by being aggressive.

- **Transitions.** Is the structure of the day predictable enough? Are transitions difficult for them? Allow enough time for them to finish what they are doing. Make sure they get enough free, unstructured playtime.

- **Releasing their nervous system.** Refer to page 195 for ideas on relaxing their nervous system, such as deep massage or big bear hugs.

WHAT IF THE BABY IS CLINGY AND WON'T LET US PUT THEM DOWN? WHAT IF THEY HAVE SEPARATION ANXIETY?

Some babies are more independent, and some babies will cling to us. Sometimes we play with children a lot and they start to depend on us to entertain them. So it becomes a combination of their character (that may not necessarily change over time but where we can start to give them skills) and what we do as the adult (which we do have control over).

In a Montessori approach, we see babies as capable beings, if we let them be. We try to give the baby time to see their effect on the world, from the noises they make, to the movements of their arms and legs, to reaching out to touch or strike something.

First we can see if we are an obstacle to their development. Are we interfering in their play? Are we doing a lot to get them to eat and sleep, and entertaining them during waking hours?

Instead, can we observe them to see how much help they need (if any)? This can change every week, every day, and sometimes every hour, so we need to keep observing.

If we are used to entertaining them, can we gradually shift from entertaining to being together? From being together to following their lead?

If they always want to be held, can we gradually show them they can also be on the ground playing for short periods? We can lie down next to each other. Then, over time, we might move from being right beside them to maybe 4 inches (10 cm) farther away. To popping to the kitchen to put the kettle on, letting them know where we are going, and then coming right back. To letting them discover a newfound interest without interruption. They will also be experiencing the reality of object permanence—that when we go away, we come back again.

Babies pick up our own energy. If we are starting to feel frustrated about needing to hold them all day, the baby may sense we are uncomfortable and cling even tighter. If we have any doubts about letting them be on the floor to play or letting someone else care for them for us, the baby may also pick up on this and again cling more. We need to work on ourselves to help our children so that we can confidently show them they are already so capable, and find that fine balance between attachment and separation.

From around 6 months to 16 months, babies can experience separation anxiety. They are still learning that when we go away, we will come back again—and they are beginning to feel a preference for having us nearby. It is difficult to see our baby upset, but there are some ways we can help them get through this stage:

1. We can give them a verbal cue as we are leaving: "I'm going to the kitchen;" from the kitchen we can call out to them: "I'm in the kitchen;" and when we get back we can tell them: "I'm back from the kitchen. It's so nice to see you!"

2. We can be positive in our communication when we have to leave as the baby will pick up our feelings of concern or trepidation.

3. When introducing them to a new caregiver, we can first invite the caregiver to the home while we are still there so our baby can get to know them, and so they become a new point of reference for them. We can then practice being in another room while the caregiver is with our baby, building up to leaving the house for longer periods of time.

4. We can keep other points of reference consistent—the order of the room, their daily rhythm, their food, etc.

5. If they are starting at a new day care, we can sit on the side of the room with them between our legs until they are ready to crawl or walk away from us to explore.

6. We can leave something nearby that has our familiar scent.

When our baby has a secure attachment and we choose other caregivers we trust, our baby also learns trust in others and themselves. (See page 96 about secure attachment and page 235 about saying goodbye to our baby.)

HOW CAN I STOP THEM FROM TOUCHING THINGS? WHEN WILL THEY STOP PUTTING THINGS IN THEIR MOUTH?

We can't stop babies from touching things or putting things in their mouths. Babies are born explorers—they need to move and explore the world around them, and the best way for them to do this is by touching what they see and bringing it to the most sensitive part of their bodies: their mouths.

The nerves in their mouth are one of the earliest parts of the body to be *myelinated* (where the nerves are able to allow signals to pass through more effeciently) so that they can feed effectively from birth. This makes the mouth the most sensitive and most suitable body part for exploring everything in the baby's path.

At the end of the first year to around 16 months, the hands will become more sensitive as myelination extends to the peripheral parts of the body, and the oral phase of development usually starts to come to an end. If a 14-month-old brings a coin to their mouth, we can usually show them how it goes through the slot in the coin box, and then they become more interested in completing that activity than putting the coin into their mouth.

Some babies stay longer in the oral stage of development if they like to suck, for example, babies who use a pacifier a lot or suck on a bottle. So the oral stage of development will ease once the pacifier and bottle are no longer being used.

WHAT DO WE DO WHEN WE NEED TO GET THROUGH OUR DAILY TASKS?

Montessori is a child-focused approach to raising children. We treat them with respect, we try to follow their needs as much as possible—yet we also have things we need to get done like cooking, cleaning, running errands, and other things we need to do or simply enjoy doing.

In the symbiotic period (the first 6 to 8 weeks after birth), it can be useful to have our partner (if we have one) and some extra hands (family, friends, a cleaning person if that's available to us) to manage the daily tasks of the home and give us time to form the connection with our new baby, establish feeding, and to rest. We may have some pre-prepared food in the freezer if we are super organized too.

In the symbiotic period and beyond, even with the best of help, there will be many times when we need to do things around the home, like cooking and washing, as well as looking after the baby. We can get some of that done during nap times, although it is a good idea to spend a lot of these nap times to rest ourselves, something many of us have difficulty with. Rest assured, the tasks will wait for us, and these special days will speed by.

As the baby becomes more wakeful, they will enjoy absorbing aspects of our daily lives. In Montessori we like to involve children in our daily life, and this can start from birth by keeping them close by as we do our own things. At first they will watch from our arms, or play on a blanket on the floor nearby, or be carried in a baby carrier. Then they will reach out to touch and explore, and over time they will be able to participate in the process. Some examples:

- We can talk to our babies about what we are doing, show them everything, and let them touch.

- Preparing a meal is like we are preparing a gift for our family, and our baby will absorb our intention, our language, and our connection.
- On a trip to the supermarket, if they are awake, we can look for the items together, count things as they go into the shopping basket, and sing songs.

These tasks and errands can become times of connection, not just something to be rushed through or something we have to do.

HOW CAN YOU DO MONTESSORI ON A BUDGET?

Often people think that Montessori is synonymous with expensive wooden toys. However, it's less about the Montessori materials and more about seeing our baby as capable and finding ways to treat our baby with respect, love, and gentle hands.

We can involve our baby in daily life and use what we already have—no need for new toys. They love to be alongside us and perhaps explore what's inside the kitchen cupboards while we cook. Instead of buying an expensive set of stairs for climbing, we can practice on the stairs to a front porch. Instead of buying a set of swings, we can hang an old tire from a tree.

When we are looking for some Montessori materials, we can try making them ourselves, for example, the Montessori mobiles can be made with supplies found in a local craft store, or sometimes even with things we have around the home.

We can buy secondhand. Find local thrift stores where we can get some pre-loved wooden toys, baskets, and baby-friendly furniture.

We can repurpose furniture and some materials as our child grows, for example, a low shelf can become a bench to sit on, and a low cube chair can become a stool.

We can rent toys or buy them together in a community where we share more expensive materials.

We can get out into nature. We can take our baby for a walk in a baby carrier or stroller, we can lie on a blanket together in the park or on the beach or in the woods, and we can pass time watching the tree leaves and branches moving.

As we learn more about Montessori and its true principles, it becomes clear that it doesn't have to cost a lot of money to do Montessori at home.

PART FOUR

OTHER SITUATIONS

SIBLINGS

If there are older siblings in the family, the arrival of a new baby may make them feel like they have been replaced or that they are receiving less attention or love.

Adele Faber and Elaine Mazlish write in their book *Siblings Without Rivalry* that the arrival of a newborn in the family is the same as our partner telling us that they love us so much that they are getting another partner. And that the new partner will sleep in our old bed and wear our old clothes, and we have to make them feel welcome and help to look after them. No wonder having a new baby in the home can be quite a transition for some children.

Preparing an older sibling

Books with realistic pictures about a new baby in the home are especially helpful to prepare an older sibling. We can let them talk and sing to the baby in the belly and begin to build a connection. We can let them help prepare the baby's space. And we can make a point of enjoying our last days together in our current family configuration.

One tip for siblings is to have the older sibling sing to or talk to the baby while they are still in utero. They can sing the same song every time, and the baby will recognize it from birth and will find it soothing. The topponcino is also great for allowing older siblings to cuddle the new baby.

When it's time to introduce our older child to the new baby, if they have not been present at the birth, we can put down the baby before the older child enters the room so our attention is solely on them. This can be easier than walking in to see us holding the new baby in our arms.

As much as possible, keep the early weeks at home simple, and if possible, ask other adults for extra hands to help. We can ask them to help with the newborn for some of the time, so we can have time to be alone with the older child or children. Some older siblings like to be involved in caring for the new baby—fetching a clean diaper or getting soap for the baby's bath. Some won't be interested, and that's okay too.

We can keep a basket of books and some favorite toys on hand while we feed, so that our other children can be occupied while we feed the baby.

When the older one is playing and the baby is awake, it can be fun to talk to the baby about what their older sibling is doing. The baby will benefit from our conversation, and the child will like being the topic of discussion.

We also don't have to give the older sibling the role of being the "big kid in the family." This can be a lot of responsibility for a young child or toddler. Instead, we can give all the children in the family responsibility, for example, saying to them, "Can you look after each other while I go to the bathroom?"

Junnifa introduced the idea of her children caring for each other. If the new baby was crying, she'd ask one of the other children to go and check on their brother or sister. This taught them that they all look after each other, not by age, but as part of being a family.

Note: For tips for setting up the home with more than one child, see page 66.

If the older sibling is upset

Often our response to an older sibling saying "I hate the baby" is that we say, "No you don't. We love the baby." However, in that moment, the older sibling needs to express how they are feeling.

Instead, we could guess how they might be feeling: "Right now you look pretty angry/sad/frustrated with the baby. Is that right?" We can give a listening ear or a cuddle, so they feel understood. And we would also be okay with limiting any physical attacks on the baby, like hitting or biting. **Allow all feelings, not all behavior.**

Then, at another neutral time, we can show the older sibling how to handle the baby: "We are gentle with the baby." And we can translate for the baby: "The baby is crying. I think they are saying that is too rough. Let's use our gentle hands."

Make special time with each child

It's important to schedule some time with each child when we can. If the baby is napping and the older child is awake, this is a perfect moment to connect and do something special together. On the weekend, if there is a partner or family member to help, we can plan a small outing with the older child—to go to the playground, to go to the supermarket together, or for a short walk to chat.

By filling each child's emotional bucket, we can help reduce the cries for attention at other times during the week. And when tempers flare and things don't go their way, we can write down in a notebook what they wanted to do but wasn't possible right then, to remember for our special time together later in the week.

Adjusting to a bigger family

Sometimes we are the parent who needs to prepare for the growing family. Will we love the baby as much as the older sibling? How will we manage with more people to look after? How can we get rid of the guilt we feel that we're not spending as much time with the new baby as we did when their sibling was young?

In his book *Thriving!* Michael Grose suggests that we parent siblings as if we have a large family with four or more children. Parents of large families can't solve every argument and entertain every child. We are the leaders of the family. We lay the foundations of the family's values and oversee the running of the ship.

And love will grow just as a candle can light another candle or another five candles without losing its own light. So our love can be shared with ourselves, a partner, and any number of children. The love keeps growing.

One last thing: Feel free to use the phrase "happy handfuls" when people say we must have our hands full. A friendly reply can be very helpful to staying positive when times are indeed "full."

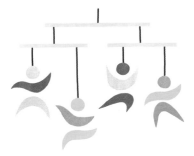

TWINS

There are very few resources about Montessori for twins. However, parents who have come to Simone's classes with twins have found that the Montessori approach is invaluable, with the biggest advantage being the children become more independent as they grow. With two of them at the same age, this is priceless.

Some suggestions for twins are:

- treating each child as unique, for example, looking at their needs individually and calling them by their names rather than "the twins"

- setting up the home so the babies can explore as independently as possible

- involving children in daily life and slowly building skills so they can manage steps for themselves

- sharing by taking turns—rather than having two of every toy in the home, the babies learn to take turns or become creative in finding a way to play together

- it's possible to breastfeed twins simultaneously, and it's okay if that is not manageable for us

- when we are busy with one twin, we can tell the other that we'll be available soon— they learn that when their turn comes, they will have their needs met

- after they can sit without support, they can enjoy sitting opposite each other while eating at a weaning table; look for chairs with arms that will keep them tucked in against the table and low seats so their feet can be flat on the floor

BOOK RECOMMENDATION

For those with twins, *Raising Your Twins: Real Life Tips on Parenting Your Children with Ease* by Stephanie Woo is written by a Montessori-trained parent of twins.

PREMATURE BABIES

We can still connect with babies who are born prematurely and need to be in an incubator in a neonatal intensive care unit.

We can pump milk to offer breast milk if possible. We can talk and sing to our baby when they are awake, and our scent will be familiar to them. We can place our hands on our baby in the incubator and, once our baby is strong enough, we can practice kangaroo care, where the baby is placed on us in an upright position, skin-to-skin. We can also learn special massage for a premature baby that is not too rough on their delicate skin. We observe to see if they are content or if it's too much for them.

And even through the sides of the incubator, we can make deep eye contact with our baby. We can let them know they are loved.

BEING AN ADOPTIVE PARENT

Adoptive parents will have a different experience. We don't have those nine months to get used to the idea of becoming a parent and being able to already connect and bond with the baby through points of reference from the womb (our voice, our heartbeat, our movements), and the baby may come into the family after a drawn-out process of adoption and at any age.

Imagine meeting a baby at, say, 6 months old. Already the baby is starting to move, wriggle, and slide. They may be interested in starting solids as well as milk feeds. And they may come to us feeling emotionally unstable from a difficult situation.

As adoptive parents, we become their rock when everything else in their world has been unstable.

We can create our own type of symbiotic period (see chapter 3), lasting for 6 to 8 weeks, when we limit our social responsibilities and focus on becoming a family. We can establish a home that feels safe, with predictable rhythms and reliable points of reference—places to sleep, feed, and play, as well as our smells, our voices, and our gentle way of handling them.

As mentioned previously in the section for feeding, supplemental nursing systems are available, which adoptive parents can use to induce lactation. If we cannot or choose not to breastfeed our baby, feeding with a bottle while holding the baby close and making eye contact is still a time to create strong bonds.

PHYSICAL DISABILITIES OR NEUROLOGICAL DIFFERENCES

People often ask if there is anything written in Montessori about children with special needs or who are differently wired. There are now Montessori training courses for children with special needs. While it's beyond the scope of this book, we have had children in our classes who have hearing difficulties or physical disabilities like cerebral palsy and children who have selective mutism, ADHD, or autism. We have family and friends whose babies have had heart surgeries, a hip brace in the first year, or needed helmets for head shaping and other reasons.

We treat every child as unique. We observe to see what they are capable of. We give them as much help as needed and allow them to challenge themselves. We look into their eyes with the same love and respect as every other child.

Their timeline may look different. But they are no less capable of being treated as the beautiful human they were put on Earth to be. Let's look at capability. Not disability.

BOOK RECOMMENDATION

For families of a baby with neurological differences, we recommend *Differently Wired* by Deborah Reber and her *TiLT Parenting* podcast.

TO PRACTICE

1. Is there a clear rhythm to our day for our baby?
2. Are we remembering to use moments of physical care as moments for connection?
3. How can we support our child's eating and sleeping? Can we let go of our anxiety in these areas? Can we help as little as possible and as much as necessary?
4. Do we want to make any changes to support our baby:
   - if they are hitting/biting/throwing/pushing?
   - when traveling in the car?
   - to limit or get rid of a pacifier?
   - when they are teething?
   - to learn early skills around sharing?
5. How can we help prepare an older sibling for the new baby?

PREPARATION
OF THE ADULT

8

OUR ROLE AS THE ADULT

One of the great things Montessori teaches parents is that we are not responsible for imparting every single piece of knowledge or idea to our child.

Children are not empty vessels needing to be filled. Dr. Montessori believed that children have the potential to learn most things if put in the right environment. This relieves parents of the responsibility of having to know everything and be everything for our children.

Children—even our tiny babies—are already capable of so much. All we do is prepare conditions that allow all that they carry to blossom. They are like seeds, and parents are like gardeners. We prepare the soil and provide nurturing, and they do the blossoming.

In many ways it is us adults who frame the way our children see and approach the world. The way we speak to them and to others, the opportunities we provide for them, and the environment we prepare for them all have a significant impact on the people they will become.

So even though we don't have to teach our babies everything, everything we do teaches them something, and this can feel like a huge responsibility. It is big work. The kind that we can be intentional about.

We start this work by first preparing ourselves.

"Every generation of children is destined to change humanity—their mission is to transform humanity to ever greater levels of awareness and sensitivity of what is good for everyone. That is why all cultures see in their children the 'hope for tomorrow,' the expectation being that they will be able to make all things better—especially in how we treat each other. But that can never come about if children incorporate our hates, our prejudice, and our petty pride. We must help them adapt to the inherent goodness of humanity and not to the present evils of society."

—Eduardo J. Cuevas G., 2007, "The Spiritual Preparation of the Adult," Montessori Conference China

PREPARING OURSELVES

We talked about preparing the environment in chapter 4—our homes and our baby's space. But there is another very significant part of the environment that we also need to prepare: ourselves!

We need to prepare ourselves physically, intellectually, emotionally, and spiritually for this work of guiding our children. The airplane warning to put on your own oxygen mask first before helping others is such an apt analogy for parenting.

We have to care for ourselves in order to care for another human. Eating, resting, filling our emotional and spiritual tanks—this is what helps us to stay regulated and objective in dealing with our baby. Parenting, especially in the early days, can be very taxing and draining. Our babies are relying on us for so much, and if we do not make conscious efforts to meet our own needs, we might find ourselves so depleted that we go into survival mode. In this mode, we will be less able to respond positively to our babies. In this mode, our baby's cry, which once was just a cue, might become a frustration.

We want our baby to have a fulfilled parent, rather than a resentful parent (putting everyone else's needs first) or a selfish parent (ignoring the needs of others). We need to look after ourselves as well as our baby.

Intellectual preparation

We need to be knowledgable about our child's development, their needs, and how to support them.

This book is a start. We can continue to build on the knowledge by being open to new research and continuing education (such as podcasts, seminars, and workshops) related to parenting, positive discipline, and other related tools that improve our knowledge of the child and equip us with tools for parenting.

Observations are also a good way to increase our knowledge of our child.

With this comes a caveat though: There are so many options now and it can become overwhelming, so we can **be selective and limit our exposure to a few options that resonate with us.**

We can also be open to learning opportunities outside of parenting or Montessori. For example, learning to play an instrument, trying a new sport, or reading something that has nothing to do with parenting but fills our soul. Anything we learn and open our heart to is something that we can model for, or share with, our child.

Physical preparation

Caring for a baby involves a lot of energy, both physical and mental. We need to be in good physical condition to be able to optimally care for our babies.

Good nutrition is so important. Every day we can hydrate often and nourish our body with healthy meals, fruits, and vegetables. As we make this conscious effort for our children, but we need to do the same for ourselves. We can set reminders on our phone to make sure we don't miss a meal. Or we can prepare meals in advance or make sure to have simple ingredients on hand that we can easily throw together.

Exercise. It can be as simple as taking walks with our baby or setting aside time to stretch or work out. This can make all the difference for our well-being and mental health.

Rest. Get as much rest as we can. Lack of sleep can affect our immune systems and also our brains. We don't need to feel bad about asking for help or getting a nanny or babysitter to give ourselves a break.

If we are the child's primary caregiver, we may feel that we have to do everything ourselves or always be there. In the very beginning, it helps to be there as much as possible and form that strong attachment with our baby, but it is okay to take breaks and ask for help as needed. Once the child has formed that strong attachment and has begun trusting the environment, thanks to consistency of care and routines, breaks can be positive for both adult and baby.

Physical care of oneself is so important because it addresses our basic needs. When we are dehydrated, hungry, tired, or sick, it is almost impossible do our best as a parent. Most of the time our brain is in a survival state, so most of our reactions will be freeze, fight, or flee responses. We can monitor ourselves for the following kinds of reactions: feeling overwhelmed, wanting to abandon ship and run away, or anger toward the baby or to the whole situation. If we feel these things, we probably need some time to nurture ourselves physically.

The other advantage to caring for ourselves physically is that we are modeling it for our baby—remember, they absorb everything they see us do.

How do you relax? Find moments to enjoy. (See our list of suggestions on page 220.)

Emotional and spiritual preparation

A support system is so important when parenting. This journey is so much nicer when it is done while walking alongside another person, whether in the form of a partner or co-parent, grandparents, caregivers, or friends.

An extra set of hands is so helpful in the first few months—someone to help make meals, take care of other children, hold the baby, or give the parents a break. (See page 224 for more ways this person can support new parents.) This can be a family member or a friend or, if within our means, a postpartum doula or mother's helper who brings with them some experience of the needs of mother and new baby and understands how to support the family physically and emotionally. Dr. Montessori and Adelle Costa Gnocchi saw a need for this person and envisioned the Assistant to Infancy—a trained Montessori guide—as one who can serve in this role. (Professional help may not be attainable for all families, though in some countries the government will send a mother's helper to assist a new parent in the early weeks.)

Other parents with babies around the age of ours or a little older can also help. Talking to friends can remind us that we are not alone and that whatever we might be experiencing is normal or is a phase that will soon pass. Many parenting struggles are transitory, and we need someone who has gone through that stage to remind us of this.

We can take time to appreciate ourselves, count our blessings, and consciously acknowledge and document the things that are going well. One of the things that can lead to an emotional breakdown is not feeling appreciated for our efforts or not feeling loved. Babies are not using words, so after a day of poopy diapers, little sleep, and lots of crying, we can feel emotionally drained and unappreciated. We can be our own cheerleader and take time to pat ourselves on the back for every day. We can get a pedicure, go out with our friends, or find a simple way to take care of ourselves. It is hard work to be responsible for another human. We want that acknowledgment from others, but we can give ourselves the gift of acknowledging it first.

Taking pictures and documenting the stages is helpful. Review some of the pictures at the end of the day, and often; even seemingly insignificant moments can trigger a memory or a smile. Do remember to enjoy the moments though—we don't need to catch every single one on camera. Also remember to be in some of the pictures, not always behind the camera. Right now we might not feel like being in a photo, but we will look back and cherish these moments.

For those who may be struggling to find the joy in the baby days, there is help available. Postpartum depression is a dark place to be and is experienced by around one in seven mothers (sometimes only after a second or third child). Seek support from a doctor or a health professional we trust.

Self-trust and forgiveness

When we have a baby, there are so many voices telling us what to do and what not to do. Many times they can be conflicting. We believe that parents are gifted with an instinct that they can trust and follow.

We can forgive ourselves when we come up short and know that every one of us has these moments. We learn and grow from our mistakes. And there will be many mistakes—that's okay.

PREPARATION OF THE ADULT

OUR INTELLECTUAL PREPARATION helps us cultivate trust in our babies: We can trust that they know what they are doing and that they have all that they need. And that they will follow their unique paths and timelines given the best conditions, which we do our best to provide.

OUR PHYSICAL AND EMOTIONAL PREPARATION allows us to come to the child with a loving attitude. We can accept our baby unconditionally and love them in spite of any flaws, ours or theirs. Love is void of anger, pride, and ego.

OUR SPIRITUAL PREPARATION allows us to adopt a posture of humility. It is this humility that allows us to constantly work on preparing and improving ourselves for the baby. It allows us to see the baby's potential, to not see them as empty vessels or even as reflections of us or any ideas or aspirations we have for them, but instead as the unique, special beings that they are.

Our own childhood and the way we were parented can affect our parenting. For some of us, we may idolize the way we were raised and often feel like we don't measure up; for others, we may not like the way we were parented and want to do things differently, but we still often find ourselves repeating the patterns; or for some, the balance is just right. In preparing ourselves to be Montessori parents, it helps to take time to revisit what we liked or did not like about our own childhood. To make peace with it and let go as much as we can, knowing that we are starting our own journey.

Instead of feeling like we are falling short, we can acknowledge our efforts and commit to doing the best we can and let that be enough.

We have talked about observing our babies and the environment, but part of preparing ourselves is observing ourselves. Observing our needs, our feelings, our reactions or responses. Often this happens as reflection. Sitting back at the end of the day and thinking about our needs.

TO OBSERVE

Here are some questions we can use to observe and reflect on ourselves. Remember that this should be a growth tool and not a judgment of self.

Did I drink enough water?

Did I eat?

Did I take a break when I needed it?

How did I react to different events during the day?

How might I have reacted differently?

What drove or triggered my reaction?

Are my tanks full?

What did I do well?

What am I thankful for?

49 IDEAS FOR STAYING CALM

How we prepare ourselves physically, emotionally, and spiritually is a personal thing. Yet so many people ask how we can stay so calm in the classroom and at home.

So here are forty-nine ideas to inspire you. These are the things that have helped us show up as the best parents and teachers we can be, and we hope that they help you too.

1. Have a morning ritual for ourselves. Get up before our baby to have some "me" time.

2. Have an evening ritual for ourselves. Enjoy the quiet.

3. Exercise. Yoga. Running.

4. Meditation.

5. Nature. Head outside.

6. Dance.

7. Enjoy our cup of coffee/tea.

8. Meet up with friends with kids.

9. Meet up with friends without kids. Perhaps drink wine.

10. Practice presence.

11. Practice gratitude.

12. Journal.

13. Write down one thing today that would make us happy.

14. Write down one thing today we'd like to remember.

15. Cook (preferably alone while someone is looking after the baby).

16. Video-chat with a friend.

17. Invite friends for a meal.

18. Bake something.

19. Arrange a night out (by ourselves, with our partner, or with friends).

20. Do a babysitting swap with friends.

21. Travel. A weekend away. An overseas adventure.

22. Say "no" to things that don't light us up, or suggest something that you'd enjoy more.

23. Use observation as a tool for being objective about a situation.

24. Be our baby's guide. We are there to support, but cannot make them happy all the time. We can offer a hug though.

25. Set up our home in a way that helps relieve some of the work. A place for everything and everything in its place.

26. Have someone to care for us. An osteopath. Chiropractor. Doctor. Psychologist. Friend.

27. Sleep.

28. Own our choices. Change what we can (be creative), and accept what we can't.

29. See things from our baby's perspective. "Are you having a hard time?" "You're one year old, and you're probably hungry/tired/had a busy day."

30. Go to bed early. Take a nap.

31. Read a good book.

32. Be aware of our thoughts and feelings without judgment.

33. Laugh.

34. Eat cake.

35. Listen to music. 432hz or 528hz frequency music can be particularly healing.

36. Take the dog for a walk.

37. Schedule some alone time.

38. Count down in our head to create a pause and respond rather than immediately react.

39. Have a bath. Every night.

40. Listen to or play music.

41. Nourish ourselves. Notice when we are sluggish, scattered, or pushing ourselves too hard. Make adjustments to balance ourselves.

42. Slow down. Allow enough time. Stop overscheduling.

43. Forgive ourselves when we make mistakes. Model making amends.

44. Celebrate where we are. We are doing our best.

45. Be self-aware and notice when we are being triggered. Make a note to meditate on why. Work on healing.

46. If we feel depressed or burned out, see a doctor or talk to a friend.

47. Practice compassion for ourselves, others, our baby.

48. Stop taking ourselves so seriously.

49. Keep practicing.

DOING OUR BEST

The wisdom from the book *The Four Agreements* by don Miguel Ruiz sums it up so well:

1. **Be impeccable with our word.** Our baby is watching us. Let them see us speaking the truth. In a sensitive way.

2. **Don't take things personally.** Our baby will cry. They are telling us something. We are there to listen. But we don't need to blame ourselves.

3. **Don't make assumptions.** If we are not sure, check. It's amazing how many times we make assumptions about something someone said that was not their intention.

4. **Always do our best.** Even when we have had very little sleep, what is the best we can do today? Perhaps today we will parent from bed, put on some music, postpone some appointments, lie down next to our baby, and let go of everything else.

In the end it is not about perfection. It's about presence. So let's aim for connection over perfection.

TO PRACTICE

- Can we build time for a self-care activity into our daily routine?
- Can we start a daily gratitude routine where we celebrate one thing that we did?
- Can we do something that is just for ourselves at least once a week?
- Can we forgive ourselves for the moments that don't go well and embrace our efforts more than perfection?

"The baby's fundamental need—precisely because he is a human being—is to be loved. But it takes a mature person to love a baby, because love takes time, love takes patience, love takes fortitude, love even requires a certain kind of humility: to love another better than one's self. The baby needs time to be understood: he needs time in everything he does."

—Taken from a speech given by Dr. Herbert Ratner, editor of *Child and Family*, to the American Montessori Society in 1963

WORKING
TOGETHER

9

WE DON'T WALK ALONE

Parenting can be filled with connection. And at times it can be filled with enormous isolation. We might realize that old friends have different priorities and perspectives, that our family helps too much or too little, or we feel the loss of special family members who will never get to know our baby. Also, the wonders of the internet can make us feel guilty that our lives aren't picture-perfect, like everyone else's seem to be. (You know, having casual picnics on the beach with a large group of easy-going friends with babies in arms, children running wild and free as the sun sets.)

It's time for us to build a village for our families. Because our children can learn so much from the vast array of people who make up the fabric of the world. And they will learn to trust the caregivers we choose for them.

Here are some people that can be part of our village:

- Our partner (if we have one)—we can work toward maintaining the connection, we can spend time together one-on-one, we can spend time together as a family, and we can allow each other alone time while the other bonds with the baby.
- Family (nearby)—they can have a special time in the week to come and be with the baby while we take time to be a version of ourselves before "mother" or "father" took over.
- Family (far away)—we can regularly connect over a video chat, read books together despite the miles apart, and sing sweet songs or play music; maybe they can visit us from time to time to help ground the online connection with real-life connection.
- Friends who parent in the same way—it's never been easier to find like-minded families either online and, even better, in person. These can be some of the fastest connections. Parents who meet at Simone's Montessori playgroup often have long-lasting friendships.
- Friends with whom we don't have to talk about parenting—conversation and connection with these friends can feed our soul and give us new inspiration, helping us be a better parent.
- A well-selected babysitter, nanny, au pair, or a day care—to give us some extra hands (or we can arrange a babysitting swap with another family).
- A cleaning person—if funds allow for a once-a-month deep clean to really scrub those places we don't always have time for.

- A professional caregiver—an osteopath, doctor, psychologist, chiropractor, massage therapist, or the like; to help care for us when we are caring for everyone else (again, if resources allow.
- People who live on our street or people working in our local stores—these people play a small part in our daily lives but become part of our extended family as the years pass.

It's okay to ask for help

We might ask for help with the baby. We can also ask for help with other things so that we can spend time bonding and building a connection with the baby.

Sometimes we are so tired, even with people offering to help, that we don't know what needs to be done or how to ask for help. Here's one idea: We can hang a list on the fridge of things that need to be done around the home or for the baby. Then anyone visiting can choose one of these things and help with it. How helpful would that be?

Working with our partner

In some families, there will be a primary caretaker and secondary caretaker. In other families, parents may take on a shared role. Whatever the balance, we can work to stay connected with our partner even once the focus shifts to be "all about the baby."

In families where one person's focus is largely on the baby in the early weeks, our partner can find their own unique ways of bonding with the baby. During pregnancy, they can talk, sing, and play music to the baby, rub our belly, form a deep connection, and lay a foundation for the coming months. Once the baby is born, they can hold and talk to them, their voice being a strong point of reference from being heard in the womb. They can bathe the baby, sing to the baby, change diapers, play music for the baby, have moments of silence together, and spend time gazing lovingly into the baby's eyes. They can also feed the baby from a bottle (with expressed milk or formula).

The partner can work on providing protection and support for the family unit during this symbiotic period—taking phone calls, managing family and friends who want to visit, preparing meals, and picking up supplies at the store. If there are other children, the partner can be the one who helps and supports them—taking them to the park or listening if they are having a hard time with the transition to being an older sibling.

The partner can provide emotional support. Mood-altering hormones rage and recede during pregnancy and the months after birth (pretty much a year after birth, to be honest), such that it can be helpful for the partner to check in daily: "How are you today? Can I get you anything?" It may be some time before the mother has the space in her head to be able to return this support as she adjusts to her new role—physically, emotionally, and spiritually.

This kind of daily check-in during pregnancy can continue once the baby is born. How can we stand together? How can we keep the partnership strong—the thing that created this special human in the first place? And how can we keep this partnership going long after birth, childhood, adolescence, and when they leave the nest?

Working with grandparents and other caregivers

Grandparents and others can help in many ways too.

They can help by giving us a break. They can offer to cook a meal or three. They can share their stories with the baby. They can enrich our family with their music, craft, history, and culture. They can run errands for the family. They can pass on news to friends to give us space. They can do some washing, fold some clothes, wipe down some surfaces, sweep a floor.

They can love us. And we can be grateful and receive at this time.

It can take some time to get on the same page as the grandparents and other caregivers. Raising children in a Montessori way can be quite different from the way they may have raised their own children and what worked for them. So grandparents may feel criticized if we reject the way that they parented us (or our partner). For some creative ideas on educating people about Montessori principles and getting them on the same page, see page 228.

Recognizing that grandparents and caregivers are not setting out to upset us will get us a long way. There are so many ways to raise children, and they are offering their best with their experience and knowledge.

That is the blessing of living in the world with other humans. Understanding that we are all trying to do our best. And how we might all be acknowledged, seen, and have our needs met.

BEING A SINGLE PARENT
OR CO-PARENT

There are so many different family constellations. We may not have a partner, or we might be a co-parent. Every type of family constellation is perfect for our child.

We may worry that our baby is growing up without two parents in the home. That they will be missing out. If we are a single parent, we can find other role models that we want our baby to grow up around. If we have a co-parent, then the baby does have two parents; they live in separate homes and the baby gets to have two houses to grow up in.

When we own our situation, we find that people accept it and don't judge us for our choices. Accept what we can't change, and change what we can. It is far healthier for people to be happy than to stay living together in an unhappy (or potentially dangerous) situation. And sometimes we didn't choose to be a single parent, but we will own it and be the best parent we can be to our baby. That is what we do have control over.

As a co-parent, we aim to be kind about the other parent when in front of our baby and as they grow. If we are having a hard time with the co-parent, find a safe place to discuss this (with a friend or therapist or the co-parent) when the baby is not around. We may not still be together with our partner, but with a baby we will always be family. As much as possible, it's important for the baby to spend time with both parents (unless the baby's safety is at stake). There is good research to support these points, and, in some ways, we need to get along even better when separated to make arrangements to care for the baby in a loving way.

GETTING ON THE SAME PAGE

Sometimes when we feel strongly about the ways in which we want to raise our baby, it can be frustrating when people in our life and our family aren't on the same page. Imagine the following scenarios (probably common for many of us):

- People in our life have a lot of wisdom and want to share it with us, where we may want to discover these things for ourselves.
- People might show love by bringing us gifts, where we prefer less in the way of material offerings.
- Family and friends we were hoping would support us may not have time to come to see us, call us, or offer to help with the baby.
- Our partner or our family may not support our decision, say, to try a floor bed.

Educate by dripping information

We may be lucky enough to have others in our lives who will sit down and read this book with us.

For most of us, we can operate more stealthily—not in a manipulative way, but slowly over time, sharing different information, in different formats, depending on how others take in information. In this way we aim to educate others about the Montessori approach, and while their views may not shift immediately, they will merge with ours over time.

Look for ways that they like to receive information—a video, a blog post, a newsletter, an article, a research paper, a podcast episode. Share stories of what has worked for other people applying the Montessori method. Talk to them about what we are trying and how things are going.

There are now so many different ways of sharing information, so find one in a format that might resonate for them.

Choose our battles

We may not get agreement on all sides about all matters. So we can decide what is the most important to us and make that the priority, the one thing that we will be firm on.

We can be kind and clear, not aggressive. We could say, for example, to our partner, "I love you. I want to show you something that is important to me. I know you don't care about this stuff, but you care about me, so will you work on this with me/listen to me/hear about it? I will lead the way, but I would love your support. Could we make a time to look at it together? When would work for you?"

We love the phrase "It's important to me." Use it in moderation. But use it. It's a way of expressing something without blaming another and requires us to be enormously vulnerable, sharing something we might otherwise choose to avoid discussing.

Communicate in a way that we will (more likely) be heard

When someone feels judged, there is little connection. We close the door to conversation and possibility.

When we correct someone, they can get defensive. They cannot hear what is important to us, and they get lost in justifying themselves.

When we think there is only one way, they might feel like they have no choice. We can look for ways to make requests rather than demands.

What should we to do instead then?

Everyone has thoughts, feelings, and needs, and we need to be creative to find ways that everyone can have their needs met. No one is right. No one is wrong. We find ways to make it work.

The following incorporates some ideas from *Nonviolent Communication* by Marshall Rosenberg for communicating in a way that will make it more likely that we will be heard by the other person. And it opens up a conversation for creativity rather than conflict.

How does it work?

When we have judgment or a thought, we must first look at our feelings. For example, say we are watching a grandparent hover nervously over our baby. We may think, for example, "Why are they always so overprotective of the baby? Why don't they let them explore?" This might make us feel frustrated, maybe even angry, as this is something we've already discussed with the grandparent.

Before we jump in to critcize, first we must ask ourselves why we are feeling this way.

What need of ours might not be being met? It might be that freedom is important to us (leaving the baby to explore freely). It might be respect, that we want others to accept the way we are choosing to raise our baby.

Only when we have explored this for ourselves and are no longer raging can we let the other person know we'd like to talk about it.

How do we communicate our feelings?

- Agree upon a good time for a conversation (not a lecture). Touch on what it might be about and that we are wanting to come up with an acceptable solution for everyone.
- Meet at the agreed-upon time.
- Make an objective statement and use neutral words: "When the baby was playing with the ball near the small step, they were trying hard to make it move and you picked them up saying 'Be careful.'"
- State how that makes us feel and express our need: "I feel upset when I see that. It's important to me that they learn to move freely and learn the limits of their body."
- Seek to understand their perspective: "Is it that you were worried about them being safe?"
- Make a request, not a demand: "Is there a way that we can let the baby explore and you won't need to worry about them being safe?"
- Look for possibilities together. Be open to creativity. It's not always a compromise—many times there is an even better outcome than we could have imagined. "Maybe you could choose to sit between the baby and the step if you are worried?" Or they might offer, "Would it be okay if I took them outside to the park instead?"

An area of conflict can end up leading to connection with people important to us despite our differences. It sounds formulaic at first, but with practice it will become more natural, we will find our own words to express ourselves, and our intentions behind the conversation will be clear—we really want to find a way to have everyone's needs met.

Tip: If someone asks us to talk about something and we are not ready to talk about it (like feeling triggered, tired, emotional, or distracted), we can say, "I'd really like to explore that with you. I'm noticing that I'm not feeling up to it right now. Could we come back to it at eight o'clock, once I've had time to process my feelings and thoughts a little more?" Make it a specific time. And stick to it.

Come from a place of shared values

If we are able to have a conversation, we can find that we have some common values, for example, that we all want the baby to grow up to feel secure, confident, and loved. Coming from this place, we can come up with creative ways to work with each other instead of resenting each other.

The objective is to share our vision and parenting ideas, or at least to find a middle ground.

We can stay calm without getting upset. We can remember not to take it personally.

The important thing is to maintain our relationships. And see that others are coming from their own experience.

What is beautiful is that often we find ways that grandparents and other caregivers can incorporate Montessori with our baby, for example, by sharing their gifts with them, like their love of gardening, hiking, crafting, or baking.

Schedule a regular parenting chat—with partner or caregivers

It can be super tiring to have parenting conversations all week long. Or there can never be a good time to talk about these things. The best partnerships we know have one time in the week (say, a Wednesday evening) where they can really listen to each other, touch base, check in with how they are both doing, and come up with a plan for the week ahead.

We can keep a list on the fridge where we can write down things that come up during the week. We can look at the calendars to see what is coming up and who will cook, pick up groceries, care for the baby, etc. We can discuss things that are coming up for us and find some creative solutions.

And the following week we can check in about how it went, what went right, and what we might need to tweak in the following week.

Make it fun—add some wine, or tea, or candles, or music. Make a plate of snacks to enjoy. And follow up with watching a movie on the couch, playing a board game, or singing along to the guitar. People on Instagram seem to do that, so it must be a thing.

If we have a grandparent or other regular caregiver, we can also schedule a regular chat at least once a month to see if we are on the same page for the care we offer the baby. Or at least on the most important things.

Seek to understand others

Be curious and understanding about the other adults too, just as we are with our children, rather than correcting them. Sometimes we criticize another parent or grandparent or teacher or carer and speak to them in a way that we would not speak to our children.

Our children pick up how we treat others, so we can keep modeling this respectful approach with everyone in our lives.

"When you shouted at them earlier about _____ , it sounded like it was important to you. Can you tell me more about it?"

Express appreciation and have fun

We can remember not to take things too seriously. At its best, raising a child can be full of joy. So let's laugh. We know they will grow out of their tricky phase (and into a new one). And we are all doing our best.

So let's give appreciation to those working with us to look after our baby. It may not be in the way that we would do it, but we can find something to appreciate.
The way they left us some extra food, folded the baby's clothes, danced with the baby, kept them company.

Say thank you and mean it. And we know who will be watching: our baby.

Our baby will learn that we are all different

We are not always going to get everyone to agree with the way we would like to raise our baby. We all come with our own history, and what we learned was right and wrong, and we know how hard it is to change years of ingrained behavior. And who says we are right in any case? Everyone sees the world from their own perspective.

Aim as much as possible to agree on the big picture. And then accept that our baby will learn that different caregivers will respond in different ways—one may be more organized, another more playful. And, as they grow, they will also learn who to go to in order to have their needs met.

WHAT TO LOOK FOR IN A DAY CARE OR CAREGIVER

When parents need or want to return to work, we want to find someone who is able to care for our baby in the same caring way we are choosing to raise our child.

It can be ideal to find someone who can look after our baby one-on-one: a grandparent, nanny, au pair, or similar person. Then our baby will have a rich language environment, one point of connection, and sick days will be less of a problem.

However, we recognize this is not always available to everyone.

A Montessori program for babies up to around 16 months is called a *nido* (Italian for "nest"). Then the child moves into an infant community around 16 months until 3 years.

The *nido* is beautifully prepared following the Montessori principles: well-selected materials arranged for the babies to explore, laid out to be calm and attractive.

In a *nido*, the importance of the staff/caregivers is fundamental. Each one is a unique and special person who:

- is loving, but does not need to be loved by the baby
- has a lot of patience
- can use slow movements
- offers rich language to the baby
- does not get upset when the baby is crying but is able to respond to, and prioritize, crying babies
- understands parents and supports, listens, and provides advice when needed

Ideally the baby has a few dedicated caregivers—their points of reference—who feed them, change them, and with whom they can establish a secure attachment. Research shows that what is important is that the caregivers show sensitivity to the child, understand the child's signals, and that there is consistency (little turnover). So it's also ideal if the child has the same caregivers for the first 3 years (with 8–24 months being a particularly sensitive period for this consistency).

While it would be lovely to have every child in a Montessori *nido*, with a loving carer, a *nido* may not be located near where we live or fall within our budget. So here are some things we can look for when looking for a day care or caregiver:

- The caregiver holds the baby and make eye contact during feeding (as opposed to propping the baby with a bottle or being on their phone).
- The environment is relaxing and attractive for the baby.
- There are age-appropriate materials for the baby to explore—made from natural materials if possible.
- The sleeping area has floor mattresses for the baby to be able to get up from when they wake up.
- Once the baby is eating solid foods, they have access to nutritious food. The baby can feed themselves and sit at a low table or chair to eat (rather than a high chair).
- The caregiver understands the importance of making time for conversation, using gentle hands when handling them, and asking their permission before handling.
- They have an established ratio of one adult to three babies. Babies do not need large social groups. They are still bonding with just a few people as their primary caregivers.
- Absence of televisions

Even these things may be hard to find in a day care or caregiver. Then we do our best to find a cozy place—a place our baby will feel secure, where there is loving staff to care for them.

What if the day care has different values than at home?

This is one of the most difficult questions we get asked. We recognize that we do not live in a utopia and we are asking a lot from these caregivers.

The most important thing is to select a nursery where we feel comfortable leaving our baby. If nothing changes, will we be okay with how it is right now? Sometimes we think that they'll come around to our way of thinking. Many day cares have been around for many years, and these things take time to change, if they ever do.

Look at what they do offer. An outside space, other babies, warm meals, or someone who enjoys laughing and being with babies.

Some caregivers will be stricter than others. Even the Montessori principles can be applied in different ways. Again, it comes back to whether we feel that all the other things outweigh this, for example, beautiful activities to absorb and a cozy space—or if we would rather be in a non-Montessori nursery where the care is warmer.

Once we have a warm relationship with the day care, they may be open to reading some articles on the Montessori approach or pages from this book, or arranging a positive-discipline workshop for the caregivers and/or parents. See the tips for getting on the same page earlier in this chapter.

And if we still don't feel comfortable, then it may be best to take them out of the day care and look for another one that fits our family better. Or come up with a creative solution like changing our working hours, looking after another family's baby one day while they look after ours another, or finding a small group of likeminded families who could share a caregiver.

SAYING GOODBYE TO OUR BABY

When we have someone else to help care for our baby, we will need to practice being confident in saying goodbye. Because remember that they are sensitive too, and pick up how to feel from us.

The first step to saying goodbye to our baby is to make sure we are happy with the care we have chosen. We need to be able to give our baby the message that this is a safe person whom we trust with their care.

Also, babies like predictability, so we can say goodbye in the same way every day. Trina from DIY Corporate Mom told us that she would always tell her baby that she would be home by the time the sun went down. Then she would read a book about goldfish. She would say goodbye. And the caregiver and baby would go to feed the fish. Finding such a connecting activity can be a great idea.

We can also practice hugging for as long as our baby needs to when we say goodbye. We can hug our baby until we feel them release their hold. Trusting this will happen is harder. And so is allowing enough time for it. Some days we may need to tell our baby that we understand they might be feeling sad and we need to leave. And we pass them carefully to their grandparent or caregiver. But most days, if we can allow the time, it will get easier. Maybe even record how many minutes they are upset each time we say goodbye so we can see how they are progressing.

(continued on page 238)

NOTES FOR OUR VISITORS FROM OUR BABY

Dear grandparents, friends, caregivers:

Thank you for visiting me. You are special to me.

Please handle me gently. Ask me if I'm ready before you pick me up, and wait until I respond. Check with me if I'd like a hug or a kiss. And you can tell that I need a little more time if I arch my back, turn away, or cry. Don't take it personally. Sometimes I need more time to warm up.

When changing my diaper, feeding me, or bathing me, talk to me and tell me what you are doing. Touch my body as if it was the first time you had been touched. This is still very new for me. And there is no rush. I love these moments for connection.

Talk to me—if I make a sound, you can copy me. Tell me about all the things around me—the names of those trees, flowers, and vegetables. I want to know everything. I like a bit of a sing-song voice, but it doesn't have to be over-exaggerated and you don't have to use nonsense words like "goo, ga, ga, ga"—copy my sounds, but otherwise talk to me as if I understand everything. Because I am taking it all in.

I know I said talk to me, but I also like quiet when I'm concentrating on something. Let me finish exploring my hands or toes, that leaf, that rattle, that mobile, that ball. My concentration is just as important as yours when you are focused on your favorite thing, so please don't interrupt.

If I fall down and cry, wait a moment before rushing to pick me up. Let me feel it. I am discovering how things work. Sometimes I'll be okay and get back up as if nothing happened. If I do need some comfort, you can check if I'd like a hug. Don't tell me not to worry or not to cry or try to distract me. I want people to allow me to process these feelings. Maybe just ask me if it was a shock.

When I am crying, I am trying to communicate something. Please don't ignore me. I don't just cry because I am hungry. I cry when I am having trouble falling asleep (a comforting hand is sometimes enough). I cry when I'm overstimulated from our day (soothing me and removing stimulation helps). I cry when I want to try something new (perhaps we could try a different space or a different activity). I cry when my stomach hurts (I'm pulling up my legs; please check the section on reflux and colic on page 196 to make some notes). I cry when I have wet or soiled my diaper (it feels so strange against my body). I cry when I'm wearing some clothing that is scratching me (please use soft clothing with few seams or tags that can irritate me), or when there is a crease in the blanket I am lying on (I know it seems small, but it feels like I'm lying on a scratchy log right now). I cry when there is a lot of movement in the house (I love my siblings but can we find a quiet place right now?). I cry when there is little movement in the house (I'd love to lie under the trees and watch the leaves move). I cry when I have drunk too much milk (and my stomach needs time to digest that last feed). And some days I just feel cranky for no apparent reason and I'd like you to love me anyway.

Help me as little as possible and as much as necessary—if you help me too much, I'll never be able to make these wonderful discoveries for myself; but if you don't help me at all, I may give up on the world around me. I know you'll find the right balance.

Let me be close to you.

And let me down on the ground to explore.

Or take me outside. Nature is the best present.

Please share your personal gifts and talents with me. Sing to me, play an instrument, take me out in the garden as you plant the bulbs, show me how you knit or carve wood, teach me your favorite sport or card game, tell me about the old days.

I don't need a lot of physical gifts. I prefer simple toys that don't flash or sing noisy songs. I like ones where I need to think and interact with them. There are lots of ideas in chapter 6 of this book. And they are often not what you find in toy and baby stores. I don't like those screens—the light makes it hard for me to sleep. And I'd rather be able to touch real objects and put them in my mouth.

And speaking of my mouth, that is how I observe the world right now. So let me put things in my mouth, and remove things that won't be safe for me.

Smile at me, laugh with me, look deep into my eyes.

Love me. I love you right back.

So, as hard as it is, this means not sneaking out so that they don't notice us leaving. We are building trust—the baby should know what is happening, where we are going, and when we'll be back. And we do our best to be back at the time we tell them.

We may also need to discuss with the caregiver how to deal with the crying after we leave. It is a lot to take if a baby cries uncontrollably when the parent leaves. We can try to help the caregiver find ways to stay calm when the baby's crying gets too much for them.

Studies show that babies take their emotional cues from the people around them. So if they see we like and trust a caregiver, they will too. It can be ideal for a caregiver to come and spend time looking after the baby in the house when the parent is also there. When our baby sees the caregiver in their home, they will learn that this is someone our family trusts. Similarly, if we are settling them into a day care, we may be able to sit off to the side and allow them to watch us for as long as it takes for them to lose interest and crawl away.

TO PRACTICE

- Can we be creative in finding ways to build our (small) village? There is a lot our baby can learn from others.
- Can we find ways to work with our partner or others so we can all have our needs met?
- Can we practice communication, which fosters connection rather than conflict?
- Can we communicate what is important to us in a way that will (more likely) be heard?

WHAT'S NEXT?

10

THE TODDLER YEARS

As we will quickly notice, just as we are starting to get used to one stage, the baby changes again and we are left catching up. So as our baby approaches the toddler years (from 1 to 3 years), here are a few things to know about toddlers to make this transition a little easier.

Toddlers develop a strong sense of order. Toddlers start to get quite particular about the way things happen. They like things to be done in the same way every day with the same rhythm. The same order getting dressed; the same routine at bedtime. Perhaps even the same spoon every time they eat. They are not trying to make our life difficult. This is important to them. They like to know where things belong and thrive on having a place for everything and everything in its place. Once we know this, instead of battling them, we can work to give them a sense of order and consistency. Research shows that children who grow up in homes with rituals and routines will be the most adaptable in the long run (that goes against the idea some hold that variety will make them more adaptable).

Toddlers do not share easily. Toddlers are busy with mastery. While babies share things easily, most toddlers are so focused on the task at hand that they don't like to give anything up until they are finished with it. Knowing this, we can help them by showing them how to take turns. If they are having a hard time waiting for their turn, we can tell them, "It will be available soon." And, when it is their turn, once they have repeated and repeated until they are finished, another child can have a turn.

Toddlers say "no." As a young toddler, our once easy and accommodating baby will start to show strong preferences. This is an important stage of their development. As they practice being physically independent from us—maybe they start to say a few words or begin to walk or feed themselves—they are asserting themselves as their own person and beginning to use the word "I." Once we know this, we will understand why they are saying "no" and not take it personally. And we will try to find ways to work with them to cultivate cooperation together in a respectful way.

Toddlers need freedom. Toddlers need limits. If there are too many rules, a toddler will fight us at every step. And without any rules, they feel lost; they need some boundaries for security, to feel that someone loves them and will keep them safe. Knowing this, we can decide what limits are important to us and set them with kindness and clarity, maintaining connection with our toddler. Instead of using time-outs or bribes, we will be clear with our expectations: "I won't let you keep hitting me. I'm going over here to calm down, and I'll be right back when I'm ready to talk."

Toddlers can master more steps in a sequence and need increasing challenges. If we don't challenge them, they will challenge us. So we can continue to observe our toddler to see what they are working to master and offer more challenging activities. As they gain mastery, we can also add more steps to add more difficulty, for example, getting an apron first before washing an apple or finding more vases so they can keep arranging flowers.

Toddlers need our help to process a lot of emotions (and yes, they need tantrums too). Toddlers don't hold in their feelings. They need to get them out, otherwise we'll find them bubbling up again and again during the day. Our first response is not, "Don't be silly," but instead, "Oh. Tell me about it," or "Really? Come show me how angry you feel on this pillow," or "Do you wish you could stay at the park and we are leaving now?" Once they've calmed down, then we are ready to leave the park or we can help them to make amends if they've hurt someone or made a mess. They feel safe to let out everything with us and know that we love them at their worst.

Toddlers want to try to do things for themselves. Our toddler's cry of "Me do it" is equally exciting (our toddler wants to learn more) and frustrating (things seem to take four times longer than they should when we are in a hurry). We can set up even more parts of our home so they can manage more and more themselves, for example, so they can help set the table, prepare their own snack, clear the table, and maybe even wash the dishes (the last is a favorite at around 2½ years old). We take time to give them as little help as possible and as much as necessary when they are learning to dress and feed themselves, and all throughout the day. And they are so delighted to manage more and more for themselves over time.

Toddlers are enormously capable. They pick things up easily (the absorbent mind continues). They will make more and more connections in the world around them. They take in everything seemingly without effort. They will start to express themselves and start to move with more and more refinement and coordination.

Toddlers go slowly. They need time to master skills. They need time to process what we say (we can count quietly to ten in our heads to give them time before repeating ourselves). And we need to—as much as possible—slow down to their pace. Rather than rushing them every morning to leave the house, we mostly go slowly and reserve rushing for days when we can't miss the train or we have an important appointment and time has slipped away.

Last, yet most important, toddlers are brilliant. They live in the present moment and are not worried about the past or future. They say exactly what they mean (not trying to be nice or polite), so there's no guessing what they are trying to tell us. They can already do so much for themselves and want to be part of our daily life. They want to help us cook, sweep the floor (really!), and wash the windows with a spray bottle again and again. They hug us and love us like no other.

THE COMING YEARS

Dr. Montessori's theory of childhood is nothing short of remarkable when we see that her overview of childhood development from the ages of 0 to 24 years is now being backed up by research about the brain. Who would have ever conceived in the early 1900s that childhood continues up to the age of 24 years old? Yet now research confirms that the prefrontal cortex (the decision-making center of the brain) is still developing into our early twenties.

She also identified *four planes of development* within this period, each 6 years in length, where there were similar characteristics being shown.

The child from 0 to 6 years

Infancy (0 to 1 year), the toddler years (1 to 3 years), and the preschool years (3 to 6 years) are what Dr. Montessori referred to as the *first plane of development.*

In this plane of development, the child is becoming physically independent—they go from a baby who is completely dependent on the adult to a child who can walk, talk, and do a great deal for themselves.

It is a volatile period with ample change. Never does so much development take place in one plane. So the child will be more emotional as they experience reams of physical, emotional, and social growth in these years.

The child has an absorbent mind across this whole plane, taking in everything in their environment effortlessly.

Where we saw that a baby and then a toddler had an *unconscious absorbent mind,* taking in everything without deliberate effort, a preschooler becomes a curious participant in the process and starts to want to understand more consciously everything they see around them. We call this the *conscious absorbent mind.*

The child begins to ask "What?" and "Why?" and from 3 to 6 years they seek to crystallize everything they absorbed from 0 to 3 years. Around 3, children start to see that symbols can be representations, sometimes showing interest in letters and numbers at this age.

The child from 6 to 12 years

The elementary child becomes a citizen of the world. This is the *second plane of development*. Their curiosity begins to reach beyond the world in front of them, and they want to know more about distant places, ancient civilizations, and the universe and beyond.

Rather than simply accepting and absorbing things as true, the 6- to 12-year-old child will ask questions about the gray areas. They might ask why our family approaches things differently than another family, for example, our religion or our family constellation. They are busy with concepts like right and wrong, good and bad, fair and unfair, and other moral questions.

They also have more complex thinking and can make amazing discoveries for themselves, if we allow them. As their parent or teacher, we can stimulate an interest just enough to draw them in, then leave them to make connections, develop theories, and sometimes explore questions that one might generally discuss in high school, at university, and beyond. It is limitless.

Parents may also be reassured to know that these years are less volatile than other years. With less explosive growth and fewer changes, the child is in a more stable period.

The child from 12 to 18 years

Teenagers have been largely misunderstood. We think that they want to rebel, they don't listen, and are characterized as being moody and grumpy. We can assure you that teenagers are lovely humans to be around. Yes, they have enormous changes going on in their bodies and hormones that can lead to a lot of emotional volatility. Yet they are not so dissimilar from toddlers—they need our support when they are having a hard time. And they need to pass through an important development stage of increasing *social independence*, moving socially away from their family and closer to friends.

This is the *third plane of development*. It's a time of big feelings. But it's also a time when children start to use their imaginations to solve social problems (from climate change, to poverty, to the availability of food, and more). They'll mostly want to spend time with friends, but they also need the security of a solid home base where they can return when they need our support.

FOUR PLANES OF DEVELOPMENT

FIRST PLANE	SECOND PLANE	THIRD PLANE	FOURTH PLANE
0–6 years	**6–12 years**	**12–18 years**	**18–24 years**
We are planting the seeds.	The stem is growing tall and strong.	Leaves and blossoms unfurl, nearing maturity.	The plant is fully grown.

FIRST PLANE — 0–6 years

- physical and biological independence
- absorbent mind
- concrete understanding of the world
- sensorial learner
- working in parallel with small amounts of collaboration
- rapid growth and change

SECOND PLANE — 6–12 years

- mental independence
- developing moral sense (right and wrong) and exploring how things work and connect
- movement from concrete to abstract learning
- mode of learning through imagination
- collaboration in small groups
- less growth, more stable period

THIRD PLANE — 12–18 years

- social independence
- developing social policy (how they would change the world)
- sharing ideas and ideals with others
- enormous physical and psychological changes (similar to the first plane)

FOURTH PLANE — 18–24 years

- spiritual and moral independence
- giving back to society
- reasoning, logical mind
- more stable period (similar to the second plane)

The child from 18 to 24 years

In the *fourth plane of development*, the child is between childhood and adulthood. They are curious about what is ahead but do not feel like an adult quite yet.

They are finding their place in society. It may be that they go on to further study. They may join the Peace Corps. It is often a time of volunteering. And it is a time of enormous freedom.

Dr. Montessori said that if everything in the first three planes of development has been done, the final plane of development takes care of itself.

And now it's time to let our children go. They will always keep the roots we have given them; now they can spread their wings wider and farther.

TO PRACTICE

- What can we prepare for the coming toddler years? How can we adjust our home to meet their changing needs?
- Can we recognize the stages of the four planes of development from our own childhood?
- How can we apply the principles of love, understanding, and respect we learned in this book to others in our lives? Our partner? Other children in our family? Our parents? Neighbors? Siblings? And those who think differently?

THE PATH TO PEACE

Back in the first chapter, we referred to our baby as a hope for the future. Yet we are not waiting for them to solve the problems that we have helped create.

It is together, with our baby, our child, our teenager, our young adult, that we can create a better world.

If we can raise them with this love, respect, and gentle hands, this is how they will learn to treat others. They will love, not hate; they will build bridges, not walls; they will work with nature, not use it up or destroy it.

Let's walk together with our family, with the next family, with our neighbor, with someone who thinks differently. Let's see and accept each other. Let's find ways to work together to meet all our needs.

Let's join Dr. Montessori in her wish for peace in all humankind.

> "I beg the dear all-powerful children to unite with me for the building of peace in Man and in the World."
>
> —inscription on Dr. Maria Montessori's grave in Noordwijk aan Zee, the Netherlands

BONUS
REAL STORIES

We are delighted to share some stories from families around the globe who are incorporating Montessori principles with their babies. Enjoy!

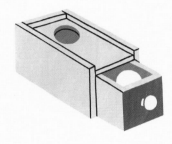

INDIA/UGANDA
(LIVING IN NEW ZEALAND)

Jaya, Nikul, and Anika
Forest Montessori

"I absolutely loved the 'symbiotic period.' We kept visitors to a minimum and just bonded one-on-one at home with Anika. This was our most special time together.

"I was amazed that a baby could concentrate for so long. [The] dancer's mobile, Gobbi mobile, and the wooden bell chimes mobile were her absolute favorites. She also loved grasping her rattles and play silks; she danced with joy every time she could see trees or rain; she loved seeing high-contrast pictures during the first few months; and we read lots of books from birth.

"Long days and nights pass by fast, but the trust they receive from you in the first year will lay the foundation for their secure attachment and their personality. You will reap the fruits of your endless love and hard work in the first year, for the rest of your and their life.

"Routines are very important for a baby—they like to know what to expect. We had a well-defined, but still flexible, rhythm to our day, and Anika thrived knowing what to expect next. I even made us a weekly calendar with pictures, and I would show Anika exactly where we were going before heading out in the car each day. This made car rides much more bearable for her."

UK

Charlie, Maria, and Lukas
Montessori Chapters

"I loved observing the new things he was learning constantly. From noticing the first time he started to focus on an object (our window shutters fascinated him!), to seeing his determination to wriggle himself to get somewhere, before he could crawl, to the first time that he rolled over on his own—they were all such exciting moments to see as a parent!

"We spoke to him as a real person from the moment he was born, letting him know what was happening when we were changing and feeding him and also what we were doing in our day-to-day lives, so he could learn to understand.

"Lukas has loved having the freedom to move around, and we have tried to offer this to him as much as possible—in the house and outside in nature. The day that he learnt to roll, we decided to move our sofa to open up our lounge space in order to give him the opportunity to move around as much as he could with minimal obstacles in the middle of the room.

"I think so much of Montessori is about the mindset, and you can learn lots as you go. Accepting that it is, and always will be, an ongoing process and not putting any pressure on yourself—enjoying it as much as possible.

"I mainly looked out for light cotton clothing that allowed his hands and feet to be uncovered so that Lukas had the opportunity to experience all of the textures around him. We looked for loose, stretchy trousers and tops that enabled him to move easily and as much as he wanted to. We kept the main rooms in the house warm so that he could have fewer layers on, and, whenever possible, we would go outside so that he could feel grass and leaves, roll around, and explore being in nature."

USA

Theresa, Chris, D, and S
Montessori in Real Life

"Montessori has allowed me to give my baby the space and tools to discover, communicate, and realize his own capabilities. It has also helped me to see him as a beautiful and unique individual, with different interests, strengths, and challenges than his sister.

"My favorite moments were the quiet and calm minutes spent nursing, when we'd simply gaze at each other. There was nowhere we needed to be but right there. I still can't get enough of that look of contentment right after nursing, when he stretches his arms and beams up at me.

"Both of my children were captivated by the butterfly mobile between two and three months of age. Once they began to grasp, they adored hanging tactile mobiles, such as ribbons, bells, and teething rings. A long-time favorite in the second half of the first year has been household objects of any kind, boxes that open and close, and simple DIY shakers!

"Our home has played a role in allowing for freedom of movement and natural gross-motor development. Since birth, we have placed our infant on a soft mat or rug on the floor to allow him to stretch and move without constraints. With a low mirror, he has also been able to see his own movements as he learns to move and work in new ways, connecting the mind and body."

TOGO (LIVING IN JAPAN)

Ahoefa, Gabin, Yannis, and Kenzo
Raising Yannis

"Montessori has allowed me to be intentional with my children. It was the guide we needed as first-time parents who were looking for a different parenting style.

"With the newborns, the talking stage was my favorite. My boys are very vocal. It started with the baby talk, so we followed their lead and continued the conversation.

"I wished I'd taken the time to embrace our Montessori journey at home. During our first year, I was very focused on making our home identical to a Montessori classroom. This caused a lot of confusion and difficulty for us and my child, until we decided to embrace this journey from our home. Montessori at home is amazing and very flexible.

"Montessori is a lifestyle; if used properly, it can help establish a healthy bond. My advice to new parents would be to live what you want your children to learn."

SPAIN (LIVING IN USA)

Neus, John, and Julia
Montessorian By Heart

"I observed the magic of Montessori for babies, and it keeps amazing me every day. The freedom of movement helped my daughter love to play and explore independently. She is a baby eager to engage with the world by moving, batting, rolling, grasping, and using all her senses. The Montessori-prepared environment for feeding, changing, and sleeping also helped her feel calm and safe and look forward to new and exciting adventures.

"A quiet, calm, and safe home environment is key to help a baby settle and start engaging with the world around them. We set up designated spaces for sleep, eating, and play, and that helped her anticipate these routines and give her a sense of security.

"I stressed too much in following the presentation timeline of Montessori materials instead of focusing more on my own daughter and her own development. That hit me when I was setting up the Gobbi mobile, and I observed in her facial expression that it was not what she was interested in at that moment. This observation allowed me to pause my mom self and go back to my Montessori self and follow her lead."

NIGERIA

Junnifa, Uzo, Solu, Metu, and Biendu
Nduoma Montessori and
Fruitful Orchard Montessori School

"Montessori helps me to notice and celebrate the effort my children have made, no matter how small. It could be trying to turn over or figuring out how to get a ball into a hole. I never cease to be amazed by how persistent and resilient they can be. Observing them is my favorite thing to do, and it is what allows me to notice. I don't celebrate it in an external way, but I allow it, and give time and space for it. This is a celebration for me, and these little moments add joy to my parenting.

"One of my favorite stages was when they'd wake up from their floor bed and without waking up crying, they'd quietly crawl over to my room, pull up on the side of our bed, and wake me up by rubbing my face with their hand or making small sounds. It happened many times with all three of my babies, and I still smile at the memories. I loved this stage when they were mobile and starting to independently explore. Using a Montessori floor bed definitely contributed to their independence in this regard.

"Having a baby with older siblings comes with its own challenges but is also beautiful to watch. I was lucky to discover Montessori before my first child, and all the work I put in him flowed over to my next child and again from both of them to my third child. They do have times when they disagree or when one interferes with the other's work, but even these moments are opportunities to learn how to express themselves kindly and how to resolve conflict.

THE NETHERLANDS

Simone's parent–baby classes
Jacaranda Tree Montessori and
The Montessori Notebook

"The wonder in a baby's eyes when they realize they made something happen— the way the ball rolled, the sound of a bell when they shake a rattle, or reaching their toes for the first time. These are the simple moments of discovery that will lay the foundation for their love of learning and the belief that they can have an effect on the world.

"I love to see the babies exploring the space in their unique way. One baby will be busy practicing crawling, another sitting to repeatedly drop a ball into a hole, and another lying on their belly to watch another baby in the class.

"The parents can do less than they think. If their baby is concentrating, they can sit to observe. And respond when the baby calls out to them. It's actually a more relaxing way to parent than feeling like we need to entertain the baby all day."

APPENDICES

MONTH-BY-MONTH MILESTONES AND PREPARATION

DURING PREGNANCY

The baby in utero is already absorbing everything.

IMPORTANT IDEAS IN THIS PERIOD

We have 9 months to prepare ourselves to become parents. This gives us time to fully comprehend that we are growing a special human with whom we can already connect. For those of us who are not carrying our baby, there are ways we can prepare to connect (see page 209). We prepare our space so that when they arrive, they will know we have been waiting for them. We communicate that they are loved, accepted, and wanted.

BOND WITH OUR BABY

- Massage the belly.
- Talk to the baby in the belly.
- Our partner (if we have one) can also talk to the baby in the belly and rub the belly.
- Communicate to the baby that they are wanted.
- We are creating points of reference for the baby to help them transition from the womb after birth.
- For adoptive or non-gestating parents, see page 209.

PREPARATION OF PARENT(S)

- Good nutrition
- Emotional/spiritual preparation
  - Make space for a baby in our lives.
  - Speak to others about being a parent.
  - Find like-minded families.
- Keep the emotional environment as stable as possible.
- If we have a partner, create a ritual of being together and checking in with each other that can continue after birth (e.g., having a cup of tea/glass of wine at the end of the day or spending some time in the morning sitting outside together).
- Look into birth options.

PREPARE CLOTHING FOR OUR BABY

- Soft clothing without seams and labels
- Made of natural materials, if possible
- Kimono-style tops or buttons at neck to make it easy to go over the baby's head
- Cloth diapers, if available

PHYSICAL PREPARATION OF OUR SPACE

- Keep the baby's space attractive and simple, with essentials at the ready.
- Cestina (Moses-style basket) and floor mattress for sleep
- Movement area with horizontal mirror
- Adult chair for feeding (if space allows)
- Changing pad
- Baby carrier and stroller
- Topponcino (thin, quilted pillow) to hold the baby during the first weeks
- Baby bath
- See chapter 4 for more details.

MONTHS 1 TO 2

The symbiotic period

IMPORTANT IDEAS IN THIS PERIOD:

1. **SECURITY.** We are building trust with our baby during the first hours, days, and weeks; we respond to their cries; we cradle them with gentle hands; we address them before picking them up.

2. **ADAPTATION.** During this period, the baby is adjusting to life outside of the womb and getting to know us, and we are getting to know them. We can make this transition as smooth as possible by keeping things simple.

3. **ORIENTATION/POINTS OF REFERENCE.** The baby learns to orient to us; we can help them with this by having a limited number of caregivers at this time and by providing consistent areas for feeding, sleeping, playing, and changing/dressing.

4. **ATTACHMENT/SEPARATION.** These early weeks are critical for the baby's attachment. We begin laying the foundation for strong attachment in the first months (with attachment happening around 8 months).

5. **TOUCH.** We use gentle, respectful touch when handling the baby. Confident, efficient movements give the baby a feeling of security and prevent us from startling the baby with unexpected movements.

6. **PHYSICAL CARE.** A lot of time will be spent feeding, changing diapers, establishing sleep patterns, and bathing the baby. We can use this time mindfully as moments of connection with the baby.

BOND WITH OUR BABY

- Hold the baby, looking into their eyes.
- Have simple conversations.
  - While nursing
  - While bathing the baby
  - During diaper changes
  - Through gentle baby massage
- Sing/dance/play music
- Skin-to-skin

PREPARATION OF PARENT(S)

- Partner can provide "protection" for family unit.
- Ask for help from partner, grandparent, caregiver, cleaner, or friend with cooking, cleaning, picking up groceries, looking after older siblings.
- Get as much sleep as possible; rest when the baby rests.
- Observation: Learn to understand our baby's needs, their ways of communication, and their unique development.

DAILY RHYTHM AND CARE

- The baby will wake to feed, then take some brief time to play/get changed/be held/have conversation, and then go back to sleep.
- Follow the baby's natural rhythm.
- Feeding on demand and many naps
- Choose clothing for free movement that is gentle on skin and easy to put over the baby's head or kimono-style.
- Ask permission from the baby before handling them—always with gentle hands.
- Keep the baby's hands free—a point of reference from the womb.

PHYSICAL PREPARATION OF OUR SPACE

- Keep space a little warmer and dimmer in the first days to help the baby adjust from the womb.
- Feeding area—try to keep consistent; at night, sit in a chair in the bedroom if space allows.
- Sleeping area—a cestina on floor bed
- Changing area—a changing pad used in the same place every time
- Movement area—a floor mat where the baby can stretch and see themselves in a mirror
- Topponcino to use as a point of reference and to remove overstimulation when the baby is being held

ACTIVITIES FOR OUR BABY

- Visual development—the baby can focus around 12 inches (30 cm); make eye contact; follow shadows from trees; interact with Montessori mobiles (Munari, octahedron, Gobbi); track older siblings
- Physical development—movement mat; let the baby stretch and learn about their body, studying their hands and feet
- Language—conversation (give them time to respond); read simple books to them; and from birth, speak to the baby in multiple languages if you have a multilingual family
- Aural development—our voices, bells, wind chimes, gentle music (especially the same music played while the baby was in the womb)

MONTHS 3 TO 4

More wakeful and alert, and trying new skills

IMPORTANT IDEAS IN THIS PERIOD:

We continue to lay the foundation for security, adaptation, orientation, attachment, touch, and physical care from the first two months. The baby is more wakeful and alert and seeks more information from their "environment"—the people, activities, and our spaces. We can see them respond to sounds and track with their eyes and reach out to the world—sensorial explorers. They are working on visual development, aural development, coordination of their limbs (to bat something with their hands or feet), and can perhaps hold something in their grasp.

BOND WITH OUR BABY

- Moments of physical care don't have to be rushed through—they can be moments of connection with the baby.
- Time for singing, playing music, moments of silence, making eye contact
- Gentle massage
- Interest in faces and watching our mouth
- Involve them in daily life around the home (and take them on simple outings).

PREPARATION OF PARENT(S)

- Take time to rest when the baby sleeps.
- Observe our baby's unique development— what is our baby like? What are they interested in? How can we support their development right now?
- Find ways to continue to connect with our partner (if we have one)—e.g., having a morning cup of tea, foot massages in the evening, lying together in bed.
- Separating: Some parents may be returning to work at this time and this is also a time to take little breaks away to refresh one's self. Always tell the baby where you are going and when you'll be back.

DAILY RHYTHM AND CARE

- Clothing—ensure free movement; uncover head, feet, and hands whenever possible
- Pacifiers— generally not used in Montessori, limit to sleep time if used
- Limit time in "buckets," meaning containers like car seats or bouncers, and allow free movement.
- Continue to ask permission to handle the baby.

PHYSICAL PREPARATION OF OUR SPACE

- Most areas will be the same as months 1 to 2.
- Once the baby is too big for the cestina, they can sleep on the floor bed or in our bed if co-sleeping.
- Play area—includes movement mat, mirror, and a low shelf with simple grasping toys

ACTIVITIES FOR OUR BABY

- Visual development—the baby can continue to use mobiles, make eye contact, and track movement in the space
- Gross-motor development—with time to explore, the baby may try rolling and will show interest in their hands and feet
- Fine-motor development—they may start to bat at the mobiles, so we can then add grasping toys for them to pull on and kick; provide interesting things for them to touch
- Language—increased vocalizations; continue to provide rich language, books, and conversation with the baby; they may practice bubble-blowing with their lips
- Aural development—think of sounds for the baby to explore

MONTHS 5 TO 6

Increasing awake time, movement, and vocalizations

IMPORTANT IDEAS IN THIS PERIOD:

The baby may wake without being immediately hungry. They can play for increasing periods of time, and they become interested in things that move, roll, and can be manipulated. Order remains important in their physical space and with their caregivers and the rhythm of their day. When they begin to eat solids, they are beginning to move from collaboration to independence as they bring food to their mouth by themselves, for example, pieces of bread or well-cooked vegetables. They may express preferences.

DAILY RHYTHM AND CARE

- 3 to 4 naps a day
- Allow time to play/explore without interrupting
- Introduction of first solid foods at 6 months

PREPARATION OF PARENT(S)

- Give as little help as needed and as much as necessary when the baby is playing—a little frustration can lead to a positive sense of mastery.

ACTIVITIES FOR OUR BABY

- Grasping toys—made of beautiful natural materials, items that fit in their hand, can include a bell/small beads inside to give aural feedback
- Treasure or discovery baskets to explore
- Language—babbling and practicing sounds

PHYSICAL PREPARATION OF OUR SPACE

- Largely the same as previous months
- Weaning table and chair

MONTHS 7 TO 9

World opening up, food exploration begins, and baby starts to seek some independence

IMPORTANT IDEAS IN THIS PERIOD:

The baby often begins to crawl and pull up to stand in this period. There is an increasing interest in food and feeding themselves. They seek independence (and then return to us). The baby begins to explore further in an expanded area beyond "their room." We can leave their door open while they nap or play (as long as it's safe). When they wake or are done playing, they find us by following our voice or sounds. When we are together, they may crawl farther and farther away from us, check to see that we are still there, and continue exploring. We can help these explorations by keeping our home environment consistent and predictable. In those moments when we notice them exploring farther than usual, we can remain where we are, a point of reference and refuge that they can come back to as necessary. Separation anxiety can begin around this time. We can tell the baby where we are going when we leave them and reassure them on our return.

DAILY RHYTHM AND CARE

- Introduction of solids continues to three meals a day
- Breastfeeding/bottle-feeding
- Two or three naps during the day

PREPARATION OF PARENT(S)

- Ensure safe spaces to explore.
- How to handle difficult behavior, for example, during diaper changes or when put in a car seat. When we view these processes as collaborative ones and involve the baby, we find that it becomes less difficult. We notify them, "I am going to change your diaper/put you in the car seat. Please lift your leg/put in your arm or I am going to help you lift your leg/put in your arm." We follow a consistent process, and our baby knows the process and feels like part of it.

ACTIVITIES FOR OUR BABY

- Grasping toys—made of beautiful natural materials
- Opening and closing
- Posting objects like balls
- Threading bangles/rings onto a stick
- Language—can begin introducing a few signs if doing sign language
- Basket of balls—to crawl after, roll between us, encourage movement

PHYSICAL PREPARATION OF OUR SPACE

- To allow more space to move, remove movement mat when the baby starts crawling.
- Provide places to pull up on—low, heavy furniture like ottomans or a bar in front of a mirror.

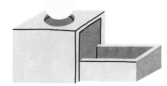

MONTHS 10 TO 12

Our explorer

IMPORTANT IDEAS IN THIS PERIOD:

The baby is often pulling themselves up to stand during this period—their world is opening up. Fine-motor skills are developing, including full-hand grasping, grasping between thumb and fingers, and the pincer grip. The baby's independence is increasing—moving away from the parents to explore the world around them. Baby is moving faster and farther, and then coming back to check in. There is more independent play. Language efforts begin to increase—babbling as if speaking in sentences, possibly repeating words or sounds, and making sounds of animals and single words can start at around 12 months. It takes so much neurological effort to learn to walk and talk that we often find that one will plateau as the other takes off; we may see a child walk before talking or vice versa. There is an increasing trust in self.

DAILY RHYTHM AND CARE

- Take time to explore the world around us—outdoors, supermarket, library, the beach or forest; show them our daily life.
- Around two naps a day
- Breakfast, lunch, and dinner—solid food they feed themselves
- Breast milk/bottle—morning and night
- Toileting—we can introduce some of the skills that will be required for toileting. We can introduce a potty, the baby can spend time in training pants instead of diapers, and we can observe and note their toilet patterns.
- Dressing—moving from collaboration to some independence

PREPARATION OF PARENT(S)

- Offer a firm foundation as their secure place, while giving them the emotional message that it's okay to explore places farther from us.
- Continued observation to see where they are developing
- Acceptance of their uniqueness and particular timeline of development
- The baby can be worn in a baby carrier while also allowing a lot of time out of the carrier for free movement. Once the baby is walking, we can let the baby walk when going out (at first small distances, then gradually increasing).

ACTIVITIES FOR OUR BABY

- Post a ball into a hole—the ball comes straight out; put a ball into a hole—open a drawer to find it again; ball hammering
- First puzzles—putting a wooden egg into an egg cup; a pop-up toy; nesting cups; simple one- to two-piece puzzles with large knobs
- Basket of balls—to crawl after, roll between us, encourage movement
- A wagon to push—once they can pull themselves up
- Rich language—books, conversations and naming *everything*
- When the baby takes their first steps, their hands become free to carry things and they see the world again from this higher perspective—try to avoid being tempted to hold both their hands to allow them to walk before they are ready.
- Allow time and space for climbing, and show them how to climb down backward, e.g., using stairs in the home.

PHYSICAL PREPARATION OF OUR SPACE

- Create a "yes" space for them to explore freely.
- Avoid playpens at any age but particularly now that they are on the move.
- Have low furniture for them to pull themselves up on and cruise—an ottoman, a bar on the wall, low shelves, the couch.
- Low shelf with simple activities that challenge their growing abilities
- Low table and chair—for eating and to bring an activity to
- Potty

ACTIVITIES LIST FOR BABIES

Ages listed below are to be used as guidelines only. Activities should be chosen based on the baby's individual interests and what skills they are currently developing. Follow your child. See which activities keep their attention, and remove those that are too hard or too easy.

BABIES UP TO 6 MONTHS

AGE	ACTIVITY NAME	DESCRIPTION	AREA OF DEVELOPMENT
All ages	Music/dance/ movement/ singing	• Play musical instruments • Listen to beautiful music (preferable to listen actively, not just as background music). • Dance with the baby • Movement—starting from birth, and on a mat with a mirror hanging lengthwise on the wall; time to move, stretch, and explore the body • Sing—starting from birth	• Music and movement
All ages	Books	• A collection of realistic books that are of interest to a young child; should relate to the life a young child is living • Begin with books that have one picture on one page, then move on to a picture with one word, next a picture with a simple sentence, building to simple stories and finally, more complex stories. • Arranged so that children can see their fronts and access them easily, perhaps in a small basket for a few books or on a small bookshelf • Start with board books and move on to hardcover and paperback.	• Language
All ages	Rhythmic language	• Simple, short poetry; songs; rhyming ditties • If it is too long, it is overwhelming for the child. • Be fairly realistic. • Finger and body movements that go along with the stories, songs, or rhymes or create your own • Examples: action rhymes, finger rhymes, haiku, patty-cake	• Language

AGE	ACTIVITY NAME	DESCRIPTION	AREA OF DEVELOPMENT
From shortly after birth	Self-expression	• In moments of care during the day—diapering, dressing, eating—we can allow the baby to respond to our conversation. • When the baby is non-verbal, conversation can be sounds, facial expressions, or poking out their tongue. • As the baby becomes verbal, they will use first words, then later phrases and sentences. • The adult gets down to the baby's eye level, maintains eye contact (if culturally appropriate), and is present. • The adult transmits that they are very interested in what the baby is sharing; for example, through body language, like nodding, or through affirming language, using words like "Really?," "Yes!," "Is that so?" "Sounds interesting."	• Language
Newborn	Munari mobile	• A black-and-white mobile • Hang it at the baby's focusing distance, no more than 12 inches (30 cm) away (generally newborns can focus the distance to their parent's face when held).	• Visual development
From 2 to 3+ weeks old	Music box	• A hanging music box with a string that the adult or child pulls to activate (or with a crank suitable for an older child) that plays a classical piece of music • Initially, the adult starts the music box for the baby. Once the child is sitting, the music box can be attached to a wall and the child can be shown how to pull cord to make it play. • Can also become a postnatal point of reference if used as part of a routine, e.g., diaper changing	• Auditory development
Around 2+ months	Octahedron mobile	• Has three different colors; light reflects on reflective paper • Introduces primary colors • Hang at a height the baby can focus on; this may now be a little higher than at birth.	• Visual development
Around 2+ months	Interlocking circles	• One full circle and one with a slot card that is half the diameter of the circle • Initially, place it in the baby's hand so they can use their reflexive grasp. • As reflexive grasp changes to intentional grasp, the baby will reach and grasp with their whole hand, a finger, etc. • An older baby will do hand-to-hand transfer, roll along the ground, etc.	• Grasping materials

AGE	ACTIVITY NAME	DESCRIPTION	AREA OF DEVELOPMENT
Around 2 to 3 months	Gobbi mobile (see page 135)	• A single color gradation of five to seven balls • Arranged from lightest to darkest in increasing lengths of cotton or coming to the lowest point in the middle • The thread used to hang each ball is the same color as the ball.	• Visual development
Around 3+ months	Mobile with stylized paper figures, e.g., reflective paper dancers (see page 136)	• Figures made of reflective paper which would realistically move, e.g., dancers, fish, pinwheels	• Visual development
Around 3+ months	Other mobiles	• Make mobiles by hanging small objects from an embroidery hoop, then hanging the hoop parallel to the ground. • Examples: pictures of faces, reflective paper, or leaves	• Visual development
Around 3+ months	Mobile with stylized wooden figures	• Three to seven different wooden figures that can move realistically, e.g., dolphins, birds, waves • Eye-catching colors to attract attention	• Visual development • Stimulus for reaching, grasping, and batting
Around 3+ months	Rubber ball with protrusions	• A nontoxic rubber, vinyl, or plastic sphere with raised protrusions • Initially hold the ball near the baby's hands; easy for the child to grasp, manipulate, and suck on. An older child will do hand-to-hand transfer, bang on surfaces with the ball, and explore other movements.	• Grasping materials
Around 3 to 3.5+ months	Three colored spheres	• Three colored balls suspended at an angle or in a triangle, with the longest thread in the middle • Red, blue, and yellow are a good start, or else another color combination, with the darkest color on the longest thread. • Balls should fit in the baby's hand but not be too small (which would be a possible choking hazard) (see page 107).	• Visual development • Stimulus for reaching and grasping and batting
Between 3 and 4+ months	Grasping beads	• Five wooden beads threaded and knotted onto leather cord or rope or sturdy cotton cord • The baby holds, manipulates, and mouths the beads.	• Grasping materials

AGE	ACTIVITY NAME	DESCRIPTION	AREA OF DEVELOPMENT
Around 4+ months	Bell on a ribbon	• A bell threaded onto a ribbon that hangs from elastic, allowing the baby to pull the bell toward themselves	• Auditory development • Visual development • Stimulus for reaching and grasping and batting
Around 4+ months	Ring/bangle on a ribbon	• A ring/bangle made from bamboo, metal, or wood and suspended on a ribbon with elastic at the top • The ring should be big enough for the baby's hand to fit through and grasp.	• Visual development • Stimulus for reaching and grasping and batting
Around 4+ months	Interlocking rings	• Three or four rings that interlock • Made of metal or wood—different materials produce a different sound • Place close enough to the baby for reaching, grasping, and manipulating.	• Grasping materials

Around 4+ months	Home objects	• Examples include:
		  ○ Honey dipper (with the handle cut short and sanded)
		  ○ Doll made from a wooden clothes pin
		  ○ Spoon
		  ○ Belt buckle
		  ○ Bangle bracelets
		  ○ Keys on a keyring
		• Provide grasping and manipulating experiences for the child to explore using their hands.
		• Check for safety, e.g., choking hazards or sharp edges.
			• Grasping materials

Around 4+ months	Bamboo cylinder rattle	• Rice, tiny pebbles, or grains placed inside a piece of bamboo, with the ends plugged with non-toxic wood putty • The baby holds it, shakes it, and experiences the sound it makes.	• Auditory development • Tactile experiences
Around 4+ months (or earlier when baby has reflexive grasp)	Cylinder rattle with bells	• A piece of doweling sanded smooth with a bell safely attached to each end or hollow with a wire inside to hold a bell at each end • Check for sharp bits that could cut the baby. • The baby holds it, shakes it, and experiences the sound it makes.	• Auditory development • Tactile experiences
Around 4+ months (or earlier, with reflexive grasp)	Commercial rattles	• Look for rattles that are wooden or made of natural materials. • Should be ones that are easily grasped and not too big, so the baby can hold it to make a sound • For shaking and experiencing sound	• Auditory development • Tactile experiences

AGE	ACTIVITY NAME	DESCRIPTION	AREA OF DEVELOPMENT
Around 4+ months	Cube with bell	• A hollow cube with rounded corners and a bell inside • For shaking and experiencing sound	• Auditory development • Tactile experiences
Around 4+ months (or earlier, with reflexive grasp)	Bells on leather strap	• Three bells attached to a leather strap • The baby can grasp and manipulate it.	• Auditory materials • Tactile experiences
Around 4+ months (or earlier, with reflexive grasp)	Silver rattle	• A lightweight silver rattle • The baby can grasp and manipulate it.	• Auditory development • Tactile experiences
Around 5+ months	Other sound objects	• Simple musical instruments like maracas • Gourds filled with beans, rice, etc. • For shaking and experiencing sound	• Auditory development • Tactile experiences
Around 5+ months or once sitting	Toy on a suction-cup base	• An object that will rock when it is hit but stay attached to surface • For example, a clear ball filled with lots of tiny balls on a rubber suction stand • The child bats, reaches, and attempts intentional grasping without material moving away.	• Activities for eye-hand coordination
5 or 6+ months	Basket with known objects	• Place two or three of the child's most frequently used toys in a small soft basket • The adult can change the objects as their favorite ones change. • The baby lies or sits and chooses one of the objects.	• Activities for eye-hand coordination
5 to 7+ months	Knitted or crocheted ball	• A pliable, soft knitted or crocheted ball • When the child grabs it, they can get a good hold on it with their fingers. • Placed near the baby to encourage movement	• Activities for gross-motor movement
Around 6 to 8+ months	Cylinder with bell	• This is a wooden rattle that rolls with a bell inside. • Placed near the baby to encourage movement	• Activities for gross-motor movement • Auditory stimulus as a movement incentive
Once baby starts to pull up, from 7+ months	Ottoman	• A heavy, stable ottoman that does not tip when the baby pulls to standing • The height of the ottoman should be at stomach height for the baby.	• Activities for gross-motor movement • Offers the baby an independent means for pulling to standing and cruising

AGE	ACTIVITY NAME	DESCRIPTION	AREA OF DEVELOPMENT
Once the baby starts to pull up, from 7+ months	Bar on wall	• A bar secured safely to the wall to enable the baby to pull up and cruise • About one inch (3 cm) away from the wall to allow the hand to wrap around the bar • Should be at chest height for the child • Could put a mirror behind the bar	• Activities for gross-motor movement • Offers the baby an independent means for pulling to standing and cruising
Between 7 and 9+ months	Egg in an egg cup/cup with ball	• A wooden egg cup with a wooden egg inside, or a large ball in a cup • To practice removing and releasing an object into a container	• Activities for eye-hand coordination
Between 7 and 9+ months	Box with cube	• A wooden cube that fits into a handmade box • To practice removing and releasing an object into a container	• Activities for eye-hand coordination
Around 8+ months	Box with tray and ball (object permanence box)	• A rectangular box with a tray attached with a hole in the top of the box for posting the ball (see workman.com/montessori for a tutorial on making this) • The ball should have a nice sound to it, like a wooden ball or table tennis ball. • To practice posting and intentionally releasing an object • To help the child understand object permanence • You can observe the child's different grasps on the ball, such as a whole-hand grasp, four-finger grasp, or two-finger grasp.	• Activities for eye-hand coordination
Once child is creeping, around 8 or 9 months	Basket of balls	• A collection of balls that are different sizes and textures • Examples: rattan ball, ball with protrusions, mini football • The baby can kick, roll, chase, manipulate, and feel the balls with their hands.	• Activities for gross-motor movement
From creeping until walking well, around 8 or 9 months	Stair	• Three stairs with a railing to hold on to on either end of a bridge • The stairs are wide but not very high.	• Activities for gross-motor movement
From creeping, around 8 to 10+ months	Ball tracker	• A series of ramps in a frame with a small ball • A hole at top left for dropping in the ball and another hole at the end of each ramp for the ball to drop onto the next ramp (instructions online at workman.com/montessori)	• Activities for gross-motor movement • Visual tracking • Auditory tracking from the sound of the ball in the tracker

AGE	ACTIVITY NAME	DESCRIPTION	AREA OF DEVELOPMENT
When the child pulls to standing, around 8 to 10+ months	Low, heavy table	• A low table made of very heavy wood for the baby to grasp and pull up on	• Activities for gross-motor movement
Once the child is able to sit stably, around 8 to 11 months	Rings and peg on rocking base	• This can be the classic Fisher-Price toy or a smaller five-ring model, with rocking base. • Initially, use it with the largest ring only. • A rocking base is used so it won't fall over.	• Activities for eye-hand coordination
8 to 12+ months (depends on skill level of previous activity)	Rings/peg on stable base	• A wooden base with a peg and a ring • Initially, the ring should have a very large opening.	• Activities for eye-hand coordination
Around 8 to 12+ months	Spinning top	• A traditional tin spinning top with a handle to pump to make it spin • Babies enjoy moving after it and eventually will be able to make it spin.	• Activities for gross motor movement
Between 9 and 11+ months	Box with drawer and ball	• A box with a hole in the top for posting and a drawer that pulls out • To practice posting and intentionally releasing an object • To help the child understand object permanence	• Activities for eye-hand coordination
Between 9 to 12+ months	Box with knitted ball	• A square box with a hole in the top slightly smaller than the knitted ball and a drawer • To practice posting and intentionally releasing an object • To help the child understand object permanence	• Activities for eye-hand coordination
Around 10+ months	Box with balls to push	• A rectangular box with three holes and balls on top • To practice posting and intentionally releasing an object • To help the child understand object permanence	• Activities for eye-hand coordination
From 10+ months	Furniture with keys	• Any piece of furniture with a lock and key that the child could work to open • Attach the key to the furniture with string.	• Activities for eye-hand coordination
10 to 12+ months	Wagon	• A wagon that is heavy enough so it does not tip as the child pulls up on it; a sandbag can be used to weigh it down	• Activities for gross-motor movement

AGE	ACTIVITY NAME	DESCRIPTION	AREA OF DEVELOPMENT
10 to 12+ months	Cabinet doors and drawers	• Cabinet doors and drawers, vanity cupboards • The adult places room-appropriate items for the child to find, for example, plastic pots and pans in a kitchen cupboard or items such as hairbrushes or clips in a bathroom drawer.	• Activities for gross-motor movement
10 to 12+ months	Basket with rings and peg	• Two or three rings in a basket and a base with a peg • The thickness of the rings can be the same or varied for an additional challenge.	• Activities for eye-hand coordination
11 to 12+ months	Spindle with napkin rings	• A spindle with two or three round metal or wooden napkin rings of identical size • On a shelf, with the rings sitting on the spindle, OR it could be on a tray with a basket for the rings	• Activities for eye-hand coordination
12+ months	Using chalk, crayon, or pencil	• A block crayon or chunky pencil (like a Stabilo woody 3 in 1 pencil) • Paper in a variety of shapes, colors, and textures • Use an underlay to protect the table.	• Art/self-expression

12+ months	Easel with chalk	• A chalkboard that is any of the following:
		  ○ On the other side of a painting easel
		  ○ A very large piece of plywood mounted low on the wall covered with chalkboard paint
		  ○ A small chalkboard that sits on a shelf
		• For chalk, start with white and gradually introduce colors and different types.
		• A small eraser
			• Art/self-expression

Able to stand unaided	Easel with paint	• An easel • Paper cut to completely cover the surface of the easel • Start with one color of (very thick) paint in a paint pot. Gradually introduce other colors one by one. Can use two or more pots for an older child. • A chunky paintbrush with a short handle for small hands to hold easily • A painting smock/apron • A cup hook to hang the smock/apron • Extra paper placed in a bin • A wet cloth to wipe up spills	• Art/self-expression
12+ months	Base with rings of dimensional gradation	• A base with spindle and four or five rings of varying gradation, ideally alternating colors • The bottom ring should not be bigger than the child's hand span.	• Activities for eye-hand coordination

AGE	ACTIVITY NAME	DESCRIPTION	AREA OF DEVELOPMENT
12+ months	Nuts and bolts	• One or two large bolts with a corresponding nut; start with the nut on the bolt.	• Activities for eye-hand coordination
12+ months	Opening and closing	• A basket with two or three common household objects for opening and closing, e.g., a decorative box, tin, purse with snap fastener, makeup container (such as a powder compact or lipstick case), toothbrush holder	• Activities for eye-hand coordination
12+ months	Vocabulary objects	• Classify real or replica objects; three to six objects • Examples: fruits, vegetables, clothing, zoo animals, farm animals, pets, insects, mammals, birds, vertebrates, invertebrates	• Language development • Expands vocabulary
12+ months	Peg box	• A wooden box with six holes and an inset tray area for placing pegs removed from the holes	• Refinement of eye-hand coordination and grasp
12+ months	Cubes on a vertical dowel	• A base with three cubes on one dowel; cubes stored in the basket or on the dowel • Preparation for bead stringing	• Refinement of eye-hand coordination and grasp
12+ months	Puzzles	• A collection of puzzles starting with one-piece knobbed puzzles and progressing to greater and greater difficulty • The kinds of subject matter depicted on puzzles need to be realistic and appealing, e.g., animals, construction vehicles.	• Refinement of eye-hand coordination and pincer grasp • Develops the ability to recognize a background shape
Around 13+ months	Locks and keys	• A lock and key placed in a basket	• Activities for eye-hand coordination
Around 13+ months	Slotted box with chips	• A box with a slot cut into it • A latch on the box adds a challenge for the fingers. • Examples of posting items include large coins, small letters (laminated), and poker chips. • Use a tray to hold both the box and the basket of posting items.	• Refinement of eye-hand coordination and grasp
Once a child can walk	Table wiping	• A tray or basket with a sponge/drying mitt • A supply of replacement drying mitts	• Care of environment

PRIMITIVE REFLEXES

MORO: involuntary startle reflex

BAPKIN: movement of the mouth and tongue when the palms of hands are stimulated

ROOTING: when the cheek or lip is touched, baby faces toward the stimulus and makes sucking motions with the mouth

TONIC NECK, ALSO KNOWN AS FENCER: baby's head is turned to one side and the arm on that side stretches out; the opposite arm bends up at the elbow

BABINSINKY: when the sole of the foot is firmly stroked, big toe moves upward and other toes fan out

AGE	REFLEX
BIRTH	Moro Sucking Bapkin Grasping Rooting Tonic neck Walking Babinsky
2 MONTHS	Moro Grasping Rooting Tonic neck Babinsky
4 MONTHS	Moro Tonic neck
6 MONTHS	Moro Tonic neck
8 MONTHS	Moro Tonic neck
10 MONTHS	Moro Tonic neck
12 MONTHS	Moro Tonic neck

FURTHER READING

BOOKS BY DR. MARIA MONTESSORI

The Absorbent Mind: A Classic in Education and Child Development for Educators and Parents,
Holt Paperbacks, 1995

The Child in the Family, ABC-CLIO, 1989 version

Maria Montessori Speaks to Parents: A Selection of Articles, Montessori-Pierson, 2017

BOOKS ABOUT THE MONTESSORI APPROACH

The Joyful Child: Montessori, Global Wisdom for Birth to Three, Susan Mayclin Stephenson,
Michael Olaf Montessori Company, 2013

The Montessori Toddler, Simone Davies, Workman Publishing, 2019

Montessori from the Start: The Child at Home, from Birth to Age Three (1st Edition),
Paula Polk Lillard and Lynn Lillard Jessen, Schocken, 2003

Understanding the Human Being: The Importance of the First Three Years of Life
(The Clio Montessori Series), Silvana Quattrocchi Montanaro, ABC-CLIO, 1991

Montessori: The Science Behind the Genius, Angeline Stoll Lillard, Oxford University Press, 2008

BOOKS ABOUT BIRTHING

*Birth Without Fear: The Judgment-Free Guide to Taking Charge of Your Pregnancy, Birth, and
Postpartum,* January Harshe, Hachette Books, 2019

Ina May's Guide to Childbirth, Ina May Gaskin, Bantam, 2003

Spiritual Midwifery, Ina May Gaskin, Book Publishing Company (TN), 2002

BOOKS ABOUT BABIES

*Baby's First Year Milestones: Promote and Celebrate Your Baby's Development with Monthly Games
and Activities,* Aubrey Hargis, Rockridge Press, 2018

Dear Parent: Caring for Infants with Respect (2nd Edition), Magda Gerber, Resources for Infant
Educarers (RIE), 2003

Your Self-Confident Baby: How to Encourage Your Child's Natural Abilities—From the Very Start,
Magda Gerber and Allison Johnson, John Wiley & Sons, Inc., 2012

Elevating Child Care: A Guide to Respectful Parenting, Janet Lansbury, CreateSpace Independent
Publishing Platform, 2014

60 activités Montessori pour mon bébé (365 activités), Marie-Hélène Place, Nathan, 2016

POSITIVE PARENTING

*Positive Discipline: The First Three Years, Revised and Updated Edition: From Infant to Toddler—
Laying the Foundation for Raising a Capable, Confident Child,* Jane Nelsen, Ed D, Cheryl Irwin, MA,
and Rosyln Ann Duffy, Harmony, 2007

How to Talk So Little Kids Will Listen: A Survival Guide to Life with Children Ages 2–7, Joanna Faber and
Julie King, Scribner, 2017

Nonviolent Communication: A Language of Life, Marshall B. Rosenberg, PhD, Puddledancer Press, 2015

GRATITUDE AND APPRECIATION FOR...

EACH OTHER—This book could not have been written without the magic of having each other as writing partners. To be able to collaborate on this book was a dream. We are so grateful for the opportunity to birth this book together with ease and grace.

OUR DESIGNERS—Our enormous thanks to Sanny van Loon for her beautiful illustrations that bring the book to life. Sanny has been so patient with our requests to ensure everything is accurate and clear, and she delivered such delightful artwork, which we adore. To Galen Smith for your genius in laying out the book and making it easy to read, and also for putting up with all our requests. And we are so happy to use the book design of Hiyoko Imai who designed Simone's first book, *The Montessori Toddler*.

THE PUBLISHER—To the Workman Publishing team for jumping on board with a resounding YES! at the idea for this book. Thanks to Maisie for the always thoughtful feedback and questions; to Sun for your help editing; to Kate for your careful eye; and to Moira, Chloe, Rebecca, Cindy, and the team for getting this book into readers' hands. A small but mighty team.

OUR CONTRIBUTORS—Thank you so much for being part of this project. Your contributions make this book even richer. Big thanks to Nicole, Ahoefa, Jaya, Maria, Neus, Theresa, Pilar, Amy, and Pamela for sharing your Montessori experiences with us. And to Karin for being the voice of the newborn—your work is so important.

OUR SUPPORTERS—We'd love to thank our sisters and friends who supported us through this writing process, read through and shared feedback. Thank you Florish Echefu, Rahma Yelwa, Zoe Paul, and Sophia Ohuabunwa. And to Jackie and Tania and also to early readers Julia, Mila, Meghan, and Chloe for all the valuable insights and encouragement. Thank you so much to Angeline Stoll Lillard. Your kindness in offering to read the book, your support—and like an added gift, your meticulous comments—are all so appreciated.

OUR MONTESSORI FAMILY—we both receive so much support and love from the Montessori community. You truly fuel us. Judi Orion helped Simone see the world through the eyes of the infant; Ferne van Zyl;

An Morison and Annabel Needs were responsible for Simone falling in love with the Montessori approach; Heidi Phillipart-Alcock introduced Simone to the wonders of Amsterdam as well as being a Montessori mentor over the years; Julia Preziosi and her school Northern Kentucky Montessori Academy introduced Junnifa to Montessori and caused her to immediately fall in love. Pilar Bewley and Jeanne Marie Paynel guided Junnifa to take the AMI 03 training. Patty Wallner's training inspired Junnifa and prepared her to understand and support babies. And to all the Montessori friends who have been such a sounding board from Instagram to Facebook groups and beyond.

FAMILIES AT JACARANDA TREE MONTESSORI and **FRUITFUL ORCHARD MONTESSORI**—Simone feels very grateful to work with the amazing families who come to her classes at Jacaranda Tree Montessori in Amsterdam. She loves learning from these families every day. Junnifa is honored to be entrusted by the families at Fruitful Orchard with their most precious possessions. It is a constant joy to watch the children blossom and see the parents grow and transform along with their children.

OUR FAMILIES—To our own families for being patient with us as we jumped on Zoom calls, edited into the evenings, and discussed colors of illustrations until we were completely satisfied. Your support means so much. Uzo, Oliver, Emma, Solu, Metu, and Biendu—you collectively are our inspiration. To our parents who have never doubted us and always supported us. We love you so much.

ALL THE THINGS—For freedom, for knowledge, for connection, for nature, for cycling through the city and the fields, for cups of tea and sweet treats, for cabins and blankets, for nourishing food and simple pleasures, for museums and photography. The things that feed the spirit for us to do the work we do with such joy. Junnifa would also like to thank God and Jesus Christ, the author and finisher of her faith.

A special mention to Grazia Honegger Fresco who has continued Dr. Montessori's work in Rome and who passed in her sleep on September 30, 2020. Thank you for your unending and rich work for all the children.

INDEX

ONLINE RESOURCES
Visit Workman.com/montessori for DIY Montessori mobile templates and other bonus material.